THE EDUCATION
OF AN IDEALIST

THE EDUCATION
OF AN IDEALIST

A Memoir

Samantha Power

DEY ST.
An Imprint of WILLIAM MORROW

Unless otherwise noted, photographs are courtesy of the author.

Insert 1: p. 6, top:, Cuny Family; p. 10, top, Geoffrey W. King; p. 12, top left, Jason Maloney; p. 12, center: Hiroko Masuike/*New York Times*/Redux; p. 12, bottom: *Des Moines Register*/USA Today Network; p. 13, top: Peter Yang; p. 14, top and bottom: Pete Souza/The Obama White House; p. 15, bottom: Courtesy Barack Obama Presidential Library; p. 16, top: AP Photo/Carolyn Kaster; p. 16, bottom: Pete Souza/The Obama White House.

Insert 2: p. 1, top: Pete Souza/The Obama White House; p. 1, center: Elliot Thomson; p. 1, bottom: AP Photo/Cliff Owen; p. 2, top: Presidential Materials Division, National Archives and Records Administration; p. 2, center: UN Photo/Evan Schneider; p. 2, bottom: Pete Souza/The Obama White House; p. 3, top: Michelle Nichols/Reuters; p. 3, center: Emmanuel Dunand/AFP/Getty Images; p. 3, bottom: AP Photo/Sergei Chuzavkov; p. 4, top: United States Mission to the United Nations; p. 4, middle: Michelle Nichols/Reuters; p. 4, bottom: AP Photo/Abbas Dulleh; p. 5, top: Courtesy Barack Obama Presidential Library; p. 5, bottom left: Stephanie Sinclair; p. 6, bottom: Elliot Thomson; p. 7, top and bottom: United States Mission to the United Nations; p. 8, top: United States Mission to the United Nations; p. 8, bottom: AP Photo/Julie Jacobson; p. 9, top: AP Photo/Rukmal Gamage; p. 9, center: AP Photo/Andrew Harnik; p. 9, bottom: United States Mission to the United Nations; p. 10, center: Brian Harkin/*New York Times*/Redux; p. 10, bottom: Randy Haniel/AFP/Getty Images; p. 11: United States Mission to the United Nations; p. 12, top: AP Photo/Bryan R. Smith; p. 12, bottom: Chip Somodevilla/Getty Images; p. 13, top: Jim Watson/AFP/Getty Images; p. 13, bottom: Andrew Harrer/picture-alliance/dpa/AP Images; p. 14, top: UN Photo/Isaac Billy; p. 14, bottom: Bullen Chol/Anadolu Agency/Getty Images; p. 15, top: AP Photo/Seth Wenig; p. 15, bottom: United States Mission to the United Nations; p. 16, top: Gilbert King

FIRST EDITION

Designed by Paula Russell Szafranski

Library of Congress Cataloging-in-Publication Data has been applied for.

ISBN 978-0-06-282069-3

19 20 21 22 23   DIX/LSC   10 9 8 7 6 5 4 3 2 1

For Cass, Declan, and Rían

CONTENTS

PREFACE

On a bright Saturday in September of 2013, I was sitting in a crowded diner in midtown Manhattan with my husband, Cass, and our kids, four-year-old Declan and one-year-old Rían. My cell phone rang. The White House switchboard was on the line: "Ambassador Power, please hold for the President of the United States."

I took two long sips of water and walked out of the restaurant's clamor toward the corner of 50th and Lexington.

I had first met Barack Obama eight years before, when he was a newly elected US senator. Although he was already considered a bright young star in American politics, I would not have predicted then that within a few short years he would become president. And I would have found it unbelievable that I—an unmarried Irish immigrant, obsessive sports fan, journalist, and human rights activist who had not served a day in government—would, within that same period, gain a husband and two children and be named United States Ambassador to the United Nations.

And yet there I was, with a security detail hovering, about to confer with the President while my family sat nearby.

Obama was not calling for a Saturday-afternoon chat. Syrian president Bashar al-Assad had recently unleashed chemical weapons against his own citizens, killing 1,400 people, including more than 400 children. This atrocity crossed the "red line" that the President had drawn when he threatened the Assad regime with "enormous consequences" if it used chemical weapons. In response, Obama had initially decided to order air strikes in Syria, but Congress—and most of the American public—had not supported him.

Then the unforeseen happened: Russian president Vladimir Putin, Assad's ally, offered to work with the United States to destroy Syria's large chemical weapons stockpile.

Locking down the specifics was left to me and my Russian counterpart at the UN. If we failed to negotiate a Security Council resolution, President Obama did not have a Plan B.

"Hey!" Obama said when he came on the line. Despite the gravity of the situation, he used the same airy inflection as when we first met in 2005.

I had only become UN ambassador the previous month, and Obama understood that I was facing a high-pressure diplomatic assignment. He was checking in to be sure we were on the same page.

"I just want you to know I have complete confidence in you," he said.

I started to thank him.

"But . . ." Obama interrupted.

At that moment I did not need a "but."

"But in these negotiations with the Russians," he continued, "I want to make sure you don't overshoot the runway."

The Syrian government was notorious for unspeakable acts of savagery against its own people, and Obama knew I was skeptical that Assad would ever relinquish his chemical weapons. He was concerned I would demand too much from the Russians and cause them to walk away.

"But don't undershoot the runway either," he quickly added.

"Yes, Mr. President," I said.

We hung up and I began walking back toward the diner, security agents in tow.

Don't overshoot. Don't undershoot. Looking up to the cloudless sky, I found myself wondering something more fundamental: "Where the hell is the runway?"

I HAD SPENT DECADES thinking about moments such as this, critical junctures in American foreign policy where lives were at stake. Studying the manual, however, is not the same as flying.

In 2002, I had published my first book, *"A Problem from Hell": America and the Age of Genocide.* In the book, I criticized US officials for doing too little to stop the major genocides of the twentieth century. Now I found myself in the President's cabinet as the Syrian regime was murdering hundreds of thousands of its own people.

"What would the old Samantha Power say to the current Samantha Power?" reporters often asked. "How does the author of a book on atrocities defend the US government's inaction in the face of mass murder in Syria?"

My standard answer rejected the implication that my past and present selves were in conflict. "The old and new Samantha know each other quite well," I would reply. "They talk all the time. And they agree . . ."

The full answer, of course, was more complicated.

I had gone from being an outsider to an insider—from being a critic of American foreign policy to a leading representative of the United States on the world stage. From within government, I was able to help spur actions that improved people's lives. And yet we were failing to stop the carnage in Syria. I was at risk of falling prey to the same mode of rationalization I had assailed as an activist.

In January of 2017, I concluded eight years in the Obama administration and became an outsider once more. As I tried to get my bearings, President Obama's successor began to turn the country in a radically different direction. Like many Americans, I vacillated between feelings of disbelief, outrage, and anxiety about the future. I had long taken for granted the importance of individual dignity, the richness of American diversity, and the practical necessity of global cooperation. Yet suddenly, these core values were under assault and far more vulnerable than I had recognized.

I set out to write a book that explored what I had learned thus far in my life and career. I returned to my early childhood in Ireland, the circumstances that brought me to the United States, my high school years in Atlanta, Georgia, and my time as a journalist in Bosnia. I delved into experiences that had moved and even altered me—as a human rights advocate, on a presidential campaign, in the White House, and at the UN. And I examined painful losses and setbacks, both in my private life and in the public glare.

We make sense of our lives through stories. Regardless of our different backgrounds and perspectives, stories have the power to bind us. In my Irish family, being able to tell a lively story has always been a means of fitting in and drawing people together. As a war correspondent, storytelling was the most effective tool I had to bridge the vast space between those suffering the wounds of distant conflict and my American readers. As a diplomat, when foreign officials refused to budge in negotiations, I would try to shake up stale debates by sharing authentic, firsthand stories about the many people who were being affected (for good and bad) by our decisions. And as a woman in national security and the mother of two young children, I used stories to make bearable the tensions inherent in balancing a demanding career and a fulfilling family life.

This story is one of sorrow, resilience, anger, solidarity, determination, and laughter, sometimes jumbled together. This is also a story of idealism—where it comes from, how it gets challenged, and why it must endure.

Some may interpret this book's title as suggesting that I began with lofty dreams about how one person could make a difference, only to be "educated" by the brutish forces that I encountered. That is not the story that follows.

PART ONE

IRELAND

W hat right has this woman to be so educated?"

My mother, Vera Delaney, had not broken any laws, yet she seemed to be on trial. As she made the case for why she should be allowed to take my brother and me to America, her fate appeared contingent upon the whims of the Irish judge who posed this question.

I was eight; my brother, Stephen, was four. Neither of us was present that day in the Dublin courtroom. But the story of what transpired there is so emblazoned in my psyche that I can see the judge's face, shaped like the map of Ireland, his skin blotted with what looked like my granny's blush. I can visualize the mahogany wood paneling behind the bench where he presided. I can smell the boiled ham that wafted off of his black robes. I can even make out the intricate white threads of his juridical wig.

I've often wondered how my mother channeled her anger: Did she start to respond to the judge's provocation, only to get a knee under the table from her lawyer? Did she feel her cheeks burn—as mine are prone to do—despite the chill of the courtroom? I imagined the voice inside her head: "Keep it together, Vera. He wants you to react. Don't give him an excuse to deny you custody."

It was far from inevitable that my mother, the person I have always admired most in this world, would end up "so educated." She came of age at a time when less than 10 percent of married women in Ireland were part of the workforce. Her father, a policeman in Cork City, was an incurable, high-stakes gambler who bet his paychecks on horse and dog racing. My mother, her four sisters, and her younger brother grew up under the constant threat of foreclosure. While none of her three older siblings went to college, my mother decided early on that she would be the first of the Delaney children to do so—indeed, she would become a doctor.

Because the Catholic girls' school my mother attended did not offer science courses, she had a problem. When she tried to apply to the University College Cork's medical program, the registrar told her she lacked the background to manage the curriculum. Undeterred, my mother registered anyway. When she got home, one of her sisters lit into her because of the lengthy program's cost. My mother responded by dumping her plate of bacon, cabbage, and mashed potatoes on her sister's lap. But she marched back to the college and, livid but shamed, changed her registration to the shorter Bachelor of Science program. After earning that degree, she went on to pursue a PhD in biochemistry in London. But caring for patients was what my mother had always wanted and would never stop wanting; while writing her dissertation, she finally decided to apply to medical school. Thirteen years after first attempting to enroll, she achieved her lifelong dream of becoming a medical doctor.

Yet in that courtroom years later, my mother was forced to answer for her career—for being "so educated"—because she was trying to move with her children to the United States, a country she had never visited, in order to get advanced training in her area of specialization, kidney transplantation.

She was also hoping to run away with the man she loved—a man who wasn't my father.

MY DAD, JIM POWER, was an epic figure—brilliant, dashing, and charismatic, yet intimidating and witheringly sharp-tongued. At six foot five he towered over his Irish contemporaries. Even as a child, I could tell he was the man in the room that people most wanted to please.

My parents met in London, where my mother was studying medicine and my dad was working as a dentist. Mum first spotted him leading a sing-along for a group of Irish exiles in the Bunch of Grapes pub in Knightsbridge. After long fending off girlfriends, my dad pursued her avidly.

Mum was a slender, stylish young woman with a lively sense of play, who could place a tennis serve or hit a squash forehand better than almost all her male peers. She liked my father's constant teasing, which kept her off balance. She was amazed by his talent for the piano and his ability to launch into whatever songs the bar patrons requested.

My father initially encouraged and helped subsidize Mum's medical school pursuits. A scratch golfer, he applauded how quickly she picked up his sport, and cheered her on as she ascended the ranks of British athletics in squash. As a teenager and college student, she had played competitive tennis and field hockey—first for her home province of Munster and later for Ireland. At squash, she was relentless: speedy to the front of the court and agile from side to side. When Mum was off in the library or on the squash court, Dad was at the pub, boasting to his friends about her latest feats. After an impassioned courtship, they wed in September of 1968.

"This is the third of my children getting married this year," her father told his mother, "and I would not put my money on this one." For a man who bet on anything and everything, this was saying something.

While my grandfather adored his daughter, his traditional views on gender roles made him worry that Mum would prioritize her career above her marriage. My grandfather accurately saw his new son-in-law as a man who needed to be taken care of. My dad had been idolized and sheltered by his own mother, but despite this coddled upbringing, he was deeply drawn to women with opinions and ambitions of their own.

While the accomplished duo initially charged forth, their interests soon began to diverge. My mother studied constantly, partly to make up for all she felt she didn't know. And having grown up fearing that any knock on the door might be a lender seizing the family home to pay her father's gambling debts, Mum was determined to take control of her own path. In contrast, my dad's achievements had always come effortlessly. His photographic memory allowed him to look at a blank wall and visualize words as he had previously read them on the page.

Because my father never felt the passion for his career that Mum had for hers, he lacked focus. Despite being an established dentist, at the age of thirty-five he decided to take the unusual step of returning to school to get a medical degree of his own.

I was born in September of 1970, while Mum was still studying to become a doctor in London. When my dad began the six-year course at University College Dublin shortly thereafter, we moved back to Dublin, where Mum would finish medical school. Although my dad breezed through his program, when he finally became Dr. Jim Power, MD, he showed no interest in practicing medicine—an attitude Mum couldn't fathom. His older sister came to refer to him as "the eternal student."

My father had always been a drinker, but after Mum threw herself deeper into her medical career, his drinking became something of a vocation. His second home was Hartigan's, a pub ten minutes away from where we lived. Known for its highbrow political debates, no-frills decorum, and the taste and pour of its pints, Hartigan's felt like a village pub in the middle of Ireland's bustling capital. My father was one of the regulars.

Guinness—the dark brown, silky stout with the thick, pillowy head—was not just his drink; it was his craft. Known as "mother's milk," Guinness had adopted the tagline "GUINNESS IS GOOD FOR YOU" in the 1920s, and most of us believed it. For decades, Irish mothers had been served Guinness after giving birth because of its iron content and perceived health benefits.

Like many of his contemporaries, my father hailed the delicacy of the drinking experience, stressing the proper "two-pour" approach: tilting the tulip-shaped pint glass at a 45-degree angle, filling it halfway, pausing so the stout could settle, and then—and only then—pouring the rest. "Pulling a pint" properly, my dad insisted, should take at least two minutes. "Good things come to those who wait," he would say, mimicking the satisfied customers in the Guinness television ads. Once the pour was complete, my dad—usually an impatient man—waited with unencumbered anticipation for the barman to smooth the creamy head with a butter knife. He relished the first taste of every pint, pausing before clearing his upper lip of Guinness's signature foamy residue.

By the time my brother Stephen was born in 1974, the cracks in our parents' relationship were widening. The pub would become at once a sanctuary for my dad and an accelerator of his faltering marriage.

BOTH MUM AND DAD included me—and, when he was older, Stephen—in what they were doing, carving out time to be alone with each of us. I would often spend large parts of my afternoons and weekends accompanying Mum to the squash court, watching her smack the tiny black ball with a wooden Slazenger racket. She was unfailingly gracious on the court, but also fiercely competitive. Sitting in the wooden bleachers and watching her seemingly endless rallies, I would cheer as she wore down her opponents with her trademark grit.

Swimming together in the Irish Sea at the Blackrock beach, we would laugh as we both turned purple, teeth chattering in the frigid water. She often brought me on road trips to her hometown of Cork to visit with her parents and my many aunts, uncles, and cousins. Driving in her tiny Mini on Ireland's bendy roads, we blissfully belted out songs of my choosing—"It's a Long Way to Tipperary," "Molly Malone," and "She'll Be Coming 'Round the Mountain." On occasions when we hopped the train in Dublin and settled in for the three-hour ride, she would unfurl tinfoil-wrapped cheddar cheese and butter wedged between two Jacob's Cream Crackers, followed by a Cadbury Flake chocolate bar or Kimberley biscuits. I loved the feeling of curling up next to her as she devoured her medical journals, and from around the age of six, I too would sink into a book.

Mum gave people she met a quality of attention that I would come to associate with the most gifted politicians. When making a new acquaintance, she would cock her head to the side and peer earnestly at the other person, digging for details and drawing connections across time and space. She laughed with her whole body, or—if someone's tale was a sad one—sagged with the weight of the other person's anguish. I never knew my mother to have an ulterior motive as she listened; she was simply curious and intensely empathetic. She had no airs and eschewed sentimentality, conveying her love not through expressive words—which to her would have sounded maudlin—but through intense, affectionate focus.

Early on, I saw that my mother had a gift for cramming as much life as possible into a day. She arose before dawn, often completing her six-mile morning run before I began groggily pouring my cereal. The only time I saw her sitting still was when she watched professional tennis. When the Wimbledon coverage began, she would park herself in front of our television for hours, contentedly taking in the juniors, the bottom seeds, the doubles, and her favorite, Björn Borg.

Mum was a terrible sleeper. She worried about her patients, with whom she formed deep attachments. But above all, she fretted about my younger brother, who spent the first six weeks of his life in the hospital. When he was born, Stephen suffered a collapsed lung and then quickly contracted meningitis. When he was unable to hold down food, the doctors realized he had a severe intestinal blockage that required surgery. He recovered from the operation, but didn't talk for his first two years. While my dad thought he would speak when he felt like it, Mum thought the meningitis might have caused him to go deaf.

Dad proved correct. Stephen became an adorably loquacious troublemaker who got great laughs out of laying intricate traps throughout the house for his unsuspecting parents and older sister. At school, though, he struggled, rarely showing interest. My mother spent many nights awake, wondering if he would ever apply himself.

My father always seemed carefree. His dental practice was desultory; he appeared to only work when he felt like it. We would play tennis in the cul-de-sac outside our home, or I would tag along as he pounded golf balls on the driving range. He was close with his parents, whom we often visited two hours away in the town of Athlone. His mother was a force of nature—as a young woman in England, she had built a school from scratch and later made a comfortable living playing the stock market. His dad, whom I and all the grandkids called "Bam Bam," was a former Irish soldier with a sunny outlook on life, often proclaiming, "Never trouble trouble unless trouble troubles you." Having retired from the military years before, Bam Bam seemed to have no higher priority than kicking around a soccer ball with Stephen and me or taking us for ice cream.

Thursdays were especially precious to me, as they were reserved for my weekly "day out" in Dublin with my dad. He would pick me up from Mount Anville, the Catholic school I attended, take me for a hamburger, and then help me stock up on candy before we landed at Hartigan's. Our arrival at the pub was usually a welcome escape from the lashing rain or, on short winter afternoons, the damp darkness. As soon as my father was spotted, he was greeted with cheers of "Jimbo!," "Jimmy!," or "If it isn't the fine doctor himself!" My dad was such a regular patron that he had a designated chair—known as the "Seat of Power"—at the bar.

From around the time I was five years old, I viewed Hartigan's as a kind of oasis. Without a fuss, I would make my way down a half-flight of stairs from the main pub room and take a seat at a seldom-used bar that mirrored the busy one upstairs. My dad would bring me a bottle of 7 Up—if Stephen was with me, he would get a Coke—and I would contentedly dig into whatever mystery I was reading. I never went far without an Enid Blyton ("The Famous Five" or "The Secret Seven" series), Nancy Drew, or Hardy Boys book under my arm.

Over the course of the many hours I spent in Hartigan's basement, I disappeared on far-off adventures with intrepid child detectives, combating thieves and kidnappers. On the weekend, when I finished a book I had brought to the pub, I would march upstairs, and my dad would dash to the car to retrieve my coloring books and markers for the next phase of the afternoon. When my dad's friends brought their children, we would play board games or make up our own entertainment while our fathers laid down sports predictions in the room above.

When I was on my own, I made small talk with the pub guests who ventured downstairs to put change in the cigarette machine or to use the bathroom. Sometimes, I would stand outside the "Gents" toilet, singing songs. I told Stephen that I offered these performances so that my musical talents (which I had yet to realize were lacking) would be "discovered," but I was probably just pining for attention. For a while, the pub maintained a slot machine downstairs, which I enjoyed because it drew occasional pub patrons. On slow days, I often stood next to the machine's display screen for the extra reading light.

Hartigan's was not clean; the downstairs, where I read, played, and sang, had a smell that mingled urine, chlorine disinfectant, and the swirl of barley, malt, and hops. I couldn't have liked these smells, or playing near a pub's toilets, but I never complained. Years later, when I mentioned to an Irish diplomat that Hartigan's had been a big part of my childhood, he claimed that once, while drinking there, he had approached the bathroom door and spotted what he thought was a sack lying across the threshold. "I went to step inside," he told me, "and then suddenly, to my horror, the sack moved. It was a person!"

I froze, thinking for a second—absurdly—that it might have been me, before he revealed that it was, in fact, a small man who had passed out. I have my doubts that this story is true, but it speaks to the way many who visited Hartigan's thought about the place I called my second home as a young girl.

Although I must have occasionally experienced boredom or loneliness down in the basement, when I think of that time, I only remember my father, the first man I loved, loving me back. While many Hartigan's regulars seemed to leave thoughts of their families behind when they entered the cocoon of the pub, my father brought me with him. I was his sidekick. I could find him any time I needed him, with a long row of drained pint glasses beside him. Instead of shaking me off when I bounded up the stairs, he often picked me up and sat me down beside him. I grew preternaturally comfortable chatting with adults and people of different backgrounds, particularly about sports.

While my dad must have been well above the legal limit when he drove us home, he seemed in complete command of our little universe. On school nights when he came home late from the pub, even if it was after midnight, he would come to my room and wake me up. Often, he just wanted to chat about my day, but sometimes he would take Stephen and me for a drive around the neighborhood in his white Mazda—the backseat of which was covered with sheaves of discolored piano sheet music, broken golf tees, loose change, greasy wrappers from the local fish and chips shop, and months-old newspapers.

Hartigan's was such a vital part of our family routine that when my aunt bought me an elegant blue raincoat and observed, "This will look lovely on you when you go to Mass on Sunday," I responded, "No—it will look lovely on me when I go to the pub with Dad on Sunday."

MY PARENTS LOVED LIFE and learning, they loved sports, and they loved me. They just found loving each other a struggle.

I craved harmony between them. On one family vacation, I interrupted lunch to present them with a fifty-pence piece I had been saving. "Whichever of you doesn't argue with the other will get this," I declared. "I will be watching, keeping careful track." But my early efforts at diplomacy did not succeed. Although my mother had fallen for my dad watching him play piano in the pubs of London, she didn't hide her disapproval of his drinking or his embrace of leisure time. But when she complained that Hartigan's was no place for kids, my father countered that if she was so committed to our well-being, she should find a way to work less and be home more.

He started to nag and even taunt her. "Where have you been?" he would say when she came home late, physically poking her with his index finger.

"None of your business," she would answer, before shutting herself in a room where he couldn't disturb her studies.

One evening, when he found her at the kitchen table reviewing for an exam, he swept her medical notes and books into his arms, and, though it was pouring rain, marched into the back garden and threw them into a walled-up boiler pit where she would be unable to retrieve them.

Sober, perhaps, my dad might have pulled back from a confrontation, but having packed away a dozen pints, he would raise his voice at her, and she would give as good as she got. Lying in my twin bed above the living room, I would listen as the arguments grew nastier and as plates from the kitchen were hurled. When I got out of bed to spy from the landing atop the stairs, I would alternate between straining to decide who was at fault and blocking my ears with my hands so I could make out nothing but the sound of my heart pounding—a sound so deafening I was sure my parents could hear it below.

Sometimes, I would get down on my knees beside my bed, make a hasty sign of the cross, and then try to drown out the noise by saying as many Hail Marys and Our Fathers as it took for the din to subside.

WHEN I WAS SEVEN, Mum left Ireland for a year to help set up the first kidney transplant and dialysis unit in Kuwait, leaving Stephen and me in the care of our dad and wonderful housekeeper and live-in nanny, Eilish Hartnett. While a year was a long time to be separated, during the summer, Mum brought my brother and me to Kuwait for a six-week visit.

There, Stephen and I experienced heat of a kind that was literally unimaginable for two Dublin kids. We wore miniature dishdashas, which kept us as cool as possible, and lathered ourselves in sunscreen before spending long hours on the beach, swimming alongside Bedouin and Kuwaiti boys—but no local girls. I was fascinated by the minarets that dotted the horizon and the mixed dress of women—some in Western clothes, others in abayas or hijabs. Alcohol was illegal, but the Irish expatriates circumvented the rules at their parties. Although my mother was never a big drinker, she liked to join in, and even contributed beer that she home-brewed in a green plastic barrel using a kit she had brought from Dublin.

The deepest impression of our stay was made less by the sights and sounds of Kuwait than by the man with whom Mum had become romantically involved: an Irishman with a wide mustache and thick, prematurely graying hair. Dr. Edmund Bourke, or "Eddie," was a pioneer in the science and practice of nephrology (the branch of medicine that deals with kidneys), and had been Mum's supervisor at the Meath Hospital in Dublin during her medical residency. Although Eddie had a wife and four children of his own back in Dublin, he and my mother were now living together in a high-rise apartment, acting as if they were married.

Before Mum brought Stephen and me back to Ireland, she asked us not to tell our dad about Eddie. If we needed to mention that there was an "Eddie" in Kuwait, we were told to identify him as "Eddie McGrath," an Irish doctor who apparently also worked in Kuwait City.

To a seven-year-old, this seemed like high-stakes mischief. I was invigorated to have been let into an exclusive club with grown-ups who now trusted me with a secret. I could tell that whatever was happening between Mum and Eddie was making her happier than I could remember seeing her with my dad.

Unfortunately, not long after we returned to Ireland, my father asked me point-blank whether my mother had been with Eddie Bourke in Kuwait. I answered truthfully that she had, presuming that Mum would not want me to lie in response to a direct question. She reassured me later that I had done the right thing. But when she moved back to Dublin from Kuwait, although she returned to live at home with us, she slept in the guest bedroom. She and my father began leading separate lives.

My dad, then thirty-six, had himself become involved with Susan Doody, a twenty-five-year-old teacher at a Dublin primary school, another welcome new presence in my and my brother's lives. While Susan showed more tolerance for pub life than my mother, she still preferred luring Dad away from Hartigan's to the latest Bergman or Fassbinder film, rugby match, or golf tournament. "He could spend hours watching any ball move on any surface," she marveled.

In Catholic Ireland, Susan kept quiet about her relationship with my dad, believing that the nuns who ran the school where she taught would come under pressure to let her go if they found out that she was dating a married man. Still, in the coming years, she would play a leading role in prodding my dad to change his lifestyle, appealing to him to find a job that was more fulfilling than his part-time dental practice. "Let's have a drink and talk about it," he would say heartily, changing the subject.

Even when Eddie emerged on the scene and my father and Susan became more heavily involved, it never occurred to me that my parents' marriage could end. To be fair, I had the facts on my side: marriages in Ireland weren't *allowed* to end. The Catholic Church was extremely influential, and the priests made sure that Irish law prohibited not only contraception and abortion, but also divorce. And if marriages were to start ending because of "the drink"—known across the land as "the good man's fault"—it seemed to me that few families would remain intact.

Despite the turbulence around me, I thought life was good. My father projected a sense that he lacked for nothing. He drank too much and clearly didn't do much work, but he had infinite time for me— a child's only true measure of a parent. My mother worked feverishly, but when we were together, she managed to make me feel as though time were standing still.

However, not long after she returned from Kuwait, Mum told Stephen and me she was hoping to move with us to the United States. Before she did so, she told my father about this possibility, stressing that she would not make the move if he would get help for his drinking problem. He refused.

My father battled Mum in an Irish court, trying to gain sole custody of us. Each depicted the other as unfit to raise kids: my father because he drank too much; my mother because she worked too much and was having an affair. My father didn't help his cause when he appeared in court once after "a liquid lunch," giving my mother more ammunition for her claim that he was incapable of taking care of two children.

When my father lost in the lower court, he appealed the case, which made its way to the Supreme Court. Once again, the court ruled in her favor. My dad didn't prepare properly, and his itinerant career left him unable to demonstrate that he had the means to financially support his family. Despite the judge's condescension to Mum about her education, in 1979 the court granted her permission to leave Ireland with my brother and me.

Given Irish tradition and the stigma associated with separating from one's spouse, it is remarkable that she was awarded custody. But the state attached three conditions if Mum wanted to take us to the United States. First, my brother and I were to be raised Catholic. We were to continue attending Mass and studying religion so that we would receive the sacraments (communion and confirmation for my younger brother, confirmation for me, and regular confession for us both). Second, my mother would home-school us in the Irish language. And finally, we were to return to Ireland to stay with my dad during the summers and over holidays like Christmas and Easter.

I did not experience the news of moving to America as a bombshell announcement. Mum must have casually introduced the idea, herself not then expecting that the move would be permanent.

We boarded a plane bound for the United States in September of 1979. I was just nine years old, but I had a clear sense that Mum would do important medical work and then bring us back to Dublin, our home.

It would be years before I understood that we had immigrated to the United States.

2

AMERICA

When Mum, Stephen, and I landed in Pittsburgh, Pennsylvania, I was dressed for the occasion in a Stars and Stripes T-shirt. Mum, then just thirty-six years old, was wearing brown corduroys and a form-fitting turtleneck. All these years later, I remember her face at the airport as we awaited our luggage: she was exhausted. Yet somehow, she was going to start her American medical career the next day.

What must she have felt when we landed? Relief that she had somehow pulled off the move? Trepidation at a new life? I imagine that she was probably just thinking: "Where in God's name are the bags? Sam and Steve need sleep."

For my part, I knew that my mother had left my father behind in Ireland. But that she had left him for good—that they would never again even argue over dinner together—had not entered my nine-year-old consciousness. It wouldn't for a very long time.

I scoured the conveyor belt for our suitcases, crammed with everything we could fit from our lives in Ireland: the components of my Irish school uniform; "runners" that would become "sneakers"; a stash of mystery novels; and "Teddy," my long-suffering teddy bear. Mum had shipped several Dunlop tennis rackets, her squash racket, her most important medical reference books, and my maroon Raleigh bicycle. She would go to great lengths to reassemble the bike—only for me to quickly disown it as out of fashion in a neighborhood where dirt bikes were all the rage.

As we exited the baggage area, I recognized the middle-aged, medium-built man with a large crop of silver-gray hair who greeted us; it was Eddie Bourke, with whom Mum had told us we would be living. By then, she had been seeing Eddie for five years and he had separated from his wife.

During our time in Kuwait, Eddie had been a playful companion, taking Stephen and me to the beach and teaching me the basics of chess, as well as a few Arabic phrases. But what stood out most was his ability to lighten our days with ridiculous rhymes. He would recite:

> There was an old lady from Clyde
> Who once ate an apple and died.
> Inside the lamented,
> The apple fermented,
> To cider inside her inside.

Or he would teasingly urge us to join in:

> Way up on the mountain,
> Green grows the grass,
> Down came the elephant,
> Tumbling on his . . .

Just as I was about to scream out the risqué swearword "ass," Eddie would plow ahead with great animation:

> Don't misunderstand me.
> Don't you be misled.
> Down came the elephant,
> Tumbling on his head.

While my dad was quick with a cutting barb and flaunted encyclopedic recall, Eddie had a warmer, more inclusive kind of wit and an intelligence that extended well beyond the field of medicine. He would sit for hours with a pencil, marking up dense history books covering everything from Qing dynasty China to the origins of the universe.

Eddie was also a once-in-a-generation storyteller. As the drinks flowed among friends, he played the role of the old Irish *seanchaí*, who offered jokes and tall tales. He would gesticulate dramatically, acting out each of the characters in his stories, his entranced audience holding their sides with laughter well before the punch line. The humor was in the telling, and Eddie delighted in other people's delight. I sometimes had the sense that, as he went about his day, he was thinking less about what was happening around him than about how he would later stage his comic reenactments.

Eddie made Mum laugh—and laughing always seemed the most important part of their life together. During my childhood, I saw my mother's face shine in two predictable circumstances: watching my father play the piano and Eddie winding up for a joke or story. She loved them both at different times, and they both drove her mad.

Eddie had been raised in a strict, staunchly nationalistic household, and had attended an Irish school where even calculus was taught in "the medium"—the Gaelic language. The Irish nationalism around him was so intense that, if a boy in his school mistakenly used his head on the Gaelic football field (as one does in the "English" sport of soccer), the match would be suspended, and the ball confiscated. Rugby and soccer were seen as sports for Protestants and Anglophiles. Despite his cerebral day job, Eddie could get choked up singing Irish rebel songs or reciting Irish insurgent Robert Emmet's last words before he was hanged by the British in 1803.

Years later, I would hear Irish novelist Colm Tóibín speak about how, growing up in Ireland, there was simply nothing worse than "being boring." "You could be smelly, you could be ugly, you could be fierce dumb," he said, happily, "but you could *not* be boring." This had been the sensibility in our home in Ireland, and so it came to be in America as well. Eddie was as far from boring as Pittsburgh was from Dublin.

When we passed through customs, I gave Eddie a huge hug—what he called a "Squasheroni"—and shouted hello in my pidgin Arabic, *"Ahlan wa Sahlan!"* *"Ahlan bik, Alhamdulillah!"* he answered, welcoming me.

Like many intellectuals, Eddie frequently had difficulty focusing on real-world tasks. But having lived in Pittsburgh for nearly a year before our arrival, he had made impressive preparations, drawing on the help of his close Irish friends in the area. He had found a two-story house for us to move into together, and purchased a yellow Renault Le Car for Mum—to complement the charcoal Le Car that he drove.

In Ireland I'd had little exposure to America. The three channels on our Dublin television had played mainly Irish and British programs, so the little I knew about the United States came mostly from American exports like *The Incredible Hulk* and *Charlie's Angels*. The few Americans I had actually encountered were tourists in Ireland on their golf holidays, most of whom seemed to be tanned men with straight teeth and loud opinions.

I didn't arrive in the US until after the local public elementary school year had already started. When Mum walked me inside and introduced me to my new teacher, I was wearing the outfit I had worn to my Catholic school in Ireland—a navy and green skirt, knee-high lace socks, black leather dress shoes, and a white golf shirt. Immediately, I felt out of place next to my classmates in their blue jeans and docksiders. Within a couple weeks, Mum took me shopping at Kaufman's Department Store, and I chose what I saw around me: a Pittsburgh Pirates T-shirt, a #12 Terry Bradshaw Steelers' jersey, a Steelers' sweatshirt, a green Izod golf shirt, green Izod pants, and a pair of light tan corduroys. This selection would tide me over until our next shopping outing many months later—although I quickly learned from my classmates that if I wore my all-green Izod outfit on Thursdays, it obviously indicated that I was "horny." While I had no idea what this meant, I did know melting into my surroundings necessitated avoiding green on Thursdays.

Relatively self-assured in Dublin, I now felt self-conscious in Pittsburgh. I had a thick Dublin accent, long red hair in a ponytail, and pale skin. My freckles suddenly seemed to stand out against the backdrop of a complexion that had seen more rain than sun. Unable to do much about my wardrobe or my Irish looks, I dedicated myself to changing my accent, rehearsing a new American way of speaking in the mirror.

I also acquired a new vocabulary. My Sunday "brekkie" of rashers, black and white pudding, and burnt sausages became an American "breakfast" of bacon and eggs. My "wellies" gave way to "snow boots." The older kids weren't smoking "fags" behind school, they were merely sneaking "cigarettes." And if we needed medicine, we no longer got it from the local "chemist," but from the "pharmacy."

Quickly seeking to master the preferred profanity of the locals, I noted that a combative classmate was no longer a "right pain in the arse," but a "royal pain in the ass." I made a particular point of brandishing words and phrases that I was told were unique to the Pittsburgh dialect, like "yinz" (for "you all"), "pop" (for "soda"), and "jagoff" (for "jerk").

Of course, other differences abounded. After years of bland cornflakes, I had infinite cereal choices, though I usually landed on Cocoa Krispies or Lucky Charms. The bus I took to school was no longer Irish green but mustard yellow. In Ireland, when I misbehaved (hiding out in the girl's bathroom, for example, to avoid ballet class, which I detested), I had been asked to produce my hand and was given a lashing with a belt or ruler. In the United States, however, I soon saw that punishment merely consisted of sitting in a corner removed from one's classmates.

Young boys lived in almost all of the houses on my street. For a tomboy like me who loved sports, the neighborhood was a dream. In Ireland, Mum had taught me to play tennis, soccer, and a bit of field hockey. But the boys on Hidden Pond Drive played—and talked about nothing but—baseball. The game seemed slow, as it does initially to foreigners. But once I mastered the rules and key statistics (batting averages, RBIs, and ERAs), every pitch thrown during every at-bat seemed like a vital part of my day.

Mum adapted to her new life, showing no discernible nostalgia for the country she left behind. Despite her deep empathy for others, she focused far less on exploring her own feelings. When I pointed out this inconsistency when I got older, she either changed the subject or just ended the conversation with a dismissive "Arragh sure, I can't be bothered."

Despite completing her medical residency back in Dublin, Mum was required to redo her training in the United States, a three-year ordeal. Yet during the same period, she somehow managed to master the new American sport of racquetball (quickly winning the local club championship). She also regularly took Steve and me to Three Rivers Stadium for the baseball games of our new hometown team, the Pittsburgh Pirates. Unlike most of my new friends' parents, she never even considered leaving before the last out. And remarkably, she attended most of my school and sporting events.

But there was no mistaking the Irishness of our family. While our neighbors ate pizza and grilled hot dogs, we rarely went a night without "spuds," and corned beef and cabbage were a staple. Eddie's version of a date with Mum was a night spent at The Blarney Stone, a local pub owned by an Irish footballer from County Kerry. When they could, they sat among fellow immigrants, ate Irish stew or bangers and mash, and joined the traditional music sing-alongs, enjoying the "craic."

THE MAIN CONSTANT between Ireland and the United States was God. In Dublin, though some of the nuns at school terrified me, being a Catholic was a source of comfort, and, I suppose, an affirmation of my Irishness. Given the unpredictability of my home life, I was soothed by the familiarity of the prayers and hymns. When Irish television and radio paused three times a day (at six a.m., noon, and six p.m.) to broadcast the slow and steady chimes of the Angelus bell, I had felt calm—not unlike the effect of the call to prayer I had heard five times a day in Kuwait. The United States was the first place I had been that didn't seem to want its people to pause and reflect during the day.

Mum stuck with her promise to the judge, driving my brother and me to Catholic Sunday school and Mass. But my main religious practice was (and still remains) private prayer, appeals to God to look after the people who mattered to me, and—even without the reminder of the Angelus bells—prayers of gratitude. I prayed when I was tying my shoes, having a bowl of soup, or riding the bus to school. I ran through long lists of all the people and occurrences I was thankful for. I prayed that "my daddy and all my aunts and uncles and grannies and grand-dads and cousins are happy." And I devoted inordinate prayer time to the fortunes of my new hometown baseball team.

My interest in the Pittsburgh Pirates quickly became fanatical. During the team's magical 1979 playoff run, which began soon after our arrival in the United States, Mum, Eddie, and I would sit on the new couch in our den and watch Captain Willie "Pops" Stargell light up the field with his smile and reliable bat. I was distraught when, during the World Series, the Pirates lost three of their first four games to the Baltimore Orioles. As my new team faced elimination in each of their next three games, I ducked into the bathroom during tense moments, got down on my knees, and prayed for a change of fortune.

I remember telling God that I knew from television that the Pirates' players did all kinds of work in the community for vulnerable people. I tried to bargain with Him, pledging to treat my five-year-old brother better in exchange for a late-inning double off the wall, each time rounding out my prayers by softly singing the Irish National Anthem. Why I viewed this song as relevant to the Pirates is unclear to me now, but when they ultimately won the Series four games to three, I was convinced that my well-leveraged negotiations and patriotic chorus were factors in convincing God to turn the contest around.

I began spending my weekly pocket money—now "allowance"—on Topps baseball cards. I was a skilled trader, doing complex multiparty deals with my neighbors, such that I ended up with the entire 1980 collection, minus two elusive cards. As a medical resident, Mum was earning little money, and because Eddie had bought the house and the cars, she was hesitant to impose her children's expenses on him as well. Thus, when I nagged her to buy me baseball cards so that I might luck into one of the two players I was missing—for me the equivalent of *Charlie and the Chocolate Factory*'s "golden tickets"—she usually turned me down.

Whenever I had saved up my allowance, I would ride my bike up the steep hill on Hidden Pond Drive and down a busy road to the convenience store a mile away. I would buy as many packs as I could afford, tearing open the waxy paper right there at the cash register, inhaling the smell of the pink gum, and checking to see whether I had landed a winner.

In my mind, Ireland was still my home. But this new place felt a bit like a wonderland. And while I was looking forward to my first trip back to Dublin, which I would take in December of 1979, I was going to gobble up all things American for as long as I could.

3

LOSS

Few memories are more seared into my psyche than the moment my father told me he would not allow my mother to take Stephen and me back to America.

Returning to Dublin for the first time since we had moved away in September, Stephen and I were spending the Christmas holiday of 1979 in our old home. Mum had traveled with us and was staying nearby with her close friend Geraldine. I was lying in my pajamas next to my dad on the king-sized bed he had once shared with my mother. He was teasing me for "sounding like a Yank" and for adopting a boy's haircut, which I had done to look as much like my Pittsburgh friends as possible. Stephen was asleep in the next room.

I was sucking on a peppermint I had raided from a stash in his nightstand when he informed me—as matter-of-factly as if offering up his golf tee time—that he planned to keep Stephen and me in Dublin.

He wanted us around, he explained, and thought it was a grave injustice that the courts had allowed Mum to take us so far away. He waited a few minutes and then telephoned my mother to inform her of his decision. In this short period of calm before I heard Mum's reaction, I felt affirmed to my core by my dad's willingness to defy the judge's ruling. All children covet signs of their parents' love, and I liked knowing that Stephen and I were worth a fight.

Once he had reached Mum, he handed me the phone so I could say hello first. Almost immediately, I blurted out the news. "Daddy's keeping us!" I exclaimed, my heart beating madly as I found myself at the epicenter of a high drama.

"What?" Mum asked. When I repeated myself, she said she would be coming to collect us immediately and told me to pass the phone to Dad. Her fury was barely contained.

"Mum's coming," I announced, handing the phone over to him.

"No she's not, pet," my dad said.

In the ensuing minutes, I could hear Mum's voice rising sharply through the receiver. Still, I figured they would have another argument—maybe even the fiercest of all their arguments—and then would sort things out.

When Mum didn't show up that day or the next, I happily settled back into my father's Hartigan's routine, with my brother by my side. I loved being back home. For all the novelty that America offered, I had missed even the rain of Ireland.

On Christmas Eve, Stephen and I watched *The Sound of Music* on a small black-and-white television in the living room where my father and Susan had decorated a Christmas tree and hung our stockings (in Ireland we used our actual socks rather than the enormous red and white American stockings that were the size of Santa's boots). My father had rented a keg from Hartigan's and his pub friends were in a jovial mood.

Stephen and I ignored the revelry, happily tugging on Irish Christmas "crackers" until they snapped in two and revealed the small plastic toy. My dad cooked us steaks in a frying pan—his specialty—and took his place at the piano, playing Hoagy Carmichael numbers and our favorite Christmas carols.

At around ten p.m., the doorbell rang. Following my dad to the door and peering around him, I saw Mum and her friend Geraldine standing there. She would not allow Steve and me to stay in a den of booze, she told my father. She had come to take us.

I stood on the threshold, snuggled against my father's leg. My brother and I watched the two people we loved most speak to each other in subdued tones, but their rage was unmaskable.

"Look at this," my mother said, gesturing to the scene inside. "Do you really think this is an environment for children?"

When Mum insisted that we were leaving, I walked a few steps toward her. My dad told me to come back, and I froze. Stephen, who had followed me to the door, shuffled forward into Mum's embrace. But I stood between my parents, paralyzed by the impossible choice.

My mother's voice grew sterner as she told me to get into her nearby car, its engine running. I did as I was told. And before I had fully processed what was happening, we were driving away.

I turned to look out the back window—a scene I later saw reprised in Hollywood movies—and in the doorway I saw my dad, deflated, watching our car depart. He grew smaller and smaller until we turned the corner and he vanished from sight.

That night, we drove from Dublin to Mum's hometown of Cork, where we stayed with her sister, Anne. Over the next few days, my father and a friend from Hartigan's, a member of the Irish parliament, began calling my mother, threatening to secure an injunction to prevent us from leaving the country. As their warnings grew more convincing, Mum began to worry that another legal battle would delay our return to the United States, where she was expected the following week to resume work. In a panic, she asked my uncle Gary, her brother-in-law and the high-spirited family fixer, to drive us to Shannon Airport.

The nighttime drive was harrowing. Uncle Gary ran red lights and drove so far over the speed limit that I felt we were in a car chase. Mum's constant checking of the passenger-side mirror was a telling sign that the grown-ups were worried. Only now—forty years later—do I realize the meaning of that frenzied drive: although she was in the right, my mother must have had no faith that the Irish courts would see the situation similarly. If my dad had appeared before a judge sober while we were still in the country, she could have lost us.

When we arrived at the airport, as the clock ticked slowly toward the hour of our departure, Uncle Gary bought Stephen and me heaping Irish breakfasts. But my mother neither ate nor took a proper breath until our flight was in the air.

Once we were back in our suburban Pittsburgh home, Mum telephoned Dad to tell him that he couldn't be trusted to put our welfare first. Not only was he drinking too much, she said, but he had effectively threatened to kidnap us. She couldn't take time away from work to chaperone our time together, she informed him, so if he wanted to see us, he would need to fly to America.

DURING THE YEARS THAT FOLLOWED, I threw myself into my new American life and began to thrive in school. My baseball skills improved, and I started learning the basics of basketball. No longer the awkward new girl with the Dublin accent and the pleated skirts, I developed a fresh set of friends. Their families brought me to barbecues in the summer and skiing and ice-skating in the winter. Although Mum was working long hours as a doctor, she would get home most summer nights in time to grill us corn on the cob as Pirates games played on the radio. Gradually, as she was able to take vacations, she and Eddie took us white-water rafting and to American historical sites like Gettysburg.

Although she said my dad had forfeited the custody agreement, my mother fulfilled the rest of its terms by taking me to Mass and continuing to teach me Irish. Nothing was worse than being summoned on a sunny day to improve my Gaelic. "Mum," I would declare, "this makes no sense. Even if I lived in Ireland, I wouldn't speak this language. And in America it is even more useless." This logic did not move her. She forced me to review flash cards and write out sentences as if I would soon be back at Mount Anville, taking an exam.

Although my dad and I exchanged letters, and I sent him my unimpressive color-by-numbers artwork, he did not visit. When Susan nudged him, he had a ready response: "I just need to get sorted." But he was never able to admit he needed help to overcome his drinking, and he never did get sorted.

I have no conscious memories of pining for my father, but even as I lapped up the American experience, a large part of me was waiting. I was waiting for word that he would visit, waiting for him to telephone (which he did, but rarely, as he kept misplacing our number), and waiting for him to once again be my companion. Mum never spoke ill of him, instead describing his "brilliance" and athletic gifts; but she made clear that he was an alcoholic, a verdict I accepted. Slotting my dad in this category was tidy. The designation allowed me to blame the separation on something other than my father. And yet, because I couldn't comprehend the true nature of addiction, I thought that if my dad simply tried harder, he could recover.

I believed that the magnetic bond between us would motivate him to get his act together—that *I* would motivate him. But as I waited, I did not feel anger at him for staying away. Instead, I began to mentally replay the Christmas Eve scene on the steps of our Dublin home. My dad hadn't been the one to leave me, I reasoned. He had been willing to break the law to be with me. I was the one who had left. I had made a choice that night when I heeded my mother's call.

Even as a feeling of regret and shame began to gnaw at me, I felt sure I would have the chance to set things right between us. So many Irish alcoholics lived well into old age that I never associated drinking with poor health. While four years had soon passed and my father still hadn't come to visit, I was still positive that we would be reunited. My dad would make sure of it.

IN 1983, MUM AND EDDIE moved us from Pittsburgh to Atlanta, Georgia. After my mother was recertified as a nephrologist, they joined the faculty of Emory University School of Medicine. We packed up and made the move south, arriving at our new home a few days before I began eighth grade—which then marked the beginning of high school.

One afternoon, more than a year after our move, I lay sprawled out on the gray carpeted floor of my bedroom, doing my history homework. My walls were plastered in pictures of my idols—everyone from Mike Easler of the Pittsburgh Pirates to Jack Wagner, the hunky actor who played Frisco on the soap opera *General Hospital*. From the sound of footsteps in their bedroom, I realized that both Mum and Eddie had arrived home earlier than usual. Behind closed doors, Mum talked quietly on the phone and had hushed conversations with Eddie. Just the family was present—Eddie, Mum, Steve, and me—but the house seemed crowded with tension. I sensed that something bad had happened.

Finally, Mum knocked on my bedroom door and sat down beside me on the floor. Her voice tight, her eyes red, she said, "I have bad news." I couldn't conceive of what might be coming, but I didn't have to wait long. "Your father has died."

I did not react. I looked at her blankly, refusing, with my entire being, to process what she had said.

"The funeral is Monday," she continued. "I don't think you should go."

I asked her how my father could have died—so suddenly, so inexplicably—at only forty-seven.

"The drink," she said.

"But I didn't know," I said slowly.

"None of us knew the extent of it," she said.

In recent years, my dad had apparently dramatically increased the amount of alcohol he was consuming, arriving at Hartigan's as soon as it opened in the morning. By the end, he had amassed such large drinking debts that the owners had finally refused to serve him. The alcohol had so ravaged his body that he had stopped eating. He and Susan had broken up, but my mother told me that Susan had been the one to find his body.

I needed to be alone. Mum walked out, closing the door behind her. As she entered the adjoining room to tell my brother, I sat by myself, numb with shock, unable even to cry. I crawled into bed and prayed that what she had just told me was not true. If it was true, I told God, I needed to see my father again in heaven, where they would surely have pubs.

Now, in addition to mentally replaying the last time I had seen my dad, I was pierced with a new realization: for five years I had been waiting for him, but he had also been waiting for me. "He wanted me to come," I thought. "And I never came."

I could not understand why an inquisitive fourteen-year-old girl like me had not asked enough questions to learn that her father's health was slipping. Why had I stupidly assumed the grown-ups would do what was best? Why hadn't I insisted on flying over to see him? Why hadn't I shown him that, despite the fact that I had gotten in the car with my mother that Christmas Eve, I was still his girl? Why hadn't I found a way to help him? I seemed to have been thoroughly passive as my dad wasted away, by himself, across the wide Atlantic.

I buried myself under the covers—the duvet quilt from my old bedroom in Dublin—and shivered with a feeling of cold so deep that it felt as though my bones were being chilled from the inside.

I later learned that Susan had gone looking for my dad after she hadn't heard from him in more than a month. When she opened his unlocked front door, she was overcome by the smell of what would turn out to be my dad's decomposing body amid the stench of vomit and human waste. The derelict, filthy house—my former home—retained only the beds upstairs and the piano in the living room. The rest of the family belongings had been stolen or pawned off—even the kitchen cutlery and our toys.

Susan bravely made her way upstairs and found my deceased father, dressed in a suit as if ready to head out on the town.

He was lying not in his bed, but in mine.

I DID NOT TRAVEL back to Ireland for my father's funeral in December of 1984. Mum was concerned that his friends and family would blame her—and me—for the downward spiral that ended in his death. She went alone, thinking that if I didn't attend, I would be spared. This was a reasonable assumption: my dad's younger sister did, in fact, verbally attack my mother just after the memorial service, screaming, "This is your fault!"

But by returning to school the day after I learned that my dad had died, I did not honor the pain that was tearing at me. By not flying back to Ireland, I took on another cause for regret. "You're really not going to your father's funeral?" one of my high school classmates asked me. Standing in front of my locker, holding a geometry textbook and a spiral notebook, I realized the mistake, but my mother had already departed.

My teenage brain had quickly established a clear, causal sequence. Nothing that a grieving family member yelled at me could have been worse than what I already believed. When I left Ireland, I left my dad; I didn't visit my dad; and *thus*, he died. Had I not left, or had I at least returned to Dublin regularly, he would still be alive.

In my chain of logic—or responsibility—my mother didn't really make an appearance. To this day, despite various therapists' insistence that I must be repressing anger toward her, I don't fault Mum for what happened. I have read widely on how children are quicker to blame themselves than to acknowledge their parents' flaws and bad decisions. But for as long as I can remember reflecting on Mum's actions, I have felt that several things were true at once. Yes, she should have actively sought out information about Dad's health, and she should have brought my brother and me back to Ireland to see our father. But at the same time, she made her decisions with our well-being in mind. It wasn't until I had my own family that I began to appreciate how *young* Stephen and I actually were when we had loitered in Hartigan's, and how dangerous that environment would have seemed to my mother.

Mum knew our father—his virtues and his vices—as only one who had loved him deeply could. It had taken her years to reach the point where she was able to disentangle herself from him and their marriage. She knew that children can almost never give up on their parents, and she did not want Stephen's and my image of Jim Power—large and luminous—to be replaced by something diminished. Years later, Susan would tell me about my dad's emaciated condition in the final two years before he died. "Jim was no longer staring at the abyss," she recalled. "He was in the abyss."

Carrying around the grief from my father's death made me more appreciative of the fact that Mum was healthy. I may have suffered a terrible loss in a terrible way, but I gave thanks to God for my good fortune—even though I now feared losing her too, I still had a mother I adored.

During the summer following my dad's death, I traveled back to Ireland for the first time since that Christmas of 1979. I visited my paternal grandfather, "Bam Bam," who was living with my aunt. Bam Bam had just turned ninety, but was still mentally and physically agile, driving a car and following sports and politics.

Not wanting to upset him, I rarely raised the subject of my dad's absence from our lives. But over the years that followed, without any conscious decision on my part, I built the relationship with him I had wanted with my father. I would faithfully visit him for several weeks each summer; we would watch Irish football together and hurl complaints at the TV. And because he gave me the gift of living until the age of 101, I would share the ups and downs of my life with him in an exchange of letters that lasted for eleven years.

On the same visit that I laid this new foundation with my granddad, however, I got a jolt from my seventeen-year-old cousin, who had revered my father. She described how lonely he had been the last few times he had come to visit her mother. "You and Stephen were all he talked about," she said. "The doctors won't ever say it, but he died of a broken heart."

It never dawned on me at fourteen to ask my cousin why, if my dad missed my brother and me so much, he had so rarely called, or why he had never gotten on a plane to visit.

He meant to. I was certain of it.

4

DIGNITY

I started at Lakeside High School in Atlanta, Georgia, in 1983, about a year before my father died. Once again, I was showing up at a new school in a new city where people spoke differently than I did—this time with Southern drawls. When Mum dropped me off, however, I quickly realized that I wasn't the only new kid arriving that day.

Reporters hovered in the vicinity, waiting to see whether angry white parents would try to impede the arrival of hundreds of new African-American students. As I approached the main entrance, these students—who ranged in age from twelve to seventeen—were filing off a long row of school buses.

Some walked into the school seemingly determined to ignore the uproar that their arrival at Lakeside was causing. A few wore headphones and swayed to music as they disembarked, perhaps shielding themselves from the commotion. Others, less bold or armored, looked like they wished they could retreat back onto the buses.

When Mum and Eddie had moved to Atlanta, they had chosen our suburban neighborhood based on the reputed quality of this two-story public high school, known to be one of Georgia's best in both academics and athletics. They hadn't realized, however, that Lakeside was caught up in a long-running fight between black and white Atlantans about the area's public education system. Just as we made Georgia our home, this conflict erupted into a racially charged firestorm.

While the Supreme Court's 1954 ruling in *Brown v. Board of Edu-*

cation had found racial segregation in public schools unconstitutional, the DeKalb County School System, like many school districts in the South, had remained largely segregated in practice. After a 1972 lawsuit challenging the district's practices, DeKalb launched what it called the "majority-to-minority" (M-to-M) transfer program. The program allowed African Americans who were a racial majority in their local schools to transfer to schools outside of their neighborhoods, where they would be in the minority. Because DeKalb school officials had initially done little to encourage black students to participate in the program, there were few takers, and the student body of Lakeside remained more than 80 percent white.

Not long before we moved to Georgia, however, the district court ordered DeKalb schools to begin providing free busing across the county. This transportation made participating in M-to-M more viable, and hundreds of African-American students applied to transfer out of lower-performing schools. Black parents sought out Lakeside for the same reason my mother had: they wanted their children to have the opportunity to thrive in a school with a stellar reputation.

In 1983, when more than three hundred African-American families signed up to send their children to Lakeside, the school district turned most of them down. The district's rationale—backed by vocal, impassioned white parents—was that Lakeside needed to maintain its student/teacher ratio of 26 to 1. To our newly arrived family, however, it seemed clear that the opponents wanted to prevent Lakeside from being more racially integrated.

Several hundred white parents mobilized to create a group they called Parents Demand Quality, which supported the district's decision to turn away a substantial number of the African-American transfers to Lakeside. In turn, their parents filed a motion with the district court, claiming that blocking their children from transferring was "based on race, not space." The DeKalb NAACP raised the case with the Justice Department's Civil Rights Division, which agreed to investigate. In the end, the African-American parents won their appeal; my class, Lakeside High School's class of 1988, became the first in the school's history in which black students outnumbered whites.

While Lakeside offered my African-American classmates more experienced teachers and better-maintained facilities, getting to know the students in the M-to-M program offered a lesson in the denial and assertion of dignity. I had heard priests talk about dignity at Mass: the Catechism insisted that the "dignity of the human person is rooted in his or her creation in the image and likeness of God." And my years in Ireland, complemented by Eddie's history lessons, had taught me plenty about British occupiers' attempts to trample Irish dignity.

While the M-to-M program gave my black classmates great opportunities, it also placed heavy burdens on their dignity. By the time I arrived at school in the morning, rolling out of bed around 7:30 a.m. and taking a quick ten-minute walk to school, most of my black peers had been up for several hours—first waiting for a neighborhood bus that would take them to a transit hub, then catching a second bus that brought them to Lakeside. I played on the school basketball team and ran cross-country and track. Due to afternoon practice, I started on homework "late"—after six p.m., when I would arrive home. The African-American students on my teams, however, had to wait around for an "activity bus" that did not even leave Lakeside until seven p.m., ensuring that they were rarely home and able to start studying before nine p.m. Crazily, students who sought out extra help from a teacher or stayed after school to use the library weren't even permitted to ride the activity bus and had to find their own way home, which meant navigating a complex Atlanta public transportation system that would have daunted most teenagers.

To this day, when I hear people judge students on the basis of their test scores, I think of my sleep-deprived African-American classmates as we geared up to take English or math tests together. We may have been equal before God, but I had three more hours of sleep, vastly more time to prepare, and many more resources at my disposal than those who were part of the busing program.

During the eighth grade, when the dramatic shift in Lakeside's demographics occurred, I occasionally heard my white classmates complain about "grease" they claimed to have found on their desks—a dig at African-American students who wore Jheri curls. A friend of mine

overheard a group of teachers crudely joking that the English department should begin teaching Ebonics, "so that we can properly communicate in *their* language."

As the school's black population expanded, the court ordered more
black teachers to be hired, a decision that prompted a number of white
parents to complain that they did not want their kids taught by African
Americans. Others went so far as to pull their children out of Lakeside
entirely, transferring them to the private, largely white Catholic schools
in the area. Some members of the faculty embraced the changes; those
entrenched in their views did not budge. One defiant white teacher,
who had been open about her opposition to the large number of
African-American transfers, was overheard in the faculty lounge saying that it was impossible to get through to her black students. "They
say prejudice is learned," she griped to her colleagues. "Well, trying to
teach blacks here, I have certainly learned it."

Mum and Eddie saw similar bigotry at Emory University, where
they had taken up their jobs as nephrologists. When Eddie attempted
to recruit a talented Haitian-American doctor who had graduated from
Harvard Medical School, one of his colleagues expressed his opposition, telling Eddie, "Down here, they park cars." At the kidney dialysis
unit, the same senior physician replaced a photograph of Martin Luther King, Jr., with that of a Ku Klux Klan leader. My brother became
friends with an African-American boy named Dorian who often came
over to our home after school. On one occasion, a neighbor called my
mother at work to warn her that she had seen a "darky" at our house.
Both Mum and Eddie made clear to Stephen and me how horrified
they were by the prejudice they encountered, and they encouraged us
to speak up when we heard such racist barbs.

I did not discuss with my black friends the more entrenched symbols of racism around us. Some Lakeside students thought nothing of
affixing Confederate flag bumper stickers to their cars. School field
trips made their way to Stone Mountain, Georgia's 1,600-foot-tall
granite behemoth, into which the Confederate leaders Jefferson Davis,
Robert E. Lee, and Stonewall Jackson had been carved. Only decades
later did I learn that the monument had been commissioned by seg-

regationists and was the scene of numerous Klan gatherings over the years. Georgia's history of lynching and violent racism was routinely ignored or minimized in our school history lessons.

For all of high school, I sat next to Preston Price in homeroom. Preston, who became a good friend, was black and gay, a rough combination in a staunchly conservative school in a white, suburban, evangelical neighborhood. By our junior year, my best friend, Sally Brooks, and another dear friend, Nathan Taylor, had also come out, meaning that three of my closest high school friends were gay. From today's more progressive vantage point, it is hard to convey just how unusual these revelations seemed at the time—and how brave my friends were. I saw how each of them agonized as they tried to figure out how to tell their family members and classmates; and I saw the excitement and heartbreak of their crushes and romantic foibles as they lived them, just as they witnessed and coached me through my own.

These early exposures didn't dim my wonderment at the United States, but they opened my eyes to my new country's struggle to manage difference.

WHATEVER THE CLASHES OF IDENTITY going on around me, I generally did what my life had taught me to do up to that point: I rolled with events and did my best to adapt. I was a conscientious student, doing homework on time and performing reasonably well on tests. I knew that getting into a top-tier university would require high standardized test scores, so I threw myself into expanding my vocabulary, preparing flash cards with unfamiliar "SAT words," and eventually getting a score high enough to give me a chance in selective admissions processes. Although I later developed into a strong student, my drive was then more evident when playing sports. Lakeside was an athletic powerhouse, sending prospects to Division I college teams and occasionally even to the pros. As the starting shooting guard on the basketball team, I spent entire afternoons and weekends shooting thousands of baskets.

I juggled my immersion in school and sports with part-time jobs, starting at the fast-food chain Del Taco, followed by stints at Sizzler and Frëshens yogurt. Lakeside also had an avid party scene. A few basketball teammates introduced me to 7-Eleven Big Gulps of Fanta soda spiked with vodka, which I consumed with enthusiasm, although I let nothing jeopardize my game-time performance.

Luckily, my high school antics never got me into any lasting trouble. Mum, however, incessantly reminded Stephen and me that alcoholism was "in our genes." And although I never came close to developing a drinking problem, my dad's excessive consumption had so warped my frame of reference that I viewed myself as a teetotaler by comparison.

What it meant to be an alcoholic was also no longer solely defined by my father's destructive habit. Eddie, too, was afflicted with the "good man's curse." Back in Pittsburgh, my mother had tried to rationalize his drinking as being very different from my father's. "He just has pathetically low tolerance," she would say. While my dad had drunk far larger quantities, Eddie's inebriation was more demonstrative. He loudly recited Irish poetry and sometimes passed out after just a couple glasses of wine ("Oh no," my mother would mutter, "the head is going down!"). The worst smell of my childhood—which to this day I associate with the pungency of my disappointment at his relapses— was Eddie's breath on nights when he tried to cover up the odor of spirits with Listerine.

My dad never really admitted he had a problem, but Eddie recognized his. He made repeated efforts to stop drinking. For years, he climbed on and off the proverbial wagon. After my dad's death, and because of Eddie's challenges in staying sober during those years, I became hawkishly vigilant for signs that "the drink" might be acquiring power over me too.

Although Stephen had spent only five years in Dublin, he had inherited many of our dad's traits and habits. He was growing up to be strikingly handsome, with ocean-blue eyes, dark hair, a lanky, athletic build, and a wide—and selective—smile that melted hearts. In 1988, after I graduated from high school, Mum and Eddie moved with my brother to Brooklyn, where they had found new jobs. There, Stephen would occasionally get stopped on the street and asked whether he had considered modeling.

Although Stephen did not start drinking or using drugs until after

I left for college, he began to withdraw from Mum and me while I was still at Lakeside. If I was a joiner, like my mother, embracing new challenges and people, Stephen had just two great passions: dogs, which he said were more reliable than people, and fishing, which he did for hours by himself. He had long ago declared to me, "I'm not like you," and, despite his probing mind, never studied much in school. Despite this, he cheered me at my basketball games and never seemed to resent Mum's and Eddie's celebration of my academic successes.

After basketball practice one day during my senior year, I arrived home to find Stephen, then thirteen, beaming at our dining room table. He had laid out the half dozen response letters from the colleges to which I had applied. I could see in an instant that the letters from Stanford and Princeton were thin, but I was focused on the much thicker, ivory envelope with the navy "Y" and a New Haven return address. I had unexpectedly gotten into Yale University, a dream destination. "Congrats, sis!" Stephen said, grinning, as I jumped up and down and stole a rare, if awkward, hug.

Despite coming at a heavy cost, Mum's decision to move to America had opened up a whole new world for me. I knew that attending Yale would do the same. But almost as soon as I ripped open the envelope and confirmed my acceptance, I began to imagine all that could go wrong. While I could adapt to any new environment, I did so with the latent conviction that nothing great could last.

5

TANK MAN

During the summer of 1989, I came home to Atlanta after my freshman year at Yale to intern in our local CBS affiliate's sports department. After covering women's basketball and volleyball for the college newspaper, I had decided to pursue a career as a sports journalist.

My print dispatches demonstrated little natural talent. My first published article in the *Yale Daily News*, appearing in September of 1988, had begun: "Volleyballs aren't the only things high up in the air this week for the women's volleyball team; so are expectations and spirits." Another article had described how the campus a cappella group Something Extra had sung the national anthem before that weekend's Yale–Cornell women's basketball game. I then proceeded to observe that "the Blue were well aware that it would take 'something extra,' or rather, 'something extra-ordinary' for them to win."

Broadcast journalism, I thought, might be a better fit. In the coming years I offered play-by-play and color commentary for the Yale men's and women's basketball teams and joined a rotating group of students on a nightly radio talk show called *Sports Spotlight*.

On June 3rd, I had been instructed by my supervisor at the Atlanta station, WAGA, to "shot-sheet"—or take notes on—a Braves baseball game against the San Francisco Giants. I had to mark down on my clipboard the precise time at which memorable events occurred—a home run, an error, an on-field brawl, a funny dance in the stands—in order to help assemble the sports highlights for the evening news. As

I sat inside a glass booth, I was surrounded by other screens showing CBS video feeds from around the world.

On the feed from Beijing, where it was already the early morning of June 4th, I saw a startling scene playing out. Students in Tiananmen Square had been demonstrating for more than a month, urging the ruling Chinese Communist Party to make democratic reforms. The protesters had used Styrofoam and plaster to build a thirty-foot-high statue called the Goddess of Democracy, which bore a close resemblance to the Statue of Liberty. They had lined her up directly opposite the portrait of Mao Tse-tung, making it look as though she was staring down the founder of the repressive Chinese state. But the day I happened to be working in the video booth, the Chinese government was cracking down. I watched as the CBS camera crew on the ground filmed soldiers with assault rifles ripping apart the students' sanctuaries. As tanks rolled toward Chinese protesters, young people used their bicycles to try to flee the scene and transport the wounded.

In the raw, unfiltered footage playing in front of me—much of which would not be broadcast—I could hear the CBS cameraperson arguing with the authorities as he was jostled. At a certain point, the monitor went black; the feed from China had been terminated. I sat in the booth, aghast at what I had seen. I found myself wondering what the US government would do in response, a question that had never before occurred to me.

That week, the front pages of all the major American newspapers printed a photograph of a man in Beijing who became known as "Tank Man." The man wore a white shirt and dark pants, and carried a pair of plastic shopping bags. He was pictured standing in the middle of a ten-lane Chinese boulevard, stoically confronting the first tank in a column of dozens.

The stark image arrested my attention. *That*, I thought, was an assertion of dignity. The man was refusing to bow before the gargantuan power of the Chinese military. His quiet but powerful resistance reminded me of the images of the sanitation workers in Memphis whose strike Martin Luther King, Jr., had joined shortly before he

was assassinated in 1968. They had carried signs that simply read
"I AM A MAN."

Although Tank Man's subsequent actions received less attention,
video footage showed him taking an even more remarkable risk: he
climbed onto the tank's turret and spoke with the soldiers inside. After
he stepped down and the tank attempted to move past him, the man
moved with it, daring the soldiers to run him over. A few minutes
into this grim dance, men in civilian clothes dashed onto the road and
hustled Tank Man away. The convoy barreled ahead; the man disappeared. He has never been identified. An untold number of Chinese
students—likely thousands—were killed that summer in the government crackdown.

I did not respond to these events by suddenly proclaiming a new-
found intention to learn Mandarin and become a human rights lawyer.
But while I knew little about the protests before they started, or even
about China itself, I could not shake my discomfort at having been
contentedly taking notes on a Braves game while students my age were
being mowed down by tanks.

For the first time, I reacted as though current events had something
to do with me. I felt, in a way that I couldn't have explained in the
moment, that I had a stake in what happened to the lone man with his
shopping bags.

Where did this reaction come from? Was it just the natural awakening of a political conscience—an inevitable progression after spending a year on a socially aware college campus? Maybe, but never before
had I considered involving myself in the causes that consumed some of
my classmates. If my political views were developing by osmosis, I had
not been aware of the transformation.

My best friend from college, Miro Weinberger, happened to be
visiting me in Atlanta that week. Since Mum and Eddie had moved
to New York the previous fall and our Atlanta house was up for sale,
I had rented a room in a shared apartment. Drinking beers on the
stoop, I told my friend about the footage from China. Miro—who
today is in his third term as mayor of Burlington, Vermont—was the

son of anti–Vietnam War activists. Miro and I had bonded over our shared love of baseball, but unlike me, he had always been equally interested in the world around him. "What am I doing with my life?" I asked. When Miro looked puzzled, I explained, "It just feels like I should be doing something more useful than thinking about sports all the time."

When I returned to Yale that fall, I became a history major, throwing myself into schoolwork and studying with far greater intensity than during my freshman year.

TWO MONTHS AFTER I RETURNED to campus, the Berlin Wall came down, ushering in the collapse of communist regimes across Eastern Europe. I had subscribed to *USA Today*, practicing what I called the "clip and shake" method—clipping the red sports section and shaking the rest of the paper into the recycling bin. Now I switched my subscription to the *New York Times*, eager to understand the monumental developments abroad.

The names, places, and events described in the *Times* were so obscure to me that I underlined key facts and figures, quizzing myself after I finished an article. With the fall of the Iron Curtain, commentators were reappraising the United Nations and wondering whether the dream of international cooperation might finally be realized. I took the train from New Haven to Manhattan for a guided group tour of UN Headquarters. I liked the concept: a single place where all the countries of the world sent representatives to try to resolve their differences without fighting.

Back at Yale, I still played sports more than I did anything else. After getting cut by the varsity basketball team, I tried my hand at every intramural sport known to humankind (from water polo and soccer to Ultimate Frisbee and touch football). Perhaps inspired by all the hours I had watched my mother play, I also picked up squash, eventually making the varsity squad. While other students received awards in a year-end ceremony, for being "Most Social" or "Most Likely to Succeed," I was such a fierce competitor that my residential college classmates created a new category for me: "Most Likely to Come Back from the Intramural Fields with Bloody Knees."

Nevertheless, reading the international news and taking political science and history classes had significantly broadened my interests by the time I finished my second year. Combining a gift from Mum and Eddie with money I had saved working in various restaurants, I was able to fund a summer-long trip to Europe.

John Schumann, whom I had started dating at the end of my freshman year, would be my traveling partner. Known as Schu, he had a mop of dark brown curly hair and an open and warm manner that made him a beloved figure on campus. A class above me, Schu had gone to high school in Cleveland and shared my preoccupation with sports. But unlike me, he was also a voracious reader of history, making him a ringer in Trivial Pursuit and a fascinating companion. We became so close that our identities seemed to merge into a single entity that our friends referred to as "Sam and Schu."

The centerpiece of our trip would be newly democratic Eastern Europe, where mass protests and political transitions were capturing daily headlines in the United States. We loved the thought of exploring a part of the world that had not yet been overrun by Western tourists and where history was being made every day.

Before we departed, the always well-read Eddie thrust an article from a little-known publication called *The National Interest* into my hands. Authored by Francis Fukuyama, and titled "The End of History?," the article argued that with fascism and communism soon destined to land in the dustbin of history, economic and political liberalism had won the ideological battle of the twentieth century. "The West," Fukuyama concluded, had triumphed.

Although I vaguely recall my Irish hackles being raised by his tone toward small countries,* Fukuyama's core claim that liberal democracy

---

* Rereading the article again recently, I think the language that put me off was: "For our purposes, it matters very little what strange thoughts occur to people in Albania or Burkina Faso."

had proven the better model seemed convincing. The foreign policy commentators I had begun reading gave little hint that issues of tribe, class, religion, and race would storm back with a vengeance—starting in the Balkans, but decades later spreading to the heart of liberal democracies that had seemed largely immune.

In June of 1990, Schu and I set out to see firsthand the region where the demand for democratic accountability had helped bring an end to communist rule. But before venturing east, we traveled to Amsterdam, where we visited the Anne Frank House. I had read about the Holocaust in high school, but it was during my travels that summer that the horror of Hitler's crimes hit me deeply. Just as observing Tank Man—a single protester—had helped me see the broader Chinese struggle for human rights, so too did visiting Anne Frank's hiding place bring to life the enormity of the Nazi slaughter. I learned a lesson that stayed with me: concrete, lived experiences engraved themselves in my psyche far more than abstract historical events.

When I had read Anne Frank's story the first time, I did not focus on the fact that she and her family had been deported on the *last* train from Holland to Auschwitz. Nor had I been aware of the stinginess of America's refugee quotas, which prevented Anne's father from getting the Frank family into the United States. Struck by these details in Amsterdam, I began keeping a list of the books I would read upon our return to the United States—specifically, books that focused on the question of what US officials knew about the Holocaust and what they could have done to save more Jews.

Next, Schu and I traveled to Germany, visiting the Dachau concentration camp, where Nazis had killed more than 28,000 Jews and political prisoners. The air around us felt heavy, as though the evil that had made mass murder possible still lurked nearby. Seeing the barracks, the crammed sleeping quarters, and the crematorium reduced us to silence for the first time in our relationship.

Although the museum exhibit at the camp made for an extremely bleak day of sightseeing, we lingered in the section that told the story of Dachau's liberation by American troops in April of 1945. For all our criticisms of what the United States may have failed to do for European Jews, Schu and I wondered aloud how the modern world would look if President Roosevelt had not finally entered the war.

When we took the train to what was then Czechoslovakia, we happened to arrive just a few days before the country held its first free election. A college classmate connected us to a middle-aged woman named Tatjana who had joined the dissident movement in 1968, after Soviet-led forces crushed the Prague Spring. Tatjana invited us for tea and showed us the trove of opposition leaflets that she had circulated as a member of the underground. Then she brought us to accompany her to the neighborhood polling station. We watched as she asked her young daughter to place her first democratic ballot in the box. Tatjana choked up as she talked about the exhilaration she felt regarding her country's political future. Again, I was struck by the importance of dignity as a historical force. "What was horrible about the communist rule," Tatjana told us, "was that the man in front of you ordering you around was very stupid, and you had to listen to him." Even amid jailings and torture, these smaller humiliations ground people down.

Schu and I then traveled north to Poland, which had experienced its first free election on the same day in June of 1989 as the Chinese crackdown in Tiananmen Square—a coincidence that would cause the landmark Polish vote to go almost unnoticed in the American media (a cold competition among world events that I would learn more about later on). Our most inspiring visit of the summer was to the Gdańsk Shipyard, where, in 1980, Lech Wałęsa had organized workers in a strike that would launch the Solidarity trade union. Solidarity turned into an opposition movement that eventually counted nearly a third of the country's 35 million people among its members.

Yugoslavia, a country in southeastern Europe bordering the Adriatic Sea, was the one place that Schu and I did not warm to that summer. While we had been blessed to form new friendships in the other countries we visited, in Yugoslavia we struggled to make connections. The trains and buses were crowded and hot, and the Cyrillic alphabets in Serbia and Macedonia made finding our way more difficult. "It just seems there isn't much laughter here," I wrote in my journal.

Before we visited, Schu and I had thought of Yugoslavia as a single entity. But in Croatia, one of its six republics, the people we met expressed little allegiance to the confederation. Given that the country's dictator, Josip Broz Tito, had died a decade before and that communism had now collapsed, it was not clear what or who would unite the country's diverse inhabitants. "I wonder if the state will have a reason to exist," I wrote to myself at the time. While fissures were evident even to an ill-informed tourist like me, I could never have imagined that the beach resorts where Schu and I swam would soon be subjected to intense bombardment by the Serb-led remnants of the Yugoslav Army. Indeed, the fall of the Iron Curtain had left us with the impression that the world was on its way to becoming more democratic, humane, and peaceful.

THE TRIP SCHU AND I TOOK to Europe cemented our relationship. But the closer we became, the more I worried about him. In the eight years since my father's death, I had been trailed by a morbid fear that my loved ones would suddenly die. If Schu was even an hour late returning to our dorm, I was often in a full state of panic by the time he arrived.

I also began to suffer bouts of what Schu called "lungers." Whether on campus or on our travels, every few weeks I would find myself struggling to breathe properly. I could identify nothing tangibly wrong, and I never rasped for breath or experienced asthma-like physical symptoms. I just felt, moment to moment, as though my lungs had constricted and I simply could not take in enough air.

Because I never experienced lungers when I was in a tense situation—playing for the team collegiate national championship in squash, or taking final exams, for instance—I dismissed Schu's gentle suggestion that my breathing problems might be related to anxiety. After a few days during which I could think about little else, the feeling would usually pass. Instead of seeking professional counsel and delving more deeply into the roots of this occasional phenomenon, I began pushing away the person closest to me.

The summer after my junior year, I lived with Schu in Washington, DC, taking up an internship with the National Security Archive, a listing I came across at Yale's career services office. As I read about the Archive, I momentarily thought it was a quasi-governmental outfit given that it shared an acronym with the National Security Agency. But far from being a cloak-and-dagger intelligence enterprise, the National Security Archive was, in fact, a progressive nongovernmental organization (NGO) whose scholars and activists spent their days submitting Freedom of Information Act requests to secure the declassification of US government records. They then used the previously classified information they unearthed to better understand US involvement in events like the 1973 coup against Salvador Allende in Chile.

The Archive's senior researchers were skeptical about US conduct abroad and determined to hold American officials accountable by exposing their deliberations. I found it fascinating to wade through piles of declassified transcripts of government meetings and telephone calls and to study decision memos and talking points that US officials had relied on to carry out their business. Much of what I read was intensely bureaucratic. But I recognized that these sterile pages were the vehicles by which American policymakers made decisions that, in some cases, impacted the lives of millions of people.

As I grew more interested in US foreign policy, Schu was beginning to consider a career in medicine. Having been a history major at Yale, he returned after he graduated to his hometown of Cleveland to take the preparatory science classes he needed to apply to medical school. After three years together, we decided to go our separate ways, though at the time I felt sure that we would find our way back to each other.

As I looked ahead, I envied the clarity of Schu's professional plan. He would have to break his back taking vexing science classes, but he knew the steps required to one day be able to treat patients. I was interested in trying to find a career that would allow me to work on issues related to US foreign policy. Although I would not have dared express my hopes aloud, I wanted to end up in a position to "do something" when people rose up against their repressive governments—or when children like Anne Frank found themselves dependent on the actions of strangers.

But I did not see a clear path ahead.

6

DOERS

Mort Abramowitz and Fred Cuny were in some respects an unlikely pair. When I met him in December of 1992, Mort was a fifty-
nine-year-old retired diplomat who had spent more than three decades
abiding by the strictures of the US government in roles that included
ambassador to Thailand, ambassador to Turkey, and Assistant Secretary of State for Intelligence and Research. The son of Lithuanian
immigrants, he had grown up in New Jersey and held degrees from
Stanford and Harvard. Mort lived in his mind and sometimes lost
sight of practical details, arriving in the office wearing mismatched
shoes or a woman's coat he had mistaken for his own after a breakfast
meeting.

Fred was a six-foot-three, forty-eight-year-old Texan who had been
kicked out of Texas A&M and, as a young man, had listed sailing a
Chinese junk ship across the Pacific as one of his life goals. Eventually trained as an engineer, Fred had become renowned as the Master
of Disaster for his relief work in more than thirty crisis zones. Wearing his trademark cowboy boots, Fred had responded to famine in
Ethiopia, an earthquake in Armenia, and war in places like Biafra, Sri
Lanka, Guatemala, and Somalia.[1]

Mort was the ambassador to Turkey when he and Fred had first
worked together in an effort to aid Iraqi Kurds who had been attacked
by Saddam Hussein and were huddling as refugees on the Iraq-Turkey

border.* Fred's methods were unorthodox—Mort recalled fielding calls from US military commanders in the area asking "Do you know what that goddamned Fred Cuny is doing?"—but the US-led operation helped save some 400,000 people. From then on, Mort provided Fred with credibility among Washington decision-makers, while Fred inspired Mort with his resourcefulness and daring.

I had the good fortune to get to know both men when, as a recent college graduate, I took up an internship at the Carnegie Endowment for International Peace, a Washington policy institute. I had heard about Carnegie from a friend at Yale, and I had applied because several of the interns served as editorial assistants with *Foreign Policy*, the Carnegie Endowment's quarterly journal. This seemed the perfect way to combine my experience in a different kind of journalism (sports) with my burgeoning interest in foreign policy. I could not think of a more perfect first job out of college.

I had pulled my grades up at Yale and written a senior essay on foreign policy that the history department gave an award. I wrote essays for the application and was invited for an interview with one of Carnegie's senior associates. A few weeks later, I was told I was one of ten graduating seniors who had been admitted to the program, and I had been assigned to *Foreign Policy*. I was thrilled.

Unfortunately, shortly thereafter, the head of the program called to tell me that the president of the Carnegie Endowment, Mort Abramowitz, had reassigned me to his office. Imagining an administrative internship from which I would learn little, I pleaded with the program head to revert to the original plan. She was firm. "Samantha," she said in a thick Southern accent, "you can't turn down the

---

* In 1991, as the US Ambassador to Turkey, Mort had been influential in convincing President George H. W. Bush to use the US military to enforce a no-fly zone protecting displaced Kurds in Northern Iraq from Saddam Hussein's attacks. In the wake of the Cold War, the United States and Russia raised hopes that they would be able to work together on ambitious new initiatives, voting together on a unanimous UN Security Council to authorize the mission.

president." What felt like an unlucky turn of fate would end up being a tremendous stroke of fortune.

In December of 1992, six months after graduating from college, I moved to Washington, DC, transferring my dorm room furnishings to a studio apartment near Dupont Circle. I had long ago framed the *Time* magazine "Tank Man" cover, and I now placed it on my book shelf, along with photos of Mum, Eddie, Stephen, Bam Bam, and my now ex-boyfriend Schu.

Mort was the first person I came to know well who had helped make foreign policy at such rarified levels, and over time he would drill into me a simple truth: governments can either do harm or do good. "What we do," he would say, "depends on one thing: the people." Institutions, big and small, were made up of people. People had values, and people made choices.

I would learn later that Mort was famous in the diplomatic corps for eschewing hierarchy and tracking down the best-informed officials in his embassies, irrespective of their rank. He also took care of "his people"—making phone calls on behalf of junior officials whose work he admired. But none of this was apparent to me in the first couple of months I served as his intern. When I offered edits to drafts of his speeches and op-eds, he would say, "Very helpful, Susan," and then incorporate almost none of what I had proposed.

My tasks at the outset were as administrative as I had feared: making sure Carnegie's public materials did not have typos and helping seat the VIP guests who attended Carnegie events—from former defense secretary Caspar Weinberger and legendary journalist Bob Woodward to Tom Lantos, a human rights champion who was the only Holocaust survivor in Congress. Although I didn't yet work closely with my boss, people whose names I had underlined in the newspaper during college were suddenly handing me their coats—and occasionally even looking me in the eye.

I was especially intrigued by Carnegie visitor Jeane Kirkpatrick, President Ronald Reagan's first UN ambassador, and the first woman in the United States ever to hold a national security cabinet position. Strangely, Kirkpatrick had first come to my attention when I was a child in Pittsburgh in the early 1980s and had somehow noticed a photo of President Reagan's senior team in Eddie's copy of the *New York Times*. Amid all the suits, the diminutive Kirkpatrick stood beaming at the center of the shot—the only woman among Reagan, Vice President Bush, and the seventeen other members of the cabinet. I had been far too young to follow her career at the UN, but the moment I glimpsed her, now a private citizen, at Carnegie, I immediately flashed back to the picture I had seen more than a decade earlier.

During Kirkpatrick's visits, she would offer acerbic commentary on the foreign policy of President Bill Clinton, who had just taken office. As I watched from the back of the room, I was struck by her bluntness, which seemed to puncture the otherwise clubby, polite atmosphere. Men usually dominated the proceedings, but she was a notable exception.

Mort seemed to respect people like Kirkpatrick who had served in government and could offer informed views. But he was impatient with the "blowhards" who circulated in the think-tank world. "These people speak so much," Mort said about the proliferation of self-styled experts in Washington, "and yet they manage to say so little."

He was even harder on himself. After he had chaired a meeting or published an op-ed that I found persuasive, I sometimes made the mistake of complimenting him. "What a load of horseshit," he would respond. I was never sure if this referred to his work or my praise. When I once thanked him for publicly challenging a visiting head of state, Mort looked at me blankly and said, "You do know I don't have any idea what I'm talking about, don't you?" His humility often manifested itself as self-criticism, which seemed an extremely uncommon—but to me a very appealing—trait for a person so respected in Washington.

Mort's standoffishness did not deter me, and his cutting commentary was familiar from years of watching my dad in action at Hartigan's. But I wondered whether I had what it took to win his confidence. I saw in him someone who could help teach me how the world *really* worked. He seemed to be guided by only one criteria, the question he would ask every time I approached him with an idea (as I often would in the coming decades): "Will it do any good?"

I noticed that Mort always rearranged his schedule to see Fred when he was in town. "He is a practical man," Mort said of the Texan. "He doesn't just tell us 'something must be done.' He tells us what should be done and how we should do it. I've never known anybody like him."

Fred was useful. And Mort valued usefulness.

IN EARLY 1993, both men were working to improve conditions in Bosnia, where a savage war had begun the previous April.

The core of the conflict arose from the collapse of Yugoslavia, whose six republics each contained a range of ethnicities and religions: Serbs, Croats, Slovenes, ethnic Albanians, Macedonians, Bosnian Muslims, and others. Tito, who had ruled the country for decades, had tried to forge a single Southern Slavic identity among the people and had stymied ethnic and religious expressions of difference.* After Tito's death in 1980, however, nationalism—of the kind Schu and I had witnessed on our trip to Croatia—had surged among the country's various ethnicities. After the Berlin Wall fell and the Soviet Union itself headed toward collapse, four of the six Yugoslav republics took steps to secede.

While the eventual outbreak of fighting had many causes, Serbian president Slobodan Milošević bore the greatest responsibility. As Yugoslavia's largest single nationality, Serbs had enjoyed plum jobs and privileges. But as the Croatian and Slovene governments moved toward declaring independence from Serb-dominated Yugoslavia, Milošević used state media to whip up fear over what he portrayed as the coming existential struggle.† If Serbs were trapped as ethnic minorities in newly independent Croatia or Bosnia, he warned, they would become second-class citizens.

In 1989, Milošević had notoriously declared "No one will ever dare

---

* The Serbo-Croatian term *"Jugo"* means "Southern," while *"slavija"* can loosely be translated as "land of the Slavs."

† Slovenia, home to almost no Serbs, secured its independence in 1991 without much of a fight. Croatia, which was 12 percent Serb, also won independence in 1991, but armed Croatian Serbs, supported by Milošević, seized control of a quarter of the country, maintaining a self-styled breakaway republic for several years.

beat you again!" to a crowd of Serbs in the predominantly ethnic Albanian province of Kosovo, shrewdly tapping into the once-dominant group's fear that they would become the losers if people of other ethnicities gained more power. Using tactics common to strongmen past and present, Milošević told the Serbs that their "enemies outside the country are plotting against [them], along with those inside the country." He capitalized on his followers' nervousness about their place in a rapidly changing world.

In 1992, Bosnia was the most ethnically mixed of all of Yugoslavia's republics. After following Slovenia and Croatia in declaring independence, it descended into the deadliest and most gruesome conflict in Europe since World War II. Milošević funneled soldiers and guns from Serbia to support Bosnian Serb militants, who quickly seized some 70 percent of the country in what they called Republika Srpska, their own ethnically "pure" republic. Bosnia's capital of Sarajevo had hosted the Winter Olympics only eight years before, but by April of 1992, Bosnian Serb rebels, backed by the remnants of the powerful Yugoslav National Army, began bombarding the city. Across the country, Bosnian Serb Army snipers and heavy weapons began firing at Bosnian Muslims, Croats, and others.

Not long before I joined Carnegie, a group of intrepid journalists had uncovered a network of concentration camps where Serb guards were starving and beating men to death, and disposing of their bodies in mass graves. The Bosnian Serb militia also set up rape camps where they sequestered Muslim and Croat women and systematically brutalized them. For the people of Bosnia, history had not "ended," and the "New World Order" had brought terror and misery.

Campaigning for president, Bill Clinton had compared the atrocities in Bosnia to the Holocaust, promising that he would "stop the slaughter of civilians" if elected. Mort's top priority was to use his platform at Carnegie to pressure the Clinton administration to translate those words into action. He turned the redbrick building at the corner of 24th and N Street into a hub where the most influential voices from the former Yugoslavia shared their perspectives with Washington's top officials and journalists.

By then, Fred was doing humanitarian work on behalf of philanthropist George Soros's foundation with the goal, as Fred modestly put it, of "breaking the siege of Sarajevo." But he made a point of visiting Washington every few months, and Mort would invite key influencers to hear his insights on the humanitarian conditions and what could be done to improve the situation. Mort's perennial sense that he did not know enough fueled his curiosity and caused him to pose fundamental questions that few were asking. He never seemed afraid of looking uninformed—which, to me, seemed to be the highest form of confidence.

As I dug into the news reporting and listened to what visitors from the region said, the war started to feel closer. The more I heard from Bosnia's crusading representative at the UN or Serbia's human rights lawyers, the more unnerved I was by the atrocities being committed.

This response marked a change for me. Between my college graduation and taking up my Carnegie internship, I had taught English in Berlin for six months. I had seen the gaunt faces of Bosnian families as they arrived at German bus and train terminals, but I had not been moved to action by their suffering. It never occurred to me that I personally could do anything for them. Although I had felt horror toward the Tiananmen massacre several years before, in Berlin I had gone about my business, teaching and exploring the city, despite encountering the war's survivors.

Now, just a few months later at Carnegie, I was devouring the dispatches from Balkan war correspondents. I was working for someone who believed he could make a difference; if I could help him, I felt I might be making a modest contribution of my own.

As I learned more, Mort began asking me to fact-check his opinion pieces for the *Washington Post* and other publications. I slowly started developing views and tried my hand at writing editorials. At first, all I did was read the drafts to Mum and Eddie over the telephone. When I finally got up the nerve to show one to Mort, he eviscerated what I had written, decrying my "purple prose" and telling me to "tone down" the language. Crestfallen, I reflected on the rejection in my journal. "I think what Mort detests—and I can't say I blame him—is my voice.

I'm too young, too lacking knowledge and experience, to assume such airs."

Even if I didn't yet have a knack for such writing, Mort was exposing me to a different mind-set. I now shared his impatience with commentary that detailed the contours of a problem without offering realistic, concrete ideas for how the United States and other actors might improve matters. And I now understood why Mort had all the time in the world for Fred, someone who was a font of constructive ideas for how to respond to the Bosnian Serb Army's devastating siege of Sarajevo.

In addition to terrorizing and killing civilians, Bosnian Serb soldiers had cut off gas and water supplies to the city, sapping the will of its inhabitants to resist. Fred and his team of humanitarian engineers had resuscitated a natural gas line, thereby enabling some 20,000 Sarajevans to restore heating to their homes during the frigid winter. But the Serbs had also cut off the power to pumps that delivered water into the capital, a tactic that had even more dire effects. In order to get water, thousands of Sarajevans were hauling large plastic containers from their homes to the town's main river or its other water sources. The river was polluted and terribly exposed to sniper fire. Because the queues at the water distribution points often stretched whole city blocks, the waiting crowds spent hours vulnerable to shelling.

"What is the most powerful weapon the Bosnian Serb extremists have?" Fred asked me and the other interns one day on a visit to Washington. "Their siege," he answered, explaining, "If we can find a way to restore water, they can still shoot people, but the city will not surrender. We will foil their plans and give the Bosnians the time to muster the means to fight back."

Fred's plan was audacious in the extreme. He planned to smuggle water pumps and other large machinery past the Bosnian Serb gunners and then jury-rig a vast water purification plant inside a Sarajevo tunnel, where it would be shielded from Serb fire. If the plan worked, Fred said, 120,000 gallons of water would flow, giving a third of the city's residents water around the clock.

Fred was just one person with a small team. His idea seemed unbelievably risky. "If this is doable," I asked, "why wouldn't the United Nations do it?"

Fred dismissed the question, telling me, "If the UN had been around in 1939, we'd all be speaking German." He was galled by UN peacekeepers' neutrality in the face of what to him seemed clear-cut aggression.

As Mort deepened his advocacy and Fred began to implement his bold plan to restore water, I also got to know Jonathan Moore, a sixty-year-old former US official based at Carnegie who had been Mort's colleague in President Richard Nixon's State Department. Jonathan had a rumpled look. When I first met him, he was wearing brown corduroys and a light green Oxford shirt under a maroon V-neck sweater—attire from which I rarely saw him deviate. For many months, he held together his Rockport shoes with silver duct tape.

A Republican for most of his life, Jonathan had served as a Senate aide and as a presidential campaign adviser. Working under six presidents, he had also held positions in several governmental agencies, including the Departments of State; Defense; Justice; and Health, Education, and Welfare.* Most impressive to me at the time, he had coordinated the US response to refugee issues under President Reagan, and had gone on to work as one of George H. W. Bush's top officials at the US Mission to the UN, helping to create the position of a full-time UN coordinator for humanitarian emergencies.

When I marveled at the variety and significance of all Jonathan had done, he downplayed his achievements. He stressed that he owed his "herky-jerky" career to finding himself in the "right place at the right time," emphasizing how much each job had given him rather than what he had contributed. He was the first person I met who talked about public service with boundless delight—as a source of camaraderie and fun. To him, even government officials who got themselves into trouble were objects more of fascination than of judgment. "He was so devious, it was neat to watch!" he would exclaim.

---

* In 1979, Congress split this agency into the Department of Education and the Department of Health and Human Services.

Jonathan keenly weighed the moral ambiguity inherent in high-level decision-making.

My first substantive conversation with him occurred after he poked his head into my office to discuss the Bosnian war. "Do you think what is happening in Bosnia is because of the absence of good or the presence of evil?" he asked.

I was carefully tracking developments in the Balkans, but I had no adequate answer to his question. That didn't stop him from continuing to drop by my office, recommending readings from scripture or leaving on my chair a news article he had clipped. Jonathan reminded me of Eddie—he had insatiable curiosity.

I realized that—with Mort, Fred, and now Jonathan—I was surrounded by people from whom I could learn a seemingly infinite amount. But I asked myself what a mere intern could do to support them. I raided Kramerbooks in Dupont Circle, immersing myself in the history and literature of the Balkans. I bought Serbo-Croatian tapes and listened to them on my yellow Sony Walkman as I walked to and from the gym. And at the end of the day, when the office began to empty out, I stayed on, poring over the reports on Bosnian concentration camps and trying to understand how such depravity had befallen the place Schu and I had visited just a couple of summers before.

Leaving the office each night, I was usually so shaken by what I had read that I did not feel steady enough to ride my bike home, choosing instead to walk with it by my side.

As I read back issues from the early 1980s of public news sources like the Radio Free Europe digest, the *Washington Post*, and the *New York Times*, I began compiling a detailed chronology of the road to Yugoslavia's destruction. My timeline was a straightforward collection of dates and events, but one that nonetheless showed Yugoslavia's downward spiral. I had started it so I could keep the sequence straight in my mind and help Mort with his op-eds and speeches. But one night it struck me that such a chronology might find a broader readership. Just as Mort was trying to make himself a quick study on the conflict, so too were many journalists, NGO advocates, members of Congress, and Clinton administration officials.

Five months into my internship, I went to Mort with a lengthy printout of my timeline, held together with a large black paper clip, and asked him if he thought it might be worth publishing. He was focused on something else and didn't seem to process my question—but he assented. Over the next several weeks, through all-nighters and weekend labor, I tried to improve its quality. In June of 1993, reasoning that speed was as important as substance, I took my floppy disk to a printer and asked them to make one thousand copies.

When I turned up to collect the order a week later, I was taken aback by the sight of a half-dozen large brown boxes that would nearly fill my small office. My amateur creation had been artfully compressed into a small book with a gray cover bearing my name and the title I had landed on: *Breakdown in the Balkans*. When word got out that such a chronology was available, the Washington think tank, diplomatic, policy, and media communities quickly emptied the Carnegie stock. I soon heard from Fred, who called on a satellite phone from Sarajevo to congratulate me on publishing the "hugely useful" *Breakdown*, which he said he was passing out to government officials and aid workers.

I felt immense satisfaction—of a kind I had never experienced personally or professionally before. But now that people were actually reading it, I began obsessing about all that I had left out. "The gaps, the gaps," I would say, deflecting compliments that came my way. Simultaneously, I chastised myself for craving the recognition I was starting to get. "Clearly, I am out, as always, for me, myself, and I," I wrote in my journal. "I need so much to remember why the book came about in the first place." I knew that conditions in Bosnia were deteriorating rapidly, and that if my chronology was to land in the hands of Fred's besieged Sarajevan neighbors, they would likely burn it along with their other books to keep warm.

The war raged unabated. Four US diplomats—George Kenney, Marshall Harris, Jon Western, and Stephen Walker—had already resigned to protest what they saw as the weakness of the US response to the Bosnian war, the largest wave of resignations over US policy in State Department history. I read about these men in a lengthy *Wash-*

ington Post profile and was gripped by their testimonies. Jon Western, a thirty-year-old intelligence analyst, had sifted through hundreds of photos and videos of what he recalled as "human beings who look like they've been through meat grinders." As he told the *Post*, the intelligence he needed to consume for his job described preteen girls raped in front of their parents, a sixty-five-year-old man and his thirty-five-year-old son forced at gunpoint to orally castrate each other, and Serb torturers who made Muslim prisoners carve crosses in each other's skulls.

Western and the other US officials who resigned had initially tried to change policy from within, but having made no headway, had finally quit. They felt they could no longer be part of a US government that wasn't doing more, reasoning that they could at least draw media attention to what they saw as America's moral abdication.

After reading the *Post* profile, I grandiosely wrote in my journal: "My only regret is that I don't work at the State Department so I can quit to protest policy. Instead, I sit impotent and incapable."

Following my summer at CBS in Atlanta, when people had asked what I wanted to do with my life, I had begun answering that "I wanted to make a difference." But at Carnegie I saw that this was an abstraction. Now I had a focus—a specific group of people in a specific place who were being pulverized, and I wanted to do someting to support them.

As a liberal arts major who had no particular knack for foreign languages, I still worried I had little to contribute. But I had managed to assemble the chronology, and I was seeing up close the vast number of ways researchers, columnists, journalists, government officials, and aid workers were involved in the enterprise of American foreign policy. All seemed to be struggling with how to define the US role in the world now that the Cold War was over, as well as how to manage a sudden flurry of nationalist and independence movements.

I remained acutely aware of all that I lacked—I wasn't an engineer like Fred, a trained diplomat like Mort, or a doctor like Mum and Eddie. I was focused, but I did not know how to channel my interests. A frustrated journal entry from the time ended simply: ". . . Act, Power."

7

RISK

Ben Cohen, a British journalist and activist, was the person who gave me the idea of traveling to the Balkans. "You should see the war up close," he told me. "And you should write something."

After I met Ben at a Carnegie event, we struck up a fast friendship. A Sephardic Jew whose ancestors escaped to Bosnia during the Spanish Inquisition, he was more knowledgeable about the country's politics, history, and literature than anybody I knew in Washington. Though he was devastated by all that had happened, he brought a dark humor to our discussions.

Ben arranged an invitation for me—the "author" of *Breakdown in the Balkans*—to attend a conference being held in peaceful Slovenia, the newly independent former Yugoslav republic. After the conference, he insisted, we should drive to Bosnia.

Given my chronic expectation that something terrible was bound to happen whenever life was going well, I feared heading into what appeared to be a blazing inferno of a war zone. I also didn't see what I could add to the existing coverage of the war, as the experienced reporters in the region were doing phenomenal work. But Ben kept pushing. And with my internship nearing its end, I had begun considering what jobs would enable me to keep working on issues related to the conflict.

Thanks to Ben, I already had one published article. Not long after we first met, he had proposed collaborating on an op-ed critiquing the direction of international diplomacy on Bosnia. Joined by George Stamkoski, a Macedonian friend of Ben's who became our third co-author, we produced what in retrospect seems a rather pedestrian essay and began "shopping" it to various newspapers.

We tried every mainstream publication in the United States, and when each one turned us down, we sent it to outlets in the United Kingdom, Australia, and Canada for which we could find fax numbers. Eventually, Ben called me with "good news and less good news." Our piece had finally been accepted, he said. "But it might be hard to find." The essay would be appearing in Pakistan's *Daily Jang*, but he wasn't yet sure if it would be in the Urdu or English edition.

I didn't care: I faxed an illegible copy of the op-ed (in English!) to Mum's office, and stuffed it into Mort's mailbox.

When I called Fred Cuny in Sarajevo to get his advice about traveling to Bosnia, he agreed with Ben: I should experience what was happening myself. He also invited me to watch his team in Croatia preparing for the water restoration mission he was planning to undertake in Sarajevo.

"I will explain more when I see you," he said cryptically, not wanting to reveal on the phone how he intended to sneak the necessary machinery past trigger-happy Bosnian Serb soldiers.

Fred's encouragement was all the motivation I needed. I worked at a think tank. I was published in a widely read newspaper. Well, okay: I *interned* at a think tank, and the paper was read widely in Karachi. But I was already going to be in the region, so I decided to add two stops after the conference in Slovenia: Bosnia, where Ben promised we would visit someplace safe, and neighboring Croatia, to see Fred in action.

As it happened, Carnegie's offices were located in the same building as *U.S. News & World Report*, a weekly magazine with a circulation of more than two million readers. I asked a journalist friend to introduce me to Carey English, the magazine's chief of correspondents. Three days later, I found myself entering his small cockpit of an office with a copy of my Balkans chronology in hand. As he thumbed through it, revealing little, I asked whether *U.S. News* would consider running an article from me once I got to the region.

Carey was tough but patient—far more patient than I would have been in his shoes. He asked me about my past journalistic experience, and I pulled out the *Daily Jang* op-ed and several sports clips from the *Yale Daily News*. He shook his head. "You are going to a war zone, you know." I assured him I understood and would not take dumb risks.

"Define a smart risk," he said.

I blanched, but he continued. "Look, I'm skeptical," he said as he handed me his business card. "But see what you come up with when you're over there, and call me collect on this number if you have a story."

I thanked him and soberly shook his hand. When I left the *U.S. News* office and the doors to the elevator closed behind me, however, I let out a joyful scream.

"Whoo-hooo, I'm going to be a foreign correspondent!"

Ben was elated at the news and immediately began filling me in on the practicalities, including that I would need a UN press badge in order to pass through checkpoints and enter Bosnia. This meant that a news organization had to sponsor me. He suggested I head back downstairs to *U.S. News* to procure a letter vouching that I would be reporting for them.

But this was an impossible ask. Carey had said he would take my call if I had a story to propose; that was a far cry from *U.S. News* sponsoring me as its correspondent. The magazine had a regular freelance contributor in the region already, and Carey was not about to undermine him by adding an untested second.

Crestfallen by the realization that our fledgling plan might already be falling apart, I sat at my desk staring at the ceiling, unsure what to do next. But when two of my fellow interns who worked at *Foreign Policy* walked by, an idea popped into my head. Back then, the *Foreign Policy* journal mostly published work for academics and policy scholars.* Its content was nothing like that of newsmagazines like *Time*, *U.S. News*, or *Newsweek*—and it certainly did not employ foreign correspondents. But I doubted the UN knew that.

---

* It was not until 2000 that *Foreign Policy* was reinvented from a quarterly journal into a bimonthly magazine for a wider audience. In 2008, the Washington Post Company purchased the magazine from the Carnegie Endowment and further expanded its reach into the online and print publication it is today.

I waited until the *Foreign Policy* editorial staff had headed home and the cleaners had completed their nighttime rounds on the floor. Once the suite was completely deserted, I walked into the office of Charles William Maynes, the journal's editor, picked up several sheets of his stationery, and then hurried back to my desk.

Hands shaking, I began typing a letter impersonating the unwitting Maynes. I was committing a fireable offense, but to me it felt like a felony. All these years later, I still feel terrible for having violated the trust of a program that was giving me so much. But determined to get to Bosnia, I went ahead and wrote to the head of the UN Press Office, asking that the UN provide Samantha Power, *Foreign Policy*'s "Balkan Correspondent," with "all necessary access."

I had a guilty conscience, but I also had what I needed to obtain my press pass.

IN AUGUST OF 1993, Ben, his friend George, and I met up in peaceful Slovenia. After participating in the conference, we made our way to the Avis car rental agency. Knowing that Avis would prohibit us from taking one of its vehicles into a combat zone, Ben told the salesclerk that he and I were planning a romantic getaway to nearby Venice, Italy. He threw himself into the part, describing our courtship and love of the coast.

Our route to Bosnia took us through Croatia, and when we arrived in Zagreb, the capital, we headed to the Bosnian embassy to collect our visas. We found a grim scene. Dozens of Bosnian refugee families huddled in a long line around the block. Several of the men and women waiting had shaved heads and crosses etched into their faces. One of them told us that they were Muslims whom the Serbs had tortured and marked.

None of my graphic late-night reading at Carnegie had prepared me to see scars cut into human flesh. I asked a man whose right leg had been amputated above the knee what he thought of the current UN peace plan, and he put his thumb down to signal his disapproval. For good measure, he directed the only English words he seemed to know at the Western negotiators: "FUCK OFF."

A proper journalist would have asked him and the other Bosnians to recount what they had gone through, but I could not bring myself to probe for details. Forcing them to rehash what had happened seemed cruelly voyeuristic. Instead, after George (who spoke Serbo-Croatian) translated some small talk, we shuffled inside to get the visas we would need in order to cross into Bosnia.

Our next stop was the local UN headquarters, where the press official told us that he did not have the passes for which we had applied. My imagination began running wild. I visualized a vast team of forensic specialists conducting an exhaustive verification process—including a call to *Foreign Policy* asking Maynes to confirm the contents of "his" letter. In reality, the UN official responsible for laminating the badges had simply taken an extra-long lunch break.

With our visas and paperwork finally in hand, we drove our rental car several hours in the direction of Bihać, a small Muslim enclave in the northwest corner of Bosnia that was surrounded on all sides by Serb militants. Ben had sold me on this destination by reminding me that Bihać was the only one of six UN-declared "safe areas" actually living up to its name. But while Bihać was not experiencing the brutal fighting going on elsewhere, the risks of visiting were real. The UN press officer had explicitly warned us not to travel there and had cautioned that many of the roads along the way were mined.

We placed a handwritten "PRESS" placard in our car window as a precaution, but it offered uncertain protection. Many Serb rebels believed they were being unfairly villainized by Western journalists—all it would take for our trip to turn deadly was one renegade soldier deciding to seek revenge. I was scared for my physical safety and knew that the trip was placing great stress on Mum and Eddie.

After passing through Croatian army and Croatian Serb rebel checkpoints, we saw the royal blue, white, and gold flag of Bosnia. A minute later, a group of very thin Bosnian soldiers welcomed us with smiles and high fives. Most of them looked no older than twenty. We drove further, into a landscape of bucolic green hills. So far, Bosnia looked nothing like the bombed-out ruins for which I had prepared myself. Around every bend I half expected the summer cheer to be shattered by gunfire, but the only sounds of war we heard were a comfortable distance away.

Over the course of our three-day stay in the Bihać area, we learned that the relative calm had a great deal to do with a wealthy Bosnian Muslim businessman named Fikret Abdić. Abdić ran a food-processing company that was the region's chief employer, which gave him bargaining power with the Serbs encircling Bihać. If they let supplies in and didn't attack, Abdić agreed to provide continued access to the food his company produced.

Because Abdić's main focus was his own profits, and because Bosnian Serb forces were killing Muslims and Croats elsewhere in the country, the Bosnian government denounced him as a traitor. He was also wanted in Austria for allegedly pilfering money intended for refugees. But the civilians we met, who had been able to keep working and sending their children to school, described Abdić as a hero. I interviewed a young pharmacology student named Nedzara Midzic who had lost twenty-two pounds when she had lived in besieged Sarajevo earlier in the war. In Bihać, she was no longer scrounging for food. "He may profit," she said of Abdić, "but at least we profit too."

Listening to Bosnians express their gratitude to Abdić was a reminder of how little I actually knew about the country's complex dynamics. I wasn't sure how I would get to the bottom of what was really happening. But at a minimum, I knew I would need to spend much more time in the region and take greater risks.

When we left Bosnia and crossed back into Croatian territory, I was immensely relieved. We had not been attacked *and* I had managed to interview civilians, soldiers, and government officials as if I were an actual reporter. Back at our hotel in Zagreb, I telephoned Mum at her Brooklyn hospital to let her know that everything had turned out all right.

Ben and George then took me to the Zagreb home of Richard Carruthers, a BBC correspondent with whom they were acquainted. Richard's smoke-filled flat was everything I had ever associated with the romantic life of a foreign correspondent. Several rugged-looking reporters in cargo pants were drinking whiskey and playing poker at a coffee table. Carruthers himself was thumbing through a vast collection of LPs in search of just the right jazz record for the steamy afternoon. And Richard's girlfriend, Laura Pitter—an American from Laguna Beach, California, whose byline I knew from *Time* magazine and the *Christian Science Monitor*—was on the porch in a red bikini, cooling off in a paddle pool and drinking a margarita.

Sitting among these journalists, I was mesmerized by their lively back-and-forth on Balkan politics. After inquiring about the Serbs' territorial ambitions, I asked them which news outlets they worked for. They told me that they all filed stories for multiple publications and networks. Because most American and British outlets did not have full-time correspondents permanently based in the region, they often relied on "stringers," regular contributors who were not on salary but were paid for each article or broadcast piece that was accepted.

When I asked whether a newcomer like me would be able to find work, though, they quickly shot me down. "The strings are all taken," one said definitively.

Laura, the only woman in the group, did not contradict her colleagues in the moment, but she pulled me aside before I left. "I don't know what these guys are talking about," she said. "There is plenty of work to go around. You should move here and give it a try." Looking around, she grabbed a cardboard coaster out from under a beer and wrote down her email and phone number.

"You can totally do this," she said as she handed me the coaster. "Write me if you're coming back. I'll show you around."

MY LAST STOP BEFORE RETURNING to the United States was to see Fred. I took a cab out to Zagreb Airport, where he and his engineering team were staging dry runs to prepare for their upcoming mission in Sarajevo. The plan called for landing C-130 transport planes in the besieged city, quickly unloading mammoth water purification modules from the cargo bays, and then whisking the modules into the city before the Serbs realized what was transpiring.

The lives of those on Fred's team—and the survival of the equipment—depended on being able to maneuver the freight onto trucks with lightning speed at Sarajevo Airport. Since the Serb soldiers manning artillery around the airport were using the siege—and the cut-off of water—to try to force the Bosnian government to surrender, they were expected to try to prevent the water equipment from being delivered, including by barraging Fred and his team with shellfire.

Watching Fred in action, I was struck not by the grandness of the enterprise, but by the tedium and the minutiae necessary to coordinate the pilots, the crewmen, the forklift operators, the engineers, and the drivers. The orchestration of every movement consumed him—any lapse in the assembly line could spell disaster.

"If we don't get the details right," he observed to me when a mix-up brought the exercise to a halt, "people are going to die."

The offloading did not go well in the trial runs I watched. Fred had calculated that the contractors would need to land the plane and unload in ten minutes or less, but the first attempt I watched took a whopping thirty-five minutes. The temperature on the Zagreb tarmac was scorching; tempers seemed to be flaring. I was worried. Fred insisted he was not.

He planned to travel to Sarajevo the next day. "You should come with me," he said offhandedly. My heart leaped. Now that I had made it to Bihać and back, I had crossed the Rubicon and visited a war zone. Though it was irrational, I was now less afraid. If I were to accompany Fred, I thought, I could give readers back home the inside story of America's humanitarian "MacGyver." I would have full access, and in showing what just one person could do, I could show how much more the United States could be doing.

I telephoned Mort with excitement, but he was having none of it. "You're coming home," he said. "You work for me." I was twenty-three years old and hardly indispensable at Carnegie, so his adamancy surprised me. Only when I got back did Mort's devoted secretary share why he had been so firm. "He was worried sick about you," she said.

While my boss had introduced me to a humanitarian cowboy, he did not want me to become one.

I PITCHED *U.S. News* a story on Bihać—the moral complexity of Fikret Abdić and "why one Bosnian safe area is actually safe." Carey told me the foreign editor was intrigued. "Give it a try," he said, asking for six hundred words.

Back in Washington, I read through my notebooks dozens of times, circling and recircling the most vivid quotes from my reporting. For days, I stared at my desktop screen at work, unable to settle on the right beginning. I joked with Eddie that I felt like the character Grand in Albert Camus's *The Plague*, who, for the duration of the novel, obsessively tries to craft the "perfect" sentence, as the plague kills off his neighbors.

After trying hundreds of alternatives, I finally settled upon, "The most jarring sound in Bihać, a Muslim enclave of 300,000 in the northwest corner of Bosnia, is not the reverberation of machine-gun fire, but the splashing and chatter of children playing in the Una River."

Two weeks later, attending the US Open tennis tournament with Mum, I called *U.S. News* from a pay phone at a prearranged time. The foreign editor told me that he planned to run the piece. I pumped my fist and gave Mum a thumbs-up. During the call, her expression had been as tense as it was when she was watching her favorite tennis players during their final set tiebreakers, but at my signal, her whole bearing relaxed.

When *U.S. News* faxed me the edited draft, however, I was horrified by their changes, which I felt misled readers. "They oversimplified my oversimplification!" I complained to Mum and Eddie that night. The next day, I delivered a long exposition contesting what the editor had "done" to my prose. I was surprised to discover that he was not wedded to his edits.

"I just didn't have space for what you gave me," he said curtly. "Make it right. But I need it quickly." In the end, *U.S. News* ran my 478-word article in a box alongside a much longer piece by their regular stringer.

Seeing my name in print in a mainstream newsmagazine felt like the greatest triumph of my life. The experience also gave me a burst of confidence. I had proven to myself that I could learn about a foreign crisis and get paid to write about it. I sent my clips—the *Daily Jang* op-ed and the newly published *U.S. News* article—to Bam Bam, then ninety-eight years old and still a prolific pen pal. "My future is very uncertain. I love working at Carnegie, and I love my boss, Morton Abramowitz. But I feel I've expired here," I wrote in an accompanying letter.

Although I didn't say so to Bam Bam, I also realized that I had picked up some unappealing habits. I had never been without opinions, but my certitude previously had to do with seemingly trivial issues like an umpire's bad call in a baseball game. Now, as I researched and reflected on real-world events, I seemed unable to contain my emotions or modulate my judgments. If the subject of Bosnia came up and someone innocently described the conflict as a civil war, I would erupt: "It is genocide!"

While I made an effort to divest myself of sanctimony—among my least favorite qualities in others—I tried to look at the upside: in the span of less than a year, I had gone from hardly thinking about serving others to constantly thinking about what I could do to be "useful"—the quality Mort, Fred, and my mother valued most.

Since the summer, I had also begun marking my place in whatever I was reading with a new bookmark: the coaster on which Laura Pitter, the war correspondent, had written her phone number.

8

HEARTS OF DARKNESS

My mother supported everything I had ever done—until I decided to become a war correspondent.

"Journalism is a fiercely competitive business," she told me in late 1993 when I called to inform her that I planned to move to Croatia. "Very few people who try actually make it."

Her conservative counsel was out of character for someone whose every major life choice—from becoming a doctor to running away with Eddie to America—had defied the odds. "Mum, since when have you ever decided whether or not to do something based on an assumption that you will fail?" I asked. "If I think everyone else will be better than me, then you're right, I shouldn't try. But if that is my approach, maybe I should just preemptively admit defeat and retire now."

The back-and-forth grew heated and unpleasant, and the conversation finally ended when one of us hung up on the other.

I knew that the real source of her worry was my safety. But I thought I could bring her around if she could see my growing interest in US foreign policy as something resembling the passion she had for medicine. Thirty years into her career, though her hours remained punishing, Mum seemed almost to skip to work—such was her love of caring for patients. I had always longed to find a job that would likewise allow me to find joy in the task itself. Before working for Mort, I wasn't sure I was capable of such dedication. But now I was beginning to feel differently.

Within a few weeks, I found myself standing beside her at a Manhattan electronics store as she handed her credit card to the clerk to buy me my first laptop computer. "I can't believe I am facilitating this," she mumbled.

Part of my strategy to wear Mum down had been projecting an air of inevitability about the entire endeavor. But as I exited the store, toting my new Toshiba laptop, I was racked with self-doubt. Was she right? Would I fall flat on my face, run out of money, and return home in defeat? Worse, would I allow myself to get sucked into life as a war correspondent and end up getting killed?

Mort was initially skeptical of the move, but knowing he didn't have a job to offer me after my internship ended, he came around; indeed, he dedicated an entire afternoon to telephoning all the newspaper editors he knew to tell them I was going. He also connected me to the foreign editor of National Public Radio (NPR), who told me, as *U.S. News* had done, that she would take my calls if I had a story idea.

Working for Mort had made me realize just how American I had become. Beyond my accent, which no longer bore traces of a lilt, I now thought like an American, reacting to problems in the world—like the Bosnia war—by asking myself, "What, if anything, can *we*, America, do about it?" I also wanted to vote, which, still an Irish citizen, I had been unable to do in the 1992 presidential election.

During high school, I had failed the driver's test several times (hitting various cones), and I still felt the sting of humiliation from admitting to my classmates what had happened. I was determined to avoid a similar embarrassment on my citizenship test, and wildly over-prepared, using a Barron's citizenship guide to create flash cards with every conceivable question I might be asked about American government and civics. Unlike many of those applying, English was my first language, and I had the benefit of learning US history in school. Still, I felt relieved when, in the fall of 1993, I learned I had passed.

Mum and Eddie had been sworn in as Americans the previous year, and, because they had made no fuss about their naturalization ceremony, I didn't think to invite them to the courthouse in Brooklyn to see mine. However, the other new Americans participating treated the day like the momentous event that it was, donning their finest suits and dresses and surrounding themselves with family.

During our collective Oath of Allegiance, we pledged, "I will support and defend the Constitution and laws of the United States of America against all enemies, foreign and domestic." Looking around the courtroom, seeing emotion ripple across the faces of those whose hands were raised, I was struck by what America meant as a refuge, and as an idea. All of us gathered that morning had reached the modern Promised Land. We weren't giving up who we were or where we came from; we were making it American. I hugged an elderly woman from Central America on my left, and a tall man from Russia to my right. We were all Americans now.

AS MY DOUBTS about whether to move to the Balkans lingered, I devised a test for myself that I have used many times since. The test, as I put it then, was as follows: *If I end up not making it as a journalist, will something else I learn in the process make it worth trying?* I would come to call this the "in trying for Y, the most I accomplish is X" test, or the "X test." This was a kind of self-protective exercise—designed to minimize my sense of risk by preemptively establishing a positive spin on even a negligible potential outcome.

Since I was fascinated by Balkan history, I had my answer. If the most I achieved by moving to the former Yugoslavia was to learn the history and language of the region, I thought, it will have been worth it (provided I did not die).

The Irish people are a famously emotional bunch, but tend to avoid displays of sentimentality. Frank McCourt, who spent his childhood in Ireland, wrote in his magnificent memoir *Angela's Ashes*:

> If I were in America I could say, I love you, Dad, the way they do
> in the films, but you can't say that in Limerick for fear you might
> be laughed at. You're allowed to say you love God and babies and
> horses that win but anything else is a softness in the head.

When I read this passage a few years after my move to the Balkans, I dog-eared the page, as I felt it unlocked one of the mysteries of my childhood in which love was tacitly communicated but almost never directly expressed.

Nonetheless, at the airport with Mum and Eddie before I boarded my flight to Europe, we all teared up as we said goodbye. In the back of our minds, we knew that relatively peaceful Zagreb would not hold me long. The human toll of the Bosnian war—and the possibility of being able to do something to draw more attention to it—would be too great a gravitational pull.

I DECIDED NOT TO DIVE IN as a freelance journalist from the start, but instead to sign up for an intensive Croatian language and culture program. I would pay a small fee to live with a host family in Zagreb rather than immediately having to find an apartment of my own. If I could get a handle on the language, I thought, I would need to spend less on expensive interpreters when I started actual reporting.

My arrival in Zagreb was not unlike that of an American college student in a study abroad program. My Croatian host family greeted me at the airport. They encouraged me to try out my rudimentary Croatian,* and I went out for drinks with their daughter, a vivacious university student who offered tips for exploring the city. But within no time, I found myself put off by the family's nationalism and the way the parents denigrated Serbs. This was not the first time I had seen how kindness toward a favored "in-group" (I was Catholic like them) could coexist with bigotry toward those who were not included. The situation reminded me of my experience as a new Lakeside student when the parents of a few of my white high school friends had gener-

---

* Serbo-Croatian was the primary language in Yugoslavia, but when the country broke up, Croatians, Bosnians, and Montenegrins claimed their own languages, purging certain words (with Croatians and Bosnians using the Roman rather than Cyrillic alphabet). Today, despite linguistic variations, the four languages are mutually intelligible versions of what had been Serbo-Croatian.

ously embraced me while disparaging the other newcomers, the African Americans who were bused to school.

I soon learned that expressions of anti-Serb animus were fairly commonplace around Croatia. Croatians had felt subjugated by Serbs in the former Yugoslavia and had very recently suffered ruthless Yugoslav Army bombardments. When I tried to argue that the whole ethnic group could not be blamed, several said out loud, "The only good Serb is a dead Serb." I eventually dropped out of my Croatian language class because my teacher refused to use words that originated in Serbia, and I began the familiar practice of building my own flash-card library. Luckily, I would later find a wonderful teacher in Bosnia.

Laura Pitter was the person who most eased my transition. She proved every bit as bighearted as she had seemed when we first met the previous summer. She immediately invited me to accompany her to interviews. "You are going to do great here," she said, as if reading my doubts. "Remember, you know the story."

After I had been in Croatia for two weeks, I telephoned NPR, using the number the foreign editor had given me before I left Washington. I tentatively asked the person who answered if she would be interested in "something" on a cease-fire between Bosnia's Muslims and Croats that had just been brokered by US diplomats. The voice on the other end seemed practiced in fielding calls from strangers. "Sure," she said, to my shock. "How about a forty-five-second spot? We will call you back from the studio within the hour."

Before I had a chance to inquire about specifics, I heard a dial tone.

I turned to Laura, who was sitting cross-legged on her couch, writing her own story on a laptop. "What's a spot?" I asked.

When NPR called back, Laura said, they would conduct a sound check and then would expect me to do three things: get listeners' attention with my opening, describe my nugget of news, and efficiently conclude.

I practiced and practiced, ducking into the bathroom so Laura wouldn't hear my affected inflections. I found the sign-off the most difficult: "For NPR, this is Samantha Power reporting from Zagreb." I just could not believe that NPR would want me to say this; they barely knew me! But Laura insisted it was standard. When the phone rang, I tried not to let my nervousness show and successfully delivered the "spot" on my third try.

I telephoned my mother later that evening, but she beat me to my news. "I nearly crashed my car on the way home!" she told me, clearly overjoyed and amazed by the speed with which I seemed to have gotten settled. Whatever her misgivings, she had never strayed from my corner. Eddie, meanwhile, had already contacted NPR to secure a copy of the tape. "They said your name twice!" he declared.

Not long after, Fred Cuny passed through Zagreb and welcomed me to the region by inviting me to dinner with a few of his friends. He told us that his team had completed the dangerous operation at Sarajevo Airport. "We got our time down to seven minutes!" he boasted, explaining that the specially designed equipment they had snuck into the city was already filtering and chlorinating previously undrinkable river water. When he and his team opened the pipes for the first time, he recalled, they were accidentally doused in five hundred gallons of water. He described a jubilant scene of soaked engineers, arm in arm with Bosnian staff who laughed merrily as they imagined what running water would mean for their families and neighbors.

I was in awe of what Fred had done. By improvising a water system, he had helped blunt the impact of one of the cruelest tactics in the Bosnian Serb siege. He had also enhanced his relevance in Washington, giving him more sway in the ongoing debate about whether the United States should use military force to try to end the carnage. Because of the Bosnian Serb Army's terror tactics and what he saw as the minimal risk to US forces, Fred believed it should. He seemed to know more than most US officials about the location and capabilities of Bosnian Serb heavy weapons. While other humanitarians avoided contact with the US government in order to show their independence and neutrality, he relished sharing all he knew.

The day after our dinner in Zagreb, Fred returned to Sarajevo. He was driving with ABC News anchor Peter Jennings when they heard a shell crashing into the main market two blocks away. Sixty-eight people were killed in what was the deadliest massacre of the war. Fred was incensed. He raged against the US government, telling Jennings on camera that two American fighter planes had been flying overhead when the Bosnian Serb Army struck. "They were stunting up there, just flying around in circles and playing," he said. "They could have done something."

I was getting a complicated introduction to American power. Since April of 1993, the United States and its NATO allies had been patrolling a no-fly zone that prevented Serb fighter jets from carrying out aerial bombardments over Bosnian territory. US-piloted F-16s were frequently visible in the sky, and their overhead passes—with sonic booms like those heard at a baseball game on the Fourth of July—were awesome displays of might.

Yet the UN Security Council resolution authorizing the no-fly zone only permitted NATO to shoot down aircraft that were dropping bombs from the air; its pilots did not have permission to attack those who were using their artillery and mortars to slaughter people.

Fred called me the night of the market massacre, his voice still trembling as he spoke: "This is a failure of humanity," he said. "They will not stop until they are stopped."

Sitting in my Zagreb apartment and watching CNN footage of market vendors carrying away the bloodied remains of their mutilated friends, I found myself rooting for the first time in my life for the United States to use military force.

Despite President Clinton's promises during the 1992 presidential campaign to stop the killing, the deaths of eighteen American soldiers in Somalia during the first year of his presidency left him deeply concerned about US forces becoming entangled in messy, peripheral conflicts around the world. He was fearful that even limited action in Bosnia would lead to "another Somalia," or, worse, "another Vietnam." This reminded me of the peril of applying analogies in geopolitics, best encapsulated in Mark Twain's line: "A cat who sits on a hot stove will never sit on a hot stove again. But he won't sit on a cold stove either." The conflicts in Somalia, Vietnam, and Bosnia had little in common with one another. In addition, the UN Security Council had imposed an arms embargo on Bosnia, which disproportionately impacted Bosnia's Muslims, as they did not have access to weapons from Yugoslavia's vast national army arsenal. They could not rescue or defend themselves. American planes were already flying overhead. I did not believe Clinton should deploy ground forces to Bosnia, but I thought he should tell Bosnian Serb soldiers to leave their positions and should order US planes to destroy their weapons, so they could not kill civilians with impunity.

I called Mort and awakened him at four a.m. in Washington. I urged him to contact all the people he knew in the Clinton administration—but mainly, I just needed to hear his voice.

"What will it take?" I pleaded.

"I don't know," he said. "But this may finally get them to move." He was referring to Clinton and his national security team. He paused. "Then again, it may not."

The fact that Fred was so close to the market when the massacre occurred was an uncomfortable reminder of what I was getting myself into. While Westerners were not targeted nearly as frequently as they later would be in places like Afghanistan and Iraq, journalists, aid workers, and diplomats still faced serious risks, and could easily be hit in "wrong place, wrong time" incidents. I could tell myself Fred knew the ropes and I would be safe with him. But any feeling of security in Bosnia was deceptive. Who lived and died in the war was viciously random.

MY FIRST SPRING IN THE REGION, I traveled with two male colleagues to the towns of Prijedor and Banja Luka in the so-called Republika Srpska. The local Serb authorities had made non-Serbs turn over their properties and businesses before gunmen forced many to flee and herded thousands into concentration camps, where they were tortured, starved, and killed. The paramilitaries had instructed Serb residents to mark their homes to denote the ethnic "purity" of those within. So many Muslims and Croats had been expelled or murdered that we referred to the area as the "heart of darkness."

As the three of us absorbed the desolate, almost apocalyptic sight of roads lined with gutted, bombed-out houses that had once been owned by Muslims and Croats, we did not speak. The homes that remained flew white flags or had Serbian nationalist symbols spray-painted near their front doors. These marked, lit residences—bustling with life, but often wedged between the carcasses of what had been the homes of their neighbors—gave off a sinister glow.

We checked into a gloomy, virtually empty hotel near the main road and went up to our separate rooms. Just as I was drifting off to sleep, I heard a sudden banging on the door. Before I had the chance to answer, several large armed men barged in, shouting at me to get up and go with them.

They reeked of alcohol, and my hands shook so much that I had trouble packing. One of the creepiest and most commanding of the lot led me outside into the backseat of a car, where, to my great relief, my male colleagues were already sitting. As I tried to settle my nerves, I watched out of the corner of my eyes as the Serb soldier who had taken me to the car began flicking through my passport.

"Sam-an-ta," he leered in a tone of mock admiration. I looked away, fearing that eye contact might increase the risk of physical contact.

"Sam-an-ta," he said again. "Are you virgin?" My head began to spin. I thought about trying to bolt from the car.

"I said, are you virgin?" he repeated. I stared out the window, determined to pretend I was not hearing what I heard.

"Sam-an-ta, answer me," he said sharply. "Are you virgin?" Lacking recourse, I snapped back at him, "It is none of your business. Leave me alone."

He asked again. "Stop," I said with as much conviction as I could muster.

He came closer, and I could see he looked puzzled—and slightly wounded. He held up my passport and said, "You born September twenty-one. I thought you virgin."

I felt suddenly faint. "No, no, no," I said, "you mean Virgo. You mean, 'Are you Virgo?' Yes! My birthday is September twenty-first. I am a Virgo."

We were soon released without physical harm. Bosnian women and girls were not so lucky. Some 20,000 of them are estimated to have been raped during the conflict.

Being a woman covering the war affected my experience in other ways. The culture that female reporters confronted in the Balkans was traditional and patriarchal, with deep-rooted sexism. That said, those with power may well have viewed women as less threatening than men, sometimes offering us better access to the people and events we wished to cover. I cannot pinpoint the difference gender made, and other female correspondents may not agree, but I found some of my sources underestimated me—and thus may have been more forthcoming than with male reporters.

One night I joined my friend Stacy Sullivan, *Newsweek*'s freelance correspondent, on an outing across Sarajevo to try to find water for a long-overdue bath. We were pulled over, arrested for violating the curfew, and confined to a Sarajevo prison cell. When I got permission to make a phone call, instead of calling the US ambassador, I telephoned the Bosnian prime minister, whom I had often interviewed and who was a notorious flirt. He seemed to enjoy flexing his muscles to secure our release, and we headed home within several hours. A couple of months later, I agreed to meet the prime minister for an interview at a Zagreb hotel as he passed through on his way to lobby the Clinton administration in Washington. When I arrived at the hotel room that the prime minister's aide had directed me to, I expected to be greeted by his entourage. Instead, the prime minister himself met me at the door—barely dressed.

I was so shocked that instead of fleeing immediately as I should have, I crossed the threshold into his suite as if on autopilot—only to spend the next fifteen minutes dodging his repeated efforts to embrace me while I futilely urged him to commence our scheduled interview. Finally, when he made clear that he had little interest in being questioned about the war afflicting his people, I left.

I do not know a female correspondent who wasn't caught off guard by an aggressive sexual come-on from a source. Because we women had become such close friends, we often traded stories and warned one another away from particular people. "Ewwwwwwwww . . ." was the subject we gave the emails we sent to one another recounting our latest experiences with unwelcome male attention. We even found ourselves occasionally expressing gratitude for those local and international officials who *didn't* make lewd comments or direct advances.

Now, however, I am struck by the fact that we didn't publicize these incidents. Perhaps this was because such aggressive acts were so run-of-the-mill that they didn't seem noteworthy. We may also have compared our experiences to those of Bosnian women whom we interviewed who had been raped and brutalized. Mainly, though, I think we believed that the burden was on us to evade harm.

9

"TELL CLINTON"

Just after US diplomats helped broker a cease-fire between Bosnian Muslim and Croat fighters in central Bosnia, *Time* asked Laura to report on the nascent peace, and she invited me along. Laura and I ended up spending several weeks traveling around the ravaged area, which had been inhabited mainly by Muslims and Croats before the war. The Bosnian Serb paramilitaries had first introduced the chilling term "ethnic cleansing" in places like Banja Luka to describe how they sought to "purify" the land they controlled of its Muslim and Croat residents. But it hadn't taken long for Muslim and Croat militias to adopt the same sinister strategy of purging the "other" from the territory they controlled.

As we drove through the areas where the US-brokered cease-fire was taking effect, we could often tell which ethnic group held an enclave only by noting who was being insulted in the graffiti scrawled on apartment building walls. Sometimes our best clue as to who had been victimized was either a church's cross or a mosque's minaret poking out from a large pile of rubble. The scenes reminded me of a Macedonian satirist's brilliant summation of the ethos behind the killing: "Why should I be a minority in your state when you can be a minority in mine?"

After ten months of ferocious fighting, the civilians we met were shell-shocked, blinking in the afternoon winter sunshine like people who had just emerged into the daylight after watching a horror movie in a darkened theater. One woman stood in her front yard looking at her home, which had been in enemy hands for more than a year, trembling at the sight of what little was left. I asked a group of soldiers how they had gone so quickly from firing grenades across a front line to tossing their rivals packs of cigarettes. "Our commanders told us to fight," one soldier said simply. "Now they are telling us to stop."

My time in central Bosnia deepened my understanding of American power, which I could now see encompassed far more than fighter jets. The United States had brokered the cease-fire not by resorting to military action, but by exerting unrelenting diplomatic pressure on both sides. Although almost everyone we met had lost a loved one in the fighting, the new agreement allowed people to dare to hope that the war—or at least their experience of the war—might end. The superpower had made a horrific situation much better.

I felt an immense sense of privilege at being able to chronicle the experience of men and women being reunited with their elderly parents who had been too infirm to flee. And I was moved by the elation of children who relished the simple pleasure of playing outside again. With the pause in fighting, a motley crew of journalists from the UK, the US, and France had rushed to the area to cover this breaking—and rare good news—story. We drove ourselves hard during the day, interviewing dozens of people and crossing front lines that hadn't been traversed in months. With regular phone service to the outside world cut off across Bosnia, we ducked into UN bases to file our stories—an exercise rarely without technical hassle. We had to first connect our computers to a regular phone jack and then dial up a number in Austria that would, on a good day and after some suspense, let off a long beep indicating that a virtual "handshake" had occurred. Then, when our stories had been uploaded, we went for drinks.

I felt like I stood out as a novice among veterans. Emma Daly of the British *Independent* accompanied Laura and me on our interviews. Although Emma was also making her first trip to central Bosnia, I seemed perpetually cold and wet while she was somehow prepared for all weather contingencies, pulling the necessary attire from her compact suitcase—whether fleece, down jacket, or raincoat. In a belt wallet under her shirt, she also kept rolls of small bills, which were essential in towns where banks had long since been destroyed. "How did you know to bring all that?" I asked enviously.

Initially, I wore a camouflaged vest and helmet given to me by George Kenney, the first of the US officials to resign from the State Department to protest the government's Bosnia policy. I thought it would protect me from stray bullets and shrapnel, but when I saw what the battle-hardened journalists wore, I realized that Kenney's vest lacked the lifesaving ceramic plates of a standard flak jacket. It would be largely useless in the face of gun- or mortar fire.

Luckily, my colleagues were so focused on gathering material for their own stories that, at first, they paid me little mind. By the time they began teasing me for the goofiness of my flimsy vest and the inappropriateness of my Nine West boots (no match for this war zone's winter mud), I blushed more with a sense of belonging than with shame. I felt exhilarated by the camaraderie; the press corps offered a solidarity I had felt before only on my sports teams. This was a club to which I very much wanted to belong.

Much of my life over the nearly two years I spent in the Balkans would entail pitching story ideas to editors in major American cities like Boston, Washington, and San Francisco. I would end up with more than a dozen different employers, from the wire service UPI to regional newspapers around the United States like the *Dallas Morning News* and the *Baltimore Sun*. But my core relationships were with the *Boston Globe*, *U.S. News & World Report*, and later, *The Economist*, *The New Republic*, and the *Washington Post*. Whenever I had a piece published, the newspaper or magazine kindly cut out the clipping and mailed it to Mum and Eddie's Brooklyn home, my only American address. Once I started taking frequent trips from relatively peaceful Croatia into Bosnia, Eddie dedicated himself to intercepting mail that included articles with a Bosnian dateline so that Mum would not realize my location.

Mort had convinced me that the only way President Clinton would intervene to break the siege of Sarajevo was if he felt domestic pressure to do so. As a journalist, therefore, I believed I had a critical role to play. I wanted not only to inform members of Congress and other decision-makers, but to try to make everyday readers care about what was happening to people thousands of miles away.

Many journalists in Bosnia brought a similar focus to their work. High-minded though it sounds, we wanted our articles to matter and our governments' actions to change. I was aware that this aspiration was more reminiscent of an editorial writer's ambition than that of a traditional reporter, whose job was to document what she saw. But when I wrote an article—no matter how obscure the publication where it appeared—I hoped President Clinton would see it. I wanted him to do more than he was doing to help the people I was meeting, most of whom were desperate and believed that only the United States could save them.

When I reported my heart out and my editors weren't interested, I was crushed. I blamed myself for not figuring out how to bridge the distance. The editors did their best to remind me of the US context so I could keep my readers foremost in my mind. They drilled into my head one of the basic truisms of reporting: if I did not make the stakes of the issue clear and compelling, most people would not read past the first paragraph.

While I despised trying to "sell" the suffering around me, the experience helped refine—in a way that would prove valuable later on—my own sense of what animated Americans or, alternatively, what was likely to cause their eyes to glaze over. As the months passed and I became a more capable reporter, I went back and forth about whether I should pursue journalism as a permanent career. Since nothing we were writing had thus far managed to sway Western decision-makers, I wondered if I could find a different path that was less about describing events and more about directly trying to shape them. Once, when I reported on a diplomatic gathering that included European foreign ministers and Secretary of State Warren Christopher, I noted in my journal: "I would like to be one of them." On another occasion, after covering a massacre of children who were struck by a shell while jumping rope in a Sarajevo playground, I wrote to myself that I wanted to "be on the other side of the microphone," in a position to make or change US policy.

I TOOK A SHORT TRIP back to Washington in September of 1994. I was twenty-three years old and had lived in the former Yugoslavia for less than ten months. Encouraged by Mort, who often seemed blind to hierarchy and propriety, I contacted two people that I still cannot believe I had the gumption to engage.

First, I called Strobe Talbott at his home. Strobe was a longtime *Time* magazine correspondent who had become Deputy Secretary of State in the Clinton administration—the second in line at the State Department. I had his number only because I had met him through Mort before he entered government. The conversation was then—and remains now—cringeworthy in the extreme:

"Hello, Strobe, you may not remember me. This is Samantha Power."

"Yes, of course, how are you?" he said warmly.

"I'm good, but I actually spent the last year in Bosnia, and I was wondering if you'd like to have a chat."

There was a long pause.

"I suppose you'd like to offer recommendations," he said dryly, filling the silence.

"I may be presumptuous enough to phone you at home at nine o'clock at night, but I'm not so presumptuous to think I could make informed recommendations. I just know what I see . . . but it might be useful to meet," I offered.

"I would like to, but I'm kind of busy with Haiti right now," Strobe replied.

I put my face in my hands and mouthed to myself, "Haiti! Of course he's busy with Haiti!!" The newspapers were then filled with reports that Clinton's national security team was meeting around the clock, preparing a large military deployment to help restore the country's democratically elected president to power.

Strobe hurried off the call. But I was not finished making a fool of myself on my homecoming visit.

Thanks again to an introduction from Mort, I met the next day with Steve Rosenfeld in his office at the *Washington Post*, where he was the editorial page editor. He understandably assumed I was interested in career advice. "So you want to be a journalist?" he asked. "No," I answered. "Or maybe," I said, not wanting to offend him. I shifted the topic. "I hear you are sort of a dove on Bosnia," I began.

As Rosenfeld looked over my shoulder at CNN's Haiti coverage on a nearby television, I tried to make a persuasive case for why he should write editorials urging Clinton to do more to stop the Bosnian atrocities. He was surprisingly polite, but also firm that the United States should stay out of the conflict.

After half an hour, when he tried to end our meeting and get back to work, I persisted.

"I know you have to go," I said. "Just two or three last points, if I may." Fifteen minutes later, I was still talking.

While I was becoming a decent reporter, I was a woefully ineffective advocate.

IN 1994 AND 1995, I traveled regularly to Sarajevo. Doing so was to be transported into another galaxy: the dystopian landscape was burned and broken, yet people went on living as if no longer noticing the plastic sheeting on their windows or the charred cars turned into barriers to shield them as they crossed the road. Parts of the city felt instantly familiar—Mum and I had watched the 1984 Winter Olympics together in Atlanta, cheering for "Wild Bill" Johnson, the daring American skier, as he captured his gold racing down hills that were now teeming with Serb heavy weapons. Scott Hamilton had skated to gold in the Zetra Stadium, which was now destroyed and surrounded by graves.

Only once inside the city could I feel how close the attacking Serbs were, and how claustrophobic the trapped inhabitants must have felt. The mountains seemed to grow out of the river that split the city in half. By holding the high ground, the Bosnian Serb Army was able to choose its targets at will. I found it hard to believe that men who called themselves soldiers were setting their rifle sights on women carrying their water jugs home. But by the time the siege was finally brought to an end, the Bosnian Serb militants would end up killing some 10,000 people in the city.

By 1994, the cemeteries in Sarajevo had already been so overwhelmed that the town's biggest parks and football fields had been converted into graveyards. Since few families who lost loved ones could afford a proper cement marker, they used simple wooden plaques, often scavenged from a table or bookshelf. I felt sick when I saw, at the Lion Cemetery, the relatively recent birthdates on the grave markers—children, teenagers, and twentysomethings seemed to account for the majority of the deaths. And alongside the Bosnian Serb leaders' determination to kill the city's residents came a desire to humiliate and torment those who survived. They bombed libraries, concert halls, and universities. As businesses closed or were destroyed, unemployment soared.

To pay for food, English professors sought out jobs as interpreters for the UN. Engineers turned to rummaging among destroyed cars for batteries with a charge. Poets and medical students who had never dreamed of holding a gun joined the army so they could defend their city and all it represented.

Back in 1992, in the early months of the war, Sarajevo residents had opportunities to be evacuated and become refugees. But many stayed because they expected that the war, which they had never believed would happen in the first place, would end quickly. Others remained because, irrespective of whether they were Muslims, Croats, Serbs, or Jews, they knew that the Serb extremists' primary goal was to destroy the spirit of tolerance and pluralism embodied in the city's multiethnic character. "If we leave, they win," Sarajevans would say defiantly. Unfortunately, once they had passed up the chance to depart, they did not get another opportunity.

As dangerous as the Bosnian capital was, I knew I was in a privileged position compared to the residents scrambling for safety around me. I had a UN press badge and thus permission to leave as well as enter; almost everyone else was stuck.

While some Western officials talked about the conflict as if it were historically preordained—"they have been killing one another for centuries"—the lives of the young people before the war were not dissimilar from those of the average young American. They would meet up for an espresso or a beer after work, and would dance at raves or to the music of popular bands like U2. The values they learned were the same as those we had been taught. Mosques, Catholic churches, Orthodox churches, and a synagogue dotted the downtown. One in every five marriages in Bosnia (and one in three in Sarajevo) had been ethnically mixed.

My childhood in Ireland had coincided with the period of sectarian tensions and terrorism known as "The Troubles," which had started shortly before I was born. The people of Northern Ireland would ultimately endure thirty years of conflict in which some 3,600 lives were lost. The deadliest attack in the Irish Republic's history occurred in 1974, a couple of months before my brother's birth, when Loyalist paramilitaries set off a series of rush-hour bombs in my hometown of Dublin, killing twenty-six people, including a pregnant woman. As the conflict escalated, a growing number of refugees from the North—more than 10,000 overall—poured across the border.

These events did not affect my life in any immediate way. Even after violent incidents in Dublin, I do not recall ever fearing that my mother would not make it home from the hospital or my dad from the pub. At the same time, my early years in Dublin meant that I never saw civil strife as something that happened "over there" or to "those people."

When I spoke with my friends and family back in the States and in Ireland, I tried to translate what Bosnians were experiencing, but I must have sounded preachy as I urged my friends to put themselves in different shoes:

> Imagine if you were sitting at home and you suddenly found that your telephone line had been cut. You couldn't even call your parents to tell them you were okay. Imagine having to sleep in every layer of clothing you owned to survive without heat. Imagine not being able to send your kids to school because it was safer to keep them in your dark basement than for them to take a short walk down the block. Imagine hearing your child's tummy growling and not being able to help because the next UN food delivery was not for another week. Imagine getting shot at by

people whose weddings you had attended. This is what is happening right now to people like us.

When I first visited, although the war had already been under way for nearly two years, I spoke to many Bosnians who still held out hope that the United States would rescue them. Their knowledge of the political dynamics in Washington was striking. The columns of American opinion writers (particularly Anthony Lewis and William Safire of the *New York Times*) were translated and, despite the shortage of paper and ink, widely circulated. Electricity was intermittent, and smuggled batteries for shortwave radios were only sold at exorbitant prices. Nonetheless, many residents knew which members of the US Senate were pushing for air strikes, while some even tracked when these politicians were up for reelection. Often my Bosnian neighbors informed me of obscure happenings in the Clinton administration. "Have you heard Steve Oxman is out and Richard Holbrooke is in?" a waiter in a café asked in 1994, alerting me to the news that Clinton had replaced his assistant secretary of state for European and Canadian affairs.

Some days, when President Clinton seemed on the verge of using military force, and the Bosnian Serb Army was afraid of provoking him, the atmosphere was so calm that I went jogging. Other periods were extremely dangerous, and I could do little more than pray the shells would not find me. On occasion, when it felt like the mortars were landing closer and closer, I was too frightened to do more than seek shelter in the bathtub of the hotel or apartment where I was staying. The most lethal days started peaceful and turned deadly: daring to trust the early quiet, people would venture outside, and Bosnian Serb forces would then hit crowded bread and water lines, markets, and school playgrounds.

Despite these horrors, for the first several years of the war, Sarajevans treated Western visitors with immense magnanimity. Even after losing loved ones—that very day—they would insist on pouring their hearts out in order to alert the world to their suffering. They would share their most intimate memories.

"Tell Clinton," one bereaved father said as he ushered me to the door after describing the loss of his son. It was a phrase I heard often.

Amid the darkness, the resilience of the people of Bosnia was inspiring. They asserted their dignity in large and small ways. People scraped together resources to stage elaborate weddings. They went on having babies, perhaps aided by the fact that birth control pills were hard to get in the besieged city. Women who walked to work did so in high heels, even though their impractical shoes would impede their escape when bullets started flying. As Bosnians waited hours in line for their turn at the water pump, they imposed rules and created penalties for those who cut the queue or took more than their share. Poets, novelists, and musicians kept writing. Though the main theaters had been reduced to rubble, artists found places to perform plays and music.

And while there was much to cry about, Sarajevans did not lose their sense of humor. At the start of the war, the Serb militants frequently graffitied areas they claimed should be theirs with the words *"Ovo je Srbija!,"* or "This is Serbia!" When they did this to a post office in Sarajevo, a resident famously responded in spray paint: *"Budalo, ovo je pošta,"* or "Idiot, this is a post office." And when the siege of Sarajevo officially outlasted the siege of Leningrad, becoming the longest in modern history, a pirate radio station blared the Queen song "We Are the Champions." The heart of the country refused to stop beating.

10

THE SECRET TO A LONG LIFE

In May of 1995, as I was traveling into Sarajevo with Roger Cohen, the *New York Times* bureau chief for the Balkans, I nearly lost my life. Serb militants had shut down the airport, so we had no choice but to enter via a dirt road over Mount Igman, the one patch of land around Sarajevo that remained in Bosnian hands. What was little more than a steep mountain goat trail before the war had become the lone land route by which people, food, and arms could still make it into the Bosnian capital.

The Serbs had attempted to take Mount Igman, and the Bosnian Army had suffered significant casualties defending the narrow eighteen-mile road that snaked through the mountain. The entire pass remained vulnerable to Serb artillery, with the last fifteen miles in the line of sight for Serb heavy machine guns and cannons. People who used the road often drove at breakneck speed around sharp bends without any idea what might be coming in the opposite direction. Honking in a blind spot was ill-advised because it would attract attention from Serb gunmen. Yet when a car veered even one foot off the path, there was no guardrail to prevent it from slipping off the shoulder. The drop was precipitous, and the Bosnian Army had mined the side of the mountain to prevent Serb soldiers from staging a stealth attack on foot.

Many people died on Mount Igman, including a number of peacekeepers and, later that summer, three US officials: President Clinton's Bosnia special envoy Robert Frasure, National Security Council aide Nelson Drew, and the Defense Department's Joseph Kruzel. The

French soldier transporting the American diplomats into Sarajevo had been driving at a rapid clip when he accidentally veered off the side of the road while trying to avoid an approaching convoy. The diplomats' armored personnel carrier went tumbling more than three hundred yards down the mountain, causing anti-tank rockets in the vehicle to explode.

From the relative shelter of a Bosnian government checkpoint at the top of the mountain road, Roger and I braced ourselves for the perilous journey. As we set off, we could see the hulks of vehicles hit by Serb gun-fire or destroyed after drivers had taken the hairpin turns too quickly. Driving the heavy armored vehicle provided by the *Times*, Roger was aiming for the unachievable combination of speed and maneuverability at once. Whenever we shaved the edge of the road, I turned my body toward the gearshift—as if I could personally avoid the land mines that the outer part of the vehicle might accidentally set off.

As we hurtled down the mountain at a velocity that we hoped would outpace the Serb gunners who might have us in their sights, Roger began to lose control of the vehicle. Our downward momentum from the steepness of the descent caused the steering wheel to elude his grasp and spin wildly. Sweating profusely, all I could do as we lunged from right to left was press my hand against the roof of the five-ton vehicle as Roger tried to keep hold of the violently shaking steering wheel and force the car toward the center of the road. At one point in particular, I felt sure we were about to plunge down the mountain as the car careened out of control toward the edge—but somehow, in a mystery that neither of us understand to this day, Roger managed to haul us back onto the trail.

I WAS BY THEN SPENDING most of my time in Sarajevo, the epicenter of the war. The situation was deteriorating badly. While I was work-ing there in June and July of 1995, an average of three hundred shells rained down on the city each day. With no end to the war in sight, I was starting to feel increasingly like a vulture, preying upon Bosnian misery to write my stories.

Even when my articles received prominent placement in a newspaper or magazine, potentially bringing my reporting to the attention of millions of people, I had a nagging sense that I was falling short. I grew practiced at interviewing survivors of violence, but I still couldn't shake the feeling that by asking questions designed to elicit appalling detail, I was exploiting someone's personal trauma for "my story."

There would come a moment in every interview where I would feel a rush of recognition—"I have what I need"—and then would hasten to wind down the conversation so I could get to a power source for my laptop and start writing. I would then begin to feel guilty for having invaded someone's home, drunk (at their insistence) their scarce coffee or tea, and left.

Once, after I rose to end an interview with an elderly Muslim woman in Serb-held territory, she hugged me goodbye. Writing later that night in my journal, I noted, "She squeezed me like I was one of her own. I was ashamed." I don't know now if I was ashamed because I had been practicing my new craft while she was sobbing in pain at the loss of her sons, because I felt the United States was not doing enough to prevent such devastation, or some combination.

When I drove with Stacy Sullivan of *Newsweek* to UN headquarters for the daily press briefing in Sarajevo, we typically passed a cluster of photographers in an expectant scrum at the entrance to the main road, which was known as Sniper Alley. The still and video photographers had their cameras ready, knowing that someone was likely to get shot by a Bosnian Serb sniper as he or she made a mad dash across this exposed portion of road. Elizabeth Rubin, a writer with *Harper's* who would become a close friend, once saw a woman who managed to survive the crossing yell back at one of the perched photographers, "No work for you today, asshole. I made it alive."

Until that summer, I had believed that if my colleagues and I conveyed the suffering around us to decision-makers in Washington, our journalism might move President Clinton to stage a rescue mission. This had not happened. The words, the photographs, the videos—nothing had changed the President's mind. While Sarajevans had once thought of Western journalists as messengers on their behalf, they had now begun to see us as ambassadors of idle nations. No matter how many massacres we covered, Western governments seemed determined to steer clear of the conflict.

Even if Clinton and his advisers did not think it reasonable to get involved to prevent atrocities, I thought they should have seen how failing to shore up a fragmenting part of Europe would impact traditional US security interests. The occurrence of such a conflict in the heart of Europe made NATO look feckless, and the failed state gave unsavory criminal elements—like arms traffickers and terrorists—a foothold in Europe. I knew that thousands of foreign fighters were making their way to the country, including the battle-hardened mujahedeen from Afghanistan. But I only later learned that a still-young terrorist group known as al-Qaeda was active there, and that two of the September 11th hijackers as well as attack architect Khalid Sheikh Mohammed ended up fighting in Bosnia.[2]

On several occasions during the long summer of 1995, when I dropped by the home of someone who had lost a loved one in the capital, I was shooed away. "Why should we talk to you?" one woman screamed at me before slamming her door. "The world knows, your government knows, and you do nothing."

Just as the war had come to feel normal, so too had the idea that nobody would stop it.

At the same time, I noticed that I had gradually lost my fear. While once I had shivered for hours after evading Serb shelling or sniper fire, now I no longer worried about the crack of gunfire or the crash of a mortar exploding nearby. Three years into their agony, Sarajevans were joking, "If you run, you hit the bullet; if you walk, the bullet hits you." I had begun to feel a similar fatalism, gradually giving up the superstitions that I had originally seized upon for safety—my Pirates baseball cap, my back-street route to the press briefing, and my ritual beer as I pounded away on my laptop after a long day's work.

I knew I had been lucky—every reporter had close calls, and mine were nowhere near as hair-raising as those of others. But they began to add up. As I was driving in Serb territory along an icy road, my car turned 180 degrees and spun into a ditch that was surrounded by mines. Once, in Sarajevo, shrapnel burst through the window and landed on the desk where Stacy and I often worked side by side. In the same month, a large mortar attack flattened a house several doors from where I was charging my computer. One day, as Stacy, Emma, and I exited our car near the Bosnian president's office, Serb snipers fired on us repeatedly, forcing us to race across the parking lot in a panicked search for cover. Our assailants were just a few hundred yards away, and certainly could have hit us if that had been their goal. Instead, they seemed more interested in amusing themselves.

The spike in violence weighed heavily on Mum, Eddie, and Stephen, who were each tracking the news from New York. When I called home, my brother, who was back for the summer after his junior year in college, grabbed the phone. Stephen and my mother had a fraught relationship: she struggled to get him to focus on school and to lay off drugs and alcohol, while he insisted he didn't need her advice, saying he took after his father, which was just what she was worried about. At the same time, he was protective of her. If one of the patients she was close to died, he was tender, assuring her she had done all she could and frying her up a fish he had caught for dinner.

Stephen and I were not especially close, but we were always warm with each other. So it shocked me when he confronted me about the risks I was taking.

"What you are doing is so selfish, sis," he said on the phone, asking, "Don't you ever think about Mum?"

My brother had a point. For all the time I'd spent trying to convey to others what it was like to be a Bosnian under siege, I had not really stopped to imagine what it must have been like to be the parent of someone who had chosen to go live in a war zone.

The call with Stephen reoriented me. "Maybe it's time," I thought, and the words of folk singer/songwriter Michelle Shocked sprung into my mind: "The secret to a long life's knowing when it's time to go." I began to think seriously about an exit strategy.

Like many of my contemporaries who had graduated college but were not sure what they wanted to do in their careers, I had considered applying to law school and had taken the LSAT during my year with Mort at Carnegie. The prospect of actually becoming a lawyer hadn't much appealed to me at the time, and I never followed through with submitting applications. After a few months of working in the Balkans, however, the idea had resurfaced.

The one area where the so-called international community seemed to be making progress was in building new institutions to promote criminal justice. A tribunal was being assembled in The Hague to punish war crimes, crimes against humanity, and genocide. Self-conscious about simply recording what was happening around me, I wondered whether, if I became a lawyer, I could do something more concrete to support the victims of atrocities or to punish wrongdoers. Immersing myself in lessons on the rule of law seemed an antidote to the violence and impunity around me.

After a year in the region, I had sent an application to Harvard Law School along with several of my press clips. I thought Harvard's prestige might add credibility to my writings and policy recommendations, and the law school brochure described a wide range of international law offerings. I also liked the prospect of being just a train ride from Mum and Eddie. In the spring of 1995, I was notified that I had been admitted.

Still unsure of whether I actually wanted to attend, I reached out to Mort for advice. He was vehemently opposed. "Why would you stop doing something valuable in order to go sit in a classroom for three years?" he asked.

He then called his friend, Assistant Secretary of State Richard Holbrooke, whom President Clinton had recently asked to lead the American effort to broker peace in Bosnia, and asked him to use his negotiating skills to talk me out of going to law school. When I answered the phone and heard Holbrooke's nasal voice, which I knew only from television, I was startled. He told me that he knew many women who had mistakenly gone to law school because they felt they needed a credential to be taken seriously. "You do not need a piece of paper to legitimize yourself," he said, before adding—to my amazement—"Mort says I should hire you."

The prospect of working as a junior aide to Holbrooke as he tried to bring the war to an end was tantalizing beyond words. I thanked him for calling and told him I would seriously consider what he had said. After we hung up, I called Eddie and told him about the conversation. "If I work for Holbrooke," I exclaimed, "I can eliminate all the middle men!" What I meant was that, in order to influence US policy, I would no longer need to convince editors to accept my stories. I could make my case directly to the top decision-makers in government.

Eddie loved the idea, and, in a spontaneous burst of lyricism, immediately launched into one of Shakespeare's best-known monologues, from *Julius Caesar*:

> There is a tide in the affairs of men,
> Which, taken at the flood, leads on to fortune;
> Omitted, all the voyage of their life
> Is bound in shallows and in miseries.
> On such a full sea are we now afloat;
> And we must take the current when it serves,
> Or lose our ventures.

Knowing I didn't always grasp precisely what he was getting at, after he finished his oration, he declared, "Go for it!"

But something held me back from taking this fantasy job with Holbrooke. I had begun to fixate on the notion that in law school I could acquire technical, tangible skills that would ultimately equip me to make a bigger difference than I would by putting words to paper, even as an aide to the US envoy. I decided to send in a letter of acceptance to Harvard in order to hold my place, but continued to internally debate whether to attend, self-conscious about the luxury of privileged indecision.

In July of 1995, however, all of this faded from mind as the Bosnian Serb military commander Ratko Mladić launched an all-out assault on the UN-declared "safe area" of Srebrenica, and in the ensuing days orchestrated the largest single massacre in Europe since World War II.

THE DAY BEFORE SREBRENICA FELL, I borrowed a satellite phone from colleagues in Sarajevo and called Ed Cody, the foreign editor of the *Washington Post*, to pitch a story on the Bosnian Serbs' march to-ward the town. Cody said he didn't deem another Bosnian Serb Army incursion newsworthy, especially as readers had seen a lot in recent months about attacks on UN safe areas.

I argued with him, pointing out that some 30,000 Muslims in Srebrenica had no protection. But I knew that American readers were fatigued and that I had to clear a higher bar to place a story in the West-ern press than in the early days of what was already a three-year-old conflict.

As I rambled on, hoping to persuade him that this crisis was differ-ent, Cody cut me off. "Well," he said, "it sounds like tomorrow, *when* Srebrenica falls, we'll have a story." I was stunned by the cynicism in his words, but I failed to change his mind.

Twenty-four hours later, Bosnian Serb forces stormed into the town of Srebrenica; on July 12th, my article ran on the front page of the *Post* under the banner headline: BOSNIAN SERBS SEIZE "SAFE AREA." When I called Mort, he was disconsolate. "This is the pits, the lowest moment yet," he said.

Western reporters like me were unable to get access to Srebrenica in the days that followed. The best we could do was speak with alarmed UN officials and Bosnian government sources, and report what was being broadcast on Serbian TV—primarily, images of Mladić in the town, carting Bosnian Muslim men and boys away on buses while as-suring them, "No one will harm you." Still in Sarajevo, I began report-ing unverifiable claims that Muslim prisoners like those we saw on TV were in fact being executed. On July 14th, I wrote an article in the *Bos-ton Globe* titled MASSACRES REPORTED NEAR SREBRENICA, which relayed the Bosnian government's allegations that hundreds of prisoners had already been murdered. I also quoted an eyewitness saying that "while the TV cameras were there, the Serbs were good. Then the media dis-appeared, and the soldiers started taking people off the buses." The whereabouts of some 10,000 people were unknown.

Ten days after Srebrenica's fall, I heard ever more terrifying reports about what was happening out of sight. Bosnian foreign minister Mu-hamed Sacirbey claimed that 1,600 Bosnian men and boys detained in a stadium near Srebrenica had been shot. Meanwhile, Bosnian Serb radio openly reported that of the Muslim fighters who had fled Srebrenica, "most were liquidated." I shuddered at what I was hearing. But blocked by Bosnian Serb forces from getting to Srebrenica, neither I nor my colleagues had any way of corroborating the claims. I hoped they were exaggerated or false. I had also already begun reporting on the brazen Serb assault on a second UN "safe area" around the town of Žepa. There, some 20,000 civilians were trapped, protected by just 79 UN peacekeeping troops.*

On August 10th, at the UN in New York, US ambassador Madeleine Albright presented evidence to the Security Council that Bosnian Serb soldiers had executed as many as 2,700 people, burying them in shallow mass graves. Albright circulated a set of US satellite images showing a small farming village fourteen miles west of Srebrenica. The "before" photos, grainy though they were, clearly showed prisoners crowded into a soccer field, along with pristine fields nearby. The "after" photos were taken a few days later; the prisoners were gone, and the earth in the neighboring fields had been disturbed in three areas, creating what looked like mass graves.

Albright linked the photos to firsthand testimony from a fifty-five-year-old Muslim who said he had been in a group of men who had been machine-gunned there. The man had miraculously survived, hiding among the corpses of his friends and relatives. At nightfall he had escaped to Bosnian territory before the bodies around him were bulldozed into one of the large graves that lay waiting.

MY FRIEND DAVID ROHDE, the *Christian Science Monitor*'s Eastern Europe correspondent, was on vacation in Australia visiting his girlfriend when the Serbs took Srebrenica. In the weeks that followed, he read horrific testimonies disseminated in the media from survivors like the one Albright quoted. Without permission from the Bosnian Serb

---

* Serb forces seized Žepa in late July, and burned much of the town to the ground. The majority of civilians fled or were evacuated to Sarajevo, but Bosnian Serb soldiers killed hundreds who were unable to escape.

authorities, he managed to elude the military and police and spend two days around Srebrenica searching for evidence of the alleged executions.

On the first day, he entered an abandoned building on the grounds of a local soccer stadium—the same place Foreign Minister Sacirbey had referred to in his alarming speech about mass executions. David found human feces, dried blood, and several dozen bullet holes up and down the walls.

On the second day, using a faxed copy of one of the blurry US satellite photos, he found the fields Albright had referenced. There, he discovered empty ammunition boxes, Muslim prayer beads, photographs, and various personal items. Finally, and most tellingly, as he would write in the *Christian Science Monitor*, he saw "what appeared to be a decomposing human leg protruding from the freshly turned dirt."

In addition, in a dozen interviews with Serb soldiers and civilians in the area, he met not a soul who reported seeing or hearing about Muslim prisoners. Thousands of Bosnian Muslim men and boys seemed to have simply vanished.

After writing a story on the graves, David traveled back to Bosnian-held territory, where he found nine Muslims who said they had played dead in the fields of Srebrenica where the mass executions occurred. When he showed the survivors the items he had found in the fields, one man gasped after seeing the 1982 elementary school diploma of his brother from whom he had been separated. He asked David where he had found the document, and David said he had picked it up fifty feet from a mass grave. The man, David wrote in the *Monitor*, "stared blankly and then quietly faded into a crowd of soldiers."

David emailed me after his encounter with the survivors, writing:

> I cannot articulate the combination of sadness and disbelief that washed over me when these men would accurately describe the soccer field I visited . . . and then go on to talk about 1,000 people being gunned down. I kept asking them more and more detailed questions, hoping they would get things wrong, but they didn't . . . These people aren't lying.

The evil of what transpired in Srebrenica, which David did more than any other reporter to expose, helped me decide what I should do next. I could continue to write articles about the Bosnia carnage in an effort to move President Clinton. I could pursue a possible job with Holbrooke and work from within the US government to push for the same outcome. Or I could attend Harvard Law School and, although it would take a few years, try to become a prosecutor who could bring murderers to justice. Working at the war crimes tribunal in The Hague now seemed like the worthiest goal, and the one that would ultimately have the most impact. We would not bring back the men and boys who had been executed, but we could make sure that Bosnian Serb general Ratko Mladić and others like him faced justice.

Jonathan Moore, the former US diplomat and refugee expert I met working at Carnegie, had become someone I turned to at critical moments. With school beginning at the start of September, I needed to make a final decision, so I telephoned him and asked what I should do.

Jonathan didn't hesitate. "Get the hell out of there," he urged me. "You need to break out of the compulsion for power, glory, ego, relevance, contribution. Get out. Get out before it gets you, and you forget what got you in."

I didn't think self-consciously about power, glory, and ego, but Jonathan knew I didn't mind seeing my name in print. He also knew that I was drawn to joining the US government's Bosnia team because I couldn't bear to move away from the center of the action.

"But Holbrooke—" I tried.

"Forget Holbrooke," he said. "There will be other jobs. Reading books will do you good."

THE PERSON WHO I KNEW would be on the other side of the argument—echoing Mort's conviction that I stay—was of course Fred Cuny. But once Fred had gotten the water flowing in Sarajevo, he had gone in search of his next ambitious project. A few months later, he had ended up in Chechnya to assess how he could help people being subjected to a comprehensive Russian carpet-bombing campaign. But I couldn't get Fred's perspective because he had gone missing.

In early 1995, I had been visiting Mum and Eddie when Fred happened to be coming through New York after his first visit to Chechnya. When he walked into the sports bar he had chosen as our meeting place, he exclaimed "Sammie!" and embraced me in a large Texas hug. When we talked about what he had seen, however, he was uncharacteristically despairing.

"The Serb forces in Bosnia are cruel," he said, "but they are always trying to figure out how they can get what they want without provoking US intervention. They bomb, they probe, they watch, they pause, they bomb again. Russia's forces in Chechnya know they are free to do anything they please. They know nobody will stop them. There are no lines they won't cross. I've never seen anything like it."

While Sarajevo had recorded as many as 3,500 heavy detonations per day, he said, the capital of Chechnya had counted that number each hour. He said that some 400,000 Chechens had been displaced in three months of fighting, and as many as 15,000 Russian and Chechen civilians had been killed.

Yet instead of being deterred, Fred saw a problem to be tackled. In what seemed to me a complete non sequitur from his descriptions of slaughter, he concluded, "I think we can help broker a cease-fire."

My eyes widened. "By 'we,' do you mean you?" I asked, hoping I had misheard. He smiled self-consciously. "Yeah, I guess so."

Fred also thought that, by visiting, he would be in a stronger position to get the Clinton administration to do more to pressure Russia to desist. He had long impressed upon me one of his core beliefs about influence: "The only way to move people in Washington is to tell them things they don't already know, and that requires seeing things for yourself."

Even for Fred Cuny, who had often managed to pull off what entire governments and humanitarian agencies deemed inconceivable, getting the Russians to cease their assault in Chechnya seemed delusional. He was the expert, though, and while I teased him about his excessive confidence, I felt I didn't know enough to challenge him.

Fred spent the next month publicly blasting the Russian government for its actions, testifying before Congress and writing a lengthy critical essay about Russia's conduct in the *New York Review of Books*. His advocacy exposed how badly the Russian efforts were going and, indeed, how some 5,000 Russian soldiers had already been killed. It also encouraged greater scrutiny of the Russian military's atrocities. By going public with his criticisms of Russia's war, however, Fred made himself a target. For his safety, Fred's coworkers pleaded with him not to return to Chechnya, but nobody could say no to Fred Cuny.

In March of 1995, Fred traveled back into Chechnya with two doctors from the Russian Red Cross, a Russian translator, and a local driver. When Fred's delegation entered territory held by Chechen separatists, they were apprehended. Fred sent a calm note to the Soros Foundation, his funder, saying that his group had been delayed. His Russian translator added a postscript with a wholly different message: "We, as always, are in deep shit . . . If we're not back in three days, shake everyone up."

Then the delegation had disappeared.

Fred's twenty-eight-year-old son, Craig, and his brother, Chris, quickly flew to the region to begin searching. They got shot at, shelled, and robbed as they spent much of the summer of 1995 trying to find him. Mort excitedly called me in Sarajevo one day with word that Fred had been found—and I was euphoric. But the report proved incorrect, one of several false sightings. Still, I clung to the belief that Fred would turn up.

In mid-August, Craig and Chris announced that Fred had been executed by Chechen rebels not long after being taken captive. Chris said that while Chechen gunmen had pulled the trigger, it was the Russian government that had loaded the gun, spreading false information that Fred was an anti-Chechen Russian agent. "Let it be known to all nations and humanitarian organizations," Chris declared at a press conference, "that Russia was responsible for the death of one of the world's great humanitarians."

I was devastated, both by the loss of someone who had been so exceptionally kind to me, and by the death of a humanitarian hero, whose expertise and can-do spirit seemed so necessary in a world increasingly racked by ethnic and religious conflict.

No matter how much cruelty I had seen in Bosnia, a stubbornly na-ive part of me could not accept the truth. For weeks, I had vivid dreams about Fred showing up at my door with a big smile and a six-pack of root beer. "You didn't really think I could die, did you?" he would tell me. I did everything I could to fend off thoughts about his final hours. And I resorted to my time-tested approach to blunting the pain I felt at losing someone important to me: I kept moving.

Fred's death cemented my decision to duck out of the "real world" and decompress. In late August, I packed up my belongings and booked my flight back to the United States to begin law school.

BACK IN AMERICA, I saw that David's reporting on Srebrenica had landed like a bombshell in Washington, yielding just the kind of im-pact I had hoped to achieve through my own writing. Suddenly, lead-ing members of Congress were pushing President Clinton to intervene militarily to end the war and prevent "future Srebrenicas."

The final straw for Clinton came in late August. As I pulled myself together at Mum and Eddie's home in Brooklyn, I heard the news that Bosnian Serb gunners around Sarajevo had struck again, hitting the same market they had attacked in February of 1994, this time killing forty-three people. Once I had established that nobody I knew had been killed, I fumed that the United States continued to allow the slaying of innocents. And in truth, I wished I were still there to cover a story that was leading the news around the world.

The day before law school began, I loaded up a Ryder truck in Brooklyn with two suitcases, a bicycle, and my laptop, and drove to-ward Boston. Just as I reached my new hometown, NPR cut into its ra-dio program with a breaking news bulletin: "NATO air action around Sarajevo is under way." I let out tears of relief.

By my second week of law school, US air strikes had broken the siege of Sarajevo and brought the Bosnian war to an end.

Fred and Mort had been right about what a US rescue operation could achieve, but tens of thousands of lives had been lost.

11

"GO REMEMBER"

From the moment I arrived at Harvard Law School, I feared I wouldn't last. While in Bosnia, I had imagined how satisfying it would be to learn the law and eventually hunt down Balkan war criminals as a prosecutor at The Hague. But as I struggled to adjust to my new life back in the United States, all I could think about was the place I had left behind. Had I remained just a few weeks longer, I kept thinking, I would have witnessed history.

As I began classes, the US-led NATO bombing campaign quickly wiped out the Bosnian Serb Army's heavy weapons and communications capabilities, leaving Serb forces unable to defend many of the towns they had ethnically cleansed over the previous three and a half years. Jubilant Muslim and Croat soldiers took advantage of the friendly warplanes in the sky and reclaimed lost territory. For the first time since 1992, my Bosnian friends in Sarajevo could get in their cars and leave the capital, visiting loved ones they had not even been able to speak with by telephone.

My new, shared apartment was in Somerville, the next town over from Cambridge. I amassed a steep phone bill, frantically calling my reporter friends in Bosnia and making them hold their phones in the air so I could hear the background sounds of honking horns and celebratory music. I surrounded myself with reminders of what I had left behind, hanging on my bedroom wall a map of Sarajevo that showed the gun emplacements around the city, and placing on the living room mantel a 40-millimeter shell that had been engraved and turned into a decorative sculpture.

My instincts continued to reflect the fact that I had spent the better part of the summer living in a city under fire: the loud scrape of a desk being moved or a library cart being pushed sent me ducking for cover. Meanwhile, simple conveniences—like a light switch—suddenly delighted me. When I visited the local supermarket, I was now paralyzed by all the options. In Sarajevo, I had counted myself fortunate to find a carton of juice priced like a bottle of Bordeaux, but in Cambridge, I was confronted by more than a dozen flavors of Snapple alone. For two years, my journal reflections had been decidedly grim, but trivial discoveries now passed for big news: "We have cantaloupe Snapple!" I marveled in one entry soon after school started.

My reacclimation to America happened slowly, and it didn't help that I spoke to Mort daily to discuss developments in Bosnia.

"I wish Fred were here to see this," I told him a few days after NATO brought the fighting to an end.

"He would ask why the hell you're in law school," Mort answered.

I wondered the same thing.

I didn't lack the ability to focus—I could bury myself in the library for hours without noticing the setting sun. But while I admired the poise of my classmates who threw themselves into Socratic debates with their peers and professors, I just couldn't make myself care about the topics we were studying. In *1L*, Scott Turow's memoir of his first year at Harvard Law School, he compares studying case law to stirring concrete with his eyelashes; this description seemed a perfect encapsulation of how I felt reading Civil Procedure cases late into the night.

I was also not that quick a study. I became flustered when called upon in class, stammering answers that other students quickly tore apart while a hundred pairs of eyes drilled into my back. When my professors interrogated me, I tried to keep my composure by making an insistent mental note, "This professor is not Ratko Mladić, he's not

Ratko Mladić, he's not . . ." But hours after class ended, my cheeks often still felt flushed with embarrassment.

ON OCTOBER 29TH, 1995, nearly two months into law school, I picked up the Sunday *New York Times* at the bottom of my Somerville stoop. There, in the upper left-hand corner, was a huge headline: SREBRENICA: THE DAYS OF SLAUGHTER.[3] A reporting team had spent weeks preparing a special investigation that contained previously unpublished details of the systematic murder of Srebrenica's men and boys.

As I sat reading—clenched in what felt like a full-body grimace—I understood what writers reflecting on the Holocaust meant when they described the human capacity to "know without knowing." I had covered the fall of Srebrenica and had read all of my friend David Rohde's articles about it. Laura, who had left journalism to attend graduate school, had spent her summer working for Human Rights Watch, gathering the testimonies of people who had survived the massacres. Yet my reaction to the *Times* exposé confirmed how wide the chasm can be between holding out hope that something is not true and actually absorbing devastating facts in all of their finality. I had experienced the brutality of the war up close. Yet before reading the *Times* piece, I had somehow believed that Srebrenica's missing men and boys were no longer alive, and yet had not necessarily believed that they were dead.*

I looked back at my own actions and wondered why I hadn't done more. "I don't know how that could have been me there," I wrote in my journal. "I was the correspondent in Munich while the bodies burned in Dachau . . . I had power and I failed to use it." In beating myself

---

* I am paraphrasing Holocaust historian Walter Laqueur, who, describing Germany in late 1942, wrote, "It is, in fact, quite likely that while many Germans thought that the Jews were no longer alive, they did not necessarily believe that they were dead." The other fitting analogy to my mental state was Supreme Court Justice Felix Frankfurter's response in 1942 to Jan Karski's eyewitness account of one of Hitler's concentration camps: "I can't believe you." When told that Karski was telling the truth, Frankfurter, who was himself Jewish, added, "I did not say this young man is lying. I said that I cannot believe him. There is a difference."

up, I was clearly exaggerating my actual power back in Sarajevo. I was a freelance journalist, running my laptop off of a jury-rigged car battery. President Clinton led the most formidable superpower in the history of the world. He had a vast intelligence apparatus at his disposal. And he certainly knew more contemporaneously than I did about the crimes Mladić and his executioners were carrying out in Srebrenica. The President of the United States had not needed my help if he was to be spurred to action.

Nonetheless, I felt at sea. My law school classmates and I were of a generation that had unquestioningly embraced the slogan "never again." Yet I was sure very few of my peers were actually aware of the *Times* investigation that had sent me spiraling, and even those who had seen it would probably have considered it "too depressing" to read. Powerless to affect the fate of men already killed, I decided that I could at least raise awareness on campus about what had happened.

In a move that at the time felt as bold as choosing to live under siege in Sarajevo, I asked my Contracts professor for permission to make an announcement before class. "I apologize for using this forum," I said nervously after taking the floor. "But I just wanted to draw your attention to something that will be in your mailbox later." I previewed the article, which documented "the largest single massacre in Europe in fifty years." My lips quivered as I rushed to try to finish. "So please read it. Thanks."

After class I met up with a new friend, Sharon Dolovich, who had done her PhD in political theory at Cambridge University and was seemingly curious about all subjects. While most of our classmates had shied away from discussing the upsetting events in the former Yugoslavia, Sharon pumped me for details on my recent experiences and seemed genuinely moved by the revelations about Srebrenica. Sharon and I dropped by the law school copy room to collect the five hundred Xeroxes I had ordered earlier in the day. Together, we solemnly stuffed a stapled copy of the article into the mailbox of each first-year law student. I knew enough not to linger and watch our classmates sift through their mail, which also included notices for an upcoming ice cream social, various law journal meetings, and book discounts at the Harvard Coop. If the Srebrenica article was to be tossed into the nearby blue recycling tub, I did not want to see it. A few of my classmates approached me later to thank me for alerting them to what had happened. But I got the feeling that most found me off-puttingly intense.

After saying goodbye to Sharon, I made my way to the law library. I had already fallen behind in my Property reading and needed to prepare for the next day's class. After a restless hour in a carrel, I wandered to the nearest phone to collect my answering machine messages. I heard the voice of my friend Elizabeth Rubin, who had just returned to New York from Sarajevo.

"Power, I don't know if you've heard," she said. There was a pause, and then what sounded like muffled crying. "It's David."

Another pause. "Um . . . he's been abducted."

I flashed back to all that my friend David Rohde had written, doing more than any reporter to uncover Ratko Mladić's summary executions. My mind jumped to Fred Cuny and his last days. "No! No! No!" I said, holding back tears as I raced to the bike rack and began fumbling with my lock so I could get home.

When I reached my apartment, I stood in the kitchen with no idea what to do. What more could I contribute to finding David that the US government, the UN, and the press corps weren't already doing? I defaulted to what I usually did when I was in a bind, calling Mort.

He was constructive and typically specific. He told me to call Richard Holbrooke—who, in a fortunate coincidence of timing, had just arrived in Dayton, Ohio, for peace talks with the warring factions. He also told me to call Strobe Talbott and Steve Rosenfeld—both of whom I had haplessly lobbied the year before. "Get the *Post* to write something," Mort advised.

Unable to get through to Holbrooke, I (somewhat absurdly) asked the hotel receptionist in Dayton to pass on a message—verbatim:

David Rohde has been abducted in Serb territory. Please make him the lead item in the peace talks.

I was able to reach Strobe, who started our conversation as courteously as ever. He told me that Secretary of State Warren Christopher had that day raised David's case with Serbian president Milošević in Dayton. Instead of expressing gratitude, though, I snapped, "That's not enough."

Strobe continued, "Milošević understands that he will bear the consequences if anything happens to David."

"The consequences!" I said, sarcastically. "What consequences?!" Strobe must have wondered why he ever took my calls.

"Well, if you're going to take that view, then there's nothing more I can say," he responded, and the call quickly ended.

When I connected with Rosenfeld, I begged him to write an editorial demanding that the US government secure David's release before proceeding with the Dayton talks. "He's the only Western eyewitness to the mass graves," I implored. "He's in profound danger."

Rosenfeld explained that the next day's paper had already gone to press. "Well, if we don't do something quickly, it will be too late," I warned. "You have to understand: people don't just disappear in Bosnia. We have a short window to shame David's captors into not harming him, but it is closing."

Rosenfeld gave me an opening. "If you want to write something," he offered, "we will run it."

Less than thirty-six hours after I heard Elizabeth's message, the *Washington Post* ran my op-ed, the first opinion piece I had penned since the *Daily Jang*. The essay, printed November 3rd, 1995, concluded: "I relay David's odyssey because he is my colleague and my dear friend. American officials claim they can do no more than 'raise the issue at the highest levels.' David did more. Why can't they?"

I went to class and tried not to think about the barbaric treatment my friend was likely suffering—if he was even still alive. When I returned home a few hours later, I saw that the tape on my answering machine had been filled. Strangers—lower-level State Department officials, Hill staffers, journalists, and *Post* readers from all walks of life—had located my home number through directory assistance and left messages asking how they could help. One man moved me immensely with his simple words of support. "Howdy, my name is Bill," his message began. "I am a truck driver. I just wanna know what I can do for David."

Much more importantly, by nightfall, the Serb authorities acknowledged that David was in their custody. Had they planned to kill him, they would never have admitted to detaining him. I now believed that his family, who had staged a protest outside of the Dayton airbase where the Bosnia peace talks were taking place, would get him back.

David was released ten days after he was seized. Once free, he revealed that a source had given him a map with the exact location of four additional mass graves near Srebrenica. Blacklisted from entering Bosnian Serb territory because of his reporting in August, he doctored the date on his expired press pass and drove into Serb territory, where he found the first of the gravesites and evidence of murder: piles of coats, abandoned shoes, Muslim identity documents, even canes and shattered eyeglasses.

But as was David's wont, he had pushed his luck, trying to find even more. He was arrested at rifle-point at the second grave, just as he was preparing to photograph two human femurs he had discovered. Because he was carrying a camera, a map with suspected gravesites circled, and film stuffed into his socks, the Bosnian Serbs labeled him a spy.

"Mr. David," his interrogator repeatedly asked him at the remote police station where he was held, "What is your rank? Who is your commander in the CIA? And what is your mission?"

His captors forced him to stand through the night, denying him sleep. They threatened him with a lengthy stay in a Bosnian Serb prison camp, and even with execution. After three days of threats, fearful that he would be shot if he continued to hold out, David considered telling the interrogators whatever they wanted. But a friendly guard whispered in his ear that he knew David was a journalist. He urged him to stand firm. This gave US diplomacy and public advocacy time to succeed.

I was thrilled by David's release and rushed to Logan Airport to be part of the crowd that welcomed him. After the dark discoveries of the previous months, the sight of David being reunited with his family felt like a sudden burst of light.

Close to midnight, I heard a knock on the front door of my Somerville apartment and saw David outside. We stayed up until daybreak, talking about what he had seen and gone through. We also began a debate, which we continue to this day, about when journalism is most effective in prodding change.

The evidence David gathered was a factor in helping convince the Clinton administration to launch the bombing raids that so quickly ended the war. Even though I was now stuck in law school, I told him that he had single-handedly given me a new appreciation for the power of the pen. He later considered attending law school because, despite being one of the most decorated reporters in the business—winning two Pulitzer Prizes—he often wished he could personally do more about the injustices he was exposing.

David's release also showed the impact of concentrated public pressure. He was the beneficiary of the so-called identifiable victim effect—the human tendency to be more helpful to those with a name and face than to anonymous victims. As Mother Teresa famously said, "If I look at the mass, I will never act. If I look at the one, I will."[4]

But I knew David had another factor working in his favor: he was American. The photo that the *Washington Post* used with my op-ed depicted a bespectacled young man wearing a fleece. For all of my heartfelt reporting and writing when I lived in the Balkans, I had managed to generate a far more intense outpouring for my friend than I had for Bosnia's thousands of victims. Readers could relate to him. They could *see* him. And because he was one person, they could imagine that their actions could conceivably help him. Not so for the people of Srebrenica. An identifiable American life would almost always be more galvanizing than thousands of faceless foreigners in a faraway country.

I HOPED THAT THE GOOD NEWS of David's release would help cure me of my all-consuming focus on Bosnia. When I lived in the Balkans,

I often thought about how lucky I was relative to the people around me. But once back in the United States, I sometimes acted as if I had personally suffered the losses of war. Changing that would take time.

Jonathan Moore had moved from Washington back to his home in Massachusetts and was now based at the Harvard Kennedy School. I often confided in him about my struggles readjusting to life as a student in placid Cambridge. Occasionally, my self-absorption— a constant—would devolve into self-pity, and Jonathan would stop me in my tracks. "Oh, I'm sorry," he would say, teasingly but firmly. "Have *you* been ethnically cleansed?!"

The first time I recall being able to make fun of myself came, strangely, during the 1995 New York City Marathon, a few days after David's release. Before living in Bosnia, I had never loved running, always preferring what I called "real sports"—games like baseball or basketball that required strategy and skill with a ball. Living in encircled Sarajevo had changed my attitude, making me appreciate the freedom running provided. After returning to the United States, I had trained for the marathon for ten weeks, with Bruce Springsteen's "Born to Run" and John Barry's cheesy movie theme "Born Free" on heavy rotation on my Walkman's mixtape. Going for ten-mile practice runs wasn't exactly fun, but I enjoyed no longer feeling caged up.

The night before the race, I ate a heaping pasta supper with two college friends who were also running. Afterward, we decorated plain white Hanes T-shirts with words designed to draw shouts of moral support from the crowd. Miro, who had been with me in Atlanta at the time of the Tiananmen massacre, wrote "MO" in huge block letters as a kind of pick-me-up nickname.

Instead of "SAM," or even "POWER," I scribbled "REMEMBER SREBRENICA."

Then, for good measure, I added on the back, "8,000 BOSNIAN MUSLIM MEN AND BOYS, MURDERED JULY 12–13, 1995."

As we set off the next day, crossing the Verrazano Bridge, I heard the crowds yelling, "Go Mo!" Seeing the energy that the cheers gave Miro, I immediately regretted the decision to splash a morbid Public

Service Announcement across my chest. Many people along the way made a spirited effort to root for me in spite of myself, albeit while mangling their attempts at pronouncing "Srebrenica."

"Remember Srebedeedeedee!" I heard, or "Remember Srebre-oh-whatever."

With two miles to go, a group of rowdy spectators, seeing my pace slowing, tried to urge me on, chanting, "Go Remember! Go Go Remember!" In my heavy-handedness, I had managed to turn myself into someone with the name "Remember," which kept me smiling until I crossed the finish line. It seemed fitting.

I RETURNED TO SARAJEVO twice during my first year in law school, once over Christmas and then again for summer break. Mort had been the driving force behind creating the International Crisis Group, a new nongovernmental organization dedicated to conflict prevention, and he asked me to help launch their first field office in Bosnia to monitor the implementation of the peace agreement that Holbrooke had negotiated at Dayton. I loved being back among my friends, seeing the universities reopened, and watching the markets and cafés bustling with life. Witnessing even a flawed peace gave me a sense of closure, which I had craved.

Unfortunately, almost as soon as I arrived back in Cambridge for my second year of law school, I found myself struggling to breathe properly. The ailment that my college boyfriend Schu had called "lungers" was back with a vengeance. In college, these bouts of constricted breathing were a nuisance, an inconvenient background occurrence that never interfered with my life. But now I was unable to concentrate on anything other than whether I would be able to take a proper breath.

On the advice of friends, I tried yoga; but like a child who has just noticed her blinking, and suddenly begins to do it intentionally, this activity only caused me to focus more on my breathing, a huge impediment to regularizing it. For the first time, I grew so rattled by this mystery ailment that I could not sleep. Even when I managed to doze off for a few hours, when I awoke, I would experience a split second of deep, regular breathing before recalling the debilitating constriction of my lungs, which would promptly return.

After several weeks of mounting torment, I took a long run along the Charles River in the hopes that it would necessitate inhaling large amounts of air. Still running after an hour, I maneuvered along the paved roads near MIT to head back to my apartment, trying to take extra-deep breaths as I ran. I was so focused on my breathing that I didn't look where I was running and tripped on an uneven sidewalk slab. I was lucky not to spill into the oncoming traffic, but I did land in a pile of shattered glass. Both of my knees were lacerated and began bleeding profusely.

I hobbled as quickly as I could, in significant pain, to the University Health Services. When the doctor asked what had happened, I told him I had been struggling to breathe and had not paid proper attention to where I was stepping. He asked if I was experiencing anxiety.

"No," I said, "the complete opposite. I was a journalist in Bosnia, and I think I find the *lack* of stress here on campus very hard to get used to."

He asked if I would like to be prescribed something to settle my nerves. I told him I was completely fine and needed nothing other than a good knee cleaning so as to avoid an infection. As I was speaking, I glanced down and saw that my knees bore shards of gravel and glass and my white running socks had turned crimson with blood.

"On second thought," I said sheepishly, "I'll take whatever you recommend."

Within forty-eight hours, the anti-anxiety medicine worked wonders; once I started breathing normally and focusing on my classwork, I pushed the incident—and my lungers—to the back of my mind. It would be years before I would begin to explore their source.

12

"A PROBLEM FROM HELL"

During law school, I came across the transcript of a US government press conference that had occurred while I was working as a journalist in Bosnia. On April 8th, 1994, a mid-level US diplomat named Prudence Bushnell spoke at the State Department's daily press briefing. She described the horrific killings that had just broken out in Rwanda—a genocidal murder spree that over one hundred days would result in the deaths of 800,000 people.

When Bushnell left the podium, Michael McCurry, the State Department spokesperson, turned to the next item on the agenda: criticizing foreign governments that were preventing the screening of *Schindler's List*, Steven Spielberg's movie about a German businessman who saved 1,200 Jews during the Holocaust.

"This film," McCurry said, "shows that even in the midst of genocide, one individual can make a difference." He continued: "The most effective way to avoid the recurrence of genocidal tragedy is to ensure that past acts of genocide are never forgotten."

What struck me was that neither the US officials speaking nor the journalists listening drew a connection between the slaughter being perpetrated in Rwanda and McCurry's appeal to act in the face of genocide. This disconnect seemed to illustrate the perplexing coexistence of Americans' purported deep resolve to prevent genocide, and our recurring struggle to acknowledge when it is happening in our midst.

Like many Americans, I had read Anne Frank's *Diary of a Young*

Girl and Elie Wiesel's *Night* as a teenager. But it was only after visiting Anne Frank's home and the Dachau concentration camp with Schu that I focused on the question of what more the United States could have done as Hitler set out to exterminate Europe's Jews.

Looking for answers, I had turned to well-known books that examined the Roosevelt administration's response—David Wyman's landmark *The Abandonment of the Jews: America and the Holocaust, 1941–1945* and Arthur Morse's *While Six Million Died: A Chronicle of American Apathy*. I admired President Roosevelt, but I could not wrap my mind around why his administration had not admitted more Jewish refugees, or at least bombed the train tracks to the death camps to disrupt Hitler's extermination networks. These steps would not have ended the Nazi's efforts to destroy the Jewish people—it would take winning World War II for that—but at the very least the United States could have saved thousands of lives.

My experiences in Bosnia deepened my original interest in the Holocaust.* While I was in law school, I scoured the weekly campus event bulletins for lectures on the subject. Not long after the Srebrenica revelations, I watched Claude Lanzmann's devastating nine-and-a-half-hour documentary *Shoah* for the first time. I roamed the stacks of Harvard's Widener Library, checking out so many books on Hitler's crimes that I dedicated my entire bookshelf to the topic. I traveled abroad, visiting the former Treblinka death camp in Poland, as well as Yad Vashem, the Holocaust museum in Israel. Although at the time I wouldn't have been able to verbalize the connection, I think I was looking for ways to put what had happened in Bosnia in historical context.

I also took advantage of Harvard's wide course offerings and signed

---

* To be clear: what happened in Bosnia was not "like" the Holocaust in the sense that Bosnian Serb militants did not set out to murder every Bosnian Muslim or Croat, as Hitler had tried to wipe out all of Europe's Jews. Serb nationalists pursued what they called "ethnic cleansing," murdering thousands of civilians because of their ethnicity and expelling the rest. But what happened in Bosnia was, in fact, genocide. The UN Genocide Convention had deliberately defined genocide as *destruction*, rather than extermination, as its authors believed that requiring a showing of intent to exterminate a whole group would ensure that action to halt genocide would invariably come too late.

up for classes across the university, including a seminar on Holocaust-related literature and film and a broader course called "The Use of Force: Political and Moral Criteria," taught by Professor Stanley Hoffmann, a legendary scholar of international relations, and Father J. Bryan Hehir, a Catholic priest and theologian. After reading the writings of Thomas Aquinas, Saint Augustine, Reinhold Niebuhr, and Michael Walzer, we were asked to apply their ideas to the war in Vietnam, the Persian Gulf War, and the 1992–1993 US intervention in Somalia.

The course introduced me to a range of questions I hadn't considered before but that would help shape my thinking for years to come. For example, when is military force justified? How do the moral and religious traditions of nonviolence coexist with the moral imperative not to stand idly by in the face of suffering? How does one (particularly one who lacks sufficient information) measure the risks of action and inaction before deciding what to do? What would it mean if any country could take upon itself the decision to use force without any rules? Who should write these rules?

For the first time, a question that I had initially seen in fairly black-and-white terms—should the United States intervene militarily to stop atrocities in Bosnia?—took on a much more complex texture. I also began to interrogate the stark, simple power of the slogan "Never again."

My thinking was powerfully influenced by Philip Gourevitch, an American writer who had traveled to Rwanda in 1995 and then published a series of haunting articles on the genocide in *The New Yorker*.[5] Gourevitch's first article about Rwanda, which I read during the Hoffmann–Hehir course, began, unforgettably:

> Decimation means the killing of every tenth person in a population, and in the spring and early summer of 1994 a program of massacres decimated the Republic of Rwanda. Although the killing was low-tech—performed largely by machete—it was carried out at dazzling speed . . . the bloodletting in the former Yugoslavia measures up as little more than a neighborhood riot.

The dead of Rwanda accumulated at nearly three times the rate of Jewish dead during the Holocaust.

It was impossible for me to comprehend that the pace of killing in Rwanda was faster than Hitler's mechanized annihilation of the Jews. Nor could I fathom that the Bosnia atrocities so seared into my consciousness could have constituted "little more than a neighborhood riot" in comparison.

I had a pretty clear recollection of being in Sarajevo in April and May of 1994, hearing about massacres in Rwanda, and assuming—just as many were doing at the time about Bosnia—that they were part of a long cycle of recurring "tribal" violence. Only when I read Gourevitch's work did I begin to appreciate the top-down, organized nature of the killings.

I was struck that, fifty years after the Holocaust, the world had stood by during both the Bosnian and the Rwandan genocides.

I decided to write a paper for the Use of Force class that would allow me to look at these and prior cases of genocide—such as the Armenian genocide, Pol Pot's slaughter in Cambodia, and Saddam Hussein's campaign to destroy the Kurds of Northern Iraq.

In the course of my research, I discovered a gap that surprised me. The books written by journalists and academics covered the atrocities, but generally did not investigate what US policymakers *themselves* were thinking when they responded to these genocides. American decisions and nondecisions seemed to have gone largely unanalyzed. The reference books I had sought for my research simply did not exist.

By the time I turned in my paper, in January of 1997, it had swelled from the required twenty pages to more than seventy. Yet I felt that I was barely scratching the surface. I had done little more than sketch, in the most general terms, the US government's responses to genocide in the twentieth century. I did not delve deeply into the question of why—despite rarely doing much—Americans continued so buoyantly to embrace the pledge of "never again." When my professors praised the paper for introducing them to a tension they had not considered before, I wondered if maybe I should try to expand the paper into a monograph or short book.

WHEN I DISCUSSED with a law school friend the pattern of non-responses I had discovered, he said, "I'm surprised at your surprise." And looking back, it is clear—maybe because I carried an immigrant's optimism—that an unmistakable innocence or credulousness helped fuel my inquiry. It was as if I had believed our resolve and then felt almost personally betrayed when I saw the promise being broken.

Regardless of whether the feeling I had was as naive as it seemed to some, the fact that "never again" still carried such force in our culture suggested I was not alone. This contradiction intrigued me. Unlike the way I felt toward my assignments in core law school courses, I was overcome with a seemingly inexhaustible need to learn everything I could about my new subject.

Because I had developed the instincts of a reporter, I was determined to gain an understanding of past events by talking directly to US government officials. I made a list of dozens of former policymakers, and started reaching out to them individually to ask about how they had experienced events in Cambodia, Iraq, Bosnia, and Rwanda from inside the government bureaucracy. Remarkably, very few former officials refused to talk to me, and most provided me with the names of other people whom they urged me to contact. I knew how differently people often remembered the same events and recognized that I would need to speak to a wide range of officials if I was going to credibly piece together what had happened.

I took a year off from law school to focus on the project, and Elizabeth Rubin kindly put me in touch with her literary agent, Sarah Chalfant. I had not written a book before, and Sarah generally represented well-known writers. But because my subject interested her, she agreed to take me on as her client. She became a spirited champion, arranging meetings with various New York publishers, and in the end, I signed a contract with Random House to write a book based on my paper. At the same time, Harvard Kennedy School professor Graham Allison contacted me after hearing about a campus talk I had given about the war in Bosnia. Allison was looking to hire someone to manage a new human rights program and offered me a job running what was then called the Human Rights Initiative. Eager for a salary that would help me pay for law school and drawn to the field of human rights (which I did not then know well), I accepted. Together, with funding from American tech entrepreneur Greg Carr, we built the Carr Center for Human Rights Policy, which became the driving force behind much of the Kennedy School's human rights programming.*

After this productive year away, I returned to law school and graduated in 1999. Many of my classmates were pursuing jobs as legal clerks or law firm associates. But I planned to stay put, splitting my time between working at the new human rights center and doing research for my nascent book project.

Wanting to put some distance between myself and Harvard, I used my modest book advance to make a down payment on an apartment a half-hour drive away in Winthrop, a blue-collar beach town. My new home allowed me relative seclusion, as well as proximity to Logan Airport, my gateway to the various countries I planned to feature in the book.

Over the next several years, I began teaching courses on US foreign policy and human rights at the Kennedy School. Initially, because many of the students were around my age or had experience working for governments or the UN, I found teaching nerve-racking. But I soon saw that preparing my courses helped me formulate a broader set of ideas on foreign policy. And I was gratified to see students stirred (as I had been) by what they learned about the Bosnian war, the Rwandan genocide, and other recent crises.

My main focus, though, was my reporting and writing. I spent nights and weekends working on the book, leaving my apartment only to pick up the *New York Times* on my stoop or to go for a run by the ocean.

I was never as disciplined as I intended to be, but early on, I learned to forgive myself. I came to understand that writing a book would ul-

---

* I served as its executive director until 2002.

timately require thousands of hours on the phone, on the road, and at my computer. I realized that it was okay to read *Sports Illustrated*, watch a baseball game, or spend a few hours talking on the phone to my parents, Mort, Jonathan, Laura, or other friends.

While I still loved the Pittsburgh Pirates, they played in the National League, and I now closely followed the Boston Red Sox, listening to every pitch live or on replay. As I drove home along Storrow Drive after a day at the Kennedy School, I was often drawn by the bright stadium lights of Fenway Park. When I pulled onto Commonwealth Avenue, if I found street parking, I would duck into Fenway for a few innings, revving myself up for the long night of writing ahead.

These were exciting times for the Red Sox, and particularly for their future Hall of Fame pitcher Pedro Martinez, who dominated batters in a way I had not seen before. Unfortunately, I was so consumed with my project that, when I had the chance to meet Martinez at a charity fundraiser, instead of talking baseball, I gave him a long account of the genocide book I was writing.

When the organizers sent me the photos from the event, there I was, in a black evening gown, gesticulating wildly as a dazed Cy Young winner occasionally looked over my shoulder for bullpen relief. It was no different for the few friends I managed to see regularly. They teased me, with little exaggeration, that I had become "all genocide, all the time."

THE TRUTH WAS that I was lonely. I longed to find the kind of companion that Eddie was for Mum. They had their ups and downs, but he had made significant headway battling his alcoholism, joining AA. And he continued to challenge her, and to make her laugh until her sides hurt. But I tended to fall for older, accomplished men who had a habit of evading real intimacy, and I remained single.

My close woman friends were godsends. We shared many of the same bad dating instincts. At one point, Elizabeth Rubin started calling the men we became involved with "lizards" because of their predictable tendency to seem available, only to slither away as soon as we made ourselves vulnerable to them. When one of us would end a relationship with a lizard, the man would inevitably come back, promising to change. We all knew rationally that true transformation was innately difficult—if not impossible. "Look how hard it is for any of *us* to change!" I would exclaim. But giving up on a cause did not come easy, so we would dig in, wasting precious months or even years in and out of doomed relationships. When we relapsed with one of our reptilian suitors, we would guiltily email the others a coded confession: "I lizarded yesterday." The solidarity among my single women friends was fierce, and experience as a war correspondent was not required for membership. When I introduced Amy Bach, a lawyer and writer friend, to the Bosnia gang, they embraced her. Amy joined us in making stories out of our misadventures, which—through the telling—reduced the sting. Once Amy called to tell me about a bout of writer's block brought on by a bad breakup. "I'm lying on the floor, Power," she said. I responded cheerily, "I love the floor!"

Not all the men I dated were irreparably cold-blooded. Yet when I would get involved with somebody who wanted to get close to me—somebody who started talking dreamily about what we might do together in the future—I would suffer immediate bouts of lungers. Instead of simply ending the relationships in an honest way, I would head off to Rwanda or another war-torn country to do interviews for my book, hoping that, by the time I returned, the person I had begun seeing would have moved on.

My friend Miro urged me to try therapy. I ridiculed this suggestion, saying, "Let me guess? My screwed-up dating life is all about my father."

Miro just looked at me for a long while, letting my words hang in the air. Finally, after a minute, he said, "You were willing to live in a war zone. It is strange that you won't even explore talking to a therapist."

In the coming months, my rationales for avoiding Miro's recommendation shifted. Therapy would take too much time away from my genocide book, which was already well overdue. It would cost a ridiculous amount of money. And, above all, it would offer, as I put it, "predictable psychobabble." But finally, after I got back together for the third time with a man I knew was bad news, I caved and asked a friend for the name of his therapist.

A few days later, I took the T to Davis Square and walked up a small hill to the therapist's home, where she saw patients in a side studio. I shook her hand and sat down on the couch.

"Tell me about your father," she began, and in that instant, I burst into tears, crying for at least five minutes, stopping only to make clear that—despite appearances—I was on top of the situation: "I'm crying for the following three reasons . . ." I explained, waving off the box of tissues she offered.

Over the next five years, therapy opened me up a bit. I learned how deeply responsible I felt for my father's death, and realized I was scared of making myself vulnerable to a loss so large again. But even as I came to better understand my actions, I continued to be drawn to men who resembled my dad—larger-than-life, roguish characters who were often struggling in some way with addiction. No amount of therapy seemed to rid me of my tendency to ignore flashing red lights in relationships.

When my first therapist moved away, I found another—this time, a straitlaced doctor. I had always maintained my physical fitness, and he urged me to make my emotional well-being as much of a priority. As the months passed, though, my patience waned for a dialogue that didn't seem to have much effect on my behavior. I started forgetting sessions I had scheduled and—not wanting to break away from my writing—began booking them more sporadically.

One day, having again forgotten an appointment, I called the doctor at the last minute to see if he could hold the session by telephone, and he agreed. I sat on my couch in Winthrop as I talked through my latest relapse with an ex-boyfriend who was separated from his wife but making no move to break permanently free. As I spoke, I suddenly heard a "beep-beep-beep" in the background. I thought I recognized the noise, but could not quite believe it, until I heard it again.

"What's that sound?" I asked.

The therapist didn't answer.

"Are you at a fucking ATM?" I asked, indignantly.

From the moment he admitted that he was, in fact, multitasking at the bank, I renounced therapy and resolved that I would "figure myself out" after I finished my book. Though I took offense at the time, the therapist was clearly mirroring my own ambivalence toward probing too deeply.

THE BOOK PROJECT DRAGGED ON. I wondered if I would ever feel it was finished. The combination of the heavy subject matter and my endless solitude might have caused me to wallow. However, thanks to the voluminous Freedom of Information Act requests filed by the National Security Archive, the Washington-based NGO where I had interned while in college, I was able to draw upon revealing, declassified documents that detailed what had been happening behind closed doors in the US government as genocide occurred. I felt privileged to be able to highlight the vivid—at times jaw-dropping—government paper trail on Iraq, Rwanda, and Bosnia.

Every time I saw a declassified cable that demonstrated the cold logic of US decision-making, a swirl of conflicting emotions arose inside me. I was simultaneously horrified and invigorated by the new understanding I got into how policymakers rationalized their decisions in real time. The answer to the puzzle of how we pledged "never again" and then looked away from genocide seemed enshrined in these sterile records.

Someone in the State Department's Near Eastern Affairs regional bureau had written about Iraq: "*Human rights and chemical weapons use aside*, in many respects our political and economic interests run parallel with those of Iraq" [italics mine]. On Rwanda, a discussion paper from the Office of the Secretary of Defense warned against characterizing the mass murder as "genocide," advising, "Be careful. Legal at State was worried about this yesterday—Genocide finding could commit [the US government] to actually 'do something.'"

Yet for every stomach-churning cable I processed from the Archive's files, I would come across an American who had risked his career—or, occasionally, his life—to lobby for action. Henry Morgenthau, Sr., the US Ambassador in Constantinople during the Armenian genocide, had sent blistering cables back to Washington, begging his superiors to do more to respond to the slaughter. Raphael Lemkin, a Polish Jewish lawyer who fled to the United States in 1941, had invented the word *genocide*, convincing himself that if such a crime had been understood and outlawed earlier, the world might have prevented the Holocaust—which killed his parents and forty-seven other family members. William Proxmire, an idiosyncratic senator from Wisconsin, stood on the floor of the US Senate 3,211 times—over a span of nineteen years—appealing to successive presidents and congresses to ratify the UN Genocide Convention, which Lemkin had helped draft.

Even stories I thought I knew gained texture when I delved deeper. I had met Peter Galbraith for the first time in Croatia, where he was US ambassador. But before that, in the 1980s, he had been a staffer on the Senate Foreign Relations Committee. Upon hearing reports that Saddam Hussein (then a recipient of US aid) had gassed Iraqi Kurds, Galbraith bravely traveled into Northern Iraq to collect survivor testimonies, hoping to use what he found as evidence to convince Congress to suspend assistance to the Iraqi government.

The first person to resign from the State Department to protest US inaction in the face of Serb atrocities was George Kenney, who had given me his flak jacket and helmet before I left for Bosnia. But until I talked to the former US officials who resigned, I didn't appreciate just how wrenching they had found leaving their dream jobs. The emotional scars of what they had seen—and what their government had not initially wished to confront—were still evident years later. I believed their actions were noble, but they were focused only on their impact, which they deemed marginal.

After five long years of obsessive sleuthing and more than three hundred interviews, I delivered what I felt was a solid draft of the book. However, I soon learned that my publisher, Random House, wanted nothing to do with it.

My original editor had left the company, so the book (actually a thick pile of paper held together with a rubber band) was up for grabs. The manuscript had three strikes against it: it had no champion at the publishing house, it was six hundred pages long, and it dealt with the gloomy topic of genocide. The book passed from one person to the next until Random House informed my stalwart agent Sarah that it would be a good idea to take the book elsewhere.

Sarah shopped the manuscript to a vast array of New York publishing houses, only to receive a stream of rejections that I took very hard. Over the span of three months, several times a week, I would rush to answer the phone every time Sarah's New York number lit up my caller ID. But the responses were all the same: Houghton Mifflin? "Pass," Sarah said. Picador? "Pass." Farrar, Straus? "Pass." Simon & Schuster? "I'm so sorry," Sarah said, "also not interested." This rejection went on and on.

I despaired at the idea that a book on which I had labored for half a decade might never see the light of day.

At one point, I received word that my original editor had decided to return to Random House. He telephoned me and exclaimed, "I want you back!" I was beyond thrilled. But a few weeks later, after reviewing the book, he changed his mind. "I'm sorry," he informed me. "The book has been passed over by so many people here that there is just no enthusiasm for it. And if we publish it, we will not do your work justice."

I told him that, if his concern was his colleagues and their enthusiasm, I would find a way to promote the book myself. I just needed them to put a few copies in print. "I will do the rest," I said. "I'm sorry," he answered. "I can't." When I hung up, I knew he meant "I won't."

As always, Jonathan Moore brought me perspective, telling me that I had been delusional to think that it would be easy to publish such a book. "The miracle is that you ever had a publisher!" he said cheerfully. "And because you thought you actually had one, you wrote the book!"

I had one hope left. I had written for *The New Republic* when I lived in the former Yugoslavia, and Marty Peretz, the magazine's owner, also oversaw its small book publishing subsidiary. Marty had read my law school paper several years before and had been unhappy with me when I signed with Random House instead of New Republic Books. I telephoned him at his home and nervously explained that the book he had last seen in its infancy had "become available again."

Marty took a long pause, but then said that he would not hold my past lapse in judgment against me. He would be "delighted" to publish the book.

Secretary of State Christopher had once tried to explain the Clinton administration's reluctance to do more to prevent atrocities in Bosnia by claiming that the "hatred" among the warring groups was "centuries old" and by saying memorably, "That really is a problem from hell." This so aptly reflected the mind-set of many senior US policymakers that I chose to title the book *"A Problem from Hell": America and the Age of Genocide.*

When it finally hit stores in March of 2002, I often recounted to audiences all the rejections it received. It wasn't that I felt sorry for myself. Quite the contrary. I felt immensely blessed that the book found a home, which so many authors never managed.

I simply felt it was essential to convey (particularly to young people) that just because someone attains a measure of success does not mean that they were destined to do so. I had experienced bouts of hopelessness in which I wondered whether I was crazy to believe anyone would ever read what I was writing. I wanted to stress that the path would almost always be winding, but that one had to forge ahead and act *as if* one had faith things would work out. One could not give up in the face of rejection. And undignified though it felt, one had to fiercely advocate on one's own behalf.

What I did not know then was how consequential my refusal to take no for an answer—and Marty's decision to take a chance on me— would prove for my life's trajectory.

13

UPSTANDERS

I had heard the saying "You don't read a book; a book reads you," but the truth of these words did not sink in until I traveled the country and began meeting people who had read *A Problem from Hell.*

Many had marked it up with yellow highlighters or plastered it with Post-it Notes for quick access to the parts they found most important. Activists told me they were reading the book to think through how they could better influence Washington decision-makers on a host of different issues. Synagogue congregations grappled with the book's invocation of the false promise of "never again."

People who hadn't followed the Rwandan genocide when it happened said to me, with great earnestness, "I should have at least called my congressman." The book had quoted Colorado congresswoman Pat Schroeder describing the reaction to the Rwandan genocide in her district. "There are some groups terribly concerned about the gorillas," she had said in 1994, noting that a Colorado research organization studied Rwanda's endangered gorillas. "But—it sounds terrible—people just don't know what can be done about the people." The paucity of domestic political awareness and pressure were key reasons even low-cost US policies went untried.

The reaction I least anticipated came from those who had no connection to the specific countries I wrote about, but who were drawn to questions about the nature of individual responsibility in the face of injustice. I found that readers from all walks of life identified with the quests of Lemkin, Proxmire, Galbraith, and the officials who resigned from the State Department. College professors assigned excerpts in broad survey courses on leadership and ethics. I received numerous emails and letters from people who said that these stories had inspired them to see how to be more active in social causes.

Somewhere along the way, I began describing the book's protagonists—those who tried to prevent or otherwise "stand up" against genocide—as "upstanders," contrasting them with bystanders. I noted that very few of us were likely to find ourselves the victims or perpetrators of genocide. But every day, almost all of us find ourselves weighing whether we can or should do something to help others. We decide, on issues large and small, whether we will be bystanders or upstanders.

Thanks initially to teachers who began to use the idea of upstanders to engage their students, the term started to catch on. Many years later, when I was UN ambassador, I was stunned—and profoundly gratified—to be informed by a reporter that the *Oxford English Dictionary* had added the term *upstander*, which it wrote was "coined in 2002 by the Irish-American diplomat Samantha Power." Of course, it proved far easier to coin the term than to know exactly how to *be* an upstander in my own life.

Beyond the grassroots interest that developed around the book's themes, real-world events expanded its audience. I was editing the page proofs six months before publication when al-Qaeda terrorists murdered nearly 3,000 Americans on September 11th, 2001. These attacks, and the political reorientation they caused, changed the entire context in which most Americans thought about US foreign policy. The sense of isolation from global threats that the United States had enjoyed for so long had been shattered, and people began to discuss America's responsibilities around the world in new ways.

The devastation of September 11th was followed by an intensifying domestic debate over whether the United States should go to war with Iraq. Although the crux of President George W. Bush's argument for removing Saddam Hussein from power was the national security threat posed by his alleged weapons of mass destruction, Bush and others in his administration often seized upon the fact that Saddam had "gassed his own people" as proof of the Iraqi regime's dangerous tendencies.

Articles assessing the merits of an invasion in the *New York Times* and *The New Yorker* cited *"A Problem from Hell"* in their descriptions of the Iraqi campaign of genocide against the Kurds. I was uncomfortable seeing my writing about atrocities used in a way that might help justify a war. In my interviews, I tried to remind people what I had actually written.

I had made several arguments. First, I noted that when crafting foreign policy, US officials naturally think through the possible economic and security consequences of their choices, but they needed to do far more to factor the human consequences into their deliberations as well.

Second, I emphasized that the United States has a large toolbox when it comes to preventing genocide. I described the many options short of military engagement at the disposal of a powerful country like the United States: public and private diplomacy, public shaming, negotiations, deploying intelligence and technical resources, international peacekeeping, arms embargoes, asset freezes, and more. Although I sometimes heard people describe the book as an extended argument for US military action in response to mass atrocities, I had actually written that the United States "should not frame its policy options in terms of doing nothing or unilaterally sending in the Marines."

As the *New York Times* noted a month before the invasion of Iraq, "Ms. Power bridles at critics who interpret the book as a simplistic call for military intervention in cases of humanitarian crises. Her point, she said, is not that the United States failed to intervene in Cambodia, Iraq or Rwanda, but that it failed to do anything at all."

While Saddam was a merciless dictator, I did not see that as sufficient reason to go to war. I believed that neither the Kurds nor the American people faced an imminent threat of the kind that justified the use of force. Some of our closest allies opposed the war, and I was also concerned about the repercussions of going it alone. These countries would hardly be eager to help rebuild Iraq in the aftermath of a US invasion.

Although I abhorred the prospect of Saddam remaining in power,

I ended up speaking out against the Iraq War on a number of occasions. As I told *Newsweek* in early March of 2003, roughly two weeks before the war began, "[The invasion] will ratify and fuel the bubbling resentment against the U.S., and this anti-Americanism is the sea in which terrorists thrive."

Yet the coincidence of publishing the book in relative proximity to the start of the war made *"A Problem from Hell"* liable to misinterpretation. A year after the war began, I again registered my frustration in an interview with the *Financial Times*, remarking, "The book is the furthest thing from a plea for American military intervention . . . [or] for unilateral military intervention on a whim or on a subjective set of excuses and justifications." To this day, however, I am still approached by people who ask how I could have supported the Iraq War.

A MONTH AFTER THE US INVASION, my publisher called and informed me that *"A Problem from Hell"* had won the Pulitzer Prize for Nonfiction.

"Are you sure?" I said, my knees buckling beneath me.

I left a message for Mum to call me back and managed to reach Eddie. My voice caught as I said softly, "I just won the Pulitzer Prize." Eddie had fostered my love of history. He had read and edited easily a dozen drafts of the lengthy book. After its publication, he had traipsed across New York City each week, stopping at various Barnes & Noble stores to move copies from the less visible history section to the displays at the front of the store, hustling to his next location whenever he was caught by a store clerk.

"What?" he said. When I repeated my news, he said, "Jesus, Mary, and Joseph." Then, clearly in a state of shock, he asked, "For what?"

"What the hell do you think?" I asked, laughing. He told me to call the publisher back: "They need to get the Pulitzer sticker on the paperback!" he exclaimed.

When Mum called from the hospital a few minutes later, I paused before picking up, just to prolong the moment. When I told her the news, she said, "Ahhh, isn't that just marvelous, Sam. Marvelous. And to think, you were having such a hard time with that bloody article . . ."

I had talked to her the previous night about my struggles with a magazine piece I was writing. For my mother, a major perk of winning the Pulitzer was that it would cheer me up. But I later learned that she was so excited about the news that she told all of the hospital nurses she worked with, as well as her favorite patients.

IN TRUTH, I FELT a profound disconnect between my personal good fortune and the state of the world. Around the time the American occupation of Iraq began spiraling out of control, the Western media started reporting about mass atrocities in a place called Darfur.

Most notably, *New York Times* columnist Nicholas Kristof traveled to the Chad-Sudan border, writing ten impassioned columns in less than a year to draw attention to the massacres being perpetrated by the Arab-led Sudanese government against African ethnic groups. The more I read of Kristof's reporting, the more I suspected that the Sudanese military and affiliated militia were perpetrating genocide. The Sudanese government, led by Omar al-Bashir, seemed intent not only on crushing a nascent rebellion in Darfur, but also on destroying the lives of many Africans there. I felt compelled to investigate what was happening.

Articles about the atrocities in Sudan frequently quoted a former US official named John Prendergast. John had previously served as an Africa adviser to President Clinton, and was now working as an analyst with the International Crisis Group, the nongovernmental organization that Mort had helped create back in 1995 (and that I had briefly worked for during law school). Although the organization generally tailored its recommendations for policymakers, John seemed more focused on convincing Americans at the grassroots level to pressure their elected officials to take action to stop atrocities. He argued, just as I had in my book, that because genocide was rarely seen to implicate "traditional" national security interests, citizens would need to make political noise if they wanted Washington to do more.

When I finally had the chance to hear John speak at an event in New York, I approached him after the Q&A and asked if he would be willing to give me a tutorial on Sudan. He had first visited the country

in 1987 and had traveled there on many occasions, often for months
at a time. After establishing that we were both lovers of baseball, we
agreed to meet up in May of 2004 for a Kansas City Royals–Boston
Red Sox game. Our outing ended up launching what would be one of
the most important professional collaborations—and friendships—of
my life.

As we sat side by side along Fenway's third base line, we talked
about how our desire to fit in as kids had helped spark our love of baseball. We also discussed the role that tenacity—and serendipity—had
played in our respective careers. The son of a frozen-food salesman,
John is a six-foot-one former high school basketball player with a pe-
rennially unshaven look and shoulder-length hair that began turning
silver in his twenties. He moved around a lot as a child and attended
five colleges before graduating from Temple University. In 1984, when
he saw television footage showing the famine in Ethiopia, he decided
to make his way to Africa. Traveling around the continent, John began
writing reports for UNICEF and Human Rights Watch on government and militia abuses against civilians.

Over the years, as he documented crimes that powerful perpetrators didn't want exposed, John was taken hostage in the Congo, survived mortar fire in Somalia, and was imprisoned in Sudan. But he was
upbeat when he talked about Africa and its potential. He predicted
that we were entering a period in which Americans—especially young
people on college campuses—would rise up to demand a different kind
of foreign policy from Washington. "It's all about pressure," he said.
"Governments will do the right thing, or less of the wrong thing, if
people make clear that they care."

We also plunged right into talking about our personal lives, each of
us quickly sizing up the other as incurably single. John had a magnetic
personality, and I had been advised that women flocked to him. He
told me he had ended a short-lived marriage and was now dating several women at once. My most lasting relationship was still with Schu
in college, and I saw nothing on the horizon likely to change that. We
didn't verbalize that day what we later realized we had decided: this

was a friendship that was going to last forever. We were not going to endanger it with a romance neither of us could sustain.

We did, however, almost immediately begin brainstorming about how we might collaborate. I floated the idea of traveling to Darfur together, telling him about the "X test."

"If the most we're able to do is bear witness and use what we see to activate more Americans to care," I said, "it will be worth it, right?"

John did not need convincing. By the time the final out of the game was recorded, we had decided on a date for the trip.

THE EASIEST WAY TO REACH DARFUR was not via the Sudanese capital of Khartoum, but by crossing the border from neighboring Chad. John and I traveled there during the summer of 2004 and spoke with dozens of Darfuri refugees about the horrors they had endured. The woman who made the deepest impression was Amina Abaker Mohammed, a twenty-six-year-old Muslim mother of six who was a member of one of the three ethnic groups being targeted by the Sudanese government. As John and I sat cross-legged in the sand under the shade of a tree, Amina stoically recounted what she had experienced. What she said defied belief.

Amina lived in a Darfuri farming village near a town called Furawiyah. The previous year, she had begun to hear that the Sudanese government and nomadic Arab bandits known as *janjaweed** had begun attacking non-Arab ethnic groups, including hers.

Amina reported that, six months before, a Sudanese military aircraft had fired four rockets near her home. Although one rocket failed to explode, she said, the others left large craters in the ground. She and her husband refused to abandon their land, but they dispatched five of their six children to the nearby mountains for shelter. Amina's oldest child, ten-year-old Mohammed Haroun, remained with her to help take care of the family's precious livestock.

Shortly after dawn on January 31st, 2004, Amina said, she and Mo-

---

* *Janjaweed*, roughly translated, means "evil horseman."

hammed arrived at the wells to draw water for their animals. They heard the sound of approaching planes, and fifteen minutes later, Sudanese aircraft began bombing the area. She and her son were separated. Amina saw Sudanese soldiers come tumbling out of trucks and Land Cruisers, followed by hundreds of menacing *janjaweed* on camels and horses. Most of the *janjaweed* wore turbans around their heads and mouths so that only their eyes were visible. In the initial onslaught, she saw dozens of her neighbors and hundreds of animals killed.

Amina scrambled with several donkeys to a red-rock hillock 300 yards away. Though she thought Mohammed had escaped, when she looked behind her, she saw that he had remained at the wells to try to wrangle the family's panicked sheep. As a circle of several hundred *janjaweed* tightened around her son, Amina ducked behind the hillock to pray.

By nightfall, the sounds of gunfire and screaming faded, and Amina returned to the spot where she had last seen Mohammed. She found a grisly scene. Rummaging frantically around the wells by moonlight, she saw the dismembered bodies of dozens of people she knew, but was unable to find her firstborn.

Suddenly, she spotted his face—but only his face. Mohammed had been beheaded. "I wanted to find the rest of his body," she told me. But she was afraid of the *janjaweed*, who remained nearby, celebrating their conquest with a roast of stolen livestock. She carried what she found of her son to the mountain where her other children were hiding. "I took my child's head, and I buried him," she told John and me, dabbing her tears with the tail of her headscarf. A week later, Amina and her five remaining children made the seven-day trek to Chad, where we would meet them.

Although we had only recently become acquainted, John and I hardly had to discuss our next move. We hired a Darfuri driver to take us across the Chad-Sudan border to Furawiyah, where we would do our best to confirm what Amina had told us and assemble proof of the Sudanese government's crimes.

Advancing at less than ten miles per hour, we drove in 130-degree heat through the inhospitable terrain of western Sudan, where virtually all human life seemed to have been forced into exile or hiding. We felt utterly alone.

As we drove deeper into Darfur toward Amina's hometown, we passed through the village of Hangala, where we found the charred remains of huts that had been set ablaze. Each had been reduced to stone walls and mounds of ashes. Amid the debris, we came across the remnants of a jewelry box, a bicycle, and women's slippers. Of the 480 people who lived in Hangala before the attack, we were later told, 46 were murdered. The rest were now homeless, scattered throughout Sudan and Chad.

In the ransacked village next to Hangala, we found a child's backpack and his "Duckzilla" notebooks, which contained exercises in mathematics, Islamic studies, and Arabic. In another house, we found small packages of beans and nuts, a sign that the inhabitants had fled in a hurry. As we left one hut, where pots had been overturned and valuables looted, we spotted three toothbrushes tucked into the thatch in the roof. Nestled next to them was a sheet of paper that had been folded into a tight square. Upon opening it, we found a few lines of handwritten Arabic script. Our translator told us that it was a prayer from the Koran, urging Allah to keep watch over the family home.

When we finally reached Furawiyah, we asked to be directed to the wells. As a local resident steered us, we passed a large gray rocket that was partly lodged in the sand; this was the undetonated Sudanese Air Force ordnance that Amina had described. We also passed an enormous crater, at least twenty-five feet in diameter and five feet deep, where another bomb had exploded.

"Here are the wells," our guide said as we pulled up to the area that Amina had depicted on a map she had drawn for us. I saw only more Sahara sand.

"What wells?" I asked.

The guide kept pointing to the same patch of desert, and, frustrated, we stepped closer. There, barely visible beneath the pale-yellow sand, were the faint outlines of the rims of one large stone well and two smaller ones. This was where Amina and her son had watered their animals, and where Amina had later found Mohammed's severed head.

The *janjaweed* had stuffed the wells with bodies and buried their victims beneath mounds of sand. In so doing, they had destroyed water sources vital for the survival of people in the area. Among the twenty-five wells around Furawiyah, we learned, only three still functioned— and those would surely dry up soon due to overuse.

The young man who showed us the wells then took us on a short drive outside Furawiyah to the base of a slope. We climbed out of our Land Cruiser and started to ascend on foot. The stench of decomposing flesh hit us before the rotting bodies, in gullies on either side of the hill, finally came into view.

Fourteen men, in bloodied traditional white djellabas or in shirts and slacks, were lying dead in the sand. I counted seventeen bullet casings scattered around them. It looked as though the men had been divided into two groups and lined up in front of the ditches. They had all been shot from behind, except for one man. His body lay not in a ditch, but in the center of the slope. One of his palms was outstretched, as if he had been pleading for mercy.

WHEN JOHN AND I RETURNED to the United States, we publicized what we had learned as widely as possible. He wrote an op-ed in the *New York Times*, and several weeks later, I contributed a long article to *The New Yorker* called "Dying in Darfur," which opened with Amina's story. Together, we also did a TV segment that aired on *60 Minutes*. We each had full-time jobs—I was still teaching at the Kennedy School, and John was writing reports for the International Crisis Group on a broad range of African conflicts. But we joined others in trying to pressure the Bush administration to take meaningful action to do more for the people of Darfur.

Thanks in part to John's relentless activism, which brought him to college campuses, churches, and synagogues around the country, an unusual coalition of students and religious groups began to coalesce. The US Holocaust Memorial Museum strived to be a "living memorial" that would use the history of the Holocaust to educate—and motivate—future generations. The museum had already hosted me,

John, Nick Kristof, and other speakers to talk about Darfur. In July, it officially issued a "genocide emergency" warning on Darfur, the first time it had ever made this designation. The same month, the museum and the American Jewish World Service teamed up to establish a broad network of faith-based, advocacy, and human rights organizations, which eventually included 190 groups and operated under the banner of "Save Darfur."

John and I donated the children's schoolbooks and backpack, the toothbrushes, and the crumpled prayer to the Holocaust museum. We were not sure the people who owned these items were still alive, and, if they were, we assumed they would not be returning to their razed homes anytime soon. The museum staff turned our photos and artifacts into a gripping exhibit, which generated additional public interest.

Evangelical Christians had a history of protesting mass atrocities in southern Sudan (which was home to a substantial Christian population), and now they began raising money for Muslim survivors in Darfur. In August of 2004, thirty-five evangelical leaders, representing fifty-one denominations and 45,000 churches, called for "swift action" from President Bush to "prevent further slaughter and death." When I reached out to a prominent evangelical leader to better understand what was driving the community, I received a refreshingly straightforward response. "Killing is wrong, whether you're killing a Jew, a Christian, or a Muslim," he said. "God made the people there in Darfur. For us to ignore them would be a sin."

Private citizens and students across the country threw themselves into the Darfur campaign. A piano teacher in Salt Lake City donated two weeks' of her earnings. The pastor of a Methodist church in Ohio asked congregants to spend half as much on Christmas presents as they usually did, and to contribute the rest—raising $327,000 for relief efforts. At Swarthmore College in Pennsylvania, a group of students heard reports that a tiny African Union monitoring mission in Darfur didn't have the budget to afford flak jackets. They raised $300,000 to help equip the beleaguered African Union personnel. Other college students formed an organization called Students Take Action Now for

Darfur (STAND), which, within three years, had established chapters at six hundred universities and high schools across the United States.

Back in 2001, I had written an *Atlantic* article describing the Clinton administration's inaction during the Rwandan genocide. I later heard from a US official that President Bush had scribbled "Not on my watch" on a memo summarizing the article. Having always hoped to reach senior policymakers with my writing, I was moved by this, even as I wondered what it would mean practically. Inspired by the Livestrong anti-cancer bracelets, a group of activists created green wristbands inscribed with "Not On Our Watch," which John and I joined thousands of people in wearing in an effort to raise awareness about Darfur. The year 2004 also happened to be the ten-year anniversary of the Rwandan slaughter, and, when the film *Hotel Rwanda* hit theaters, powerfully telling the story of Paul Rusesabagina, the hotelier who sheltered thousands during the genocide, many viewers looked to apply the lessons of Rwanda to the crisis under way in Darfur.

In September of 2004, as this pressure was building and the killings in Darfur continued, Secretary of State Colin Powell testified before the Senate that the Sudanese government's actions amounted to "genocide."[6] This was the first time that the US government had issued such a finding. Far from satisfying the activists, however, Powell's genocide declaration inspired them to push even harder.

The Bush administration responded, appointing a special envoy and imposing new sanctions on the Sudanese government. It also greatly increased aid to displaced Darfuris and support for the peacekeeping forces deployed by the African Union and the United Nations. Unfortunately, because the war in Iraq was going so poorly, the administration had lost substantial influence abroad, which weakened its ability to mobilize a united, global coalition to pressure Khartoum to end its atrocities.[7]

Darfur exposed the limits of what one country could do—even one as powerful as the United States. The perpetrators of genocide knew they could still rely on powerful players in the international community, like China, to defend them. Nevertheless, the outpouring of attention forced the Sudanese government to allow food aid and foreign peacekeepers into their country. The movement also kept Darfuris fed and sheltered with the donated funds. This unique network of students, faith groups, and others, in which I had only a small role, helped save lives.

WHEN GEORGE W. BUSH WAS REELECTED in November of 2004, I was despondent. The result seemed to affirm Bush's decision to invade Iraq, his introduction of torture, and his use of the Guantánamo Bay prison for indefinite detention of prisoners of war, among other deeply problematic, harmful policies. A few days after the election, I had coffee with Peter Galbraith, whom I had profiled in my book. He urged me not to wallow, but to do something constructive.

"What would you have me do?" I said, grasping at one of the few positive national stories to have come out of the election. "Go work for Barack Obama?"

I had never heard of Obama before his speech at the July 2004 Democratic National Convention. Before he took the stage, I had been toggling between an evening Red Sox game and the various speeches from Democrats criticizing President Bush. But as soon as Obama began his oration, I was transfixed by his soaring, inclusive message.

Peter brightened when he heard me mention the senator-elect from Illinois. "Would you do that?" he asked.

"Do what?" I answered, not even sure what I had just said.

"I know a good friend of Obama's. Let's send him your book," Peter replied.

"Why would Obama want a six-hundred-page book on genocide?" I asked.

Peter shot me an exasperated look. "Do you want me to engage my guy or not?" he asked.

That week, I inscribed and mailed a copy of *"A Problem from Hell"* to the address that Peter had given me. I did not expect to hear back.

But nearly five months later, in March of 2005, I received an email from Obama's scheduler saying that the senator was interested in meeting for dinner the next time I was in Washington, DC.

14

GOING TO WASHINGTON

When we met for dinner at a Washington steakhouse in the spring of 2005, Senator Barack Obama introduced himself with a distracted handshake and apologized in advance for any interruptions from lobbyists that would come during the course of our dinner. The whole restaurant seemed to be staring at the forty-three-year-old freshman senator as we sat down, reflecting the unprecedented attention that he had drawn since his keynote address at the 2004 Democratic convention. With one speech, Obama had propelled himself onto the national stage. Before even being sworn in as a senator, he had signed a million-dollar book deal and appeared on the cover of *Newsweek*.

Because Peter Galbraith had connected me to Obama and his advisers with an eye toward getting me a job in his Senate office, I had come to the dinner expecting that to be a main topic of conversation. But Obama gave no indication he was even aware of the possibility.

He started by making clear that he couldn't stay long, but tactfully reassured me that we would have other opportunities to speak. "I really hope over the next forty-five minutes we can start what will be a longer conversation over time," he said.

I made a mental note not to order an appetizer and to speak quickly.

But once Obama settled into our conversation, his various curiosities seemed to override his plan for a rapid exit.

"Where do you come from?" he asked, starting us off. I gave him my story: Ireland, Pittsburgh, Georgia, Bosnia, Winthrop. At thirty-four, I had a time-tested encapsulation of my life.

"Because there was no divorce in Ireland, my mother decided to move to America."

"After I saw images of emaciated men behind barbed wire in Europe, I became a war correspondent in the Balkans."

Obama refused to follow my script. "What the hell does 'no divorce in Ireland' have to do with ending up in Georgia?" he asked, interrupting me as I tried to speed through the chronology. Or, "What do you mean, you just went and became a war correspondent?"

His interjections took me by surprise. I thought a life like mine would have been familiar to him, given his own itinerant upbringing. I knew he had lived in Indonesia as a boy and had moved to Chicago after college without really knowing anyone. "You know how it is when you turn up someplace new," I said. "You figure it out."

Obama looked skeptical. "Well, you are more entrepreneurial than I am," he replied disarmingly. "Chicago is not Sarajevo."

He had published a memoir at age thirty-three, but he seemed almost bored by the topic of himself and eager to focus on someone else for a while. His manner was at once regal and relaxed.

I had brought a long list of questions for him, but he kept drilling down on my experiences, asking me to elaborate on just about everything I had grown used to discussing in shorthand. Mort ("What is it about him you most admire?"). Basketball ("Were you any good?"). Harvard Law School ("After Bosnia, was it crazy to be in a place where people were worried about grades and small things?"). The craft of storytelling ("When you start, do you think more about character or plot arc?"). The only topic we didn't touch on at any length was the one that I was probably the most interested in given my own background: his father.

I knew from his memoir *Dreams from My Father* that Barack Obama, Sr., had met and married Obama's mother, Ann Dunham, when Obama Sr. came from Kenya to the University of Hawaii on a scholarship. I knew that when Obama was three, his dad had gone back to Kenya, returning to visit his son just once, seven years later. I also knew that, when he lost his position in the Kenyan government, Obama Sr. had begun drinking heavily, eventually dying in a car crash when Barack was twenty-one. Probing this topic further seemed presumptuous, especially given all that Obama had already put in the public record, and I was hesitant to mention my own alcoholic father. Instead, when we alighted on the topic of his upbringing, I simply said, "Your mother was one brave woman."

He smiled and remarked, "In many ways, the book I wrote about my father is all about my mother."

Obama eventually brought the conversation around to US foreign policy, but through a personal lens. I told him about my drive to law school in August of 1995 when I cried upon hearing the radio announcement that the United States had finally intervened to try to end the killings in Bosnia.

"Why the tears?" he asked a bit coolly.

"I guess relief that America had saved all those people," I said.

"Hmm," he responded, giving little away about his own view.

He asked me about the massacre in Srebrenica. He wanted to understand what had happened, but also what the episode could teach Americans about how to improve the responsiveness of the US government and the UN to future such crises. Because the United States had ended the Bosnian conflict without incurring combat casualties, President Clinton's use of military force was hard to argue with in retrospect. But Obama expressed sympathy with decision-makers, noting how hard it must be to predict in advance exactly how local actors will respond to US involvement in a conflict.

I was familiar with the speech he had given at a Chicago anti-war rally. "I don't oppose all wars," he had said in October of 2002 as the Bush administration moved closer to invading Iraq. "What I am opposed to is a dumb war." I asked him about it, noting that he had taken this position at a time when most Americans supported going to war. I wondered if he had considered the possibility that he was committing political suicide. At the same time, he had not pandered to the progressive crowd, making clear that he was not a pacifist and that some wars were worth fighting.

Pivoting away from the speech, Obama said he found it maddening that Bush administration officials had simply presumed that our soldiers would be welcomed as liberators in Iraq. For him, it seemed like malpractice to judge one's prospects by one's intentions, rather than making a strenuous effort to anticipate and weigh potential consequences.

Over the course of our dinner, Obama posed questions that I had never considered, wondering aloud whether the controversial "broken windows" theory of policing might be strategically applied to shoring up failing states like Sudan.[8] "I can honestly say I've never thought about that," I said, resolving to do my homework and get back to him.

When I explained how idle I had felt reporting on the bloodshed in Bosnia while hoping that others would do something to stop it, he acknowledged that he had experienced a similar feeling of futility as a community organizer in Chicago. This frustration of attempting to address symptoms and not causes, he told me, had convinced him to get into politics, where he could pursue systemic change. "Now I have different frustrations," he noted dryly.

When I finally succeeded in moving the conversation away from myself, I asked him how he was handling his meteoric change in fortune—going from an ugly defeat in his first run at Congress in 2000 to handily winning a seat in the Senate four years later.

He acknowledged that an awful lot had broken in his favor in recent years. Yes, he had won his Senate seat by 43 percentage points. But, he stressed, his opponent, Alan Keyes, had never even lived in Illinois and had entered the race only after the Republican primary winner dropped out amid a sex scandal. And even before that, Obama reminded me, he had been trailing in the Democratic primary before the front-runner faced his own damaging scandal involving an allegation of domestic violence.

The hardest part of his demanding new life, Obama reflected, was being away from his two young daughters, then ages three and six. He had a routine that generally allowed him to tuck them into bed at home in Chicago on Monday nights, fly to Washington, and be back in time to say good night on Thursday—but he admitted, "My wife is carrying us . . . I just can't miss those flights."

When I asked him how, with such intense media attention, he kept

from getting "too big a head," he gave an answer I would hear him repeat often in the coming years: "It has never really felt as if it is about
me as such. I've become a vehicle. People hunger for something they
aren't getting—authenticity, a willingness to speak one's convictions,
aspirations that transcend party affiliation. I guess I'm filling some
kind of void."

Obama spoke with unusual precision about his strengths and weak-
nesses. "I'm not some big original thinker," he said. "But I listen well,
I synthesize ideas, and I can generally figure out how to communicate
what we need to do."

We discussed the fact that people were already urging him to run
for President in 2008. On this issue, Obama was adamant: despite the
buzz generated by his arrival in Washington, he would not enter the
race.

"If I ran for president," he said, "I would have to start fundraising
and building an organization two years after becoming a senator. How
presumptuous would that be? It would take a lot of nerve. I'm going to
keep my head down."

After John Kerry's bruising defeat in the 2004 election, Obama
said he wanted to help spearhead the development of a fresh, affirmative vision for the Democratic Party. He was reaching out to foreign
policy thinkers like me, and to former US diplomats, he said, because
he wanted to brainstorm with people from different backgrounds about
America's role in the world. He was doing the same with health care
experts, environmentalists, and economists to spur his thinking on domestic policy.

"I have no power as the ninety-ninth senator," he underscored, referring to his lack of seniority in the Senate. "But I find myself in this
surreal position where almost nobody in this town has a bigger platform. I don't know how long that will last, but I'm going to try to
use my influence while I can." He thought Kerry had lost the election
because voters had not been sure what he stood for. "I have learned,"
Obama told me, "that if you are truthful, people respond, even if they
don't agree with you. We have to find our truth and not be afraid to be
straight with people."

After four hours, our "forty-five-minute" dinner began to wind down. Obama had mentioned that Mark Lippert, a Navy reservist and experienced Hill staffer, was his senior foreign policy adviser. I had known in advance that he already had a full-time aide, but hoped I might be able to help him develop broad strategy. Yet even though the dinner was going well, he seemed to think of me as an academic with whom he might occasionally share his ideas, not somebody who might join his team. I began to worry that the conversation we were wrapping up would prove to be a onetime event.

I wanted more than that. Although the Republicans controlled both the Senate and House, I still held out hope that Congress could play a role in forcing the Bush administration to abandon its ruinous approaches to Iraq and counterterrorism. Even though I had interviewed hundreds of US policymakers for my genocide book, I thought I would be a better teacher at the Kennedy School if I were more familiar with Congress's role in foreign policy. And above all, I was now not only inspired by the kind of leadership Obama had espoused publicly but also by the kind of person he actually seemed to be.

As Obama asked the waiter to bring the check, I ran over my time-honored "X test" question in my mind. In this context, the question seemed to boil down to: "If the most I am able to do is learn more about how Congress works, will moving to Washington have been worth it?" But in this case, the truth was that Obama had a background, optimism, and vision that I hadn't encountered in another public figure. Yes, I would learn. But I was also energized by the prospect of being part of whatever he did.

Despite this conviction, I felt self-conscious about raising my own future with him. And since he showed no sign of recruiting me, I would have to force myself to raise a question that had been on my mind, but didn't seem to be on his: Might there be a place for me on his team?

After he paid, Obama stood up and I quickly followed. We continued chatting as we walked slowly toward the door of the restaurant, which was now nearly empty. He had seemed in such a hurry at the beginning, but now he chatted easily, as if the time pressure had lifted.

I did not want to look back and feel I had missed the moment, so

I decided to risk rejection and take the plunge. "You know, if you think I could be helpful, I could come down to Washington and work with you," I offered.

He asked me what I meant, and I explained that since he wanted to develop a broader foreign policy platform, I could take a leave from Harvard and help him do that. He asked if I was sure that would make sense for me. "You've got books to write and courses to teach," he said.

I was firm. "Even if you don't change the world overnight," I said, "I will learn something, right?"

At 11:15 p.m., as we stood on the deserted street, his driver's engine idling, he jotted down his email address and cell phone number. He would work out the details with his chief of staff, but would love to bring me "on board."

I RENTED A SMALL CARRIAGE HOUSE apartment a short walk from Capitol Hill. If Washington, DC, thought of itself as the center of the universe, the 288-foot-high dome of the US Capitol building seemed—and in fact was on street maps—the center of the center. When I worked for Mort at the Carnegie Endowment back in 1993, I had taken long runs on the Mall, looping around the Lincoln Memorial and climbing the hill toward the Capitol dome, which was always lit up in the humid night. I had seen it so often in movies and on postcards that, from the outside, it had come to seem more like a cardboard cutout than a building where real work was done. But as an aide to Barack Obama, I felt I would actually have the chance to influence the direction of US foreign policy. I imagined myself drawing up legislation in eighteenth-century nooks, as George Washington and Thomas Jefferson gazed down approvingly from murals above.

The first indication that I was not to be a twenty-first-century incarnation of James Madison came as soon as I showed up for work. It turned out that Obama's office was located not in the Capitol building, which is reserved for House and Senate leaders, but in the gray-white marble Hart Senate Office Building adjacent to the Capitol. Opened in 1982, Hart had a large atrium with the feel of an ice-skating rink, while the nondescript Senate chambers encircling it resembled dentists' offices.

The only sign that Obama's Senate office housed a rising star was the sight of school groups waiting for hours in the small reception area in the hopes that they might catch a glimpse of him. African Americans came from all over the country for this privilege, as if needing proof that an African-American senator (only the third since Reconstruction) really existed. I felt for Obama. Overnight, millions of people had invested their hopes in him.

My role was not well defined. I would be paid a small stipend (not by his office but by the Council on Foreign Relations) to serve as a "foreign policy fellow" on his Senate staff.* I was given a cubicle, a badge, and a key to the office so I would be able to work on weekends.

It didn't take long to discover why Obama wasn't crazy about his job. The 109th Congress, already under way when I arrived, would end up meeting for fewer days than any in more than fifty years. This was fewer even than the Congress of 1948, which was famously assailed by President Harry Truman as the "do-nothing Congress"—and it still managed to pass the Marshall Plan to rebuild Europe. "It's worse than the UN!" Obama vented as we spoke on the phone one evening.

As I trailed Obama and his aide Mark Lippert to committee hearings around the Capitol, the congressional debates I observed seemed detached from actual human life. Many members appeared to be motivated less by John F. Kennedy's call to service than by a self-serving parody of that famous exhortation: "Ask not what your representative can do for the issue, but what the issue can do for your representative." Unsurprisingly, the legislative branch was suffering a major drop in popularity. At the outset of the new session in January of 2005, Congress had a 43 percent approval rating among Americans. By December of 2006, that figure had dropped to 21 percent.[9]

Obama had come to Washington having served for eight years as a

---

* In the year 2000, CFR had awarded me a fellowship, which I had deferred for several years, but which helped support a yearlong stint in Senator Obama's office.

legislator in the Illinois State Senate, where he had helped pass laws on campaign finance reform, an earned-income tax credit for the working poor, and a requirement that police interrogations be videotaped. Yet in the far grander US Senate, he was stymied. On foreign policy, he had been inspired by the program built by Indiana Republican senator Richard Lugar and Georgia Democratic senator Sam Nunn, which over two decades had help secure and eliminate more nuclear weapons than those in the combined arsenals of China, France, and the UK. Obama and Lugar would go on to work together to pass a bill that expanded funding for nonproliferation initiatives, but the spirit of bipartisanship that animated the Nunn-Lugar partnership—and that appealed to Obama—was rapidly fading. Often surprisingly transparent about his thinking, Obama told an interviewer after his first year, "I think it's very possible to have a Senate career here that is not particularly useful."

Occasionally, Obama tried to poke fun at the disconnect between his star power and his limitations in achieving actual results. "I've been very blessed," he quipped in a speech at the Gridiron dinner. "Keynote speaker at the Democratic convention. The cover of *Newsweek*. My book made the best-seller list. I just won a Grammy for reading it on tape . . . Really, what else is there to do?" he asked, pausing for effect. "Well, I guess I could pass a law or something."

When I saw him in the office, Obama seemed to resent many of the new demands on his time. In his past life, he had enjoyed great freedom, shuttling between representing his district and teaching constitutional law at the University of Chicago. He now bristled at the vast number of people who had access to his calendar and all the obligations that encroached on his independence. Before I made the move to Washington, Obama told me that he planned to force me to go on walks with him, allowing us to escape staff scrutiny and talk through the ideas he was exploring for his next book. But, he added, "I may just put my headphones on and chill while we walk."

His temperament definitely did not fit the profile of Senate legends like Lyndon Johnson, who, when he first came to Washington as a junior Hill aide, got a room in a hotel where fellow staffers stayed and took four showers a day just so he would bump into people in the shared bathroom. Obama, by comparison, was a recluse.

He just didn't seem to need the affirmation that Johnson, Bill Clinton, and so many other highly successful politicians famously craved. It often seemed as though part of him was floating above the fray, judging what he and his colleagues were doing below.

I occasionally sat behind Obama at Senate Foreign Relations Committee hearings in a row of seats allocated for Senate aides so they could answer their members' questions. As the senators engaged witnesses, they seemed less interested in changing minds than in scoring points with the media, special interest groups (who I was shocked to learn actually wrote many of the senators' questions), and, on a good day, their constituents back home.

"Here we go again," Obama told me as we entered one hearing in which Secretary of State Condoleezza Rice was testifying. "We will faithfully pretend to be asking questions, but we will instead give statements. She will faithfully pretend to answer our questions, but will instead answer questions we didn't ask so as to deliver talking points we've all heard before. And the hearing will end, and we will walk out of here, calling it 'democratic accountability.'"

Once, as one of the hearings dragged on, Obama tilted back in his chair and motioned to me to lean in. I hunched forward eagerly, thinking he was looking for counsel. He held his binder up to shield his mouth so his colleagues could not hear him, and said, "I'm sorry you have to witness this." With Republicans in the majority, Congress seemingly had little appetite to influence the Bush administration's actions.

The most important foreign policy issue then was the direction of the war in Iraq, where US troops were confronting a worsening insurgency and the prospect of an open-ended military occupation. When I arrived in DC, more than 1,500 members of the US military had been killed, and another 11,000 wounded. Close to two years after President Bush had declared the end of major combat operations, the American public was increasingly questioning a continued military presence in Iraq. Since taking office, Obama had visited Iraq to hear from the troops and had held sobering meetings with men and women who had sustained serious injuries on the battlefield. In a decision that disappointed Obama's anti-war supporters, though, he voted against a proposal requiring that US troops leave Iraq within a year. Instead, he supported an amendment that called on President Bush to begin a phased troop withdrawal. (Neither measure passed.)

Despite his desire to bring our 140,000 troops home, Obama did not believe that Congress was equipped to micromanage the war. He was also frustrated by the binary way in which pundits, administration officials, and members of Congress chose to discuss Iraq, as if the only options available were "staying the course" or "cutting and running."

Obama often formulated his own views on important policy questions by bringing people with disparate perspectives together and listening as they debated what to do. He did this on several occasions regarding Iraq, gathering Lippert, communications director Robert Gibbs, chief of staff Pete Rouse, me, and others. I was heartened every time he reminded us that he wanted to determine the right approach "on the merits," and only afterward "worry about the politics." But even with worthy intentions, it wasn't easy to know what to recommend. As we deliberated, I was reminded of President Johnson's famous observation that a leader's problem was not in "doing what's right, but *knowing* what's right."

AS WAS PROBABLY FITTING, I received my first taste of the politics of politics while working in the Senate. Although Lippert had seemed welcoming at the start of my tenure, he was not enthusiastic about my continued presence. I tried to put myself in his shoes. He had been Obama's chief foreign policy adviser, and suddenly I had shown up in what was a surprisingly small office. I understood it might be initially awkward. But instead of coming around and welcoming an extra pair of hands, he seemed mostly to resent the intrusion upon his turf. I proposed speeches, op-eds, and Senate resolutions on topics I had discussed with Obama, but Lippert generally responded by saying that other senators had already cornered the market on the issue, or by questioning how Obama's input would "add value." Disheartened,

I began to ration my time in the office, just trying to do good work whenever Obama or Lippert threw an assignment my way.

One day when I was in the office, my computer froze as I was attempting to print a news article for Obama. After I jumped on a colleague's desktop and pulled up the story to print it, an Outlook message alert popped up in the lower right-hand corner of his computer screen, showing that he had received an email from one of Obama's top advisers. The message notification was followed by several others—all of them appearing quickly and then melting away, so I caught only the gist. I don't know the full context to this day. But even from the partial messages that momentarily appeared on the screen, I could see that—to my horror—the emails between two senior colleagues I respected were about me.

"You'll LOVE this," the first one began, suggesting that I was exploiting the genocide in Darfur to promote myself. Those that followed continued in the same vein.

As each notification popped up and then vanished, I felt guilty that I was inadvertently seeing portions of a coworker's personal messages, but also clueless for having failed to recognize the extent of my colleagues' resentments. From the familiar, chummy tone of the exchange, it was clear that I had stumbled into an ongoing back-and-forth in which I was a regular topic.

Instead of getting angry, I felt wounded. I also didn't know what I was doing to come across in the way I was being described.

I went for a walk outside to compose myself and then called my friend Debbie Fine for some support. Debbie, a Washington lawyer I had recently gotten to know, went to great lengths to reassure me. She asked me to imagine a scenario in which the senior men in the office ganged up on a *man* that Senator Obama had personally invited to work with him.

"They hate that you have your own channel to him," she said. "And because you're a woman, they think it's okay to tear you down."

Working alone for years as a journalist and an academic, I had mostly been spared the petty office dynamics that many people deal with every day. I had also never been so proximate to "power," which seemed to have earned its reputation as a corroding force. I still don't know whether I was being undermined because my relationship with Obama existed independently of the normal office hierarchy, because I was a woman, or some combination. Regardless, I realized that sharing the same general political loyalties does not mean that people are kindred spirits.

And I now knew that I would need to keep up my guard.

15

THE BAT CAVE

Because I didn't feel secure in my new work environment, I found myself more distracted at work than I had been before. When I told John Prendergast about how I was feeling, he appropriated the concept of the Bat Cave from Bruce Wayne, giving it new life.

The Bat Cave, John explained to me, is inside each of our heads—either a place of great stillness, or, on other occasions, a place where bats fly around, flapping their wings in sometimes frantic ways. Being "in the Bat Cave" thereby became our shorthand for times when self-doubt was intruding.

The bats fluttered wildly in my head when I worked in Obama's Senate office, and while I tried to slay them by reminding myself "it's not you; it's them," that mantra rarely worked. Eleanor Roosevelt wrote movingly about having her own equivalent of a Bat Cave, but in the end, she found consolation by telling herself, "Great minds discuss ideas; average minds discuss events; small minds discuss people." I agreed with this, but I still couldn't get the small things or people out of my head.

EVENTS IN MY PERSONAL LIFE required me to understand better where my "bats" were coming from. Alongside my breathing issues, ever since the publication of *"A Problem from Hell,"* I had begun to experience regular episodes of sharp, debilitating back pain. Every few months, I would find myself writhing on the floor with back spasms and would spend the day wrapped in a heating pad.

I initially attributed the pain to cramped travel on too many airplanes and to punishing squash and marathon training sessions. But
the episodes continued even when I eased up on international trips and
competitive sports. Next, I thought I was hurting my back by spending too much time hunched over my computer, so I ordered a stand-up
desk and an ergonomic keyboard, which also didn't help.

Ultimately, although I despised sitting still for the treatments,
I tried massage therapists, chiropractors, and acupuncturists. I also saw
orthopedists who X-rayed me from every conceivable angle, but who
could not find the structural damage that I insisted was there. While
I could generally make the back inflammation go down after a few
days, nothing seemed to resolve the underlying issue. And once I was
working in the Senate, my back spasms grew even more frequent.

Even though I remained convinced I had dislocated something in
my lower back, I soon came to understand that the pain might have a
different source. A few months before I had moved to Washington,
something unexpected and wonderful had happened: I fell in love.

The man in question was a thirty-eight-year-old actor from the
midlands of Ireland, whom I met while he was performing on Broad-
way. A mutual friend introduced us after learning that I admired his
acting and that he both loved baseball and had read *A Problem from
Hell*." Our first date was at a Mets game in New York City, where we
started a conversation that seemed destined never to end. A week into
our relationship, we heard ourselves talking about marriage, and I felt
as though I had found the person I wanted to share my life with. "I feel
like myself, only more so," I wrote in my journal.

My new great love was a recovering alcoholic and deeply involved in
"The Program," or AA. Eddie and my brother, Stephen, were also both
active in AA, and, given my father's inability to get help, I had great
admiration for people who invested themselves in trying to hold the
demon of addiction at bay. I attended several open AA meetings with
him, and saw the power of his community in deepening his determination not to fall back into old habits. His vulnerability was every bit as
appealing to me as his strength. I had excessively scrutinized my prior
relationships, assessing and reassessing their pros and cons. But for the

first time, I was out of my head and carried away by feelings of great joy. I couldn't imagine the relationship ending.

But then it did. The pace and intensity of our courtship, which I found thrilling, threw him off-kilter. A creature of routine in New York, he suddenly found himself taking trips to visit me and, when we were apart, staying up late to talk with me on the phone, departing from the rituals he used as his guardrails for staying sober.

For me, the only negative aspect of our romance was that I quickly began to imagine the slew of terrible mishaps that could befall him. When I heard about a construction accident in New York, I called him in a panic, virtually positive that he was buried under the scaffolding. When he decided to purchase a motorcycle, I became hysterical, begging him not to.

For him, though, as we plunged deeper into our relationship, the negatives quickly began to add up. His recovery was his priority. He needed to control his surroundings and his emotions. The first sign that we were heading in a bad direction was an email he sent in which he wrote: "I have never felt this way before. I don't know what to do." Within days of introducing doubt into the relationship, he told me he could not see me anymore and refused even to take my calls.

I was blindsided and crushed. Whether because he was an Irish alcoholic who left me, or because he was a person I loved who left me, the breakup surfaced a sadness that I had not been fully aware I was carrying. For weeks, I was unable to work, eat, or sleep. John, who lived in my Capitol Hill neighborhood, stayed close to me, calling multiple times a day and taking me to shoot baskets at the local YMCA. He encouraged me to mourn and come to terms with the end of the relationship, but he also urged me to use what had happened to try to understand the role my father's death was playing in my turmoil—as well as in my lungers and back pain.

John himself was the child of an alcoholic. He too was then going through a difficult breakup, and he suggested that we try attending Al-Anon meetings, which are for the family members of alcoholics. At these sessions, we listened to other people describe their histories, the ways they had sought to compensate for their loved ones' drinking, and the corrosive residue of their experiences. John and I related to these stories and tried to understand the feeling of rejection and the longing for control we had both developed. We allowed ourselves to be defenseless with each other, and we pushed ourselves to dig deeper.

Since I was not contributing meaningfully in the Senate office, I decided that for the first time in my life I would make my emotional health my top priority. Instead of trying to repress my fears, I had to identify and talk about them.

I found a new therapist and threw myself into our sessions in a way I had not done before, arranging to speak twice a week. With my heartbreak so close to the surface, the feeling of loss I had experienced as a child became easier to reach. The therapist questioned why I had gone to live in a war zone and why I was so drawn to other people's suffering, speculating that this focus allowed me to continue minimizing my own pain, which naturally "paled in comparison" to genocide.

I resisted his analysis. While acknowledging that my loss may have expanded my ability to empathize, I said I knew plenty of people who hadn't lost a loved one and yet still dedicated their whole selves to improving the lives of others. I felt I was drawn to writing about atrocities not because of childhood trauma, but because understanding and preventing mass murder was intrinsically important. However, I admitted—to him and to myself—that my parents' breakup and father's death continued to tear at me. Even though these formative events of course did not compare to the suffering of Rwandans, they nonetheless left their own scars.

At the time, I was also writing my next book—a biography of the late UN diplomat Sergio Vieira de Mello, whom I had known in Bosnia and who was killed by a suicide bomber in Iraq. This project also oddly raised issues of abandonment. When I wasn't in my cubicle in Obama's Senate office, I was in my carriage house conducting phone interviews with US soldiers who had tried to rescue Sergio from the bombed-out rubble of UN Headquarters. Because of the absence of planning by the Bush administration and the looting of Iraq's fire stations, the would-be rescuers didn't have the equipment that they believed would have saved him. The more I learned, the clearer it was that Sergio, one of the world's great humanitarians, had ended up dying a preventable death. Unearthing these facts stirred up imagined visions of my father's last hours.

In therapy, I became aware of a deeply submerged, misplaced certainty that if my brother and I had remained at home in Dublin, our father would not have died. For years, it seemed, I had been subconsciously blaming myself for my dad's death. Because I had long accepted that alcoholism was a "disease" over which my father was powerless, I believed that it had been my job to save him. But now, with the help of John, Al-Anon, and therapy, I saw that my child-self had not been a capable agent in a grown-up world; I finally recognized that I had been helpless. For the first time in my life—at the age of thirty-five—I began grieving over the monumental loss and rupture that I had experienced. And I started to stop seeing that loss as my fault.

I also came to understand just how unwittingly determined I had been to never be vulnerable to such a loss again. And the only way to avoid such pain had been to choose men who themselves resisted sustained closeness.

EVEN AS JOHN AND I CONTINUED to push each other to explore our pasts, the original spark for our friendship—our work in response to the genocide in Darfur—was now part of something larger than either of us could have imagined. The anti-genocide movement, which started in 2004, had continued growing.

Major universities—including all of the University of California campuses, Yale, and Harvard—divested their endowment portfolios of stocks belonging to companies doing business with Sudan. Don Cheadle (the lead actor in *Hotel Rwanda*) and George Clooney had traveled to Darfur with John, and both resolved to throw their celebrity into publicizing the atrocities. Cheadle and John coauthored a bestselling book with strategies for how citizens could get involved, while Clooney and Elie Wiesel lobbied the UN Security Council to devote more resources to addressing the crisis. And after intense pressure from activists who were critical of China's support for Sudan, Steven Spielberg withdrew from his role as artistic adviser for the opening ceremony of the Beijing Summer Olympics. John recognized the shallowness of much celebrity activism, but he also saw that when celebrities were serious about an issue over a long period of time, they helped expose large numbers of people to the cause. This would end up being the case with Cheadle and Clooney, whose advocacy seemed to put Darfur into the public consciousness and onto the radar screens of policymakers more directly than many experts had been able to achieve on their own.

To capitalize on this wave of attention, the Save Darfur Coalition planned a rally on the National Mall for April of 2006. Because of the sacrosanct office rule that weekends were Obama's family time, his schedulers declined the invitation for him to appear. However, a few days before the rally, Obama told me he wanted to make an exception. "I have to go, don't I?" he asked. "I mean, I care about this issue. I can't not go, right?"

Obama had been outspoken on Darfur since joining the Senate. He and Kansas senator Sam Brownback had published an important op-ed in the *Washington Post* warning that the situation in Darfur was likely to "spiral out of control" without a significant shift in US policy. His partnership with Brownback, a conservative Republican, helped demonstrate that the movement had bipartisan support, and his presence at the rally would be a huge draw.

To generate as much attention for the event as possible, Obama, Brownback, and Clooney held a joint press conference at the National Press Club, where they argued for turbocharging the few thousand peacekeepers in Darfur into a much bigger and better-equipped UN-led mission. After encouraging more countries to take responsibility for stabilizing hot spots around the world, Obama urged that this new UN force be comprised of troops from Western countries. He also gave me a shout-out for my work on the issue, saying, "I've got to give a special acknowledgment to the person who's technically on my staff right now . . . because she actually thought that I might be able to do something on issues that she cared about . . . She's a wonderful friend and has written a book that I'd recommend to everybody." I was surprised to find how much I needed a bit of recognition after such a rocky stretch.

John and I had spent hours on the phone preparing for the rally.

We shared drafts of our respective remarks with each other, and we made plans to deliver them on the stage side by side. Still, we kept our expectations in check. "Do you really think ten thousand people will show up for this?" I asked, citing the optimistic figure the organizers had given the National Park Service. "I have no idea," John said. "But if they don't, we will just have to be extra grateful to those who do come."

On the eve of the rally, the buses began arriving—student groups, churchgoers, people in hijabs and yarmulkes. President Bush graciously met with activist leaders in the Oval Office. "For those of you who are going out to march for justice," he told them, "you represent the best of our country."

The speakers were a mix of celebrities and public officials, including Clooney, Wiesel, Nancy Pelosi, Al Sharpton, Olympic speed-skater Joey Cheek (who had donated his $40,000 in medal earnings from the 2006 Winter Games to Darfur relief), and Paul Rusesabagina, the Rwandan hotelier Cheadle played in *Hotel Rwanda*. In the end, more than 50,000 people showed up, including Mum, Eddie, and Laura.

The loudest applause of the day went to Obama. I had sent him an email with a few ideas for his speech. But after looking out at the swelling crowd—a heartening sight to a former community organizer—he started with Scripture:

> In the Book of Proverbs, Chapter 24, Verses 11 and 12, it reads as follows:
>
> *Rescue those being led away to death,*
> *Hold back those staggering toward slaughter!*
> *If you say, "But we knew nothing of this!"*
> *Does not he who weighs the heart perceive it?*
> *Does not he who guards your life know it?*
> *Will he not repay each person according to what he has done?*

Obama proceeded to take note of how tempting it often is to look away, and how complex modern challenges can seem:

There are problems in the world that sometimes seem over-whelming. There's so much misery, so much want, so much con-flict and cruelty, so much violence. And at times there's lack of moral clarity.

We look across the span of the globe and we can't always tell who the good guys are and who the bad guys are. We don't always know what the proper course of action is. And so we're some-times tempted to withdraw into our own private lives, our own private struggles and ambitions, our own private gardens.

But this is not one of those times.

Today we know what is right and we know what is wrong. The slaughter of innocents is wrong. Two million people driven from their homes is wrong. Women gang raped while gathering fire-wood is wrong. Silence, acquiescence, paralysis in the face of genocide is wrong.

The whole audience seemed to be hanging on Obama's every word. For all of his deflections about being just "a vehicle" for Americans wanting to transcend the stale politics of the time, he was captivating people of all races and religions, young and old. Even his closing plea for American leadership sounded different from the normal platitudes one heard from a politician.

"I know that if *we* care, the world will care. If *we* bear witness, then the world will know. If *we* act, then the world will follow!" he said. "And in every corner of the globe, tyrants and terrorists, powers and principalities, will know that a new day is dawning and a righteous spirit is on the move, and that all of us together have joined hands to ensure that never again *will* these kinds of atrocities happen."

The crowd went wild. I was moved and exhausted. The solidarity I had advocated for over so many years had found a powerful and com-passionate champion.

That night, as I applied heat to my back, Obama called after landing in Chicago.

"That was quite something," he said. "You should feel really good about what happened out there."

"I do," I started. "But now . . ."

"I know, I know," he said. "The genocide in Darfur rages on. But you know what? Sometimes you just have to take the time to appreciate a good thing, even if it doesn't necessarily bring you exactly what you want. If you don't savor moments like today, you won't have the fuel you need to keep going. Take it from me."

I told him how much his involvement had meant, and, after hanging up, slept for twelve hours.

I LEFT WASHINGTON WITH LITTLE FANFARE in the summer of 2006. Although I had never considered myself a particularly partisan person, I came away immensely frustrated with the way Republicans often forced debates over US policy into a false dichotomy between an overreliance on military force on the one hand, and what they called "appeasement" on the other. I was also struck by how unprepared our national security institutions were for responding to unconventional threats like climate change. To deal with cross-border challenges, we needed to build coalitions, a prospect that required having credibility with foreign publics—and the Iraq War had cost us dearly in that respect.

Seeing all of this up close was deflating. But I did not consider the year a loss. My personal ups and downs in Washington had finally forced me to start addressing the unconscious forces inside me—forces that may well have been preventing me from finding a lasting romantic relationship. And despite the difficulties I experienced while working for him, I did feel that I had gotten to know Senator Obama.

During the time I lived in Washington, Obama had spent nights and weekends writing his second book, which he was calling *The Audacity of Hope*. He would email me, usually late, after watching ESPN's *Sports Center*, which I had generally watched as well. I would immediately mark up his drafts with edits and suggestions before returning them to him. I had come to realize that these exchanges were more valuable than anything I was doing for him in the Senate.

When I called Obama to tell him that I was heading back to Massachusetts, he cut me off. "Yeah, I never expected you to be useful to me here." Having spent a year of my life trudging to and from the Hart Senate building, I was taken aback.

"I don't mean to hurt your feelings," he said. "Let me rephrase that: I don't have the power to use you properly. I was actually wondering what took you so long to bolt."

I stared at the phone incredulously. Had he known all along how pointless the year in his office had often felt?

Although I didn't share this with him at the time, my experiences with the Senate had left me with one conviction: Obama needed to get out of there. Even though Democrats had taken both the House and Senate in the 2006 midterm elections, I did not think Congress was where he belonged.

Like millions of other people, I believed that he should run for President.

DURING THE MONTHS AFTER I MOVED back to Winthrop and resumed teaching at Harvard, I spoke with Obama often.

"How's your Sergio book going?" he asked me in one call. I offered him more detail than he needed, as always, and then, assuming he wanted help on something, asked, "So what's up? What can I do for you?"

His response surprised me. "What do you mean? I'm just calling to see how your book is coming and how you're doing. I know how hard it is."

I asked him about his recent trip to Kenya, his first since becoming an internationally known figure. He told me about the intensity of the crowds who lined the streets wherever he went.

"Goodness," I said. "How did that feel?"

"Pardon?" he replied.

"How did it *feel*?" I repeated.

"What do you mean?" he asked.

"Barack!" I exclaimed. "Feelings! Remember those?"

"I don't know," he said. "I guess I felt the way I feel about all of this. People are hungering for something, and they see that something in me. I can't take it too seriously."

In October of 2006, *The Audacity of Hope* was published to a historic reception. Supporters wearing "Obama for President" paraphernalia mobbed his events, and tickets to free book readings were sold by scalpers online. With crowds overrunning the bookstores, Obama's publicity team laid down rules: no photos, no personal conversations, and no more than three books to sign per person.

Obama told me that he had begun to think seriously about a presidential run, but he was worried about the time away from his daughters and Michelle. He knew that he would be sacrificing his privacy and that the campaign trail would be grueling. "I just don't know if I want the aggravation," he told me.

I urged him to go for it. "There's nobody else who can break through. And even if it won't be fun for you, and you don't need it, the issues you care about need you."

"Yeah, yeah," he said, "I get the argument for doing it. I just need to know that we can manage this as a family. And I need to know that I can win."

I was acutely conscious of how little I knew about political campaigns or his prospects against the financial juggernaut that seemed ready to line up behind Hillary Clinton, the presumptive Democratic front-runner for 2008. I also couldn't conceive of what it would be like to weigh pursuit of the highest office in the land against missing one's spouse and young children. I didn't bring up the topic again. Instead, I scrutinized his public statements just like the rest of the country. All I knew was that if he did decide to run, I wanted to be there with him.

As I waited, I had a lurking fear that I would make a mistake that would somehow foil his ascent. Now that my intensive therapy had helped me recognize the misplaced sense of responsibility I felt for my dad's death, I had begun experiencing telling dreams.

In one dream, I had brought Obama to sunny Yankee Stadium for Opening Day. As we watched the Red Sox defeat the Yankees, he told me that if he raised the money that he expected during a fundraiser that night, he would announce the next day that he was running for President.

During this dream conversation, his communications director kept calling, reminding Obama that he needed to get back to Manhattan for what the campaign was calling the "mother of all fundraisers." Obama put his hand over the phone and said, "You'll get me there on time, right?" I gave him a thumbs-up.

When the game ended, we climbed the stairs to board the subway back into the city. No sooner had we started moving than I realized I had accidentally led him onto a northbound train, traveling away from Manhattan. I rushed to the conductor.

"Sir," I said. "I'm here with Senator Obama, the next President of the United States. Could you tell me what the next stop is?"

"Yes," the conductor said. "It's Albany, New York, in three hours."

In my subconscious, Obama's mistake of trusting me had cost him the presidency.

Of course I kept this inner drama to myself, and continued to hope he would announce he was running. In November of 2006, I had just returned from a run when the phone rang.

"I have some great news," Obama said when I answered. I held my breath. "I wanted to call to share it with you," he said.

"Yes?" I managed.

"My news is . . . WE BEAT JOHN GRISHAM!!" he exclaimed. "*Audacity of Hope* is number one on the *New York Times* bestseller list!!"

My heart sank. He was clearly thrilled that he had edged the hugely popular writer from the top spot. But I wasn't sure whether he took more pleasure in his book news or in messing with my head.

"Congratulations, Barack," I said quietly.

Several weeks later, on December 12th, 2006, I finally got the real call. "We're pulling the trigger on this thing," he told me. "You can't tell anyone. We'll probably announce in mid-January. It'll be fun."

16

YES WE CAN

As I worked at my computer in Winthrop in the spring of 2007, I received an email that was clearly not intended for me. Cass Sunstein, a University of Chicago law professor and an Obama campaign adviser, had written:

> Martha—Isn't this law group a disaster? As in, worse than, say, anything?

I had met Cass once before at an academic conference. We had struck up a lively conversation, and I had learned that, like me, he was an avid squash player. But we hadn't kept in touch.

Cass had seemed almost incurably cheerful during our brief interaction, so the sour tone of his email surprised me. But since it was addressed to Harvard Law School professor Martha Minow, I deleted the message and went about my day. I soon realized, however, that I was not the only accidental recipient of Cass's private lament.

Neither Cass nor I were full-time or paid campaign advisers. We were professors who contributed policy ideas by telephone and email to candidate Obama's campaign and who spoke publicly on his behalf. Obama's staff had assembled a working group comprised of legal scholars to inform his views about an assortment of pressing issues, including how to go about closing the Guantánamo Bay detention facility and reversing President Bush's licensing of torture. Obama and Cass had been colleagues at the University of Chicago, where they both taught classes on constitutional law. With a possible Obama speech on the rule of law approaching, the group had produced nothing.

In expressing his frustration to Minow via email, Cass had mistakenly autofilled the entire senior staff of the Obama campaign. His criticism of the law group caused wide offense. Danielle Gray, the immensely capable lawyer in charge of domestic policy, took it as an insult to her leadership and forwarded the email to me, saying, "Can you believe this asshole?" A friend of hers converted part of Cass's email into a large poster and hung it on the wall at campaign headquarters: DANIELLE GRAY . . . WORSE THAN, SAY, ANYTHING?

I felt for Cass. Like most mortals, I had suffered my own email mishaps. Not long before, I had been set up on a blind date by Tom Keenan, a friend and fellow professor whom I had come to know through his research on mass atrocities. The date had not gone well. I wrote to Tom with a rundown of all I did not like about his friend, asking how he could have conceivably thought we might get along. I stressed that the incompatibilities were deep, signing off the email, "I think, as the old saying goes, you can only make them dress better!"

As soon as I hit send, I heard a ping in my inbox: it was the message I had just sent, freshly delivered as an incoming email.

Within seconds of that first ping, I heard a second. I had received a note from Tom, which simply read: "You didn't?"

I put my head in my hands, then slowly typed: "I did."

Tom and I were part of a listserv of thousands of genocide activists, scholars, and survivors, and I had accidentally sent the note savaging the blind date to that whole list. Years later, when I was serving as US Ambassador to the UN, people who had received my email would still exuberantly quote my words back to me: "You can only make them dress better!"

After triple-checking the "To," "Cc," and "Bcc" fields, I wrote to Cass, telling him not to lacerate himself, as just about everyone had either made a similar technological slip or soon would. When he was next in Cambridge, we met for coffee and brainstormed about what Obama should actually propose in order to reverse Bush's problematic policies. I also learned that, like me, he was a compulsive Red Sox fan.

In the coming weeks, Cass gave me helpful comments on a draft of my biography of Sergio Vieira de Mello, and I offered feedback on his forthcoming book, *Nudge*. As we got to know each other, I found myself wondering how he might respond to an article I was reading or lecture I was attending.

When the Red Sox began their triumphant 2007 playoff run, we started texting each other managerial advice during the games: "This pitcher has nothing left—sit him down!"; or, if a runner got on base, "Send him, NOW." At first, I didn't attach special significance to the fact that I was taking an inordinate amount of time to craft these texts.

I LOVED EVERYTHING ABOUT CAMPAIGNING for Obama and leaped at the tasks his full-time team in Chicago assigned me. I spoke at fundraisers. I traveled to critical early primary and caucus states like Iowa, New Hampshire, and Nevada to fire up volunteers. And I went on television to debate surrogates for Hillary Clinton, the odds-on favorite among the eight candidates competing for the Democratic nomination. Not only did my values strongly align with Obama's, but I had found the collegial community that I had hoped for when I worked in the Senate office. Cass's email venting notwithstanding, the Obama campaign volunteers were joined by a deep sense of kinship.

In the early months of the Democratic primary contest, Obama's candidacy was a long shot. He still started many of his campaign rallies by acknowledging that voters sometimes confused his name with "Yo Mama" and "Alabama." But the first sign that the campaign might be more than just a feel-good journey came in April of 2007, during the first of what campaign insiders call "mini-primaries," moments when competing candidates announce how much money they have raised. David Plouffe, the hyper-disciplined campaign manager, had given no public indication of how we were faring, coyly waiting until Clinton publicized her numbers—$19.1 million raised in the first quarter—before releasing Obama's total. Our campaign had raised $24.8 million, shattering all prior first-quarter records. OBAMA RAISES $25 MILLION, CHALLENGES CLINTON'S FRONT-RUNNER STATUS, read CNN's headline. "Not bad for a rookie," Obama emailed me.

One of the Democratic primary's most important moments—and one that would be a harbinger of Obama's eventual foreign policy as President—occurred during an early debate in July of 2007. A voter who submitted his question via YouTube asked if Obama would be willing to meet without preconditions with the leaders of US adversaries such as Iran and Cuba.

"I would," Obama answered. "The notion that somehow not talking to countries is punishment to them . . . is ridiculous." Clinton disagreed with Obama on the spot, and the next day attacked his position as "irresponsible and frankly naive." The press and pundits joined the Clinton campaign in ridiculing the novice candidate for his "gaffe."

"How are you holding up?" I asked Obama when we spoke the evening after the debate. My tone was that of someone gingerly checking in with a friend after a personal tragedy.

"Never better," he said. "This whole controversy is absurd. But it is orienting. These people really do believe that they can keep following the same herd mentality, and that they will get different results. What is it they say about the definition of insanity?" he continued. "We can't only try diplomacy *after* countries have done what we want."

Instead of backpedaling, Obama made diplomacy and engagement with adversaries a centerpiece of his candidacy going forward. He grew more outspoken about how his views differed from conventional wisdom on foreign policy. In the week after the July 2007 debate, he publicly ruled out using nuclear weapons against terrorists, a stance that commentators ridiculed as "soft." He also promised to pursue Osama bin Laden into Pakistan—if necessary, without permission from the Pakistani government. Clinton and Obama's other primary opponents criticized this position as reckless.

With the foreign policy back-and-forths heating up, the Obama campaign sought "validators" who would defend his positions in public. There were almost no takers. Indeed, when Obama wanted to argue for diplomatic engagement with Iran in a speech on terrorism, even members of our in-house foreign policy group bristled.

I got a call from Ben Rhodes, Obama's twenty-nine-year-old foreign policy speechwriter, who was at his wits' end as he tried to mobilize support for his boss's positions. Ben had been an aspiring fiction writer, but the September 11th attacks had led him to parlay his writing talents into the realm of US foreign policy. Prior to Obama's campaign, he had spent five years working for former Indiana congressman Lee Hamilton and helped draft a congressionally mandated report on how to fix US policy in Iraq. He thought Democrats lacked creativity on foreign policy and, like me, appreciated Obama for his willingness to challenge Washington orthodoxy.

"I need your help on something," he said when we spoke in early August of 2007. "We need to make a clean argument, pulling all the strands together, as to why we need fresh thinking."

Ben and I spent the next day going back and forth on an ambitious memo that the campaign would send under my name to media outlets, supporters, and donor mailing lists. Titled "Conventional Washington versus the Change We Need," the memo took on the Bush administration, the Clinton campaign, the editorial pages of the major newspapers, and majorities in both houses of Congress—all of whom had supported the Iraq War.

"It was Washington's conventional wisdom that led us into the worst strategic blunder in the history of US foreign policy," I began. Those who were attacking Obama's foreign policy ideas, I wrote, were using the same labels—"weak, inexperienced, and even naive"—that they had used against those who had the good sense to oppose invading Iraq.

"American foreign policy is broken," I argued. "It has been broken by people who supported the Iraq War, opposed talking to our adversaries, failed to finish the job with al-Qaeda, and alienated the world with our belligerence."

The response to the memo was decidedly mixed. Despite turning down Richard Holbrooke's job offer during the Bosnian war, I had stayed in touch with him. He had championed my genocide book and even become a friend. He was also a staunch Hillary Clinton supporter. "Sam, Sam, Sam," he said when he called to give me his take on the memo. "Did you really think it was necessary to insult *everyone* in Washington?"

While Obama became increasingly sure-footed on foreign policy, his campaign as a whole appeared to be flagging. Even his increased national exposure during the debates was not putting a dent in Clinton's nearly 30-point lead in the national polls. By the fall of 2007, Obama's top donors were asking where their money was going. Obama tried to calm his supporters, reminding them that he was the insurgent running against the Democratic Party favorite: "I was the unlikely one, remember?" he pointed out. "This is supposed to be hard."

In 2004, I had followed the primaries the old-fashioned way—by watching debates and reading national polls to figure out who was "leading." But now that I was immersed in a campaign, I realized that victory would have little to do with these metrics.

Obama's campaign strategy boiled down to a simple mantra: "Iowa, Iowa, Iowa." To win the Democratic nomination, Obama had to win the January 2008 Iowa caucus, the first primary contest, and use the momentum from that victory to leapfrog into national contention. Plouffe judged every request that came to the campaign by a simple standard: Will this help us win in Iowa?

"We are running for President of Iowa," I explained to Cass, whom I was now talking to several times a day.

Obama decamped to the state for much of 2007, meeting Iowans in person and trying to convince those who had never participated in Democratic caucuses to get involved. Personally, I didn't know whether winning Iowa was feasible, but I did recognize that it was his only viable pathway to the presidency. With three months to go before the caucus, the *Des Moines Register* poll—the one poll that actually did matter—had Obama trailing Clinton by seven points. I began to worry that his improbable candidacy might flame out. If Obama didn't win in Iowa, we had no backup plan.

While I never heard Obama express doubts about his campaign strategy, I did hear him begin to entertain the prospect of losing. In one phone call, sounding exhausted, he told me how worn down he was by being away from his wife and daughters.

"This campaign is win-win," Obama said. "Either we win, and that's great. Or we lose, and I get my life back." A few weeks later, just after an interview I had given aired on television, I was surprised to see an email pop up from Obama. "Your candidate needs to do better in the polls so you don't have to be so defensive," he wrote.

I couldn't stand the thought of a defeated Obama going back to the US Senate. And, if I were honest with myself, I also couldn't bear the idea of leaving Team Obama and returning to the routine of academic life.

FORTUNATELY, SOMETHING SHIFTED IN OBAMA during the final days before the Iowa Democratic Caucus: for the first time, he seemed to be having fun.

Having survived what he called the "public colonoscopy" of almost a year of campaigning, he could finally focus on the two dimensions of the contest that he had a real knack for: grassroots organizing—and winning.

The campaign's ground game in Iowa was breathtakingly comprehensive. Seeing the young campaign staff's relentless efforts during a trip to Iowa, I commented in my journal, "something is building, something unstoppable, something deeply affirming." Plouffe and Iowa state director Paul Tewes had deployed 159 field organizers to all of Iowa's 99 counties, a strategy that was then unheard of. These paid staff were supported by 10,000 volunteers—all for a state where only 124,000 caucus-goers had participated in the previous Democratic primary. Tewes and his team were so thorough that the campaign contacted one undecided voter—in person, on the phone, and through mailings—a whopping 103 times.[10]

When I met Obama's young volunteers, I rarely had the sense that they were involved in order to land Washington jobs or even to add an experience to their résumés. The Iowa field organizers pulled countless all-nighters in their genuine desire to see Obama win. And their passion began to carry over into Obama's own approach.

During rallies, Obama was alone among primary candidates in calling his young organizers up on stage to thank them. He became a more determined, more inspiring version of himself. As he later put it, "Iowa really belonged to those kids . . . you just didn't want to screw up. You wanted to make sure that you were worthy of these efforts."[11]

I hadn't known Obama long, but my experience offering edits for *The Audacity of Hope* had demonstrated that he could crank up his energy when facing the pressure of a deadline. David Axelrod, Obama's top strategist, likened him to Michael Jordan, who once said, "When the game gets close and something big is on the line, it all slows down, and I see things better."

Obama had been long-winded in the early primary debates. Privately, he had described debating—with its emphasis on camera-ready putdowns and sound bites—as a "trained seal act." But once he started connecting with Iowans themselves, he sounded punchier and less professorial. He also grew more motivated, becoming livid at the Clinton campaign's failure to crack down on campaign staffers who had circulated emails casting doubt on his Christian faith.

When I sent him positive feedback after the final debate before the Iowa caucus, he wrote back "Just gimme the ball." For the first time since I met him in 2005, he seemed to be exactly where he wanted to be.

As the day of the Iowa caucus approached, Obama's entire network seemed to be descending on the state. Senior policy advisers and high-powered donors were spotted helping shovel snow from driveways and committing to babysit so that Iowan parents could participate in the evening caucus. I sat in a cubicle, dusting off my Serbo-Croatian as I placed calls to those with Slavic names on the campaign phone list, hoping to make the very specific case for why Obama was the right candidate to manage ongoing divisions in the Balkans.

Economic adviser Austan Goolsbee, Cass, and I were handed a list of likely caucus-goers who lived an hour or so from Des Moines, and told to go "get out the vote." At the outset, we were proud of the fact that, together, we could answer questions from voters about even obscure economic, legal, and foreign policy issues. But most of the people on our list had already been contacted dozens of times by the campaign and wanted to be left alone. When they actually did come to the door, they most commonly asked for the address of their local caucus site—the one question that sent us scrambling for answers from headquarters.

Although we were ineffective canvassers, Cass and I still managed to have a blast together. He was exactly sixteen years older than me—we happened to have the same birthday. He had once been married (to his college girlfriend) and they had a daughter named Ellyn, who was in her late teens. As soon as Cass knew he was interested in me, he called Ellyn, with whom he shared everything. Once we started dating, she asked to speak with me to express how happy she was for her dad.

Cass was a complete original. His hunger for discovery, so evident in the dozens of books he had written, was a quality he brought to every moment he was awake. He was as fresh in the world as the world was to him. I never heard him repeat himself. He wrote about serious things, but his open face always seemed ready to laugh. I found myself answering questions about myself that he hadn't asked. I wanted him to know everything.

My back pain had been worse than ever that year—so bad that it felt like I was spending more time at the chiropractor than anywhere else. Elliot Thomson, a close law school friend, had long believed that my back pain stemmed from psychological and not physical ailments. When I told him how bad it had gotten, he mailed me a copy of John Sarno's *Healing Back Pain*, which I read cover to cover. Sarno argued that pain of the sort I had been experiencing could stem from a failure to grapple with deep distress that then gets "somatized"—lodged or manifested—in the body as physical pain.

Since none of my MRIs had turned up any actual spinal or nerve damage, I thought that it was possible Sarno's theory applied to me. I discussed the possibility with Cass and then poured out as much of what was bottled up in me as I could access, leaving myself more exposed than in any prior relationship.

On our first weekend away together, I popped Advil and tried to stretch my back on the floor of our hotel room. But at the same time, I told Cass about the "Bat Cave," explaining that, in the early days of a relationship, I tended to go on a "scavenger hunt for the fatal flaw" of the person I was dating. My brother, Stephen, liked to tease me for having once broken up with a guy because he didn't have an EZ-Pass. And I described what I was learning in intensive therapy, revealing my lingering concern that I would try to push even an ideal partner away. Despite gaining a rational understanding of my behavior, I remained subconsciously terrified of letting someone come too close for fear they would leave me or die.

Instead of running away from my red flags, Cass told me, "I am listening. But you should know that I will not let you ruin this."

His confidence was bracing. Following that first trip together, my back pain disappeared after six years of regularly incapacitating me. Something had lifted.

"This is a man completely in my corner," I wrote in my journal. "I feel scary calm." It didn't hurt that, with the campaign heating up, I did not have as much time as usual to disappear into my head.

Still, to be safe, I told Cass to call John (whom he didn't yet know) if I started pulling away. I had seen my brother and Eddie use their buddies in AA to help keep them sober; I was asking John to mediate between me and Cass, to try to prevail on Cass not to come on too strong too soon, but also not to give up on me.

Since Obama knew us both, I wrote to tell him I had "romantic news." Although he was in the last stretch of his Iowa campaigning, he called me almost as soon as I sent the email.

"This better be good," he said.

"It's Cass," I revealed.

"Cass?! Cass Sunstein? He's a total slob," Obama said, and the phone line dropped.

I knew how messy Cass was. His office at the University of Chicago was so cluttered that it had been photographed for various campus publications. Piled high on his desk—and a foot deep on the floor—were law review journals, students' blue book exams, old editions of *Baseball Prospectus*, Milk Duds boxes, crusted Diet Coke cans, squash rackets, men's ties, squeaky dog toys, socks, and much more. I was horrified when I visited, but I rationalized that perhaps this disorder, like dressing better, was something that could be fixed.

Now Obama was giving me a more negative take, and his blurted reaction rattled me. Feeling old reflexes suddenly rising, I knew I didn't need anyone's help in talking myself out of a relationship. As I sat in my apartment in Winthrop and furiously dialed Obama, I kept getting voice mail. I wondered if Obama, who had known Cass for at least a decade, knew something I did not.

Finally, after fifteen minutes, he called back, apologizing profusely for having left me hanging on a matter so important. He explained that he was in rural Iowa and had lost his cell phone signal.

"What I should have said is: This is wonderful news! Cass is one of the most brilliant, creative, and kind people I have ever met. Congratulations."

Before he hung up, Obama also offered some parting counsel: "Don't fuck this up."

ON THE DAY OF THE CAUCUS, one of the coldest of the year in Iowa, Cass arrived at campaign headquarters in Des Moines bearing a gift: an unfashionable woolen Chicago White Sox hat he had picked up at O'Hare Airport on the way. "I didn't want you to be cold," he said, simply. In that instant, I realized how long it had been since I had let anybody take care of me in the way that Cass was doing.

As we drove around together and encouraged Iowans to participate, we met young caucus-goers who looked fresh out of high school and many other first-time participants—including Republicans and Independents.

At around 7:30 p.m., we were in the backseat of a friend's car driving to the Iowa Events Center, where we expected to watch the results trickle in on the big screen over the course of a long evening. To our surprise, we heard on the radio that MSNBC had already projected Barack Obama as the winner. Some 240,000 people had turned out to caucus, nearly double the number from 2004. Cass and I could hardly process what we were hearing, but we embraced and raced inside to wait for Obama to appear. I emailed him from my BlackBerry, "Um, congratulations on changing everything forever."

Many political experts—and surely millions of voters—had believed that an African American could not be elected President in a majority-white country with deep racial fault lines. In a single night, Americans in one of the whitest states in the country had changed our understanding of what was possible. The resounding triumph had also underscored how large a difference young people make when they turn out.

Many years later, Obama would say of his Iowa caucus victory, "That's my favorite night of my entire political career . . . a more powerful night than the night I was elected President."[12]

Cass and I took up seats, along with Austan Goolsbee, on bleachers behind the podium where Obama would eventually speak. Ensconced among Iowans, campaign volunteers, and donors, Austan and I began to lead our section in a series of unsophisticated chants.

"Give me an *O*!" I shouted. Austan wrapped his arms above his head in the shape of an *O*. The bleacher roared, "OOOOOOOOO!" The next morning, a picture of us making the large *O* sign and shouting at the top of our lungs was splashed on the pages of the *Des Moines Register*. We looked like drunken members of a fraternity rather than senior advisers to a potential president, but the photo captured the exaltation of the night.

Never before in my life could I recall so much going right at the same time. My loved ones were healthy. I was part of a team of people I cherished. I had worked for three years with the person who could well become the next leader of the free world. And I was falling in love with a remarkable man who appeared to love me back.

When Obama walked onto the stage, he seemed incandescent with delight. Instead of basking in the roar of the crowd, he began by applauding his supporters, campaign staff, and volunteers.

Then, as he prepared to step up to the podium to deliver the victory speech that almost nobody outside of Iowa had predicted, he scanned the crowd. Most politicians—or public speakers, for that matter—look out at audiences without actually absorbing the individual faces. To my astonishment, however, when Obama looked to the bleachers behind him, he spotted me and then saw Cass.

He pointed from me to Cass and Cass to me, as if to say, "Now *this* is the real news!" He offered up a wide and mischievous smile, turned to the podium, and, a few seconds later, began: "They said this day would never come . . ."

17

MONSTER

I was in Dublin, Ireland—the place where, to paraphrase Yeats, all my ladders had started—when the politics of politics caught up with me.

On March 6th, 2008, two months after Obama's surprise win in Iowa, I was on the international leg of the publicity tour for my book about Sergio Vieira de Mello. After a few days in London, I had arrived in Ireland and spent a glorious evening at the University College Dublin, where I gave a lecture. A group of my former Dublin school friends, whom I hadn't seen since we were children at Mount Anville, suddenly appeared at the table where I was signing books. I remembered most of their names immediately and, though thirty years had passed, was transported back to our school days together.

My late father's family and friends—including his buddies from Hartigan's Pub—turned out in force, as did members of Mum's family. The bitterness of the rupture from long ago was drowned out by the pride they each felt in "Jim and Vera's daughter." The whole evening had been an emotional one.

Adding a surreal dimension to the day, U2's Bono, hearing I was in town, had invited me to join him and the musician Brian Eno for a drink at the Shelbourne Hotel. Bono had just departed when my cell phone rang. I heard the voice of Denis McDonough, the foreign policy coordinator for the Obama campaign.

"Have you seen *Drudge*?" he asked, referring to the right-wing news website with a large readership.

"*Drudge*? No, why?" I asked.

"They have you saying all kinds of crazy shit about Hillary to the *Scotsman*," Denis replied tersely.

I felt my face flush. Denis read aloud what the *Scotsman* had me saying:

"We fucked up in Ohio . . . In Ohio, they are obsessed and Hillary is going to town on it, because she knows Ohio's the only place they can win. She is a monster, too—that is off the record—she is stooping to anything."

Denis paused to get my reaction.

I assured him there had been a mistake. "No way I said that. I haven't even been to Scotland on this trip."

Denis went on. "It gets worse," he said. "They quote you saying, 'You just look at her and think, *Ergh.*'"

I could not imagine denigrating the appearance of the first competitive woman presidential candidate in history. Hecklers in New Hampshire had yelled at Clinton to iron their shirts. Tucker Carlson, then an MSNBC host, had remarked, "When she comes on television, I involuntarily cross my legs." Clinton was the only person running whose opponents critiqued her wardrobe and the tone of her voice. I wanted Obama to win—but I admired Clinton and could see that many of the attacks against her were sexist and unfair.

"I did not say those things," I assured Denis.

"Great," he said. "It's getting a lot of play here. So let's just snuff it out. The campaign will demand a retraction."

"Thanks," I said as I hung up, eager to get out of the news as quickly as possible.

My hand trembled as I put the phone down. After I recounted to Eno what was being reported by the American media, he asked if I was sure I had been misquoted. "I couldn't have said those things," I insisted, "because that's not what I think."

But as I reflected on the four days I had spent in the UK during my book tour, I realized I had little memory of *anything* I had said. I had appeared on radio and television morning and evening news shows. I had engaged students at Oxford University and done a slew of back-to-back, indistinguishable print interviews. Of those, I recalled only being pinned into a windowless hotel suite and managing to stay awake by alternating Diet Cokes and coffees before each interview.

I tried to recall the different stops on the British press junket. Through the cobwebs, I suddenly remembered a phone call from Austan Goolsbee that had interrupted one of the many interviews.

Austan had telephoned seeking advice on "how to deal with the media"—a request that would soon seem painfully ironic. He had been quoted in the press as having told Canadian officials during a private meeting that Obama's campaign pledge to renegotiate NAFTA was only "political positioning." The Clinton campaign had pounced, publicizing the report to paint Obama as duplicitous. The campaign dubbed the episode "NAFTA-gate," and Clinton said Obama was misleading American voters while Austan gave "the old wink-wink" to Canada.

In these critical months of the Democratic primary, significant acrimony existed between our two campaigns. Obama had gained front-runner status in February, after winning ten consecutive victories over a two-week period. Distressingly, Clinton had started making statements that seemed to favor the presumptive Republican nominee John McCain over her Democratic rival. "I have a lifetime of experience I will bring to the White House," she told reporters at one point. "I know Senator McCain has a lifetime of experience he will bring to the White House. And Senator Obama has a speech he made in 2002."

In a *60 Minutes* interview, when asked whether there was any truth to the rumor that Obama was a Muslim, Clinton had responded, "I take him on the basis of what he says," and then, when pressed, deftly added, "No, there is nothing to base that on, as far as I know." Clinton had also recently released her most memorable ad, which depicted children sleeping safely while an emergency phone rings in the White House at three a.m. "Who do you want answering the phone?" the voice-over asked, implying that Obama did not have the experience needed to handle a national security crisis. Obama had fired back. "We've had a red phone moment," he told a gathering of the American Legion. "It was the decision to invade Iraq"—a decision, he reminded his audience, that Clinton had supported. Still, I worried that swing voters would be influenced by Clinton's negative depiction of Obama if he made it to the general election.

In fact, Clinton's strategy to introduce doubt about Obama's readiness for the job even seemed to be paying off with Democrats. Two days before I arrived in Ireland, she snapped Obama's streak by winning primaries in Rhode Island, Texas, and Ohio. She called it a turning point in the race.

My doubts began to tug at me. Which reporter had I been with when Austan called? Had he or she listened in on our conversation, or embellished something I had said? Then, the person's face and manner suddenly came back to me. Young and eager, she had spent a good ten minutes before our interview asking me for advice on how she might become a foreign correspondent. I quickly called Denis back and asked him to hold off on issuing a denial until I was absolutely certain it was warranted. I said good night to Eno and rushed up to my room, enveloped by a sudden feeling of dread.

I rummaged through my bag and pulled out a copy of my UK book tour schedule. There, on the first day, after my red-eye, was a listing for an interview with a reporter named Gerri Peev. She was the woman I was with when Austan called—and, to my horror, although she was not Scottish, the publication she worked for was the *Scotsman*.

Peev's telephone number was right there on the schedule, so, although it was after midnight, I called her. I blew past the pleasantries when she answered.

"Hi, this is Samantha Power, and you have quoted me saying things I didn't say."

"I wouldn't do that," she said.

"But you did, Gerri," I said, practically yelling. "You did. I would never have called Hillary Clinton a monster."

Then she explained what happened. "I wrote a story about you and your career and your Sergio book, but I went back to the desk and they said, 'That's awful dry, don't you have anything better?' And I went back through the tape and there was that stuff. And I thought, 'Hey, well, that's lively.'"

"But I couldn't have said the things you have me saying," I repeated, even as an icy sensation crawled up my spine.

I assumed she had made up quotes loosely based on whatever she had written in her notebook, so I asked her if she had a tape. She fumbled on the other side of the phone with her recorder, and then I heard my voice.

The next few minutes were miserable. From what I could tell, she and I had almost wrapped up our interview when Austan called. Once I had ducked into the hallway to speak with him, he told me that the Clinton campaign was taking out ads featuring him as the centerpiece. When we hung up, instead of taking a few minutes to cool off, I returned, agitated, to the couch where Peev and I had been sitting.

As I explained why I had interrupted the interview, I vented in frustration, using the kind of hyperbole and profanity I typically reserved for Fenway Park umpires. I naively assumed that this part of my conversation with Peev would not be for publication, given that it had nothing to do with the subject of our interview, which was my new book.

Had I really used the word "monster" to describe Clinton? The tape recording confirmed that I had. But listening to our back-and-forth, I heard that it was actually Peev who had said, "You just look at her and think, 'ergh.'"

I had then repeated her prompt in the process of making my own point. "*You* just look at her and think, 'ergh,' but . . ." I said, going on to add that, regardless of Peev's view of the candidate, many voters in Ohio believed Clinton's warnings about Obama's trade policies.

Peev's inclusion of my use of her words made it sound like I was disparaging Clinton's physical appearance. However, in addition to saying "monster," I had made another critical comment, charging that "the amount of deceit she has put forward is really unattractive."

I told Peev that because of what she had published, I would have to leave the Obama campaign. "No, you won't," she said, seemingly oblivious to the roiling controversy occurring on the other side of the Atlantic. "Nobody reads the *Scotsman*."

I called Denis back, dejected, explaining what had happened and the box in which I found myself.

"Dang, Sammy," he said. "This is bad."

I was distraught by the thought of having damaged Obama and dashed off an email to him, detailing, blow by blow, what had happened and ending with:

> I am so, so sorry. I cannot tell you how badly I feel or how boneheaded I know I was. Please feel free, at any point of this awful process, to throw me under the bus, if it will ever help protect you from such damage.
>
> I hope you're holding up. And again, my deepest apologies.

Obama responded an hour later, telling me to be more careful but not to worry about it.

"You are absolved," he wrote. "Rule of thumb—nothing is off the record when you're part of a presidential campaign. Thought you were great on Charlie Rose, by the way." My misstep probably seemed like child's play given everything else he was confronting on the campaign.

BY THE TIME OF MY ILL-FATED TRIP OVERSEAS, I had been seeing Cass for two months—which was about the time my antibodies against commitment generally kicked in. John was encouraging me to stay out of the Bat Cave and to avoid overthinking the relationship. I was trying, but my anxiety reemerged as I once again began awakening with lungers.

Frustrated by a week of phone calls in which I was growing increasingly distant, Cass decided to book a flight from Chicago to Dublin so we could spend the weekend together. By the time I learned about the *Scotsman* article, Cass was already in the air. It was too late to tell him to go home—which I wanted desperately to do. When I faced problems, I faced them on my own. And this problem seemed likely to get worse before it got better.

I stayed up throughout the night, hitting refresh on a Google search of my name. This gave me the unusual life experience of watching what I hoped would prove a small screw-up turn into a large, global scandal.

Cass, who remained unaware of any of this as he flew over the Atlantic, received a despairing email from me on his BlackBerry when he landed:

> Hey darlin,
>
> It's 4 am in Ireland and I'm still up because I made the biggest mistake of my rookie career. See today's Scotsman for the worst ever SP fuck up. I feel so very badly.
>
> Look forward to seeing you later. I'll be the one who was up all night.
>
> Xosp

Reading my message, Cass thought I was overreacting. "So sorry sweetheart—hoping this is smaller than you think," he wrote from the airport.

When he got my email, he told me later, he pulled up a few stories on his BlackBerry and assumed the controversy would be a blip. When he arrived at my hotel, I had departed for my day of Irish book tour events. He opened his laptop and did a more comprehensive search. When he logged on, he could hardly believe what he saw. As he later described it, "You were everywhere."

The websites of American publications paraded my quotations beneath banner headlines. SAMANTHA POWER THINKS HILLARY CLINTON IS A PROBLEM FROM HELL, wrote *New York* magazine. The New York *Daily News* assailed my "slime-time politics" with a cover that screamed MONSTER BASH. Clinton campaign staff inflated my importance on Obama's campaign, seeking to portray me as the candidate's alter ego, while the Obama campaign sought distance, saying I was one informal adviser among many.

I had the delusional notion that I could get through that day without the Irish public learning of my sins. I made it through one Ulster radio show and a second Dublin program. But half an hour into my third appearance, the host relayed a question from a caller: "Is Samantha on your show the same Samantha who recently called Hillary Clinton a monster? If so, shame on her." The radio host, Pat Kenny, looked confused until his producer ran into the studio with a printout of a news story, which he then summarized on air. "Is it the same?" he asked.

I looked down. "I wish there were two Samantha Powers out there," I said apologetically to the live Irish audience. "I wish there was a double who had been my imposter."

The only consolation came from Cass, who wrote to me as I shuttled from one venue to the next: "So glad I'm here amid this—got your back."

As soon as New York woke up Friday morning, I telephoned Richard Holbrooke to get his sense of the situation. "Well, Sam," he said as soon as he picked up, "you've outdone yourself this time."

When I asked how bad it was, he asked me to hold so he could check the morning news. "Well, you're leading the *Today* show"—I could hear the sound of the channel changing. "You are leading *Good Morning America*, and"—he paused while he flipped to CBS—"Good news: you're only the second story on CBS."

"Shit," I said.

"I'll say," he said.

The *Weekly Standard* mordantly observed that mine "might have been the most ill-starred book tour since the invention of movable type." *New York Times* columnist Maureen Dowd wrote, "While we've seen book tours that set up a presidential run, we've never seen one that tore one down."

The previous year, I had been profiled in *Men's Vogue*. As part of a photo shoot, the artistic designer had given me stiletto heels, which I had refused because I couldn't stay upright. I ended up wearing them while uncomfortably sitting on a simple wooden crate. That photograph now appeared on the cover of the New York *Daily News* with the headline: PRETTY DUMB!

Clinton campaign surrogates went into full attack mode. Terry McAuliffe, the campaign's chairman, sent out a fundraising email that urged supporters to donate because of my remarks: "A contribution now will show the Obama campaign that there is a price to this kind of attack politics."

I had given the Clinton campaign a priceless gift. Obama prided himself on running a clean campaign, above negative tactics, but my interview with Peev suggested otherwise. Clinton was also portraying Obama as inexperienced, and what I had said—both in substance and in my clumsy effort to assert that it was off the record—implied that he was surrounded by amateurs.

Texas Congresswoman Sheila Jackson Lee, the national co-chair of Clinton's campaign, called for me to be fired, as did three other prominent Democratic representatives. "It's really a test of Senator Obama," Jackson Lee said. "It's a test of character."

I did not expect the attacks to let up, but I knew I had to get in touch with Clinton to apologize and explain that I didn't actually hold the view of her captured in the *Scotsman*. I wrote a letter to her and sent it to one of her top aides, whom Cass knew.

Cass and I then began the drive from Dublin to Belfast, where I was slated to give a Friday-afternoon lecture at Queen's University. I was leaning against Cass in the backseat when David Axelrod—Obama's political maestro, and my designated executioner—called.

"Hey Sam, you know we love you," Axelrod began. "You have been amazing for us, on TV and behind the scenes. Barack really values you." Even in my semi-catatonic state I knew that this was a ritualistic prelude to the blow he was about to deliver. "But we can't afford to associate with you right now," he continued. "You are radioactive. Even if we kept you on, we couldn't use you. So we might as well get the benefit of asking you to resign."

All of his words blurred together and I just heard "resign, resign, resign, resign." I asked gingerly if I could perhaps take a leave of absence instead. Axe said that a hedged departure would risk causing a "slow bleed," bluntly concluding, "We need to cut this off"—meaning, "We need to cut *you* off."

Obama called me a few minutes later, telling me how sorry he was. He made me feel temporarily better by assuring me that I just had to sit in the "penalty box" for a while. He promised to bring me back "as soon as things have settled down." I tried again to explain what I had done, how Austan had called, how I normally erred on the side of publicly praising Clinton when I did interviews.

He agreed. "Yes, I know. I saw that on Charlie Rose."

What I found remarkable about our conversation was how present he was and how much time he gave me. He acted as if no useless explanation or tangent from me was too irrelevant.

When we hung up, a campaign press aide sent me a draft resignation announcement to edit, which I did, painstakingly. The same aide subsequently informed me that someone had accidentally sent the press an earlier draft. Frazzled minds tend to fixate on the small instead of the large; likewise, I found myself focusing more on the detail that they had used the wrong version of my resignation statement than on the fact that I was no longer part of the campaign.

"They didn't use my edits," I groaned to Cass as we made our way to Belfast.

As the pain of what had transpired sunk in, I curled up in Cass's arms for the rest of the journey and tried to face the immutable fact that my time on Team Obama was over. After spending the previous fourteen months promoting Obama's candidacy, the campaign had come to feel like a second family. I wished Cass and I could just drive up and down the Irish coast for the rest of time.

When we pulled up to the campus in Belfast, I saw, for the first time in my life, paparazzi staked out for my arrival. In the backseat of the car, Cass advised me to just walk right past them, but I said that I was probably incapable of not explaining myself. And when I exited the car, the journalists' gentle, Irish way of posing questions prompted me to answer.

When I watch the video of that brief interview all these years later, I am immediately transported. Ghost-pale, my lips chapped, without a hint of makeup, I am attempting to ensconce myself in my favorite green hoodie—a strange choice of attire for a university lecture. When a cameraman asked if I regretted my statements, I rambled on for two minutes, apologizing profusely. The reporter interjected: "It is coming at a very crucial time for both campaigns." I agreed, resisting the impulse to say "No shit, Sherlock," and instead responding, "Yeah, it's not good." I continued:

> It is one hundred percent thoroughly my fault . . . I think I'm a bit of a political rookie. I'm a policy person, a scholar, and new to campaigning, and perhaps maybe the heat of it got to me a little bit and I overreacted to something that I heard. But again, there is no excuse.

The fact that my very public fall had occurred while I was in my home country—where many people had expressed pride in a Dublin girl making good on the big stage of America—made me feel deeply ashamed.

Even though I had resigned, reporters remained interested in what several called my "Icarus-like descent." A little cottage industry even developed over the coming weeks in which transcripts of my previous interviews were scoured for other potential mistakes. Some journalists found prophecies from me predicting my own downfall. The year before, I was reminded, I had told *The Chronicle of Higher Education*, "The one thing that terrifies me [is] that I'll say something that will somehow hurt the candidate."

More recently, I had commented to a *Financial Times* reporter in London that politics attracted two different kinds of people—those "in it for the game" and those who had a list of problems they wanted to address. "People who treat it as a game usually do better," I had said.

If I sounded like I was holding myself apart from the famously cutthroat world I had joined, I probably was. But I resolved that if I ever got to work in the political sphere again—and it did not then seem likely that I would—I would make myself as uninteresting and unavailable to the press as possible.

TRYING TO LIFT MY SPIRITS, Cass bought us scalped tickets to a sold-out Irish football match at Croke Park. For once, however, I tuned out at a sporting event. I hadn't slept in forty-eight hours and was over-come by the useless longing to go back in time.

After the match, we walked around Dublin. Though I was paying little attention to our route, I looked up at one point and realized that we were on the outskirts of St. Stephen's Green, near Hartigan's Pub, my childhood home away from home.

When we entered, the smell was the same—some irremovable blend of Guinness, peanuts, and disinfectant. We took seats at the bar, where a woman who could have been eighty or forty polished the glasses. Cass blurted out, "Did you know Jim Power?"

The woman didn't blink, but looked at me and said, calmly, "Hello, Samantha." I had not been back to Hartigan's in three decades.

As Cass and I sipped our sodas, the woman, known as Ma Mul-ligan, described to Cass how I used to tear through stacks of mysteries as I passed the time downstairs. She told me that my dad had framed one of the color-by-numbers drawings I had sent him from Pittsburgh. Since I had talked to so few of his friends and associates from that time, I took advantage of the opportunity to ask the question that con-tinued to gnaw at me. "So many people drank here, and drank a lot, but my dad was the one who died. Why do you think that was?"

Ma answered simply, without drama or sentiment: "Because you left."

I had thought it impossible to feel worse, but my heart was reveal-ing its elastic power to absorb more pain. Cass laid down a crumpled pile of euros and quickly ushered me out of the bar.

NOT LONG AFTER WE RETURNED to the hotel, I saw the Wyoming caucus results on the news. Obama had won 61 percent of the vote to Clinton's 38 percent. I realized that I had been holding my breath, carrying around the utterly irrational fear that I was single-handedly going to cost Barack Obama the Democratic nomination. The fact that only 5,378 Wyomingites had voted for Obama—compared to Clinton's 3,312 voters—didn't matter. Feeling a strange mix of delight, relief, and exhaustion, I slept for the first time since the *Scotsman* article ap-peared.

The next day, Obama sent an email, asking about my morale:

> Wanted to check in with you to make sure you're ok. I know
> this whole thing is shitty. But I hope you know how much I love
> and appreciate you, that all this will blow over, and that we are
> going to change the world together. In the meantime, enjoy your
> travels, make sure Cass spoils you, and let me know if you want
> to talk at all.

By the following week, unable to keep down solid food since my
name appeared in the headlines, I had lost seven pounds—along with
the ability to think about anything other than myself. When Eliot
Spitzer, the governor of New York, became ensnared in a prostitution
scandal, I opened the *New York Times* to see a large pull-quote from
Spitzer's call girl that read: "I just don't want to be thought of as a monster!" When I saw her defense, I tossed the newspaper aside. "Cass,"
I insisted, "I have changed the way we talk. Now everyone is saying
'monster.' It is the new definition of the most terrible thing you can be."

Cass thought this was nonsense. I was suffering, he insisted, from
what behavioral scientists called the "Spotlight Effect"—the overwhelming human tendency to believe that others are noticing one's
actions far more than they are. This seemed a fancy way of stating what
was true: becoming a headline news story was causing me to exaggerate
my own importance.

Not all the ongoing coverage was negative. I awoke one morning
to find Cass on his laptop, his eyes welling with tears. After reading
about my resignation, an Irish doctor named John Crown had realized
that I was the daughter of a man he had once watched hold forth at
Hartigan's. In an essay in the Irish *Independent*, he wrote intimately of
the sociology and poignancy of the pub scene:

> Dr. Jim Power was the intellectual alpha male of the Hartigan's
> herd, a fearsomely formidable pub debater and commentator on
> the human condition, with a brilliant if acerbic turn of phrase, a
> man who saw off challenging younger bucks, leaving them stag-

gering into the bush with one swish of his tongue. Sitting regally
on a stool reading *The Daily Telegraph*, he would deflate egos,
demolish myths and dispense well-informed editorials on the affairs of the day. Those who knew Jim recognised the melancholy
that many separated fathers have, the sadness of separation from
children . . . I think that Ireland could never have allowed [his
daughter] to thrive and grow the way that America did. Sad for
Jim, but thank God she emigrated.

There was a richness to this description of my father that pierced
(and pierces) me. Any child who loses a parent covets even the smallest
details, but because my mother felt guilty about not having been able
to help my dad, I had rarely heard about his life in anything more than
broad strokes. I read John Crown's words so many times, I practically
committed them to memory.

WHEN I GOT BACK to the United States, I was bombarded with media
requests, which I turned down. I also canceled upcoming book tour
events so as to stay out of the news. Obama sent an email, urging me
to reconsider:

> I don't think you should be avoiding interviews! I think you
> should go out there and talk about your wonderful book . . . Do
> not crawl under a rock. It's not good for you, and it's not good
> for me.

Obama and I had always bonded over basketball, and his emails
and phone calls were so well timed during this particularly low period
that I began to refer to him as "my Robert Horry." Horry was an itinerant NBA player who had a knack for hitting improbable, last-second
jump shots during key moments in the playoffs, earning him seven
championship rings and the nickname Big Shot Rob. "Every time I'm
slumping toward self-immolation," I wrote Obama, "you land that
22-footer from the corner as time expires."

Obama himself was going through a searing period where old tapes of sermons by his pastor Reverend Jeremiah Wright were forcing him to explain his views on race and patriotism. Yet throughout my exile, he was reliably available by phone and email anytime I needed him. When I wished him luck, just hours before he would deliver what became known as his "Race Speech," he joked: "This whole Reverend Wright thing was an elaborate ruse to take people's attention off you!"

His empathy and sense of perspective were extraordinary.

Before my book was published, I had agreed to appear on Stephen Colbert's Comedy Central show to promote it. When I called Colbert's office to cancel, the producer urged me to use the show to try to put what had happened behind me. Inspired by Obama's encouragement not to hide, I decided to do my first live interview since having to bow out of the campaign.

As I sat in the green room getting made up, I heard Colbert film the show's opening. "With us tonight is Samantha Power, Barack Obama's former foreign policy adviser. Who says he's inexperienced? He already has a *former* foreign policy adviser!"

I found myself laughing for the first time in days.

DAY BY DAY, LIFE SLOWLY NORMALIZED. I had clung to Cass in the weeks following the scandal in a manner that made it hard to separate from him when his travel schedule required us to part. I had never allowed myself to depend on anyone in this manner. He held me, fed me, and even served as a human screen for me on airplanes, enabling me to walk down the aisle to the bathroom without being recognized.

From the start, I had known that Cass was brilliant, kind, and hilarious. But now his strength and capacity to care deeply stood out. I could find no excuse to run away from him.

Although we had not been dating long, Cass had flown to Dublin with an engagement ring in his pocket, hoping to propose. Three weeks after I resigned from the Obama campaign, he laid the ring awkwardly between us on the couch of his Chicago apartment and asked if I would marry him. I accepted immediately. I had never come close to marrying anybody before, but I had never met anybody even a little bit like Cass. "I like, love, and admire you," I told him.

When a friend asked him why he had proposed so early in our relationship, he said, "I love sitting next to Samantha. And it occurred to me that, if she married me, I would be able to sit next to her for the rest of my life."

When I called Obama to tell him the news of our engagement, he was thrilled. I tried to convince him that his main area of concern about Cass had been addressed, writing soon after:

> Cass is no longer quite the same slob you knew. We have an agreement: on each occasion he leaves his apartment each day, he has to carry at least one item with him to the dumpster (eg, argyle sweaters and "Members Only" jackets, Red Sox season guides from the pre-steroids era, his prior tenant's water color paintings, 1993 University of Chicago environmental law exams . . .)

Cass was content anywhere. Whether hanging out in an airport lounge or waiting at the dentist, he needed only his laptop to feel at home. I came to understand why he was one of the most prolific scholars in the world—he used every nook and cranny of the day, no matter where he was, to write. As soon as he had turned on his MacBook Air and pulled up a document on the screen before him, he simply picked up where he had left off ten minutes, an hour, or the day before. Whenever he received thoughtful criticism of his articles or books, it usually brought a smile to his face. "I love this," I heard him say once. "His points are devastating."

But amid his general contentment, he seemed to value our relationship more than anything. We worked sitting side by side, with Johnny Cash or Leonard Cohen playing in the background. Like me, he had to be peeled off the floor after athletic outings. Our version of a romantic evening entailed hitting the squash ball. And since neither of us cooked, we ordered in. His staple as a bachelor had been Panda Express; I convinced him to make modest upgrades.

As I planned a large Irish wedding, I also discovered my inner bride, a stranger with surprisingly strong views. I told Cass I wanted to get married in Loher Church, a small white Catholic church on a cliff overlooking the Atlantic. The church was near Waterville, a secluded beach town at the foot of the Kerry mountains where my mother's younger sister, Patricia, and her husband, Derry, lived. Mum had brought Stephen and me to Waterville many times before we moved to America, and Patricia and Derry's home had become my favorite place of retreat in my adult life. I went there to read, write, listen to Irish music, and hear the wild stories of my aunt, uncle, and cousins.

Because so many of our friends were traveling vast distances to get to Waterville, I arranged activities for guests, such as hiking up the craggy mountains around the village and taking what proved to be a very rough sea journey out to the sixth-century Christian monastery on the spectacular Skellig Michael Island (later made famous as Luke Skywalker's hideout in *Star Wars: The Last Jedi*). I also orchestrated a soccer game on the town green several hours before I was expected at the church, horrifying the hair and makeup stylists when I arrived in my hotel suite caked in mud.

I felt intense joy and certainty marrying Cass, and the day carried added layers of emotion. At the reception, my dad's side of the family raised glasses alongside my mother's. Cass's daughter Ellyn delivered a beautiful toast. And I was touched immeasurably when Eddie, who had raised me for so much of my life, pulled me aside before he walked me down the aisle, to say "Drop the 'step.'"

Although it took me a few seconds to decipher his comment, I realized Eddie wanted me to drop the "step" in "stepdad." And from then on, I did.

HOLBROOKE HAD GIVEN ME the wedding present I most wanted: he arranged a face-to-face meeting for me with Hillary Clinton. I conveyed the depths of my regret in person, and she graciously accepted my apology. We did not make the meeting public, but Obama—who deemed it a strange wedding gift ("Don't most people get toasters?" he teased)—decided that this was enough to end my exile.

The night he clinched the number of delegates needed to seal the Democratic nomination, he sent me a note. "Best part is, now I can get you back on the team!"

On August 19th, the day I returned to work at campaign headquarters in Chicago, five months after I had resigned, I wrote to Obama to say, "THANK YOU FOR YOUR HUMANITARIAN INTERVENTION. It turns out you have some pull!"

He wrote back: "You were never off the team . . . just taking a break to find true love."

Obama's words spoke to a strange truth on which I had not really reflected. Making such a large and public mistake left me feeling defenseless and massively vulnerable. Forced away from the work I longed to do, I allowed a man I might otherwise have pushed away to take care of me.

My regular "X test" formulation now had a new twist: if all I achieved in becoming an overnight media scandal was marrying Cass, it was perhaps the best deal of my life.

18

VICTORY

I had assumed that when I left the "penalty box," or what my Irish relatives called the "sin bin," life would return to the way it had been before my slipup. It didn't.

In the fall of 2008, I split my time between teaching two days a week at the Kennedy School and serving as one of Obama's foreign policy advisers, this time based at campaign headquarters in Chicago. Despite receiving my official campaign badge and BlackBerry when I rejoined the team, I felt I bore a large scarlet letter—an *M* for Monster, or maybe an *L* for walking campaign Liability.

The higher-ups told me to keep a low profile, as they believed my presence would dampen Obama's appeal with women voters and impede the reconciliation under way with Clinton's primary supporters. In turn, I began to shrink from activities that might garner attention in order to protect Obama from his association with me. I wore my green hoodie to headquarters in an effort not to be recognized by visiting reporters. And I tried to avoid eye contact with David Plouffe, the campaign manager, whose jaw I swore tightened whenever he saw me.

In October, I learned that I was pregnant with a baby boy whom we would name Declan and who was due the following May. I was ecstatic about becoming a mother, but I suffered from acute morning sickness. My constant trips to the women's bathroom required me to walk past the offices of the senior campaign leadership, whose cold stares sent me tumbling back into self-absorption.

Still, I didn't blame them. "If I were Plouffe," I thought, "and the stakes were this high, I would shun me too. Why take a risk?"

ON NOVEMBER 4TH, 2008, Cass and I sat on plastic chairs in a white tent in Grant Park, Chicago, among Obama's friends, advisers, donors, and a host of politicians and celebrities. Just outside—in the same spot where police had mauled protesters at the Democratic National Convention forty years before—240,000 people of all races, religions, and generations watched the election results on a Jumbotron showing CNN. Win or lose, Obama would speak on the stage beneath the big screen later in the evening.

Everything we were hearing from the campaign was positive, but none of us could bring ourselves to believe what was transpiring until Wolf Blitzer made it official. "This is a moment that a lot of people have been waiting for," he said as soon as polls closed on the West Coast, at ten p.m. Chicago time. "CNN can now project that Barack Obama, forty-seven years old, will become the President-elect of the United States." A checkmark appeared beside Obama's picture.

In every corner of the tent, people jumped up and down. I levitated, lunging into Cass's arms like a World Series–winning pitcher embracing his team's catcher. Everyone around us seemed to be crying. My phone was ringing off the hook. Cass—not normally a hugger—was enfolding any friend or stranger in his path.

Many of my relatives in Ireland had either stayed up all night or set their alarms for five a.m. Obama (or, as my Irish cousins liked to say, "O'bama") had done what nobody—even most of his closest supporters—thought possible. His six-point margin of victory was a modern-day landslide. He had taken Virginia and Indiana, states that had not gone Democratic since President Johnson had won them in 1964. The possibilities ahead seemed infinite. I waited in a line of friends and family to congratulate the new President-elect.

"This is something, huh?" Obama said, giving me a deep hug across a rope barrier. I answered truthfully, "It's too big to comprehend. Do not compute, do not compute."

The man before me was outwardly the same person I had worked with since 2005. But everything about his manner seemed altered by what had just happened. He had always been a solitary person, but now, even as he and the future First Lady made their way down the line in a seamless communion, he seemed well and truly alone.

It was as if he had been suddenly encased in a glass box, the only man in the world who would be *President of the United States.* He alone would make the call on when to go to war, and, more immediately, he alone would be responsible for saving a US economy that was in free fall.

Obama had joked in the past about the dangers of the "dog actually catching the bus." Now he would face the bleakest economic forecast for the United States since the Great Depression. On a night that brought unmediated bliss to the rest of us, Obama's big smile was there, but the usual spark of mischief in his eyes seemed to have vanished.

Although the election had been called only hours before, and he would not formally occupy the presidency until January, the burdens of decision-making already seemed to be crashing down upon him. This was a momentous night, but for the President-elect, it did not seem a particularly happy one. Even as he focused on his friends like a laser, telling Cass he was looking "more dapper" than he had ever seen him, Obama was reserved, seeming to be saying his goodbyes rather than hellos.

OBAMA HAD MADE CLEAR to Cass and me that he would want us to join his administration if he managed to win. The memory of my struggles in the Senate office made me wonder whether I—who had flown solo my whole career before that fateful dinner with Obama in 2005—could find a place in a huge bureaucracy, having to constantly jockey for access. But Cass and I both believed in him, and we were eager to try to work on issues that we cared about. I knew I was tired of being a professional foreign policy critic, opining and judging without ever knowing whether I would pass the moral and political tests to which I was subjecting others. I wanted to be on the inside, to try to influence this new administration's actions. We never seriously discussed the downsides of upending our lives; we just began making plans to move to Washington.

Determining what I should *do* in government, however, was an entirely different matter. Prior to election night, every time Mum or Eddie had raised the question of what role I would want if Obama became President, I would hush them, saying they would jinx the whole election. But now I needed to figure that out.

A few days after we saw Obama in Grant Park, he wrote to say that he was giving up his personal email account. First, though, he asked what my dream job was. I had planned to work wherever he told me, naively assuming that he would have a fixed idea where I belonged. But he was busy filling out his cabinet and developing strategies to address the skyrocketing unemployment rate; he had no mental space to come up with a job description for me.

With nothing to guide me, I thought about how I could be useful, drawing on my years of extensive reading about US foreign policy, along with the interviews of US officials I had conducted for my books. The role I described in my email reply to Obama was convoluted. I thought my specialty could be big picture—articulating American grand strategy in language that people could digest. I also hoped to take up perceived lost causes, conflicts in countries that didn't make the headlines, to find ways of leveraging the President's personal interest to improve a situation.

I pored over every word of my proposed position, not wanting to come across as presumptuous, but also believing that Obama might be willing to define a job in the terms that I laid out. Cass googled prior administrations so we could use the correct nomenclature for a title, and we settled on proposing "Assistant to the President for Special Projects." Mum and Eddie, whom I ran everything by, offered feedback on the tone and substance of the note, as did my aunt Patricia and uncle Derry, with whom Cass and I had gone to stay for a few days in Waterville just after election night. I enlisted the views of John, Mort, Jonathan, and Holbrooke—all of whom had served either on the National Security Council (NSC) or with the State Department. I ended the email to Obama by stressing that we would need to define any job in a manner that appealed to National Security Advisor Jim Jones,

Deputy National Security Advisor Tom Donilon, and Mark Lippert, whom Obama had named NSC chief of staff.

I heard nothing back for weeks. Obama now occupied an entirely different orbit from mine. The size of the Secret Service team around him had increased exponentially. Even close confidants like Valerie Jarrett and David Axelrod no longer called him "Barack," "Obama," or "BO." He was now the President-elect, or the "PE."

When Obama walked by, people who had known him for years jumped to their feet, practically saluting. A forbidding mystique pulsed out of any room he occupied. I wanted to talk to the PE, to see how he was doing and how I could support him during these precious weeks. But I saw that the most prized commodity of all now was his time, and I certainly didn't *need* to see him. I just wanted to check in on my friend.

Because Obama, my biggest champion in the political world, was no longer reachable via email, I was now at the mercy of the people he had deputized to manage his personnel choices. Lippert was coordinating the hiring for Obama's national security jobs. Even though he never seemed a fan of mine, I admired his decision to leave the campaign at its height to deploy as a Navy intelligence officer to Iraq, where he had earned a Bronze Star for his service.

When my emails seeking clarity went unanswered, I checked occasionally to be sure my cell phone was working. When I finally managed to reach him, he demanded to know why I had proposed the "assistant to the President" title in my note to Obama. "Jim Jones, the National Security Advisor, a decorated American Marine general, will be an assistant to the President," he said. "You think you're in his league?" I was mortified.

When Cass and I had done our online research, we had seen the designations "assistant," "deputy assistant," and "special assistant" to the President, and had somehow jumbled up the order, thinking that "assistant" was the lowest rank of the three—when, in fact, it was the most senior. My limbo continued. "I'm being treated like I'm a problem to be solved," I told Cass, "not a person anyone actually wants."

My new husband, by contrast, was given the job he coveted. On one of our earliest dates, I had asked him, if he wasn't a law professor, what he would most want to be. I imagined he might answer playfully "bass guitarist for Bruce Springsteen." Instead, he gazed off into the distance, his eyes practically misting up with emotion, and said, dreamily, "OIRA." I responded, "What the hell is OIRA?" When the head of the transition team informed the President-elect of Cass's ambition, Obama reportedly asked the same question.

It turned out that the Office of Information and Regulatory Affairs (OIRA) was known around Washington as "the most powerful job nobody has ever heard of." OIRA oversees regulation on issues as diverse as civil rights, health care, the environment, worker safety, transportation, food safety, and veterans affairs. Obama told Cass that he intended to nominate him for the post, and Cass spent the transition weeks between November and January giddily mapping out what the new President could do on regulation during his first hundred days.

Once Obama announced his choices for the big national security jobs, I hoped that someone high up would focus on the next level down. Strobe Talbott generously called, having forgiven me for lobbying him rudely on Bosnia more than a decade before when he was President Clinton's Deputy Secretary of State. Strobe was close to Hillary Clinton, whom Obama had just nominated to become Secretary of State. A few days later, after inquiring whether she would consider me for a position, Strobe forwarded me a blunt message from a Clinton insider: "I think she should go with the NSC."

Cass tried to console me. He insisted something would work out, quoting Nobel Prize–winning psychologist Daniel Kahneman, who wisely wrote, "Nothing in life is as important as you think it is when you are thinking about it." But even when I managed to focus elsewhere, my mind ran wild, reminding me of how scarred I was by my recent public disgrace.

In one of my many dreams during this period, I was overjoyed because I was about to interview for a job with Clinton at the State Department. As the meeting time approached, I looked frantically for my car keys, but couldn't find them. After rushing to the State Department in a cab, I was told that the meeting had been moved to her office on Capitol Hill. When I got there, I realized that although I was already half an hour late, I needed urgently to use a restroom—as pregnant women often did. The bathrooms had long lines of women beside them, and, as I waited, my cell phone rang, telling me I had to get to the meeting or it would be canceled. When it was finally my turn for the bathroom, I stepped forward, inching past a woman who had just arrived. As I walked by, she began whacking me with her hand-bag. Doggedly continuing forward, I heard her fall behind me. When I turned, she was lying on the ground and jabbing her cane upwards at me, saying, "You, missy, will pay for this. I recognize you. You are Samantha Power. I am going to tell all the newspapers that you hit an old lady trying to go to the bathroom."

This was my mental state as I waited for a job offer.

I was also determined to keep my pregnancy hidden from my colleagues on the transition team. I lived a strange duality. On the one hand, the very thought of the baby—"half of Cass!"—made me smile throughout the day. But on the other hand, I reflexively feared I would get a lesser job if senior people found out, so I wore oversize Irish woolen sweaters and wide scarves, often keeping my winter coat on indoors.

The irony of my subterfuge was not lost on me. The President-elect was the progressive son of a trailblazing mother. He had married a woman who had once been his mentor, and they had two young daugh-ters. Yet here I was, one of his female advisers, petrified it would cost me if the people around him discovered I was pregnant.

Obama had nominated Susan Rice to become US Ambassador to the UN. Rice had been a national security aide during the Rwandan genocide, and I had been critical of her in *A Problem from Hell*. But after some initial awkwardness, we had grown friendly over the course of the campaign, and she had been one of the few people to go out of her way to stay in touch during my exile. Strong-willed and scrappy, she laughed easily and was quick to break out dancing at social events.

Having observed the UN in Bosnia and written about it for much of my career, I offered to help her prepare for her new role. When I mentioned the job that I had pitched to the President-elect, she thought it was idiotic. "What you say you want is all mush," Susan explained, drawing on her decade of experience at the National Security Council and State Department. "Who will report to you? What will you be responsible for? If you are responsible for nothing, nobody will call you. You will be a floating person, irrelevant to what is happening day to day."

Susan advised me to seek the job of Senior Director and Special Assistant to the President for Multilateral Affairs at the National Security Council. This was the President's senior adviser on all matters related to the UN. "From the White House," she said, "you can see the full field." She would help show me the ropes, and I could serve as a bridge between her team at the US Mission to the UN in New York and the White House, which tended to develop its own insular political culture from which even cabinet members felt excluded.

Convinced by Susan's bureaucratic wisdom, I told the President-elect's foreign policy gatekeepers that I would like to be considered for this specific multilateral affairs position. I was finally speaking a language that White House personnel staff could act on, as the job had existed in the Bush administration, and it had been allotted a salary. Lippert, who had been inundated with demands from former campaign staff, seemed genuinely relieved to be able to slot my name into the traditional organizational chart.

Much as I wanted to change the system and fantasized about doing so for Obama, my embrace of an established, conventional role would be the first of many concessions I would make to immutable realities. I had also never before relied so heavily on someone for career advice. I was grateful to Susan and would soon learn that, as a Washington novice and as a woman in national security, I needed to ask others for support.

Even when Lippert and I had settled on the job, I still had to get the formal okay from National Security Advisor Jones, who would be my new boss. As I awaited my interview with him, I drove to the FBI field office in downtown Boston to be fingerprinted for the investigation that was required before I could obtain a security clearance. I also started making my way through a mountain of government paperwork. I had to complete forms for ethics, medical history, and financial disclosure, but it was the SF-86, the national security background questionnaire, that stunned me with its breadth. The form had twenty-nine separate sections, each with a detailed subset of questions. It also came with a bold warning that those who submitted false information could be charged with a federal crime and face up to five years in prison.

Among its requirements, the form asked applicants to go back fifteen years and list any "close and/or continuing contact" with a foreign national, along with *any* contact with the representative of a foreign government. My entire family besides Mum, Eddie, Stephen, Ellyn, and Cass lived in Ireland, so I had to list each of my relatives. I sent emails to my Irish cousins telling them to alert the rest of the family that the FBI might soon be in touch. "Don't worry," I told them. "I'm not in trouble." I had also traveled widely in Asia and Africa as a journalist, interviewing dozens of foreign officials, so I spent a number of taxing days going through my old reporters' notebooks to track down the dates and locations of each of those interactions, as required by law.

In January of 2009, I learned that I had been granted the top security clearance I needed to be able to participate in classified discussions and receive intelligence products. Now all I needed was General Jones's approval.

A few days before Obama's Inauguration, my cell phone rang, and I was surprised by the voice I heard on the line.

"It's Obama," he said.

"You're kidding," I replied.

"Who else would it be?" he teased.

"You don't call yourself the 'PE'?" I asked.

"It sounds like a ratty gym class," he joked. "I prefer Obama."

We discussed my job limbo, which he said he'd been inquiring about constantly. "It will be fine," I said, knowing the unfathomable pressures he was under. He described the logistical nightmare of ensuring that all of his friends and family felt appreciated during the festivities. "It's like a wedding," he observed.

I praised the draft of his Inaugural speech I had read, especially the line in which he would tell dictators that America "will extend a hand if you are willing to unclench your fist." Cass took the phone with a big smile.

"We've come a long way from the University of Chicago," said Cass.

"Maybe I should have taken Douglas Baird's offer," said Obama, referring to the University of Chicago Law School dean who had urged Obama to pursue a tenure-track professorship.

"Well, if you keep up the good writing, I'm sure something can be arranged," said Cass.

Obama signed off, saying, "I'd like to get together with you two, soon, to bat some ideas around."

We would quickly learn that such a meeting was a luxury the forty-fourth President of the United States could scarcely afford.

THE NEXT DAY, CASS and I boarded the US Air Shuttle in Boston, ready to take up our new life in the nation's capital. Mum and Eddie would be meeting us in DC so we could attend the Inauguration together.

I was struck by the Americanness of it all. When they came to the United States three decades before, could Mum and Eddie have imagined that their adopted country would elect an African-American President? Or that their daughter would get to work at his White House?

After the plane took off, we flew over Winthrop. I glanced at my home out the window before the land below us faded quickly into the distance.

PART TWO

19

NO MANUAL

Three days after President Obama's inauguration, National Security Advisor Jim Jones invited me to interview for the position of Senior Director for Multilateral Affairs at the National Security Council. His administrative aide told me to bring a government ID in order to get past security, but out of an abundance of caution I brought my driver's license, social security card, passport, and birth certificate. I was not going to be denied.

After clearing the Secret Service checkpoint and metal detectors, I found myself on West Executive Avenue, the narrow lane that runs between the White House and the Eisenhower Executive Office Building (EEOB). The stately, nineteenth-century EEOB is where most of the President's staff have their offices, and where, as a journalist, I had interviewed US officials for my articles and books. But never before had I set foot in the West Wing, where I would be meeting with Jones. I didn't know Obama's new National Security Advisor, and I was sufficiently nervous about the impending interview that I did not really take in how momentous it was to be walking under the familiar portico of the White House.

After a short wait in the visitors' reception area, where I tried unsuccessfully to focus on the *New York Times* lying on the coffee table, Jones's assistant guided me into a narrow passageway that led almost immediately to the cramped "Suite" of offices belonging to America's top national security officials. Four aides were packed into cubicles, while the hugely influential Deputy National Security Advisor worked in a room roughly the size of a broom closet.

"Location, location location," I thought to myself. And, as if on cue, I heard Obama's voice beckoning someone down the hall.

Jones was a six-foot-four former Georgetown basketball forward and decorated Vietnam War veteran who had risen through the ranks of the military to become a four-star general. He kept his hair trimmed short and had the lean physique of someone still ready to suit up for battle. Although he cut an imposing figure, he was wonderfully informal as he escorted me into his office.

"Pretty cool here, isn't it?" he said.

His shelves were already lined with photos of his grandchildren and dozens of "challenge coins" bearing the insignia of the various US military detachments he had served in or visited over the course of a forty-year military career.

I had first heard about Jones from Fred Cuny, who had spoken glowingly about the general's provision of US military protection to Kurds in Northern Iraq after the Persian Gulf War. As we sat down at Jones's conference table, I mentioned that Fred had helped inspire my early career choices. Jones broke into a broad smile and, for the next ten minutes, talked about their partnership and the gaping hole left by Fred's death.

I had rehearsed a detailed set of arguments for why I would make a trusty NSC aide, but after throwing out a few perfunctory questions about what my priorities would be, Jones asked, "Can you start next week?" He didn't seem to notice my pregnancy, which did not show clearly and I did not bring up.

Mark Lippert's assistant called me later in the day to say that the NSC had earmarked an office for me in the EEOB.

"Really?" I exclaimed. "So this is real?!"

"Yes," she said warmly. "But I want to warn you, the space is really small."

I said I didn't care how big my office was, reminding her that I had worked out of a backpack for years as a reporter, requiring only a notebook, pen, and laptop. But then I hesitated.

My mother (bottom row, center) at age sixteen with her secondary school field hockey team.

On their wedding day in 1968, my parents, Jim Power, age thirty-one, and Vera Delaney, age twenty-four, outside the church in Cork City, Ireland. They are flanked by her sister Patricia Delaney and his brother-in-law Vincent Pippet.

My early years in Dublin, with Mum and Dad.

Mum and Eddie in the late 1970s.

With my younger brother, Stephen, in 1978, the year before we left Ireland for the United States.

19 · TRADER · 83

After arriving in Pittsburgh in 1979, I chopped off my red hair, practiced an American accent, and quickly immersed myself in the foreign sport of baseball.

In 1983, not long after after Mum and Eddie moved Stephen and me to Atlanta, Georgia.

With Eddie, who was full of mischief and who raised me to appreciate the power and magic of storytelling.

As the starting shooting guard on the Lakeside High School basketball team, I spent countless afternoons and weekends in solitude shooting baskets.

With my college boyfriend Schu during our trip through Europe in the summer of 1990.

Mum, Stephen, and Eddie at my college graduation in 1992.

Fred Cuny, renowned as the "Master of Disaster" for his relief work in more than thirty crisis zones. He would successfully engineer a dangerous operation to restore water to besieged Sarajevans.

Jonathan Moore, a former US official who served under six presidents, and Mort Abramowitz, a retired US diplomat who became my first boss when I interned at the Carnegie Endowment. They became two of my most important mentors and influences.

In August of 1993, en route to Bosnia for the first time, with journalist George Stamkoski and my friend Ben Cohen (not pictured). The handmade "PRESS" placard in the window of our rental car was intended as a safety precaution.

I joined George and Ben in interviewing a group of Bosnian military officers in Bihać, a small Muslim enclave in the northwest corner of Bosnia that was surrounded on all sides by Serb forces.

On a reporting trip to central Bosnia with Laura Pitter, who was instrumental in encouraging me to move to the Balkans to become a foreign correspondent.

Traveling with Croatian journalist Hrvoje Hranjski on a UN flight from Zagreb, Croatia, to Sarajevo, Bosnia, in April of 1994.

Interviewing UN Force Commander Michael Rose in Sarajevo in 1995.

Writing a story in
Sarajevo in 1995.

My closest friends in Bosnia were a small group of female
reporters, including (from left) Laura Pitter, Elizabeth Rubin,
Emma Daly, and Stacy Sullivan.

Journalist David Rohde and I interviewing a survivor of the 1995 Srebrenica massacre.

Crossing the finish line of the 1995 New York City Marathon. My decision to splash the morbid public service announcement "Remember Srebrenica" across my chest created some confusion along the route.

Cornering bemused Hall of Fame Red Sox pitcher Pedro Martinez at a charity event, where I couldn't stop myself from giving him a long account of the genocide book I was writing.

With US diplomat Richard Holbrooke. Despite turning down his job offer during the Bosnian war, he eventually became a trusted friend and counselor.

Eddie and Mum, who have edited dozens of drafts of each of my books, beside piles of chapters that they've marked up.

One of my most important professional collaborations—and friendships—has been with John Prendergast. In 2004, we crossed the border from Chad into Darfur, Sudan (left), to investigate the genocide there and then, along with Gayle Smith, became involved in the Save Darfur campaign.

Speaking at a Women for Obama event in the early months of his presidential campaign.

Leading cheers with Obama campaign adviser Austan Goolsbee after Obama won the Iowa Caucus in January of 2008.

Cass and I started dating in early 2008, spending time writing side-by-side in my Winthrop, Massachusetts, apartment. We were married on July 4th, 2008, in Waterville, Ireland.

After pulling an all-nighter to work on his Nobel Peace Prize acceptance speech, President Obama summoned me and his speechwriters Jon Favreau and Ben Rhodes to discuss his new handwritten draft.

Declan Power Sunstein was born in April of 2009, and two months later, he met President Obama for the first time.

Mum and Eddie visiting the White House in early 2009.

President Obama and members of his national security staff discuss Sudan in September of 2010.

At the memorial service for Richard Holbrooke, who died of a heart attack in 2010. In the years ahead I would find myself constantly wishing I could pick up the phone to seek Holbrooke's advice.

With President Obama, Senior Advisor David Plouffe, National Security Advisor Tom Donilon, and Deputy National Security Advisor Ben Rhodes, discussing Obama's upcoming trip to the 2011 UN General Assembly.

"Is it a lot smaller than the other Senior Directors' offices?" I inquired. There was a long pause.

"For now, yes," she said.

Something similar happened when the NSC Human Resources Department informed me of my salary. I did not question the figure they presented, knowing that I would take a pay cut from working at a private university. The following day, however, I learned from a male colleague, also a Senior Director, that he would be paid five thousand dollars more than me.

Instead of demanding a pay raise, I emailed Lippert, saying I had learned of the two salary tiers for Senior Directors. I asked what I would need to do to earn the higher pay. Lippert called immediately, and, since I wasn't home, apologized to Cass. He said the mix-up would be corrected, which it was, but I wondered if I was experiencing bad luck or something more deliberate.

The next week, at long last, I showed up for work at the White House, feeling elated to be a part of Obama's team. My office in the EEOB was located inside a SCIF—a Sensitive Compartmented Information Facility. This meant that I worked inside the equivalent of a room-sized safe. If I was the first to arrive in the morning, I had to enter a combination by rotating a palm-sized dial on the heavy door. NSC offices lacked natural light because the blinds on the windows had to be kept closed to impede foreign spying. The computers at our desks didn't allow us to access personal email, and we were required to leave our BlackBerries and cell phones on a table just outside the SCIF door.

In my orientation briefing on security, I was warned that countries like China and Russia had sophisticated capabilities, so it was essential that I only talk about sensitive matters in spaces like my office that were designed for confidential discussions. I was also told to be wary of people working for foreign governments, as they sometimes tried to manipulate or blackmail US officials to gain access to classified information.

When I got an overview of the health benefits for government employees, I learned that my three months of maternity leave would be unpaid. I would be able to use whatever sick days and vacation I had accrued to continue receiving my salary for a short while after Declan's birth. But, because I was due in May, I would not have been in the job long enough for much of my leave to be covered. I was fortunate—I had savings, and I had Cass. But it seemed outrageous that other people might feel compelled to return to work before their parental leave was up simply to resume being paid. Thanks to Congress's refusal to change the law, America was then one of only two high-income countries in the world that did not guarantee paid maternity leave.[1]

Cass would soon be nominated as the head of OIRA and was already happily ensconced at the Office of Management and Budget as a senior adviser. On my second day, he invited me to lunch at the West Wing's Navy Mess. A set of color-coded badges denoted which parts of the White House grounds staff could access, and Cass and I were glad to receive highly coveted blue badges, which enabled us to enter the West Wing without an escort.

The Mess was much fancier than it sounded. I had expected a cafeteria-style canteen, but a Navy steward in a dark suit and tie escorted us to our table, where our food was served on White House china. Because of the maritime images on the windowless walls, we had the feeling of being in a ship's miniaturized grand dining room.

"It's like the *Titanic*," I observed, referencing the only nautical dining visual that sprang to mind.

"Let's hope not!" said Cass.

He insisted that we mark the occasion of our first week on the job by indulging in the White House's signature desert, the Chocolate Freedom, a brownie cake that oozed hot fudge and was topped with vanilla ice cream and chocolate syrup. The past year—campaigning, resigning, marrying, getting pregnant, and relocating to DC—had been a whirlwind, and we were finally pausing to celebrate. We clinked our dessert spoons as if they were champagne glasses and luxuriated in the sudden calm.

Later that afternoon, I joined a half dozen NSC officials in the office of NSC Executive Secretary Mara Rudman to discuss the drafting of a document outlining Obama's strategic priorities in foreign policy. As soon as the meeting began, I felt a surge of queasiness and clamminess. I was five months pregnant, so feeling nauseous wasn't unusual. But this felt different.

As the sound of my colleagues' voices receded, I started to shiver and then quickly lost consciousness, my head drooping against the tall shoulder of the yellow Victorian armchair where I sat. Because somebody else was speaking, no one noticed that I had fainted. I came to on my own and quickly excused myself. The sugar surge from the Chocolate Freedom must have done me in.

Prior to starting at the White House, I had fainted only twice in my life—once when I was eleven years old, standing at the back of church during Mass, and once in law school when I was dehydrated from a severe bout of flu. But I would soon match that total in my first week as an adviser to the President of the United States.

The second time, I was alone in my office, sitting at my computer. I recognized the onset of nausea just in time to use my arms as a cushion before I collapsed on top of the keyboard. Since my first fainting, I had avoided large sugar intakes, but that day I had not yet made time for lunch. When I came to, I resolved to keep a stash of crackers nearby to avoid working on an empty stomach.

Looking back, I cringe at how hard I was pushing myself through the most hectic and demanding workdays I had ever experienced. But my doctor didn't see a health risk, and I saw women further along in their pregnancies moving at the same frenetic pace—just as I had seen my mother do years before when she was pregnant with my brother.

AS A NEW NSC EMPLOYEE, I had anticipated that I would get some kind of tutorial on how to do my job. But while I found directions on my desk for how to set up my voicemail, there was no manual on how to help shape US foreign policy.

President Obama's NSC served as a central coordinating hub to inform and advise his decision-making on national security, and to ensure that his foreign policy was implemented across numerous executive branch agencies. Senior Directors were the core of the President's NSC staff, and we held roughly the same "rank" as Assistant Secretaries at the State Department. We prepared background papers and talking points, and we offered advice to President Obama, National Security Adviser Jones, and Deputy National Security Adviser Tom Donilon on what the United States should do vis-à-vis particular countries, emerging threats, and sudden crises. On key matters, we would lay out before the President the pros and cons of pending choices. These "decision memos" were liable to cover everything from whether to provide Pakistan additional military assistance to whether Obama should meet with the Dalai Lama over Chinese objections.

The NSC had "regional" Senior Directors for every part of the world, "homeland" Senior Directors for threats like natural disasters and cyberattacks, and "functional" Senior Directors for issues that cut across different parts of the globe, such as nuclear nonproliferation, climate and energy, and international economics. As the functional Senior Director responsible for multilateral affairs, I advised the President on US relations with international organizations, especially the United Nations.

My portfolio was broad. On a typical day, I might review a UN Security Council draft resolution ratcheting up sanctions against Iran or I might assess whether the United States should support deploying UN peacekeepers to a conflict zone. I also got Jones's permission to serve concurrently as Obama's Senior Director for Human Rights, since no other Senior Director had been assigned that responsibility.

In theory, my human rights role meant that I would be able to generate discussion within the NSC and across the government about possible US actions to combat political repression, anti-Semitism, crackdowns on religious minorities, human trafficking, or mass atrocities. In practice, however, I needed support from the appropriate regional Senior Director when I wanted to influence policy toward a particular country where abuses were occurring. Some colleagues were more enthusiastic than others about my involvement in "their" countries.

Because of "optics"—a term that I heard constantly—I even needed sign-offs from regional Senior Directors to hold certain meetings. For example, if I hoped to see a critic of the Egyptian government to learn about worsening conditions in the country's prisons, I first had to check with the Senior Director responsible for the Middle East. My colleagues were sometimes concerned about the "message" that holding meetings with dissidents would send to governments whose cooperation the United States sought. Occasionally, I would be asked to delegate a meeting to a lower-level person at the State Department to avoid raising the ire of an American ally. They had a point: foreign governments could in fact get upset when they heard that White House officials had taken meetings with opposition figures, but the irritation would quickly pass. I argued (unsuccessfully) that routinizing such non-official contacts would make us better informed and render each specific meeting less noteworthy, as it would be interpreted as part of a larger, systemic approach.

My first months on the NSC in some ways reminded me of moving to the United States thirty years before. I had once again arrived in a foreign land. In Pittsburgh, I had self-consciously appropriated the idioms and expressions I heard my friends use. Now, I was exposed to a whole new bureaucratic lingo. I had to anticipate "pushback" from constituencies that I had never even known existed. I saw government officials "foot-stomping" points they felt strongly about. When the President was meeting with another head of state, we had to agree in advance on what "the ask" and "the deliverables" would be. When the bureaucracy was mired in gridlock, one hoped for an "action-forcing event" like a high-level official's testimony before Congress or an upcoming meeting with a foreign minister that would create pressure to make a decision.

Sports metaphors, which I readily understood, were ubiquitous. When we secured what we wanted at the UN, for example, it was generally not a good idea to "spike the ball" and boast about our success. When we couldn't decide on the best path forward, we needed to "tee up" the issue for higher-level decision.

The gendered metaphors made my skin crawl. In advance of laying out the full scope of our strategy for Iraq, "we needed to show some leg" to foreshadow what we were about to do, or we needed to go in "open Kimono" and be fully transparent. When we landed on an option in the middle, avoiding a hard choice, we might find ourselves "half-pregnant," a phrase I'm embarrassed to say I heard myself using while more than half-pregnant.

WORKING AT THE NSC seemed a little bit like conducting an orchestra. I had one very important power: I got to choose the "music" within my area—that is, the issue on which to spur a government-wide debate about what the United States should do. I then chaired meetings in the Situation Room,* gathering people from the intelligence community, the State Department, the Defense Department, the Treasury Department, USAID, and other agencies to explore whether we could agree on a desired strategy.

These meetings were rarely harmonious. Even representatives from the same government agency often disagreed on an appropriate approach. State Department country experts, for instance, might differ from their colleagues focused on war crimes prosecutions over how to hold a government accountable for large-scale civilian deaths. A few of Obama's political appointees in the Defense Department embraced my recommendation that the United States join the international treaty banning land mines, while long-serving, uniformed officers staunchly opposed the idea. The discussions could be raucous, tense, and unpleasant.

---

* The Situation Room refers to the secure complex built by President John F. Kennedy in 1961. It includes both the main conference room, known from countless movies, and several smaller breakout rooms, such as the one depicted in the now-famous photo of President Obama and his top advisers tracking the Osama bin Laden raid in 2011.

When a decision was especially important or we could not reach consensus about next steps, Donilon would convene the "Deputies," the number-two officials of each government agency, or Jones would gather the "Principals," the heads of the agencies like Secretary of State Clinton and Defense Secretary Robert Gates. When Obama wished to discuss an issue, he would summon the Principals or relevant NSC staff so as to hear competing perspectives and offer direction.

The flow of paper—and the so-called clearance process—from one official to the next was the lifeblood of government policymaking. If the White House was going to issue a statement (for example, to condemn a crackdown on protesters in a foreign country), an NSC country specialist would write the first draft. He would then circulate it by email to others on the NSC for edits. Among the recipients would be members of our press team, lawyers, and liaisons to Congress. Every NSC official who was seen to have "equity" in a statement had to be "looped in" so that they could "chop on," or edit, the words that went out into the world under President Obama's name. I was stunned by the number of cooks in the kitchen—and not at all surprised by how blandly the resulting White House statements often read. Anything sharp or interesting was likely to be edited out somewhere along the line.

And this wasn't just true of official statements. Everything US officials did seemed to need clearance from someone else, creating countless internal veto points before an idea would be raised with the President. Even First Lady Michelle Obama needed the National Park Service's sign-off before she could plant a vegetable garden on the South Lawn.

I was chastised several times during my first month because I sent material directly to Lippert and Donilon without first getting approvals from other Senior Directors, who had their own views on the topic. This sin of bypassing colleagues with equities was termed a "process foul," and being guilty of it felt akin to committing a crime. Over time, however, I came to appreciate the importance of fidelity to "process"—especially when colleagues tried to send the President material that didn't offer a perspective on how a decision might impact human rights.

I saw early on how few voices in high-level government discussions highlighted the nexus between human rights and US national security. Although government officials did not brand themselves with the labels that academics obsessed over (like "realist" or "liberal internationalist"), the realist view—which downplayed the importance of "values"—was dominant. Many US officials considered prioritizing human rights to be in tension with, if not antithetical to, our traditional security concerns.

My view was that the way governments treated their own citizens mattered, and could have a direct impact on American national security interests. Countless studies showed the importance of the rule of law to sustained economic development, and the strong causal links between government repression and civilian susceptibility to radicalization and extremism.[2] Nonetheless, it was rare for participants in NSC meetings to identify respect for individual dignity as central to a country's long-term stability. I would try making these points, but I didn't get the sense I was denting the entrenched skepticism that I encountered.

I was not an absolutist. Sometimes, of course, US officials did face a stark, short-term choice between promoting human rights and pursuing competing interests—for example, seeking partnerships with the authoritarian Chinese government in order to confront major shared threats like the North Korean nuclear program and climate change. Sometimes it was unwise to be publicly vocal about human rights concerns, as more progress might be made behind the scenes. Regardless, I was frustrated that we didn't more often internalize the implications of the truism that countries that treated their citizens with respect made far more reliable partners over time.

ALTHOUGH I WAS NEWLY ENDOWED with a responsibility to mobilize action, I did not yet know how to move the US government. And from the start, I was aware that very bad things were happening in the world.

As I wrote in my journal in February of 2009:

> Sudanese troops massed around Darfur. We were told 30,000
> people had gathered at the UN base in Darfur . . . The UN was
> packed up to leave. And Samantha Power, upstander, had no
> fucking idea how to write a decision memo.

I wasn't sure what I needed to do. Was I senior enough to guide
the rest of the administration on an issue that didn't warrant the President's attention? Who among the other Senior Directors did I need
to consult? If one of my colleagues disagreed with my approach, who
would break the tie? How would our guidance eventually be dispensed
to US diplomats out in the world? These questions would take time for
me to sort out.

My multilateral portfolio required me to make recommendations
to President Obama and others on, for example, whether the United
States should run for a seat on the UN Human Rights Council. This
was a body that I felt we had a clear interest in joining, because participating would allow us to push for broad-based human rights actions.
But because the Council dedicated a disproportionate number of its
resolutions to denouncing Israel, President Obama would be attacked
by some if we ran for a seat.

Unsure of how to proceed, I sought out Denis McDonough. Denis
was now a top adviser to Obama who saw the President several times
every day.

"What does Obama want to do about the Human Rights Council?"
I asked.

"What do *you* think, Sammy," he answered back.

I was confused. I had thought the President would provide us
with direction. But it turned out that with the crashing economy, the
wars in Iraq and Afghanistan, and all the active plotting by terrorists, he was concentrating primarily on high-stakes issues. On other
foreign policy matters, Obama would be briefed on what we were doing and would sometimes tell us to change course. But he understood

from the start that he would not be able to do his job if he did not delegate.*

Obama's thinking departed in important ways from that of the foreign policy establishment. During the presidential campaign, he had taken stances that differed from most Republican and Democratic candidates. However, once in office, he would draw on recommendations from his cabinet and NSC staff in making foreign policy. Because of this more bottom-up process—and because Obama selected a four-star general as National Security Advisor, retained President Bush's Secretary of Defense, and made someone whom he had sparred with on foreign policy his Secretary of State—his bolder instincts were not always reflected in day-to-day decisions.

This was especially true in the early months of the administration, when Obama's mid-level political appointees were awaiting confirmation from the US Senate and not yet in place. Indeed, when I chaired meetings in 2009 to consider whether our administration should take a fresh position on something, I often heard one of two entrenched views: "We never do that," or "We always do that." The past was prologue: those who had conceived of policies in a certain way were ill disposed to try something new.

Truthfully, though, I was often facing a more fundamental problem than dealing with an internally conflicted bureaucracy and ingrained views. On many of the challenges that crossed my desk, I had a hard time answering Denis's vital question: What *did* I think?

---

* We ran for, and won, a seat on the Human Rights Council in 2009. Through our leadership in the Council, over the course of President Obama's time in office we helped authorize international commissions and rapporteurs that exposed human rights abuses in many repressive places, including Iran, Syria, Sudan, Russian-occupied Crimea, and North Korea. Our spearheading of a UN Commission of Inquiry on Human Rights in North Korea allowed us in 2014 to mobilize the necessary votes to put North Korean human rights violations on the Security Council agenda for the first time. In response to Sri Lankan president Mahinda Rajapaksa's atrocities against Tamil civilians, we led the Human Rights Council to adopt resolutions insisting on accountability for wartime abuses. This resulted in the diplomatic isolation of the Sri Lankan government, a factor that reportedly influenced some Sri Lankans, who voted him out of office in 2015. We also succeeded in getting the Human Rights Council to reduce by half the share of country-specific resolutions on Israel.

When I held back in policy debates out of humility, I saw others—who often knew less—sound off with strong opinions, helping tip the direction of our policy. Being forceful and having others on your side often mattered more than the objective merits of one's argument.

Early on, Susan (now Ambassador Rice) warned me: "Don't let anybody there roll you, Sam." I wasn't familiar with what it meant to be "rolled," so she helpfully clued me in.

"Act like you are the boss," Susan counseled, "or people will take advantage of you."

I knew that Susan was said to have a "black belt" in bureaucracy, and, determined to accelerate my learning, I jotted down her advice in the government-issued green notebook I carried with me everywhere.

20

CAN WE GO HOME NOW?

I made my first trip to the Oval Office on March 10th, 2009, when UN Secretary-General Ban Ki-moon paid a courtesy call to President Obama.

I assumed that I would have little difficulty finding the Oval. After all, in my new universe, it was the sun around which all planets rotated. And by then, I had taken many short walks from my office in the EEOB to the ground floor of the West Wing for Situation Room meetings.

Unfortunately, as soon as I entered the White House, I realized I had no idea where to go. I rushed back to my office in the EEOB and googled "Oval Office West Wing map." I ended up printing out a small map from the *Washington Post* website that showed a floor plan. But the image, which was not drawn to scale, gave me a false sense of security. I wandered up to the second floor, while the Oval—which was tough to miss—was on the first.

By the time I found my way into the "pre-brief" with the President, the other participants were already seated, and National Security Advisor Jones was speaking. I sat down awkwardly, maneuvering my seven months' pregnant body onto the couch between my colleagues, trying to catch my breath before the President called on me.

Since my fainting episodes, I had carried a well-worn Poland Springs water bottle everywhere, and I thought nothing of setting it down on the elegant wooden coffee table next to Obama's large bowl of fresh apples. As soon as I did so, however, a butler promptly removed the unsightly item from view. Susan, who was sitting next to Jones, tried to give me an encouraging smile, but her face bore the trace of a grimace.

President Obama greeted me warmly. "How are you, Power?" he said. "Let me give you a minute to get your bearings." I tried to slow my breathing.

After he motioned for me to offer my thoughts, I told him that his meeting with the secretary-general was happening at a critical juncture. The previous week, Sudanese president Omar al-Bashir had been indicted by the International Criminal Court (ICC) for war crimes and genocide perpetrated by his forces in Darfur. In retaliation, he had just expelled thirteen international aid groups from his country, thereby crippling vital food deliveries that Darfuri displaced people needed to survive.

More nervous than I had ever been in Obama's presence, I told him that Darfur stood at a "strategic moment." I emphasized the peril faced by more than a million Darfuris, and I urged him to use his remarks to the press alongside the secretary-general to publicly condemn President Bashir's actions.

"This will be the first time your voice will be heard saying that the expulsion of humanitarians is unacceptable," I said.

"But if I say that," Obama asked, "what leverage do we have to follow through?"

The man who sat before me in the President's chair looked and sounded just like the man I had worked for in the Senate and on the campaign. However, even two months into his new job, he was different.

"Nobody is going to go in and arrest Bashir, and his own guys are not going to dislodge him," Obama continued. The NSC Senior Director for Africa attempted to respond, but the President cut her off as well.

"What do we have to make Bashir cooperate? Are the Arabs with us?"

I shook my head.

"The Africans?"

"Some," I said.

"China?"

I looked down.

The Chinese government, which was emerging as a major force in world affairs, argued that a sovereign state had the right to do whatever it wanted within its borders. This position was rooted in its own self-interest: China didn't want outsiders scrutinizing its domestic human rights abuses. And even though many African leaders had declared their intention never to allow "another Rwanda," they were not looking to confront the oil-rich government of Sudan.

"So what leverage do we have?" Obama asked again.

Susan jumped in, outlining the range of economic sanctions we could impose on Sudanese government officials, and mentioning the no-fly zone Obama had floated during the campaign. But Obama was elected President promising to wind down wars. Grounding Sudan's air force by militarily imposing a no-fly zone could entail beginning a new one.

"I'm not trying to be difficult here," the President said. "But we simply don't have that many tools to play with, and the Sudanese must know that."

With the pre-meeting winding down, I made one last effort to convince him that, even though no panacea existed, he should still speak out.

"The Sudanese government has a long history of making threats and then walking them back under public pressure," I said. "They are very eager to develop a working relationship with your administration, and your voice can make a difference."

Obama was not satisfied, but he clapped his hands together, signaling it was time to welcome the secretary-general.

In *"A Problem from Hell,"* I had highlighted the work of Albert Hirschman, the Princeton economist who published the landmark book *The Rhetoric of Reaction* in 1991. Hirschman's thesis was that those who didn't want to pursue a particular course of action tended to argue that a given policy would be futile ("futility"), that it would likely make matters worse ("perversity"), or that it would imperil some other goal ("jeopardy").

Senator Obama and I had talked about Hirschman's work, and I had admired Obama's ability both to identify the constraints the United States faced and to think creatively about ways we could transcend those barriers. Now, though, endowed with powers he had never had before, he seemed less inclined to believe the United States could get its way. The President was keenly alert to the risks, as he often put it, of "overpromising and underdelivering"—a version of Hirschman's futility concern.

Ban Ki-moon was escorted into the Oval, and he began telling Obama how much he looked forward to working with the members of his team: "Susan Rice, General Jones, Hillary Clinton, Samantha Jones . . ." Even though I had met the secretary-general several times before I entered government, I wasn't surprised that he mangled my name. What did give me a jolt was that he identified me as the fictional, sex-addicted businesswoman played by Kim Cattrall on HBO's *Sex and the City.* Three of Ban's advisers immediately leaned over to him, whispering "Power, Power."

The meeting proceeded uneventfully. Afterward, to my pleasant surprise, Obama used his joint media appearance with the secretary-general to forcefully condemn the Sudanese government's actions. Khartoum did not agree to re-admit the thirteen NGOs, but it would allow other aid groups to make up most of the lost humanitarian capacity.

After the UN delegation left the Oval, Obama approached me and asked when I was due. "I think Barack would make a great name," he joked.

I was so eager to talk about substantive foreign policy issues with him that I blurted out a few sentences about what I was working on. As soon as I did, I saw his shoulders stiffen, and he said he had to get to another meeting.

Initially stung, I thought about it later and understood his reaction. "Everyone on planet Earth wants something from him," I told Cass. "He probably just wanted one simple conversation about baby names."

In the Senate and during the campaign, my conversations with Obama could glide between the personal and the political. But now that he was President, he had the power to order officials in the government to take action on almost any issue in the world. This meant that when I raised a foreign policy topic with him, I wasn't launching an interesting discussion. Rather, I was making an implicit demand.

WHEN I HAD FIRST FLASHED my badge to gain entry to the Situation Room, I heard a kind of internal "intruder alert" go off inside my head. Given my background as a journalist, I wondered whether people would be reluctant to speak during meetings I attended.

"Will people think I'm just a reporter masquerading as a bureaucrat?" I asked Cass. He answered with typically astute behavioral wisdom. "People tend to think about themselves," he told me. "It is highly unlikely your colleagues are thinking about you at all."

But he was not entirely correct. Early in the administration, John Prendergast orchestrated the placement of a brilliant half-page advertisement in the *Washington Post* and *Politico* that caused a stir within the White House. In addition to being my close friend, John remained a leading advocate on Darfur, and his shockingly well-informed ad took personal aim at specific Deputies, the typically faceless and nameless senior officials who were making key decisions about how our administration would handle the crisis there. The ad ran the same day that they were meeting to discuss what the United States should do next, and it included their pictures and first names—"Erica, Tom, Jim, Stuart, Michèle."* In addition to publicizing the precise timing of this private meeting, John knew the content of the policy divisions among the Deputies. Many in the administration assumed, wrongly, that I was his source.

John had been best man at my wedding. He was Declan's godfather, and he had cared for me during some of my most difficult moments. But when I started in government, we had made a pact to never discuss internal deliberations. I wanted to continue to hear about what he

---

* They were, respectively, UN Ambassador Susan Rice's deputy Erica Barks-Ruggles, Deputy National Security Adviser Tom Donilon, Deputy Secretary of State Jim Steinberg, Treasury Undersecretary Stuart Levey, and Undersecretary of Defense for Policy Michèle Flournoy.

learned on his travels to Africa and his recommendations for what we should do on various issues. But having served in the Clinton White House, John understood that our work-related conversations could go in only one direction.

With John's ad and in other instances, I never knew how to address rumors of my culpability. If I marched into the offices of my higher-ups to discuss a suspected leak, I feared it would suggest guilt. But if I waited for the accusations to be leveled in person, I would be waiting a long time. Government, I discovered, was a lot like high school: people tended to dish on their peers behind their backs rather than to their faces.

Obama once pulled me aside and warned me that, because of my ties to journalists and NGOs, some in the White House suspected I was talking to the press out of school. I responded firmly and honestly, "It will never, ever be me." I kept that promise and never leaked—but since those who did were never identified, the cloud of suspicion remained.

IN MY WRITING LIFE before government, I had come to believe that the only way to understand a place was to hop on a plane and spend months digging in to what was happening. Hearing in person from the people who were affected by US foreign policy decisions seemed essential. Yet once I gained actual responsibility for helping develop these policies, I found it almost impossible to travel. Multiple NSC officials needed to approve my trips, and my early requests were almost always denied. When I asked to join a State Department delegation in a dialogue with the Burmese government, for example, I was told I couldn't go because the presence of someone seen as close to President Obama might inflate expectations of a breakthrough.

After a proposed trip to the UN offices in Geneva was deemed "nonessential" and declined on budgetary grounds, I offered to pay my own way. The NSC administrative official looked at me incredulously.

"If you are representing the United States government," she said, "the government must support the trip."

"Yes," I said, cluelessly, "but you are saying the government won't cover my trip, and I still want to go. It's worth it for me to use my own money." I did not go to Geneva.

I chafed at being cooped up in an office. "I'm like a plant in need of light," I complained to Cass. And if I was this insulated, I thought, how must President Obama feel?

On the campaign trail, I often heard Obama lament his relative seclusion. Indeed, on the rare occasions he broke free of his fixed schedule and made a spontaneous visit somewhere, campaign staff would send around an email saying, "The bear is loose."

I couldn't imagine how "the bear" was now dealing with life inside the sturdiest, most regimented bubble in the world. He had a convoy of thirty vehicles wherever he went. He could do almost nothing on a whim. Days or even weeks before he went somewhere, large advance teams would secure his intended destination and even meet with the people greeting him. Everything must have felt rehearsed.

Seeing how cloistered he was, I gained a whole new respect for the importance of the relatively obscure Office of Presidential Correspondence. Some fifty staff members and three hundred volunteers helped decide which ten letters and email messages written to the President (out of the ten thousand that arrived each day) would go in the briefing book Obama took home at night. This sampling of correspondence— the "letter underground" as the staff called it—gave the President perhaps his most authentic glimpse into the real world.

Obama had played basketball all his life, but once he became president, he seemed to prefer golf. "Eighteen holes is what passes for freedom in this job," he once explained to me. For someone pent up by rope lines and armored cars, barricades and security details, an afternoon round under an open sky must have meant much more than golf.

MY HUSBAND WAS HAVING his own issues adjusting to our new world. Unlike me, Cass needed to be confirmed by the US Senate before he could take up his dream job of running OIRA. As a former University of Chicago professor invested in ensuring that regulatory benefits exceeded costs (an approach also championed by Republicans), he was seen as too conservative for the post by some progressives. But it was right-wing pundits and politicians who waged a full-throated campaign against his confirmation.

Cass had published well over four hundred articles (most long and academic), and nearly forty books. He had never written cautiously, weighing in on contentious topics such as abortion, pornography, and animal rights. If you had tracked only Fox News, which distorted Cass's writing, you would have thought President Obama had nominated a radical, Marxist, animal-rights activist who would use his perch at OIRA to ban hunting and prohibit meat consumption.

By coincidence, Cass had just published a book called *Rumors*, about how easily lies were spread and reputations were soiled in the internet age. Suddenly, the author of *Rumors* found himself subjected to the wildest falsehoods imaginable. The Center for Consumer Freedom wrote that Cass's appointment "could spell the end of animal agriculture, retail sales of meat and dairy foods, hunting and fishing, biomedical research, pet ownership, zoos and aquariums, traveling circuses, and countless other things Americans take for granted." On the floor of the Senate, Kentucky Republican Jim Bunning warned, "According to Mr. Sunstein's logic, your dog could sue you for putting its collar on a little too tight."

Fox News's Glenn Beck developed an obsession with Cass, labeling him "evil" and calling him "The Most Dangerous Man in America" on air over a hundred times. To his nightly audience of three million viewers, Beck ranted about Cass's coauthored book *Nudge*, which discussed modest steps governments could take to improve citizen welfare. But as Beck saw it, Cass's true ambitions were much more ominous: "First it's nudge. Then it's shove. Then it becomes shoot."

I was frightened at how far Cass's critics seemed prepared to go. He got emails that ran the gamut from obnoxious ("I believe animals have rights, the right to be tasty") to menacing and confused ("Go back to Israel, you Nazi"). The US Sportsmen's Alliance called on its followers to "take up their arms" in order to prevent Cass from assuming the job.

He began receiving death threats at our unlisted home address. One, which I brought to the head of security at the NSC, read:

If I were you, I would resign immediately. A well-paid individual, who is armed, knows where you live.

I alternated between reassuring myself that these warnings were
just meant to intimidate and being unable to sleep for entire nights
as I stared at Cass and imagined someone actually harming him. No
matter how much therapy I had done to try to heal the wounds left by
my father's death, I still worried that the deep love and peace Cass had
brought me could not last.

BOTH OF US MISSED controlling how we spent our time. And early
on, we didn't feel that we were accomplishing what we wanted. As we
walked to the car at night, we would assess how we had fared during
the workday with the shorthand of whether we were "respected" or "not
respected," and whether we were "effective" or "not effective."

I would typically tell Cass that I had landed, yet again, in the lower
left-hand quadrant: "not respected, not effective."

My focus became intensely bureaucratic. In the distant past, I had
felt my blood boil confronting Bosnian Serb militiamen for the crimes
they were committing. But now, holed up in a fully secure office with
the blinds perpetually drawn, my universe shrank. Exclusion from a
meeting was enough to cause me to fume to Cass that I should just pack
up and move back to Boston. After meetings, an NSC colleague would
send around what was called the Summary of Conclusions (SOC) to
all those who attended, memorializing what had been agreed upon.
If the SOC omitted, for example, my nonconcurrence on whether we
should recognize a flawed election somewhere, I was almost as enraged
as if I had personally witnessed a soldier rough up an election monitor.

Because we were expecting a child, we had started to receive gifts,
and one of the children's books, *Alexander and the Terrible, Horrible,
No Good, Very Bad Day*, stood out. We were each so unaccustomed to
dreariness in our work lives that we felt like Alexander, mired in cycles
of complaint that were becoming self-fulfilling prophecies. Cass never
put personal sentiments in emails, but many days he would send me an
SOS in code: "CWGHN?" (Can We Go Home Now?).

It felt surreal and embarrassingly self-centered to be unhappy working in the White House. I thought about my Irish cousins and aunts and uncles who were so amazed by my place of employment that they were planning to fly a very long way to get personal tours. I was learning vast amounts about how foreign policy was made. I was being schooled by top experts on parts of the world I had not previously known much about. After soliciting the views of people across the government, I had made recommendations to the President that resulted in the United States rejoining a number of UN agencies from which President Bush had walked away. And I had successfully pushed for Obama to raise his voice against the wartime atrocities being carried out in countries such as Sri Lanka and Sudan.

But I knew I did not yet have the relationships, the clout, or the mastery of bureaucratic processes I needed to maximize my impact.

21

APRIL 24TH

Every year on April 24th, Armenians around the world, including more than one million Americans of Armenian descent, commemorate the Ottoman Empire's 1915 slaughter of 1.5 million people. Every year on this day, the US President issues a statement condemning the killing. And every year since 1981, that statement has failed to use the word "genocide" for fear of offending Turkey, an important NATO ally. As a candidate, however, Obama had promised the Armenian-American community that, if elected, he would recognize the genocide.

In *"A Problem from Hell,"* I described in considerable detail the Ottoman attempt to destroy the Armenian population. I also told the story of Raphael Lemkin, the Polish Jewish lawyer who had been so influenced by the Armenian massacres and the Holocaust that he invented the word *genocide*. After the book was published, I built strong ties with Armenian-American leaders and participated in their memorial events, where the weathered faces of the genocide survivors still reflected the intense pain of their losses. I had been unprepared for the emotion of Armenian Americans as they expressed their gratitude to me, an outsider, for taking up their cause. "Thank you for telling our story," one survivor told me. "We didn't know whether we would be believed."

These conversations often ended with some version of the same question: "What will it take to make the US government recognize our suffering?"

Shortly before I arrived in Obama's Senate office in 2005, John Evans, the US Ambassador to Armenia, had raised the ire of the State Department by publicly stating the verifiable truth that the "Armenian Genocide was the first genocide of the twentieth century."[3] The State Department subsequently forced his early retirement. In response, Mark Lippert and I had helped Obama prepare a forceful letter to Secretary of State Condoleezza Rice, criticizing the Bush administration's position.

Obama's letter cited Lemkin, as well as Henry Morgenthau, Sr., the US Ambassador to the Ottoman Empire in 1915, who had described the situation as "a campaign of race extermination." The letter to Rice also quoted the US Consul in Aleppo who reported witnessing a "carefully planned scheme to thoroughly extinguish the Armenian race." These American diplomats had been part of the same State Department that, nine decades later, was refusing to admit what had happened.

"The occurrence of the Armenian genocide in 1915 is not an 'allegation,' a 'personal opinion,' or a 'point of view,'" Senator Obama wrote to Secretary Rice. "It is a widely documented fact."[4]

The Turkish government was the big impediment to changing the US stance. Ankara was relentless in promoting the idea that no such "genocide" had occurred. Over the years, I had learned to spot the Turkish officials at my public events: they almost always wore suits, even on weekends in California bookstores, and they tended to carry a copy of my book with the Armenia chapter heavily annotated. My Turkish critics wrote colorful rants on the book's Amazon page, slamming my allegedly shoddy scholarship and giving their reviews titles along the lines of "Armenian Propaganda from Harvard."

After seeing Senator Obama and others on the Hill take such strong stands, I began to believe that official US recognition of the genocide might be within reach. In October of 2007, I wrote a column for *Time* titled "Honesty Is the Best Policy," arguing that "a stable, fruitful, 21st-century relationship cannot be built on a lie." In the piece, I urged the US government to stop acting as though it lacked leverage over Turkey. While it was true that we used the country as a supply route to our troops in Iraq, it was also the third-largest recipient of US foreign assistance, behind Israel and Egypt, and a $7 billion trading partner. Over the years, support from the US government had brought Turkey into NATO and built up its military. The United States had helped construct and maintain the strategically important Incirlik Air Base, and our continued military presence there provided Turkey an extra measure of stability. After Turkish appeals, the US government had named the Kurdistan Workers' Party (PKK) as a foreign terrorist organization, which influenced the European Union's subsequent decision to make a similar designation. I argued that the relationship between our two countries was deep enough to endure Turkish anger over a change in America's policy.

Once Senator Obama announced his bid for the presidency, his campaign sought to capitalize on the strong support he already had among Armenian Americans. Campaign staff who did voter outreach circulated the letter Obama had sent to Secretary Rice, and I made a video in which I promised Armenian Americans that Obama would not let them down as other presidents had. I framed Obama's willingness to recognize the genocide as part of his general propensity to "challenge conventional wisdom and conventional Washington," which he had already demonstrated by speaking out against the Iraq War. In the campaign video, I told viewers that Obama had reached out to me after reading *A Problem from Hell*," which documented the Armenian genocide, and I closed with the most personal endorsement I could offer:

> I know him very well, and he is a person of incredible integrity . . .
> He is a person who can actually be trusted, which distinguishes
> him from some in the Washington culture. So I hope you will
> take him seriously as you have always taken me seriously.

Although the issue was far from the minds of most voters, Obama's campaign website posted his pledge that "as President I will recognize the Armenian Genocide." On election day, by most accounts, Armenian-American voters had supported him en masse.

OBAMA'S FIRST OVERSEAS TRIP as President included a two-day stop in Turkey less than three weeks before Armenian Remembrance Day. I knew that virtually the entire national security establishment would dedicate itself to persuading Obama to avoid using the "g-word" on the trip, but I felt I could make a convincing case for why he should.

To the extent that I had imagined difficult policy debates in government, I had envisaged them as more Technicolor versions of the discussions we had in Obama's Senate office. President Obama would sit in his chair (which now happened to be in the Oval Office). He would pose questions, and we would each state our case. His trusted advisers would then duke it out in front of him. The President would make the tough decision, and we would rush off to implement it. But since I was no longer spending significant time with Obama, I had no way of knowing whether, next to the matters of life and death that he dealt with daily, the recognition question would even be brought to his attention before he flew to Turkey.

Foreign policy debates did happen after the President's daily intelligence briefing in the morning, but only the Vice President, National Security Advisor, and Deputy National Security Advisor regularly took part. The President also convened NSC staff to air disagreements, discuss major problems, and consider time-sensitive issues. But as we approached our two best opportunities for recognizing the genocide during his presidency—his trip to Turkey in early April and his April 24ᵗʰ statement—no such meeting was scheduled.

I bombarded Denis McDonough and speechwriter Ben Rhodes with emails imploring that we somehow find time to discuss the recognition question with Obama before he left for Turkey. Close aides of Obama's during the campaign, Denis and Ben both now had roles at the White House that were more senior than mine, and they generally labored to ensure that Obama's campaign promises were fulfilled.

I tried to tap the insurgent spirit that had permeated the campaign, arguing that Obama should not only recognize the genocide, but do so in Turkey.

"That would be classic Obama," I wrote Denis and Ben, even as I sensed that a more circumspect approach was creeping in.

When I didn't hear back, I urged them to at least ensure that Obama would leave open the question of recognition so we could discuss it upon his return. I pointed out that, for a man who prided himself on gathering his "Team of Rivals" before making hard decisions, the group traveling with him to Turkey held a very one-sided view of the matter.[5] Of those who would be joining him on Air Force One, Ben was the only person pushing for Obama to fulfill his pledge.

In the old days, I would have simply emailed Obama my argument, "process foul" be damned. But while he was the first president to regularly use email, I was not yet among the few people who had his address. When he departed for the trip, I had no idea how he would handle the issue when it arose.

In the President's first press conference in Ankara, Christi Parsons of the *Chicago Tribune* unsurprisingly asked about it:

> You said, as president, you would recognize the genocide. And my question for you is, have you changed your view, and did you ask President Gül to recognize the genocide by name?

Standing beside Turkish president Abdullah Gül, Obama gave a response that had clearly been scripted, and one not dissimilar from the deflections I had heard from US diplomats skirting the issue when testifying on Capitol Hill. He pointed to negotiations then occurring between the Turkish and Armenian governments as offering a channel in which the contested history could be resolved:

> Well, my views are on the record and I have not changed views . . . what I want to do is not focus on my views right now but focus on the views of the Turkish and the Armenian people. If they can move forward and deal with a difficult and tragic history, then I think the entire world should encourage them . . .

> And the best way forward for the Turkish and Armenian people
> is a process that works through the past in a way that is honest,
> open and constructive.

I flinched when I heard the phrase "difficult and tragic history," which was the State Department's preferred euphemistic dodge for genocide. But it was the words "honest" and "open" that really bothered me. How could we urge honesty and openness when we ourselves weren't being honest and open on the issue?

Obama was of course correct that it was the Turks and Armenians who needed to resolve questions about the past. But this was irrelevant. The Turkish government had no intention of truthfully delving into Ottoman history. Moreover, gesturing toward what would be ideal and even necessary didn't absolve our administration of the responsibility to make a clear decision of our own as to whether to recognize the genocide.

When the President returned to the United States, I renewed my efforts to ensure that we would at least debate what should go into the annual commemorative statement on April 24ᵗʰ, when Armenian Americans expected Obama to deliver on his campaign promise. To put the situation in government-speak, it was the best action-forcing event I would have to push the issue.

Having worked at the White House three months, I had observed that government habits and processes tended to be institutionalized reflections of human nature. In life, when we feel uncomfortable about something, we often prefer to avoid discussing it. In government, because there is so much going on, it is especially easy to escape unappealing conversations. Indeed, even when people fully intend to make time to debate a vexing issue, they often get consumed by the crises of the day. On the Armenian genocide, the key players had little incentive to schedule a meeting since any White House deliberation would be both unpleasant *and* jeopardize the status quo. Given Obama's plan to remove US troops from Iraq, and Turkey's importance to regional stability, they were extremely reluctant to upset business as usual. The matter was simply treated as decided.

As Armenian Remembrance Day approached, the National Security Council officials who advised the President on Europe and had organized his trip to Ankara wrote the first draft of the commemorative statement. Because they had "the pen," they had a significant bureaucratic advantage: deciding which edits from others on the NSC to take and which to ignore.

When the draft came to me, I used Track Changes to make significant revisions to the initial, formulaic statement—of course writing in the word "genocide." Each time the original authors circulated a revised draft of the statement, however, they dropped the word. It was a crushingly antiseptic way to realize we were going to dash the hopes of people who had trusted us.

As time ran out, I decided to offer a formulation that would at least break new ground. I inserted Raphael Lemkin and the fact that the Armenian massacres had motivated him to invent the word "genocide." But the Senior Director for European Affairs told me that this approach would be "the worst of both worlds—destined to disappoint the Armenians and enrage the Turks." I should stop trying to be "too clever by half."

I didn't give up. That year, the Holocaust Days of Remembrance ceremony fell on April 23rd, and President Obama was slated to join Holocaust survivor Elie Wiesel and others in the Capitol Rotunda. They would be speaking before a large audience of survivors, American Jewish leaders, members of Congress, and foreign diplomats. When Obama's remarks for the Holocaust memorial event went around for clearance, I tried to insert references to the Armenian genocide there, and my NSC colleagues again rejected my additions. I fell back to trying to add references to the "slaughter of the Armenians," reasoning that nobody in our administration denied that, in 1915, 1.5 million Armenians had been killed. Here too I failed. My colleagues argued that Turkey would be upset to see the massacre of Armenians included in a speech about the Holocaust.

"For them, that would imply that it was genocide," an NSC coworker explained.

"Yes, it would imply that," I said, raising my voice, "because it was genocide!"

OBAMA'S SPEECHWRITER SARA HURWITZ had integrated some of my other ideas into the Holocaust remembrance remarks, and she kindly secured an invitation for me to attend the event. Just as Sara and I disembarked from the staff van at the Capitol, we saw President Obama exiting his limousine ahead of us, making his way up a set of stairs.

When he turned to look behind him, he spotted me and gave a friendly wave, shouting "Hey Sam!" In the old days I might not have registered such a greeting as anything special. But I was grateful. I waved back and joined the group of people trailing him up the stairs.

Since I had not traveled with the President before, I had not yet experienced presidential movement, an epic affair. You go with the flow or you get left outside the fully secure zone that the President inhabits. When Sara and I reached the top of the stairs in the back of the Rotunda, we saw a VIP entrance, through which Valerie Jarrett, David Axelrod, and the other senior staff were making their way to seats. Sara told me she planned to stand in the back behind the media and encouraged me to follow the VIPs to a seat so I could rest my eight-months' pregnant body during the event. Unfortunately, as I hesitated, considering whether to follow Sara or sit, security guards sealed off both the staff and VIP entrances. I suddenly found myself alone.

A Capitol police officer appeared out of nowhere. "Can I help you, ma'am?" he asked gruffly, clearly disconcerted by the sight of a displaced person backstage at a presidential event. I had started the day in a sour mood and now I was stranded.

I resisted the urge to answer, "Yes, sir. You can help me by shouting out 'Armenian genocide' in the middle of this ceremony!" But just as I was about to explain my limbo to the officer, I heard a familiar voice.

"Hey, leave her alone! She's with me."

President Obama had left his holding area to use the bathroom, which happened to be near where I was standing. "Mr. President!"

I exclaimed, flustered, but delighted. This was the first time I had seen him alone since he became President. He gave me a warm embrace, sized up my tummy, and asked how soon I was expecting.

"How are you finding it all?" he asked.

For a split second I thought, "Don't ruin this nice moment with a man who never gets a break. He is talking to you as a friend, not as the President to be lobbied." But I couldn't help myself, as it was not too late for him to change his mind—Armenian Genocide Remembrance Day was still a day away.

"I'm really worried about the Armenians," I said.

Obama's eyes flashed—first in surprise, and then, seemingly, in anger.

I knew I was taking advantage of a chance encounter outside a men's room to try to sway the President on a question that had already been decided, but it was too late to stop now.

"They really counted on us," I continued.

"You know what," the President said, "I'm worried about the Armenians too. But I am worried about the living Armenians. Not the ones we can't bring back. I am living in the present, Samantha, trying to help the Armenians of today."

He was referring, I realized, to US efforts to support the normalization talks between Turks and Armenians. If achieved, the reestablishment of diplomatic relations would have profoundly beneficial economic effects for the citizens of Armenia, and Armenian president Serzh Sargsyan had told Obama he wanted to secure an agreement. Obama had clearly been convinced that if he recognized the genocide, the Turks would be so angry that they would abandon the discussions with Armenia.

I believed he was being misled.

"Mr. President, the talks are not going to work," I said. "We know that the Turks are engaging in the normalization process precisely in order to convince you not to recognize the genocide. But they aren't serious beyond that. As soon as they get through April twenty-fourth, they'll refuse any compromise."

"Well, you know what?" he said sharply, before walking away, "I don't have the luxury of not trying for peace."*

I felt light-headed as the police officer escorted me to a seat. After the event began, I watched Wiesel step up to the podium. He always looked so fragile and small. But as I had witnessed many times before, once he began speaking, the force of his convictions and wisdom made him project like a giant.

After describing what the Hungarian authorities and the Nazis had done to his family, Wiesel found a way to close out his remarks with a proclamation of faith. "In the final analysis," he said, "I believe in man in spite of men." He continued:

> I still cling to words, for it is we who decide whether they become spears or balm, carriers of bigotry or vehicles of understanding, whether they are used to curse or to heal, whether they are here to cause shame or to give comfort.

The power of words. I wondered how President Obama was hearing what Wiesel was saying, and whether he felt any fresh tug to use a word that mattered to so many who had lost so much. I sensed that for all his seeming conviction that he was making the right choice, he was more conflicted than he wanted to reveal. Even though the question of Armenian genocide recognition was a small one in the scope of his presidency, he knew that his decision would cause pain.

But he was the President of the United States. No matter how hard I tried, I would never be able to put myself in his shoes, or appreciate the variables he was weighing. He was getting to know Turkish prime minister Recep Tayyip Erdoğan, and had seen how emotional and erratic he could be. Erdoğan might well retaliate against the United States, even if doing so would harm his own people. And with the US

---

* Although Turkey and Armenia did sign protocols in October of 2009 pledging to normalize relations, the process fell apart by 2010, and the rapprochement never occurred.

economy still losing more than 500,000 jobs each month, and more than 130,000 US troops still stationed in Iraq, Obama must have felt he could not afford to incur the risk.

I also understood—somewhere deep down—that the debate over US recognition was over. If the President wouldn't follow through on his promise in 2009, when he had the most leeway and political capital to take a risk, I knew we would not recognize the genocide during his presidency.

Obama stepped to the podium. The theme of his speech was individual responsibility—how we each must decide whether we stand up or stand by. He talked about the range of factors that made the Holocaust possible, including "the willingness of those who are neither perpetrators nor victims to accept the assigned role of bystander, believing . . . the fiction that we do not have a choice."

I was struck by how strained Obama already looked just three months into the job. A key part of his message had always been that one individual could change lives. Now he was the leader of the free world. With a pen-stroke, he could pardon a person on death row, send American soldiers into battle, or right a historic wrong.

He asked, as one does on such occasions, "How do we ensure that 'never again' isn't an empty slogan or merely an aspiration, but also a call to action?" And he answered, inconveniently in light of the Armenian Remembrance statement that the White House would issue the next day, "I believe we start by doing what we are doing today—by bearing witness, by fighting the silence that is evil's greatest co-conspirator."

The ceremony closed with Cantor Alberto Mizrahi singing "The Song of the Partisans," aka, "Never Say That You Have Reached the Final Road," which a Vilna underground fighter wrote in 1943 upon learning of the Warsaw ghetto uprising. Several Holocaust survivors in the audience sat weeping.

AS I GOT UP to leave, emotionally drained, several European ambassadors stopped me to express gratitude for the President's remarks. Not wanting to be rude, I lingered. But by the time I looked around, I no longer saw any of the White House officials who had been part of Obama's delegation. I grew frazzled and hurried in the direction of the motorcade.

When I walked outside into an unseasonably warm April day, I saw a row of armored black SUVs and vans. I knocked on one of the SUV's windows, which the driver opened. "Is this the White House convoy?" I asked.

"No," he said pointing off into the distance, "that is."

I saw a formidable lineup of vehicles, which included the President's limo and his many police escorts, speeding away. I had been left behind.

It was all too much. Standing in the hot sun, I called Cass and asked him to leave the meeting he was in because I needed him—still an unusual admission on my part.

"It was so horrible," I began rambling. "He is not going to recognize the genocide. He is furious with me. And he actually thinks he is doing the right thing—for Armenians! And after that all the speakers talked about the importance of words and remembering history so we don't repeat it. Then they drove off without me."

Cass waited me out calmly. "I am so proud of you," he said simply. This set me off again.

"Proud of me? How can you be proud of me? I failed all those people, and tomorrow they are going to be so sad. Some of them are one hundred years old!"

Cass could probably tell I was not in the proper frame of mind to be reasoned with. "Just come back to the office," he said. I looked down and realized I hadn't brought my purse with me.

"I can't," I said. "I don't have any money." He said he would wait for me outside the White House and pay the taxi driver.

Sitting in the taxi, I felt eighteen, not eight months' pregnant. When the taxi pulled up to the corner where my husband was standing, Cass handed cash to the driver and hugged me on the sidewalk for a very long time. After we walked into the EEOB and cleared security, he held my hand and deposited me in my office.

For the next hour, I worked at my computer, making a list of the leaders of the major Armenian-American groups I would need to call in advance of the President's commemorative statement the next day. They had been checking in by email and phone for days, seeking hopeful hints about what Obama planned to say. I dreaded talking to them.

Although the air conditioner in my office was on, the room felt like it was steaming up. My clothes were sticking to me, and, when I got up to go to the restroom, I noticed that my pants were damp. I returned to the piles of work on my desk, starting to wonder if all the day's stress and emotion should concern me.

I called my obstetrician and described how I was feeling. As a precaution, he told me to make my way to Sibley Hospital. I didn't want to leave work mid-afternoon, but agreed, telling my colleagues that I needed to make a quick trip to the hospital. "I will be back in an hour or two," I said.

As soon as I arrived, a Sibley nurse ushered me in for tests. "Honey, you're not going anywhere," she soon declared. "Your water broke today."

I was stunned. I had imagined that when one's water broke it gushed forth. My official due date was several weeks away.

"But I haven't bought a stroller yet!" I cried, adding, "and I didn't turn off my computer." Even as I said these words, I knew how ridiculous they were.

I suddenly felt euphoric. The doctors could not pinpoint exactly when my water had broken, but it seemed to have happened around the time of my sharp exchange with the President, or perhaps just after, as I sat listening to the speeches.

Eighteen hours after I was admitted to Sibley Memorial Hospital—with Cass, Mum, and Eddie on hand—Declan Power Sunstein was born. He entered the world on April 24th, 2009, Armenian Genocide Remembrance Day.

22

TURNAROUND

Even though I had been firm in my intention to take three months of maternity leave, everyone who knew me insisted that I would be unable to put down my BlackBerry. I assumed that they were right. I had never not worked; from the time I was a child, my life had entailed constant motion. Whether moving among cities and countries or juggling teaching, activism, and writing, I tended to fill downtime.

But after April 24th, 2009, for the first time in my life, I became virtually still. I found myself able to sit for an eternity, simply staring into the green eyes of my redheaded newborn. In times past, when I took a break from work, I was prone to bouts of anxiety. But this time lungers did not return. As a new mother, I of course had to fight the urge to focus constantly on my son's health and safety. Since I still half expected tragedy to befall my loved ones, I tried to fixate on the present and block out fears for the future. Each night before I went to sleep, I would remind myself, "Every day is a blessing," often whispering the words to Cass.

During my time off, I also thought a lot about the early struggles I'd been having at the White House. Experiencing such a drop-off in contact with Obama had been a shock to my system—and my ego. Even before entering government, I had known that who participated in meetings was often as contested as what was decided. Still, as a long-time member of Obama's circle of advisers, I had wrongly assumed that access wouldn't be an issue for me. During my early months, I had been genuinely surprised to find myself—in the almost comical new lingo of the bureaucracy—"not manifested" for important deliberations on Iraq and Afghanistan, conflicts that I had been discussing with Obama since 2005.

Instead of recognizing the division of labor that necessarily occurs in government, I took it personally. Others around me had long forgotten about my gaffe during the campaign. My relationship with Secretary Clinton, while not close, was cordial. Nonetheless, I remained distressed by what had happened. When I was not included in meetings—meetings that, when I did get to attend, usually proved underwhelming—I began to feel as though my colleagues didn't trust me or value what I had to say. But now, with more distance from the office, I could see that perhaps I had not been invited simply because my bosses were trying to avoid overcrowding meetings with NSC staff.*

I began to focus on all I could still do as part of the Obama administration. While other national security officials weighed options for the US-led war in Afghanistan, I could try to mobilize people around initiatives of my own. Working on lower-profile issues would give me more room to maneuver and involve fewer senior people peering over my shoulder.

I would not get to travel abroad as often as I had as a journalist, but that meant I would be able to work on important foreign policy issues by day and cuddle up with "my boys"—Cass and Declan—by night. My new cravings as a mother obliterated other longings. "Declan gives me calm," I wrote in my journal. "I want to bring that calm to work with me, and retain it."

Above all, I realized that I had allowed the indignities I felt to crowd out the basic, thrilling reality that I worked at the White House for President Barack Obama. In just the short period during which he had been in office, Obama had made high-risk decisions that were helping turn the economy around. He was putting in place desperately

---

* Secretary of State Clinton and Secretary of Defense Gates were usually allowed to bring only a single aide to NSC meetings, and they understandably complained when they saw NSC staff filling the scarce seats lining the walls of the Situation Room.

needed regulations to lower carbon emissions and developing a plan that would eventually provide health insurance to more than 20 million Americans. And in foreign policy, he had banned torture and begun negotiations with Russia to reduce our respective nuclear arsenals. He had three and a half years left in his first term and no guarantee of a second term. I had never been given an opportunity like this, and I could not count on ever getting one again.

I couldn't change the fact that there would be times when the President would make a decision that I recoiled from, as had happened with recognition of the Armenian Genocide. I was going to take those moments hard. But at least I understood Obama's logic. And I certainly had not entered government expecting that it would be easy to fulfill every campaign pledge or win every battle to inject concern for human consequences into high-level decision-making. After all, I had written a book on how normal bureaucratic habits pull the system in predictable directions. I was profoundly privileged to be in a position where I could at least try to make a difference.

Of course, I still felt pangs when I saw others at the center of the action. I was in the middle of maternity leave on June 4th, 2009, when Obama delivered a major address to the Muslim world from Egypt. His speech bravely touched upon core tensions between the United States and Muslim societies—violent extremism, religious freedom, women's rights, and the Israeli-Palestinian conflict.

My only contribution to the remarks had been urging Ben to ensure that the President renounced the use of military force to bring democracy to other countries. Out of the President's mouth, I heard words I knew Obama deeply believed: "No system of government can or should be imposed upon one nation by any other." As I sat nursing six-week-old Declan at home on our red IKEA couch, I found myself wishing I were in Cairo with the President, Ben, and the others.

I scoured the internet for reactions. Most of the commentary seemed to appreciate Obama's "refreshing" and "humble" tone, but people wanted to see what concrete policies followed. Obama seemed to have a rare chance to push for reform in a part of the world where horizons were dimmed by corrupt economies and political repression.

IN JULY OF 2009, my three months of leave were up. I kissed Declan goodbye and placed him in the arms of our new live-in nanny, María Castro. María was the single reason I would be able to work fourteen-hour days in national security for eight years during the Obama administration.

María hailed from near Guadalajara, Mexico, and, from the start, she treated Declan as if she would want to spend even her days off with him. She took him to Mass and taught him to speak Spanish. She was so present in our son's life that his first word was "*lota*," short for the Spanish *pelota*, or ball. "Mama" (mercifully!) came next. And "Mima," his version of María, emerged not long thereafter.

By the time Cass and I would arrive home around nine p.m., María had usually managed to prepare dinner while also keeping Declan entertained. Even that late at night, she somehow projected the sprightliness of one who was just starting her day.

María's family and my family grew close. When one of María's daughters had children, Declan viewed them as little brothers, and María's daughters, grandchildren, and husband spent lots of time at our home while María worked. In her time off, she once traveled overseas on vacation with Mum and Eddie, while Declan stayed home with me. She was, of course, our employee, and she made tremendous sacrifices to work long hours to support us, but at times I felt as though our two families had joined forces.

Still, because my hours were so punishing, even a full-time nanny as devoted as María was not enough. When I returned to work, I also enrolled Declan in a daycare located in the basement of a government building across the street from the White House. This proximity allowed me to pop over a couple of times each day to nurse him on a rocking chair beside his crib before María came to collect him in the late afternoon.

While I had occasionally forgotten to eat when I was a pregnant White House staffer, I never forgot Declan's appetite. I did my best to prioritize visits with him over just about every other activity in my day, dashing to his daycare, nursing, and then hustling back across 17th Street. On occasions when I was unexpectedly summoned to the National Security Advisor's office for a time-sensitive meeting, it pained me to call the daycare to tell them that they should go ahead and give Declan a bottle with the milk I had left that morning. And when I was running late for a feeding, I had no compunction about sprinting in heels down the stately corridors of the EEOB and out the White House gates.

Because I was chairing so many meetings throughout the day, I had almost no margin of error for these visits. On several occasions, I caught myself mindlessly beginning to unbutton my blouse as I exited the White House grounds. Once, one of my NSC colleagues crossing in the other direction spotted me and grinned. "Busted!" I shouted out joyfully as I ran past. The moment seemed to highlight the sheer absurdity of the number of tasks all of us were cramming into each day. With rare exceptions, though, I did not feel distracted at work because I now had a child. If anything, motherhood made me more focused and efficient, given that every extra hour at the office meant another hour away from my son.

Like so many parents whose work deprives them of the time they crave with their children, I was all too aware that I would never get to redo the parts of Declan's early months and years that were whirring by. I told myself that I was "binging" in my work life and that the day would come when I would binge with my family, creating a permanent home. Still, every couple of months during my time in the administration, I tried to step back to assess whether I was getting enough done in my job to justify all the time away. Even during productive periods, I never felt great about my choices.

ONE DEVELOPMENT THAT DRAMATICALLY IMPROVED my work environment was acquiring a new set of friends. Gayle Smith, the Senior Director for Development and Democracy, occupied an office just down the hall from mine. Gayle, also a former journalist, had distinctive short silver hair styled like Grace Jones's. She had served as President Clinton's Senior Director for African Affairs, surprising herself by proving a complete natural in government. She understood my initial struggles to get situated and patiently explained the way policymaking worked. I knew Gayle was becoming more than just a work friend when I walked into her office and saw that she had printed out a photo of Declan and hung it on her wall. Gayle insisted that, if we wanted to build team feeling, we needed to take matters into our own hands. She invited me over to her home for Thai takeout, encouraging me to bring Declan, and we began plotting how we could more than double our impact.

One Wednesday, Liz Sherwood-Randall, the NSC Senior Director for European Affairs, invited the President's NSC Legal Advisor Mary DeRosa, Gayle, and me to stop by her office for a glass of wine. What was supposed to be a quick break turned into a ninety-minute release, with each of us apologetically calling our assistants to ask if they could move our next appointments owing to "urgent business." We had so much to discuss—our frustrations at the NSC, but also what we were proud of and what we hoped to achieve. This first relatively spontaneous invitation turned into a sacred weekly "girls' hour" of wine, cheese, and gossip. As women rotated onto and off the NSC staff, the participants evolved.

A few years before, when John Prendergast and I had attended Al-Anon meetings for the family members of alcoholics, we had both seized upon an Al-Anon motto that seemed profound: "Never compare your insides to somebody else's outsides." Yet before I joined what we listed on our official calendars as the "Wednesday Group," I had been doing just that with my White House colleagues. *They* strode commandingly around the office. *They* were constantly briefing the President. I felt like the odd person out. But as I got to know my fellow female Senior Directors and began peeling back the layers, I learned about their own struggles. One was trying to raise two teenage boys with a spouse who commuted from California on the weekends; another had a child who was seriously struggling in school.

When I complimented one of my new friends on the framed photograph of her briefing President Obama, she responded with sweet vulnerability, saying "I was so excited when someone told me the photographer was there." Another colleague confided that the large number of candid shots displayed of her with the President was misleading. "Basically, every single time I have been in his presence, I have requested a photo," she said. "I hang every one of them up because it makes foreign diplomats think I'm a big deal." Over time, I learned that I was not even the only one to have relied on the *Washington Post*'s map to find the Oval Office.

These Wednesday evening get-togethers became one of the few immovable parts of my schedule. As I had experienced with the female reporters in Bosnia, I felt part of a sisterhood—like these women would support me, no matter what. Each of us gave the others a quality of attention that was too often lacking in the transactional world we inhabited. When I shared my habit of always fearing the worst when I couldn't reach Cass, María, or my parents, I was amazed to learn that others leaped to similar worries. Delving deeper into the lives of my colleagues was a precious reminder of the relevance of "Never compare your insides to somebody else's outsides," a mantra I learned to keep at the forefront of my mind.

Beyond our Wednesday night sessions, a change also crept into the way we acted in the day-to-day NSC policy debates that were central to getting work done. Without ever discussing it or making a conscious shift, we reflexively engaged one another in meetings. This did not mean we always agreed with one another; some of my most heartfelt arguments were with my fellow female Senior Directors. But we took one another's ideas seriously. This meant never leaving them simply hanging in the air, which typically happened in large group discussions.

When I am asked today what it was like working in the national security world as a woman, I don't have a simple answer. Although Obama had appointed more women to cabinet-level national security roles than any president in history, his NSC was the most male-dominated place I had ever been in the United States. Men held the positions of National Security Advisor, Deputy National Security Advisor, Homeland Security Advisor, NSC Chief of Staff, Strategic Communications Advisor, and speechwriter. During that first year of the administration, this top NSC tier was supported by twenty-six Senior Directors—and only six of us were women.

I was fortunate never to experience sexual harassment of the kind I knew many other women had endured.* And while I could tell I was being condescended to at times, I could never be sure it was because of my gender. I started out as a complete novice in government, and in debates, I often advocated on behalf of human rights, which national security professionals generally viewed as a "soft," secondary priority. But being with the Wednesday Group made me feel the power of numbers.

I also came to appreciate one advantage I had: I played basketball. Soon after returning from maternity leave, I joined regular games that took place at the Department of the Interior and on a court that Obama had refurbished just off the White House lawn. Playing pickup with other administration officials gave me relationships I could never have cultivated through regular office interactions. I not only competed and joked around with my male colleagues, but also cornered them to lobby for my latest cause. I finally understood why so many men played golf, and the professional disadvantages that accrued to women (and men) who didn't.

FROM WHERE CASS AND I PARKED every morning, the most direct route to our offices was simply to stroll two blocks down 17th Street and turn west into the EEOB, where we worked on opposite sides of the sprawling building. But when I returned from leave, Cass started insisting that we enter the building through the front gate of the White House, adding five extra minutes to our walk.

---

* In November of 2017, as the #MeToo movement was unfolding, more than two hundred women in the American national security community—including colleagues of mine from the Obama administration—signed an open letter that offered a stinging assessment of how women were treated within our profession. Noting that sexual harassment and abuse was "not just a problem in Hollywood, Silicon Valley, newsrooms or Congress," the letter stated, "Many women are held back or driven from the national security field by men who use their power to assault at one end of the spectrum and perpetuate—sometimes unconsciously—environments that silence, demean, belittle or neglect women at the other."

As early as 7:00 a.m., as we flashed our badges and underwent a security screening, we would see tourists pressing their faces up to the iron gates. They hoped to spot, if not the President himself, then at least Bo, the Obama family dog, or the television reporters who were doing their morning stand-ups on the lawn.

When the workday ended late, I was so eager to be reunited with Declan that I was tempted to forgo this circuitous path back to our car. However, Cass refused to let me deviate, insisting we walk by the illuminated White House on our way out. These daily strolls became a kind of gratitude ritual for the opportunity that we shared.

At the office, I tried to follow through on the commitments I had made to myself while on leave. With Denis's support, I expanded the size of my staff from one NSC quasi-deputy (or "director") to four; with each NSC director who worked under me, we would be able to drive progress on three or four more real-world issues.

My early hires had been men, in part because many of the talented women I approached about working at the NSC told me they were turned off by the notoriously grueling hours. But for the first time, I began aggressively reaching out to women who had made an impression on me in meetings, trying to convince them to join my small team rather than waiting for them to apply. I also dedicated more energy to building coalitions with like-minded individuals across government. And I regularized the practice of holding several meetings each week with outside groups to be sure I was continually being exposed to fresh thinking.

The aspect of government that I had least appreciated before I joined was the importance—and shortage—of "bandwidth." So much was going on in the world on any given day that one could easily lose an afternoon editing language in various press releases. Mort, my longtime mentor, urged me to prioritize, helping me understand my days as analogous to my mother's when she worked in the emergency room. He advised me to start by doing triage: patients with life-threatening conditions should be seen first. At the same time, I needed to look for opportunities. Was there a place in the world that was ripe for reform? Was there a conflict or situation where, with more diplomacy, resources, or pressure, the United States could make a positive impact?

Richard Holbrooke, whom Obama had named Special Representative for Afghanistan and Pakistan, was also influential in shaping this approach. At the height of my frustrations with my new role, he had taken me to Martin's Tavern in Georgetown for a cheeseburger. He wisely urged me to change my focus. Rather than fighting to get into meetings where I would be outnumbered, he suggested I prioritize issues about which there might be no White House meetings at all.

Holbrooke summed up this advice in one phrase: "Go where they ain't." By "they," he meant senior US officials. Legions of government aides flocked to consequential issues that drew presidential attention. But all around the world, immense suffering was occurring in forgotten places. With even a modest time investment, one could support positive change in ways that would not make the evening news. Lower down in the bureaucracy, he and Mort both stessed, one could also find enthusiastic partners brimming with ideas about how to help.

If ever I sounded self-conscious that I was not working on "big-ticket" foreign policy challenges, Holbrooke would snap me out of this myopia. "Stop it, Sam," he would say. "Do good where you can do good. The people in those countries don't give a damn how high a priority what you do is to anybody else. They don't have another hope besides America."

He boosted my spirits, telling me that as long as I fixated on getting things done and "not the bullshit," I would earn a reputation for competence. I took his message to heart, telling my team that our prime asset was our doggedness. "We just have to care more," I said. Our comparative advantage would be that we would never give up.

A month after returning from leave, my attitude had been transformed. I sent Cass an email message that included just one line: "Revelation: I love my job."

IN THIS SPIRIT of constructive opportunism, I thought I could help Iraqi refugees garner stronger support from the US government. At my urging back in 2007, then-candidate Obama had pledged to expand humanitarian assistance to the four million Iraqis who had been displaced in the wake of the US invasion and to increase the number of Iraqis resettled in the United States. Instead of meeting resistance when I tried to ensure we followed through on these promises, I encountered many US officials who had themselves lived in Iraq and were especially concerned about those who had risked their lives working as translators for the US military. By the time Obama took office, at least three hundred of these Iraqis had already been murdered as retribution for assisting our soldiers.*

After some bureaucratic wrangling, I got myself designated "White House coordinator for Iraqi refugees," which would show both the Iraqi government and US officials across the administration the emphasis President Obama was placing on this issue. To see the scope of what needed to be done, I decided to try again to make a foreign trip in my official government capacity. This time, my travel was approved.

The sense of satisfaction I felt at finally being able to leave the insular world of Washington was immediately dimmed by the realization that I would be away from Declan for the first time since his birth nearly seven months before. My mind began to run wild, imagining the various ways I would die on the trip. After landing in Iraq, our vehicle would be attacked on "Ambush alley," the road that connected Baghdad Airport to the Green Zone. Or we would make it to the US embassy—a $740 million fortress larger than Vatican City—but as soon as we ventured outside to meet displaced Iraqis, a suicide bomber would ram his truck into our convoy. Here, my morbid thoughts were especially vivid, because of the year I had spent reporting on the 2003 suicide bomb attack on the UN base in Baghdad that had killed Sergio Vieira de Mello and twenty-two others.

By the eve of the trip, I had spiraled into what the intelligence community would call "moderate confidence" that I would not be returning home. Cass was not helping. He had not known me back when I traveled

---

* Some 142,000 Iraqis had worked for the US government, military, and other US-backed programs since the beginning of the war in 2003. As a result of their work, many had been branded "traitors" by Iraqi extremists and gone into hiding.

to dangerous places, and his idea of a far-flung destination was Florida. He thought the idea of willingly taking a trip to Iraq was insane. He harped on the issue for days, repeatedly urging me to reconsider.

Since I was determined to go, I decided I would write my young son a letter in case my worst fears were realized. Rereading the letter today, it is jarring—and moving—to see how determined I was to express to Declan what my father had never been able to say to me. But it is probably also not unlike the letters thousands of service members, aid workers, diplomats, and journalists have written their own loved ones before deploying.

November 12, 2009

Dear Declan,

You are reading this note because something bad happened to your mother. I have had six months and almost three weeks with you. They filled me—you filled me—with the greatest sense of peace I have ever known. When you came out, your dad cried, "He has red hair!" and from that moment we were joined as red heads—determined, proud, ferocious, observant—and this is the most important part—kind red heads. You and me Declan, two Irish beings together taking on the world.

The most important thing for you to know is that you have the best father any child could have or has had. Cass is the best father because he is the best man. He has an enormous heart. It is almost too big for this world. Sometimes cynicism and deceit escape him because he can only do goodness. You were born to more love concentrated between two people than words can really capture. Maybe you can watch the video of our wedding and catch a glimpse. The love was almost instant (though I was in denial for a while!) and it was completely unwavering. We used to have contests as to who loved each other more. Maybe you and he will have these contests together some day. Cass can love infinitely, and you will bathe in the glow of that love for the rest of your life. I have never been happier. Even the lowest moments of the last two years were life highs because I was sitting beside Cass.

The second thing you should know is that you changed my life. I used to work really hard—really long hours with a really single-minded focus—and I used to think that work to change the world was my reason for being on this Earth. I still want to change that world—this is why I'm going to Iraq—but my new reason for being is you and your daddy, our family. Every night when I rush up the back stairs and down the hall, and you hear my footsteps and crane your neck back toward the door from the red couch, I am soothed. Whatever my failures at the office, or my frustrations, I touch your soft skin, and am struck by a flash of amnesia so potent that it is literally as though the day hasn't happened at all. By the time I am grabbing you and we are dancing toward the bath, I am blissfully happy. Every minute we had together was a blessing and made my life better.

The third and final thing I would like you to know is that you have the capacity to take care of many people in your long life. Please start with your daddy, the love of my life. And then, when you're ready, look around at all the people in need around you. You, Declan Power Sunstein, will be a boy and man of many gifts. That is obvious already. Please share them with others. (But don't forget to start with daddy, and also with granny and Eddie, who taught me everything and, like Cass, know how to love fully.) And as you grow up, please know that whenever you hear thunder, that will be me. Whenever the Red Sox win in the ninth, that will be me. Whenever you and daddy dance together, know that I am there too. I will always be watching my boys. My boys, whom I love so much that I feel my heart will burst.

Love, Mum

The morning I left for the airport, Cass continued to plead with me to cancel. Then, belatedly realizing he was compounding my sadness and worry, he switched gears. As I finished packing, I suddenly heard Tom Petty and the Heartbreakers blaring on full volume from our bedroom: "You don't have to live like a refugee . . ." As Cass so often managed to do, he made me smile.

When we parted, he also came through with a wonderful saying that became our go-to phrase: "Feel the fear and do it anyway," he told me.

As compared to almost everyone else in Iraq, the truth was that I was kept remarkably safe. Unlike when I was traveling solo as a journalist, as an official US visitor I was encased in an armed bubble at virtually all times. In the old days, the security precautions would have made me feel shackled. But because of my new family, I was grateful. The flipside of this protection was that I saw just how many US service members put themselves in harm's way on behalf of civilian visitors like me. They staked out our routes and venues before we arrived, flew us in helicopters over insurgent areas, and drove convoys through congested streets.

Although I would meet with the Iraqi prime minister and his senior aides, the most important part of the trip was my dialogue with dozens of Iraqi displaced persons. Many described dire living conditions and spoke longingly of their previous neighborhoods, from which they had been expelled just because they were Sunni or Shia. I also met with US military officers who begged me to do more to help their translators reach safety in the United States.

Once I had returned to Washington, I went to work expanding support for Iraqis, whose lives the US invasion had irreparably changed. I successfully fought to increase by some $50 million the resources we could make available to those trying to return to their homes. I also pushed to resettle more Iraqis to the United States, an initiative on which the Bush administration had done far too little.[6] On average, we were able to bring some 17,000 Iraqis to the United States each year of Obama's presidency, including thousands of interpreters and other US-affiliated Iraqis, and their families. And when we discovered that the Iraqis arriving in the United States were getting so little financial support that they were quickly falling into poverty, working with Eric Schwartz, the tireless assistant secretary of state for refugees, we found a way to double the modest initial stipend newly resettled refugees received.*

DESPITE MY ENTHUSIASM for my job, when I got up each morning I did not look forward to opening the emails and alerts that had come in overnight, describing a coup, massacre, terrorist attack, or natural disaster happening somewhere in the world.

In October of 2009, I awoke to a very different form of bad news: Barack Obama had been awarded the Nobel Peace Prize. Less than a year into his presidency, Obama was receiving an award previously bestowed on Nelson Mandela, Mother Teresa, and Dr. Martin Luther King, Jr.

When I relayed the news to Cass, he looked stricken, as if I had told him someone we knew had fallen ill. The choice seemed wildly premature, as well as a gift to Obama's critics, who delighted in painting him as a cosmopolitan celebrity detached from the concerns of working-class Americans. But there was no getting around it: come December of 2009, Obama would travel to Norway to accept the most prestigious prize in the world.

Jon Favreau and Ben Rhodes, Obama's two gifted speechwriters, took on the difficult task of drafting the Nobel address. I popped into Jon's tiny office on the first floor of the West Wing, and he told me that the President had decided to directly confront the awkwardness of receiving the prize so early in his presidency. He also wanted to frame the speech around the more profound irony of winning a peace prize at the very time he was deploying 30,000 additional soldiers to Afghanistan, augmenting the force of over 67,000 US troops already there.

---

* The stipend, which covers refugees' first three months in the United States, had been $900 a month for decades. This was hardly a windfall. Most refugees arrive to the United States in extremely precarious financial situations, but they are required to reimburse the US government for the full cost of their travel, which often totals thousands of dollars and drives them into debt soon after arrival.

This could be Obama's most important speech yet, I thought, as my mind lit up with a million ideas about how he could use it to meditate on profound questions of war and peace, modern-day evil, and the ethics of responsibility. The following day, I set my alarm for four a.m., fed Declan, and then sat down at my home computer to work. I grabbed books from my shelf on the modern history of efforts to regulate warfare. I dug into the writings of the American theologian Reinhold Niebuhr, whom I had first read in law school in the class about the political and moral criteria for using force. And over the course of a few hours, I wrote a detailed memo that offered thoughts on how the President could use "just war theory" as a frame to explain his vision for what he called "our common security, common humanity." This was the most animated and assured I could remember feeling since I entered government.

I emailed my lengthy memo on warfare and morality to Jon and Ben, who, with time expiring, were too immersed in drafting the speech to look at it. Determined to get a hearing for my ideas, I brought the memo to Denis, who initially agreed to give it to Obama, but then, after I had checked on its status multiple times, informed me that the President was immersed in finalizing his decision on the new Afghanistan strategy. He would not have time to read it.

I subsequently took to carrying a copy of the memo around, wondering how I could get past the gatekeepers to the one person I thought might appreciate it. Then, in a stroke of fortune, just a few days before the speech, Obama's motorcade pulled up as I was exiting the West Wing. When he stepped out of his limousine, he saw me and shouted over the heads of the Secret Service, "We need to talk."

The day before he was scheduled to fly to Oslo, Obama summoned me to the Oval and described the outlines of the address he wanted to give. "I have the clay. I can see in it the shape of what I'm trying to do," he said. "But I just may not have enough time to execute."

As he spoke, I interrupted excitedly with thoughts, which he then riffed off. I felt like nothing had changed since the Senate days when we first discussed books and ideas. After forty-five minutes, he was given a note saying he needed to wrap up. I handed him the memo I had prepared, which included a history of humanitarianism, an account of the relationship between human rights and conflict, and thoughts on violence from Hume, Kant, Martin Luther King, Jr., Niebuhr, and Henry Dunant, the founder of the International Committee for the Red Cross.

Obama stayed up through the night, starting a new speech from scratch and developing an elaborate, deeply original, handwritten draft on a yellow legal pad. In the morning, he called Jon, Ben, and me into the Oval to walk us through what he had done. The President had produced a piece of rhetoric that embraced contradictions that most politicians blew past. He rejected pacifism in the face of evil and aggression; at the same time, he insisted that while soldiers could achieve great glory, "war itself is never glorious." He criticized the "reflexive suspicion" toward the United States and the use of military force prevalent in Europe, defending America's record in underwriting the global order and the modern-day peace in Germany, Korea, and the Balkans.

"I understand why war is not popular," Obama had written. "But I also know this: the belief that peace is desirable is rarely enough to achieve it. Peace requires responsibility."

As we walked out of the Oval, Obama put his hand on my shoulder and said, "We may just have to bring you along as a stowaway." Within an hour, I had received a formal invitation to fly on Air Force One. I raced home, packed a suitcase, and kissed Declan goodbye, calling Cass from a cab on the way to the airport to tell him that I was on my way to Norway.

Jon, Ben, Denis, David Axelrod, and I worked through the night in the airplane conference room. The President, dressed in a golf shirt and khakis, wandered in and out with his handwritten edits as we each tried to reconcile the core tensions inherent in his argument. It did not seem ideal that Obama was pulling what appeared to be his second consecutive all-nighter, so we were relieved when he retired for a few hours of sleep. When he awoke, he dove back into the speech, refining it until Denis told him he had to let it go.

An hour later, I sat in Oslo City Hall along with around a thousand others and listened to Obama deliver his Nobel address.

> As someone who stands here as a direct consequence of Dr. King's life work, I am living testimony to the moral force of non-violence. I know there's nothing weak—nothing passive—nothing naive—in the creed and lives of Gandhi and King.
>
> But as a head of state sworn to protect and defend my nation, I cannot be guided by their examples alone. I face the world as it is, and cannot stand idle in the face of threats to the American people. For make no mistake: evil does exist in the world. A non-violent movement could not have halted Hitler's armies. Negotiations cannot convince al-Qaeda's leaders to lay down their arms. To say that force may sometimes be necessary is not a call to cynicism—it is a recognition of history; the imperfections of man and the limits of reason.

He rejected the false choice between realism and idealism, saying:

> I believe that peace is unstable where citizens are denied the right to speak freely or worship as they please; choose their own leaders or assemble without fear. Pent-up grievances fester, and the suppression of tribal and religious identity can lead to violence. We also know that the opposite is true. Only when Europe became free did it finally find peace. America has never fought a war against a democracy, and our closest friends are governments that protect the rights of their citizens. No matter how callously defined, neither America's interests—nor the world's—are served by the denial of human aspirations . . .
>
> We can acknowledge that oppression will always be with us, and still strive for justice. We can admit the intractability of depravation, and still strive for dignity. Clear-eyed, we can understand that there will be war, and still strive for peace.

The crowd was taut with concentration until the very end, but once Obama finished, people erupted into sustained applause.

Barack Obama was the only President in my lifetime capable of such an address. *New York Times* columnist David Brooks wrote, "The Oslo speech was the most profound of his presidency, and maybe his life." Even predictable Republican critics of the President praised it, including Newt Gingrich and Sarah Palin.

On the plane home, I reflected on all that had conspired to produce the speech—not only Obama's willingness to confront big, hard questions, and clarifying thinking from people who lived long ago, but also bureaucratic gridlock and a chance encounter. The drafting process had been a tightrope walk, but it had come together beautifully.

23

TOOLBOX

From our earliest conversations, Obama and I had talked about the recurrence and seeming inevitability of mass atrocities. We discussed not what it would look like to eliminate evil, a utopian fantasy, but rather, how to *optimize* what the United States did in response. Now that Obama was the president and I was his human rights adviser responsible for atrocity prevention, we had a chance to actually implement the kinds of changes we had batted around.

Researching *"A Problem from Hell,"* I had observed that deliberations about how to prevent mass atrocities rarely took place in a timely way among senior decision-makers in the US government. And lower-level US officials who pushed for action lacked the power to authorize it, finding themselves mired in bureaucratic gridlock while violence spread. Partly as a result, the US government often failed to employ low-cost tools—such as sending diplomats to apply pressure or mediate, cutting off the flow of weapons to a country, or working at the UN to deploy international peacekeepers.

In my writing and activism, I had argued that US officials should respond with a sense of urgency to early-warning signs, and that they should be empowered to alert senior decision-makers to threats of violence. High-level officials should then open their toolbox, scrutinizing whether or not the benefits of employing a particular tool outweighed the costs.

People who knew me before I met Obama expected the hardest

part of my adjustment to working at the White House would be taming my outspokenness.

But when people asked, "Do you miss having your own voice?" I could barely fathom the question.

"The reason I was exercising my voice before was to influence people in jobs like the one I now have," I would say. "A voice is not an end in itself."

Now that I was a US official, I hoped to prod the system to speedily consider US and international options to mitigate violence.

PRESIDENT OBAMA LIKED TO QUOTE from a scene in *The Departed* where Mark Wahlberg and a fellow cop are on a stakeout. When the other policeman loses the man they are tracking, an enraged Wahlberg begins yelling at the officer, who indignantly shouts back, "Well, who the fuck are you?"

"I'm the guy who does his job," Wahlberg responds. "You must be the other guy."

With a similar dynamic in mind, I lobbied for the creation of the first-ever White House position to coordinate the US government's response to atrocities.[7] I was responsible for all multilateral affairs and human rights issues; I needed a single individual by my side who would think full-time about how to prevent mass atrocities. Together, we could push senior decision-makers to authorize action before violence spiraled out of hand, incurring fewer risks and conceivably saving more lives.

After consulting with President Obama, Denis McDonough (who had replaced Lippert as NSC Chief of Staff) agreed to create the position of NSC Director for War Crimes and Atrocities, which would report to me. I had a very specific person in mind for the role: a thirty-two-year-old civil rights lawyer named David Pressman, who had served as an aide to Madeleine Albright when she was Secretary of State.

I had gotten to know David back in 2005, when he worked with George Clooney to intensify public pressure on the Bush administration to do more to prevent atrocities in Darfur. He was full of contradictions. He projected ambition, and over the years had cultivated an impressive Rolodex of contacts in both political parties. He said he became a lawyer because he viewed law as a "language of power." Yet David's Machiavellian sensibility had a beautiful twist—he ruthlessly pursued the goal of protecting vulnerable people.

True to this aim, during law school he secured a clerkship on the Supreme Court . . . of Rwanda. And while David could be argumentative to a fault, he also had an endearing ability to laugh at himself. I had heard the acronym GSD—Get Shit Done—used to praise people who were effective in government, and I was confident that David's GSD score would be high. He was destined to break large amounts of bureaucratic crockery, but I could not imagine achieving the kind of change I sought without him.

Once David assumed the newly created position, I could count on finding him in the office when I arrived early in the morning, and he usually stayed well after I left late at night. I don't think I ever came in to the EEOB on the weekend without finding our office door unlocked and David pounding away on his keyboard. Because I had been unable to secure additional office space, my administrative assistant's tiny cubicle had been partitioned into two. Both she and David worked without complaint in a jury-rigged space not much larger than a mid-sized refrigerator. "You've come a long way since hanging out with movie stars," I teased him.

David and I met with people inside and outside the US government to devise a list of meaningful reforms. And we drafted a directive that President Obama soon issued to his cabinet, declaring that "preventing mass atrocities and genocide is a core national security interest and a core moral responsibility of the United States" and creating an Atrocities Prevention Board, the first White House–led structure tasked to react to early warnings of atrocities.

From there, Obama directed the intelligence community to prepare an unprecedented National Intelligence Estimate (NIE) identifying the places facing the greatest risk of mass atrocities. He licensed the creation of "alert channels" so that information about unfolding crises could more easily reach decision-makers, including him. He directed the Pentagon to incorporate the prevention of atrocities into its train-ing and contingency planning. He banned violators of human rights from entering the United States.[8] And he called on the private sector to create new technologies that could expose or authenticate violations of human rights.

But while these moves were trailblazing, the real test of the US government's seriousness about preventing mass atrocities would come, of course, in the real world.

IN 2010, ON THE FIFTEENTH ANNIVERSARY of the Srebrenica mas-sacre, I returned to Bosnia as a US official, touching down in a Sa-rajevo that had been transformed from the war zone I'd lived in as a young reporter. The Bosnian government had designated July 11th, the anniversary of Srebrenica's fall, as a day of mourning and remembrance in which families would gather to bury the remains of their loved ones. Remarkably, forensic experts were still discovering bone fragments and personal effects of the victims. Five years before, I had visited with my friend David Rohde for one such ceremony in which 610 men and boys had been interred. This year, 775 Bosnians would be laid to rest.

Before the official ceremony began in the tiny hamlet in eastern Bosnia, I ducked away from the heads of state and foreign ministers milling around and approached a woman who looked distraught. She told me in Serbo-Croatian that the previous year she had buried her husband and three of her five sons, each of whom had been murdered by Bosnian Serb soldiers. This year she was burying her fourth son.

I knew how hollow my words would sound. But I told her I had come on behalf of President Obama, who wanted to express his condo-lences and solidarity. *"Ja sam nova majka,"* I added, but as soon as I said those words ("I am a new mother") and thought of Declan, I struggled to continue.

"Ne mogu zamisliti Vašu bol," I said. "I can't imagine your pain."

The woman began speaking. "In my dreams they are there," she said. "But then I wake up and they are gone. They have vanished." What she said next shook me: "My son I am burying today was only seventeen. He was just a young boy. I didn't have time to love him enough. I didn't give him enough hugs. He wouldn't have known what he meant to me."

We never know how much time we will have with those we love. I could do nothing other than embrace the woman.

"We can't bring your sons or husband back," I said as we parted. "But we will never give up on bringing to justice those who did this to your family."

Ratko Mladić, the mastermind of the Srebrenica genocide who had been indicted by the UN war crimes tribunal, had evaded capture for fifteen years. There had to be a way to find him.

The two previous administrations had tried. President Clinton's State Department created a War Crimes Rewards Program, plastering around Bosnia and Serbia thousands of WANTED posters featuring photos of Mladić and the other leading indictee, Bosnian Serb political leader Radovan Karadžić. The posters promised $5 million for information that led to their arrests. But in Mladić's early years on the run, he had benefitted from a wide circle of protectors that included elements within the Serbian military and Russia's powerful Federal Security Service.

At the beginning of his presidency, George W. Bush had intensified the manhunt, sending more Special Forces to Bosnia than the United States had deployed anywhere else in the world since the end of the Cold War. But after September 11th, 2001, tracking down Balkan war criminals naturally receded as a priority, and the intelligence and military resources dedicated to finding Mladić were reassigned to counterterrorism efforts. Without pressure from the United States, the pursuit lost momentum.[9]

After President Obama took office, he sent Vice President Joe Biden to Belgrade to meet Serbian president Boris Tadić, a reformer who wanted to forge a closer relationship with the West. Biden encouraged Tadić to find and arrest Mladić. Our government and that of the UK offered assistance to Serbian authorities in tracking the fugitive's whereabouts. Unfortunately, concrete leads remained elusive.

Using the tools at our disposal, we got to work. Stephen Rapp, Ambassador-at-Large for War Crimes, traveled to Serbia five times to underscore President Obama's deep interest in the case. Capitalizing on the imprimatur of the White House, David also launched a new process in which he gathered government agency representatives to look for ways the United States could capture those, like Mladić, who had been indicted by international tribunals for war crimes or crimes against humanity.

David always took great pleasure in inventing new government acronyms. "Off to PIFWC!" he would exclaim as he made his way to the Situation Room, carrying a large notebook containing the latest intelligence on our government's efforts to track alleged war criminals. While I couldn't always remember precisely what PIFWC stood for (Persons Indicted For War Crimes), I regularly popped my head into David's cubicle for status updates on Mladić's whereabouts.

"Nothing yet," he would usually say. "But he's top of the list!" If David was pessimistic, he never showed it.

Bringing mass murderers to justice meant more than just providing a degree of closure for the families of victims—it advanced US interests. Finding someone like Mladić would remove a major impediment to reconciliation in a place where the US government had deployed tens of thousands of troops and invested billions of dollars in pursuit of greater stability. This logic extended well beyond the Balkans. Impunity for people who had committed unspeakable atrocities undermined fragile governments, often the same governments the State Department and the Pentagon were going to considerable lengths to strengthen. The rule of law was an essential foundation for peace and economic development, and even though the apprehension of war criminals would not itself usher in lawfulness, it could possibly deter other would-be mass murderers.

In emphasizing the importance of arresting war criminals, David and I of course understood that we would not be able to secure significant additional intelligence or financial resources. To compensate, we pursued an approach inside the government that had a lot in common with activist strategies outside: look for pressure points, identify potential allies, and work the system. And thanks to the relatively simple bureaucratic innovation of the NSC-initiated PIFWC meetings, I saw almost immediately how attention from the White House activated interest throughout the government and concentrated minds in Serbia.

In an overture that proved pivotal in demonstrating to the Serbian government that President Obama was deeply committed to seeing Mladić brought to justice, we invited the Serbian president's chief of staff, Miki Rakić, to the White House. David, who had been a theater director in college and always had an eye for the *mise-en-scène*, reserved the ornate Indian Treaty Room in the EEOB for our meeting. He thought the intricate gold and marble detailing and the kaleidoscopically tiled floor would serve as a fitting backdrop to my reciting the benefits that would accrue to Serbia if Mladić were rounded up. Rakić made clear he would take the message back to his president. This renewed dedication to the pursuit of Bosnia's most wanted took place almost entirely behind the scenes, but it successfully signaled to Serbian officials that *they* should dedicate more assets to the search.

My phone rang at six a.m. on May 26th, 2011. It was David.

"We got Mladić," he said, sounding euphoric.

I could hardly process the news. "You're kidding?" was all I could initially manage. But to my amazement, it was no joke. After fifteen years on the run, one of the world's most notorious war criminals was behind bars.

In a joint effort involving Serbian, British, and American intelligence agencies, officers from the Serbian Interior Ministry had found and arrested Mladić in his cousin's farmhouse.[10]

Hailing the arrest in a statement, President Obama applauded President Tadić and noted the long record the United States had, "from Nuremberg to the present," in pursuing justice "as both a moral imperative and an essential element of stability and peace."

Obama concluded, "May the families of Mladić's victims find some solace in today's arrest."*

I had suggested this line, thinking not just of the mother I had spo-

---

* In 2017, the International Criminal Tribunal for the former Yugoslavia would convict Mladić of war crimes, crimes against humanity, and genocide, sentencing him to life in prison.

ken with during my visit to Srebrenica, but of all the families in Bosnia who had endured unthinkable loss.

ONE OF THE FIRST MAJOR TESTS of whether we could smother a possible crisis early on, before it devolved into mass killings, came in South Sudan.

According to a peace agreement brokered by the Bush administration in 2005, South Sudanese voters were supposed to hold a referendum in January of 2011 on whether to secede from Sudan. Two decades of Sudanese government bombing raids and ground attacks were thought to have left nearly two million people dead, and the people in southern Sudan unequivocally wanted independence. But as we met at the NSC to map out possible scenarios in advance of the vote, it seemed inconceivable that Khartoum's genocidal government would allow the oil-rich south to become its own country. The most likely outcome was either that Sudan would prevent the referendum, or that it would simply refuse to recognize the inevitably unfavorable results. Both scenarios would provoke violent conflict. Warning lights from NGOs and our own intelligence community were flashing red.

The administration was filled with people who cared deeply about South Sudan, including Susan at the UN, my Wednesday Group friend Gayle, and our colleagues in the State Department and NSC who managed Africa policy. Denis sent stern messages to all government agencies that a peaceful referendum in South Sudan was one of President Obama's personal priorities. At the UN, Susan negotiated a landmark communiqué in which China and African nations joined the United States and Europe in calling on the Sudanese government to respect the referendum results. Both the United States and the UN also carried out contingency planning in case violence erupted.

In large part because of this sustained pressure and unusual international unity, the Sudanese government allowed the vote to go forward. Some 98 percent of the four million registered South Sudanese participated, with 99 percent favoring independence. The government in Khartoum begrudgingly accepted the outcome.

Knowing that the South Sudanese had experienced such endless heartbreak, I was immensely relieved as I read in the *New York Times* about their celebration—"hollering, singing, hugging, kissing, smacking high-fives and dancing as if they never wanted the day to end, despite the sun beating down and voting lines that snaked for blocks."

In Ivory Coast, the tools we employed were different, but also had important effects. There, the crisis emerged when the incumbent president, Laurent Gbagbo, lost his bid for reelection and tried to remain in power while holed up in the presidential compound. Forces loyal to Gbagbo used a large arsenal of weapons to attack civilians and shell homes in neighborhoods thought to be aligned with the winner, Alassane Ouattara. By February of 2011, the potential for mass atrocities was high, and as in South Sudan, grave warnings were pouring in.

Instead of waiting for lower-level diplomatic maneuvers to be tried, we recommended President Obama telephone Gbagbo to press him to accept the election results. When he ducked the call, we sent him a written message from Obama, conveying that he would face consequences if he refused to step down. We also imposed visa restrictions and targeted sanctions on Gbagbo and members of his inner circle, while working with other countries that had influence in Ivory Coast to see if they could convince Gbagbo to go into exile.

During the Rwandan genocide in 1994, most UN peacekeepers evacuated the country when the violence escalated. In Srebrenica in 1995, UN forces stood by while a massacre was committed. This time was different. France and the United States led a relatively collaborative UN Security Council in authorizing the 11,000 UN peacekeepers in the country "to use all necessary means" to protect civilians from attacks.

Working in tandem with 1,600 French troops who were stationed in Ivory Coast, the UN peacekeepers showed unusual firmness, striking military sites that were being used to launch attacks against civilians, and eventually targeting Gbagbo's presidential compound, from which he commanded his loyalists. Gbagbo was finally arrested in April of 2011, averting a larger bloodbath and allowing Ouattara to take office, fulfilling the will of the voters.

To combat the killers in the so-called Lord's Resistance Army

(LRA), President Obama deployed US resources in *support* of central African governments whose previous efforts had foundered. Formed in northern Uganda in the late 1980s by a young rebel soldier named Joseph Kony, the LRA had killed some 100,000 people, displaced another 2.5 million, and kidnapped at least 60,000 children. Kony and his commanders forced boys as young as six to become soldiers and made young women and girls act as sex slaves.

With broad bipartisan backing and energized by religious and student groups in the US, President Obama ordered the deployment of one hundred military personnel to provide advice, training, and information to what were largely Ugandan military efforts to hunt down and dismantle the LRA leadership.[11] Although a US military presence can often provoke a backlash abroad, when thirty of these advisers set up shop in Obo, an impoverished town in the neighboring Central African Republic, the residents were so relieved to have protection after years of LRA attacks that they reportedly staged nightly celebrations to honor the Americans.

In addition to working with the regional militaries, officials with the State Department and USAID helped build early-warning networks, using radios and cell phone towers, which communicated LRA troop movements to isolated communities. And in collaboration with the governments of the Central African Republic, the Democratic Republic of Congo, and South Sudan, the US military advisers helped airdrop one million leaflets that contained photos of former LRA fighters who had safely returned home, information about the demobilization process, and maps showing the closest sites where militia members could defect.

Through the same War Crimes Rewards Program that helped secure Mladić's capture, the State Department offered $5 million for information leading to the arrest of Kony and his two lieutenants. While Kony has eluded capture to this day, one of his top aides, Okot Odhiambo, was found dead in 2015, while another, Dominic Ongwen, surrendered to US forces and was sent the same year to the ICC. He is currently standing trial on numerous counts of war crimes and crimes against humanity.

The US-backed regional effort made a major difference. Battlefield deaths and defections reduced the LRA's fighting force by more than half, significantly eroding its ability to terrorize civilians. In 2010, before President Obama stepped up US involvement, the LRA killed 776 civilians. In 2013, it killed 76. In 2014, it killed 13.

TWO YEARS INTO THE ADMINISTRATION, I had a greater appreciation for the limits of our resources—most particularly our attention, our intelligence assets, and our senior diplomatic personnel. Nonetheless, I saw that with the President's backing, utilizing the toolbox could pay dividends on other vital issues as well.

Attacks abroad against the LGBT community called out for attention. Hundreds of LGBT people were being killed annually, and tens of thousands faced both arrest and the threat of physical and sexual violence. Seventy-six countries criminalized being gay, and five states (Mauritania, Sudan, Iran, Saudi Arabia, and Yemen) still imposed the death penalty as punishment.* Although attacks on LGBT people were not being carried out on the scale of mass atrocities, David and I set out to identify a set of tools that the US government could use to promote the safety and dignity of people being persecuted and attacked for their sexual orientation.

Supporting at-risk LGBT people in other countries was breaking new ground. Indeed, just before President Bush left office, his administration refused to support a UN General Assembly declaration that called for an end to the criminalization of homosexuality around the world, even though sixty-six other countries, including all twenty-seven members of the European Union, had signed on. A couple of weeks into Obama's presidency, our administration had reversed course and joined the declaration.[12]

Gruesome events drove home just how vulnerable LGBT people remained in many parts of the world. In 2011, a forty-six-year-old Ugandan activist named David Kato was murdered. Kato, one of the bravest

---

* Today, seventy countries criminalize being gay, and six (Iran, Nigeria, Saudi Arabia, Somalia, Sudan, and Yemen) impose the death penalty for consensual same-sex acts.

LGBT leaders in the world, was bludgeoned to death with a hammer in his home. His murder followed the publication of his photo, name, and address in a Ugandan tabloid, among a list of one hundred alleged "Homos." Kato's picture appeared next to the words "Hang them."

Devastated by the news of Kato's death, David drafted a short statement for President Obama to issue, which I pushed up the NSC's chain of command. While the Ugandan government was an ally in taking on the LRA, its stance on LGBT rights was abhorrent. Kato's murder terrified LGBT Ugandans, who understandably had no confidence that the police would protect them from violence. President Obama hailed Kato, whose name was not widely known globally, as "a powerful advocate for fairness and freedom" who had "tremendous courage in speaking out against hate." A friend of Kato's read Obama's statement at his funeral.

For a head of state—and not just any head of state, but the President of the United States—to denounce the killing of a gay activist abroad was unheard of. Yet by raising his voice, President Obama was making clear that he cared about attacks on LGBT people wherever they happened.

At the last minute, we decided to include a reference in the President's statement to five LGBT murder victims in Honduras. Even this brief mention made headlines there. And when the US embassy followed up, offering American assistance, the Honduran government agreed to establish a Special Victims Task Force of federal police and prosecutors to investigate crimes against LGBT people and other vulnerable groups. I relayed this development at our biweekly NSC meeting of Senior Directors, using these examples to make the case that US officials should not underestimate the power of their words. Not long after, we helped secure a resolution in the UN Human Rights Council, which for the first time in history recognized discrimination against LGBT people as a human rights violation.

We had to walk a very fine line in promoting LGBT rights internationally. The more vocal Obama and other Western leaders became, for example, the more we saw African leaders trying to claim that "imperialists" were foisting their values on traditional cultures. We were sensitive to the risk that the US government's vocal support for LGBT people abroad could end up being counterproductive.

At the same time, US reticence over the years had not prevented various African leaders and parliaments from propagating bigoted laws (sometimes encouraged by American evangelicals who felt they were losing ground in the United States). Nor had our silence deterred vigilantes from brutalizing gay people in their communities.

We took our cues on whether to speak out publicly or engage governments behind the scenes from LGBT activists, many of whom were bravely protesting and filing court cases themselves. Of course, among activists too one could hear a range of opinions. But by and large, they said President Obama was uniquely situated to advocate for gay rights, as he could draw on America's long struggle for civil rights—and our own country's slow progress toward LGBT rights—as he explained the importance of equality.

David started convening US officials from agencies across the government to brainstorm what the United States could do to integrate LGBT rights into our foreign policy. Knowing that *who* attended government meetings—how invested they were in an issue, or how much clout they had back in their home agency—was often a better predictor of eventual impact than precisely what was on the agenda, David handpicked the participants.

Whenever I sat in on these meetings, I would express my wonder at the enthusiasm of those at the table. "I've never seen such a beaming bunch of government officials in my life," I would tell David. Many US officials who joined our efforts identified as LGBT themselves, and they relished being part of a historic process that could help people living in the shadows elsewhere. The mere fact that each meeting began with an intelligence briefing on threats to LGBT people abroad was a rousing mark of a new era.

Every September, the President traveled to New York to deliver a kind of State of the Union on foreign policy to the world leaders gathered at the UN General Assembly (UNGA). As Obama's UN adviser, I worked with Susan and her team in New York to help plan the President's meetings with other heads of state during his three-day visit. I also offered Ben Rhodes ideas for his annual speech.

When Ben circulated a draft of the 2011 UNGA remarks to a small circle of NSC officials, I tried to add a line in which Obama would urge world leaders to respect LGBT rights. Yet every time Ben sent around a revised version of the speech, my line had been cut. As was often the case with the harried speechwriting process, he did not have time to write back to explain why he kept rejecting my suggestion.

I tried calling and emailing, even unsuccessfully resorting to parking myself in front of his door at the hotel where we were all staying. Finally, the evening before Obama was slated to speak, I spotted Ben across the lobby and began a light jog in his direction. When he saw me coming, he looked pained and hurried toward the nearest elevator bank.

"I can't," Ben said when I caught up with him. "We just don't have room. Obama's all over me to cut more."

"I understand," I said, while also positioning myself so the elevator door couldn't close. "I'll send you a much shorter version of the point!"

I hurried to my room, emailed Ben a menu of options to choose from and, having not heard back by three a.m., drifted off to sleep. I had secured a decent number of changes to the speech on other human rights issues, and I was resigned to the fact that this would not be the year President Obama took on LGBT rights at the UN.

When I woke up a couple of hours later, though, Ben had forwarded me the final version of the speech with the words "Happy Birthday" at the top of the email. My birthday (and Cass's) always fell during UNGA week. In the craze, I had forgotten it. This birthday present—like Holbrooke's wedding gift of a meeting with Hillary Clinton—was unusual, but much appreciated.

That day, sitting in the US seats in the General Assembly hall behind Secretary Clinton and Ambassador Rice, I held my breath while Obama spoke, wondering whether he would be greeted with jeers or cheers as he declared:

> No country should deny people their rights because of who they
> love, which is why we must stand up for the rights of gays and
> lesbians everywhere.

He was the first head of state ever to advocate for gay rights in the
UN General Assembly.

Owing to alphabetical happenstance, the US box was adjacent to
that of the Zimbabwean delegation, where the eighty-seven-year-old
president Robert Mugabe sat. Mugabe had once remarked that gay
people were "worse than dogs and pigs and should be hounded out by
society." And he had overseen changes to the country's criminal code
to make it illegal for men to even hug one another in public. As soon as
Obama invoked gay rights, I heard Mugabe groan, "My God!"*

Human rights advocates around the world expressed gratitude to
Obama for elevating the issue in such a forum. As the Kenyan activist
David Kuria told a journalist, "When a President such as Obama with
African roots talks in favor of gay rights, at the very least it shows that
not everyone is homophobic and that, in fact, African leaders are in
a . . . thinning minority." The following year, Kuria would become the
first openly gay person to run for office in Kenya.

After I left the General Assembly hall, I forwarded a copy of
Obama's remarks to Sally Brooks, my close friend from high school,
whom I had watched struggle for acceptance as she came out when we
were teenagers.

David Pressman's meetings with government agency representatives had generated a range of practical ideas on how to expand our
tools to help LGBT people in peril. We enshrined the best of these
in a presidential guidance document, which Obama signed. The very
existence of what became an official Presidential Memorandum on International Initiatives to Advance the Human Rights of Lesbian, Gay,
Bisexual, and Transgender Persons sent a ripple throughout the US
government, signaling to officials at every level that the President cared
about fighting anti-gay prejudice.

---

* In 2015, Mugabe would use his UNGA speech to proclaim, "We are not gays!"

Obama instructed government agencies to step up the diplomatic fight against the criminalization of LGBT people abroad. He directed the State Department to improve protection for LGBT refugees and those seeking asylum. And he encouraged diplomats to fund rapid legal defense to combat the imprisonment or persecution of sexual minorities.

During the eight years Obama was President, US embassies would open their doors to persecuted LGBT persons, with many ambassadors marching in LGBT Pride parades and pressing foreign governments to reject bigotry and protect the rights of all their citizens.

Obama's personal engagement with Brazilian president Dilma Rousseff secured the creation of both a special unit at the Organization of American States for monitoring LGBT rights in Latin America and a new position for a high-level expert (or "special rapporteur") who would advocate on their behalf throughout the Americas.

Clinton would give a landmark speech at the UN in Geneva in which she proclaimed "gay rights are human rights, and human rights are gay rights," echoing her famous 1995 speech on women's rights in Beijing. Her successor, Secretary of State John Kerry, would create the position of US Special Envoy for the Human Rights of LGBT Persons. Overall, as an administration, we would dispense more than $30 million to support frontline advocates for LGBT rights in some eighty countries.

And, in powerful acts of statesmanship and symbolism, when he traveled to Africa, President Obama would raise LGBT rights standing next to the very African leaders who ridiculed them.

Promoting these rights abroad wasn't just something that affected vulnerable foreigners. When planning to live or travel overseas, LGBT Americans had to consider whether they would be harassed, denied service, or even lynched for their sexual orientation. We were using US foreign policy to work toward a day when the rights that were finally gaining acceptance at home would not be denied abroad.*

---

* In his better-known domestic efforts, President Obama secured the inclusion of LGBT soldiers in the military, expanded federal hate crimes protections, and ultimately pushed for a nationwide right to same-sex marriage, which the Supreme Court recognized in 2015.

LEADERS RARELY GET POLITICAL CREDIT for preventing harms or for attempting to improve the lives of vulnerable people. Practically speaking, the complexities of almost every international crisis mean that even a generally positive outcome is messy and involves tradeoffs that do not resolve the issues at the root of conflict or exclusion. When the US government takes a leadership role in preventing mass atrocities, the blame is sometimes laid at our feet for not being able to prevent future human rights abuses. And unfortunately, violence frequently recurs.

In South Sudan in late 2013, for example, some of the very same politicians and generals who brought the country into existence would lead their people into a savage civil war.

In Syria, we would soon see that bureaucratic reforms and high-level discussions would not spare President Obama the wrenching dilemma of whether to risk using military force to try to prevent slaughter.

Discrimination and attacks against LGBT people still happen all around the world.

But just because we couldn't right every wrong did not mean we couldn't—or shouldn't—try to improve lives and mitigate violence where we could do so at reasonable risk.

Obama once told me, "Better is good, and better is actually a lot harder than worse"—a message he has expressed often since leaving office.

Convincing the American national security apparatus to incorporate concern for human consequences into our dealings with other countries would never be easy. And people were right to charge that, even at our best, the United States was inconsistent. But on the occasions when we did push other governments to treat their citizens with dignity—something few other governments took it upon themselves to do—US influence could be profound.

24

REVOLUTIONS

In early 2010, President Obama sent US troops on a humanitarian mission to help Haiti recover from a devastating earthquake that had killed more than 150,000 people. After a discussion in the Situation Room among top national security officials about the progress of the mission, I pulled aside Deputy National Security Advisor Tom Donilon. The participants in the meeting had seemed confused about the US military's exact mandate, and I stressed how important it was that our forces in Haiti be given a clearly defined set of tasks.

Tom had served in every Democratic administration since Jimmy Carter, and he would be elevated to National Security Advisor later that year. He often dispensed wisdom on how government worked, and told me I should not have waited until a high-level meeting had ended to make my point.

"Listen," he said firmly. "If you hear nothing else, hear this. You work at the White House. There is no other room where a bunch of really smart people of sound judgment are getting together and figuring out what to do. It will be the scariest moment of your life when you fully internalize this: There is no other meeting. You're in the meeting. You *are* the meeting. If you have a concern, raise it."

PRESIDENT OBAMA INVITED ME to "catch up" over lunch in May of 2010, a few months after US troops had safely returned from Haiti and six months before the so-called Arab Spring would begin.

Obama walked me into his small private study off the Oval, where he and Vice President Biden held their weekly one-on-one lunch. As we entered, I saw a pair of Muhammad Ali's red boxing gloves that I remembered Obama had also kept on display in his Senate office. On the walls were a nineteenth-century oil painting of Abraham Lincoln strategizing with his generals about how to end the Civil War and a seascape of Cape Cod that reminded me of the beach outside the window of my old apartment in Winthrop. Obama told me he had praised the painting when he had seen it hanging in the late Ted Kennedy's Senate office. Kennedy, who had painted it himself, then surprised Obama by giving it to him.

"I don't talk to you enough," Obama said as we sat down. "I thought it would be useful to hear what you think we are doing right, what we are doing wrong, what ideals we have betrayed lately."

For someone in his position, Obama remained refreshingly aware of how sequestered he was. Even in private, he seemed to inhabit a sphere of his own. His place had been set at the head of a table that could have seated six people, while mine was laid at the opposite end. Although we were in a small room, he felt far away.

Our conversation quickly turned to the Middle East, where the Egyptian government had just enacted a two-year extension of its harsh emergency law. I lamented the fact that the United States rarely protested how our autocratic allies in the region acted, even when they repressed their people in self-defeating ways. We got to talking about how such draconian measures could have destabilizing effects that would end up harming US interests. Obama grew animated talking about the sclerotic and out-of-touch governments ruling much of the Arab world.

"If these guys don't address the demands of young people," Obama predicted, "something's gonna give." He was clearly interested in what this combustible situation foretold for the people of the Middle East and North Africa, and in turn for US foreign policy.

Soon after our lunch, three of my NSC colleagues and I collaborated on a memo to Obama that addressed the urgent need for political and economic reforms. Working alongside Dennis Ross, the Senior Director responsible for the Middle East; Gayle Smith, the Senior Director for Development and Democracy; and Jeremy Weinstein, a political scientist who worked under Gayle, we proposed looking afresh at US policy in the broader Middle East.

While Gayle, Jeremy, and I brought expertise on democratization, Dennis had decades of regional experience that we lacked. He had been a key player on Mideast policy in multiple presidential administrations and had served as President George H. W. Bush and President Clinton's lead envoy on the Israeli-Palestinian peace process. Jeremy, who had taken leave from Stanford to work at the NSC, was the heart of our team. I was already working with him on a major global anti-corruption effort, known as the Open Government Partnership (OGP), which he had conceived of, and Gayle and I would spearhead in parallel to our efforts on Middle East reform.* We viewed the initiatives in tandem, as OGP called on governments to be more transparent, which in turn empowered citizens to hold political leaders accountable for their failure to deliver. Befitting his professorial background, Jeremy preferred making aruments for which he could demonstrate empirical support. "Here is what we know," he would say whenever we tried to drill down on some seemingly unanswerable dilemma. He would then cite academic research that spoke to the precise issues at hand.

Our memo to President Obama warned that people in the Middle East and North Africa were becoming increasingly dissatisfied with their governments. We asked him to issue a "Presidential Directive" instructing US government agencies to examine how the United States could get ahead of these brewing grievances by advancing the cause of reform.

Obama read our memo, and in August of 2010 he issued the formal directive we recommended. Using the language we had suggested, he told government agency heads that America's interest in political and economic stability was harmed by blindly supporting authoritarian Middle Eastern governments and frequently ignoring how they treated

---

* Today, the OGP is comprised of more than seventy countries, which have each made dozens of specific commitments (totaling more than 3,000) to fight corruption and improve service delivery by harnessing new technologies and incorporating citizen feedback into their programs and policies.

their citizens. The President instructed the heads of his cabinet agencies to identify leverage we could use to encourage governments in the region to be more open and responsive to the needs of their people.

The logic behind President Obama's guidance was that the United States needed to act while we still had time to support political *evolution* in the Middle East. Otherwise, we would find ourselves figuring out how to respond to *revolution*. Or, as I put it when we gathered US officials in the EEOB to brief them on the directive, "President Obama believes that if we are willing to bear more pain now, there will be less pain later."

With Jeremy sitting behind us in a large, secure conference room, Dennis, Gayle, and I began chairing biweekly meetings with Middle East experts from State, Defense, Treasury, the intelligence community, and other parts of the government. Jeremy and other NSC officials led additional meetings to develop a set of detailed plans on how to engage specific countries. We used these meetings to generate ideas for how to revamp long-standing US policies in the region, most of which had changed very little over preceding administrations.

Many of the US government's Middle East experts who attended our meetings argued that the political status quo in the region served US interests. Therefore, they warned that the types of reforms we were discussing could invite negative consequences. Despite Obama's explicit request for detailed proposals, they balked at coming up with ways to encourage Middle Eastern governments to change.

This reaction was not entirely surprising. American diplomats were our primary eyes and ears on the ground in the Middle East, and while some were entrepreneurial, managing to explore the societies in which they lived, others were out of touch with what was referred to as "the street": students and young adults, people who lived outside of major cities, and those with lower socioeconomic status. The security regulations put in place after the September 11th attacks compounded the disconnect, as diplomats were sometimes also restricted in their movements. These factors meant that they tended to over-rely on governmental and elite sources to inform their thinking. As a result, the US government heard little from citizens who were growing angry with the inequality, corruption, and repressiveness of life in outwardly stable countries like Tunisia and Egypt.

During my early days at the NSC, Richard Holbrooke had warned me that I should get used to feeling dependent on other governments for information. "US officials wearing badges around their necks run around the world trying to find foreign officials who wear badges around their necks. And they call it diplomacy," he said. "This is why we know so little about what is actually going on anywhere."

I was not a Middle East expert, and the regional specialists' fears about altering the status quo were credible. However, many of their arguments appeared not to have been stress-tested in decades. As a baseline, many seemed to reflexively assume that the status quo *could* be maintained. Conversely, Dennis, Gayle, Jeremy, and I argued that regimes that consistently failed to deliver for their people would come under growing pressure. And when citizens contested the ways they were being governed, long-standing leaders could soon find themselves backed into a corner, resorting to ever-more incendiary means to cling to power.

Polling already showed that the more repressive governments became in trying to keep a lid on brewing discontent, the less legitimacy they had with their people. When we took into account key trends—like mass unemployment, a population predominantly made up of young people, technology that increased the average person's ability to see elites' standard of living and to organize—we concluded that change was coming. Or, as Obama had forecast during our lunch, "something's gonna give."

We made the case for building US policy in the region on a foundation of principles rather than continuing to rely on particular leaders. To get our point across, we started using the biweekly sessions to challenge traditional assumptions. We reminded participants that Tunisian president Zine El Abidine Ben Ali was seventy-four years old, Egyptian president Hosni Mubarak was eighty-two, and King Abdullah of Saudi Arabia was eighty-six. Since authoritarian leaders would not live forever, we asked our colleagues what would come after these men exited the scene.

Mubarak, for example, planned to hand over power to his son Gamal. This bothered many Egyptians, who saw Gamal as corrupt and wanted to have a say in who would run their country. Yet US officials had not pushed for fair elections, fearing that doing so would jeopardize the Egyptian government's support for peace with Israel and counterterrorism cooperation with the United States. However, when we discussed what motivated the Egyptian government, we managed to secure relative agreement around the table that the country's leaders were looking out for their own security interests. Even if we challenged them on issues of governance, they had ample reasons for pursuing the policies on Israel and terrorism that we wanted to see continue.

After four months of meetings, many of the most skeptical participants seemed to embrace the need to pursue incremental but meaningful change. Together, we arrived at a set of core principles that provided the foundation for a modified approach to the region. US officials would start speaking more in public about issues that we knew resonated with frustrated citizens. Even the Pentagon would be expected to deliver the President's message on the importance of reform. And different US government agencies would bring to bear a variety of carrots and sticks to try to convince governments in the Middle East and North Africa to respond positively to our recommendations. We also developed granular reform proposals for a number of specific countries.

Once the President blessed the new strategy, which we expected he would do within a few days of receiving the plans, we would still face many hurdles. The dictators in the region would naturally resist liberalizing, and some US officials would be unenthusiastic about implementing the President's guidance. Still, the existence of a US government reform agenda for the broader Middle East represented a shift.

On December 17th, 2010, just as we were sending this large package of material to President Obama for his approval, a Tunisian fruit vendor lit himself on fire.

Mohamed Bouazizi's desperate act of protest against corruption and humiliation set in motion a cascade of revolts that would reorder huge swaths of the Arab world. These uprisings would end up impacting the course of Obama's presidency more than any other geopolitical development during his eight years in office.

The revolution had begun.

NEARLY TWO MONTHS AFTER THE TUNISIAN UPRISING started and four days after Mubarak, the seemingly permanent ruler of Egypt, stepped aside, the protests reached Libya. In the eastern city of Benghazi on February 15th, 2011, Libya's internal security service arrested Fathi Terbil, a thirty-nine-year-old lawyer who had spent years advocating on behalf of the victims of Libyan leader Muammar Qaddafi. That night, hundreds of people gathered to demand Terbil's release, and over the next two days, Libyans in other towns took to the streets.

In response, the Libyan regime's forces began shooting civilians. These attacks prompted more demonstrations—and more violence. After four days of protests, 233 people were reported dead, and Libyan Americans were frantically dialing the White House switchboard, pleading for help.

Before the Arab Spring, Qaddafi seemed like such a cartoonish character that one could sometimes lose sight of his ferocity. My only in-person exposure to him had come in 2009, when I helped organize Obama's first trip to the UN as President. Qaddafi spoke to the General Assembly immediately after Obama, rambling on for one hundred minutes and at one point theatrically throwing a copy of the UN Charter over his shoulder.

Yet alongside his flashy antics, during his forty-two years in power, Qaddafi had turned Libya into one of the most repressive states in the world. He had made it illegal to hold demonstrations or criticize the government. His regime's criminal code had made capital offenses out of various forms of political opposition, and the judiciary had once handed down a death sentence to someone for starting an NGO. Libya's security forces had become notorious for persecution, torture, and summary executions of those who defied Qaddafi's rule. Over the course of twenty-four hours in 1996, they had killed 1,270 inmates in the Tripoli prison that housed many political prisoners. The secret police, state-backed militia, and other armed elements had complete impunity to terrorize the Libyan people.

When the Qaddafi regime turned its guns on peaceful demonstrators, Obama publicly condemned the crackdown. In Tunisia and Egypt, pressure from the US President and other world leaders played a role in ultimately convincing the militaries in those countries to allow protests to continue. But with Libya, the United States had just restored full diplomatic relations in 2006.[13] With only shallow ties between the two governments, senior American officials could not call up their counterparts in the hopes of influencing the decisions being made by Qaddafi and his inner circle.

The Libyan dictator was highly unlikely to have listened anyway. Rather than show signs of relenting, he promised—and delivered—more violence. After protests spread from Benghazi, the country's second largest city, to the capital of Tripoli, Qaddafi's son, Seif al-Islam, addressed the nation. He described the "rivers of blood" that would flow if demonstrations continued. Roughly ten days after the first major street protests, the UN reported that more than 1,000 people had already been killed.

President Obama had seen enough, and on February 26th, he called on Qaddafi to step down.

In these still-early days of the Arab Spring, Ben Rhodes pointed out to me that events in the Middle East had become "watercooler issues." Americans who did not generally follow current events were captivated by the mass protests and closely tracked what Obama was doing in response. The President had been reticent when Iran's "Green Revolution" erupted in 2009, fearing that offering his vocal support would allow the Iranian government to caricature protesters as American-backed agents. With Libya, however, Obama was forceful. To convince Qaddafi that he should negotiate his political exit, he directed Donilon to get US government agencies to identify sources of leverage over the Libyan leader.

Everything we knew about Qaddafi's personality suggested that he cared passionately about his worldly possessions. If he believed his wealth was endangered, we thought, he might stop the violence and step aside, following in the footsteps of the Tunisian and Egyptian leaders. Moving quickly, we froze $37 billion of Qaddafi's assets in the United States, while our NATO allies froze an additional $30 billion.

We then rallied the world to take steps to pressure the Libyan regime. The Arab League—the main regional organization for Arab nations—suspended Libya as a member, even though it was then serving as its chair. The UN General Assembly also suspended Libya from the Human Rights Council (where it should never have been elected a member in the first place), and called an emergency session to establish a commission that would investigate Libyan war crimes. The fifty-seven-country Organization of Islamic Cooperation likewise condemned Qaddafi's "excessive use of force" for creating "a humanitarian disaster."

A powerful voice during this period was Libya's own ambassador to the UN, Abdurrahman Mohamed Shalgham. A longtime regime loyalist, Shalgham defected to join the opposition because he was horrified by Qaddafi's brutality. In an extraordinary scene, while sitting behind Libya's UN placard, he pleaded with the world to stop his president.

"Please, United Nations, save Libya," he begged. "No to bloodshed. No to the killing of innocents." Libya's deputy ambassador, who had defected several days before Shalgham, sat behind his boss in tears.

Less than two weeks after the protests had begun, the United States led a unanimous Security Council in imposing an arms embargo and economic sanctions on the Qaddafi regime. The Council also referred the war crimes and crimes against humanity being committed in Libya to the ICC. I had worked with Susan and her team in New York to refine the elements of the far-reaching resolution. When it passed in such record speed, I thought it was probably the best example in history of governments hastily using a vast array of "tools in the toolbox" to try to deter atrocities. The resolution was also notable for uniting countries like China, Russia, Germany, Nigeria, South Africa, and the United States on a complex issue of international security—a rarity in geopolitics.

The overall solidarity among nations reflected sincere horror at Qaddafi's murderous crackdown, but it also highlighted the Libyan leader's international isolation, which predated the Arab Spring. Qaddafi had funded insurgencies and supported terrorism in innumerable countries. He had also lied to or insulted a remarkably large number of heads of state. He was unique in having virtually no friends who would stand up for him. Not China. Not Russia. Not his fellow autocrats in the Arab world.

We hoped that in light of this global unity, Qaddafi would reconsider his bloody endgame and elect to negotiate an end to the crisis.* But at no point did the Libyan leader take genuine steps toward a peaceful resolution.

AS THE PRESIDENT'S HUMAN RIGHTS AND UN ADVISER, I suddenly found myself closer to the center of the action at the White House than I had been before. I avidly embraced the responsibility this carried, although it coincided with a very difficult period in my personal life.

The previous year, Cass and I had started trying to have a second child. We were fortunate to get pregnant quickly, but I miscarried several weeks later. This proved to be a pattern: we experienced three further miscarriages in succession.

One occurred when I was two months pregnant with a baby we had already decided to name "Jack" if it was a boy. At the time it happened, I was in Sri Lanka attempting to raise with the country's president the need for accountability for war crimes committed in the last stages of his government's war against the Tamil Tigers. I began to bleed just as I boarded the plane home.

After landing in Washington, I met Cass and we went straight to the emergency room at Sibley Hospital. An ultrasound technician examined me, moving the probe back and forth against my lower belly. His rhythmic pressure made it appear as though the baby were moving on the screen, and my spirits soared.

"There's your baby," the technician said.

"And his heartbeat?" I asked expectantly, craving confirmation of what I thought I had just seen.

"No, that's me making the movement," he replied with little affect. "Your baby has no heartbeat."

---

* Even though the ICC now had jurisdiction over crimes being committed in Libya, several countries that were not party to the court were prepared to offer Qaddafi safe exile.

I dug my face into Cass's chest and cried, as he did the same.

Cass was immensely supportive during these heartbreaking times, but I also came to count on the Wednesday Group—my female colleagues on the NSC. As I tried to bounce back from my multiple failed attempts to have a child while managing the intensifying demands of my job, our six p.m. Wednesday meetings became a sacred refuge. The mothers in the group lifted me up, particularly when Cass and I began in-vitro fertilization (IVF) treatments.

On a few occasions during 2011, I ended up having to slip out of high-level meetings to make it to the IVF clinic in time for a scheduled egg retrieval, or to have the doctors implant the embryos Cass and I had spent the previous weeks making together. I often felt self-conscious making my exit, but when I caught the eye of a Wednesday Group member across the room, she would wink or give me a thumbs-up, and my guilt at leaving would give way to a burst of excitement. Without this support, the combination of the pregnancy disappointments and the juggling might have led me to give up on what at times felt like a futile pursuit.

Friends who tried IVF had often complained about feeling fatigued by the stress of being poked by so many needles or by the battery of foreign drugs in their bloodstreams. While I certainly didn't enjoy the daily drug injections, I relished the opportunity to have agency over at least one aspect of our effort to have a child. I finally felt as though I was doing something concrete to contribute to our quest.

As a former reporter, I retained the habit of carefully detailing in my government notebooks what was discussed and decided in meetings in the Situation Room. During this period, however, my scribbles jumped from detailing Libyan military movements to recording specific telephone instructions from a nurse about how to adjust my IVF drug regimen. It dawned on me that future researchers of the Arab Spring who dug through the White House archives would have a hard time making sense of this juxtaposition.

I WAS BETWEEN ROUNDS of IVF when I received an invitation to accompany Secretary Clinton to Geneva, where she would be speak-

ing at an important UN Human Rights Council meeting on Libya.
I had long hoped to work closely with Clinton. Even though she made
a point of asking about Declan when I saw her at the White House,
I continued to feel awkward in her presence.

Jake Sullivan, her longtime senior aide, had orchestrated the invitation. Just thirty-four years old and even younger-looking, Jake was a
force of nature. I had never seen anybody so quickly and wisely synthesize information and transform it into strategic counsel. I felt I learned
from him almost every time he opened his mouth. I relished the chance
to discuss fast-moving events with him during the trip, and happily
said yes.

Flying to Europe on the plane her staff had christened "HillForce1,"
I handed Clinton a printout of the recent findings from the UN High
Commissioner for Human Rights, Navi Pillay:

> Libyan forces are firing at protesters and bystanders, sealing off
> neighborhoods and shooting from rooftops. They also block am-
> bulances so that the injured and dead are left on the streets. Re-
> ports from hospitals indicate that most of the victims have been
> shot in the head, chest, or neck, suggesting arbitrary and sum-
> mary executions. Doctors relate that they are struggling to cope
> and are running out of blood supplies and medicines to treat
> the wounded. Images of unverifiable origin appear to portray the
> digging of mass graves in Tripoli.

I found the last sentence particularly chilling, as it brought me back
to Srebrenica and the mass graves that had been dug for thousands of
bodies.

On my laptop, I pulled up a photo of a large protest in Benghazi.

"They've lost their fear," I said, showing Clinton the image.

She nodded, adding, "Not a woman among them."

Even though she believed Qaddafi's attacks on his people disquali-
fied him from leading Libya, she was rightly worried about what would
come next.

When we arrived at the Human Rights Council meeting, ambassadors and their aides chatted with each other and typed on their BlackBerries, barely listening as speaker after speaker read monotone statements condemning Qaddafi. But when Clinton began to speak, the crowd hushed.

Clinton reinforced President Obama's demand that Qaddafi step down, and, knowing she was speaking to ambassadors from other repressive countries, pointedly warned, "The power of human dignity is always underestimated until the day it finally prevails."

I had a mix of feelings as we flew back to the United States. On the one hand, I knew that President Obama had summoned virtually every American nonmilitary tool to influence Qaddafi, while convincing the world to do the same. On the other hand, I saw that something had been unleashed in Libya that was beyond Qaddafi's power to control—and ours as well.

For all of our hopes that the Libyan leader would step down or at least cease attacks on civilians, he repeatedly made clear that he planned to stay in power—and that he viewed those who opposed him as an existential threat to be eliminated. In a fist-pounding, seventy-five-minute speech on Libyan television, he had ranted against the opposition, calling them rats and threatening to slaughter them if they did not surrender. At one point he claimed, "I and the millions will march in order to cleanse Libya inch by inch, house by house, home by home, alley by alley, person by person, until the country is cleansed of dirt and scum."

The question of what these threats would mean for Libyan civilians took on profound urgency as Qaddafi began to seize momentum on the battlefield. By the beginning of March, his forces had recovered from early losses and were marching toward Benghazi, the home of the revolution and main opposition stronghold, and recapturing cities and towns along the way.

The director of the Benghazi Medical Center told one wire reporter that people were showing up at his hospital with "mainly gunshot wounds to the head, chest, abdomen—mostly young people under

25." He said, "The size and type of these injuries were horrific. Some were cut in half." Elsewhere, a British journalist witnessed people arming themselves with household items like hammers and axes to defend against Qaddafi's advancing forces.[14]

By this point, columnists and NGOs had begun urging Obama to use military force to prevent a wholesale massacre. On March 1st, the US Senate passed a resolution by unanimous consent urging the UN Security Council "to take such further action to protect civilians in Libya from attack, including the possible imposition of a no-fly zone over Libyan territory." Congress didn't specify what "such further action" beyond a no-fly zone might include, but even establishing one would likely require the United States to bomb Qaddafi's air defenses— something the Senate resolution failed to mention. As often happens in a crisis, members of Congress and editorial writers wanted to be seen calling for decisive measures ("Obama must act!"), but they used vague language to duck responsibility for the ensuing costs.

On the afternoon of March 15th, Obama convened his cabinet secretaries in a National Security Council meeting to discuss whether anything could be done to prevent the fall of Benghazi and other towns. In the hours before the meeting, as I digested that day's ghastly stream of reporting and intelligence, I felt like time was slowing down and speeding up at once. Every red light on my BlackBerry seemed to bring a new SOS from a Libyan saying, "Please help! They are launching an all-out offensive! They are crushing us . . ."

I had not originally been included on the list of people authorized to attend the President's meeting, but, mindful of our earlier exchange about Haiti, I wrote to Donilon, urging that he allow me to come.

An hour before the NSC cabinet meeting, I received word that I had been approved.

This was the meeting.

25

ALL NECESSARY MEASURES

President Obama was irritable as he opened the NSC meeting on the worsening crisis in Libya. "I know you have an agenda and a menu of options for us to consider," he told Donilon. "But we need to start with a baseline question: Is there going to be a Libyan opposition by the weekend?"

Qaddafi's forces were on the verge of taking back the town that provided water and fuel to Benghazi. The President was briefed that a military assault on the city of 700,000 people could begin within forty-eight hours, and would be followed by an extended siege.

Britain and France had brought a draft resolution to the Security Council to authorize the creation of a no-fly zone over Libya, and the main decision before Obama was whether the United States should join our allies in calling for this action. I had been incredulous when I learned of the European proposal. The Libyan military was retaking towns with its tanks and paramilitaries, not its air force.

Obama was equally mystified by the no-fly zone idea.

"What percentage of attacks are Qaddafi's forces carrying out by air?" he asked.

"Negligible, sir," replied the representative from the intelligence community.

Obama shook his head, frustrated that our allies would be presenting the United States with what he later called a "turd sandwich." They were pushing us to embrace an option that seemed to offer hope to desperate Libyans but would not save them. For that to happen, more than a no-fly zone would be required.

In some government meetings I saw open minds at work—men and women who came into the Situation Room willing to revise their positions if they heard a compelling argument or were presented with fresh facts. I had also seen officials who sounded entrenched in their views, but who knew (and knew that everybody else knew) that they would compromise in the end. They believed that by initially seeming inflexible, "the room" would land closer to where they started than if they "caved" early.

However, in this meeting, most participants came in with a fixed position about what to do or not do in Libya. Only the President seemed to be trying to objectively process the facts being presented and the arguments being made.

Susan, joining by video from New York, argued that we should seek a UN Security Council resolution to do what was *actually* required to save Benghazi and other opposition-held areas. This option would mean going beyond a no-fly zone and striking Qaddafi's forces and the land-based weapons they were using to attack civilians. Secretary Clinton joined by telephone from Paris, where she had just met with Libyan opposition leader Mahmoud Jibril. She threw her considerable influence behind Susan's recommendation.

Vice President Biden and Defense Secretary Gates both voiced opposition to any plan that would involve the US military. Biden, who had advocated bombing Bosnian Serb Army heavy weapons back in the 1990s, had grown dubious about using US military force. He regretted having supported the invasion of Iraq and consistently advocated for winding down the war in Afghanistan. His skepticism of a new military engagement also likely stemmed from the experience of having been the father of a soldier at war. Speaking to veterans and military families, Biden often mentioned that when his son Beau had served in Iraq, he came to understand what the poet John Milton meant when he wrote, "They also serve who only stand and wait." As for Gates, he did not believe that the United States had a vital national interest in preventing mass atrocities in Libya. The specter of becoming militarily involved in a third Muslim country hung over the discussion.

Obama seemed restless and unsatisfied as he heard from his key advisers. But he also gave little hint of the course of action he favored. If he laid out his thinking, those who disagreed might silence themselves, or what he said could land in the press.

When all of the cabinet officials had weighed in, showing a fairly evenly divided room on the question of whether to undertake military action, Obama sought out the opinions of those not sitting at the table. Recounting his mind-set at the time, the President later explained to the writer Michael Lewis that he was "trying to get an argument that [was] not being made."

Bringing the backbenchers into the conversation, he heard the powerful argument that US military action might ultimately hurt the cause of nuclear nonproliferation. Qaddafi had previously dismantled his nuclear program at the behest of Washington, so other governments—like that in Iran—might see what happened to Libya and decide to accelerate their pursuit of nuclear weapons as a deterrent against attacks.* However, several officials who favored Susan's proposal stressed that, if Qaddafi were to succeed in his crackdown, this could encourage excessive brutality by other leaders in the Arab world, setting back the peaceful, democratic gains recently made in Tunisia and Egypt.

From the start of the meeting, Obama had asked us to gauge the

---

* Qaddafi had announced in late 2003 that Libya would shut down its rudimentary nuclear weapons program. If the Libyan program had not been terminated—and if it had advanced significantly in the intervening years—it might well have deterred foreign military action in 2011. Nonetheless, in the years after the Libya military intervention, Iran still decided to go along with the US-led plan that curtailed the country's nuclear weapons program. It is possible that the NATO-Arab intervention in Libya affected the calculation of North Korea's Kim Jong-un as he assessed whether to trade away his nuclear program for sanctions relief and other incentives. The North Korean government has referenced Libya as a worrying precedent. Experts, however, cite a large range of additional reasons that the Kim regime refuses to give up its nuclear weapons. The analogy between the two countries is particularly fraught because, while Libya did not have any nuclear weapons when it gave up its program, North Korea tested its first nuclear device in 2006 and has many such weapons today. The incentives and leverage for each country diverge in important ways.

likelihood of mass killings. He demanded that we not use vague phrases like "the town will fall" without specifying what such a development would mean for Libyans.

"In the towns that the regime is recapturing, what do we know about what is being done to civilians?" he asked.

The details we had been able to ascertain as Qaddafi's forces and pro-government militias moved across the country were deeply worrying. UN Secretary-General Ban Ki-moon had relayed reports of Qaddafi supporters making house-to-house arrests and executing wounded opposition fighters in hospitals. The UN's Humanitarian Coordinator for Libya had visited the city of Zawiya the previous day, after it had fallen back under Qaddafi's control and found a partially destroyed ghost town. The regime loyalists in charge refused his request to visit the local hospital, where executions had been rumored. But journalists who had snuck into the town during the fighting reported horrific scenes. A British reporter with *The Times* spoke to a doctor who had seen civilians attacked with machine guns and rocket-propelled grenades. The doctor said government snipers had targeted him and other medics as they tried to help the wounded. A Sky News journalist described witnessing the "wholesale killing of civilians" after Qaddafi's forces arrived in a column of tanks, saying, "Doctor after doctor, nurse after nurse told us, and we could see it for ourselves, people, university professors, students, engineers, all being attacked. And there was nothing that they could fight back with."[15]

About ninety minutes into the Situation Room discussion, the President made his way around to me.

"Sam?" he asked.

I began by making clear just how little we could verify about what Qaddafi's forces were actually doing to civilians when they reclaimed territory. But I underscored that we had reason to be concerned about two kinds of atrocities.

First, Qaddafi's siege of Benghazi was sure to be savage, as his forces seemed likely to lay waste to the city in order to capture it. The regime's heavy weapons were already beginning to decimate opposition-controlled Misrata, Libya's third-largest city. A siege of

Benghazi seemed sure to entail shelling and sniping, as well as the denial of food, water, and electricity.

Second, after Qaddafi's troops eventually took control of Benghazi and other towns, they could carry out fierce reprisals against those who had rebelled against the government. The extent of the carnage that would follow was difficult to predict. However, on the basis of Qaddafi's past treatment of his opposition, the conduct of his forces since the start of the protests, his threats, and the isolated reports we were getting about atrocities, it seemed likely that his security forces would jail, torture, or murder many of their perceived opponents.

These two questions—the length and ruthlessness of the siege of Benghazi, and the relative cruelty and breadth of attacks afterward—were interwoven. Even if Qaddafi did not stage mass executions of the kind he had threatened, people connected to the opposition believed that they would be slaughtered if the city fell.[16] Fearing this, they were extremely unlikely to surrender, prolonging the siege and threatening more lives.

Speaking as Obama's adviser on multilateral affairs, I stressed the unusual international agreement up to that point. The Arab League's demand for military action, for instance, was a surprising development given the widespread distrust of the US government that existed among Arab countries. I read passages from the recent communiqué issued by these Arab governments, in which they called for the UN Security Council "to bear its responsibilities" and "to establish safe areas in places exposed to shelling . . . [to allow] the protection of the Libyan people."

I closed by arguing that we should cite this appeal as we pursued a civilian protection mission along the lines of what Susan had proposed.

The President nodded and moved on to hear other views. After nearly three hours, he ended the meeting without rendering a final decision.

He was at a crossroads. The pressures that the United States and other countries were imposing on Qaddafi's regime would take months to reach their full effect, and we had run out of further nonmilitary steps to take to try to affect the Libyan leader's near-term calculus.

On the other hand, President Obama knew that the American people were exhausted from a decade of war.[17] Although Republicans were denouncing him as weak for not stopping Qaddafi, they seemed likely to oppose whatever he did.

He had to weigh this context—and a set of unknowable reactions—against the risks of protracted siege warfare and possible slaughter.

"I want real options," Obama said, wrapping up. "If we are in for a dime, we are in for a dollar. I'm not going to do some half-assed no-fly zone. To me, that's the worst option. Either we go in heavy and fast or we should not pretend we are serious about stopping Qaddafi."

He asked a smaller group—mainly his cabinet and not including backbenchers like me—to reassemble later that evening, when he would choose among those real options.

SUSAN CALLED ME AROUND ELEVEN P.M. that night. President Obama had decided to try to prevent the fall of Benghazi and other opposition-held towns. He had instructed her to see whether she could get a resolution through the Security Council to license coercive steps to protect civilians. If she could not achieve this, he made clear that the United States would not intervene militarily.

I worked into the early morning with Susan and her team. They drafted new provisions to supplement what the British and the French were already proposing, and I ran the new language by my colleagues and bosses at the NSC. The next day, Susan formally circulated an American draft resolution to the Council with the US revisions clearly marked on the British-French draft in Track Changes. The new American language would "authorize Member States . . . to take all necessary measures . . . to protect civilians and civilian populated areas."

Susan made sure her fellow ambassadors understood what this meant. "This is an authorization to use force not only against airplanes attacking civilians," she stressed. "It is also an authorization to use military force against ground forces targeting civilians."

The text of our resolution was not original—similar provisions had been used to set up the UN-declared no-fly zone in Bosnia back in 1993 and to authorize the use of force in Afghanistan in 2001.

Some of the countries that would vote in favor of, or abstain on, this "all necessary measures" resolution would later claim that they were surprised and even outraged to see the US-led military coalition go beyond imposing a no-fly zone. But they were either lying to the world or to themselves.

The entire US government mobilized to urge countries with seats on the Security Council to support the revised text, which was sponsored not only by the United States, the UK, and France, but also by Lebanon on behalf of the Arab League. Still, we all knew that Russia's vote would be decisive.* A Russian abstention would allow the resolution to go forward, but Moscow had never been enthusiastic about licensing Western countries to use military force for ostensibly humanitarian purposes.

Meanwhile, even as it became apparent that the Security Council was seriously considering authorizing military action to protect civilians, Qaddafi announced that his forces were preparing to seize Benghazi. In the hours before the UN vote was scheduled, with his troops and militia massing just ninety miles south of the city, the Libyan leader took to the radio with a warning to residents: "It is over; the decision has been made. We are coming." To the opposition fighters, he said, "We will find you in your closets. We will have no mercy and no pity."

Around midnight in Libya—six p.m. New York time—on March 17th, thousands of Libyans gathered in Benghazi's main square, gazing up at jumbo video screens tuned to live coverage of the Security Council's vote. People were focused so intently on the UN session that when I visited Libya with Susan months later, many of those we met could recall the lime green outfit she had been wearing in the Council chamber. As one Libyan described it to me, for the crowd in the

---

* In the Security Council, the author of a resolution—the "penholder"—submits a draft for the other members of the Council to review. In order for the text to pass and become a resolution, it must receive a positive vote from nine of the fifteen members and not be vetoed by any of the five permanent members—China, France, Russia, the United Kingdom, and the United States. Because of Russia's veto power, in 1999, the Council did not authorize NATO's military campaign to prevent atrocities in Kosovo.

square, the question being posed to the international community was: "Raise your hand if you want to prevent the massacre of Libyans."

When ten of the fifteen hands on the Security Council were lifted in favor of the resolution, the people packed into the square erupted into loud applause. When five countries—Brazil, China, Germany, India, and Russia—abstained immediately thereafter, people jeered and threw their shoes at the screens. But once they understood that no country had vetoed and thus the resolution had passed, the crowd again began cheering wildly. The celebrations lasted deep into the night, as people honked their car horns and waved Libya's flag from the pre-Qaddafi era.

On March 19th, the United States, France, and the UK began striking Libyan military targets, acting under the umbrella of NATO, in a coalition that included Jordan, the United Arab Emirates (UAE), and Qatar. Benghazi and other opposition-held towns in Libya would not be allowed to fall into regime hands.

The week after the Security Council approved the resolution, Russian prime minister Vladimir Putin began publicly blaming President Dmitry Medvedev for Russia's abstention.* Medvedev, however, had almost certainly coordinated with Putin before sending instructions not to veto to the Russian Ambassador at the UN. In truth, the world was broadly united in taking military action to protect Libyan civilians. As Medvedev himself told journalists just after Putin criticized him, "the consequences of this decision [to abstain] were obvious. It would be wrong for us to start flapping about now and say that we didn't know what we were doing . . . everything that is happening in Libya is a result of the Libyan leadership's absolutely intolerable behavior and the crimes that they have committed against their own people."

On March 28th, President Obama delivered a prime-time address

---

* Russia's constitution did not allow a president to serve more than two consecutive terms, so in 2008 Putin became prime minister—and Dmitry Medvedev, his hand-picked successor, was elected president. Despite Putin's move to the prime ministership, he retained significant influence over domestic and foreign policy. In 2012, Medvedev announced that he supported Putin returning to the presidency, and Putin was again elected Russia's official head of state.

to explain US military action in Libya. "Some nations may be able to turn a blind eye to atrocities in other countries," he said. "The United States of America is different. And as President, I refused to wait for the images of slaughter and mass graves before taking action."

The United States had helped orchestrate the fastest and broadest international response to an impending human rights crisis in history.

BECAUSE OF MY JOURNALISTIC CAREER, and my resignation from the Obama campaign, I had a modest public profile before I went to work at the NSC. However, knowing which side of the government's "work horse/show horse" divide I wanted to fall on, I had kept my head down. In my days before government, Eddie had responded to luke-warm reviews of my books with the old saying, "There is no such thing as bad publicity." My view about serving at the White House was that there was no such thing as good publicity. I wanted to stay below the public radar and focus on doing my job.

Unfortunately, after Obama decided to use force to protect Libyan civilians, the *New York Times* offered a bizarre rendition of the key March 15th meeting in the Situation Room. The *Times* effectively attributed Obama's decision to "three women": Susan Rice and Hillary Clinton, both cabinet members, and me—a backbencher. The article failed to mention the fact that a far larger number of men than women argued for using force, and it depicted Obama as a mere vessel for his female advisers' designs.

Times columnist Maureen Dowd drew on her paper's news story for an opinion piece titled "Fight of the Valkyries," which began: "They are called the Amazon Warriors, the Lady Hawks, the Valkyries, the Durgas. There is something positively mythological about a group of strong women swooping down to shake the president out of his delicate sensibilities and show him the way to war." Conservative commentators had a field day, with Rush Limbaugh mocking the President and the men in the room as "sissies." Because of this coverage, journalists began writing profiles of me, making me want to disappear under the flowerbeds of the Rose Garden.

Even though I had been one of the people who recommended the course of action President Obama had ultimately chosen, I was conflicted about American military involvement. I was relieved beyond measure that Libyans had been granted a reprieve from Qaddafi's wrath. But I was simultaneously anxious about the many ways the military operation could go wrong, and I hoped that Obama would not regret his decision.

Five years before, during one of our many talks in his Senate office, Obama had noted: "You're not nearly as hawkish as people think you are." This was true. I had favored the use of American air power when I lived in Bosnia, and opposed the Bush administration's invasion of Iraq. As an NSC official, I participated in hundreds of policy debates about countless countries and global problems, and I almost never recommended using US military force.

I had seen the good that the US air campaign had done in Bosnia, effectively ending a horrific conflict. But I also knew the history of the Vietnam and Iraq wars and was familiar with how little US government officials sometimes knew about the foreign places and peoples whose fates their decisions would impact. As a young foreign service officer in Vietnam, Richard Holbrooke had clipped and shared a Peanuts cartoon strip showing a disconsolate Charlie Brown after his baseball team was thumped 184-0. "I don't understand it," Charlie Brown says. "How can we lose when we're so sincere?"[18] I used to muse over the fact that American political consultants who were paid millions of dollars to predict the behavior of the *American* electorate still frequently got their forecasts wrong—and they spoke English, talked to voters, and knew our history. Whatever our sincerity, we could hardly expect to have a crystal ball when it came to accurately predicting outcomes in places where the culture was not our own.

It was especially hard to know what dormant tendencies lay buried in a society where, for decades, the "Brother Leader" had sought to control even the thoughts of citizens. The Libyan opposition spoke of creating a constitution and an open society, but even if Qaddafi left power, who would maintain order going forward? Since Qaddafi had demolished Libya's institutions, how would the country function without a strongman at the top?

Despite these considerations, neither at the time nor presently do I see how we could have rejected the appeals of our closest European allies, the Arab League, and a large number of Libyans, including the Libyan ambassador to the UN, and stood by as Qaddafi followed through on his pledge to retake Benghazi and "cleanse" people, house by house. Still, every day of the spring and then summer of 2011 that the conflict dragged on, I worried about how the Libyan transitional authorities would manage the future.

ASSESSMENTS OF PRESIDENT OBAMA'S ACTIONS in Libya often assume that, had he made a different set of choices and not intervened, Qaddafi could have returned the country to more or less the way it had functioned before the protests and crackdown. What this view fails to take into account is the fact that Libyans had minds of their own.

Unlike in Egypt, where students played a leading role in toppling the Mubarak government, former government officials and defectors from Libya's security and armed forces helped drive the opposition movement in Libya. They were a determined, heterogeneous network that held territory and established transitional governments in towns that came under their control. Additionally, countries in the region flooded Libya with weapons and military equipment in support of various opposition factions, making them even harder for Qaddafi to snuff out. Although the Libyan regime had decisive military advantages over the opposition, the seeds for a long-term insurgency had been planted before the UN Security Council authorized the use of force to protect civilians.

Had the United States taken no further action beyond the sanctions, arms embargo, and other nonmilitary measures initially approved by the Security Council, no one can say with confidence what would have happened. Qaddafi seemed almost certain to commence an assault on Benghazi and enter into a long fight to retake and hold other areas. He probably would have retained power without regaining complete control of his vast country, which is roughly four times the size of California. At the same time, some opposition forces could have teamed up with extremist financiers and arms suppliers outside

Libya, deepening the chaos. This very scenario would soon unfold in Syria.

Had this occurred, many US intelligence analysts predicted that, since Qaddafi viewed Western governments' call for his departure as a betrayal, he would return to sponsoring terrorism as he had in the past. US counterterrorism experts therefore worried both about who would come after Qaddafi if he fell *and* about a bloody insurgency and a surge in terrorism if he remained.

In other words, from their vantage point, Libya was unlikely to become stable anytime soon.

Subsequent criticisms of President Obama's decision-making during this period that fail to grapple with these dynamics do not present a realistic picture of the factors driving his thinking. What transpired in Libya in February and March of 2011 had fundamentally changed the country. Once the revolution spread, the real question became how to use the tools at our disposal to bring about the best possible—or the least bad—outcome.

OVER THE NEXT SEVEN MONTHS, the joint NATO-Arab coalition did what it could from the air to protect Libyan civilians. Unfortunately, instead of ceasing their attacks, Qaddafi and his forces hung on, continuing to bombard populated areas. Most alarmingly, despite efforts by the UN, the African Union, and the White House itself (which sent a diplomatic delegation to meet with Qaddafi's key advisers), the Libyan leader did not credibly engage in discussions aimed at ending the war.[19]

The most consoling voice I heard during this period was that of Chris Stevens, a senior US diplomat whom Clinton had posted in Benghazi as a liaison to the Libyan opposition. Chris spoke Arabic and had served in Syria, Egypt, and Saudi Arabia. From 2007 to 2009, he had been the second in command at the US embassy in Libya.

Chris and a small team of aides arrived in Libya on a Greek cargo ship not long after NATO began bombing. They fanned out, meeting with everyone from former Qaddafi-era officials who had defected, to lawyers, doctors, businesspeople, and volunteer soldiers. Chris reported that Libyans were exuberant about building a new, free country. He sent emails and cables back to Washington about the opposition radio and television stations and the human rights and women's rights organizations that were sprouting up all over "liberated" territory. These dispatches practically crackled with the energy and optimism of those enjoying freedom for the first time.

When I met Chris on his occasional visits to Washington, I was struck by how special his brand of diplomacy was. A native Californian and former Peace Corps volunteer with a toothy smile, he gave off the feeling of someone who knew that he could learn more from backpacking through an area than meeting with dignitaries. Libya seemed to be not just a country where Chris had been posted; it was a place that he was making his home. He was also refreshingly willing to admit all that he didn't know—that none of us could know—about what went on in the minds of Libyans who had been locked under repressive rule for generations.

On August 20th, 2011, Libyans in Tripoli rose up against Qaddafi, breaking a months-long military stalemate and marking the overthrow of the repressive government.[20] I was at home with Declan, who was nearly two and a half years old. "Qaddafi is gone!" I told him, somewhat amazed.

My young son began marching around our apartment, shouting, "No more coffee! Coffee is gone!"

IN JULY OF 2012, Libya successfully held its first democratic election in nearly fifty years, with many Libyans enthusiastically flashing their ink-stained fingers in victory signs and embracing the election as a marker of the new country they hoped to build. Nonetheless, the post-Qaddafi political transition was already turning chaotic, and the country's regional, tribal, and religious* divisions were becoming more pronounced. Qaddafi himself had been brutally executed by a group of rebels near his hometown of Sirte two months after Tripoli fell to the

---

* Although almost all Libyans were Sunni Muslim, some were secular, while others wanted to see Libya governed by strict adherence to Islamic law.

opposition, and this proved a harbinger of the lawlessness and violence that would follow.

During our calls and meetings over many months, Chris's main focus was always on the need for Libyans to establish physical security. But police who had served in the Qaddafi government were largely vacating their posts, and local militias were filling the vacuum. Chris threw US support behind a nascent Libyan opposition council that tried to bring those fragmented forces under central control. But countries in the region that had supported various opposition factions during the rebellion against Qaddafi went on funneling arms into the country, urging their proxies to fight for more power.

When President Obama had decided to use military force to protect civilians in Libya, he stressed that he did not want US involvement to morph into an open-ended commitment akin to what had happened in Afghanistan and Iraq. Because the United States had spearheaded and led the military coalition, he expected our European allies to take the lead on helping Libyans manage the aftermath. In communicating this, Obama sent an unintentional signal to his senior national security team that he felt the United States had already done its share.

Perhaps no amount of outside engagement during this period could have counteracted Libya's centrifugal forces. However, once it became clear that European efforts to shore up the transition were falling short, the US government could have exerted more aggressive, high-level pressure on Libya's neighbors to back a unified political structure and cease their support for the competing opposition factions.*

Instead, in September of 2012, after terrorists attacked US facilities in Benghazi, our administration shrank further from engagement in Libya. The attacks killed Chris, whom I had so admired, along with Glen Doherty and Tyrone Woods (two security officers working for the CIA), and the State Department's Sean Smith. Following their deaths, Libyans flooded the streets in solidarity, carrying signs with messages

---

* In 2014, President Obama would instruct the State Department to ramp up US diplomacy and Secretary of State John Kerry and others would do so, making relentless efforts. But by then, Libya's fissures had hardened.

like CHRIS STEVENS WAS A FRIEND TO ALL LIBYANS, WE'RE SORRY, and THUGS AND KILLERS DON'T REPRESENT BENGHAZI OR ISLAM. But President Obama's political opponents reacted not by rallying behind the pursuit of the perpetrators, but by politicizing the attack.

And in Libya, despite the severe downturn in security, citizens seemed able to agree on just one thing: there should be no international military or police presence in their country. *Libyans* should determine the country's future, they all said. And for better and worse, in the coming months and years, they would.

26

LET'S PRAY THEY
ACCOMPLISH SOMETHING

No matter how many unsuccessful pregnancy tests I had taken over two years of trying to conceive a second child, I could never suppress my faith that two lines would appear. In my eagerness to learn immediately whether my latest round of IVF had worked, I had even taken to storing test kits in the locked safe in the EEOB where I kept classified files. For five consecutive months, I used a manila folder to hide the kit as I carried it down the hall to the women's restroom. And on almost as many occasions, after I took the test, I convinced myself that a faint, second line existed—only to have Cass, the realist, shake his head glumly.

But on the sixth time I made this walk, there was no doubting what I saw: two dark pink lines beside each other. I galloped down the stairs to Cass's office, burst past his assistant, and un-self-consciously waved the stick in the air. After four rounds of IVF and four miscarriages, Cass and I knew we could take nothing for granted—but we also knew that we now had a chance.

In the coming months, despite one major scare where I began bleeding eight weeks into the pregnancy, Eamon (Irish for Eddie's name, if it was a boy) or Rían (Irish for "king," if it was a girl) managed to hang on.

Declan worried aloud whether there would be enough of his mother to go around when a new baby came. Yet he still rested his head against my growing tummy, and, once we learned it was a girl, whispered to her, "Hi Rían, it's your brother. I will see you soon."

On June 1st, 2012, as I was texting at two a.m. with Denis McDonough about an Israeli-Palestinian issue brewing at the United Nations, I felt cramping begin. Only at this late date did I really allow myself to believe that we were having another baby. "The king is coming," I whispered to Cass, waking him.

Together, we had produced around seventy embryos through the IVF process. Only one, this little warrior Rían, was going to make it. And indeed, after she was born, everything about her seemed rooted in an irrepressible desire for life.

When I returned to work after my maternity leave, I largely retained the perspective I had first gained while caring for Declan. My moods were less affected by the highs and lows of the daily grind. During times when slights and setbacks might once have sent me off into the Bat Cave, I was usually able to access the calm I felt while caring for my kids. I also noticed that I had stopped getting nervous before big government meetings. What had once felt like the pinnacle of my week no longer held that status.

But there were exceptions—and meeting Aung San Suu Kyi was one of them.

IN OCTOBER OF 2012, a month after I had gone back to work, I found myself in Rangoon anxiously waiting to see Burma's iconic, oft-imprisoned opposition leader. For as long as I had cared about human rights, I had been in awe of Suu Kyi's courage and poise. Even as her husband lay dying with cancer, she had refused to leave her house arrest in Burma to visit him in the UK, fearing the military junta would not allow her to return home. For her pacifism and activism, she had been awarded the Nobel Peace Prize in 1991.

With the initially hopeful events in the Arab world turning violent, Burma seemed a rare bright spot. During the previous two years, its military government had released hundreds of political prisoners from jail while freeing Aung San Suu Kyi from house arrest. Most significantly, the regime had respected the results of parliamentary elections in which her opposition party dominated.

These tentative steps toward openness suggested that more progress was possible, and in order to try to accelerate it, President Obama intended to become the first sitting US president to visit Burma. Bold, principled engagement with repressive governments was exactly what the President had meant in his inaugural address when he pledged that the United States would extend a hand if autocratic leaders would unclench their fists. We knew, however, that Suu Kyi was opposed to a presidential visit, and the White House had sent me to Rangoon in the hopes that I could help change her mind.

When the military regime took its first tentative steps toward expanding political freedom, our administration had pursued what we called an "action for action" approach: US steps toward normalization followed liberalizing steps from Burma's military leadership. However, partly owing to concerns that the European Union was lifting sanctions faster than we were, benefitting European businesses, the White House had begun deviating from that playbook, rushing to lift the ban on US companies investing in Burma. Given the number of reforms the ruling generals still needed to make, I had argued for retaining more targeted sanctions until we saw more progress. I thought we were moving too briskly. "The United States government has no dimmer switch!" I vented to my staff before flying to Rangoon.

I arrived at a sterile office where the National League for Democracy, Aung San Suu Kyi's political party, hosted the stream of foreign emissaries suddenly visiting Burma. After a perfunctory greeting, Suu Kyi cut right to the chase.

"A presidential visit is a dreadful idea," she said. I had not expected her to be quite so firm and quickly grew flustered.

"I understand you feel that way," I began.

"I don't *feel* this way," she said. "I believe I know my country far better than you in Washington. This trip is a mistake."

"If I may just lay out a few of the reasons that—" I tried.

"There is nothing to be said," she interrupted. "President Obama traveling to Burma at this time will legitimize a military regime that has consistently stood in the way of democracy."

"I understand the risk," I said, "but I am here to get your thoughts on how we can use the trip as leverage to secure concessions from the military that will—"

Again, she cut me off. "This is not a good use of time," she said. "Nothing you say will alter my view."

After several more attempts to convey how we hoped to use an Obama visit to advance political reform, Aung San Suu Kyi made clear her view had not changed. "This is your decision," she said. "But the consequences will be ours to cope with."

I pivoted to discussing a topic she liked even less—the status of the country's Rohingya population. Burma was nearly 90 percent Buddhist, and the Rohingya were a beleaguered Muslim minority that the military dictatorship disenfranchised and severely mistreated. Over the previous three decades, they had been denied citizenship and conscripted into what amounted to slave labor. Government rules forbade Rohingya from traveling out of their villages, or from marrying and having children without official permission. And state security forces used rape to terrorize Rohingya women.

Incited by extremist Buddhist monks and backed by government security forces, local Burmese vigilantes had recently killed hundreds of Rohingya and burned many villages to the ground, displacing more than 100,000 people. Hatred toward this minority group was so widespread that I had even heard Burmese human rights lawyers speak about the Rohingya with contempt.

When I brought up how state forces had pushed Rohingya families out of their homes and violently attacked them, Aung San Suu Kyi had a ready answer. "Do not forget that there is violence on both sides," she said, repeating a false claim made by Buddhist radicals to justify the attacks.

Few predicted then that the persecution of the Rohingya would escalate into full-scale genocide, which it did in August of 2017.* But I was still shocked that this renowned champion of freedom was drawing an equivalence between defenseless civilians and heavily armed, state-backed mobs. I appealed to her to raise her voice to demand that the rights of all people in Burma be protected.

"It is a tragedy," she said. "It will do nobody any good for me to take sides."

"We are not asking you to take sides," I said. "We urge you to use your immense credibility to speak up on behalf of human rights, and to acknowledge all who are being abused."

I knew Suu Kyi had relied on her Buddhist faith during her years in captivity, so I asked whether she could issue even a simple message on the importance of compassion and "loving kindness." Since she was the most beloved public figure in the country, such a gesture would go a long way toward reminding her millions of constituents about the importance of nondiscrimination and nonviolence.

"You should not rely on propaganda for your information," she said tersely. "Muslim countries are hyping events. It is irresponsible, and they are making matters worse."

I was crestfallen to hear such coldness in the face of escalating violence against civilians. But above all, I was rattled by Suu Kyi's holier-

---

* During President Obama's second term, influenced by Aung San Suu Kyi's stated support for a full lift of economic sanctions, he would remove most of the remaining restrictions. I again raised objections, given the substantial democratic progress yet to be achieved and my worries about the Burmese military's ongoing abuses against civilians. But the White House made a calculated gamble that greater openness, prosperity, and exposure to the outside world would ultimately spur political liberalization. In October of 2016, several months before President Obama left office, Rohingya militants staged attacks against local police. Following this, the Burmese military carried out massive "clearance operations" in Rakhine State, destroying a number of villages, killing civilians, and displacing an estimated 94,000 Rohingya. Then, beginning in August of 2017, the Burmese military initiated a catastrophic campaign of murder and rape against the Rohingya population living in Rakhine, which led to thousands of deaths and the exodus of more than 800,000 Rohingya refugees into neighboring Bangladesh. The UN and numerous human rights organizations documented a campaign of "genocidal intent" that included widespread sexual violence, summary executions of civilians (including babies and children), torture, and the destruction of entire villages.

than-thou tone. "I must say," I said wearily, "when I was young, I never imagined that one day I would have the honor of meeting you. But had I imagined it, this is not how I would have thought the meeting would go." Suu Kyi offered the slight trace of a smile.

What I found most chilling was the fact that she was a bad listener—an alarming quality in a leader. And she demonstrated scant empathy for the plight of a vulnerable minority, despite clear evidence of the crimes being committed against them.

"What's weird," I recounted to Cass when I got home, "is that her whole life has supposedly been about human rights, but it is not clear she cares that much about humans." When I returned to the White House, I told my colleagues that, while I hoped my experience with Aung San Suu Kyi was an aberration, pinning our hopes on her leadership could be a mistake.

AS PLANNING FOR PRESIDENT OBAMA'S VISIT progressed, Aung San Suu Kyi came around to supporting it. She was focused on her own political fortunes and saw the domestic benefit of embracing the occasion. Unfortunately, her rivals in the military government refused to agree to a set of reforms that we had hoped to announce before Obama arrived. So, a few weeks after my initial trip, the President asked me to return to Burma and lock down our desired terms. I would have just three days there to forge an agreement before Air Force One touched down.

Given this compressed timeline, I felt enormous pressure, which I conveyed to Ben Rhodes, who played a key role in crafting our Burma policy and understood all that was riding on the upcoming negotiation. Ben was a lifelong Mets fan who despised the New York Yankees as much as I did. But in the days before the trip he began calling me "Mariano," for Mariano Rivera, the Yankees' Hall of Fame closer—his way of trying to give me confidence that I could deliver for our boss.

On the flight over, I carried three items of critical importance: a thick briefing book that I consumed during the twenty-hour journey; a notebook where I mapped out the concessions I would be seeking; and my breast pump, which would help prevent my milk supply for five-month-old Rían from drying up on what would be my second lengthy trip to Burma in a month.

Over three bruising days of negotiations, I secured a communiqué that contained a powerful set of commitments from the Burmese government. The final agreement included a large additional release of political prisoners, access for humanitarian workers to war-torn ethnic areas, and permission for critics of the Burmese dictatorship to return from exile or to travel outside of Burma.

After Air Force One landed at the airport in Rangoon on November 19th, 2012, I received a large hug from Tom Donilon, the normally undemonstrative National Security Advisor. He was elated with what I had secured.

"You belong out in the field," he declared.

Walking by, Obama stopped to congratulate me on the "nice work."

Having just won reelection two weeks prior, he was the most relaxed I had seen him since before Election Night in 2008. I hurriedly thanked him for making the trip and thus giving me bargaining clout, but he waved me off.

"Let's not kid ourselves," he said, "I'm only a prop."

When our convoy arrived at Aung San Suu Kyi's home a few hours later, she seemed extremely happy to see the President. He too was moved to be in the place where she had effectively been imprisoned on and off for fifteen years. She welcomed us into her book-lined study, greeting me as if we were meeting for the first time.

Obama began by expressing his admiration for all she had already achieved for democracy in Burma. "How can we be of further assistance?" he asked. Instead of answering Obama's question, Suu Kyi spoke for the next twenty minutes about the arcane procedural maneuverings that dominated the Burmese parliament. At various points I looked toward Obama, wondering if he was disappointed or bored. But he didn't seem to mind her journey into the weeds of Burmese politics.

Halfway through their allotted time together, Suu Kyi asked to meet alone with President Obama and Secretary Clinton. I was immensely relieved for an excuse to leave the room—I had not had time to pump for hours and had grown increasingly uncomfortable as the meeting went on.

I raced out to the armored vehicle where I had left my pump and asked to be directed to the nearest restroom, which was on the ground floor of Suu Kyi's home, across the hall from the study where Obama, Clinton, and she were still talking.

I perched myself on the closed lid of the toilet, assembled the breast pump, and then attached the suction cups first to a pair of small bottles and then to myself. When I turned on the pump, it began its loud, rhythmic, blare: HEEEE-HAWWWW. HEEEE-HAWWWW. HEEE-HAWWWW.

Initially, I was self-conscious about the noise, wondering if Obama, Clinton, and Suu Kyi might be able to hear it. But a large press pool from all over the world was milling outside, creating a din that I was confident would drown out other sounds.

Because I found it uncomfortable to pump, I had always disliked it. And if I didn't produce as much milk as usual, I felt like a failure. But on that day, in part because it had been so long since I had last pumped, the milk flowed freely.

I took in the utter improbability of the moment. Barack Obama, the first African-American president of the United States, had just been elected to a second term by a sizable margin. Aung San Suu Kyi was a free woman and a member of the parliament from which she had been banned for decades. And I, the mother of two children who had successfully negotiated with the Burmese military junta's representatives in advance of a presidential visit, was pumping in the bathroom of the home of a human rights giant. I looked up at the ceiling and said a short prayer of thanks.

At one point, I thought I heard the chatter of the media die down, so I assumed that Obama and Suu Kyi were about to begin their press conference. I leaned over toward the window in the bathroom, which was beside the toilet, and pulled back one of the curtains to see if this was the case.

To my surprise and horror, the window looked directly out onto the porch where the two leaders were already making statements to the cameras. Had I unwittingly drawn the curtain a few inches wider, I would have exposed myself to the world.

DURING THE FLIGHT HOME, President Obama was in high spirits after his reelection and what had become a widely celebrated visit to Burma. He summoned me to his personal cabin on Air Force One and asked me what job I hoped for in his second term.

Cass had just left the White House after three and a half years. He was now commuting between our home in Washington and a small rental apartment near Harvard Law School, where he had resumed teaching three days a week. I did not want to leave government, but I was ready to try something new. I had run a number of policy processes to their conclusion, led our efforts to improve the government's responsiveness to atrocities, and worked with Susan and others to ensure we reengaged a variety of international bodies. I thought it was time for someone with fresh eyes to take up my portfolio. I also thought I might be more effective tackling issues that our administration was struggling with (Syria being the best example) from a different perch. Susan was in the running to become Secretary of State or National Security Advisor, so I told the President that I would be interested in taking her place if she left the UN.

"What's your second choice?" Obama asked immediately.

I told him I would work wherever he wanted to put me, but I returned to the UN job. I knew the organization well, I said, and I understood its flaws. I had proven my ability to negotiate important deals. I would be a forceful advocate for American ideals, and my tirelessness would enable me to effectively rally other countries to address threats that mattered to the United States.

I had never had to sell myself to Obama before and felt awkward doing so. Indeed, the last time I had tried to convince someone to give me a job was in 1993, when I had met with Carey English at *U.S. News & World Report*. At least then I had been able to hand him my Balkans chronology and writing clips. I hated the sound of advocating for my own advancement.

Obama challenged me to justify my preference for the UN position.

"I thought you cared about making a difference," he said. I gave him a puzzled look as he continued. "You have a hell of a lot more influence on US policy from where you are now than you would from the UN." Punctuating his point, he pronounced "the UN" in a dismissive tone. For the next ten minutes, I found myself transported to Obama's law school classroom as I defended my professional qualifications and described how I would approach the job.

When Cass later asked how well I had answered Obama's questions, I gave myself a "B-," before adding, "and that's with grade inflation."

Only after I had returned to my seat in the main cabin did I think of half a dozen arguments I should have made. My motto—not just as a journalist, but also in life—had always been "show, don't tell." But given that President Obama was arguably the most preoccupied person on the planet, in this case I kicked myself for not connecting the dots.

IN MARCH OF 2013, after more than four years at the White House, I took a short break from the administration. President Obama and I had not discussed the UN job a second time. Even though Pete Rouse, one of the President's closest advisers, had told me Obama was seriously considering me, I couldn't be sure what he would ultimately decide. Eager to continue serving, I accepted an offer from the new Secretary of State, John Kerry, to become Undersecretary of State for Civilian Security, Democracy, and Human Rights. The role came with a large portfolio in which I would oversee human rights, refugees and migration, international justice and law enforcement, and conflict prevention. The position required Senate confirmation, so I submitted all of my financial and personal records to a team of White House lawyers who would scrutinize the information to ensure that I had done nothing illegal or unethical. Then, I waited.

At home, I was elated to be able to steal full days with Rían, who was already nine months old. I also taught three-year-old Declan to swim and brought him to his first Washington Nationals baseball games. Then, in late May of 2013, the main White House lawyer reviewing my files called to inform me that I had cleared the vetting process. My nomination would be announced imminently.

In a remarkable coincidence of timing, Cass and I had been invited to dine with the President, the First Lady, and a few of their friends at the White House residence that very night. In anticipation, I had recruited Eddie to make the drive down from New York to babysit, leaving him with explicit instructions for feeding Rían, who was a fussy eater.

A few minutes late, we were escorted up to the Obamas' home and out onto their balcony overlooking the National Mall. Obama was already holding forth among his guests, and as we entered, Cass accidentally knocked over a glass. Obama laughed, perhaps recalling Cass's messiness when they were colleagues at the University of Chicago.

"Leave it to Cass," the President said playfully, "to break the White House."

After half an hour of small talk on the outdoor portico, our group was called to dinner. Just as I walked back into the residence, my phone rang. Eddie was in a state of panic, unable to find Rían's pumped milk. Instead, he had settled on something white that didn't smell like milk and wasn't fitting through the small hole in Rían's bottle, causing her to complain loudly.

Realizing that he had mistakenly attempted to feed her rice water, I ducked down the hallway to try to calm my frazzled father while President Obama treated the other guests to a quick stop in Abraham Lincoln's bedroom, showing them the only copy of the Gettysburg Address personally signed by the sixteenth president.

Explaining the logistics of baby care to Eddie by phone was like trying to explain the complexities of a new tech gadget: what seemed straightforward to me just wasn't obvious to a man in his seventies. He became increasingly frustrated, I then grew exasperated, and both of us ended up practically shouting. This had happened many times before, but never in such close proximity to Abraham Lincoln's bedroom. As our conversation escalated in its inevitable way, I suddenly heard a voice behind me.

"Let me talk to him."

President Obama grabbed my cell phone. "Listen," he instructed Eddie, "this is the President of the United States. You can do this. You just need to stay calm and focus."

Obama proceeded to speak with Eddie for a good three minutes before he handed the phone back to me, saying, "He's got this." When I put the phone to my ear again, Eddie had hung up, undoubtedly to call Mum. A masterful storyteller had been gifted one for the ages. And for once, no embellishment would be necessary.

President Obama asked if he could have a word with me in a separate room. I nodded nervously, wondering what was on his mind—or what I could have done wrong. He did not leave much time for suspense.

"Tom is leaving," Obama said matter-of-factly, referring to the National Security Advisor. "I am going to move Susan down here into his job, and I want to move you to the UN."

I swallowed hard and, while I continued to watch the President's mouth move, the sound of his words grew faint, drowned out by the tumult in my own brain.

"Holy shit—I'm going to be UN ambassador," I thought to myself. "Wait until I tell Mum and Eddie!" Then, almost instantaneously, the bats in my Bat Cave went into a fluttering overdrive. "Oh no—Fox News is going to portray me as a madwoman," I worried. "This could be a nightmare . . ."

When I refocused on President Obama, he was zeroing in on my Senate confirmation.

"The lawyers are telling me that you have been vetted back to when you were twenty-three, but this is a cabinet position, so the vetting needs to go back further. I need you to think really, really hard about whether you did anything between the ages of eighteen and twenty-three that we need to know about—anything at all that could embarrass us," Obama said. "If there is something, I'm sure we can figure out a way to manage it, but whether it is sex, drugs, or taxes, *we need to know*. I just need you to think."

The joyful moment of being chosen had lasted a grand total of ten seconds. President Obama saw my face fall.

"What is it?"

"I . . . did not have an ideal romantic life in those years," I offered. "I dated a lot of the wrong guys." I was already overthinking the situation, conflating my early relationships with a few lizards with something severe enough to hurt my confirmation.

"Well," Obama said, "unless you dated Yasser Arafat, I think we'll be okay."

And with that, he walked me into the Old Family Dining Room, where the rest of his guests were seated at the table, chatting with the First Lady.

Cass was seated at the opposite end from me. He watched as I unsteadily took my seat and drained a glass of water. Our eyes met, and I shook my head in astonishment. I put my hand over my heart, signaling that something major had happened. Cass used his fingers to draw the letters "U" and "N" in the air, and I nodded back. As my husband beamed with delight, I sat silently through dinner and drinks, which went until one a.m., racking my brain to recall anything untoward I might have done a quarter of a century before.

As President Obama walked us to the door at the end of the night, I thanked him for the opportunity he was giving me. But he was not there yet.

"Think," he said, giving me a parting kiss on the cheek.

That night, instead of sleeping, I imagined how every event in my life could be most negatively portrayed.

"Pretend you are Fox News," I told myself. I had traveled to Cuba with a human rights activist to document Fidel Castro's abuses. I saw the Fox headline: "OUR WOMAN IN HAVANA."

I had been involved with a man who claimed he was divorced from his wife, but I later learned they were only legally separated. "HOME WRECKER," the New York Post would proclaim.

Finally, at around five a.m., I settled on the issue that was surely going to seal my doom—and, according to the logic of my sleep-deprived paranoia, unravel Obama's presidency altogether.

As a freelance journalist in Bosnia, I had been paid twenty cents a word for my articles (which, at around eight hundred words each, earned me $160 per piece). Was I sure I paid taxes on every single one of my Bosnia articles? "TAX CHEAT!"

My mind raced through all the publications I wrote for in my

Balkan years: the *Boston Globe*, *Miami Herald*, *San Francisco Chronicle*, *Economist*, *U.S. News & World Report*, *Washington Post*, *The New Republic*. "Rack your brain, Samantha," I commanded myself. "Were there others?"

And then, at around 5:30 a.m., I remembered the *Irish Sunday Business Post* and the *Yorkshire Post*. I wrote a couple of articles for the former and no more than a half dozen for the latter. I began to spiral downward and shook Cass, who had been sleeping beside me.

"Cass, wake up," I said. "I don't think I paid taxes on my income from the *Yorkshire Post* in 1995."

Through his haze, he asked, "Yorkshire, England? When did you live there?"

I reminded him that, in a bygone media age, smaller regional newspapers had assigned articles to freelancers around the world. He asked me how much income I had earned from the *Yorkshire Post*, and I said, as if it was a vast sum, "easily six hundred dollars." Then I corrected myself, "No, even more than that in dollars, because the six hundred would have been in British pounds."

Knowing better than to make fun of me, he turned away, saying I should go back to sleep and assuring me we would find a tax lawyer in the morning. "This *is* the morning," I said.

It would turn out that my Achilles' heel was not my taxes, which I had paid. And it certainly was not my ex-boyfriends. In the new era of permanent political and policy warfare, it was my writing and public commentary.

ON WEDNESDAY, JUNE 5TH, a beautiful afternoon five short days after the President had told me to "think" about my past, the White House announced to the press corps that Obama would be making a "personnel announcement" in the Rose Garden.

Cass happened to be overseas the day of the ceremony, so he settled for calling me what felt like every fifteen minutes. In the morning, I dropped Rían at daycare across from the White House, and deposited Declan at his summer baseball camp.

This left me with a few hours to finish preparing my remarks for the event and to track down phone numbers for the White House to contact potential validators—people who could attest to the fact that I was qualified for the position. I picked up Declan at camp around lunchtime, but, because of heavy traffic, had to scramble to change him into a borrowed toddler blazer and clip-on tie. Mercifully, María was there to help me scrub the brown baseball dust off his grimy face, print my remarks, and get to the White House in time to collect Rían and calm myself.

When we arrived, my parents, María, and the kids were quickly escorted to their seats, while I joined the President, Susan Rice, and Tom Donilon in the Oval Office.

After a few minutes of small talk, the President led us outside, and we stood behind him as he walked to the podium. The crowd—filled with our families, friends, and colleagues—greeted us with an extended round of applause, putting a lump in my throat. Mort was in the audience, and Gayle helped keep Declan in check during the ceremony.

The President began by thanking Tom for his four and a half years of tireless service. He described his confidence in Susan, who would be stepping into the government's most important, high-pressure foreign policy position. And finally, as I looked at Mum's and Eddie's faces in the audience—in the Rose Garden! At the White House!—the President introduced me as his choice to represent the United States as UN ambassador:

> One of our foremost thinkers on foreign policy, she showed us that the international community has a moral responsibility and a profound interest in resolving conflicts and defending human dignity . . . To those who care deeply about America's engagement and indispensable leadership in the world, you will find no stronger advocate for that cause than Samantha.

When I stepped up to the microphone, I recounted how I had arrived in Pittsburgh as a nine-year-old, wearing a Stars and Stripes T-shirt. "Even as a little girl with a thick Dublin accent who had never been to America," I said, "I knew that the American flag was the symbol of fortune and of freedom." I described practicing a new accent in front of the mirror "so that I too could quickly speak and be American."

The day before the Rose Garden ceremony, I had remembered that Cass's dad, Dick Sunstein (who died of a brain tumor when Cass was just twenty-five), had been on furlough from the Navy in San Francisco in April of 1945 during the founding conference of the United Nations. Rummaging through a box Cass kept of his dad's letters from the war, I found one Dick had sent to Cass's mother that seemed uncannily resonant.

"Conference starts today," the letter dated April 25th, 1945 began. "The town is going wild with excitement. It is a pleasure to be here for the opening few days. Let's pray that they accomplish something."

After reading parts of the letter in my Rose Garden remarks, I repeated Cass's dad's words. "Let's pray that they accomplish something."

I concluded by saying that I had seen the best and worst of the UN—aid workers enduring artillery fire to deliver food to people in Sudan and peacekeepers failing to protect the people of Bosnia. The UN had to do a better job "meeting the necessities of our time," I said, an objective that I believed was possible to achieve only if the United States led the way.

I knew many in my Irish family would be watching the ceremony. And I felt a twinge of sadness that my dad wasn't around to witness it. But mainly, I felt as though I was levitating. I thought of all that Mum and Eddie had done for me over the years. Mum getting on that plane to America and later buying me my first laptop before I headed off to the Balkans. Eddie keeping my love of the underdog alive with his Irish fight songs. Both of them spending an untold number of hours editing chapters of my books—even after their own long days of work at the hospital.

I had traveled a vast distance to represent the United States at the UN. And I still had one last hurdle to clear.

27

ONE SHOT

Back at our Georgetown apartment after the Rose Garden ceremony, Eddie sat transfixed on our couch, watching commentators on CNN dissect the personnel "shake-up" President Obama had just announced.

After putting the kids down for a nap, I joined him.

"How bad?" I asked.

"Nothing to worry about," he said.

"How bad?" I asked again.

"They get paid to say these things," he said.

With Eddie and Mum now sitting on either side of me, we listened to a parade of analysts predict that I was in for a lengthy, ugly confirmation fight on Capitol Hill. One of the talking heads suggested my struggle might resemble that experienced by John Bolton, the flame-throwing conservative whose 2005 nomination to become UN ambassador had proven so controversial that he was ultimately unable to win confirmation.*

"Oh dear," my mother sighed, before quietly stepping outside for a walk around the neighborhood.

Mum had once sent me a pick-me-up card in which she wrote the inscription that appears above the entrance to Wimbledon's Centre Court, from Rudyard Kipling's poem "If":

---

* Bolton would serve as US Ambassador to the UN under a recess appointment, and in 2018 he became Donald Trump's National Security Advisor.

If you can meet with triumph and disaster
And treat those two imposters just the same

This was always easier said than done—for me and for her.

I understood that for many of Obama's Republican critics, my perspective on foreign policy was intrinsically suspect. And having watched Cass go through the confirmation process back in 2009, I knew the US Senate's approval was not foreordained. Like my husband, I had amassed a voluminous body of writing that the senators' staffs would examine. As the *Washington Post* summarized, "During a long and outspoken career as a journalist, author and human rights activist, Power, 42, has provided extensive fodder for questions about her views on many US foreign policy issues."

The *Post* article also made the unwelcome prediction that "congressional Republicans looking for a foreign policy fight" could try to derail my confirmation. Senator Ted Cruz of Texas was one of the first out of the gate, calling my selection "deeply troubling" and charging that I "strongly supported the expansion of international institutions and international law . . . at the expense of US sovereignty." Soon after, the far-right Center for Security Policy (CSP) launched what Fox News called "a movement" against my nomination.*

Led by CSP president Frank Gaffney and retired lieutenant general William Boykin, a former Pentagon official from the George W. Bush administration, the group circulated a letter about Obama's "wholly unacceptable choice" that was signed by more than fifty conservative activists, retired military officers, and former government officials. "We should be proud to be Americans, and if you look at Samantha Power's track record, there is a strong indication that her attitude is just the opposite," Boykin said at a National Press Club event held to mobilize opposition.

I spent the days after the announcement contacting Republicans to try to secure their support. One of my first calls was to Senator Lindsey

---

* CSP is a "think tank" that has also been designated as a hate group by the Southern Poverty Law Center, due to its anti-Muslim stances.

Graham of South Carolina, as he was one of his party's leading voices on foreign policy. He got right to the point.

"Are you the crazy nut the blogs are saying you are, or someone who will defend US interests at the UN?" Graham asked.

"The latter, sir," I responded.

Much to my amazement and perhaps influenced by his friend Senator John McCain, with whom I had worked on human rights issues while serving at the White House, Graham immediately issued a statement praising my nomination.

Thinking I should reach out to the two Republican senators representing Georgia, I also called Sally, my high school friend, to see if she happened to know anyone connected to them. As it turned out, Sally's stepfather worked closely with a leading Republican lawyer in the state, who graciously agreed to encourage Senators Saxby Chambliss and Johnny Isakson to see me.

Chambliss had been a staunch opponent of Cass's nomination four years before, and while they had ended up working together closely once Cass had assumed his role, I was not optimistic that he would support me. Yet as soon as I walked into his office, I was bathed in a particularly Southern kind of warmth. Chambliss asked me about my basketball-playing days at Lakeside High, and then quickly eliminated the suspense about how he was leaning on my nomination.

"Look, Samantha," he said, "I'm not supporting you because of your advocacy for human rights, but I admire your genocide book. I'm not supporting you because you got into trouble on the Obama campaign for your comments about Hillary Clinton, though I must say I like a lady with a sharp tongue. I'm supporting you for one reason: your husband. There are few finer men around."

I was grateful when Republican senators agreed to meet with me, as not all of them did. Although Senator Cruz and Senator Mike Lee of Utah grilled me about the deficiencies of the United Nations and eventually voted against my nomination, our discussions were lively and respectful. I had the opportunity to explain why the world's only global organization was vital to our national interests in an era when confronting the major challenges to the United States required international cooperation.

"Of course US sovereignty is important," I told Cruz at one point during our private exchange, "but to protect US security, we need the UN to get other countries to step up to confront threats."

After these discussions, I resolved that, if I became ambassador, I would try to set aside time to meet with UN critics and those generally skeptical of America's engagement abroad. The growing number of Americans getting their news from Fox were seeing the UN falsely depicted as a threat. In debunking these fabrications and taking on the arguments of American isolationists and nationalists, I hoped to make a small contribution to sustaining support for US investments in the international system.

All told, I found that I had more support than the pundits had initially anticipated. But many senators informed me that they were reserving judgment. What I said and how I presented myself at the confirmation hearing would prove pivotal.

As my scheduled appearance approached, I was of two minds about it. On the one hand, I would be relieved to finally get to speak for myself and respond publicly to the bizarre caricatures of my views that were being promoted by Fox News and right-wing websites. On the other hand, I needed to be very sure that I did not make a mistake. My goal was to make no news.

BILL DANVERS, A SENIOR STATE DEPARTMENT AIDE, ran point on my confirmation. Bill had served in a number of national security roles in the Executive Branch and on the Hill, including as staff director of the Senate Committee on Foreign Relations, where my testimony would take place. In addition to accompanying me to meetings with senators, Bill organized a series of mock confirmation hearings (or "murder boards") for me to practice responding to the aggressive questioning of senators.

I recruited people from inside and outside the government to be my mock interrogators, including Cass, David Pressman, and my friends Jon Favreau and Tommy Vietor, longtime Obama aides who had re-

332 The Education of an Idealist

cently left the administration. Their job was to act like the most abrasive senators imaginable.

The pummeling began immediately.

"What makes you think you have the experience to represent us at the UN? What does an academic know about foreign policy?"

"You called Hillary Clinton a 'monster.' Is insulting people how you plan to win friends and influence people at the UN?"

"You have written that the United States made a mistake by not recognizing the Armenian genocide. Yet President Obama has also failed to do so. Will you, right now, pledge that as UN ambassador you will recognize the genocide?"

"You have long criticized American foreign policy and shown you would prefer the United States be ruled by world government and by international treaties. Do you plan to use your position to undermine the sovereignty of the United States?"

Everyone who participated in these sessions had before them the most controversial excerpts from my past writings and interviews, and expertly used them to back me into a corner. Someone would read a quote that sounded maximally objectionable, before asking innocently, "Is this still your view?" Cass, who played Senator Rand Paul, knew I got needlessly irritated when people mistakenly added an "s" to the end of my last name, so he upped the ante by addressing me as "Ms. Powers" every time he asked a question.

As my colleagues, friends, and spouse threw hundreds of questions at me, it quickly became apparent that I made a lousy witness on my own behalf. I had a knack for offering long, sincere, and ultimately damaging answers. I showed poor judgment even on minor issues of decorum; when "Senator Paul" called me Ms. Powers, I interrupted to correct him—"It is *Power*, Senator." I had not expected these practice sessions to go smoothly right away, but neither had I imagined them to go quite so badly.

Danvers, whose sighs grew louder the longer my answers dragged on, told me plainly:

There is something you do not seem to get: the senators are not there to listen to you. They are there to listen to themselves. They want to be on television. They want to play to their base. As you speak, most will not even be listening. You are just filler between their first comment that pretends to be a question and their second comment that pretends to be a question. So the longer your answers are, the more annoyed they will become, and the greater the chance that you say something you will regret. If you hear nothing else, just remember this: your hearing is not on the level.

I knew this from my days working with Obama in the Senate, but I struggled to internalize the implications.

In our life together, Cass had almost always found words of encouragement for me in low times. But here, instead of offering false praise for answers that could appear in a guide for how not to get confirmed by the US Senate, he just commiserated, telling me, "I'm so sorry you have to go through this."

I devoted weeks to the murder boards, drilling my answers in an effort to make them as rote and succinct as possible. State Department officials had prepared responses to various questions that might trip me up, but much of what they wrote felt inauthentic. I would stop halfway through attempting the formulaic answer and tell my interrogators, "I can't say this. It doesn't come close to answering the question."

On a number of occasions, this caused Danvers to bury his face in his hands before asking, "Do you want to get confirmed or not?"

My temper would flash. "I want to get confirmed," I once responded, "but not at the expense of becoming a Washington asshole."

We eventually managed a compromise. "Here's what will work," I told Danvers. "You don't want me actually answering the question in the detailed way I would generally respond. And I don't want to pretend that a senator didn't ask a question we all heard him ask, or mouth a bunch of drivel. Why don't we find something that isn't my first answer, but that feels responsive and which is something I actually believe?"

This became the strategy by which I prepared—finding a way not to always say what first came to mind, but to express something that, as I put it, "was *also* true."

I had an opportunity to try out this new approach when discussing an article I had written for *The New Republic* in 2003, just before President Bush's invasion of Iraq. In the article, I argued that the United States should practice what we preached to other countries. "Instituting a doctrine of the mea culpa would enhance our credibility," I wrote. "US foreign policy has to be rethought. It needs not tweaking but overhauling. We need a historical reckoning with crimes committed, sponsored, or permitted by the United States."

"For what crimes does the United States need to apologize?" Tommy Vietor asked in one of the murder boards.

"Thank you for your question, Senator," I said. "Obviously, this is a challenging issue. But for example, the torture at the Abu Ghraib prison, the . . ."

"NO, NO, NO . . ." Danvers shouted, as Cass looked down to avoid eye contact with me. "Why would you say something that somebody could paint as an insult to our armed forces? Why the hell would you pick a fight like that? You don't have to. Your goal is to get in and out of your hearing, not to establish world historical truths."

"OK," I said, defeated, and by then exhausted. "I get it. Well, what should I say?"

"Say the article was written a long time ago, and your views have changed," said Bill.

"My views have definitely changed," I said, "but I still believe we make mistakes and that we can't pretend we don't."

Bill again gave me the look of "Do you want to be UN ambassador?"

Our strategy called for saying something that was "also true," so I suggested, "I can talk about the importance of accountability, as well as how great the United States is—which I believe."

Bill did not object, so I fleshed out a detailed version of this response and practiced it for days.

I KNEW MY ANSWERS to the senators' questions had to show that I was not taking the outcome of the confirmation process for granted.

This meant prefacing most responses with caveats like, "If I am fortunate enough to be confirmed, I will . . ."

But with Susan already in place as National Security Advisor, I couldn't wait until the Senate had voted before planning how Cass and I would go about uprooting our family and moving to New York. Fortunately, Hillary Schrenell, who worked at the US Mission to the UN, took much of this burden off my plate.

I had first met Hillary a decade before, when she was a twenty-two-year-old intern at the Kennedy School. I found her so dedicated and sharp that I hired her as my full-time research assistant. In five years of working together, she became a close friend. After she graduated from Harvard Law School in 2010, I introduced her to Susan Rice, who hired her as a policy adviser. Now, if I could get confirmed, I would have the chance to work with Hillary again. But in the meantime, I asked her to come to DC to join my confirmation team. I felt it was important to have someone in my inner circle who knew both me and the practical and substantive steps I would need to take once in the job. Because Hillary was close to my family, she also volunteered to help me think through how I would get everybody moved to New York.

I was a bit embarrassed to rely on Hillary for help on household issues given that she would soon be my senior policy adviser—*if I was fortunate enough to be confirmed*—but she insisted on using her vacation time to help me.

"The whole system is geared for the old days, when a male ambassador swoops into his new job," she said. "And the faithful wife trails behind, organizing the movers and finding schools for the kids."

We both knew that Cass was not going to embrace the role of old-school spouse. Over the years, I had learned that when I assigned him domestic tasks, I often regretted it. After I gave birth to our son, I asked Cass to write Declan's name and birth date on the official form. A few months later, after I waited several hours at the Washington, DC, birth registry for Declan's birth certificate, I received one for "PECLAN POWER SUNSTEIN."

As soon as I saw the typo, I knocked on the glass window and asked

for the spelling to be corrected. But the clerk told me that such an altera-
tion would require a trip to the "amendments office." I was beside myself.

"Ma'am," I said, "I promise you I didn't call my son Peclan and then
change my mind. My husband just has horrible handwriting."

The clerk repeated directions to the amendments office and slid the
glass window shut. After waiting another hour, I received the corrected
birth certificate, which still noted that Peclan Power Sunstein was born
April 24th, and then, beside his "birth name," in inch-high black type,
the office had added the stamp, "AMENDED," and his "new" name,
Declan Power Sunstein.

The experience now seems trivial, but at the time it sent me into an
exasperated rage at my husband. "You had one job!" I told him. "And
now, for the rest of his life, Declan will have to explain to people why
his parents named him Peclan!"

When Rían was born, Cass promised I could count on him.
"I learn well," he said. Yet when I returned to the same birth registry to collect our daughter's birth certificate, it read "RTAN POWER
SUNSTEIN." Her birth certificate, like Declan's, now has an inch-
high "AMENDED" stamp, indicating that, after a few months of reflection, her parents decided that "Rían" was preferable to "Rtan."

I felt we had no margin for error when it came to settling our family in New York, and was grateful to be able to rely on Hillary. She
developed an elaborate matrix of all the local preschools and daycares so
I could begin to make inquiries. Knowing Declan and Rían herself, she
also helped me narrow the search by speaking with the administrators
of schools that she thought might be a good fit. She even helped find
computer classes for María, who had generously agreed to move with us.

When I talked through my substantive priorities with Hillary, she
urged me to decide who I would want as my chief of staff—one of
the first consequential decisions I would make. I settled almost immediately on Jeremy Weinstein, my former NSC colleague. I had seen
firsthand how effective Jeremy was in government. He brought a special combination of realism about government's limits and a drive to
nonetheless get as much out of the system as possible.

Jeremy had spent two years at the NSC and then returned to Stanford to resume teaching. I asked him to move east again for another two-year stint. My offer presented an excruciating choice: he had two young sons, ages three and six, and was a committed partner in childcare with his wife, Rachel, who worked as an environmental advocate. But Rachel heroically agreed to shoulder the child-rearing burden for two years, while Jeremy committed to traveling back to California every other weekend. The sacrifices he and his family made were enormous.

Jeremy's interest in public service was deeply personal. When he was seven years old, his father began working obsessively to expose a top-secret CIA program called MKULTRA. The program had funded esteemed psychiatrists and psychologists in the United States and Canada to administer experimental drugs and intensive shock treatments on human subjects—one of whom was Jeremy's grandfather, causing him permanent brain damage.[21] Following an eight-year lawsuit, the CIA settled with eight Canadians, including his grandfather, paying victims a woefully modest amount.

From his family's ordeals at the hands of the US government, Jeremy acquired two key convictions, both of which I shared. He believed that governments should not be able to act with impunity in the name of national security. And equally important, he thought public officials should keep in mind the individuals who would be harmed by our failure to act in the face of gross injustice.

For all I would honestly say about my love of the United States at my confirmation hearing, I never forgot how often people in positions of power fell short. With Jeremy as my partner, I believed we could assemble a team that shared both our ambition and our humility in facing the formidable challenges that lay ahead.

WITH TWO DAYS TO GO until I was to appear before the Senate Foreign Relations Committee, Cass got us a hotel room a block from our apartment so I could focus on final preparations for the interrogation that we knew lay in wait. We recognized that if I worked from home and saw so much as a small sock belonging to Declan or Rían—never mind their magnetic selves—being deferential to Rand Paul would quickly fade from my mind.

Over those last forty-eight hours, Cass and I ate three meals a day together as he fired question after question at me, and I grew more and more skilled at responding without setting off land mines.

ON JULY 17TH, 2013, I woke up in the hotel to the sound of drumbeats and a looping piano riff:

> Started from the bottom now we're here
> Started from the bottom now my whole team fuckin' here

Cass's laptop was blaring Drake's ode to beating the odds and showing up the haters. "Just the way Drake intended!" I exclaimed, wishing the computer speakers could play louder. As I showered, dressed, and recited answers to Cass's questions on climate change, world government, the Middle East, and more, I asked him to add Eminem's "Lose Yourself" to the playlist.

There we were—two nerdy professors rapping Drake and Eminem lyrics in the Georgetown Inn:

> His palms are sweaty, knees weak, arms are heavy . . .
> He's nervous, but on the surface he looks calm and ready . . .
> You only get one shot, do not miss your chance to blow
> This opportunity comes once in a lifetime . . .

Though I belted out Eminem's "his palms are sweaty, knees weak, arms are heavy" line with great fervor, the truth was that, as we made our way to Capitol Hill, I felt calm and ready.

Because of my Georgia background, Senators Chambliss and Isakson had agreed to introduce me before the Senate Foreign Relations Committee. But as soon as Chambliss began speaking, I accidentally knocked over a glass of water, which spilled across the long, wooden table in the hearing room.

"Good start, Sam," teased Isakson.

The hearing room was filled with friends and supporters. My parents, Cass, Laura, Hillary, María, Declan, and Rían sat right behind me. Other close friends sat a row behind them. Unsurprisingly, Rían became restless almost as soon as the hearing began, and María spent the next few hours roaming the halls with her. When Declan saw his godfather, John Prendergast, enter a few minutes after I started testifying, he said in a loud whisper, "Mommy, look, there's John." I tried to ignore him because I was responding to a senator's question at the time, but his whisper grew louder.

"Mommy, John's here!"

My mother tried to quiet him, but I knew he needed acknowledgment. When another senator on the dais began speaking, I quickly turned to Declan to signal that I too was pleased that John was there.

Fortunately, the hearing went well and I did not make headlines. However, I did have a tortured exchange with Florida's Republican senator Marco Rubio, who, just like in the murder boards, had a stack of my writings sitting in front of him, with the most controversial comments highlighted. Rubio spent most of his time on the *New Republic* article I had prepared to discuss.

"Which crimes [committed by the United States] were you referring to, and which decisions taken by the current administration would you recommend for such a reckoning?" he asked.

My learning kicked in, and I responded by saying something I believed . . . but which was perhaps not what Rubio was hoping to elicit:

> I, as an immigrant to this country, think that this country is the greatest country on Earth, as I know do you. I would never apologize for America. America is the light to the world. We have freedoms and opportunities here that people dream about abroad.
>
> . . . the point, I think, that I was trying to make is that sometimes we, as imperfect human beings, do things that we wish we had done a little bit differently, and sometimes it can be productive to engage . . . with foreign citizenry in a productive dialogue. And I think that is what President Clinton did [by apologizing] in

the wake of the Rwandan genocide. It had a great effect. It really meant a great deal. And that is really all I was meaning.

Rubio noted that the Rwandan genocide could be characterized as "permitted" by the United States. But he wanted to know: "Which [crimes] did the United States commit or sponsor that you were referring to?"

Coached to avoid specifics, I fell back to home base: "Again, sir, the greatest country on Earth. We have nothing to apologize for."

Rubio looked up with surprise and considerable irritation, but I kept an eye on the clock in front of me. I knew that he was allotted five minutes for questioning, and his time would soon expire. I kept hearing Danvers's words in my head. "This hearing is not on the level. *It is not on the level.*" I just had to be patient and not let my self-consciousness about my answers overwhelm my desire for self-preservation.

For two minutes we went back and forth in exchanges like this:

> **Rubio:** So you do not have any [crimes] in mind now that we have committed or sponsored?
> **Me:** I will not apologize for America. I will stand very proudly, if confirmed, behind the US placard.
> **Rubio:** No, I understand. But do you believe the United States has committed or sponsored crimes?
> **Me:** I believe the United States is the greatest country on Earth. I really do.
> **Rubio:** So your answer to whether we have committed or sponsored crimes is that the United States is the greatest country on Earth?
> **Me:** The United States is the leader in human rights. It is the leader in human dignity . . .

Rubio's time expired. I had lost my innocence. And two weeks later, the US Senate confirmed me by a vote of 87–10.

28

"CAN'T BE BOTH"

I was sworn in as the twenty-eighth US Ambassador to the United Nations on August 2nd, 2013. As we stood in his West Wing office, Vice President Joe Biden handed Cass a tattered, leather-bound Bible that had been in the Biden family since the 1890s. As Cass held the book, which had a Celtic cross on the cover, I placed my left hand on top and raised my right hand. Almost as soon as I began the oath, I got choked up. Seeing my emotion, Cass followed suit. And then, never one to be outdone, Biden's eyes welled up with tears as well.

I was overwhelmed by the momentousness of representing my country at the United Nations. Even after I watched the final Senate votes being tallied on C-SPAN, the idea that I would be the one sitting behind the placard that read "United States" had not seemed entirely real.

Now, looking into the sky-blue eyes of the Vice President and hearing myself swear to uphold the Constitution, I was struck by the gravity of embodying *America* to the world. Taking the oath, I felt what I imagined medal winners might experience as they stood on the podium at the Olympics and listened to their national anthem—a mix of pride, patriotism, and relief.

I had known Biden since my time in the Balkans, when he was a senator lobbying President Clinton to rescue Bosnians under siege. And over the past several decades, he and Cass had often discussed judicial appointments. The Vice President had shown immense warmth toward both of us.

Having observed Biden in debates in the Situation Room, and from just chatting with him during chance encounters in the West Wing, I was struck by the extent to which the man I saw up close resembled the public Biden, the person millions of Americans felt they knew. He was blunt and demonstrative. He could go on too long. But he seemed to see the value of each person he met, irrespective of their status.

After losing his wife and one-year-old daughter in a car accident, Biden encouraged people to confide their losses to him. I learned from one of his advisers that he still gave his personal cell phone number to grieving strangers he met, urging them, "If you feel low and you don't know where to turn, call me."

I marveled at how, when these people sometimes followed up, he made them feel as though they were his first priority.

Once I had concluded the oath with the familiar words "So help me God," Biden leaned toward me and said, "Don't you change up there. Be you. That's what we need."

"Yes sir," I replied, before Cass added, "She doesn't have a choice."

WHEN SUSAN WAS AMBASSADOR to the UN, I had stayed with her in the official residence of the ambassador at the Waldorf Astoria Towers, so I thought I knew what to expect. But nothing prepared me for arriving at the Waldorf in the role myself.

"Good evening, Ambassador," the doorman said as Cass and I exited my armored SUV and stepped under the blue and gold Waldorf Astoria awning.

"Good evening, Ambassador," the concierge said, after we had passed through the revolving doors.

"Good evening, Ambassador," one receptionist repeated, followed by two others.

After we rode up to the forty-second floor, the armed guard who kept watch outside the apartment around the clock added his greeting: "Welcome *home*, Ambassador."

Nobody said much to Cass.

The Waldorf Astoria apartment complex, which opened in 1931 along with the renowned hotel, had been home to every US Ambassador to the UN since 1947. After leaving office, Presidents Herbert

Hoover and Dwight Eisenhower had suites there, as did Frank Sinatra, Queen Elizabeth II, and General Douglas MacArthur.

After the guard opened the door, Cass and I entered tentatively, not quite able to absorb the fact that a palatial, nine-room, five-bathroom, white-carpeted penthouse had become our family home.

María had stayed in Washington with Declan and Rían so I would have a few days to choose their schools. When I looked into their shared bedroom, I was stunned to see that Hillary had already decorated it, lining the walls with giant floor-to-ceiling photographs of Declan's favorite Washington Nationals players and preparing Rían's crib—probably the first time a US Ambassador to the UN had needed one.

At a certain point, delighted to be alone with me for the first time in many hours, Cass exclaimed, "Let's race!," and we began doing wind sprints down the long halls.

"You may be a fancy ambassador," he shouted over his shoulder, "but I'm still faster."

Finding ourselves with a rare "date night," Cass and I pored over the stash of takeout menus left for us. "New York is the United Nations of food," I thought, before we settled on Szechuan Chinese from nearby. When we called in our order, asking for delivery to the Waldorf Astoria sounded positively bizarre.

After Cass blared Bob Dylan's "Shelter from the Storm," we capped off my first night as a fancy ambassador by watching the two-hour season finale of the crime mystery series *The Killing*.

CASS HAD BEEN so thoroughly in my corner since the moment Obama selected me as ambassador that he had not thought much about how his own life would change once I assumed the role. Because he had taken a nearly four-year leave from Harvard Law School to run OIRA, he did not feel he could abandon his teaching position again so soon. As a result, he planned to continue teaching in Cambridge three days a week during the school year, spending the rest of his time with our family in New York. He anticipated a seamless transition. But not long after I arrived at the office for my first official day on the job, he called in a panic from our bedroom at the Waldorf, where he was working for the day.

"There are too many people," he said, almost hysterical.

"What do you mean?" I asked.

"There are people in our home. People in our bedroom."

"What people?" I asked.

"All kinds of people," he said.

He was referring to the staff that cared for the ambassador's residence—a chef, an assistant house manager, and the Waldorf's cleaning staff.

After I had left that morning, chef Stanton Thomas had knocked on the bedroom door.

"I'm in here," Cass had shouted, hoping for privacy. When the knock came again, Cass trudged to the door.

"So sorry to bother you, Professor Sunstein," Thomas said amiably. "But I'm going for groceries. What does the Ambassador like to eat?"

Cass's mind, unusually, drew a complete blank. He viewed food as fuel—tuna sashimi from Nobu was indistinguishable from a tuna sandwich from a vending machine. He and I had been married five years, and he still had not dedicated mental space to logging my food tastes. However, wanting to be left alone, he knew he needed to come up with an answer, so he blurted, "Diet Coke."

Chef Thomas looked back quizzically. All that mattered to Cass was that a person who was not me was still standing there.

"And cheese," my husband added cheerfully, closing the bedroom door.

When I came back that evening, the refrigerator was filled with dozens of Diet Cokes and the largest variety of cheeses either of us had ever seen.

Every time Cass entered or exited the Waldorf, the concierge in the lobby greeted him as "Mr. Power." After a few weeks, Cass decided he should tell the man his real name.

"Good morning," Cass said. "You are so friendly to me, I just thought I would clarify . . . My last name isn't actually 'Power.' It is 'Sunstein.' But you can call me 'Cass.'"

The concierge looked mystified.

"That's incredible," he said, shaking his head.

Now Cass was the one who was confused.

"I just can't believe this," the concierge said. "You look *exactly* like Mr. Power."

WHILE MY HUSBAND NAVIGATED his first experience of being viewed as what he called a "derivative person," I adjusted to the fact that a protective detail of armed agents from the State Department's Diplomatic Security Service accompanied me virtually everywhere. Even when I went for a run in Central Park, I did so with these agents keeping pace beside me. For years, I had watched Cabinet officials disembarking from their armored black SUVs at the White House and felt the aura of importance they carried. Now, suddenly, I was one of them.

There were obvious perks. No longer permitted to drive, I did not have to jostle for parking in Washington or New York. I was prescreened for travel, so I could arrive at airports just minutes before the boarding gate closed. And because the protection officers had scoped the restaurants where I would be eating, I rarely had to wait for a table. The drawbacks, though, were not trivial: outside of our home, most conversations I had with Cass and the kids would happen in the agents' company. Although I would grow personally close to many of the individuals who served on my security detail, I frequently found myself longing for privacy.

I also had far less time alone at my new workplace, the United States Mission to the United Nations, a twenty-two-story, 147,000-square-foot building on the busy corner of 45th Street and 1st Avenue in midtown Manhattan, directly across the street from UN Headquarters.

After more than four years at the White House, I had grown accustomed to reading intelligence about terrorist threats to US government personnel and facilities around the world. Since the 1998 bombings of US embassies in Kenya and Tanzania and the September 11th attacks in 2001, many American diplomatic facilities, including the US Mission to the UN, had undergone extensive overhauls. The building had been gutted, completely redesigned and rebuilt to endure even an enormously destructive attack. The glass windows in the bright atrium lobby were tempered to withstand explosions, and a special filtration system protected against chemical and biological agents. The offices were set back forty feet from the curb, and the first six floors had no windows.

My office was near the top of the building, and it looked out on the East River and UN Headquarters. At street level, I could see the 193 flags of the UN member states, as well as school groups lining up for tours throughout the day. I could also spot the UN's most famous sculpture, known as Non-Violence: a mammoth, bronze Magnum revolver with its barrel twisted into a knot.

In 1945, after the devastation of two World Wars, the United Nations' founding charter defined the aim of the organization in stark terms: "to save succeeding generations from the scourge of war." The UN is the one place on earth that brings together representatives of all the world's recognized governments, large and small, rich and poor, in pursuit of this goal.* China, with 1.4 billion people, sits in the UN General Assembly with the Pacific island nation of Tuvalu, which has a population of 11,000. Russia, a country of 6.6 million square miles, sits alongside Monaco, which covers less than one square mile.

The UN founders recognized that conflict is often connected to economic deprivation and saw a role for the UN in helping to mitigate hardships that might fuel instability. As a result, thanks to the financial contributions of member states, UN programs over the years have lifted tens of millions of people out of poverty. Its food aid has nourished those at risk of starvation. Its refugee agency has resettled and sheltered people with no place to go. Its health efforts have eradicated smallpox and very nearly ended polio and guinea worm, while providing vaccinations to children who might otherwise have died of preventable diseases. And its environmental programs have mobilized countries to halt the depletion of the ozone layer, among other feats.

---

* When the UN was founded in 1945, it had just fifty-one members, but the number grew over the years, largely due to decolonization in Africa and Asia and the collapse of the Soviet Union. Initially, China's seat was occupied by the Republic of China, ruled by Chiang Kai-shek, who had fled with his forces to the island of Taiwan in 1949 after China's civil war. In 1971, the People's Republic of China assumed control over China's seat.

UN Secretary-General Ban Ki-moon was himself a beneficiary of efforts like these. UNICEF, the UN children's agency that has facilitated access to schooling for millions of kids, helped provide Ban with an education when he was a boy living in an impoverished, rural village in war-ravaged Korea.

And yet. On matters of war and peace, the UN has been less of an actor in its own right than a stage on which powerful countries have pursued their interests. Richard Holbrooke, who served as President Clinton's UN ambassador, once observed, "Blaming the UN for a crisis is like blaming Madison Square Garden when the New York Knicks play badly. You are blaming a building."

In 2010, Holbrooke had died suddenly of a heart attack, leaving a void in the lives of all who loved him. I missed him terribly and found myself constantly wishing I could pick up the phone to seek his counsel. Once I became ambassador, his wisdom echoed in my brain—and I often cited his analogy to Madison Square Garden, which vividly encapsulated the power and limitations of the UN.

As an organization, the UN has at its disposal whatever resources the governments within it choose to provide. It is the major players—countries like the United States, China, and Russia—that dictate how "the UN" handles crises. As a general rule, when politicians claim that a crisis is the "responsibility of the United Nations," they are diverting attention from their own impotence or lack of political will. In actual fact, in order for the UN to "act" or to "reform," a critical mass of countries must make that happen (or at least not actively block others from doing so). Much of the UN's dysfunction stemmed from the actions of particular countries, especially powerful ones. Early on in my tenure, I was given a cartoon that circulated widely at the UN. The cartoon showed dozens of people listening to a speech. In the first panel, the speaker asks, "Who wants change?" and all audience members enthusiastically raise their hands. In the second panel, the speaker refines his question, asking, "Who wants *to* change?" This time, each audience member looks toward the ground, demurring.

Measuring the impact of UN standards and laws on state behavior is difficult, but a world without UN rules or without UN humanitarian agencies would be infinitely crueler. And while divisions within the Security Council severely reduced the body's impact, doing away with the UN—or unilaterally exiting the organization, as some Republican politicians have proposed the United States do over the years—would greatly undermine collective efforts to end all conflicts.

While most countries, including the United States, sometimes balk at living by the ideals in the UN Charter, it is historically significant that none of the major powers have fought a war with one another since the UN's founding. UN peacekeeping missions have fallen far short on many occasions, but they have also helped protect huge numbers of civilians from violence and prevented conflict from spreading across borders.

Former UN secretary-general Dag Hammarskjöld may have best summed up both the UN's track record and its promise when he said it was created "not to lead mankind to heaven but to save humanity from hell."

WHEN I ENTERED THE LOBBY of UN Headquarters for the first time as US Ambassador, around two dozen reporters and photographers were waiting for me. I offered some brief comments, expressing my eagerness to make the UN work for Americans and for vulnerable people around the world. As the reporters thrust out their tape recorders, I noted that they were wearing the same UN press badge that I once wore. And they were chasing down leads in the same corridors where I had once walked as a reporter. I felt a warm connection with a group of people whose world helped shape me. But I also knew that I had to be guarded. I could not repeat the mistake I had made with the *Scotsman* during the Obama campaign.

Before I could assume my official functions, I was required to present my credentials to Secretary-General Ban Ki-moon.* For reasons I cannot now fathom, I chose to wear a striped sundress that exposed

---

* In accordance with diplomatic tradition, I would hand over a letter from President Obama that asked Ban to formally accept me as the President's representative.

both too much shoulder and too much leg. Upon seeing the official photo of me with the secretary-general, the French Ambassador to the UN, Gérard Araud, would later ask mischievously, "You wore your swim suit to present credentials?"

The picture showed me from the waist up, and, as I shook hands with Ban in his dark suit, one could have reasonably thought that I wandered into the UN from a local pool. I later heard from Kurtis Cooper, my deputy spokesperson, that a Spanish-speaking reporter had pulled him aside to ask about my attire as well, but managed only, "Samantha is very . . . hippie, no?" As a woman diplomat, I had to come to grips with the fact that, while I wished to focus on substance, my wardrobe would be scrutinized right alongside my negotiating skills.

Despite the UN secretary-general's grand title, he was named in the UN Charter as the administrator of the organization. For this reason, former secretary-general Kofi Annan described the position as "more secretary than general." In 1935, when Soviet dictator Joseph Stalin was asked to help enlist the Pope in efforts to counter the threat of Nazism, he reportedly answered, "The Pope? How many divisions has *he* got?" The UN secretary-general is in a similar bind: he commands no armed forces and has no authority over heads of state, so he lacks the means to enforce UN rules that are supposed to govern how countries behave. In all areas, he must rely on collective action by UN member states. Nonetheless, the secretary-general can use the prestige of his office to pursue diplomacy, and he can employ his bully pulpit to urge countries to respect human rights and international law. In our short meeting, which included our spouses, I told Ban Ki-moon that I looked forward to building a strong working relationship with him and warned that I had a long list of issues I hoped to raise when we next spoke.

THE KEY TO SUCCEEDING as ambassador, I knew, was to get the most out of the remarkable team of people who worked for the US Mission to the UN. Less than 10 percent of the 150-person staff were political appointees like Jeremy, Hillary, and myself. The vast majority were permanent staff, including foreign service and civil service officers who had worked previously for President George W. Bush's administration. Some civil servants had been at the Mission for more than thirty years, serving as far back as the Reagan administration. Many worked punishing hours, including weekends.

The career staff had generally internalized an unspoken (and sometimes spoken) rule of government to await instructions from those above them in the hierarchy before taking initiative. I had left my job at the National Security Council with a heightened appreciation for the importance of inclusive and transparent government processes. Yet now I urged the members of my team to show less deference to the system. Before they leaped to implement a direction, I asked them to take a moment to consider whether they agreed with the course of action envisaged.

Many had lived in the conflict-prone countries we were discussing. Some were experienced in the fields of international law or humanitarian relief. Several were Chinese, Russian, or Arabic speakers who brought invaluable insight to US negotiations. And almost all of them had institutional memories I lacked—knowing what had and hadn't worked in the past. I reminded them of the expertise they brought to their jobs and encouraged them to make their own recommendations to help shape US policy.

I knew that Holbrooke, Mort, and Jonathan had surrounded themselves with people who both challenged them and generated ideas, even if they were considered "junior." I wanted to do the same. One didn't have to be seasoned to be creative, and I needed ideas from wherever I could get them. I also tried to encourage an ethos of never being satisfied by merely raising an issue, making a public statement, or holding a meeting, stressing that we "care less about inputs and more about outcomes." When USUN diplomats committed the cardinal sin of "admiring the problem," I would handwrite on their memos, "If you were Obama, what would *you* do?"

Jeremy started organizing "deep dive" discussions during which we would carve out two hours to look afresh at policy problems, asking our in-house Africa, China, or sanctions experts to imagine formulating new policies from scratch. If we felt we had come up with something worth considering, I would talk to John Kerry to sound him out. We also urged staff to dedicate a specific time in their week to talk to someone outside government who knew about the issues they were working on. For understanding a place like Syria, where our embassy had closed down, those who worked in civil society could offer us a perspective that we could not get from within the US government. And we created a speakers' series, where academics and journalists would come to the Mission to share their experiences.

My team and I knew the danger of being overwhelmed by what we called "the tyranny of the inbox." As a result, after soliciting ideas from my staff and the four deputy ambassadors,* I settled on several human rights concerns that I would try to address without much involvement from Washington—issues that would not only help specific individuals, but also perhaps boost the confidence of US diplomats who sometimes seemed to doubt America's potential impact. We chose initiatives that I knew President Obama would support wholeheartedly, but which much of the bureaucracy beneath him did not prioritize.

At a time when American society seemed to be increasingly divided on the subject of immigration, I decided to find occasions to highlight the impact being made by refugees and immigrants in the United States. In addition, I would work with my team to embed LGBT rights within the DNA of the UN and to try to secure the release of political prisoners.

I wanted to highlight these issues from the very start. The same day as my meeting with the secretary-general, I visited a Refugee Youth Summer Academy, where dozens of local elementary and junior high

---

* In addition to the job I held as US Permanent Representative to the United Nations, the Mission had four other US ambassadors—the US Deputy Permanent Representative to the United Nations and Deputy Representative in the Security Council (Rosemary DiCarlo, followed by Michele Sison), an additional Alternate Representative of the United States for Special Political Affairs in the United Nations (Jeffrey DeLaurentis, followed by David Pressman), a US Representative for UN Management and Reform (Joe Torsella, followed by Isobel Coleman), and a US Representative on the Economic and Social Council of the United Nations (Elizabeth Cousens, followed by Sarah Mendelson).

school students who had been refugees were preparing for the upcoming school year in America. I met kids from places like Sudan, China, and Iran, and they told me about the traumatic situations they had escaped. I noted that I too had come to the United States as a young child, not knowing a soul, but had been lucky enough not to have experienced the hardships they had fled. I said that I was in awe of their courage and resilience.

After my confirmation hearing six weeks before, several newspapers had published a photograph of me with Declan, who had jumped into my arms when the gavel sounded. Since then, I had received notes from women all over the country describing how heartened they were to see someone attempting a national security cabinet role with small children in tow. I understood the reaction because, decades before, the photo of UN ambassador Jeane Kirkpatrick standing alone among so many men in Reagan's cabinet must have somehow shaped my own sense of the possible. I hoped my presence would show these young people where they could end up.

As I was leaving, one of the students, a refugee from Afghanistan, asked a question I had not been anticipating: "What do you think about communism?"

A small group of UN reporters who had accompanied me on the school visit leaned in to hear my response. Once I got over my surprise at the question, I expressed my disdain for the suffering caused by communist rule. Kurtis whispered to me as we walked out, "It is my job to be paranoid, but that was a fine answer."

Kurtis added, though, that I needed to get comfortable not answering questions. My press spokeswoman, Erin Pelton, would soon sit me down for media training, rattling off the list of "safe harbors" I could turn to when confronted with a question that was either new or difficult:

"I'm not fully familiar with what you are describing, but I will look into it, and we will get back to you with a response."

"Rather than commenting on the specifics, let me say this generally . . ."

"I'm not going to speculate on . . ."

"What we should all be focused on is . . ."

I joked with Erin that I was reminded of the scene in one of my favorite baseball movies, *Bull Durham*, where Kevin Costner's veteran character lectures a rookie pitcher played by Tim Robbins. "You're gonna have to learn your clichés . . . they are your friends," Costner advises, before sharing several favorites, like "We've gotta play 'em one day at a time" and "I'm just happy to be here. Hope I can help the ball club."

Erin and Kurtis understood that I was someone who tended to speak from the heart. I also tried to answer the questions reporters actually posed rather than the questions I wished they had posed. But we all recognized that these habits could become liabilities. Over the course of President Obama's first term, I had seen how easily administration officials' words could be taken out of context, and I did not want to supply the sound bite for the next manufactured scandal on Fox News.

I WOULD SPEND THE LARGEST SHARE of my time as ambassador in the UN Security Council. The UN founders assigned the Council the task of maintaining peace and gave it broad enforcement powers, making it the UN's most important body. The Council has fifteen members, but operates on a two-tiered structure of permanent and nonpermanent members. The five permanent members are the United States, China, France, Russia, and the United Kingdom, while the other ten seats are held by countries elected to serve two-year terms before rotating off.[22] The competition for these nonpermanent seats is fierce.[23]

The Security Council tends to be ineffective when the major powers are divided (as was true during the Cold War) and when they are largely indifferent (as was the case during the Rwandan genocide). But when the divisions can be managed or overcome, the Council has enormous influence. It can impose economic sanctions, initiate emergency mediation, and launch peacekeeping missions. Above all, it has the power to legalize actions that would otherwise be illegal under international law.*

The work tempo at the Security Council had changed a lot over the years. In 1988, the year before the Berlin Wall fell, the Council met just 55 times. In 2014, my first full year in the job, the Council met on 263 occasions—but we issued resolutions licensing concrete actions in only one-fifth of those sessions.

The presidency of the Council rotated alphabetically each month, and when I arrived in August, Argentina controlled the agenda. At my first Security Council meeting as ambassador, Cristina Fernández de Kirchner, the country's populist president, presided, and the UN secretary-general and fourteen foreign ministers attended. Kirchner, who arrived twenty-five minutes late, used her remarks to slam the United States and other permanent members for using their veto power to block important initiatives.

President Franklin Delano Roosevelt, who conceived of the UN with Winston Churchill, insisted that the Security Council's five permanent members be given the power to reject Council measures they didn't like. FDR had seen Congress vote against US membership in the League of Nations after World War I, and foresaw that providing the United States the veto as a lever of control would make it possible for the US Senate to support joining the UN, which it voted overwhelmingly to do.

Over the decades, the United States has used its veto power to prevent nondemocratic countries (which remain a majority at the UN) from joining forces to weaken international norms or to take other actions that harm US interests. That said, as of my arrival in 2013, the veto had been used more than 250 times, sidelining the Council on some of the world's most devastating conflicts.[24]

---

* After the Council passes an enforcement resolution, however, nothing happens in the real world unless the countries that belong to the UN act on that resolution. For example, when the Council creates a new peacekeeping mission, some of the 193 UN member states must contribute the troops, police, equipment, and funding that make such a mission possible.

Although I did not find my first Council meeting as ambassador terribly enlightening or practical, a head of state was presiding, and my staff advised me not to get up and leave after I had spoken. Colleen King, my new special assistant, handed me background reading for my other meetings that day, and I remained in the Council from 9:30 a.m. to 1:15 p.m., when the meeting was "suspended."

"It isn't over?" I asked the US diplomat sitting behind me. When he told me that the meeting would resume after lunch, I offered the old adage, "I guess everything has been said, but not everybody has said it."

The afternoon session, which one of my deputies attended, consumed an additional four hours and forty minutes.

Many Council sessions were far more valuable. I found those on specific crises an important means for us to mobilize global support for the US position. Their occurrence also allowed me and my team to use the days or hours in advance to urge our colleagues in Washington to reconsider what were sometimes stale US policy positions. We tried to use the Council debates as occasions to articulate fresh stances on behalf of the United States—for example, challenging foreign autocrats for doing away with term limits, or condemning human rights abuses about which the US government had not previously spoken. And of course, in my time at the UN, the Council would use its enforcement powers to condemn lawless actions in many parts of the world, to dispatch peacekeepers, and to impose economic sanctions on those who had violated international law.

Narrowing negotiating differences with other countries happened not in formal Council sessions, but in one-on-one meetings with my fellow ambassadors or in the calls and overseas visits I made to foreign ministers and heads of state around the world. With this in mind, I delegated attendance at some Council meetings to my deputies. However, even this calculation of when to show up was more complicated than it seemed. When the American ambassador made a habit of skipping Security Council sessions, it offended the country presiding and other Council members. Because each of the ten nonpermanent members of the Council would rotate off the Council after two years, and in many cases would not be elected again for decades, their ambassadors were regularly present. I would need support from them on close votes, so every decision on skipping a meeting entailed an intricate calculus involving issues beyond whatever was being discussed in the moment.

So much was happening at the UN that, when the prepared speeches went on too long, I would use the time to plow through more than a hundred pages of materials I received daily in order to deliver direction to my staff. At any given time, US diplomats working at the Mission were immersed in negotiations on issues ranging from whether to impose sanctions to how to rehabilitate child soldiers after conflict. In the General Assembly chamber, US representatives often sought to expand girls' education programs while also fending off maddening efforts to create new UN positions, which would cost money that could otherwise be spent providing assistance to people in need.

Sometimes, leaving the office at nine p.m., I would see the size of the briefing book being sent home with me for the next day and wilt in disappointment, groaning to Jeremy, "So much for catching up on *The Affair*!" But as soon as I got home, I would inevitably devour the contents—preparatory material for my meetings and events the next day, classified updates on various conflicts I was tracking, lengthy analytic reports from organizations like the International Crisis Group, and updates from staff on our longer-term initiatives. Having consumed foreign policy news since I was eighteen years old, I found homework like this riveting.

AFTER THE FIRST PORTION of the Security Council meeting chaired by President Kirchner had wound down, her team escorted those of us who participated to a large UN dining room for lunch. I found myself seated next to Bruno Rodríguez, the foreign minister of Cuba, a country with which the United States had not had diplomatic relations since 1961. Because US officials did not then have contact with Cuba's diplomats, I seized the opportunity to raise the case of Oswaldo Payá.

Payá was a fearless Cuban democracy activist who had gathered more than 25,000 signatures to press the communist government to allow basic freedoms. After mobilizing the largest peaceful movement in Cuba since Fidel Castro had taken power in 1959, Payá had been killed in a car crash in 2012. According to his family and the Spanish politician who was with him at the time of his death, government-backed thugs had run his car off the road.

The Castro government naturally denied wrongdoing, but its history of harassing and imprisoning those who pushed for reform left it little credibility. At the lunch, I pressed the foreign minister to allow an independent investigation of what had happened.

"If you have nothing to hide," I said to Rodríguez, "what are you afraid of?"

I had just started an official Twitter account. Having returned to the US Mission, I tweeted: "Oswaldo Payá stood up for freedom. Just raised with the Cuban foreign minister the need for a credible investigation into his death." Payá's daughter tweeted back her thanks and urged the UN to "help stop the #Cuban government impunity."

The *Washington Post* and newswires picked up the story, which appeared in media around the world. I was exhilarated by the seeming ease with which—from my new position—I could elevate the profile of an egregious injustice.

But a few days later, when I met the Mexican Ambassador to the UN for the first time, he chastised me for publicizing something I had discussed during a private UN lunch.

"You have to decide whether you are a diplomat or an activist," he said. "You can't be both."

"I am both," I told him, "and we should all be both. I'm not going to drink wine at a lunch with the Cuban foreign minister and pretend his government is not responsible for killing one of the country's best."

"I hear you," he said, "but people won't speak freely to you if they think you are more interested in making a media splash than engaging in real dialogue."

I explained my rationale. "Cuban government goons ran Payá off the road. They know that and will never allow a proper investigation. The closest we may get to holding them accountable for murdering a Cuban activist are a few negative headlines. I don't see how silence helps anyone."

"Talk to me in a few months," he said.

The Mexican ambassador became a friend, but I never came around to his view. I was not prepared to choose between public and private diplomacy; both have their place.

29

THE RED LINE

In August of 2013, just three weeks into my new job, I took a short family vacation back to Waterville, Ireland, where Cass and I had gotten married. We had booked the trip long before my nomination as UN ambassador, and I had considered canceling once I was confirmed. But knowing how little time I would have with Cass and our kids in the coming months, I decided to go ahead.

We descended on the tiny coastal village with my security detail and secure communications equipment in tow, along with baby food and bottles, two car seats, and a stroller. We spent our first two days going for walks by the sea and enjoying long meals with my aunt Patricia and uncle Derry.

But on the third day, August 21st, I awoke to find dozens of news reports on my BlackBerry. A multipronged Syrian chemical weapons attack on the Damascus suburbs had killed more than 1,400 people, including at least 400 children.

As Rían slept and Declan played in the next room, I watched the horrifying videos of the aftermath already being uploaded to YouTube. The ghastly montage included footage of the deceased—wide-eyed, openmouthed, and seemingly frozen—and survivors who were vomiting, tearing at their clothes, and gasping frantically for breath. Witnesses recalled the smell of burning sulfur or cooked eggs. First responders came across children convulsing and turning blue. "I went to one of the houses and found an infant who was a year and a half old," one man said. "He was jumping like a bird, struggling to breathe. I held him immediately and ran to the car, but he died."

From the way bodies were positioned, it was clear that parents had lost their lives while trying to shield their kids from the poison. Several of the girls captured in the videos were dressed in polka-dotted pants like those I had dressed Rían in the day before. In one clip, I saw twelve bodies of all ages lying side by side—victims from a single family, the narrator said.

After what felt like an eternity, I turned off my computer and put my BlackBerry aside. Ireland was five hours ahead of Washington, so I knew it would take some time before Susan would gather the President's national security team. Obama had warned the Syrian government not to use chemical weapons. Now, the whole world was waiting to see how the United States would respond.

IN 2011, THE SYRIAN REVOLUTION had begun like the other uprisings across the Arab world—with jubilant, largely peaceful protests. Given the earth-shattering developments taking place in Tunisia, Egypt, and Libya, Syrians believed they were riding a wave of history that would soon wash away their oppressive and corrupt government, which had been led by the Assad family since 1970.

During this early stage of the revolution, I was still working at the White House and had the chance to meet Syrian opposition and civil society leaders who traveled to Washington seeking US support. Often wielding large maps, they excitedly pointed out the towns that were no longer controlled by the Syrian authorities, and they described voting for the first time in free elections to choose the local committees that would govern newly liberated areas. But within a matter of months, the bright future had darkened. The Syrian regime, run since 2000 by President Bashar al-Assad, responded to the opposition's progress with violent tactics more inhumane than anything I had seen since researching the Rwandan genocide for *A Problem from Hell.*

Initially, the Syrian police rounded up critics, while government snipers shot at protesters. Before long, Syrian forces began firing on the funerals of those killed. They also filmed the mourners so that they could identify more opposition supporters to arrest. Many of those detained were tortured and some were executed. Assad's army soon increased its firepower, shelling neighborhoods thought to be sympathetic to the opposition. The military used anti-aircraft guns and incendiary weapons to destroy apartment buildings and schools. And from low-flying aircraft, they dropped large containers packed with explosives and chunks of metal, known as "barrel bombs." Before long, regime soldiers and militia were killing hundreds of people each week.

By 2012, as Assad intensified his bombardment of civilian neighborhoods, the same local committees that initially symbolized Syria's democratic flowering had taken on the task of creating impromptu field hospitals to treat the wounded. Some had also begun caring for the growing number of orphaned children.

I was in awe of the bravery of the Syrian people, remembering the vulnerability I felt trying to shelter in the bathtub in Sarajevo while the Bosnian Serb Army shelled the neighborhood where I slept. After feeding Rían one night, I wrote in my journal, "Where would I be if I were Syrian? Risking my life to try to win freedom for my family or keeping my head down so as to try not to lose my family?"

In July of 2012, President Obama received reports that the Syrian military was preparing to escalate further—this time using chemical weapons. In a speech to veterans on July 23rd, he included a carefully prepared warning that the Syrian government would "be held accountable by the international community and the United States should they make the tragic mistake of using those weapons." US diplomats also fanned out to deliver private messages of this nature to the Syrian government and its backers in Russia and Iran.

At a White House press conference the following month, the President significantly sharpened his warning. After being asked a question about Syrian chemical weapons, Obama said extemporaneously, "We have communicated in no uncertain terms with every player in the region that that's a red line for us and that there would be enormous consequences if we start seeing movement on the chemical weapons front or the use of chemical weapons. That would change my calculations significantly."

ASSAD WASTED LITTLE TIME before crossing this red line. The US government began receiving information in late 2012 that the Syrian government had begun using chemical weapons. When I saw these reports while working at the White House, I was stunned that Assad seemed to have defied such a specific warning from Obama—so stunned that I even wondered whether the allegations were true. But then, when we received reports of further attacks in the early months of 2013, my incredulity turned to a fervent hope that Obama would respond forcefully.[25]

Before anything else, the President needed to be certain that the claims were indeed accurate. Because the Syrian opposition tended to be the first to disseminate information about chemical attacks, we had to be careful. The false statements prior to the invasion of Iraq about Saddam Hussein possessing weapons of mass destruction also gave US officials pause. The intelligence community had no intention of rushing to judgment, especially knowing that their assessment of whether the Assad regime had used chemical weapons could conceivably set the United States on a path to military confrontation.

Finally, on April 25th, 2013—four months before the attack that would kill 1,400 people—the White House sent a letter to Congress reporting the intelligence community's findings. The Syrian government, the letter confirmed, had used the odorless and extremely deadly nerve agent sarin "on a small scale."*

Taken together, these chemical weapons strikes were estimated to have killed between 100 and 150 people. These fatalities did not generate significant public uproar in the context of a war that had already taken more than 90,000 lives by the spring of 2013. Still, the findings called into question whether Obama had been serious when he warned of "enormous consequences."

I had taken a short leave from the Obama administration in late March of 2013 in order to prepare for what I thought was my next assignment as Undersecretary of State. When Ben Rhodes convened

---

* By this time, the press was reporting that Israel, France, and the UK had reached the same conclusion that Assad was using chemical weapons.

a conference call with the press to discuss the letter to Congress and field questions about the administration's next steps, I combed over the transcript posted online, looking for clues.

Ben's main message surprised me. President Obama's response to Assad's use of chemical weapons was to propose that the UN now undertake an inquiry into the allegations. Obama knew that some around the world would not trust American intelligence findings. He reasoned that an on-the-ground UN investigation "above and beyond" what the United States had conducted would be accepted as more independent and objective.

Removed from the internal debates, I was disoriented. The Syrian regime had used chemical weapons. Assad was extremely unlikely to allow UN inspectors anywhere near evidence of his culpability. Was the White House in denial that the red line had been crossed? Or had President Obama decided not to enforce his threat?

A reporter on the call asked Ben the obvious question of whether or not the White House believed that Assad had violated Obama's red line. He gave a forced answer, saying, "We are continuing to do further work to establish a definitive judgment as to whether or not the red line has been crossed."

This White House language recalled the Clinton administration's hesitation in calling the slaughter of 800,000 Tutsis in Rwanda "genocide," an evasive tactic I had criticized in my writing. In both cases, an American administration had resisted making a clear determination for fear that doing so would oblige the President to undertake actions that he hoped to avoid.

Ben also delivered a new warning to Assad on behalf of the administration, but it sounded like the kind of official US statement I would have skewered in my past life. "President Assad and those around him should know that the world is going to continue to carefully monitor this issue and bring forward information as we have it," Ben said. "Were he to undertake any additional use [of chemical weapons], he would be doing so under very careful monitoring from us and the international community."

I emailed Ben afterward, knowing he had been put in a tough spot because he had nothing concrete to announce. He wrote back simply, "You have no idea."

As the senior White House national security official responsible for press engagement, Ben was what was called the "stuckee"—the person stuck publicly defending what other senior officials wisely avoided discussing.

Four days after Ben's April press briefing, the Syrian regime struck again with chemical weapons. And unsurprisingly, when the UN attempted to deploy its investigators to look into the reported attacks, Assad refused to allow them into the country.

Finally, on June 13th, a week after my nomination as UN ambassador was announced, the White House acknowledged that the red line had been crossed.

This time, Ben issued a statement saying that the intelligence community had now gathered enough evidence to have "high confidence" that the Assad regime had carried out "multiple" chemical weapons attacks. In response, Ben said, the President had decided to provide military support to the Syrian opposition for the first time—in essence, authorizing American personnel to arm and train moderate factions among the rebels fighting the Syrian government.

Ben could not offer specifics about the impact of this US policy shift because the details were highly classified. So while administration officials could say they had imposed consequences on Assad's regime for crossing the red line, they could not specify the nature of these consequences in any detail. Since even Assad didn't know the particulars of the cost he would be bearing, he seemed unlikely to be deterred from carrying out further attacks.

This remained the basic state of play on August 21st, 2013, the date of the Syrian regime's massive early morning attack on the Damascus suburbs. Watching the footage from the apartment where we stayed in Ireland, I felt sure that Assad had chosen his timing deliberately: the attack began a year to the day, Washington time, from Obama's red-line threat.

"WHAT DO YOU THINK this will mean?" Cass asked.

"Nothing," I said testily. I was sickened by what I'd just seen, and, not for the first time, my dark mood ensnared those around me.

While this attack was clearly an order of magnitude different from Assad's previous chemical weapons strikes, I did not expect that the large number of fatalities would fundamentally alter our approach to Syria.

"This won't change things?" Cass said.

"Nope," I replied. "Watch."

I dreaded the inevitable meeting where the national security team would discuss next steps. I assumed we would do little more than denounce the atrocity and impose economic sanctions on those involved in Assad's chemical weapons program.

I tweeted limply: "Reports devastating: 100s dead in streets, including kids killed by chem weapons. UN must get there fast & if true, perps must face justice."

Looking back, I see that I was doing what I had long ridiculed others for: demanding the "UN" take action, despite knowing that Russia would prevent the Security Council from doing virtually anything.

Later that day, however, I received a secure call from my deputy in Washington. To my shock, he said that the President had asked the Pentagon to draw up targets for air strikes.

I spent Wednesday and Thursday in Waterville, calling in to back-to-back classified meetings with Obama and the national security cabinet—my ear essentially glued to the secure phone. Obama was enraged by Assad's attack. Rather than debating next steps with us, as he generally did, he made clear that he had decided to punish Assad. My prediction to Cass had been wrong—the attack had brought about a major change in US policy after all.

Administration officials who had previously argued against using military force in Syria were now in full agreement with the Commander in Chief. Chairman of the Joint Chiefs of Staff Martin Dempsey, the President's top military adviser, told Obama in a National Security Council meeting two days after the attack, "Normally, I would want you to know what comes next. But this is not one of those times."

The President was not enthusiastic about risking a new war in the Middle East. But, as he explained to us, "When I said that using chemical weapons was a red line, this is what I meant." He emphasized that he saw no other way to communicate to Assad: "Don't do this again."

As all this transpired, our "family vacation" in Ireland had become one of familiar dashed expectations. I was not spending time with Cass and our kids in the way we had all hoped, and at the same time, I was not serving the President as I could if I were present at the UN.

In addition, my absence from New York had quickly become newsworthy. On the day of the attack, I had directed the Deputy US Permanent Representative to call an emergency Security Council meeting, which she then attended in my stead. Fox News contributor Richard Grenell, who would later become President Trump's Ambassador to Germany, quickly drew attention to my whereabouts, writing, "While the White House was pretending to be in urgent mode, the new US ambassador didn't think the meeting was worth her time."

When Fox reporter James Rosen grilled Jen Psaki, the spokesperson for the State Department, asking, "Where exactly was Ambassador Power?" Psaki tried to protect my privacy, saying that I was on a "pre-arranged trip" and had been in "constant contact" with the White House. But when Rosen asked if I was on vacation, she replied, "I don't have any more details for you." A rumor began to swirl that the President had dispatched me on a covert diplomatic mission.

Finally, on Friday, August 23rd, having identified the itinerary that would get me back to the United States without missing an important meeting with the President while I was in the air, the kids and I flew to New York. Cass remained in Ireland to give an academic lecture that he had scheduled months before. Because María was away on vacation with her family, I desperately needed help with childcare. Mum and Eddie answered the call, as they so often did, descending on the Waldorf within hours of our arrival.

The following day, in a meeting I attended in the Situation Room, Obama questioned Dempsey on how long it would take to launch American missiles once he officially ordered the strikes.

"If I gave the order Sunday night," Obama asked at one point, "could this be done as early as Monday?"

The Chairman said yes, stressing that everything was in place.

Obama made clear that he was likely to direct the Pentagon to commence the operation within forty-eight hours.

Before the meeting ended, Obama turned to me. "Sam, I need you to get those UN inspectors out of Syria," he said sharply. "That UN mission needs to be shut down *now*."

After months of being blocked by the Assad regime, twenty UN investigators had arrived in Damascus on August 18th—just three days before the massive chemical weapons attack—to investigate the allegations of chemical attacks from earlier in the year. Obama was concerned that the Assad regime, which was clearly capable of stooping to anything, would detain the UN officials and use them as human shields once US military strikes began.

I told him I would call UN Secretary-General Ban Ki-moon and report back.

I HAD BEEN CAUGHT OFF GUARD by President Obama's decisive reaction to the attack. For more than a year, he had expressed strong misgivings about using military force in Syria. Prior to August 21st, he had deemed the risks too high and the impact too uncertain. He had also focused on the fact that our administration would lack broad international support for enforcement action, and that Russia would inevitably prevent the UN Security Council from authorizing it.* After three Russian vetoes in the Council, it was obvious that this route for addressing the crisis was blocked. Russia even refused to allow the Council to issue a toothless press statement the day of the large Damascus attack.

---

* International law generally recognizes three circumstances in which states are permitted to resort to the use of force on the territory of another state: (1) when acting in individual or collective self-defense; (2) when the other state consents; or (3) when explicitly authorized by the UN Security Council. As veto-holders, the permanent members of the Security Council thus have tremendous say in how—or whether—force can be used under international law to confront threats to peace and security. In this case, Russia's veto prevented the Security Council from taking *any* action in response to Syria's blatant violation of international humanitarian law.

In our internal discussions, Secretary Kerry and I had pointed to the perverse circumstance in which the UN Charter effectively rendered President Putin the arbiter of legality. We and others had also cited NATO's action in Kosovo as an example where government lawyers had argued that force was "legitimate" under international law despite the absence of Security Council approval. Obama, however, was understandably worried about how a more expansive rationale would end up being abused by others.

The deterioration of the situation in Libya since Qaddafi's fall had also contributed to the President's skepticism about whether military action would achieve the desired US objectives. And for all of its chaos, Libya actually seemed far more straightforward than Syria, which had a prewar population that was three times larger and riven by deep societal cleavages. Although Syria was 74 percent Sunni Muslim, the Assad family and much of the governing class came from the minority Alawite sect. The involvement of Iran and Hezbollah on Assad's side, and Saudi Arabia, Turkey, Qatar, UAE, and others on the side of different opposition factions made the conflict dauntingly complex.

Even if the Syrian landscape had been less fragmented, Obama's actual options for responding to chemical attacks were constrained. The United States could not strike the chemical weapons storage facilities themselves; doing so would send toxic plumes into the air, risking the lives of thousands of Syrians. And since air strikes against other Syrian military targets would leave the chemical weapons intact, the Assad regime could respond to US military action by again gassing opposition-held areas—further escalating the crisis.

In our debates, Obama had also expressed concerns that what started as a "limited" military operation in Syria would expand. The Assad regime inflicted mass casualties on a near-daily basis, using all manner of weapons. Obama knew that if he opted for targeted air strikes to punish chemical weapons use, pressure would grow for him to respond to other types of deadly attacks as well, both because they were horrific and because after US strikes, American "credibility" would be on the line.

And finally, despite the clamor of leading Republicans for military action in the immediate aftermath of the August 2013 attack, Obama recognized how quickly his political opponents would abandon the cause if they deemed it expedient.

These were among the many dynamics that those of us advising the President had debated prior to August 21st and now were discussing anew as he prepared to order military action. Yet for the first time since the start of the Syrian conflict, *even when considering all of these potential downsides*, Obama had concluded that the costs of not responding forcefully were greater than the risks of taking military action. Whereas on Libya he had sought a UN Security Council resolution authorizing the use of force, here—given the stakes for Syria and for upholding the international norm against the use of chemical weapons—Obama was prepared to operate without what White House lawyers called a "traditionally recognized legal basis under international law." The lawyers suggested that, given the vast number of international obligations Assad's regime had violated, acting without the Council could, as it was in the case of Kosovo, be "justified and legitimate under international law."

My own view was that Obama was right to have decided to respond to the August 21st attack with air strikes. Indeed, I believed that he should have responded in this manner even to the previous, smaller-scale chemical attacks, once the intelligence community had confirmed them. Had he ordered limited strikes then, I wondered whether Assad's forces would have dared to stage such a large subsequent attack.

Regardless of what the United States might have done beforehand, after the brazen killing of 1,400 people, I did not believe that additional nonmilitary actions would be sufficient to deter Assad from gassing more Syrians. We were already providing military support to the Syrian opposition. We had secured the deployment of UN cease-fire observers earlier in the war. On chemical weapons specifically, we had waged a diplomatic full-court press with Russia and Iran, Syria's backers, pressing them to restrain their ally. We and the Europeans had imposed a raft of economic sanctions, but even in apartheid South Africa and Milošević's Serbia, two places where sanctions played an important role in changing government behavior, they did so over a period of years, not months. Moreover, the US and European asset freezes and banking restrictions against Syrian government officials, which had been imposed in 2011 and 2012 and could be expanded now, were not global in their reach. Russia had used its veto to prevent the Security Council from levying sanctions, which meant that the Syrian government could continue to legally transact business in many parts of the world, while still receiving weapons and funding from Russia and Iran.

If we responded with more of the same, I felt sure Assad's regime would continue with more of the same.

Assad had staged the largest massacre of the war, and he had carried out a chemical attack beyond anything the world had seen in a quarter century.[26] While I wished President Obama would consider confronting Assad's other instruments of death, I agreed with him that chemical weapons warranted a specific red line. They were weapons of *mass* destruction, capable of killing vast numbers of people at once. The nations of the world had come together after World War I to ban these weapons, and if the international consensus against their use were to break down, the lapse would almost certainly come back to haunt many more people (Americans included) in and out of conflict zones around the world.

I had no illusions that the kind of limited military action Obama was about to order would bring the Syrian war to an end. That would take sustained international diplomacy, which had repeatedly stalled. But in my view, diplomacy had been ineffective in part because Assad had become convinced that no one would stop him from using even the most merciless tactics against his own people. If the US government looked away from this incident, signaling that Assad could gas his citizens at will, I worried he would never feel sufficient pressure to negotiate. Instead, he would go on using unspeakably vicious methods to remain in power, and the war would continue indefinitely, killing countless Syrians and eventually endangering American national security.

Even if US-led action would not save Syrians from being killed in other ways, preventing any loss of life was important. And critically, the risk of Assad retaliating or US action devolving into full-fledged conflict seemed very low. As President Obama put it publicly in early September, "The Assad regime does not have the ability to seriously threaten our military . . . Neither Assad nor his allies have any interest in escalation that would lead to his demise."

For these reasons, I understood why the August 21st attack had changed President Obama's extremely fraught appraisal. And I wholeheartedly backed his plan to destroy select Syrian military targets.

WITH OBAMA PREPARING TO GIVE the final go-ahead for the strikes, I began hustling among videoconferences with Susan and the US national security team; Security Council meetings; and strategy sessions with the ambassadors from the UK and France, whose militaries planned to join us in the coming operation.

In the evenings when I got home, Declan, who was desperate for attention, would often emerge sleepily from his bedroom. Both he and Rían had a knack for wailing at high volume at precisely the moment John Kerry decided to call. When I attempted to create a sound buffer by locking myself in the apartment's secure study, the raucousness was only made worse by their determined pounding on the metal door of the top-secret vault.

Whenever I was on the verge of losing my patience, I reminded myself of my good fortune: I could put my kids to bed knowing that, when I checked on them late at night, they would be there, breathing soundly in their sleep.

30

"CHEMICAL WEAPONS WERE USED"

As soon as I arrived back in New York from Washington on Saturday, August 24th, I began engaging UN Secretary-General Ban Ki-moon in an effort to secure the withdrawal of the UN investigators from Syria. However, Ban insisted that the UN team was staying put. The Syrian government had prevented their visit for more than four months, and now that they had finally gotten in, Ban wanted them to remain so they could investigate the new attack.

As reasonable as this sounded, the UN team had no mandate to assess who had carried out the attacks. They only had the authority to ascertain *whether* chemicals had been involved. When it came to the massive attack that had just occurred, however, this question had been answered.

The victims had been videotaped and photographed displaying all the medically established bodily responses to sarin. Innumerable survivors and witnesses had described symptoms consistent with sarin. All of this evidence and testimony had been disseminated around the world. Not even the Syrian or Russian governments denied that banned chemical weapons had been used—they just denied Assad's responsibility, instead claiming the opposition was at fault.

I reminded Ban that Damascus and Moscow were now heartily embracing the UN investigation because it was a convenient stalling mechanism. The Assad regime would tightly control the investigators' every movement. And every day these UN inspectors remained in Damascus was another day for the Syrian military to destroy evidence of its crime and move its precious heavy weapons into hiding.

I expected the secretary-general to see the demonstrable ridiculousness of keeping inspectors in harm's way solely for the purpose of telling the world what it already knew.

"This is a moot mission," I told Ban. "The UN is being manipulated."

But from Ban's perspective, pulling the inspectors out would make the UN look complicit in the western military action that he and the world recognized was imminent. The secretary-general was unyielding. "We cannot *not* proceed," he said.

The presence of the UN team caused Obama to delay the US military operation he had hoped to launch on the night of August 25th. Every day for the next five days, Obama would ask me, Susan, or John Kerry whether Ban had withdrawn the flawed mission, so that he could order the planned strikes. And each day, one of us would report to the President that the UN investigators remained in Damascus. Obama was seething with frustration.

On Friday, August 30th, nine days after the attack, Ban called to relay the utterly unsurprising news that the UN team had gathered convincing proof that sarin gas had been used. They would be leaving Syria the next morning with environmental and biomedical samples (like tissue and hair), as well as weapons fragments collected from the neighborhoods they visited.

Even if the UN team had stayed too long to learn too little, I thought, its departure from Syrian territory was a major development. It would give President Obama the peace of mind he had been seeking to launch the planned air strikes, which I assumed he would do as soon as the UN team crossed the border into Lebanon the next day (and were no longer potential hostages). Knowing what was coming, the UN had evacuated its expatriate staff and paid Syrian local staff three months' advance salary.

That night, as I wearily entered the Waldorf at nine p.m., I heard my secure phone ring and hustled to the back study to answer it. Susan was on the line.

I started filling her in on the latest from the secretary-general, but she cut me off. President Obama had decided on a sudden change of course, she said. He had gone from "wanting to go and go yesterday" to deciding that he would seek authorization from Congress for the use of force before proceeding with military strikes against Assad.

I was so taken aback that I asked Susan to repeat what she had said, to be sure I hadn't misheard.

She insisted that Obama was not going wobbly on the use of force itself. "He will fight like hell to get the authorization," she explained. "He is betting his presidency and our reputation in the world on this."

When I asked if the President might be open to reversing his decision, she said we would have a chance to offer our views at a meeting early the following morning. But, she added, "His mind is made up."

I PARTICIPATED IN THE SATURDAY-MORNING Situation Room meeting from a small, secure videoconference facility at the US Mission in New York.

The President opened by reviewing the Pentagon's chosen targets, which, by necessity, were not involved with chemical weapons production or delivery.

"What if Assad doesn't stop using chemical weapons?" Obama asked. "What if this drags on?"

Obama was focused on the duration of the mission because of longstanding questions related to the President's use of force when not responding to an imminent national security threat. Although the Constitution designates the President as Commander in Chief of the armed forces, it gives Congress the power to declare war. Over the past several decades, presidents have argued that the limited nature and scope of their military operations meant they were not "at war" as such, allowing them to use military force without congressional approval. However, the 1973 War Powers Resolution stipulated that, when Congress has not authorized a military operation, the President must report the action to Congress within forty-eight hours and remove US armed forces from "hostilities" within sixty days. Presidents have generally gotten around the sixty-day requirement by arguing that US hostilities were not continuous, allowing the "clock" to stop and then reset again. Indeed, during his first term, Obama himself had contended that he was in compliance with the War Powers Resolution during the 222-day military campaign in Libya because US involvement was sufficiently limited as to not constitute "hostilities" or require the automatic sixty-day pullout.[27]

But on Syria, Obama had now decided that Congress should fulfill its constitutional responsibility and leap with him into the unknown.

The President was concerned that if he acted without Congress and the mission dragged on or took unexpected turns, his political opponents would attack his presidency as lawless and illegitimate. Republican as well as Democratic presidents had skirted the War Powers Resolution in the past. However, the partisan rancor in Washington had grown so intense that, despite these precedents, House Republicans could easily have used a dispute over whether Obama was violating the law to launch impeachment proceedings. Already, some 140 House lawmakers (among them 21 Democrats) had signed a letter warning Obama that military strikes in Syria "without prior congressional authorization" would be unconstitutional.

The President wanted to be sure that, in the event military strikes did not achieve their intended effects immediately, Congress would already have provided clear legal permission to allow the United States to finish the job—no matter how long it took.

"If Assad thinks he can wait us out," Obama said during the meeting, "that's in nobody's interest."

I found this reasoning persuasive in every respect except one: for all the drawbacks of moving ahead without congressional support, proceeding with congressional support required . . . *Congress*.

Many in the GOP seemed convinced that their most politically advantageous posture was unyielding opposition to Obama's proposals, regardless of their content. Indeed, a month later, House Republicans would shut down the government for sixteen days in a quixotic attempt to defund Obama's health care law.

Given these domestic political dynamics, and the significant fact that the British parliament had just voted not to join the United States and France in the military operation,* Vice President Biden, Secretary of State Kerry, and Secretary of Defense Chuck Hagel all raised questions about Obama's change of heart. Kerry was the most apocalyptic in his foreboding. "It is no exaggeration to say that, if you lose with Congress, having already told the world you are going to use military force, people will proclaim the effective end of your second term," he warned during the meeting.

However, after voicing their concerns, all three ultimately expressed support for the President's plan to request congressional approval. They said that, by making our case to the public and campaigning relentlessly, we would be able to mobilize the required votes. An important factor in their thinking was Israeli prime minister Benjamin Netanyahu's vocal support for US military action, along with that of the influential lobbying group AIPAC. Further, because Iran was supporting Assad, they argued that the anti-Iran animus on the Hill would help us get over the vote thresholds needed in the House and Senate.

Every fiber in my being was alarmed by Obama's proposed plan, but when I spoke up during the meeting, I phrased my apprehension as a question. "The thing I don't understand is, what happens if Congress doesn't support you?" I asked. "Does that mean Assad could just keep using chemical weapons, and they would become like a conventional weapon of war?"

Even though Obama planned to publicly stress that the Constitution provided him the authority to use force regardless of how Congress voted, I did not believe that he would launch strikes in the face of open opposition on Capitol Hill. It therefore seemed particularly dangerous to announce a decision to go to Congress without first having a well-informed understanding of where the necessary votes would come from.

---

* The day before this Saturday meeting, British prime minister David Cameron's military authorization measure had been narrowly defeated in Parliament by a margin of 285–272. The loss was a humiliating blow and a misreading by Cameron of UK politics, presaging the 2016 Brexit vote that would drive him from office.

Obama seized on my question, asking others around the table to debate it. But instead of grappling with what we would do if the House and Senate did not support us, people quickly returned to arguing that Congress could be brought on board.

Within just a few weeks, I would feel comfortable asserting a view in cabinet discussions on any subject, giving voice to whatever doubts or questions stirred inside me. But that fateful day, less than a month after assuming my new position, I felt as though I had just parachuted into a conversation mid-sentence. And on the specific issue of legislative feasibility, I believed I had to defer to Biden, Kerry, and Hagel. The three former senators brought a combined seventy-six years of experience on Capitol Hill to the discussion.

I also knew that the day before, Susan had tried to convince Obama that Congress could not be relied upon. He had not budged then, and nothing in his disposition as he chaired the meeting led me to believe he was open to changing his mind.

What I did not know in that Saturday meeting was that this would end up being the only time Obama would seriously contemplate using military force against the Assad regime. We would have countless meetings and debates on Syria over the next three and a half years, but he would never again consider taking the kind of risk he had been prepared to bear in the immediate aftermath of the August 21st attack.

THE PRESIDENT GAVE ME TWO MAIN ASSIGNMENTS once he made public his decision to go to Congress: drumming up international statements of support for American military action, and helping to mobilize domestic public opinion in advance of the House and Senate votes.

While the countries in the UN had been relatively united in the run-up to NATO's intervention in Libya, member states were divided over the right course of action in Syria. Leading the opposition to military strikes were the Russians, who wanted to forestall bombing at all costs. Syria hosted the Russian military's only base outside the former Soviet Union, and Russian arms manufacturers sold the Syrian military billions of dollars' worth of weapons. Despite the fact that only limited US strikes were planned, Putin worried that US actions would set in motion a chain of events that could result in Assad's ouster or diminish Russian influence in the region.

At the UN, Russian diplomats pointed to the 2011 overthrow of Qaddafi and his violent death at the hands of the opposition as a means of discrediting the proposed US response to the chemical attack. Russia argued that NATO's intervention in Libya had been just another American "regime change" operation under the guise of humanitarian protection, and that this time countries shouldn't be fooled about what would happen in Syria.

It was true that when Qaddafi refused to order his forces to stop attacking Libyan civilians, the line became blurred between enforcing the UN Security Council's civilian protection mandate and pushing for a political transition away from his leadership. But whenever Russian officials raised this objection, they had no answer for how Libyans were going to be protected (as was required by the Council resolution, passed without Russia's objection) if Qaddafi's forces kept attacking them. Nonetheless, these claims that the United States and our coalition partners had overstepped on Libya gave Russia another argument for why countries should not support a military operation to confront Assad.

Putin went further, rejecting the overwhelming evidence linking Assad's regime to the attack, which he called "utter nonsense." I brought US intelligence experts to the US Mission to share what we had gathered with other countries so they could judge for themselves. I invited ambassadors from key countries in Europe, Asia, and Africa to hear the grisly, voluminous details.

To those prepared to review the facts—a practice that had already begun its sharp decline around the world—Assad's regime was clearly responsible. The Syrian government was widely known to have a sophisticated chemical weapons program. Only professionals had the know-how to mix the chemical agents, fill the munitions, and strike so many opposition neighborhoods in such quick succession. The rockets used in the Damascus gas attack were used regularly by the regime and had never been seen in the possession of the Syrian opposition. Tracers from the rockets indicated that they had been launched from regime territory. Our intercepted communications revealed a senior Syrian official discussing the regime's responsibility for the attack.[28] And, of course, not a single person in regime-held territory appeared to have been injured or killed.

Put another way, a ragtag opposition would have had to acquire the chemical agents, the mixing expertise, and the surface-to-surface rockets capable of carrying sarin gas; then these opposition fighters would have had to move all of this across an impenetrable front line into regime territory so as to target their neighbors and family members back in the areas where they lived.

Despite the plethora of hard evidence, most foreign ambassadors ducked the question of who had used chemical weapons. Exasperated, I argued at a closed meeting of the Security Council, "I know the Earth is round, not flat, but I haven't personally traveled to the edge of the Earth to see if it ends abruptly. At a certain point, unless you have a reason for wanting not to believe—because you are a patron of the perpetrators or because you don't want to get in the bad books of President Putin—you would accept the overwhelming evidence."

At one point, after listening to the lead UN inspector talking clinically about the "tissue samples" his team had gathered around Damascus, I tried to bring the Council back into reality. "A sample is part of a human being," I said, by now beyond furious at the refusal of countries to take a stand.

"If we can't come together over this," I asked, struggling to keep a steady voice, "what will move us?"

I took to railing against those who condemned the sarin attack in the passive voice. "For a crime of this magnitude," I argued before representatives of the other 192 countries in the General Assembly, "it is not enough to say 'chemical weapons *were* used'—any more than it would have been enough to say that 'machetes *were* used' in Rwanda in 1994. We must condemn the user."

Yet to this day, most countries have avoided pointing the finger at the Syrian regime.

LIKE THE PRESIDENT'S ENTIRE SENIOR TEAM, I was given a list of senators and representatives to call as part of the effort to whip votes on the Hill.

Democrats wanted to support Obama personally, but they were afraid that voters would not back even a limited mission in Syria. Many began our calls by expressing remorse over the vote they had taken in 2002 to authorize the Iraq War. One Democratic House member informed me that she had received 2,400 constituent calls against air strikes in Syria, and just 60 in support. Tellingly, several Democrats plaintively asked, "Why did the President come to us?"

Because Congress was on recess, many representatives were in their districts, hearing directly from constituents. I connected with Democratic senator Al Franken, who told me that "the first, second, and third questions" he was getting from Minnesotans were all on Syria. "People are really frightened of another war," Franken reported.

When I spoke to John Boozman, a Republican senator from Arkansas, he said, "I understand the problem with the gas and all that, and we are a hawkish state." But he added, "I can't find anyone in Arkansas supportive of this, and I have been all over."

The White House was hearing these same concerns and growing alarmed about the prospects for securing congressional approval. Seeking to shore up support among Democrats, White House chief of staff Denis McDonough asked me to make the progressive case for Obama's plan at the Center for American Progress, a liberal Washington think tank. Carried live on multiple networks, I knew the speech would be the most watched that I had ever delivered.

I discarded the draft remarks that the White House provided, writing feverishly through the night before I was scheduled to speak. To the degree that I had always had a principle at the heart of my advocacy, it was simple: meet people where they are. As an administration, we had to directly address the very reasonable concerns Americans were raising and not simply talk about children frothing at the mouth, as if their suffering in and of itself should trigger military action.

I did not view America's responsibilities in the world in such simplistic terms. Like President Obama, I cared above all about consequences. I believed that the most important part of decision-making was not the justness of one's intentions but the effectiveness of one's actions. We had to have very strict criteria for employing military force— but in this circumstance, I felt that the criteria had been met.

In my remarks, I addressed the ambivalence that I knew people felt:

> On the one hand, we Americans share a desire, after two wars, which have taken 6,700 American lives and cost over $1 trillion, to invest taxpayer dollars in American schools and infrastructure. Yet on the other hand, Americans have heard the President's commitment that this will not be Iraq, this will not be Afghanistan, this will not be Libya. Any use of force will be limited and tailored narrowly to the chemical weapons threat.

> On the one hand, we share an abhorrence for the brutal, murderous tactics of Bashar al-Assad. Yet on the other hand, we are worried about the violent extremists who, while opposed to Assad, have themselves carried out atrocities.

> On the one hand, we share the deep conviction that chemical weapons are barbaric, that we should never again see children killed in their beds, lost to a world that they never had a chance to try to change. Yet on the other hand, some are wondering why—given the flagrant violation of an international norm—it is incumbent on the United States to lead, since we cannot and should not be the world's policeman.

I closed by stating as plainly as possible what was at stake:

> We all have a choice to make. Whether we are Republicans or Democrats, whether we have supported past military interventions or opposed them, whether we have argued for or against such action in Syria prior to this point, we should agree that there are lines in this world that cannot be crossed, and limits on

murderous behavior, especially with weapons of mass destruction, that must be enforced.

By taking skeptics' arguments seriously, my speech made a strong
case for Obama's plan. But I convinced few people.

For some, like Arizona senator John McCain, Obama's proposed
action was too mild to deter Assad. "How can military strikes be limited *and* enough?" he wanted to know.

But his was a minority view. While Syrian Americans tried to rally
support for Obama's initiative, most other Americans wanted no part
of Syria. The student activists, civic groups, churches, mosques, and
synagogues that had come out en masse to demand help for the people
of Darfur were largely silent.

With each passing day, outrage faded over the images of Syria's
dead. In its place, domestic and international concerns about the potential fallout from US military action increased. On September 5th,
the *Washington Post* published a whip count that found "more than four
times as many opponents of military action in the House as supporters."

Based on all the available evidence, President Obama realized there
was no point in going forward with a congressional vote to authorize
strikes. We were clearly going to lose in the House, perhaps by a sizable margin, and we would possibly lose in the Senate as well.* Yet the
Commander in Chief of the world's largest superpower had told the
world that Assad's egregious slaughter of civilians demanded a forceful
response.

With no Plan B, we were in deep trouble.

ON SEPTEMBER 6TH, a boxed-in Obama met with Putin on the side-
lines of a large global gathering in St. Petersburg. During their private
talk, Obama raised the possibility of the US and Russia working together to destroy Syria's chemical weapons program.

Putin appeared receptive to the idea, but most of us thought he was

---

* A simple majority in each house of Congress would have been needed to pass an
authorization for use of military force.

feigning interest. While our non-proliferation experts had held technical talks with Russian specialists on what the US and Russian governments could do to prevent *terrorists* from seizing Assad's chemical weapons, Moscow had shown no appetite for dismantling the program itself. Now, Putin and his advisers knew from both the US media and their own diplomatic reporting that Congress was not going to authorize bombing. They could have achieved their objective of forestalling American military action by just letting US domestic politics play out to their inevitable conclusion.

On September 9th, John Kerry gave voice to this skepticism about the prospects for destroying Syria's chemical weapons. At a press conference in London, a reporter asked him whether Assad could do anything to avert US bombing. "Sure," Kerry ad-libbed, still clinging to the hope that Obama might order the strikes. "[Assad] could turn over every bit of his weapons to the international community within the next week. Turn it over, all of it, without delay . . . But he isn't about to do it, and it can't be done, obviously."

Yet just a few hours later, to Kerry's great surprise, Russian foreign minister Sergey Lavrov called him. Having heard the Secretary of State's public comments, Putin had asked Lavrov to follow up to say he was, in fact, willing to work with Obama to rid Assad of his chemical weapons. Within four days, Kerry and Lavrov had negotiated the contours of a framework for how the chemical weapons program could be dismantled.

I was then handed the task of negotiating a UN Security Council resolution with Russia's Ambassador to the UN. We had to map out a massive, unprecedented operation and get the world on board.

WHEN I MET WITH SUSAN before taking on my new role in New York, she had conveyed one message more firmly than any other: my relationship with Russia's UN representative would be pivotal to my success.

"Invest in Churkin," she advised. "He will drive you crazy, but you will need each other."

Vitaly Churkin, then sixty-one, with a tuft of white hair and a hearty laugh, had already been permanent representative at the UN for seven years. He knew the organization's rules and procedures better than anyone—and he was famous among UN diplomats for using that mastery to Russia's advantage.

For two weeks following the Kerry–Lavrov agreement, Vitaly and I spoke or met multiple times a day about the chemical weapons resolution—at the US Mission, at the Russian Mission, and on neutral ground. Our negotiations were being so closely watched that reporters and cameras hounded us wherever we went, looking for signs of a collapse in talks that could somehow result in Obama going ahead with military strikes.

I knew all that could go wrong and all that depended on these negotiations. I expected the bats to descend. But they never came.

I felt confident. I was representing my country on an essential issue. Although I had never negotiated with Vitaly before, as an NSC staffer I had carefully tracked Susan's clashes and compromises with him. I was backed by incredibly experienced US non-proliferation officials and lawyers who were available to answer my every operational and Syria-specific question. And Susan and Kerry were just a phone call away.

I knew that in spite of the twists and turns of my first month, we still had a chance to exact a penalty for the Assad regime's monstrous war crime and perhaps prevent similar attacks in the future. I regretted that our administration had not ascertained whether we had the votes *before* the President announced he was going to Congress. Had he known he would fail, I did not believe he would have chosen the path he did. But we were where we were: if we could rid Assad of one especially deadly weapon, I thought, maybe it would dent his confidence and make him more amenable to political negotiations.

As Vitaly and I sized each other up, we also had to navigate our respective systems. Since Putin's primary objective was preventing US military intervention, I knew that Moscow was carefully vetting every provision I put forward, fearing the US government would later stretch the meaning of the UN resolution's language to claim an international legal basis for using force.

For our part, we remained deeply distrustful of Moscow's intentions. How could we possibly end up with a reliable agreement when Russian officials continued to push the preposterous claim that the opposition had carried out the chemical attacks? Wouldn't the Syrian government, which had just gassed 1,400 people without remorse, cheat on whatever we agreed to—and do so with Russia's assistance?

The negotiations were painstaking, with both of us laboriously insisting on word changes to close loopholes that one of us saw and the other insisted did not exist. The mutual suspicions ran so deep that I was reminded of a story about the contentious talks during the nineteenth-century Congress of Vienna. After the Austrian diplomat Metternich was awakened with news that an ambassador he had been sparring with had died in the night, Metternich reportedly asked, "What can have been his motive?"

Sometimes, when one of us refused to budge or seemed not to be taking the concerns of the other seriously, our conversations grew heated. On several occasions, Vitaly dramatically slammed shut his leather briefcase and stormed out of our negotiation, muttering what I assume were Russian swear words. Once, he returned sheepishly after a few minutes, saying, "Well, now that I got that out of my system, how about a drink?" A member of his staff then appeared with a large bottle of Black Label whiskey. I wondered whether Vitaly was employing some time-tested Russian tactic where the same negotiator played both the good and bad cop.

We suffered many setbacks. One day when I arrived at the Russian Mission, Vitaly told me he had "good news and bad news." The good news was that, after a delay, he had finally received instructions from Moscow on how to respond to the provisions I had proposed. The bad news, he said, was that "if I follow my instructions, you will never talk to me again."

Meanwhile, I went from being barely available to my family to disappearing entirely during the two weeks of negotiations. As I tried to sneak out of the Waldorf early one Sunday morning for a standoff with Vitaly, Declan grabbed me before I made it out the door. "Más," he said, using the Spanish he had learned from María to indicate he needed "more."

"Mommy, people don't work on Sundays," he insisted.

I told him I was going to try to stop people from doing bad things. He seemed satisfied, asking "Will you come back after you stop them?"

I nodded, but on the short, quiet drive to the US Mission, I shuddered at the inadequacy of the effort to which I was devoting every ounce of my being.

"If we do everything right, Assad will have one less weapon," I thought.

F. Scott Fitzgerald famously described the importance of being able "to hold two opposed ideas in the mind at the same time," while still retaining "the ability to function." I was quickly becoming practiced at this discomfiting balance. I wanted desperately to get chemical weapons out of Assad's hands and to uphold the norm against their use. Yet I knew that accomplishing this would not be a "victory" for most Syrians.

DURING THESE NEGOTIATIONS, I had the chance to work closely with John Kerry for the first time. He had already represented Massachusetts in the US Senate for ten years by the time I moved to the Boston area for law school, and I had crossed paths with him at Harvard events and Red Sox games over the years. I had also watched him in action when I worked in Obama's Senate office, as they both served on the Senate Foreign Relations Committee. But I could never have predicted the warmth he would show me as his colleague.

The relationship between UN ambassadors and secretaries of state is often quite tense. Strain inevitably arises from the fact that a UN ambassador's cabinet role technically gives him or her a vote equal to the Secretary of State's on matters of national security, despite the fact that the Secretary manages 276 diplomatic posts around the world and more than 70,000 personnel, while the UN ambassador runs the equivalent of one small embassy in New York.[29]

Fortunately, Kerry had one overriding objective in his role as Secretary of State: get as much done as humanly possible to prevent and end wars. He would later call his memoir *Every Day Is Extra*, quoting a phrase he and his buddies who survived the war in Vietnam used to say to one another. He acted as if each day in his job could be the last, and he seemed to see me as an ally with a similar mind-set. Once he had latched onto something, getting him to let go was almost impossible. This relentlessness was an enormous asset.

Since he had negotiated the initial chemical weapons framework with Lavrov, Kerry was hugely invested in my discussions with Vitaly. He called half a dozen times a day, usually asking "What's up?" before I detailed the state of play and we strategized about next steps.

At one important juncture, he became livid when I explained that Russia was playing a self-serving game of diplomatic telephone, with Vitaly quoting Lavrov saying that Kerry had agreed that our resolution would not be binding under international law.

"That's utter horseshit, Sam!" he boomed over the phone, "and I'm happy to call Sergey and give him hell."

I said I knew it was rubbish and that there was no need for him to engage. But Kerry being Kerry, he called back fifteen minutes later, informing me "I just read Sergey the riot act."

Between his first call and unexpected second call, I had begun nursing Rían, and she was an audible eater.

"What's that noise?" Kerry asked suddenly.

My cheeks flushed. Even though he couldn't see me, I felt as though he could, and it was not a pretty picture. The receiver on the secure phone was jammed under my right ear, Rían was draped across my bare chest, and I had a pen in hand.

"Multitasking," I said. "I'm just feeding my girl."

Kerry howled with laughter.

"That's SO GREAT, Sam. Make sure she gets a good meal, and then go stick it to the Russians."

In the end, guided by the Kerry–Lavrov framework and backed by the technical expertise of our respective arms control teams and lawyers, we came to an agreement on the text of a resolution. The final step was to put it before the Security Council for passage.

WALKING INTO THE COUNCIL chamber before the vote on September 27th, I noticed Kerry chatting with Lavrov. When I approached,

I saw the Russian foreign minister was handing out blue pins adorned with a white dove, the symbol of peace. It was simply too much, and I walked back the way I came.

Kerry was upbeat about what we had accomplished. Just after he sat in the US chair to take the vote on what would become UN Security Council Resolution 2118, he leaned back and said, "This is a pretty damn good resolution, Sam."

In one sense, he was right. We had made the best of a bad situation. The operational mission that we had created with Russia would eventually result in the destruction of equipment used to make chemical weapons at twenty-one separate Syrian sites. Meanwhile, the existing chemicals in Syria's extensive arsenal would be removed from their hiding places and loaded onto Danish and Norwegian ships. Under the protection of naval forces from Russia, China, Denmark, Norway, and the UK at various points in their journey, the ships would carry much of the chemical stockpile to an Italian port, where an American Navy vessel would receive the most dangerous of the chemicals and then neutralize them in international waters.

On a scale of one to ten, the degree of difficulty of such an unprecedented, multifaceted mission in a red-hot war zone was eleven.

And yet, over the next year, brave men and women would achieve the seemingly impossible, removing and destroying a whopping 1,300 tons of chemical agents that Assad would otherwise have had at his disposal for future attacks.

Although Russia's involvement in this effort seemed puzzling at the time, Putin likely supported the mission in order to eliminate even the miniscule near-term chance that Obama would use military force in Syria. His coziness with Assad notwithstanding, Putin may have also wanted to reduce the likelihood of his ally staging another large chemical weapons attack down the road. Even though Congress had effectively tied Obama's hands for this round, the Russian leader knew that Assad was a serial chemical weapons user. After his next attack, the United States military would have targets at the ready, and the congressional political dynamics might have shifted. By forcing Assad to renounce chemical weapons and getting him to work with the international community to destroy them, Putin was also, in a perverse sense, legitimizing Assad, who tried to portray himself as a person willing to do whatever it took for "peace."

More broadly, Putin was on a mission to restore Russian greatness. Spearheading this initiative won him accolades, with many commentators praising the Russian leader for showcasing his country's enduring influence on the world stage—and for outmaneuvering Obama.

I secured the strongest deal possible in a circumstance where our leverage had been badly dented by Congress's opposition to the President's proposed authorization. But on the day my first major Security Council resolution became law, I could not shake the concern that the Council was implicitly licensing other kinds of attacks on civilians. After all, because Russia refused to include references to SCUD missiles, artillery, barrel bombs, and even napalm, the resolution was silent on Assad's other murderous weapons.

What the United States and Russia had done together was meaningful, but we could not pretend it was remotely enough. With the threat of US military force no longer looming, the Syrian military resumed its ferocious assaults on civilians. Two days after the resolution's passage, a regime air strike would kill fourteen people, most of them children on their first day of school.

Additionally, in the months after the Syrian government issued a "declaration" of its inventory, laying out the quantities and locations of its stockpiles, laboratories, and delivery systems, we discovered that it omitted some capabilities and supplies we knew it had.[30] Several years would pass before the regime would dare to use sarin gas again. But just seven months after the Council vote, the Syrian military began weaponizing chlorine, relying on the widely available household chemical to supplant the sophisticated weapons we were destroying.

More than anything, I despaired for the future of Syria. By coming so close to punishing Assad only to pull back, the US government had moved farther away than ever before, telegraphing that we would likely never do so. Assad could reasonably conclude that, going forward, he could starve his people into submission, carpet bomb hospitals and schools, and eventually even resume chemical weapons attacks, all without the United States doing much to stop him.

Although the effects of this red-line episode were hard to measure, a large number of foreign diplomats told me afterward that America's "flip-flopping" had damaged President Obama's global reputation. I found much of this criticism maddening, given that many of these same ambassadors represented countries that would never have stood publicly with the United States had we gone ahead with air strikes. But it is undeniable that the perception of the "unenforced threat" shadowed our administration's subsequent efforts to influence Assad and other actors in the war. This moved us further away from the President's aim—and the regional and global necessity—of achieving a negotiated settlement to end the conflict.

Despite making the best of a terrible predicament, there was no getting around the fact that President Obama's own public statements prior to going to Congress reflected a firm conviction: what Assad had done merited using military force. As Obama had asked in his speech to the nation on August 31st, "What message will we send if a dictator can gas hundreds of children to death in plain sight and pay no price?"

Obama went to Congress because he believed that legislators would heed what their Commander in Chief called "a serious danger to our national security." They didn't. Assad still paid some price—giving up chemical weapons—but he subsequently used the rest of his arsenal with even greater abandon.

The costs—to Syrians, the United States, and the world—would continue to grow.

31

WHEN AMERICA SNEEZES

Early on in my tenure as UN ambassador, I attended a Security Council session dedicated to addressing mounting violence in the Central African Republic (CAR), an impoverished, landlocked country of 4.6 million people being engulfed by Muslim-on-Christian and Christian-on-Muslim terror. At the session, CAR's UN ambassador, Charles Doubane, pleaded with the Council to come to the rescue of his "bewildered, helpless people." He told us that fifty-three years after independence, his country had "totally collapsed."

I was startled to hear Doubane describe himself as the "Ambassador of a failed state." I was also horrified by the litany of graphic examples he offered of the savagery that CAR's people were suffering. Despite the work I had done on mass atrocities over the years, I knew almost nothing about the situation Doubane was describing. I arranged a meeting with him so I could begin to get educated.

The Permanent Mission of the Central African Republic to the United Nations, like that of many small countries, was located in an unassuming office complex a block from UN Headquarters. When I arrived, a diminutive, elderly, French-speaking man answered the door, exclaiming happily, "Bonjour Madame l'Ambassadrice!" Upon walking in, I was struck by the fact that the CAR "team" consisted of just two people—Doubane and this cheerful man whose suit hung off his frail limbs.

While the US Mission to the UN contained nearly two hundred offices and cubicles spread across twenty-two floors, the CAR Mission amounted to the entryway where I found myself standing and a tiny adjoining room. The Mission carried the pungent smell of cologne and was inordinately tidy. In fact, it had so little clutter that I wondered if the two diplomats had just moved in.

As I processed the scene, Ambassador Doubane strode into the entryway, where his associate now stood holding a bulky camera. The ambassador was dressed spiffily in a navy suit with a royal blue silk handkerchief in his blazer pocket to match his royal blue shirt. He shook my hand warmly. Then he stiffened, stood between his country's flag and that of the United Nations, and—as his colleague snapped photos and I listened—spoke with great formality, declaring:

> Madame Power, since the Central African Republic declared independence in 1960, no greater honor has befallen our humble Mission than to have the chance to welcome you here. We have checked our records, and we can find no evidence that a US Permanent Representative has ever before visited the Central African Republic's Mission to the United Nations.
>
> By taking the time out of your busy schedule to be with us here today, you have shown us that the world's superpower cares about what happens in our small, suffering country—that the Honorable Barack Obama knows our pain. My country will remember this visit forever. You have given us the first hope we have felt in a very long time.

I stood awkwardly as the ambassador delivered his homage. Amid all that President Obama was juggling, I was not sure he was carefully tracking the violence in the Central African Republic, and, new to my job, I had not intended to raise expectations with the CAR government about what the United States might do to help. When Doubane had finished, I said I was very touched by what he had said and thanked him for taking the time to meet with me. I knew every minute of his day was precious, as his people were counting on him to rally the world. I added that I would do my best not to disappoint him.

He walked me toward a chair in his office, and on the small glass coffee table, incongruous against the spartan office furnishings, I saw a lush collection of fresh white and yellow roses. I knew that the CAR government was so short on funds that it had fallen behind on its negligible UN dues and was struggling to pay the rent. Catching my gaze, Ambassador Doubane explained, "This is a very special occasion for us. Ever since your scheduler called last week, we have been preparing our office for your visit."

With the formalities behind us, he asked how he could be of help. I said I had no agenda. "I have just come to learn," I said. "Tell me more about your country."

He began to speak but quickly stopped. I initially thought he was struggling to find the proper English word to convey his meaning, but then I realized he was tearing up. I touched his arm and told him I was sorry about the horrors befalling his people. He said quickly, "No, it's not that, Ambassador. What is happening in my country is terrible— more terrible than anything that has ever happened to us before. But I am emotional because you are here. The United States of America is the greatest country in the world, and you, America, are here."

MY ENCOUNTERS WITH AMBASSADOR DOUBANE influenced me in at least two important ways. First, after human rights organizations and UN officials in CAR began echoing his warning of a coming genocide, I took the first of four trips to Doubane's country—a country that no US cabinet official had ever visited. Convinced that the potential for genocide was real, I reached out to Rwandan president Paul Kagame and got his agreement to send Rwandan peacekeeping troops to CAR. My team in Washington then worked with the Pentagon to get the fast-moving US military to equip and fly Burundian and Rwandan soldiers into the inferno as part of a beefed-up protection force.

My French counterpart, Gérard Araud, was already elevating the issue at the UN, where many other conflicts were competing for attention. I joined him, lobbying humanitarians to help stranded civilians who wished to leave their religiously mixed communities because they were afraid of being butchered.

The Obama administration's engagement over the next several years did not solve the crisis in the Central African Republic. Far from it. Thousands have been killed and one out of every four Central Africans remains displaced. As a detailed study produced by the US Holocaust Memorial Museum's genocide prevention center later noted, "Although the forces the United States helped deploy may have proven to be among the most effective peacekeepers in CAR, they represented only a tiny fraction of what was needed to stop the violence."[31]

Nonetheless, when the international forces arrived, the Christian-Muslim atrocities were spiraling out of control. The troop influx gave some people the ability to remain in their homes and others the means to escape. With time, the peacekeepers brought down the level of violence. Under President Obama, the United States would also become the world's most generous country toward CAR, providing more than $800 million in funding for humanitarian aid and peacekeeping operations during his second term. My team and I were able to bring attention to the crisis and help galvanize efforts that may have prevented the worst-case scenarios from coming to pass. Our actions led some to claim that we helped avert a genocide. I had gone into government hoping to be a part of efforts like this.

The second consequence of visiting Ambassador Doubane and hearing his story was that I decided to try to meet with each of the UN ambassadors to learn theirs. Partly, this decision was strategic: for the big, challenging votes in the General Assembly, where the United States was often outnumbered, the relationships I built could turn my colleagues into unlikely allies. But even if these so-called courtesy calls did not win extra support for the United States, I believed in the importance of conveying a sentiment I often heard from Vice President Biden, quoting his own mother: "Nobody's better than you, but you're better than nobody."

The UN Charter says that the UN is "based on the principle of the sovereign equality of all its Members," but almost nothing at the UN conveyed equality between the United States and, say, the Democratic Republic of Congo, the most destitute country in the world. So few people worked at the missions of small or poor countries that they often missed important votes and negotiations. If the ambassadors had conflicting doctor's appointments or traveled home for consultations, for example, they often lacked backup to ensure someone would take their place.

The United States, on the other hand, was the host country to the United Nations. We were the most powerful and richest country in the world. At times, this privilege led us to take other countries for granted. But when we recognized the inherent worth of nations and the individuals who represented them, we were valuing their dignity. By visiting the other ambassadors rather than having them travel to the US Mission to meet me (as was traditional), I was able to see the art my colleagues wanted to showcase, the family photos on their desks, and the books they had brought with them all the way to America. Most significantly, regardless of their size, wealth, or geopolitical heft, I could show them America's respect.

The role model I looked to for how to engage my colleagues was Eddie. In the three decades I had watched him, no taxi driver, medical patient, or person at the local café with an unusual accent seemed to be immune to his charm—or his questions. "You wouldn't happen to be from Uzbekistan?" he would ask, before sharing his love of silks from Samarkand. When he spotted a very tall, thin African with facial scars, he might ask, "Do you come from the Dinka or the Nuer ethnic group?" These conversations often ended with an exchange of telephone numbers and an agreement to meet for coffee later in the week. Eddie read more than anybody I had ever met, but he supplemented what he learned in books by engaging the walking, talking libraries that populated our daily lives: the people around us.

During my three and a half years as the US Ambassador to the UN, I was able to visit with the ambassador of every member state in the UN, except North Korea. When I mentioned to friends what I was doing, they would sometimes gasp, thinking I was planning to visit the other 192 *countries* in the world. In fact, my ambition was modest: I never once had to leave the island of Manhattan to access representatives from every corner of the planet.

My twenty-four-year-old scheduler, Megan Koilparampil, took full ownership of this effort. She had read *"A Problem from Hell"* after college, and during her job interview, she made clear that her interest in atrocity prevention drew her to the position. She understood that the operations work she and others in the US Mission did—scheduling, logistics, and event or trip planning—was every bit as important as the work our diplomats did negotiating through the night. Indeed, the operations team had mugs made with the acronym "GSD" (for "Get Shit Done") on the side.

Megan devoured the task of scheduling courtesy calls. Some of the people who answered at the offices I hoped to visit did not speak English, so Megan canvassed our team to find people with the necessary language skills. At the small, understaffed missions, days of attempts were sometimes required before someone answered the phone. Often, it was the ambassador who eventually picked up. When I had concluded my visit to a foreign colleague's office, very often he or she would bid me farewell with a request to "say hi to Megan." On occasion, when urging a country to take a tough vote, I would invoke the person they would least want to disappoint. "I am really counting on you," I would say. "And so is Megan."

The one-on-one meetings were eye-opening and often inspiring. Usually, when I reached out to a foreign diplomat, I did so because I needed something: I might want their country to support our position in a tense budget negotiation, for instance, or to send its soldiers to protect civilians in a crisis zone. But I tried not to use these individual visits to make such "asks."

Instead, I inquired about the ambassadors' upbringings, how they became diplomats, what they missed most about their countries, and what challenges they found most daunting. Around 50 of the 191 ambassadors I visited reported that no US Permanent Representative had set foot in their mission before. Many treated "America's visit" as a very special occasion, dressing up more formally than usual, bringing national delicacies from home to offer me, and having a camera at the ready to record the moment for posterity.

Developing these relationships obviously did not mean smooth sailing for me or for US objectives at the UN. But just as President Obama's personal popularity was a major asset in getting other countries to share information with the United States or to spend money on something the US government deemed important, so too did my personal relationships help turn ambassadors into advocates for our causes. And it was a two-way street. They introduced me to challenges their countries were facing that I would not have known about otherwise. This information allowed me to reach out to my colleagues at the State Department to see if the United States could be doing more to lend a hand.

I was struck on many of my visits by the extent to which the UN-based ambassadors and their citizens back home were intertwined with the United States. The ambassador from Eritrea, then the most isolated country in the world aside from North Korea, had been educated at Bowdoin College in Maine and American University in Washington, DC. The Somali and Bruneian ambassadors had attended the Fletcher School of Law and Diplomacy at Tufts University in Massachusetts. I heard constantly about connections like these. A half dozen of my fellow ambassadors began our meetings expressing "personal thanks" to the United States for educational support they had received through various State Department programs, which they said had made it possible for them to become diplomats.

And the connections extended well beyond higher education. Most Americans appreciate the vast cultural and immigration connections the United States shares with countries like China, Ireland, Israel, Italy, Mexico, or Poland. But it was only through these courtesy calls that I learned of more obscure ties. For example, although Cape Verde is a country of just 546,000, some 400,000 people of Cape Verdean descent live in the United States. Likewise, more than 15,000 people from the Marshall Islands, which only has a population of 53,000, reside in Springdale, Arkansas, with most of them working at the Tyson Foods headquarters.

The ambassadors' personal stories—which I could learn only through these visits—were often gripping. The Cypriot ambassador, who had an enormous Chicago Bulls banner hanging in his office, had been ten years old when his family fled the Turkish invasion. He had returned home only once. Although he despised the sight of Turkish settlers living in his childhood house, he expressed appreciation for the fact that they had returned two photo albums left behind decades before—one of his parents' wedding, and one of him and his brother as kids. Like so many who had been displaced, he longed to go back permanently. We discussed the UN-brokered Cypriot peace talks, which had stumbled partly over property issues. Knowing the ambassador's connection to the home he had lost humanized what was at stake in the negotiations.

The Zambian Ambassador to the UN had previously worked as a pediatrician in Lusaka, her country's capital, treating children with HIV. She spoke about the powerful impact of President George W. Bush's multibillion-dollar anti-AIDS program, which had successfully slowed the devastating spread of the disease. "Before PEPFAR," she said, "there was nothing I could do to help my babies." New HIV infections in Zambia had been cut in half since the program's inception in 2003.

The Somali ambassador had spent his career as a journalist with the BBC until 2015, when he had narrowly survived a double car bomb. "Many times I wept like a child because of the news," he said. "I decided that I couldn't continue to stand by like an outsider. I had to do something to try to help my country." He decided to join the fragile Somali government to do his part to combat terrorism.

Bhutan's ambassador had been raised in a family with six children in a rural part of the country. When her father decided that she and her sister were going to be educated, they had walked an entire day to reach a paved road, where they boarded a bus bound for a school in India. The Tajik ambassador was one of thirteen children, and his father had sent all the surviving siblings to the capital for their education. The ambassador, who learned to speak seven languages, ended up getting his PhD from Johns Hopkins University and working with political scientist Francis Fukuyama.

The Lao and Vietnamese ambassadors each had lost close family members in wars with the United States, and they had traumatic memories of fleeing their homes and sleeping in trenches to avoid US bombing. However, both said they wanted desperately to "turn the page" on relations with their former antagonist. They reported that their populations were fiercely pro-American.

When the ambassador from Antigua and Barbuda was four years old, he told me, he had been playing in the cotton fields when another child had poked his eyes with a stick. Because Antigua had no ophthalmologists, he lost sight in both eyes, but eventually became the first legally blind person in the Caribbean to attend university. During his time at the UN, one of his children was working at a center for the blind in Massachusetts.

While I looked forward to most of my courtesy calls, I was unenthused about some, including my meeting with the Cambodian ambassador, a man who in UN gatherings mumbled his country's turgid prepared statements and betrayed no charisma. True to form, he began our meeting by delivering a set of rote talking points. But when I asked him what life had been like for him as a boy growing up under the Khmer Rouge, his manner was transformed.

He said that the Khmer Rouge executed his father "for being a teacher," but when they murdered his sister, a housewife, he said, "they did not have to give a reason." The ambassador noted matter-of-factly that he and his surviving siblings nearly starved to death. "I am surprised by how much food is wasted at the UN," he said, simply.

The ambassador from Swaziland—a repressive, landlocked monarchy in southern Africa—told me that his mother was the corrupt king's sister, raising my hope that he would have influence with his government back home. However, his next comment quickly brought me back to reality: "Oh the king has soooo many brothers and sisters. I was already in this job before he even realized we were related!"

One of the biggest surprises came when I met Mamadou Tangara, Gambia's ambassador. Tangara reported to Gambian president Yahya Jammeh, a vindictive dictator who had been in power for more than two decades. When I dropped into Tangara's office, he told me he had never been paid such a visit and quickly opened up.

"I'm worried," he confessed, explaining that Jammeh was growing increasingly erratic. "Things are getting worse every day," he said. "He is pushing away anyone who tells him the truth."

A few months later, I saw Tangara at the annual Fourth of July reception I hosted on behalf of the United States at the Central Park Zoo. After posing with him for a photo in the receiving line, I pulled him aside and whispered, "Mamadou, I'm starting to think your president is a bit crazy." When his face darkened, I worried I had crossed a line.

"That's not true, Ambassador," he said, his voice rising. "My president is not a bit crazy. My president is *completely* crazy." Tangara became a friend, and someone who volunteered to help me try to secure the release of political prisoners languishing in Gambian jails.

When Jammeh was unexpectedly defeated in elections in 2016 and refused to give up power, Tangara took a stand. Risking his life and that of his elderly father back home, he declared allegiance to the legitimate, newly elected president, and refused to take further instructions from Jammeh. Promptly fired, Tangara made plans to pack up his family and leave New York. But thankfully, unrelenting pressure from African leaders, the United States, and the broader international community forced Jammeh to recognize the election results. He gave up power, and Tangara was eventually reinstated.

In June of 2017, after I had left office, I received a text from Tangara informing me that he had just been named foreign minister by the new president. "Your support and friendship gave me the courage to stand strong in defense of truth and justice," he wrote. What was striking to me was how little it had taken to make him feel that way.

Occasionally, in the privacy of these one-on-one meetings, an ambassador would confide that he or she would like to support the United States on a particular issue but couldn't because of problematic instructions from their capital.

"I am with you," they would say, "but I need help. Can John Kerry call?"

At such times, the ambassadors would identify the minister or deputy minister responsible for the objectionable voting guidance. This would enable me or other US diplomats to reach back to our embassies on the ground to get them involved. I was awestruck by America's reach, and by the eagerness of our ambassadors around the world to leap into action.

Nothing was more unsettling than my conversations with ambassadors whose countries were threatened with extinction as a result of climate change. I arrived at the UN at a time when the UN-sponsored process was stalemated and acrimonious. When countries convened in 2013, more than two years before the eventual Paris Agreement, the Philippines's lead delegate went on a hunger strike to protest the lack of urgency among negotiators, and a bloc of 132 countries staged a walkout. Similar frustrations, as well as abject fear, dominated my meetings with representatives of the most vulnerable nations.

The Cape Verde ambassador told me that in the previous year, his country had not seen a single drop of rain. "Do you know what it means for it never to rain at all?" he asked. For island nations around the world, the huge spike in extreme weather events was destroying whatever economic or developmental gains they had made during the previous decade.

The ambassador from the Marshall Islands informed me that every two weeks, high tides on different parts of the islands caused around a thousand people to relocate inland. Since she was based in New York, she had allowed her family residence to be converted into a home for "climate refugees." She explained that four families were crammed into the residence at any given time, but most people she knew were looking to emigrate. Many indigenous communities, meanwhile, could not even contemplate the pain of leaving behind the bones of ancestors or forgoing sacred traditions tied to the land.

The islands that formed Kiribati had a combined population of 112,000 people. Among them, the highest elevation was just six feet. The ambassador was skeptical his country would survive. "We are falling into the sea," he said. His government was encouraging citizens to consider moving elsewhere under a plan it called "migration with dignity." It had even gone so far as to purchase land 1,200 miles away in Fiji, where Kiribati residents could relocate when their country became unlivable. The only plot the Kiribati government could afford, however, was forested and swampy, and unlikely to support the livelihoods of their entire population.

The inhabitants of island nations felt trapped. Even though they knew they needed to make plans to live elsewhere, they did not have the visas required to move. "We didn't cause this problem," the ambassador from Tuvalu said. "But when a hurricane hits the United States, your people get warned and they have some chance to move to higher ground. When we get warned, there is nothing we can do. We don't have high ground—the only place to go is up a coconut tree."

But how, I asked, could an elderly person get up a tree?

"Exactly," he replied.

These countries were counting on the United States to lead the world in finding a solution. Their ambassadors encouraged people who denied or doubted the global scientific consensus on climate change to visit their homelands. "We are losing so much time," one said. Each full year that I was in my job at the UN was hotter than the one before, and each was hotter than any single year in recorded history. If the United States did not show leadership to combat these trends, they warned, they and their families were doomed.

When I visited the ambassador from Grenada, she summed up the dynamic with a phrase I heard often: "If America sneezes, people in my country catch a cold."

32

UPSIDE-DOWN LAND

With its towering ceiling and large, ornate mural depicting a phoenix rising from the wreckage of war, the Security Council chamber always exuded the aura of a grand and timeless stage set. But in February of 2014, when I looked around the room, I momentarily felt that I had actually been transported to a prior age.

The chamber was packed in anticipation of a US–Russia showdown.

Using tactics similar to those of the Soviet Union, Vladimir Putin's Russia was attempting a vicious land grab in Ukraine. Furthermore, he and his representatives were lying about their aggression to the world, acting as if the abundant evidence from photographs, satellites, and live witnesses did not exist.

The UN press gallery, often a sleepy locale, was brimming with foreign journalists. Photographers jostled one another for the best vantage to cover the expected drama. As I entered the chamber, the initial flurry of camera flashes was blinding.

I was not alive during the Soviet invasions of Hungary in 1956 or Czechoslovakia in 1968. When the Berlin Wall fell in 1989, I was only nineteen and just beginning to immerse myself in foreign affairs. In the years that followed, I had mistakenly assumed that Russia had left behind the era of brutalizing its neighbors.

As our emergency meeting was gaveled to begin, I sat in the US chair and reflected on the fact that just as in 1956 and 1968, only one country could lead the world in standing up to Moscow on the international stage: the United States.

Then it hit me: Wait! That's me. I'm America here. *I'm* the one who has to respond.

DURING PRESIDENT OBAMA'S FIRST TERM, he had orchestrated a "reset" with Russia, and his partnership with President Medvedev resulted in a number of significant national security achievements. The United States and Russia had successfully negotiated the "New START" treaty and slashed our respective nuclear stockpiles. We had worked together on Iran, imposing multilayered sanctions that would soon cause Tehran to surrender its potential nuclear weapons program. And perhaps most remarkably, given the history between our two countries, Russia had granted the US military access to a critical land route for supplying our troops in Afghanistan.

Even when we were on good terms, however, nothing came easily with Russia. Whether Vladimir Putin was prime minister or president, the Russian government locked up and even murdered its critics. At the UN, Russia played the spoiler, impeding American efforts to promote human rights and to secure various reforms within the organization.

Nonetheless, I had invested long hours in forging a constructive working relationship with Vitaly Churkin, Russia's Ambassador to the UN. Because Russia held one of five vetoes at the Security Council, its vote was critical if we were to get the Council to send peacekeepers to conflict areas, impose sanctions on wrongdoers, or even just condemn a coup. In order for the UN to have a meaningful impact on issues of war and peace, the United States and Russia had to be willing to make deals. Our two countries did not have the option of remaining at arm's length.

Vitaly had only recently gotten to know me during our negotiations over the Syria chemical weapons resolution. But I had known him far longer, having watched him in action when he served as the Russian envoy to Bosnia in the 1990s during the war. I had occasionally been in the pack of journalists surrounding him in Sarajevo, notebook and tape recorder in hand. Vitaly always seemed to relish these engagements, eloquently delivering a predictably pro-Serb line while simultaneously insisting upon his own complete objectivity. I remember being struck by the fact that his English was so fluid that he quoted lines from American movies and songs and even made English puns.[32]

But something else impressed me more. After the February 1994 massacre of Sarajevo market-goers, Vitaly had reportedly been pivotal in convincing the Bosnian Serbs to move their heavy weapons away from the Bosnian capital. This brought Sarajevans a reprieve of many months. When the Serbs subsequently resumed shelling the city and began assaulting the UN-declared "safe areas," Vitaly was also the rare Russian official who publicly criticized them, saying they were "afflicted with military madness." To me, this indicated a promising independent streak.

Vitaly became UN ambassador in 2006 and seemed a permanent fixture. He had sparred with Susan Rice when she had been ambassador, but they had also become friendly. In their last UN meeting together, she had roared with laughter when he presented her with a mock Security Council statement expressing "relief" at her departure. The mock-up also sent condolences to "that other Security Council," the National Security Council she would soon chair in her capacity as National Security Advisor.

I had already come to respect Vitaly's talents as a negotiator. He had brought procedural wisdom and textual creativity to our Syria chemical weapons discussions, but above all he listened with careful intensity. When he wasn't melodramatically storming out of a meeting, he was good at bridging gaps.

Significantly, he also valued US–Russia cooperation. From his time as an interpreter in arms control negotiations during the Cold War, Vitaly drew a lesson: even when Russia's overall relationship with the United States was strained, our two countries could carve out discrete areas for progress and try to build constructive momentum. I knew he often pushed for compromises that Moscow was disinclined to make. Vitaly and I always took each other's calls. And for the three and a half years we worked together, we would do our best to reconcile positions that on their face looked irreconcilable.

As I got to know Vitaly, I naturally wondered how he could stand working for Putin and why he hadn't resigned somewhere along the way. Even though people who crossed Putin often ended up jailed or even killed, I didn't think he stayed because he was intimidated. Instead, the most memorable stanza from Tennyson's "The Charge of the Light Brigade" (one of Eddie's favorite poems) would often come to my mind: *"Theirs not to make reply, Theirs not to reason why, Theirs but to do and die."*

Vitaly had been a child actor in Soviet films and had come of age during the height of Cold War competition with the United States.[33] After the collapse of the Soviet Union, he despised what he saw as the American tendency to take Russia for granted. Like many proud Russians, he embraced Putin's goal of "raising Russia from its knees." Even if the Russian leader's actions made him uncomfortable, he would go on serving his country.

Mutual interest alone could have produced a civil and professional working relationship between us. But over time, Vitaly and I developed something resembling a genuine friendship. UN culture was drearily buttoned up. Whether diplomats bloviated or spoke in monotone, they hewed closely to generic talking points. Some had strong views but were prevented by their governments from airing them. Others had been receiving "instructions" from their capitals for so long that they seemed to have suspended thinking for themselves. Vitaly was different.

He had a point of view—on everything from the sources of Alexander Ovechkin's greatness as a hockey player to what China's rise would mean for the world. Even when discussing issues on which Russia had scant Council support, he seemed to delight in playing the role of the underdog. He was also a masterful storyteller with an often irreverent sense of humor. When I once went on too long speaking before the Council, he responded, "After hearing all that the Permanent Representative of the United States felt she needed to share with us today, I am tempted to read my statement twice." On another occasion, when we were arguing after a Council session, I told him that I knew he had mixed motives—"half sincere and half ulterior."

"No," he countered, "we are fully sincere about achieving our ulterior motive."

Vitaly and his wife, Irina, a French teacher and translator, were avid theatergoers. I had established an unusual partnership with Oskar Eustis, the artistic director of the Public Theater in New York. Oskar would contact me when a new production was premiering, and we would brainstorm about whether it made sense to invite foreign diplomats. I considered these nights a wonderful means of employing American "soft power," and the plays often transmitted subtle messages about the importance of human rights. Unlike some other foreign colleagues, Vitaly accepted every one of my invitations.

When I brought a dozen ambassadors to the Public Theater's performance of Shakespeare's *Cymbeline*, he was the first to leap out of his chair to ignite a standing ovation. He did not hold it against me when the press covered his presence at the LGBT-themed musical *Fun Home*, an unusual night out for the representative of a famously homophobic government. At the intermission of *Hamilton*, he interrogated Cass, a professor of constitutional law, about whether creator Lin-Manuel Miranda had accurately depicted the Founding Fathers' debates.

Vitaly and I both loved sports, and the only times he didn't answer his phone were when Russia was competing in the Olympics or the World Cup. We brought each other to games (he favored hockey and tennis; I could never convince him that my favorite sport, baseball, was interesting, so we settled on the NBA). I also introduced him to FX's Cold War drama *The Americans*, which he claimed was "a bit ridiculous," but nonetheless watched compulsively.

Most memorably, I invited him and Irina to my parents' home in Yonkers for Thanksgiving, making him the only United Nations colleague who ever entered my wild Irish family sanctum. When they arrived, Irina immediately sat down on the carpet and began playing with my children, while Eddie and Vitaly talked Russian history and literature. When we went around the table to describe what we were most thankful for, Vitaly said, "Peace between our two countries. Whatever happens, we must preserve that. It was no fun before."

I liked and respected Vitaly. But I also spent much of my time at the UN in pitched, public battle with him.

IN LATE 2013, VIKTOR YANUKOVYCH, the Russian-backed president of Ukraine, walked away from a wide-ranging economic and political agreement with the European Union that he had been planning to sign. His about-face prompted protests from hundreds of thousands of Ukrainians. Moscow had leaned hard on Yanukovych not to sign the deal, and young people who saw their future in Europe took to the streets in significant numbers. They were joined by Ukrainians of all ages who were fed up with pervasive government corruption.[34] Together, gathered in Kiev's Maidan Square, they shouted out *"Hid-nist! Hid-nist!"*—"Dignity! Dignity!"

As the protests swelled, Ukraine's security forces began firing on the demonstrators, killing more than one hundred people in January and February of 2014. Eventually, intense pressure from the Ukrainians who had taken to the street, Yanukovych's political allies, and foreign governments (including EU countries, the United States, and even Russia) convinced the Ukrainian president he needed to contain the unrest. Yanukovych signed an agreement with the opposition for early elections and democratic reforms, but fearing for himself and his hoarded wealth, he then abruptly fled his own country, eventually resurfacing in Russia.

In late February of 2014, Russia invaded Ukraine, seizing the Crimean peninsula. Three months later, it sent its forces into eastern Ukraine, waging full-blown war. Russia's military takeover of part of its neighbor was a flagrant violation of international law, which prohibits one country from forcibly taking another's territory. In 1990, when Iraq invaded and attempted to annex Kuwait, the Security Council demanded Iraq's withdrawal and ultimately authorized a multinational military coalition to restore Kuwaiti sovereignty. But now, because Russia was a permanent member of the Security Council, it was able to use its veto to prevent a united international stand against its blatant aggression.

Still, the Council became important. It was there that the United

States and other countries fought in the court of public opinion over truth and culpability. Following Russia's illegal land grab, it became the main venue in which the United States and our allies exposed Russian deceit and emphasized its isolation in the world.

Some of the most storied diplomatic showdowns in the post–World War II era had occurred in the Council, as countries sought to define their positions as indisputable facts. During the 1962 Cuban Missile Crisis, as television cameras rolled, US Ambassador Adlai Stevenson interrogated his Soviet counterpart about whether the USSR had deployed missiles in Cuba. "I am prepared to wait for an answer until Hell freezes over, if that is your decision," Stevenson said. When the Soviet representative hedged, Stevenson theatrically unveiled images of the missiles at Cuban bases, proving their existence to the world. More notoriously, in 2003, when the Bush administration wanted to convince a skeptical international audience that Saddam Hussein's alleged weapons of mass destruction posed an imminent danger, Secretary of State Colin Powell used the Security Council as the stage on which to make his now-discredited presentation.

More directly applicable to the Ukraine crisis was the 1956 confrontation between the United States and the Soviet Union over the Soviet attempt to crush Hungary's democratic uprising. When I had first read about this episode as a college student, I was flabbergasted by the Soviet ambassador's contradictory and desperate claims in his face-offs with US Ambassador Henry Cabot Lodge, Jr. He denied the facts of what the USSR was doing, insisting that Soviet troops were not entering Hungary despite film footage showing they were. He billed Soviet actions as humanitarian, claiming that the United States and its allies had created "a state of terror" inside Hungary and that Soviet forces had intervened to prevent a "fascist dictatorship." And he pointed the finger at events or sins committed elsewhere, invoking the Suez Crisis in Egypt to muddy the waters about Soviet wrongdoing.

Close to sixty years later, at the initial emergency Security Council session on the Russian land grab in Ukraine, I found myself sitting two seats away from Vitaly, listening as he used identical tactics to deny that the Russian military had invaded Ukraine.

Ignoring the extensive evidence of Russia's aggression, he claimed that the Russian military was not even in Ukrainian territory. He painted a false picture of neo-Nazis and fascist sympathizers terrorizing Russian speakers. Then, he dramatically held up a letter from Yanukovych, Ukraine's discredited and absent president. "The lives, security and rights of the people . . . are under threat," Vitaly read out loud from Yanukovych's "request" for Russian intervention in words likely scripted by Putin himself. "I therefore call on President Vladimir Vladimirovich Putin of Russia to use the armed forces of the Russian Federation to establish legitimacy, peace, law and order and stability in defense of the people of Ukraine."

In formulating my response, I had to speak to multiple audiences. In addition to directly confronting the Kremlin, I needed to appeal to other countries to join us in pressuring Russia to reverse its military takeover. I also had to consider the Ukrainian people. Ukraine's ambassador had informed me before the meeting that millions of Ukrainians would be watching the session on prime-time television, gathering in their homes, in bars, and before storefront windows. I wanted them to know that America stood with them, and to feel the depth of that solidarity.

Additionally, with Fox and CNN carrying my remarks live, I had to bear in mind the American domestic audience, including Republican members of Congress who were portraying our administration as soft on Russian aggression. I had to vent our outrage while also establishing the truth about what was actually taking place in Ukraine.

And I absolutely had to win the argument with Vitaly.

Complicating matters further, Susan had called just before I left my office with instructions not to be "too hot." The words of the UN Ambassador speaking on behalf of President Obama could inadvertently provoke Putin to launch attacks in other parts of Ukraine. I assured her that I would not overdo it.

I started by laying out the facts about Russia's actions in painstaking detail. Russian military forces had taken over Ukrainian border posts. They had surrounded Ukrainian military facilities in Crimea. They were blocking cell phone service. Russian ships had moved into the waters off of Sevastopol, Crimea's largest city. Russian fighter jets and helicopters had repeatedly violated Ukrainian airspace, and a number of Russian troop transport planes had landed in Crimea.

After I heard Vitaly speak, I decided to go beyond my prepared remarks to respond extemporaneously to the falsehoods I had just heard.

"Listening to the representative of Russia," I declared, "one might think that Moscow had just become the rapid response arm of the High Commissioner for Human Rights."

The Russian takeover was not about self-defense or restoring calm, as Vitaly had alleged. It was a military invasion of territory that the Soviet Union had made part of Ukraine in 1954, but which Putin and many Russian nationalists wanted to be part of Russia.

"Russia has every right to wish that events in Ukraine had turned out differently," I concluded, "but it does not have the right to express that unhappiness by using military force or by trying to convince the world community that up is down and black is white."

A few days later, as I walked my kids back from a playground near the UN, several Ukrainians came over to thank me for exposing Russia's lies. One distraught elderly woman said, "We were afraid we would be alone."

Afterward, Declan asked me what the women were so upset about, so I told him about Putin, searching for terms a five-year-old could understand. "It's like someone entering our apartment, taking two of your favorite stuffed animals from your toy corner, and then saying they used to belong to him," I explained. "How would that feel?"

He looked at me with a pained expression and shook his head incredulously as we resumed our walk home.

ALTHOUGH PUTIN ATTEMPTED to depict the Ukraine conflict as one between the United States and Russia, I tried to focus on the Ukrainian people whom Russia sought to airbrush from history. Having fought for democratic reform, these Ukrainians were now suffering the devastating effects of a conflict that would go on to kill more than 10,000 people and displace two million.

In order to see the impact of the conflict firsthand, I traveled to Ukraine to meet with young reformers who had joined the new government that succeeded Yanukovych's. I also visited with families who had been forced to flee eastern Ukraine because of the Russian-sponsored violence. One mother told me how her husband and two-year-old child were killed when their home near the town of Debaltseve was shelled during a Russian separatist offensive. She and her five surviving children escaped in a van whose roof and doors had been blasted out by shelling, eventually arriving in the Ukrainian capital of Kiev, where locals took them in.

And yet Vitaly continued to act as though none of this was happening, giving voice to the deceptions of the Russian government. When I presented the facts, he simply pretended they were not true. "I have the impression that Ms. Power is taking her information from United States television," he said during one of our confrontations. "Then of course everything in Ukraine must seem just wonderful."

My speechwriter Nik Steinberg and I tried to use my remarks at each session to convince fence-sitting countries to condemn the Russian government's actions. Nik had been a student and teaching assistant of mine at the Kennedy School, where he had stood out as a gifted writer. He had gone on to work for Human Rights Watch, documenting disappearances and extrajudicial killings in Mexico. He had never served in government or written a speech before he came to work for me. But when I hired him, he took to it instantly. He anticipated and preemptively rebutted counterarguments. He was prescriptive about what needed to be done and who needed to do it. And he eloquently told the stories of specific individuals whose lives were on the line, something that human rights NGOs excelled at, but which government speeches rarely tried.

Critically, Nik brought an outsider's perspective. He would interrogate claims made by US officials that did not seem to have strong backing and reject the bureaucratic impulse to soften sharp, potentially arresting arguments. Ever the field researcher, when he wanted to include a personal story in one of my speeches, he would try to obtain additional details from the relevant individuals (or people directly connected with them), regardless of where they were in the world.

Nik also kept his cool when foreign government officials made outrageous claims in his presence. Once, when we met together with a Mexican official who said that most of the victims of Mexican disappearances were criminals, I slipped Nik a note that said, "You must want to throw yourself out the window." He glanced at it, and then calmly went on to ask a series of questions, exposing the speciousness of the official's claims.

For important national security remarks, like those I began frequently giving on Ukraine, Nik often had to consider contradictory edits and comments from more than twenty faceless officials within US government ranks. After experiencing this process for the first time, he came into my office looking exhausted.

"Make sure you also run my statement by Susan and John," I reminded him.

Despite momentarily appearing dazed by my request—as if I was asking that he telephone President Obama for line edits—he quickly recovered, and within the hour had figured out how to get speeches before the National Security Advisor and Secretary of State. On fast-breaking, high-stakes issues, we needed to ensure that both were comfortable with what I was going to say on behalf of the United States.

Keeping my remarks current for each Ukraine session demanded that I present evidence of Russian misdeeds in real time. But because the information on which we were relying was highly sensitive, the intelligence community had to continually decide which details it was prepared to declassify for use in my remarks. Sometimes that process broke down or different intelligence agencies disagreed on what should be disclosed. I often found myself beginning a Council session with Nik still on the phone, trying to ascertain whether I had license to expose the details of particular Russian troop or weapons movements.

During one televised meeting, I still had no speech in hand when the Council president turned in my direction and said, "I now give the floor to the representative of the United States." As my microphone light turned red, signaling my time to begin, I felt my special assistant Colleen breathlessly swoop in behind me. I reached my hand back like the anchor in a relay race awaiting a baton, Colleen handed me a green folder, and I opened it and immediately began to read, feigning calm.

The flurry of Russian provocations, followed by emergency Security Council and high-level Washington meetings on Ukraine, meant my kids saw me even less than usual.

One night, arriving home at ten p.m., I did what my dad had done with me in Dublin after returning from Hartigan's: I roused Declan from bed for some fun.

"Let's go get a burger," I said, taking him to The Smith on 2nd Avenue.

Cass was in Cambridge, and I longed to share with someone how I was doing my small part to stand up to Putin, who Declan had asked about regularly since our sidewalk exchange with the Ukrainians. As my son dug into the bacon from his cheeseburger, I regaled him with my best lines from earlier in the day. I proudly recounted how Vitaly had seemed to stumble in our back and forth. And I told Declan that I had made clear that just because Putin had big weapons did not mean he could take what belonged to other people.

"Did it work, Mommy?" he asked innocently, dipping his French fry in mayonnaise.

"Did what work, Dec?" I said.

"Did Putin leave Crimea?" he asked.

I smiled. Declan, in all his wisdom, was focused on the one result that mattered—not who won the public debate, but whether the aggressor had retreated. My son had brought me down to earth.

"Not yet, Dec," I said. "But a Power never gives up, do we?"

"Never!" he said, his face bright with possibility. "And tomorrow you can try again."

WHEN RUSSIA ATTEMPTED to formalize its military conquest of the Crimean peninsula, I saw an opportunity to do something concrete.

Russia had announced a plan to stage a referendum for the Crimean people to vote on their future. What the Russians were doing, however, was a sham. Putin only gave Crimeans the choice between joining Russia or becoming independent. He refused to give voters the option of remaining part of Ukraine. Moreover, the atmosphere before the poll was terrifying. Russian soldiers in unmarked uniforms and ubiquitous Russian-backed paramilitaries were flaunting their heavy weapons and abducting, beating, and torturing activists, journalists, and minorities.

I huddled with the lawyers and regional experts at the US Mission, and we came up with a practical plan to preserve Ukraine's legal claim to Crimea. Prevented by Russia from mobilizing international action through the Security Council, we decided to run a resolution in the General Assembly that rejected the upcoming referendum and the redrawing of Ukraine's borders.

Many votes in the General Assembly were purely symbolic. But, in this case, if we could win the vote, Russia would at least not be able to alter the boundaries on official maps.[35] No matter what "facts" Russian forces created with tanks and terror, Crimea would remain legally part of Ukraine. This was an unconventional approach, and we would need the majority of the other 192 UN members to get on board, but it was the best way we could use the UN to enshrine Ukraine's right to recover its own occupied territory.

We fanned out, as only America's diplomats can. My deputy, Rosemary DiCarlo, a thirty-year veteran of the Foreign Service and a fluent Russian speaker, drew on her contacts around the world to get US ambassadors to take the issue directly to heads of state, while I tapped the relationships I had forged through my courtesy calls. "Every small country in the world needs the protection of the UN Charter," I argued. "Think of what it would mean if international borders suddenly became optional. Think what the world would become if your neighbor got to unilaterally decide that a peninsula in your country should become part of theirs."

Nonetheless, on the day of the vote, I was worried. I knew that Russia's closest allies would take its side, and we presumed that many countries would abstain in order to avoid angering Putin. We had also heard from several developing countries that Russian diplomats were offering cash in return for their support.

In the General Assembly, each country's representative presses a button and his or her vote instantaneously appears on a digital jumbo screen beside the country's name: green for YES, red for NO, and yellow for ABSTAIN. The green YES votes of the United States and Ukraine—voting for the resolution and rejecting the validity of the referendum—were among the first to appear. Russia was naturally first among the NO votes. Other countries seemed to be taking their time, and my heart beat wildly in suspense.

One by one, the votes appeared. In the upper right of the screen, I saw a flash of green, followed by another flash of green in the lower left, then another in the upper left. For thirty seconds, flash after flash came up green. So many of the countries that had been undecided—that had privately confessed their fear that Russia would retaliate against them if they sided with the United States and Ukraine—came through.

The final vote on whether to reject Russia's referendum proved a rout: 100 YES votes with the United States and Ukraine, just 11 NO votes, and 58 ABSTENTIONS.* The Associated Press described the result as "a sweeping rebuke of Moscow."

This success did not mean I could answer Declan's question in the affirmative. Putin had not left Crimea, and he was unlikely to do so. In fact, despite having denied his forces were there, the Russian president soon signed a treaty annexing the peninsula.[36] But at least the UN maps would continue to depict Crimea as part of Ukraine.

That was not a lot in light of the gravity of the harm inflicted, but it was not nothing. Putin would not be able to erase his crime, and Ukrainians would know that most of the world supported them.

After the vote, I spoke directly to Russia—and Vitaly: "You do not get to choose your own facts and your own law. *The law* tells

---

* Twenty-four UN member states did not vote, either because of their small staffs or in order to avoid alienating either the United States or Russia.

us your actions are unlawful. *The facts* tell us you are taking territory from a sovereign neighbor. And *the vote* here tells us all you are alone."*

A FEW MONTHS LATER, on July 17th, 2014, Russian-backed rebels who had seized parts of eastern Ukraine fired a surface-to-air missile that hit a Malaysian Airlines passenger jet, flight MH17. The plane was making its way from Amsterdam to Kuala Lumpur in an established flight corridor 33,000 feet above Ukraine. The strike incinerated all 298 people aboard.

We again convened an emergency session of the Security Council. Before anybody spoke, all fifteen ambassadors stood for a moment of silence. The losses were heartbreaking. Joep Lange, a Dutch scientist and a giant in the field of AIDS research, had been traveling with several colleagues on their way to an AIDS conference. One couple had been on a family vacation in Europe with their three kids—ages twelve, ten, and eight—and had decided to stay on for a few days while the children and their grandfather returned home on the flight. Overall, eighty children had been killed.

Thinking about the passengers, I snuck a glance at Vitaly and found myself wishing there was a bottom to the depths he would stoop to defend Russia. But I did not expect this to be the day he broke ranks. He would do his job as he understood it.

Since having Declan and Rían, I had noticed that I risked losing my composure whenever I tried to speak publicly about harm done to children. I learned that I could improve my chances of holding it together by reading a speech out loud multiple times before I gave it publicly, allowing me to spin a web of distance and separate my heart from its content. If I had time to read a speech five times before delivering it, that web would be five times as thick as if I read it once; if I managed

---

* In addition to Russia, the NO votes came from Armenia, Belarus, Bolivia, Cuba, North Korea, Nicaragua, Sudan, Syria, Venezuela, and Zimbabwe. This meant that Russia, while technically not "alone," did not win any support beyond the "who's who" of repressive states that generally voted together irrespective of the substance of the resolutions. Even China did not vote with Russia.

to read a speech a dozen times, I could almost guarantee that I would get through the remarks, no matter the subject. But in the case of flight MH17, I had not had time to fully inoculate myself.

"As we stared at the passenger lists yesterday," I began, "we saw next to three of the passengers' names a capital 'I.' As we now know, that letter 'I' stands for 'infant.'"

As my voice cracked, I paused. I had the sudden impulse to leave the chamber, sprint a block, barge into Rían's preschool class, and hug her and never let her go. Instead, I glared at Vitaly and found a way to keep going, locating an emotion I could rarely find: rage.

The facts were obscene. Proud of having acquired a powerful new weapons system, Russian separatists in eastern Ukraine had posted to social media sites numerous videos that showed them moving around the very SA-11 surface-to-air missile system that we assessed had shot down the plane. The separatist leaders, initially thinking they had hit a Ukrainian jet, had even boasted about the strike online, saying, "We have warned everyone not to fly in our skies."

In the days ahead, Russian separatists casually wandered through the wreckage, trampling on human remains and carting away evidence. In videos, they could be seen tossing around children's toys and rummaging through luggage. They also removed from the crash site the missile parts they feared would incriminate them.

The Russian government, of course, simply denied any involvement, rejecting evidence that the missile system came from the Russian military.* Meanwhile, the Russian disinformation apparatus, which had been distorting events in Crimea and Eastern Ukraine from the start, went into overdrive. Russian news and internet sources simultaneously pushed stories blaming the crash on the Ukrainian military (for mistakenly believing the aircraft was Putin's and trying to assassinate him)

---

* In 2018, the Joint Investigative Team (JIT) responsible for investigating what happened to MH17 concluded that the Russian military's 53rd Anti-Aircraft Missile Brigade was responsible for providing the Russian separatists with this missile system. The JIT—comprised of criminal investigators from the governments of Australia, the Netherlands, Belgium, Malaysia, and Ukraine—also documented that the system in question returned to Russia after the attack.

and the CIA. One macabre theory held that the plane had been surreptitiously filled with dead bodies prior to taking off.

The Russian government weaponized social media, using trolls and bots to bring these wild-eyed conspiracy theories into wider circulation. One year later, a poll would find that only 3 percent of Russians believed Russian separatists were the perpetrators of the attack, while more than 60 percent thought the Ukrainians or Americans bore responsibility. The Russian lies even made their way to the American mainstream when, in October of 2015, CNN asked presidential candidate Donald Trump who was behind the missile strike. Trump repeated Putin's denials of Russian involvement, adding, "to be honest with you, you'll probably never know for sure."

Russia's success in obscuring its crime likely encouraged Moscow to think bigger.

33

US AND THEM

By sheer coincidence, several of my Security Council appearances coincided with President Obama's public statements on Ukraine. The visual of me speaking out against Russian action in the presence of the Russian ambassador naturally carried with it the drama of an in-person altercation. Obama, conversely, tended to deliver his statements at a podium in more sterile settings. My rejoinders were often spontaneous because I was reacting to Vitaly's claims in the moment. Obama's were prepared well in advance and read from a script.

Had the President resorted to fiery language like mine, he would have seemed unpresidential. Nonetheless, the press decided to play up the contrast, and President Obama's critics began using me to attack my boss.

A number of networks juxtaposed clips of Obama and me speaking on Ukraine, in an effort to show that the President's heart was not in his condemnations. Ralph Peters, a retired Army lieutenant colonel and national security analyst on Fox News, told Sean Hannity, "I heard Samantha Power, who seems to be the only real man in the administration."

"She served up red meat," Peters said, while Obama "served up lukewarm waffles."

On *Meet the Press*, NBC's Andrea Mitchell contended, "They had the same intelligence, the same evidence. Samantha Power was a more forceful presentation at the United Nations than the President."

In the *Washington Post*, columnist Charles Krauthammer criticized

Obama's "rote, impassive voice" when talking about Ukraine, claiming that it "borders on disassociation," while "Samantha Power delivers an impassioned denunciation of Russia."

Two colleagues of mine at the NSC sent me back-channel messages that the President's senior staff wished I would "dial it back." Although such criticism now seems thoroughly inconsequential, at the time I found it dismaying. I almost never second-guessed myself when I was in a high-stakes negotiation with Vitaly or when I was challenging him extemporaneously in the Council. And even when I visited danger-ous conflict zones, I felt completely in my element. Yet the politics of politics, the internal sniping that occurred within the government, still rattled me, as if I were back in Obama's Senate office. I never found a way to fully slay those bats.

I reached out to Ben, who had written the statements for which Obama was being faulted. He reassured me, saying that he had seen the President shut down those who were complaining.

"Why the hell do you think I put Samantha up there?" Ben re-ported Obama saying. "She is doing exactly what she should be doing."

That same calm spirit in our President that some found frustrating served to protect me at times when others became petty. I could imag-ine Obama saying, "Our problem, last I checked, is not our outspoken UN ambassador. It is Putin. Can we kindly focus on what we are going to do about that?"

AUTHORITARIAN LEADERS FREQUENTLY MANUFACTURE and demon-ize "enemies" to shore up support from their political base. Vladimir Putin was no exception. Since returning to the presidency in 2012, he had signed a law designating NGOs in Russia as "foreign agents" to be monitored. He had expelled USAID from the country (falsely claiming it was interfering in elections), ending two decades of work that had delivered more than $2.5 billion in funding for programs on such issues as education, the environment, and strengthening democratic institu-tions. Seeking to portray himself as the keeper of "traditional" values, Putin also took aim at LGBT people in Russia, championing laws that criminalized supporting LGBT rights and that banned same-sex couples from adopting children. With the 2014 Winter Olympics in Sochi about to begin, Putin had claimed he would welcome gay spectators to his country, before adding, "Just leave kids alone, please."

Not content to simply persecute gay people in Russia, Putin insisted that his representatives take action at the UN as well.

In 2014, Secretary-General Ban Ki-moon had decided to use his narrow administrative authority to do something bold for LGBT UN staff. Ban granted the spouses of all UN employees in same-sex marriages the same benefits as their heterosexual counterparts. The secretary-general's administrative order was less important for its practical impact, which was small, than for the important message it sent about equality.

This was precisely the message to which Russia objected. Vitaly called me a few days before Christmas. "We are taking this to a vote in the General Assembly," he said. "It cannot stand."

I doubted that LGBT people suffering persecution around the world would have heard about the UN's inclusive new policy. But if Russia succeeded in repealing it, I could already see the international headlines—UN VOTES TO STRIP GAY PEOPLE OF BENEFITS.

Although I told Vitaly that we would fight and win, I was bluffing. Given that homophobic policies were widespread among governments represented in the UN, I did not see how we could rally the votes to defeat the Russian repeal effort. Russia started with support from the fifty-seven countries in the Organization of Islamic Cooperation, as well as those in the then-fifty-four-nation African Union. We could count on the governments of Europe, and we would look to Latin America, which had become remarkably progressive on LGBT rights, to give us a chance at leveling the playing field.

After hanging up with Vitaly, I walked out of my office to tell my schedulers that I would not be doing last-minute Christmas shopping for my kids that evening after all. We were in for a fight and needed to mobilize quickly.

Hillary Schrenell, my friend and senior adviser, and Kelly Razzouk, a career civil servant who was a lead US negotiator on many human rights issues, became co-captains of our new campaign. Hillary was the person at the US Mission who knew me best, so she started analyzing my relationships with various ambassadors to pinpoint where we might find opportunities to flip a vote. I then began calling foreign diplomats to gauge their support. Kelly and Hillary, who listened in on the calls, kept a spreadsheet to mark down what was said and by whom, tracking every relevant word my interlocutor offered to explain how his or her country was planning to vote. These details allowed us to strategize what arguments would be most convincing in our follow-up calls.

The four deputy US ambassadors at the UN also threw themselves into lobbying for votes. One of them was David Pressman, whom I had recruited to the US Mission from Washington. When he took up his position in 2014, David had become the first openly gay American ambassador at the UN. The five of us divided up the world map and, with Megan and others in the front office helping, tried to reach every persuadable ambassador before they returned to their home countries for the holidays. Isobel Coleman, the ambassador for UN management and reform, had only just been confirmed by the Senate, but she threw herself into the task of cold-calling diplomats she had never met to try to earn their support. Michele Sison had taken Rosemary's place as the senior-most deputy, and, having been US Ambassador in Lebanon, Sri Lanka, and UAE, she had a vast web of connections to draw on at the UN and abroad.

As was typical, most countries we pushed on the issue hoped it would disappear so they could escape the vote. We made clear that ignoring Russia's anti-gay campaign was not an option the United States was willing to consider.

"This is not going away," I told my foreign colleagues. "If you don't like that it is happening, take that up with President Putin. But we need your support."

We practically begged those ambassadors who were LGBT friendly to cancel their vacations to attend the vote, which we expected the Russians to spring on us between Christmas Eve and New Year's Day. Separately, we also asked US ambassadors posted in key swing countries like South Africa, Rwanda, and Vietnam to convey to the leaders of these countries how much their vote would matter to the United

States. US ambassadors overseas knew the White House was fully behind our initiative, so they picked up the phone or requested urgent, high-level meetings. As a result, we were able to apply pressure both on UN ambassadors in New York and on their bosses back home.

Diplomats at the US Mission followed my lead and expressed supreme confidence to their Russian counterparts about our ability to marshal significant support. In the face of our bluff, Russia grew unsure of the solidness of its coalition and decided to postpone the vote. A Russian diplomat explained his government's thinking in an email that accidentally got forwarded to us:

> We were very upset how the group was outwitted by the USA . . .
> Now we think the numbers will be worse . . . It will be much
> worse . . . It is better to have good preparation for March.
>
> —Russia

I enlarged the text of the email and printed it on glossy paper, inscribing notes of thanks to all the US officials who had sacrificed precious family time around the holidays to thwart Russia's designs.

Unfortunately, when bigotry is part of the equation, people rarely give up without a fight.

As they had promised, Russia's diplomats rededicated themselves to overturning the UN's benefits for same-sex partners. And in response, the US Mission team again fanned out, cornering our foreign counterparts in the various chambers of the UN and phone-canvassing them until they gave a firm answer as to how they planned to vote.

If a country told us they would abstain, we urged them to find a way to vote no on Russia's resolution. If they said they supported Russia's repeal because it was the "African position," we pointed to South Africa's progressive Constitution, which explicitly recognizes LGBT people as a protected class. "There is no African position," we argued. African countries could abstain without departing from unanimity, we assured them.

As I looked for any angle to pull countries to our side, some calls produced distasteful exchanges. "I know you believe homosexuality is immoral," I heard myself saying. "*This is not about that*. This is about a Russian campaign to narrow the administrative authority of the secretary-general."

When the day of the vote finally arrived, we were not sure where we stood because a number of ambassadors had not yet received official guidance from their capitals. Sitting in the US chair in the nerve-racking final moments before I would press the button to vote, I watched the ambassadors from Panama and Haiti on their cell phones, animatedly lobbying to secure a change in their instructions. The Panamanian ambassador spotted me watching her in tense anticipation. When she put down her phone, she flashed me a grin and a thumbs-up, mouthing the word "No!" The Haitian ambassador followed suit.

Kelly, holding a clipboard with her latest spreadsheet, went in search of one of the supportive African representatives she realized was missing from the hall. She waited outside the men's room until he emerged and then beseeched him to run in order to vote on time (which he just managed to do).

In the end, thanks to the widespread, relentless lobbying of US diplomats and spirited leadership from the Netherlands and Latin American countries like Argentina and Chile, the resolution to rescind benefits to LGBT couples failed. In fact, it failed by a margin of almost two to one.*

Close to every swing country in Africa and Asia went our way. The bravest votes came from Liberia, Malawi, Rwanda, Sierra Leone, and the Seychelles, who all voted NO. Many other ambassadors from African countries—twenty-eight in total—either abstained or made the intensely personal choice not to show up to the vote because they didn't like the instructions they received from their capitals. Sri Lanka, which was liberalizing after a period of repressive rule, boldly stood with democratic countries in rejecting Russia's measure.

That evening, those of us involved in the effort gathered with some

---

* In the end, Russia managed just forty-three YES votes to remove LGBT partner benefits, receiving support from countries like Saudi Arabia, China, Iran, India, Egypt, Pakistan, and Syria. We secured eighty NO votes to preserve them. Thirty-seven countries abstained, while thirty-three countries did not vote.

of the other staff at the US Mission. We went around the room and each reflected on what had happened. David, who had helped me push LGBT policies at the White House, shared what the day and the entire campaign had meant to him. He reminded us that not so long ago, being gay and serving in the State Department had been a terrifying experience. In the 1950s and 1960s, homosexuality was classified as a national security risk, and more than 1,000 people were fired or forced out due to suspicions of being gay. It was not until President Clinton's first term that Secretary of State Christopher finally put an end to the practice of vetting employees as potential threats solely on the basis of their sexual orientation. David had come to work at the State Department around when Clinton nominated James Hormel to be ambassador to Luxembourg, the first time an openly gay person had been put forward for an ambassadorship. Key Republican senators had blocked Hormel's confirmation because of his sexuality. David asked us to imagine how he now felt seeing US diplomats all around the world working tirelessly to advance the cause of LGBT equality.

When it was my turn to speak, I gave voice to something I had learned in government: sometimes, preventing a bad outcome is what passes for victory.

"We won," I told the team, "because we cared more and we worked harder. Never forget how much that can matter."

THE MORE THE US AND RUSSIAN GOVERNMENTS were at loggerheads, the more I had to compartmentalize in order to work productively with Vitaly. We were continuing to authorize peacekeeping missions in Africa together. Along with those of four other governments, diplomats from the United States and Russia were close to finalizing a nuclear deal with Iran. And yet in countless Security Council sessions, Vitaly was defending the indefensible, repeating lines sent by Moscow that he was too intelligent to believe and speaking in binary terms that belied his nuanced grasp of what was actually happening.

Then, to my surprise, at the height of the Ukraine crisis, I began receiving text messages from him, asking to meet "not at my mission or yours."

We settled on a booth in an empty, darkened restaurant in the basement of the Millennium Hilton across from the UN. The hotel, which I found creepy even when it was bustling, reminded me of the kinds of places I had frequented decades before in the desolate heartland of the Bosnian Serbs' ethnically-cleansed, breakaway state.

Vitaly, it turned out, was making contact without Moscow's blessing. He said he wanted to brainstorm about how our countries could find a way out of the Ukraine crisis. In our first private meeting he told me—wrongly it would turn out—that Putin did not intend to occupy eastern Ukraine.

"If we did that, it would only spoil his Crimea victory," he said. "You can't do better than 80 percent approval ratings . . . it would be all downhill."

I reminded him that at the start of the crisis he had initially told me that Putin would not seize Crimea, either. "You have a habit of conflating your hopes with your forecast," I said.

He shrugged: "I choose to be an optimist."

I said I understood why, and quoted my favorite line from the late psychologist Amos Tversky, who had said he preferred optimism because "as a pessimist, you suffer twice."

At a later one-on-one meeting in the same basement restaurant, Vitaly gave me a list of individuals in the United States and abroad whom Putin was "inclined to listen to." He thought the people on his list might be able to convince Putin to pull back from eastern Ukraine. I passed the names to the White House, which explored those and other back channels in the coming weeks. Unfortunately, none bore fruit. Around this time, I wrote in my journal: "It seems massively likely that this will be war, a real war, a big war, a war whose consequences will be felt well beyond Ukraine."

Vitaly and I continued to meet discreetly, and he tried to give me insight into Putin's mind-set. Invariably, though, the ideas he offered for "big bang" constitutional reform proposals to guarantee the rights of Russians in eastern Ukraine proved to be ones that the Ukrainian government had already floated. Every time Ukraine made a proposal that Vitaly thought might be sufficient, the next time we met I would hand him a news article detailing the fact that Russian separatists had already rejected it. Putin was deft at pocketing the concessions from Ukraine and then moving the goalposts on his demands. He was not serious about making peace, and ultimately Vitaly's ideas went nowhere.

President Obama directed the US government to invest in stabilizing the Ukrainian government. We provided more than $1 billion in foreign assistance over the next two years in an effort to strengthen the country's military and economy and to reform corrupt political institutions. These steps would bring Ukraine closer to the US and Europe, as the majority of its citizens desired. To impose costs on Russia, President Obama also levied targeted sanctions on wealthy individuals close to Putin and on state-connected entities in the energy, financial, and defense sectors. In order for sanctions to be effective, we needed to convince the countries of the EU to mirror them, which, given the financial blowback many of them faced, required relentless diplomacy.[37]

But the conflict in eastern Ukraine continued. And in turn the US relationship with Russia further deteriorated. It became increasingly difficult to hive off the acrimony from Ukraine and Syria and to keep finding common ground responding to matters in other regions of the world. Vitaly and I tried to keep working together, but Putin began personally involving himself in a growing number of issues—including, to my shock, the twenty-year commemoration of the massacre of 8,000 Muslim men and boys in Srebrenica, Bosnia.

The United Kingdom had been negotiating a fairly bland Security Council resolution that condemned the Srebrenica genocide and stressed the importance of accountability. But as the vote drew near, my team sounded the alarm: Russia was striking references to "genocide" from the draft text.

The objective facts about Srebrenica had long been established. In 2007, the International Court of Justice had found that Bosnian Serb soldiers had perpetrated genocide there, and Serbia itself had extradited Slobodan Milošević to stand trial for genocide at the UN war crimes tribunal in The Hague. However, a few days before the 2015 anniversary, Russia's diplomats made clear that they would not allow a resolution to pass if it mentioned "genocide." Incredulous, I called Vitaly.

"What are you doing on the Srebrenica text?" I demanded. "You were there then. You can't deny this history."

He paused. Then, choosing his words carefully, he said coldly, "I take it you will not accept our text, and we cannot accept yours."

"What is going on?" I asked, worry setting in. I imagined how the mothers of Srebrenica would react to hearing that the UN rejected the full truth of what had happened to their sons. "Come on, talk to me. You've met those families."

He began to soften. "I have my instructions, and they are not flexible," he said.

"Are you kidding me? You really can't call the genocide 'genocide'?" I asked.

"You know me well enough to know when I am kidding," he said.

"Shit," I replied. "Can we try to be creative? Those people will be devastated if we can't figure this out."

Over the next forty-eight hours, Vitaly and I ducked out of Security Council meetings and huddled in different corners of the UN, in search of compromise language that would make clear that the Security Council recognized the genocide while allowing Putin to agree to abstain.

We stripped "genocide" references throughout the text, replacing them with euphemisms that reminded me of the annual White House statements on the Armenian genocide that I despised. To compensate, we inserted a reference recalling the "judgment of the International Court of Justice of 26 February 2007," and we attached the court's written finding of genocide as an appendix.

I did not feel good about what I had negotiated. But our draft met two important standards: it made clear that the Security Council saw the events of 1995 as "genocide," and it had a chance of being acceptable to Putin, who Vitaly had indicated was carefully reviewing our drafts.

In the end, my own misgivings about the language Vitaly and I had agreed upon proved moot. The morning of the vote, he sent me a one-line email verdict on our compromise text: "It didn't fly."

Knowing Russia was going to veto even the watered-down text, we reverted back to the draft that properly and frontally recognized genocide. I felt for Vitaly as he raised his hand to veto a resolution he knew his country should have supported.

I began my remarks after the vote by drawing on my personal history. I recalled being a twenty-four-year-old reporter in Sarajevo when a colleague first told me about reports of mass executions. Not wanting to believe what I was hearing, I told the Council, my reaction at the time had simply been "No"—it was not possible.

When I had learned earlier that day that Russia was planning to veto the Srebrenica resolution, I recalled to the Council, my incredulity and disappointment had prompted the same reaction: "No."

I had invited David Rohde, who had uncovered the massacre, to the session, along with Laura Pitter, who had chronicled it for Human Rights Watch and encouraged me to move to the Balkans in the first place. I looked in their direction as I spoke.

I described the mother I met in 2010 who was burying the fourth of her murdered sons. "She was still searching for the remains of the fifth," I said. "It is that mother's truth and pain that was vetoed by Russia today . . . This is a veto of a well-established fact documented by hundreds of thousands of pages of witness testimony, photographic evidence, and physical forensic evidence."

Because Vitaly knew exactly what had happened in Srebrenica, he had not denied the facts in his statement defending Russia's vote. Instead, he had said that dwelling on the past would impede reconciliation between Bosnians and Serbs. I tore into this rationale, arguing, "Imagine being the mother of those five sons killed in the Srebrenica genocide, and being told that a denial of the genocide will advance reconciliation. It is madness . . . There is no stability in genocide denial."

In the end, I knew—and Vitaly must have known as well—that Putin saw the world in us-versus-them terms.

If Ukraine was with the West, then Russia would punish Ukraine.

If Western countries embraced LGBT rights, then Russia would try to deny them.

If the West was critical of the Bosnian Serbs, then Russia would side with even those responsible for genocide.

And no matter what, Vitaly would try to sell what Russia was doing to the world.

A WHILE LATER, ON THE MORNING we were set to elect new members of the UN's forty-seven-nation Human Rights Council, I opened a red folder on my office desk and began reading from the cable inside. What I saw was not unexpected, but it still caused me to shake my head. "What on earth will it take?" I wondered.

I hated my voting instructions from Washington.

Being on the Human Rights Council gave the United States important influence over the direction of international human rights investigations, but the elections themselves were an unseemly exercise. Nominated by their respective regions, infamous human rights abusers always appeared on the ballot (and thus on the Council). In this election, three countries—Russia, Hungary, and Croatia—were competing with each other for the two Eastern European seats.

Russia had invaded Ukraine. It was backing the Assad regime in Syria at all costs, contributing to some of the worst carnage the world had seen in a half century. Putin had shuttered independent media, banned various nongovernmental organizations, and imprisoned dissidents. Yet the instructions I received from the State Department about how to vote were timeless and impervious to these developments. In the General Assembly later that morning, I was directed to vote for Russia.

Russia and the United States were permanent members of the Security Council, and for as long as anyone could remember, it was our practice to vote for one another in UN elections as a "courtesy." This was a self-interested, reciprocal deal we had with each of the four other permanent members, meant to assure the United States of four reliable votes in every election we ourselves entered.

As I walked across 1st Avenue to the United Nations, I asked my elections officer, a young US diplomat, if he expected a close race for the Eastern European seats. "Russia has it locked," he explained. "The last time they ran, they won 176 votes, even more than France and the UK."

I made my way into the US box in the General Assembly hall and ruminated. One of the immensely gratifying aspects of being a senior official in President Obama's administration was that I almost never received direction from Washington that I did not have a chance to shape or challenge. Looking around the chamber at the other ambassadors, I knew that I was likely the only person in the hall who enjoyed such independence.

I understood the logic of the US government's long-standing deal. But this day felt different. Too much had happened since I arrived at the UN not to vote my conscience. After the secret paper ballots had been passed around, I wrote the names of Croatia and Hungary in the Eastern European section, folded the paper over three times, and placed it through the slit in the brown wooden box that a UN official carried down the aisle.*

Occasions when the majority of UN ambassadors milled around in one place at the same time were rare. As the votes were tabulated by hand, I crisscrossed the chamber, trying to gin up commitments from my colleagues on issues that ranged from releasing a political prisoner their government had locked up to voting to condemn Iran's human rights record in the General Assembly.

Election winners were normally announced in less than half an hour, and, as the clock ticked well beyond that, the chatter in the room began to fade.

"What is taking so long?" my Uruguayan colleague murmured.

My elections expert hustled down to the front of the chamber and returned to explain that one region's vote was too close to call, so UN officials were doing a recount. "Probably Hungary and Croatia battling for the last slot," he said.

Finally, around two hours after we had handed in our ballots, the

---

* It gave me no pleasure to vote for Hungary, where Prime Minister Viktor Orbán had attacked political rights and civil liberties, stacked the judiciary, and moved aggressively to silence critical voices. He and his political party had also taken to demonizing refugees and the Hungarian-born investor George Soros, using rhetoric with anti-Semitic undertones. Still, compared to Russia—which was facilitating mass atrocities in Syria and had invaded Ukraine—Hungary was the better option.

president of the General Assembly took the microphone and read the names of the fourteen countries that had won seats on the Human Rights Council. Russia was not among them.

In the Eastern European region, Hungary, which had more money to invest in its lobbying campaign than Croatia, had received 144 votes. Croatia snagged the second seat with 114 votes. Russia had received only 112 votes. A collective gasp of shock rippled through the hall. Had there been one more vote for Russia and one fewer for Croatia, the two countries would have tied. If this had occurred, Russia would have bullied and bribed during the run-off, and walked away with the seat. As it stood, Russia had lost—the first time in history that its government had been defeated in a major UN election.

I looked over at the Ukrainian ambassador. His face was cupped in his hands. I wasn't sure if he was weeping with relief or smiling.

On one level, of course, the outcome was not a big deal. Russia's loss in this election would not bring about the removal of its troops from Ukraine. But it was a rare repudiation of Putin on the global stage and a tiny measure of accountability for a country that had enjoyed impunity for its actions.

34

FREEDOM FROM FEAR

In July of 2014, a doctor named Kent Brantly became the first American diagnosed with Ebola. Brantly had contracted the virus treating patients in Liberia, and when he returned to the US for medical care, CNN, MSNBC, and Fox News all broadcast live footage of a police-escorted ambulance transporting him from an Air Force base to Atlanta's Emory Hospital. As news choppers filmed his arrival from above, he exited the ambulance in a large white biohazard suit and walked into the hospital, where highly trained Ebola specialists would treat him in a special isolation unit.

Three days later, another American named Nancy Writebol also arrived at Emory for treatment. Writebol had worked alongside Brantly in Liberia, where she too had been exposed to the disease. The arrival of a second Ebola-infected person in the US generated more breathless news coverage. Although infectious disease experts emphasized that the broader public was not at risk, fear and misinformation about the potential for a domestic Ebola outbreak ricocheted around the internet.

"Officials are importing Ebola into the U.S.," warned the popular far-right website *InfoWars*. Donald Trump, less than a year from becoming a candidate for President, tweeted:

> The U.S. cannot allow EBOLA infected people back. People that go to far away places to help are great—but must suffer the consequences!

And:

> The U.S. must immediately stop all flights from EBOLA
> infected countries or the plague will start and spread inside our
> "borders." Act fast!

Trump would play a significant role in hyping the possibility of a mass Ebola outbreak in the US, firing off more than fifty tweets on the topic and raising it during his TV appearances.[38] Thanks to the care provided by Emory's experts, Brantly and Writebol were declared Ebola-free and released soon after receiving treatment—a development that generated far fewer headlines.

I had first heard about the outbreak of Ebola in West Africa several months before Brantly and Writebol were infected. At the time, I had instinctively viewed it as a horrible medical calamity that would be conquered with the help of public health professionals. This is what had occurred in every previous Ebola outbreak.

Only when I spoke with the UN's top humanitarian official, Valerie Amos, did I realize that this time was different. Amos told me people were so scared of the disease that the UN was having trouble getting even its fearless humanitarian emergency staff to deploy to Guinea, Liberia, and Sierra Leone.

"Ebola is winning," Amos said, with unusual panic in her voice. "We are not close to stopping it."

I asked my mother, who at seventy was still a practicing physician, if she would consider doing a medical mission to West Africa. She answered with an emphatic—and unexpected—"no." As she explained to me, "I want to be around to see Declan and Rían grow up."

Only then did I appreciate the reflexive conclusion that even seasoned medical professionals were drawing: go near Ebola, and you could die.

SEEING THAT THE EPIDEMIC WAS SPIRALING out of control, in August of 2014, National Security Advisor Susan Rice assembled the

President's top advisers in the Situation Room to discuss how our government should respond. Gayle Smith had ably managed the US response from the White House up to that point, but she made clear that rapid action was needed, requiring decisions that could only be made by the individuals who *ran* the major government agencies. Tom Frieden, the director of the Centers for Disease Control and Prevention (CDC), briefed us that more people had already died from Ebola in Liberia alone than in the twenty previous Ebola outbreaks combined.

Frieden then passed around a single-page CDC handout we would soon begin referring to as "The Slide." It showed a simple graph: the x-axis listed dates through January 2015, and the y-axis had the cumulative number of Ebola cases. The CDC was predicting an eye-popping spike in infections. Unless the doctors and aid workers attempting to prevent and treat the disease ramped up their response, The Slide indicated that the number of Ebola infections would continue to double every three weeks. This exponential spread would result in up to *1.4 million* infections within five months.[39]

A full thirty seconds passed before anyone spoke. Perhaps sensing that the entire national security cabinet was in a state of shock, Frieden pivoted. "Ebola has always been beaten. Ebola *will* be beaten," he told us. Frieden explained that Ebola patients needed to be temporarily quarantined from their communities so they would not infect their relatives and neighbors. If 70 percent of those with the virus could be isolated, we could bend—and ultimately end—the devastating curve of the epidemic.

Looking around the room, I noticed that almost everyone was still staring at The Slide.

In the flurry of meetings that followed, Susan surprised many of us by reporting that President Obama wanted to explore involving the US military in the response. He saw that those attempting to fight the epidemic in Guinea, Liberia, and Sierra Leone were overwhelmed. These countries had endured horrific conflict and made significant strides toward lasting peace, but they remained fragile, lacking the resources and expertise to contain the epidemic on their own. Obama recognized that unless their governments received help, Ebola would spread to additional countries in the region, causing a humanitarian catastrophe that would kill hundreds of thousands, including Americans who lived and worked in Africa. And, ultimately, Obama was concerned that without significantly more aggressive action, unsuspecting travelers with Ebola would end up making their way to the United States.

The Ebola mission being contemplated was like none undertaken before. But with talk of sending troops, Defense Secretary Hagel and Chairman of the Joint Chiefs Dempsey did what the military sensibly does when any new troop deployment is being discussed: they questioned whether soldiers would be given clear tasks that they had the mandate and means to accomplish.

"I keep hearing you all saying, our soldiers will 'suit up' and do this and that," Hagel said in one meeting. "Suit up? What does that even mean? My guys have never even seen these HAZMAT suits, apart from in horror movies."

Frieden and his staff at the CDC were big proponents of involving the US military because of its singular logistics and rapid deployment capabilities, but Dempsey pressed the public health experts to define precisely what the soldiers would *do* day to day once deployed to West Africa. Frieden responded that they would rapidly assemble what were called Ebola Treatment Units, the specially designed, tented field hospitals where patients could be treated.

"Hire the circus if you want to put up tents," Dempsey said, demanding that the health officials offer more specifics.

Ultimately, Dempsey and the Pentagon planners devised a brilliant operation that the Chairman presented to the President—"a logistics mission with a medical component," he stressed, "not the other way around." President Obama then announced that he was sending some 3,000 troops to Liberia and ramping up each component of the US response. Drawing on the expertise of hundreds of USAID and CDC staff deployed to West Africa, the United States would facilitate the training of tens of thousands of local health workers to care for Ebola patients. We would create an air bridge to fly doctors, nurses, and supplies to the region quickly. And we would build the Ebola Treatment Units, which would allow up to 1,700 patients at a time to receive treatment.

Obama was providing an awesome demonstration of US leadership and capability—and a vivid example of how a country advances its values and interests at once.

In his remarks announcing the operation, the President made clear that the burden of responding could not just fall to the United States; other countries needed to do much more. His decisiveness gave those of us who worked for him what we needed to mobilize this international support. I invited the other UN ambassadors to the US Mission to hear from Frieden, who once again explained the stakes in his mild-mannered yet terrifying way. He described how Ebola had jumped across national borders, penetrated urban areas, overwhelmed clinics, and caused businesses and schools to close. He detailed how local burial customs had helped it spread. And most unnervingly, he walked the ambassadors through The Slide depicting the path to 1.4 million infections by January of 2015.

"I have never seen an infectious disease of this lethality spreading so fast," Frieden said plainly, as diplomats from around the world transcribed his most quotable lines for the cables they would send back to their capitals. In his presentation, Frieden let nobody off the hook. His message, which I reinforced with the foreign ambassadors, was that each of us had a responsibility—no matter how big or small our country, no matter how substantial or minimal our financial means.

In January of 2000, during Richard Holbrooke's tenure as ambassador to the UN, he had helped shift the public debate on AIDS in Africa by placing it on the regular agenda of the UN Security Council. Inspired by Holbrooke's initiative, I gathered my team and floated the idea of convening an emergency session of the Security Council on Ebola. Many of my staff were skeptical that other countries would support the idea: the Security Council grappled with matters of war and peace—it did not generally address public health emergencies. Because Russia and China typically objected to expanding the Council's writ,

I turned to the individuals who represented the imperiled West African countries.

After the ambassadors from Guinea, Liberia, and Sierra Leone filed into a small conference room at the US Mission, I expressed my sympathies and asked them how they were holding up. Some 23 million people lived in their three countries, and the epidemic did not discriminate; the ambassadors' immediate families were in grave danger. I told them I was considering convening the Security Council on the epidemic, and that the US was prepared to introduce a resolution declaring Ebola a "threat to international peace and security." We would use this resolution, the first of its kind, to call on countries to provide more money and health workers to combat the outbreak.

The three ambassadors swiftly embraced the proposal. "This can only help," said Vandi Minah, the ambassador from Sierra Leone. "Anybody who says otherwise isn't seeing their country—and their people—disappear before their eyes." No UN member state would dare defy these ambassadors and protest the emergency meeting.

The diplomats and staff at the US Mission dropped whatever other work they were doing to get other countries to join Guinea, Liberia, and Sierra Leone as cosponsors of the US resolution. After securing one country's agreement to sign on, I would try to create a friendly competition by immediately relaying the news to ambassadors from that country's geographic rivals. "Chile and Brazil are cosponsoring," I told my Argentine counterpart, whose foreign minister was generally suspicious of US-led initiatives. The ambassador soon called to tell me that her minister had instructed Argentina to become a sponsor too.

When I entered the UN Security Council chamber on September 18th, just two days after President Obama's dramatic announcement that he was sending troops to the region, every red seat in the diplomats' gallery was filled with ambassadors and high-ranking officials. Senior diplomats even sat scrunched together on the steps in the aisles.

I had reserved seats on the floor for Mum and Eddie. My mother's love of medicine was so fervent that she had always hoped that Stephen or I would feel the same pull. Back when Eddie was still a practicing physician, he had championed the medical contributions made by the

African diaspora. Since Ebola struck, he had been taking advantage of the fact that he had retired to lend his support to my African UN colleagues by helping them fundraise. In convening the meeting to appeal to the doctors and nurses of the world to help, I felt closely connected to my parents and their passions, and I hoped they felt their hand in our efforts.

After I sat down and prepared to gavel the meeting to a start, I scrolled through a stream of text messages that were pouring in to my phone: "We want to cosponsor." "We are in." "Count on us." "Thank you for US leadership." I showed the texts to Rabia Qureshi, the foreign service officer at the mission who covered West Africa. She shook her head in disbelief and told me that, at last count, we had a breathtaking 100 country cosponsors. Ten minutes later, we had 20 more. By the time the sponsors' list closed, we had 134, the largest number of cosponsors for any Security Council resolution in the sixty-nine-year history of the UN.

I HAD WORRIED before the session that nothing we said or did in the meeting would succeed in conveying the gravity of the moment. "We have to find somebody to speak who can drive this home," I had told my deputy chief of staff Sarah Holewinski. "We need somebody who is from there, who *feels* this." Sarah had delivered, tracking down a thirty-nine-year-old Liberian health worker named Jackson Niamah who was working with Médecins Sans Frontières (MSF, or Doctors Without Borders) in Monrovia, the Liberian capital.

Niamah's face appeared on a large video screen that descended from the ceiling of the Security Council chamber. The picture was blurry, the audio scratchy. One had the sense that the connection could go out at any time. But when this man on the other side of the world spoke, my fellow ambassadors—who usually multitasked during briefings—stared up at the screen, rapt.

Niamah said that when Ebola came to Monrovia "people began dying," including his niece and cousin, both nurses, who passed away in July of 2014. "So many of my friends, university classmates and colleagues have died in recent months," he said. "They die alone, terrified, and without their loved ones at their side."

Niamah had signed up to work for MSF out of a sense of patriotism. His job was to assess patients and then help care for those diagnosed with Ebola. He described what it meant to have more infected people than the MSF clinic had beds. "We have to turn people away, and many are dying at our front gate," Niamah said. "Right now, as I speak, there are patients sitting at our front gates, literally begging for life."

He then went on:

> One day this week, I sat outside the treatment center eating my lunch. I met a boy who approached the gate. His father had died from Ebola a week ago. I saw him with blood at his mouth. We had no space, so we could not to take him in . . . When he turned away to walk into town, I thought to myself that that boy is going to take a taxi, and he is going to go home . . . and infect his family.

Because Ebola was transmitted through fluids exchanged during physical contact, anyone the boy touched would likely become a casualty of his return.

Niamah pleaded for help. "There are still homes in Monrovia that do not have soap, water, and buckets," he said. "Even those simple things could help curb the spread of the virus."

Finally, he closed with an ominous warning: "We do not have the capacity to respond to this crisis on our own. If the international community does not stand up, we will be wiped out."

The phrase echoed across the chamber, where diplomats sat without making a sound. "We will be wiped out."

Niamah had made an abstract threat strikingly human and real. Still, each government was doing a cost-benefit calculus about the specifics of what they would contribute. For all the high drama of the moment, and all the support our Security Council resolution had earned, political leaders had experienced few costs for running away from Ebola. Even The Slide, by far the most powerful weapon I had in attempting to convince other countries to do more, was liable to cause despair and fatalism.

Speaking after Niamah, I addressed this head on:

> These models show what could happen if we continue to let fear, inaction, or indifference drive our response . . . Models are forecasts of the future. But . . . it is *we* who actually determine our future. Individuals make history, not models. The United Nations was built for global challenges like this. That is why we are here.

As a young reporter, I had despaired over the inaction of UN peacekeepers in Bosnia. But I had come to understand that the UN was not a single entity, choosing to act or not act—it was a building where countries gathered. When confronting a crisis, individuals who helped lead those countries had to decide what they were prepared to do. If enough individuals could summon the will to chip in and work together, we could save millions of lives.

With this in mind, I urged the governments that had closed their borders to people coming from the infected countries to reconsider the implications of what they were doing. I said their reactions were understandable—driven by a desire to protect their own citizens from the spread of the virus. Rather than emphasizing the coldness of the restrictions, I focused on the fact that border closures put *every* country at greater risk. If medical personnel believed they would not be able to travel home after working in an Ebola-affected country, they would be less likely to volunteer to help. This would reduce the likelihood that Ebola would be controlled, in turn increasing the chances that the disease would spread to the very countries whose leaders were trying to keep their people safe. Like so many twenty-first-century challenges, Ebola was not a zero-sum fight in which some countries could "win" by pursuing their interests in a vacuum.

I had told the ambassadors from other countries not to take the floor if they planned only to lament the seriousness of the epidemic.

"Please don't admire the problem," I urged, repeating the expression I used with my staff and heard President Obama employ often. We needed to hear from those undertaking concrete actions.

As the session went on, there was no sweeter sound than to hear a colleague say, "I am pleased to announce today . . ." China, which was increasingly looking for ways to show off its superpower status, declared fighting Ebola "a common responsibility of all countries in the world" and pledged to send more money, supplies, biosecurity labs, and public health professionals. The UK promised an additional five hundred treatment beds in Sierra Leone (a contribution that might seem small, but that would prove important). Japan sent some 20,000 infection prevention suits for health care workers. The Swiss provided 14 tons of protective medical gear like specialized eye goggles and masks. Malaysia kicked in more than 20 million medical rubber gloves. Cuba sent its highly experienced team of 250 doctors and nurses trained in foreign disaster response. Uruguay promised not to pull its peacekeepers out of the UN mission in Liberia, as some countries had begun doing.

Our landmark session on Ebola was the most unified of my time in New York. Merely convening the meeting generated striking headlines like EBOLA DECLARED THREAT TO PEACE AND SECURITY BY UN. As US diplomats fanned out around the world and President Obama personally threw himself into lobbying world leaders, we suddenly seemed to be on a solid track. All told, the US and other countries would end up pledging some $4 billion toward supplies, facilities, medical treatments, and other components of the initial response.

However, just as we began making real progress, a person who became known as "Patient Zero" was diagnosed with Ebola in Dallas, Texas. At precisely the time when we needed to keep calm at home, act pragmatically, follow the science, and lead the world, all hell broke loose.

THE URGENT CNN BULLETIN appeared in my inbox on September 30th: BREAKING NEWS: FIRST EBOLA CASE DIAGNOSED IN U.S. My stomach sank.

Thomas Eric Duncan had recently been working for a shipping company in Monrovia. Before traveling to the United States to visit family, he had tried to help his landlord's nineteen-year-old daughter, Marthalene Williams, get to a hospital. Williams was soon expecting a baby and assumed her convulsions stemmed from pregnancy complications. Duncan and Williams crisscrossed the city by taxi in search of care, but, with the epidemic raging, they were turned away from three facilities for lack of space. Duncan helped carry her back to her family home, where she died of Ebola within hours.

A few days after arriving in Dallas, Duncan went to the emergency room complaining of "abdominal pain, dizziness, nausea, and headache." While the nurse who treated him noted that Duncan had recently arrived from Africa, this information was not highlighted to Duncan's doctor, who ended up discharging him. Two days later, when his condition worsened, he was rushed by ambulance back to the hospital. His blood tested positive for Ebola, and he died a week later. Texas health officials announced that at least fifty people whom Duncan had interacted with in the United States were at risk of contracting Ebola.

The news coverage quickly became saturated by sensationalized fear. "What's that?" Fox News host Jeanine Pirro seethed. "You don't want people to panic? You don't want us to panic? How about, I don't want us to die!" CNN ran an onscreen graphic asking whether Ebola was "The ISIS of biological agents?" while another Fox host, Eric Bolling, mused, "We have a border that is so porous, Ebola or ISIS or Ebola on the backs of ISIS could come through." In less than two days, Twitter mentions of the virus increased from 100 per minute to over 6,000 per minute.[40] And when two of the Texas health workers who cared for Duncan—Nina Pham and Amber Vinson—tested positive for Ebola, the public concern exploded into something approaching hysteria.

A teacher in Maine was placed on a three-week leave of absence because she had visited Dallas for a conference. A passenger who vomited on a flight from Dallas to Chicago was sequestered in the bathroom until the plane landed. A middle school principal in Mississippi was asked to stay home after parents learned that he had traveled to

Zambia—a country on the other side of the continent from the affected region.

The approaching midterm elections in November fed into the fear-mongering and political posturing, with Republican members of Congress compounding the turmoil by demanding a government-imposed travel ban. House Speaker John Boehner encouraged the idea, and several Democrats facing tough reelection fights also offered their support. Some of Obama's longtime critics, seeming to tap into the racist conspiracies suggesting the President was not fully American, accused him of prioritizing the lives of Africans over those of the American people.

As sensible as it may have sounded to try to contain the spread of Ebola by keeping travelers from West Africa out of America, the travel ban Obama's critics proposed would almost surely have made the problem worse. Such a ban would likely have had a dramatic chilling effect on travel *to* the countries where the infections were happening—but it would not have prevented the daily influx into our country of US citizens and permanent residents returning *from* West Africa, who could not have been legally barred from returning home.* Moreover, the experts in our government believed a ban was not even likely to prevent noncitizens from traveling to the United States. Rather, many would instead go to Canada or Mexico first and then seek to enter over one of our land borders.

With public pressure mounting, President Obama named Ron Klain, a skilled government operator with deep political connections across the country, as his Ebola "czar." Klain instructed the CDC to funnel travelers from the region through five major US airports, where he posted public health officials to conduct intensive screening of new arrivals. "We've got to bring the fever down," Obama said repeatedly in our internal meetings, which he was now personally chairing several times a week.

Less presidentially, I wrote in my journal on October 17th: "Our

---

* At the time, well over half of the 150 people entering the US on a daily basis from the affected countries were American citizens or permanent residents; the proposed travel ban could only have been legally applied to noncitizens.

ability to lead the world turns on our ability to prevent a full freak-out at home."

Although we made our case everywhere, from media interviews to congressional testimony, we were not persuading people. An ABC News/ *Washington Post* poll taken the week of October 20th found that 70 percent of Americans supported blocking entry for all people who had been in the Ebola-affected countries. A CBS News poll from the same time period showed that an even greater percentage of people—80 percent— favored mandatory quarantines for American citizens returning from West Africa, regardless of whether they showed any Ebola symptoms.

Against this backdrop, my speechwriter Nik suggested that I travel to the three Ebola-affected countries in West Africa.

LEAVING NEW YORK in the midst of our lobbying efforts had never occurred to me, but I immediately embraced Nik's idea and asked my staff to see if the White House would provide a government plane for a trip. While I still saw my primary role to be helping gin up resources from other countries, I thought my advocacy would be more credible if I could draw on what I had personally seen. A trip would also enable me to bring journalists to the sites we visited, and their stories could demonstrate to the American public that by following proper precautions, one would not contract Ebola. And, ever a believer in a worm's eye view of a crisis, I would be able to get a firsthand sense of what the US and UN needed to do differently going forward, informing my recommendations to the President and secretary-general.

USAID's highly trained Disaster Assistance Response Team was playing a major role in coordinating the American response, so I reached out to USAID administrator Raj Shah for a gut-check. He encouraged me to go. "Our partners are toiling in complete isolation over there," he said. "It will be a big morale boost."

The main skepticism I heard came from an unsurprising source: Cass hated the idea and for the first time, Declan was old enough to offer reinforcement.

Having just entered kindergarten at the UN International School (UNIS), Declan must have heard someone talking about the epidemic.

"Mommy are you going where the Bola is?" he asked me a couple days before I was scheduled to depart. I nodded, but promised I would stay safe.

"How do you know?" he asked, adding: "Those other people thought they would be safe too."

I explained how I would not do anything dangerous, but he kept pressing, saying, "Mommy, I'm certain you will bring back Bola." I had never before heard him use the word "certain," which I found jarring.

Fear continued to spread as my team made final preparations for the trip. On October 23rd, a New York doctor named Craig Spencer was diagnosed with the virus after returning from an MSF mission in Guinea. When the news broke, Spencer's cell phone rang off the hook as his former patients called to see if they could help.

Spencer had covered a lot of ground during the week between his return and his diagnosis. He had walked the High Line in Chelsea, eaten at a popular restaurant in Greenwich Village, and gone bowling in Williamsburg. Even more terrifying to New Yorkers, he had taken an Uber and ridden the subway. A tightly packed city with millions of people had its first Ebola case—the plotline of a horror film come to life.

As fear reigned during this period, politicians' reactions varied widely. New York City mayor Bill de Blasio rode the subway and dined with his wife at the restaurant where Spencer had eaten to show they were safe. Conversely, New York governor Andrew Cuomo joined New Jersey governor Chris Christie in announcing that their states would quarantine any person who had worked to combat Ebola in West Africa. It did not matter whether they showed symptoms or not—for twenty-one days, they would be wards of the state. That same day, immigration officials at Newark airport detained Kaci Hickox, who had been working with MSF in Sierra Leone, even though she tested negative for Ebola.

The combination of adding three extra weeks to health workers' time away from work—*and* the additional state-sponsored stigma—seemed sure to reduce the number of American doctors and nurses willing to travel to the region, weakening the response at just the time

when we needed a huge surge in trained personnel. Prior to the outbreak, Liberia had just one doctor for every 100,000 people. (By comparison, the US then had around 257 doctors per 100,000.)

The day of Hickox's confinement, Susan Rice, who had done a
masterful job pushing the administration to be aggressive in our Ebola
response, telephoned to urge me to consider calling off my trip. Acknowledging that she was calling more in her capacity as my friend
than as National Security Advisor, she urged me to think about my
responsibility to my kids. I said I had of course thought about my family, but I was confident in the safety protocols and felt it was essential
to show that our collective domestic panic was misplaced.

She continued to press me. "Think about it, Sam," she said. "What
if something goes wrong? Can you imagine what would happen to our
larger effort if a member of the President's cabinet had to be quarantined?"

Susan was highlighting a problem I had not sufficiently considered. The political sands were shifting beneath our feet. While we were
abroad, Cuomo, the governor of the state where my team and I lived,
could conceivably make further changes to New York's rules and declare that even individuals who had no physical contact with Ebola
patients would be isolated upon return, just for visiting West Africa.

Cass, meanwhile, remained opposed to the trip. "There is nothing you can accomplish by going that you can't accomplish by staying
home," he said. The problem with Cass's counsel was that he had made
similar arguments regarding every previous trip I had taken. Because
I wanted to go, I sought advice from others.

I reached out to Klain, who was supportive. He reminded me that
Terry McAuliffe, the governor of Virginia, was keeping Dulles Airport open and free of quarantine restrictions. I once again called Raj,
the USAID administrator, and pressed him on the question of risk.
"Look, you are not going to be touching Ebola patients," he said. "But
of course it is risky." When he had traveled to Guinea a few weeks
before, he recalled listening to his interpreter translating and suddenly
thinking, "Wait, as he is speaking inches from me, microscopic specks
of his saliva could be entering my ear right now. This is not good!"
Still, he urged me not to cancel.

I also called my mother, who had gotten educated on Ebola since her initial negative reaction. She now offered unflinching encouragement, ending our call by saying, "I wish I could come." With her vote of confidence, I resolved to go ahead.

I gathered the small USUN team accompanying me, whose physical safety was my responsibility, and delivered the spookiest sermon they had ever heard. "You could forget that you must not shake anyone's hand," I said. "And, if you shake someone's hand who has Ebola and a tiny cut, and you have the same, you could get Ebola." Unaccustomed to offering this form of apocalyptic leadership, I echoed Susan's concerns as my team looked at me gravely. "I want to make sure that each of you has thought through the risks you are taking," I said. "It is absolutely not too late for any of us—or all of us—to back out. Are you sure you still want to go?"

Hillary, my longtime aide and friend, was the first to speak. "We should go. We will be incredibly careful, and our visit can make a difference." Each of the other members of my team affirmed what Hillary had said. "'Freedom from fear,' right?" said one, citing one of FDR's "Four Freedoms," which I often drew upon.

Before leaving, Declan and I made our peace about the trip. He was then in a phase of acute empathy. At times it took absurd form, such as eating the last remaining chicken finger even though he was full, "so the chicken finger won't be left all alone." I told him that, because there was at least a chance I could help people who were really sick, I had to go. He came into my bedroom the morning our team departed and said, in a very grown-up voice, "The people in Africa are really lucky that you are going to the Bola place to try to help. I'm proud of you, Mommy."

BY THIS POINT, more than 10,000 people in West Africa had confirmed or likely cases of Ebola, and some 4,900 people had died.* The physical manifestations of the disease—fever, vomiting, diarrhea,

---

* Due to significant underreporting, these official numbers were probably far lower than the actual human toll.

bleeding, and intense pain—had left victims dying on roadsides and in overcrowded clinics. I expected the trip to be as unsettling as any I had ever taken. Instead, I found it to be a stunning tribute to American ingenuity and, above all, to the resiliency of the people of West Africa.

When announcing our stepped-up response, President Obama had assured the American public that all US personnel being deployed to the region would abide by strict protocols to ensure that they did not contract the virus. My delegation took a number of precautions—traveling with a physician, checking our temperatures regularly, giving elbow-bumps as greetings instead of handshakes, and not entering the Ebola Treatment Units we visited.*

The US commanding officer in Liberia, US Army Major General Gary Volesky, flew our delegation by helicopter from near Monrovia to Bong County, where we met US Navy technicians who had just set up an Ebola testing lab. Previously, blood samples had needed to be taken by motorcycle on often-impassable roads to the only lab in the country, which was located in Monrovia. The samples were sometimes lost in transit, and the testing queue was long. People far away from the capital, like those in the area we were visiting, usually did not get results back for at least five days. While they waited to hear whether they had Ebola, they were often kept quarantined with other Ebola patients, increasing the risk that those who did not actually have the virus would end up contracting it anyway.

At a nearby Ebola Treatment Unit, we heard that the US lab was already having a huge effect. Now that test results were provided within five hours, beds were freed up for actual Ebola patients and the infected were swiftly isolated so they did not transmit the virus. Equally important, the ability to begin early treatment was dramatically increasing survival rates.Once these recovery stories finally began to make their way back to rural communities, terrified citizens with Ebola symptoms began to come forward, suddenly hopeful that their lives could be saved. As

---

* In addition to my small group of aides from the US Mission to the UN, our delegation included Jeremy Konyndyk, director of USAID's Office of US Foreign Disaster Assistance; and Andrew Weber, the State Department's Deputy Coordinator for Ebola Response.

Albert Camus wrote in *The Plague*, "It could be said that once the faint-est stirring of hope became possible, the dominion of plague was ended."

In Sierra Leone, we visited Freetown's new Ebola response call cen-ter. The CDC had identified safe burial as the *sine qua non* of ending the epidemic, so it was heartening to learn that a robust public infor-mation campaign had finally begun spreading word among the city's residents to call 117 when a sick person had died. I could see that the message was getting through. On the wall of the call center was a map of Freetown. The Sierra Leonean volunteers were using red pins to mark the locations where deaths had been reported. When a team retrieved and buried a body, the red pin was replaced with a blue one. A week before, the Sierra Leoneans told us, only 30 percent of bodies were being collected and safely buried within twenty-four hours. By the time we visited—in no small part due to the infusion of British military and civilian experts and other international support—98 per-cent of reported bodies were being buried within a day. On the map, we saw a single red pin surrounded by a sea of blue pins. The practice had not yet been scaled in districts outside the capital, but they had developed proof of concept.

At training centers run by the United States in Liberia and by the United Kingdom in Sierra Leone, we saw young people lining up to volunteer. I stopped a number of them, asking what was motivating them to take part in the Ebola response. With the economy in com-plete free fall and unemployment surging, for some it was the lure of a day's wages. But for most, it was the simple desire to help. As one young man in Sierra Leone told me, "If we leave our brothers and sis-ters to die, who knows, it might be us next. It is a point of duty."

Were it not for the staff and security I had around me, I would have felt like I was back in Bosnia, notebook in hand, asking questions and hoping that I could convey these inspiring stories to someone im-portant. Now, thankfully, I would be able to report what I witnessed directly to the President of the United States.

One of our biggest concerns was one that had inhibited the re-sponse from the start: stigma. I met one twenty-four-year-old survivor in Guinea, a high school teacher named Fanta Oulen Camara, who told me she had lived three lives: before Ebola, in the hell of her infection, and since recovering. She said her post-Ebola life was harder than when she was battling death. Her friends had stopped talking to her, and she felt so alone that she had even considered returning to the Ebola treatment center to see if she could live there.

Back in Washington, Obama had done what he could to fight the stigma, inviting Texas nurse Nina Pham to the Oval Office after she was released from the hospital, and giving her an effusive embrace. I had taken to describing the photo of the scene as "the hug heard around the world" because everyone from Camara to Liberian president Ellen Johnson Sirleaf had mentioned how much it meant to them. "Our countries need to be hugged like Nina Pham," Johnson Sirleaf told me.

Before heading home, I visited with Jackson Niamah, the Liberian health worker who had spoken so movingly by video to the Security Council about his people's devastating plight. He was now so confident and cheerful that I hardly believed he was the same person we had heard from the previous month. Because the United States and other countries were furiously building Ebola Treatment Units across Liberia, he told me his MSF clinic could finally care for all those who arrived seeking medical attention.

As I left our meeting and reflected on all that we had witnessed, I began to believe that we would succeed in ending the Ebola epidemic—if fear (channeled through Congress) did not interfere with the US-led response.

AS IT HAPPENED, on the day we departed West Africa, President Obama decided to convene the national security cabinet to determine whether to succumb to congressional calls for a travel ban. I would join the Situation Room meeting from the plane by secure videoconference.

At the top of our meeting, President Obama pinpointed the challenge: "There is the epidemiology of this, and then there is the sociology of it." As Cass had pointed out to me, more Americans had married Kim Kardashian than had died of Ebola. But the national panic was real, and it risked crippling our response.

American politicians seemed to relish the opportunity to declare that they would not allow hermetically sealed hospital waste from Ebola patients even to transit their states on the way to a landfill. Amid such uproar for only four cases diagnosed in the United States,* the challenge before us was securing funding despite the fact that some of the very people who were fueling the frenzy controlled the purse.

As the highest-level US official to have visited the region, I was thrilled to be able to affirm from the plane that our interventions were working. I told President Obama and the rest of the national security team that I had seen US troops operating around the world in places like Bosnia, Kosovo, Kuwait, and Iraq, but that I had never witnessed such creativity and rapid returns. I described the impact of US lab technology, the increase in safe burials, and the flood of new recruits to training programs, as well as the gratitude expressed by leaders and ordinary citizens.

Knowing the President's frustration about "free-riding" in the international system, I also laid out in detail what China, the UK, France, and even small countries like Cuba were contributing. I confidently stated that we were going to end the Ebola epidemic. However, knowing the pressure he was under to announce new travel restrictions, I finished with a plea: "Mr. President, my appeal to you is to wait before making any move." Our embassies in the region had explained that they had already dramatically slowed the processing of visa requests, and I relayed the message that they could easily, *quietly*, dial back the flow even further.

"But," I said, "we lead the world no matter what we do. If we announce a new policy of visa restrictions, every European country will follow our lead, and it will have a devastating effect on morale at just the time it is finally rising."

I also argued that, no matter what we announced, Congress would inevitably demand more concessions from us down the line.

"If we can wait, even just a few weeks," I said, "we will have evidence to show that our way is working."

---

* By comparison, in 2014 more than 55,000 Americans died of flu-related illnesses, while some 32,000 Americans died in car accidents.

The President was in full agreement. His public comments had been clear. "America is not defined by fear," he had said. "America is defined by possibility. When we see a problem and we see a challenge, then we fix it." Congress would not be back in session until November 12th. Obama told us we had until that date to turn anecdotes and impressions into hard facts.

Our next stop was Brussels, where I would be lobbying the deep-pocketed European Union to expand its contribution. In my thick binder of preparatory reading materials, I came across an essay that MSF had posted on its blog the previous week from a Liberian worker named Alexander James who had been traveling around the country educating communities on Ebola. "Sunday, the twenty-first of September, is a day I will never forget in my life," James wrote:

> At that time, Ebola had come to Liberia so I tried to talk to my family about the virus and to educate them, but my wife did not believe in it. I called my wife begging her to leave Monrovia and bring the children north so we could be together here. She did not listen. She denied Ebola.
>
> Later that night, my brother called me. "Your wife has died." I said, "What?" He said, "Bendu is dead." I dropped the phone. I threw it away and it broke apart. We were together for 23 years. She understood me. She was the only one who understood me very well. I felt like I'd lost my whole memory. My eyes were open, but I didn't know what I was looking at. I had no vision.

James went on to describe how his two daughters and his brother had then died of Ebola as they tried to care for each other. Only his son, Kollie, also staying in the house in Monrovia, was still alive. James met up with his son in the northern part of the country, where Kollie too was diagnosed with Ebola. James continued:

> When the test came back positive, it was a night of agony for me. I didn't even shut my eyes for one second. I spent the whole

night just crying and thinking about what would happen now to my son . . .

I was able to see Kollie in the care center from across the fence, so I called out to him, "Son, you're the only hope I got. You have to take courage. Any medicine they give to you, you have to take it." He told me, "Papa, I understand. I will do it. Stop crying Papa, I will not die, I will survive Ebola. My sisters are gone, but I am going to survive and I will make you proud . . . "

When finally I saw him come out, I felt so very, very happy. I looked at him and he said to me, "Pa, I am well." I hugged him. Lots of people came to see him when he came outside. Everybody was so happy to see him outside . . . Since then, he and I do everything together. We sleep together, we eat together and we have been conversing a lot. I asked him, "What's your ambition after you graduate from high school?" He's a tenth-grade student. He told me that he wants to study biology and become a medical doctor. That's what he told me!

. . . He is 16 now, so I will make him my friend. Not just my son, but my friend, because he's the only one I have to talk to. I cannot replace my wife, but I can make a new life with our son.

A family of six, reduced to two, and almost to one. As I read this story, all the pent-up emotion I had been carrying during the trip came pouring out.

IN THE END, the surge of resources, from money and health workers to buckets and SIM cards, meant West Africans got what they needed to conquer Ebola.

Although the affected African countries would suffer several small flare-ups thereafter, Liberia was declared Ebola-free for the first time on May 9th, 2015. Sierra Leone rid itself of the disease on November 7th, 2015. And Guinea got a clean bill of health on December 29th,

2015.* Some 28,000 people were infected with Ebola, and more than 11,000 people ultimately died, but the curve depicted on The Slide never came to pass.

The most deadly and dangerous Ebola outbreak in history was beaten above all because of the heroic efforts of the people and governments of Guinea, Liberia, and Sierra Leone. Their national health responders were on the front lines battling the virus from the very beginning, providing care, staffing treatment units, and educating affected communities. Their citizens took it upon themselves to change the way they interacted with one another, avoiding hugs and even handshakes. The people of the region labored to track down every single contact that an Ebola-infected neighbor may have had. And, if a loved one died, they developed the discipline to avoid the burial rituals they had long cherished.

America's involvement was also crucial. President Obama ordered a mission that played an essential role supporting Africans fighting the disease. Obama's leadership also gave despairing people a reason to believe that Ebola *could* be beaten. By refusing to impose the travel ban that even prominent figures in his own party were calling for, he maintained leverage to rally other world leaders to resist as well.

In the wake of this effort, an unusual wave of confidence washed over the UN. The combination of ending the Ebola epidemic and concluding the Iran nuclear deal in 2015 made diplomats believe for the first time in a while that diplomacy and collective action could, in fact, make the world better and safer.

Despite this success, the polarization that was increasingly defining American politics and society meant that those who had objected to Obama's efforts never acknowledged how effectively he had managed the crisis. Our health workers and soldiers never got the bipartisan embrace they deserved for their bravery and sacrifice. Mostly, the United States and the world just moved on.

---

* *Lasting* Ebola-free declarations were made by the World Health Organization on March 17th, 2016, for Sierra Leone; June 1st, 2016, for Guinea; and June 9th, 2016, for Liberia.

I continued proudly to describe what President Obama and American doctors, nurses, health workers, aid workers, diplomats, and soldiers had accomplished together. I used Ebola as an example of why the world needed the United Nations, because no one country—even one as powerful as the United States—could have slayed the epidemic on its own.

Only months later did I learn about an incident that had happened while I was in West Africa. A group of agitated parents at Declan's school had urged that he be kept home under self-quarantine for twenty-one days following my return. Fortunately, the school's administrators had declined.

35

LEAN ON

Whenever I worked at home at night and during the weekend, Declan seemed to delight in making his presence felt. "Mommy," he said during one of my calls with the secretary-general, "Can I ask you something?"

I shook my head and whispered, "I'm on the phone."

"Mommy, it's important."

"This is important too," I said, cupping my hand over the receiver. "I'll be off in a minute."

"Mommy," he persisted, "what's the score of the Nationals game?"

Another time, after failing to get my attention as I participated in a White House conference call on Russia sanctions, Declan stomped away, muttering, "Putin, Putin, Putin . . . When is it going to be Declan, Declan, Declan?"

Rían, who has an unusually generous heart, tended to forgive my distractedness.

On days when I took her to the YMCA for a swim, or stayed off my phone during her weekend soccer practice, she had a habit of graciously awarding me extra credit.

"That was incredible," she would say. "You watched me play the whole time!"

María regularly packed a snack and a change of clothes in Rían's backpack for these outings. But when she was away, I was prone to leaving home empty-handed.

Rían would shake her head knowingly and ask, "Did you forget again?"

"Unfortunately, yes," I would admit. "But, remember I—"

And then, in a kind of game that developed between us, before I could finish, she would say: "I know what you are going to say, Mommy: You have *other* qualities!"

NOT LONG BEFORE I BECAME UN AMBASSADOR, Facebook executive Sheryl Sandberg published *Lean In*, her influential book about the significant obstacles that women confront on their paths to professional and personal achievement. Sandberg, who had worked in the US government before moving to the private sector, argued that women needed to raise their voices in meetings, put themselves forward for advancement, and demand more equal contributions from their partners at home.

Because I was juggling my job in the Obama administration with raising two young children, I was often asked by journalists where I came down on Sandberg's argument. In responding, I sometimes said that the weight of my balancing act often made "fall down" a more apt description of my life than "lean in." But usually I invoked Hillary Clinton, who I once heard say, "It's not so much lean in as lean *on*."

With Cass teaching in Cambridge during the week, I myself leaned most heavily on María, Mum, and Eddie. But I also depended on friends like Laura, who after working a long day at Human Rights Watch faithfully dropped by the Waldorf every Wednesday night to play with the kids. Hillary, John, my law school classmate Elliot, and a legion of other friends carved out time to act as an extended family. Without this support network, I don't know how Declan and Rían would have transitioned so smoothly to our radically different life in New York City.

My friends and family helped me adapt the ornate Waldorf apartment for the kids. We taught Rían to use a scooter by jogging alongside her as she trundled across the hardwood and carpeted floors. And we took turns pitching Wiffle balls to Declan in the spacious "great room" where I generally held receptions with foreign ambassadors and dignitaries.

"Pure power!" Declan would exclaim after whacking a Ping-Pong or squash ball the length of the room, as John attempted to make a diving stop before the ball clattered against the grand piano. Fearing a fire hazard, every few weeks Mum, María, or I would recover balls from the chandelier. Once, as I stood on top of a dining room chair and used Declan's bat to dislodge a ball that had gotten wedged among the glass pendants, I said to Cass, "I just can't see Adlai Stevenson or Jeane Kirkpatrick doing this."

Early mornings were precious because, thanks to María, I could focus on the kids themselves, rather than the frantic last-minute preparations for school. At around 6:30 a.m., before Washington or UN meetings began, Declan and Rían would pile into Cass's and my bed as María packed their lunches, and we would take turns ranking the highlights of the previous day. When Cass was in town, he would play Steve Earle's "Galway Girl" from his laptop, in honor of his dark-haired, blue-eyed daughter, and show Declan YouTube highlights of the baseball greats. Both kids would watch endless videos of dogs—German shepherds, Rhodesian ridgebacks, and yellow Labs—preparing for the choice Cass promised they would have when we moved as a family back to Massachusetts. Rían developed an all-consuming interest in ChapStick and lip gloss, slotting the different flavors into a neon pink plastic briefcase as methodically as I had once stored my baseball cards. As I got ready for work, and as María turned to getting Declan dressed, Rían would recruit me to test out her latest exotic acquisition.

After breakfast, María would walk Rían by stroller to her daycare a few blocks from the Waldorf, while I would accompany Declan to his more distant school in my armored car. On these morning trips, thanks to the fact that an agent on my security detail did the driving, I was able to sit beside Declan in the back and help him learn to read. With the agents often complimenting him when he sounded out a hard word, this regular "read-time" allowed Declan to master the Batman phonics books, graduate to chapter books, and eventually devour the whole Harry Potter series. Whenever he managed to read five pages aloud during our trip, I would buy him a donut in his school cafeteria. On days he managed even more, I threw in a bonus side of bacon.

Because so many of the agents who provided security were parents themselves, they were wonderfully sensitive to the awkwardness of people in dark suits staking out a school pickup or hovering as I pushed Rían on the swings at the playground. They did their best to be unobtrusive.

Sometimes, I was overwhelmed by the agents' thoughtfulness. From the time she was a baby, Rían had been plagued by frequent ear infections, and when she was three years old, began to show signs of hearing loss. Her doctor told us that he could fix the problem by removing her tonsils and adenoids and inserting tiny tubes in her ears. On the day of her operation, Cass and I helped her into the back of the armored vehicle just after dawn as we prepared to head to New York-Presbyterian Hospital. She squealed with delight when she spotted what was sitting strapped into her car seat: a stuffed white bunny adorned with a pink bow.

"This is the best surgery ever," she proclaimed. With all that was going on, I hadn't remembered to get her a good-luck gift—but the agents delivered.

The other UN ambassadors were similarly generous toward my family. Halfway through my tenure, Boubacar Boureima, Niger's Ambassador to the UN, told me that the African ambassadors were "all talking" about how much they enjoyed getting to know Mum and Eddie and seeing Declan and Rían race around the apartment. The inclusion of three generations of my family in large gatherings, he said, "was creating a different impression of the United States," one with which they could identify. "Family matters so much to Africans," he explained. "The big power seems much more open to us."

I had not been trying to make a statement by including Mum, Eddie, and the kids when I held events at the Waldorf apartment. With a job that didn't allow much free time, I was simply hoping to maximize every moment with them.

Animal-obsessed, Declan and Rían quickly realized they could talk to my colleagues from around the world about their home countries' wildlife. The normally reserved Namibian ambassador, Wilfried Emvula, became an effusive storyteller when he had the chance to talk about his country's cheetahs. At one reception, Declan and Rían convinced Egyptian ambassador Amr Aboulatta to leave the main gathering and visit their bedroom, where they showed off their diverse stuffed animal collection. Amr eyed the array, and then shook his head in mock outrage, affecting injury. "How can you have a pink flamingo and not have a camel?"

"I am so sorry," Declan said with great seriousness. "I will ask Santa for a camel."

Declan's favorite animals were elephants, leading him to fixate on Zimbabwe—the country that his *National Geographic* map depicted with the highest elephant concentration. When other ambassadors invited him to visit their countries, he would apologetically say that he was planning to visit Zimbabwe first. After hearing a version of this exchange several times, I decided to describe Robert Mugabe's repressive rule to Declan in accessible terms.

I told him that the leader of Zimbabwe was not terribly nice to the people who lived there. He locked up those who criticized him and gave the country's riches to his friends.

"Why don't they get somebody else?" Declan asked, leading me to explain that Mugabe would not allow the Zimbabwean people to choose a new leader. As a result, I said, we were not likely to visit anytime soon.

Declan considered this new information and, solutions-oriented, asked, "How old is Mugabe?"

When I answered "ninety-one," he broke into a large smile. "Great," he said, "so we will be able to see the elephants pretty soon."

I didn't bring up the topic again, but every few months he would ask for an update on Mugabe's health. In 2017, when the Zimbabwean president was forced out of office, I showed Declan video footage of the street celebrations. But by then he was canny enough to ask, "Is the new guy better?"

At times, I wasn't sure if I was wise to translate aspects of my work life into language the kids could understand. Declan's favorite books at the time were the British Mr. Men series. The characters each bore the names of their personalities: Mr. Mean, Mr. Chatterbox, Mr. Greedy, Mr. Lazy, Mr. Strong, and so on. I would sometimes spin the globe around, point to a country, and then describe that country's ambassador, giving him a Mr. Men nickname. In light of the many events held at the residence, though, it was inevitable that Declan would personally encounter one of these "characters" from our game. Luckily, even at a young age, he had the sense not to cause a diplomatic incident, and would only whisper to me excitedly when he realized that an ambassador he had just met was the Mr. Impossible we had been discussing a few weeks earlier.

The morning President Obama was intending to announce a plan to open relations with Cuba, I was bursting to tell someone, so I decided to disclose the news to Declan, who was then five years old. To give him context, I summarized more than fifty years of US–Cuba relations, describing how the US government had put in place something called an "embargo" to cut off the flow of goods between our two countries. In just a few hours, I told Declan, "President Obama is going to try something new." He nodded along as I spoke, seeming to absorb my simplified history lesson.

Later that day at the US Mission, I gathered my team to watch Obama's televised announcement. Just as the President started speaking, the nurse from Declan's school called to tell me that he had been playacting as an animal during recess when his friend Sawyer had accidentally kicked him in the face, giving him a bloody lip.

Declan grabbed the phone from the nurse.

"Mommy," he said, his voice conveying urgency. "We need an embargo for Sawyer."

I told myself that the exposures the kids were getting to the world beyond America's shores would compensate in a small way for the shortage of time they had with me. But I knew nothing could substitute for parental attention. I also worried that my kids would grow accustomed to a penthouse apartment and special treatment. I remembered the gratitude I felt as a child when Mum scored a seat in the upper decks of Pittsburgh's Three Rivers Stadium for a Pirates game. Yet when I took Declan to Washington Nationals' spring training each year, he got to go onto the field and meet the players. When Mum and Eddie had taken me to Disneyworld, we had queued for hours to ride Space Mountain, making the thrill all the more immense. Yet when I brought Rían back to the scene of my childhood delight, I looked at the other parents guiltily as my security escort moved us to the front of the long lines. At such moments, I made sure to tell the kids, "This. Is. Not. Normal"—a good reminder to myself as well.

"LEAN ON" ENCOMPASSED more than this invaluable support from family, friends, and coworkers. It also spoke to the importance of women having each other's backs. I saw this dynamic play out in powerful ways at the male-dominated United Nations. While men had held the majority of positions during my time working at the NSC, only when I got to the UN did I regularly find myself the only woman in the room.

When Obama had nominated me for the job, I went to see Madeleine Albright, President Clinton's UN ambassador during his first term (before she became America's first female Secretary of State in his second). Albright told me that in 1993 she had assembled the seven female ambassadors at the UN (out of 183 countries at the time) in what she called the G7—the "Girl Seven." The way she described her gatherings with the women who represented Canada, Kazakhstan, the Philippines, Trinidad and Tobago, Jamaica, and Lichtenstein reminded me of the Wednesday Group. Albright's G7 developed into both an informal sisterhood and a cross-regional lobby that managed to secure the appointment of two female judges to the bench of the UN war crimes tribunal.

Fortunately, I had far more female company at the UN than Albright. When I arrived in New York, I was the thirty-seventh woman permanent representative out of 193 countries.* Inspired by her initiative, I convened the G37 as often as I could. I invited my female colleagues to dinners at the apartment, including an evening featuring the authors Katty Kay and Claire Shipman, who discussed their book *The Confidence Code*, which argues that "success correlates more closely with confidence than it does with competence."[41] I also invited all of the G37 to the Public Theater's *Eclipsed*, a play about sexual violence in Liberia that was written, directed, and performed solely by women.

Whenever we got together, we would inevitably commiserate about how tired we were of being asked how it felt to be "one of only X women" in whatever venue we were in.[42] We would also lament how some in the broader international affairs community still dismissed the push for enhanced female participation as a form of special pleading.

We knew that advocating for inclusivity was more than just a gender or moral issue. In fact, progress toward gender equality has broad, intrinsic benefits for whole societies. One of the best predictors of a state's peacefulness is the way women are treated within that state. In addition, progress at closing the gender gap in employment significantly increases GDP, reduces income inequality, *and* leads to higher incomes for men. Learning from one another that we shared a frustration with the narrow way in which gender issues were sometimes treated emboldened us to be more outspoken.

Still, I was acutely aware that my circumstances as a woman at the UN were not comparable to those of my female colleagues. Because the United States was the most powerful country in the world, the fact that I was *American* was far more salient to UN officials and foreign diplomats than the fact that I was a woman. I suffered few of the slights endured by female diplomats from other countries.

I also knew I had it easy compared to Albright and Jeane Kirkpatrick, who President Reagan had made America's first female UN

---

* Because ambassadors came and went, the number fluctuated during my tenure, rising as high as forty-two and dipping to thirty-six.

ambassador. During my time interning for Mort, I had watched Kirkpatrick confidently interrogating guests at the Carnegie Endowment. We had vast policy differences, but I read up on her UN experience and discovered that, as tough as she looked, even she had grown weary of the constant sexism in New York and Washington.

Once, President Reagan's chief of staff, Mike Deaver, approached her with a sensitive request: Could she urge Reagan to pursue an opening with the Soviet Union?

"Everyone notices you have influence with the President," Deaver explained to her.

When Kirkpatrick shrugged, he went on. "No, no, everyone notices. He always listens when you speak. He looks at you and his eyes light up. Maybe it's because you're a woman."

"Maybe it's because he's interested in foreign policy," Kirkpatrick shot back.[43]

WHEN IT WAS TIME for the UN to elect a new secretary-general in 2016, I thought that a woman might be selected for the first time. When I mentioned this to a European ambassador, he told me that he was open to it—"as long as she is competent."

I relayed this comment to Jordan's UN ambassador Dina Kawar, who had become a close friend. She rolled her eyes. How, she asked, could anybody seriously think that an unqualified woman might just slip through the cracks to become UN secretary-general? As Dina joked to me, "Are they afraid that some woman will say, 'Oh, I was going to do my hair today, but thought I would become Secretary-General instead!'" Such qualifiers would never have been considered necessary for male candidates in the race.[44]

Of the five countries that held permanent seats on the UN Security Council, only the United States had ever appointed a woman as permanent representative, and often I was the only woman in the Council as a whole.* When school groups were escorted into the viewing gallery to listen to our debates, I wondered what the young girls thought

---

* The United Kingdom would appoint its first female ambassador to the UN in 2018.

when they saw one woman seated among fourteen men. Surely, their ambition—or at least their sense of possibility—would be influenced by such a striking disparity. The boys' sense of what was "natural" would undoubtedly also be shaped by snapshots like this.

In 2014, thanks to rotations among the ten nonpermanent members of the Council, I had the chance to serve with five other women, the ambassadors representing Argentina, Lithuania, Luxembourg, Nigeria, and Jordan. We were the largest female contingent on the Security Council in the seven-decade history of the UN.

Although we still accounted for less than half the ambassadors on the Council, and although our number would dwindle back to one female representative in 2016, the excitement around the UN was palpable. Young women would pull me aside in the restroom to say how proud they were to see the six of us duking it out in the traditionally male chamber. Our deliberations changed in subtle ways; I noticed that the female ambassadors tended to refer back to their colleagues' comments more frequently than the men did.

Having six women on the Council didn't deter male ambassadors from occasionally taking outlandish positions, such as questioning well-documented cases of sexual violence. Once, when we were discussing what to do about allegations that Sudanese Army soldiers in Darfur had perpetrated mass rape, one of my African colleagues dismissed the detailed reports.*

"Why would the soldiers have done this when they have their wives to come home to? Where is the proof?" he asked, insisting, "If these rapes really happened, the women would have spoken openly about it—even if the security forces were present."

I interjected. "Oh, are you speaking from your vast personal experience of having been raped and then being asked what happened while security forces affiliated with your rapists leer over you?"

On another occasion, Vitaly memorably criticized the UN's Yemen

---

* According to Human Rights Watch, over the course of thirty-six hours in late 2014, Sudanese uniformed and armed military personnel raped more than two hundred women and girls in a "systematic" attack in the town of Tabit.

envoy for spending too much of his precious time talking to women. "Your job is to make peace, and that is hard enough," Vitaly said. "Why are you wasting your time having meetings with women who aren't even involved in the conflict?" On such occasions the women ambassadors—and a few of the enlightened men—would fling our hands up to demand the floor in order to respond.

More impactfully, we pressed for action by the UN secretary-general to punish those who had perpetrated sexual violence, including, horrifyingly, UN peacekeepers themselves. Over Egypt's objections, we secured the passage of a Council resolution that required the UN to expel whole peacekeeping units whose soldiers were accused of sexually abusing civilians. As a result, in 2017, Secretary-General Guterres sent home the entire deployment of more than 600 Congolese peacekeepers that had been stationed in Central African Republic, following numerous accusations that a number of them were perpetrating abuses.

While I could do little to affect whom foreign heads of state selected to represent their countries at the UN, I tried to make the US Mission to the UN friendlier to women and mothers—even by making small changes like installing the US Mission's first lactation room. I also pressed to include women experts in Security Council debates—and not just on those topics explicitly branded as "women's issues." When the US ambassadorships under me opened up, I actively recruited women to apply and recommended several of them to the White House. In the end, President Obama named women to three of the four posts.

When I traveled abroad, I added a stop on each trip to interact with teenage girls. I especially loved playing sports with them—the epitome of the "lean on" ethos, in which team members set one another up for success. In Mexico, I played soccer with a group of underprivileged girls. In war-ravaged northern Sri Lanka, I played the local sport of Elle (a bat-and-ball game) in the rain with Muslim girls who had only recently returned to school after years of conflict. And in the Middle East, I played basketball with Israeli and Palestinian girls who hoped to become engineers, architects, and even politicians. In each instance, the shy teenagers who had barely spoken before we began playing began to open up once I was in my gym clothes, no longer looking like a senior US official.

When I met with young women in the United States, I erred on the side of oversharing, describing my self-doubt in the Bat Cave and the tradeoffs between my dream job and the family I longed to see more of. I did not gloss over the challenges they would face if they pursued ambitious careers in public service or foreign policy, but I encouraged them to take the leap.

I also offered a dose of perspective, highlighting the stories of women and girls who were breaking through barriers I found almost unimaginable. In Afghanistan under the Taliban, for example, girls had been denied almost all access to education. Yet by the time I arrived at the UN, three million Afghan girls had risked violence and enrolled in schools. Finally allowed to run for seats in Afghanistan's Parliament, women had won 28 percent of the positions—a higher proportion than in the United States Congress.

I often spoke publicly about the Afghan Women's National Cycling Team, which was banned under the Taliban but had been reestablished in 2011. Since then, the team had grown to around forty women. Afghan men frequently yelled at women cyclists to get off the road, and motorcyclists had even been known to grab at the women as they pedaled past (causing several to crash). Yet the women kept on riding.

I would ask my audiences—whether my fellow UN Security Council ambassadors or a group of students—to think about the impression these women left:

> Imagine just for a minute what it must feel like to be a little girl from a rural town in Afghanistan—and to suddenly see those forty women, in a single file, flying down the road. To see something for the first time that you couldn't have believed possible. Think about where your mind would go—about the shockwave that image would send through your system. Think what it

would allow you to believe possible. You would never be able to think the same way again.

Agency. Self-determination. Dignity. Solidarity. We could not discount the potential impact of even one such altered perspective on a young girl, her family, and, eventually, on an entire community.

36

TOUSSAINT

Ever since my time in Bosnia, I had believed that I could best learn about a situation by being where events were unfolding. As the Hungarian war photographer Robert Capa once said, "If your pictures aren't good enough, you aren't close enough." I tried to bring this "get close" spirit to diplomacy.

As a writer and an activist, seeking out people's firsthand experiences was of course common practice. But as a government official, it proved much more difficult. The briefing papers and diplomatic cables I consumed rarely offered raw, unfiltered points of view.

As I brainstormed with my team about how to concentrate our energies in the final stretch of the Obama administration, my top Africa adviser, Colin Thomas-Jensen, floated the idea of traveling to the forgotten parts of Cameroon, Chad, and Nigeria to meet with people on the front lines of the fight between the governments in the region and the terrorist group, Boko Haram.* Boko Haram wanted to create a purely Islamic state in the area where these three countries and Niger converged, and its fighters targeted those who did not support the group's demand for the strict imposition of Sharia law.

Boko Haram gained global notoriety in April of 2014 after it

---

* The name roughly translates as "Western education is forbidden."

kidnapped 276 girls from a school in Chibok, Nigeria. The girls had been preparing for the all-important exams that would determine whether they would gain admission to a vocational school or university. The night of the raid, the Boko Haram militia barged into the dormitories and forced the terrified girls, both Christians and Muslims, onto trucks and motorcycles, leaving their school in flames. When one of the trucks broke down, 57 girls managed to escape. But the rest were brought to rural hideouts, where their captors forced them to adopt a radical form of Islam and marry Boko Haram soldiers.

In the #BringBackOurGirls campaign that followed, public figures and grassroots groups used social media to pressure governments to devote more resources to locating the abducted students, who seemed to have vanished. The girls' mothers and fathers, I had read, were "going mad" at the lack of progress being made to find their children.

The Chibok kidnapping occurred the same year that the Islamic State of Iraq and Syria (ISIS) rose to prominence while swallowing up huge swaths of territory in the Middle East. Yet in 2014, Boko Haram actually held the dubious distinction of being the world's deadliest terrorist group. The following year, in 2015, it killed more people than al-Qaeda's core franchise had in its entire history. And by 2016, Boko Haram had pledged allegiance to ISIS, amassed thousands of fighters, and displaced 2.5 million people from their homes. Horrifyingly, the Chibok girls constituted only a small fraction of the staggering 10,000 children estimated to have been seized by the group since 2013. In some cases, girls and boys they kidnapped were drugged and forced to become suicide bombers.*

Although the Pentagon had sent three hundred advisers to support counter–Boko Haram efforts, the regional militaries that US personnel advised had not proven effective. The governments were making

---

* Boko Haram carried out 183 suicide attacks over the course of 2014 and 2015. Of these attacks, 58 were perpetrated by children, three-quarters of whom were girls.

familiar mistakes, prioritizing the killing of terrorists but giving scant consideration to the ways their own human rights abuses and economic neglect were aiding Boko Haram's recruitment.

As we discussed a possible trip to Cameroon, Chad, and Nigeria, Colin cautioned that security concerns would make a visit even more complicated than our trip to West Africa during the Ebola outbreak and our four trips to the violent Central African Republic. But making the effort to go would also break new ground. I would be the first cabinet official to visit Cameroon since 1991. I had traveled to Chad earlier in the administration, becoming the most senior US official ever to visit, and would now be returning there for the second time.

Like a good number of American "partners" in fighting terrorism, Cameroon and Chad were run by repressive presidents who had been in power for decades—thirty-four years for Cameroon's Paul Biya and twenty-five years for Chad's Idriss Déby—rendering them accountable to almost no one. Their undisciplined armed forces were committing human rights violations against a backdrop of broader state abuses against the general population. While I thought the mounting threat posed by Boko Haram made it necessary (if unappealing) to work with these governments, I also believed we needed to train carefully vetted units and use our military and financial support as leverage to try to secure reform.[45] The governments needed to begin punishing soldiers who committed torture and extrajudicial killings, and to allocate economic support to impoverished civilians in areas where Boko Haram had gained ground.

The fact that aid workers had begun warning of imminent mass starvation in some of the conflict-affected areas of Nigeria provided an even more immediate reason for making the trip. Boko Haram's attacks had so severely disrupted local trade, agriculture, and transportation that more than 50,000 people in the northeastern part of the country were believed to be experiencing famine-like conditions. Hundreds of thousands more could soon starve if they did not get relief. If we went, Colin said, we would be able to use the visit to shake loose $40 million of additional US humanitarian assistance.*

Traveling to Cameroon, Chad, and Nigeria would mean a full week away from Declan and Rían. Because I wanted my children to feel safe, I was never sure how to discuss the darker aspects of my work. But, as with most matters, I tended to err on the side of disclosure. I pointed on the map to the parts of northwest Africa where I would be visiting and told Declan and Rían about a very nasty group of bandits who were preventing children from going to school and sometimes even taking kids away from their parents. Rían was just three, but was immediately saddened.

"Are they crying?" she asked of the kidnapped children. "Yes," I answered, "lots of people are crying right now."

Declan had a different focus. Just about to play his first official Little League game, he had laid out his new uniform on the dining room table: royal blue socks, white polyester elastic-waist pants, and a royal blue and orange jersey. The sight of his beaming face reminded me of my delight when my softball coach in Pittsburgh opened the trunk of his station wagon and handed me my first uniform. I had sprinted with my new gear to the car, shouting "Look, Mum!" in my Dublin accent. Nothing had made me feel more American than donning my "Oilers" pinstripes.

Even amid the craze of being US ambassador, I had always made time for baseball with Declan, whether taking him to Washington Nationals games when the team passed through New York, dropping him each morning at a summer baseball camp in Brooklyn, or simply stealing away for a Sunday game of catch in Central Park. He could not believe I was now going to miss his debut. I explained that I couldn't control the timing of my trip and that Cass would attend in my stead.

---

* High-level trips are valuable because they often generate White House–led processes through which US government agencies find "deliverables" that, when announced, might make the host government more responsive to US requests. Travel by senior US officials is thus often accompanied by an announcement of new US funding. Without making this trip, I could not have secured the release of a similar level of additional assistance.

"He will be on his phone the whole game," Declan complained.

"Probably," I answered, "because he will be messaging me updates on your game."

This explanation seemed to put him at ease. But less than an hour before leaving for the airport, I realized that I did not have the ethernet cable I would need to connect my computer on our government plane (which could videoconference into the Situation Room but inexplicably lacked the basic cords to get online). Crestfallen, I rationalized that I would be better off poring over my briefing materials than hitting refresh on my email every fifteen seconds to follow Declan's at-bats. Consumed by last-minute packing, I did not notice that Cass had slipped out of the apartment.

Just as I went looking for him to say goodbye, he burst through the front door, his light blue Oxford shirt drenched in sweat. He had sprinted eight blocks to the Apple Store and made it back just before I was scheduled to leave.

"Make two plans, God smiles," he said, handing me a bag. "I got two cables in case one doesn't work."

I gave him a hug of gratitude, and as I held him, he repeated what he generally said before I traveled overseas: "Please don't go."

Because ISIS and its affiliates had begun attacking Western targets—murdering American journalists in Syria, shooting up hotels and tourist attractions in North Africa—I had spent a fair amount of time thinking about all that could go wrong on the trip. But I cheerfully proclaimed, "Feel the fear and do it anyway," reminding Cass that I would be back home in time for Declan's seventh birthday in a week.

Rían came running up to the door. No taller than my rolling suitcase, she sweetly demanded "five kisses and hugs." In the midst of our final hug, I said I would talk to her every day and bring her back a new flavor of ChapStick, as I tried to do from all my trips.

As we flew, thanks to my airborne internet connection, I learned in real time that Declan had reached base four times (thanks to two line-drives and some clumsy fielding by the other team), and I ordered him a Nationals youth baseball jersey for his birthday, customized with

"POWER" on the back. Then I turned my focus to preparing for what I expected would be a difficult visit.

OUR DELEGATION INCLUDED A HANDFUL of my staff from the US Mission, as well as senior officials from the State Department, USAID, and the Pentagon, among them the deputy commander of US armed forces in Africa. On our first full day in the region, we traveled to Maroua, the capital of Cameroon's Far North Region, where people who had been attacked by Boko Haram were concentrated. I always tried to visit survivors of violence before meeting with heads of state. It allowed me to hear eyewitness perspectives that I could then relay to leaders, who usually lived far removed from their people.

When our plane landed, some three hundred Cameroonian special forces stood in full combat gear at the airport. Because Boko Haram attacks were recurrent in the area, and the group's fighters could so easily melt into the local population, the security planning had been an elaborate affair. As we pulled out of the airport, the special forces stood guard about every five hundred feet. Passing by, I could see they were wearing body armor and carrying assault rifles and grenade launchers.

Cameroonian police and soldiers in camouflage set the pace and brought up the rear of our convoy. A team of US Navy SEALs, their faces shrouded in bandannas, distributed themselves among our vehicles, joining my usual security detail and an additional layer of diplomatic security from the US embassy. We had each been asked ahead of time to provide our blood type so that the ambulance in the convoy would have enough plasma in case of an emergency. A Cameroonian military helicopter flew overhead, and we were told that a US surveillance aircraft thousands of feet up in the air was also monitoring the area for approaching threats.

As a journalist, I had wandered around foreign lands with little more than a backpack, notebook, flashlight, and stash of $1 and $5 bills. When I saw American dignitaries zoom by in their ostentatious, armored convoys, I had often wondered how anybody in Washington thought such a display would enhance America's prestige.

"Do we really need all this?" I asked Michael Hoza, the US Ambassador to Cameroon. He was adamant that we did.

"Can you imagine what it would do for Boko Haram's standing around the world if they took out a cabinet official?" he asked.

Our convoy of fourteen armored vehicles rumbled along roads that the Cameroonian government had temporarily closed to civilian traffic. I looked out the bulletproof-glass window at the locals who lined the route—in some places, five people deep. Many waved and smiled. Young boys and girls peered out from behind the legs of their parents, and women in multicolored dresses carried enormous water jugs on their heads, waiting patiently for the spectacle to conclude so they could resume their routines.

The protection afforded to me and my team cast in relief the daily vulnerability of the people watching our convoy go by. Yet I knew that if I had second-guessed the security professionals, we might have been forced to cancel the visit north. Since the 2012 Benghazi attacks, the entire American security apparatus had grown even more averse to taking chances.*

Najat Rochdi, the UN humanitarian coordinator for Cameroon, was seated next to me in the armored car. A native of Morocco who had lived in Cameroon for three years, Najat demonstrated striking knowledge of the history, culture, and trauma of the place. On the plane ride over, I had scribbled down dozens of questions, and Najat now seemed to have answers for all of them. She gave me the strategic big picture, but also carried with her a list of thirty-seven children, some as young as eleven, who were languishing in a local Cameroonian jail, accused of being Boko Haram members despite an absence of evidence. I asked her to give me the list so I could show it to President Biya when I met with him the next day.

---

* As it happened, Boko Haram would stage multiple attacks while our delegation was in the region, including an assault on a Cameroonian checkpoint that killed three soldiers and a suicide bombing that killed eight people at a camp for displaced persons in Northeast Nigeria.

I also inquired about the Cameroonians who were being diverted from their livelihoods for the morning due to all the security closures.

"How upset are they about all this fuss and inconvenience?" I asked.

"Unfortunately," Najat said, "they have no experience of the government looking out for them, so this is just another day."

After a ninety-minute drive, we reached the town of Mokolo. Drummers in traditional garb gave us an energetic, celebratory welcome, and we paid a courtesy call to the head of the local administration. In our short meeting, he spoke proudly about Cameroon's self-appointed neighborhood guardians, or "vigilance committees," which were trying to rid the area of Boko Haram. He described a recent incident in which one group of locals had used stones and bows and arrows to kill a twenty-five-year-old woman who entered a market wearing a suicide belt under her clothes. In that instance, it seemed, the woman was indeed a threat, but I had read reports of these same "guardians" attacking people as "Boko Haram" so they could steal their livestock. When I steered the conversation toward this problem, the official dismissed my concerns, denying that abuses against civilians were taking place.

After I bade the man farewell, my deputy chief of staff, Gideon Maltz, intercepted me before I could head back to the car. I rolled my eyes in frustration with the just-concluded meeting, which he had skipped. Gideon had planned the trip, and I liked to tease him that all the productive meetings were my idea and all the useless ones were his fault. However, his face looked pale, his eyes dull. Something was wrong.

"What is it?" I said.

"We need to talk to you," he replied, motioning me away from a media scrum to a small, darkened room down the hall. Colin, my Africa adviser, was waiting there, his eyes filled with tears, while Kurtis, my spokesman, and Becca Wexler, my special assistant, looked at the ground.

"What?" I asked, my mouth suddenly dry. "What?"

My mind leaped immediately to all the catastrophes that could have befallen Mum, Eddie, Cass, and the kids, but I did a quick calculation on the time difference with New York and reassured myself that they were likely still sleeping.

Colin spoke, barely able to piece a sentence together.

"As we were driving here," he said, "our car hit a young boy."

"Oh my God," I said.

My vehicle had been seven cars in front of theirs, and I had heard nothing. "Oh my God," I said again. "Is he going to be ok?"

The looks on Gideon's and Colin's faces—and the fact that the boy had been hit by an armored vehicle traveling forty-five miles per hour—told me everything.

"We don't know yet," Gideon mustered.

Colin was beside himself. The father of a young daughter, he had dedicated his life to efforts to end Africa's most intractable wars. "We stopped after we hit him," he exclaimed. "But then they made us drive on."

He did not have to tell me who "they" referred to. I knew how US security officials would react in a situation like that. Along with the risk of a Boko Haram attack on stationary Americans, the officials would have immediately worried about the possibility of mob violence against Gideon, Colin, the Cameroonian driver, and the other US diplomat who was in the vehicle.

"We have to go back," I said.

Colin clarified that, though their car had been told to drive on, the ambulance in the motorcade stopped to treat the boy.

I asked if they knew how the accident had happened. "I thought that pedestrians were blocked from accessing the road," I said, uselessly.

Gideon thought the child had been looking off into the distance when he ran onto the road. Others later speculated that he had been focused on the Cameroonian helicopter shadowing the convoy.

As we each struggled to process what had happened, we discussed what to do next. Knowing that a group of survivors of Boko Haram violence had already been assembled to meet with us, Gideon and Colin recommended we follow through. Since we were awaiting word on the child's fate and could do nothing to help him, I agreed.

"But," I said, "no matter what, I am going to go see the boy's family."

On the short drive to our destination, I felt as though my insides had congealed and an intense wave of nausea came over me. Closing my eyes, I prayed that, against all odds, he would survive.

We arrived at a large dirt courtyard where small clusters of Cameroonians had gathered. Najat and I were led to a heavyset Cameroonian woman dressed in light purple, who held a toddler in her lap. We sat across from her and I asked Najat, who was translating, to begin by asking the woman where she and her daughter were from.

After Najat asked my question, the woman shook her head. "This girl is not mine," she said, caressing the child.

Najat probed in French and then suddenly broke off, saying, "Oh God. They took everybody from her. Her two kids, her husband. They killed them all. She has nobody left." The woman started to sob. A Cameroonian man who had joined our circle told her to stop crying. I cut him off.

"She can cry," I said. "We should all cry."

Each of the half dozen Cameroonians we met with over the next hour shared similar stories. They heard a "boom boom boom" when Boko Haram arrived in their village. Their attackers offered them impossible choices: leave your home or be killed; give us your daughter or we will murder your mother. One Cameroonian woman told us she had fled with her five-month-old baby, one-year-old, and three other young kids, and managed to survive a walk of several hundred miles. The woman did not say what had happened to her husband, but I had been briefed in advance that he had been set on fire in front of her.

After I finished speaking with the survivors, Becca pulled me aside. "The boy didn't make it," she told me, her voice shaking.

I had been expecting this news. But still, I felt as though my knees were wilting beneath me. Kurtis joined Najat and me in our vehicle, and for a long while none of us spoke.

Over and over in my mind, I heard, "First, do no harm. First. Do. No. Harm."

We had brought $40 million and the promise of high-level American attention. We were pledging enhanced information-sharing and military training. And we had invited journalists from outlets like ABC News, National Public Radio, the Associated Press, and the *New*

York Times, whose coverage would call attention to the plight of Boko Haram's victims, almost certainly bringing more money to buy medicine and food.

But whatever good we managed to do, I thought, could never compensate for what had just happened. Had we not come, a six-year-old boy would still be alive.

Kurtis, who was trying to pull himself together to talk to the media, reminded me that the Cameroonian authorities were responsible for security precautions like setting the pace of our drive, erecting the barriers by the road, and keeping people off the streets. The vehicle that hit the boy belonged to the United Nations, and the driver had been a Cameroonian UN employee.

None of these details mattered. Kurtis's comments melded together, as the same four words kept blaring in my brain: First. Do. No. Harm.

When I told Najat that I wanted to go and see the boy's family, she tried to dissuade me, saying it was impossible to know how the family's village would react to our visit. Carlos Johnson, the head of my New York–based security detail, chimed in to agree. But I think no decision in my life up to that juncture seemed like less of a choice than the question of whether to pay our respects.

"This is not negotiable," I said. "We can't not do this."

After a pause, Najat admitted that she would probably make the same call. Carlos said he would "work it" with the Navy SEALs and Cameroonian security officials, but that they would need some time to "secure the site." Colin joined Carlos in getting the embassy's top security officer to quickly develop a plan for my vehicle to stop at the boy's home while keeping the rest of our large, heavily armed convoy at a respectful distance.

As Cameroonian and US security officials mapped out the new itinerary, we stuck with the next part of our original plan, driving nearly an hour to the Minawao refugee camp, home to some 60,000 Nigerians who had poured across the border in search of safety from Boko Haram.

I called Cass to tell him what had happened, asking him to tell Mum. I did not want her to hear about the accident on the news. We could not talk long because the line was bad. But he just kept repeating, "I'm so, so, sorry Samantha." For the next several hours, every time we drove back into cell phone range, I would receive a flurry of one-line emails from my husband—simple messages such as, "Heartbroken here as well."

Judging from the number and tempo of the emails he was sending, I could tell he could not concentrate on his work. This was the first time I had known him to be unable to focus.

When we arrived at the camp, we were greeted warmly by refugees gathered at the entrance. As television cameras rolled, I waved inertly, forcing a smile and eye contact with the children along our path. I told Najat I needed to use the restroom before we began our meetings. I had not been alone since I had heard about "the boy"—whose name, we had finally learned, was Toussaint Birwe.

I was escorted to a small plastic portable hut that encased a hole in the ground. I knew that this was the only place in the camp where I could find solitude—the only place I could escape the probing gaze of the media and the anguished looks on the faces of my team members, themselves in desperate need of consolation. I lifted the latch on the fiberglass door, ignored the overwhelming stench, and stepped inside.

I looked at the time on my phone and gave myself two minutes.

I imagined Toussaint's smile, as he pointed eagerly to the motorcade. I imagined his small body lying on the road. And I imagined someone running to tell his parents and his siblings. I heard their searing cries upon learning what had happened. I thought of them in that moment, praying as they prepared for his burial. I let go of all the emotion I had been suppressing and sobbed with abandon. For two whole minutes, I did not have to appear strong or be strong for others.

When my allotted two minutes were up, I took a few wet wipes from my bag—the smell of which would always remind me of changing my own kids' diapers—and attempted to remove the traces of my meltdown. Then I opened the door of the toilet and walked out into the harsh sunlight.

THE DRIVE FROM THE REFUGEE CAMP back to Toussaint's village was foreboding. Although it was steaming hot in the area, my skin began to go numb.

When we arrived, I exited our vehicle and walked down a dirt path leading to Toussaint's house. I felt as though the entire village had turned up. While we had been welcomed earlier in the day, now dozens of men squatted or stood stoically nearby, silently staring at us. I concentrated on putting one foot in front of the other.

As we ducked under a low doorway into a mud-walled home, we found a very old man, probably in his eighties, who was Toussaint's grandfather. He sat beside a much younger woman named Fanta Makachi, Toussaint's mother. They were sitting on wooden crates opposite white plastic lawn chairs, where we were gestured to sit.

I shook the old man's hand first. He looked strangely serene. A Cameroonian translated his words into French, which Najat translated into English. "It was God's will," he said. "It was his time. God had a reason for taking him. We praise God."

I looked at Toussaint's mother. She was wearing a T-shirt and a floral skirt. Her eyes looked vacant. She did not speak.

Najat, Ambassador Hoza, and I went to shake her hand, but she looked away as she held out her limp palm. I longed to connect with her, to know that she saw the depth of our regret and sorrow. But she was naturally unable or unwilling to fully participate in our visit. I was thankful she had even agreed to see us.

Toussaint's two brothers and two sisters ranged in age from one to eleven years old. I watched one of the young boys, himself tear-stained, slide into his mother's lap. I tried to speak. Now, Najat translated my words into French before the Cameroonian spoke them in the local dialect.

"As a parent—" I started, but I choked up and had to begin again.

"I cannot imagine what you are going through," I said. "I am so terribly sorry."

Before I knew it, we were back outside, all of us blinking back tears as we walked toward our vehicles. Later that night, I wrote in my journal: "I think walking over that threshold was the hardest thing I have ever done in my life. I did not do it well, but I am glad I saw their faces."

ON THE NIGHT OF THE ACCIDENT, when our flight landed back in Cameroon's capital, I was scheduled to videoconference into an NSC meeting chaired by President Obama. As various senior officials wandered into the room before the meeting started, I could see them notice me on the large screen, but no one gestured my way. I had been shivering in the frigid embassy conference room, but now, feeling as if my colleagues were deliberately looking away from me, I turned hot with shame, shedding the jacket and sweater in which I had been bundled.

I saw Secretary Kerry walk in and assumed he too would say nothing. But when he spotted me, he pressed the button to unmute the microphone and shouted, "Sending you a big hug, Sam."

Becca passed me an email from Jim Clapper, the Director of National Intelligence:

> Knowing you as we do, I expect you've taken this hard. It's doubly sad, given the noble mission you had just embarked on. I choose to think now of the thousands of lives that you have saved—either directly or indirectly. Please accept my heartfelt thoughts, prayers, and a virtual hug.

I was overcome with gratitude.

I wondered if President Obama knew what had happened and whether he would say anything. Just after he entered, Susan passed him a note. He studied it for a second, then his shoulders slumped. He exhaled deeply, shaking his head as if pained. Given his job, the note could have informed him of any number of tragedies. But I had an instinct it was about our convoy's accident.

Obama launched directly into chairing a two-hour discussion of our policy on Middle East peace. I compartmentalized, participating in the meeting as if it were any other day.

I did not get back to my hotel until midnight. I tried to sleep, but kept waking up and checking my BlackBerry as if I might find a message that said: "What you think happened today did not really happen."

Instead, I received an email from the President:

> I'm so sorry about today—heartbreaking. I know you know rationally that bad stuff like this happens, and there's nothing you could have done differently to anticipate it. But given the emotions it surely evokes, it's worth hearing from your friend that I don't know anyone who cares more about people, and your work saves countless lives, and I couldn't be prouder of you. So hang in there. Much love.

"Hang in there" seemed the operative words. Knowing that Colin, Gideon, Kurtis, Becca, and others were probably just as sleepless and tormented in their own rooms, I spent the next hour sending them individual emails of thanks and support.

"I was so glad you were by my side," I wrote to Becca, "though I wish for your sake you could have been elsewhere."

OVER THE NEXT WEEK, I met with the presidents of the three countries we were visiting: Paul Biya of Cameroon, Idriss Déby of Chad, and Muhammadu Buhari of Nigeria. Because I had spoken with civilians before each of these meetings, I was able to describe not only the devastation being caused by Boko Haram but also the damage the presidents' own militaries were doing with their mass roundups and seeming indifference to the starvation that loomed.

Presidential advisers shuffled awkwardly in their chairs as I spoke, some even interjecting to claim that I was misinformed—or lying. But I was able to present a detailed litany of the facts that our delegation had gathered. I and the deputy commander of US forces in Africa each spoke with humility about the challenges of fighting terrorists. We stressed that military force alone would not solve their problems, describing how torture and civilian casualties had set back US efforts to defeat al-Qaeda in Afghanistan and Iraq.

I also held a very difficult meeting with the grief-stricken parents of the abducted Chibok girls. When I arrived at the park where they held daily vigils, I was handed a card bearing the name of Aisha Ezekiel, a teenager who had been missing for 738 days.* A woman draped head to toe in a bright red *chador* stood and declared:

> Our Chibok girls are no longer just children from Chibok. They are no longer just children from Nigeria . . . Aisha Ezekiel is now *your* daughter. As long as Chibok girls are in captivity, we are *all* in captivity. Humanity is in captivity.

A father then pleaded with us not to allow his daughter to be punished simply for wanting an education. "Take our cry to the world," he implored me. The parents could not comprehend how a country as powerful as the United States, with all of our sophisticated surveillance tools, could not find their daughters. I knew nothing I said would be satisfying, but I took the microphone that had been passed among the parents.

"What I can tell you, as a personal representative of President Obama, is that we will never give up," I said. "Just as you will never give up. We will never give up." I believed that our intensifying efforts would help, but I did not want to raise false hopes.

When I got back to New York, I joined others in the US government in pressing the leading UN humanitarian organizations to declare what is known as a "Level 3 emergency"—the highest level at the UN—in order to focus attention and resources on the severity of the looming famine. The resulting Level 3 declarations, which were made over the following months, enabled UN agencies to channel more funds to the region. I also lobbied the secretary-general to chair a high-level event at the next UN General Assembly, which he did, raising an additional $168 million in humanitarian assistance for the people menaced by Boko Haram.

---

* Since 2016, more than 100 of the 219 Chibok girls who ended up in captivity have either escaped or been freed by Boko Haram. Aisha was one of the girls released by the group in 2017 following negotiations with the Nigerian government.

Separately, I worked closely with the State Department as we sought to mobilize support for the Birwe family. Because such accidents had unfortunately happened before, an established protocol existed for how to provide funds to the families. Toussaint's family ultimately received restitution many times greater than the protocol stipulated, and the State Department also funded the construction of a well in Toussaint's honor, providing fresh drinking water for his village.

In an area of such extreme poverty, with no tradition of saving, I recognized that the infusion of money would only last so long. I wanted, in some small way, to do something meaningful for Toussaint's four siblings, so Cass and I established an escrow account in Cameroon to fund their primary and secondary schooling.

TOUSSAINT'S DEATH FORCED ME to more directly confront a charge often made against the United States—that even when we try to do right, we invariably end up making situations worse. I knew the force of this argument. In the dark days after we returned home, no matter what anybody tried to tell me, I fixated on the suffering our visit had brought about.

As the weeks passed, however, I began to think about the impact of our efforts differently. Although my sense of responsibility for the accident would never abate, I began to take pride in what our delegation had tried to accomplish. Being a public servant requires making decisions every day—decisions that can have unintended outcomes, even life or death consequences.

The road to hell is paved with good intentions, to be sure. But turning a blind eye to the toughest problems in the world is a guaranteed shortcut to the same destination.

As a young reporter watching American motorcades zoom by in Bosnia, I judged the people inside only by what they achieved in the moment. I could not fathom just how long it sometimes took to see a return on their investment. I also never considered what the former Yugoslavia would have looked like if the United States had *not* shown up.

Each member of our delegation had taken personal risks by traveling to Cameroon, Chad, and Nigeria, and had done so out of a conviction that our fates were somehow linked to those of people thousands of miles away. Every day, while nobody was watching, young boys and girls were dying in the countries we visited because of malnutrition, disease, military violence, and terrorism. We visited because we were determined to help in a way that we knew no other country would. After the accident, people in the region had gone out of their way to thank us for being there. Amid the warnings of impending famine, we had announced new humanitarian assistance, and we had pressured governments to cease their human rights abuses and better facilitate international relief initiatives. These efforts mattered and would continue to matter.

We had also gathered ideas for how to advise President Obama following our return. Thanks to a strong White House push from Susan, the United States stepped up its efforts against Boko Haram. In 2016, as the regional coalition further pushed the terrorists out of the territory they had seized, deaths at the hands of Boko Haram dropped by 80 percent from the previous year. And humanitarian organizations finally gained access to parts of the region in dire need of support.*

Toussaint's death also concentrated my focus on Declan and Rían. Since I first met Barack Obama in 2005, I had managed to get married and build a family. But my kids were not seeing enough of me. My father's sudden death during my childhood had shown me that tragedy could strike in an instant. But Toussaint's death once again brought that stark reality to the surface. So much of what happens is beyond our control.

Yet how we use the time we have is within our control. Representing the United States at the United Nations, I was doing the most ful-

---

* Progress against Boko Haram has been uneven since 2016. Despite the splintering of the group into competing factions and claims by the Nigerian government that it had been defeated, Boko Haram militants continue to kidnap children and launch deadly attacks. Although fewer people are being killed than in the 2013–2015 period and Boko Haram controls far less territory than it once did, the group still constitutes a threat to millions of people, and human rights abuses perpetrated by the regional militaries are still rampant.

filling work of my career. When the Obama administration ended in 2017, I would have liked nothing more than to find a way to continue serving as a diplomat if Hillary Clinton became president. But I knew that instead I would need to leave government and finally build a home for my family. I needed to get closer to those I loved most.

37

THE GOLDEN DOOR

One fall afternoon, I got an excited call from María. After living in the United States for seventeen years, she had received a date to be sworn in as an American citizen.

Born near Guadalajara, Mexico, María Isabel Castro Gonzalez was one of ten children. Her dad was a farmer, her mother a shopkeeper. She had married young and, in 1998, at age thirty-one, moved with her husband and four children to Virginia, where he had found work as a builder. Cass and I first met María when one of his colleagues recommended her as an occasional babysitter. But the moment I saw the way she held our then-infant Declan, I had asked if she would consider becoming our live-in nanny.

María had tremendous energy. She kept running lists in her mind of all that she needed to do in a day or week, and when she got to the end of one list, she would immediately devise a new one. She was a perfectionist about her work and managed almost all aspects of our household when I was in government. She also made time to attend daily Mass during the week. Because Declan and Rían often accompanied her, to this day they say their Our Fathers and Hail Marys in Spanish. María's faith in God's love gave her an optimism and joy that I almost never saw falter. Knowing she was watching over our kids made it possible for me to work while having peace of mind about their well-being. Her presence in our family was a profound blessing.

I had spoken previously at naturalization ceremonies and wanted to help celebrate María's big day. I offered to give brief remarks at the event where she would officially become a citizen.

Like many Americans, I was familiar with one of the verses from Emma Lazarus's "The New Colossus," the poem engraved on the base of the Statue of Liberty: "Give me your tired, your poor, Your huddled masses yearning to breathe free." But as I reread Lazarus's poem on the drive to María's ceremony, I took special note of her final line: "I lift my lamp beside the golden door!" Mum, Eddie, Stephen, and I had entered through that door, and now María would do the same.

That morning, she would take the Oath of Allegiance alongside people originating from twenty-eight countries. I could only imagine what each had been through to gain a foothold and integrate themselves into American society. And as I looked out onto the crowd of expectant new Americans, I could see the pride in their faces: they felt they had *earned* their citizenship.

The ugly political winds in the United States contrasted sharply with the earnest gravity of the occasion. Donald Trump had launched his campaign for President on a platform that blatantly stoked fear about immigrants and refugees, falsely depicting them as criminals and terrorists who were cannily masquerading as persecuted civilians. Among his proposals, he had called for a "total and complete shutdown of Muslims entering the United States," claiming such a ban would prevent terrorism.* Back in 1979, when my family moved to Pittsburgh, the Troubles were still roiling Northern Ireland and terrorists had killed civilians in Dublin, my hometown. The repulsive ideology of judging (and punishing) people collectively due to nationality or religion could have kept my family and other Irish immigrants out of the United States.

In my speech at María's naturalization, I decided to address these worrying forces. For as long as the United States had existed, I said,

---

* Terrorists in fact made use of what Trump was doing—branding all "Muslims" as a threat—to try to broaden their appeal. In 2016, for example, clips of Trump's campaign rhetoric were featured in recruitment videos for both ISIS and al-Shabaab (the al-Qaeda affiliate based in Somalia).

some people had claimed to represent "an original, pure America" and defined themselves in opposition to immigrants. Nativists had once stigmatized Chinese, Irish, Italian, and Jewish arrivals. Now they had turned on Latinos and people of Muslim faith. In the face of such fear-mongering, I urged those taking the oath that day not to hide where they came from, but to celebrate it.

The audience included not only those being naturalized, but Eddie, Declan, Rían, and several of my friends who had become María's over the years. I recounted her journey from Mexico to the United States, describing all she had sacrificed for her family and for mine.

"She's not only taught my children her language," I said, "but more importantly, she's taught them her values. How to listen. How to treat people with respect and dignity. How to live life and treasure the small wonders every day."

María had held on to all she learned in Mexico, I said, "and now my kids will carry what María teaches them for the rest of their lives."

When I returned to the US Mission after the ceremony, I was struck that the faces in a typical US government office did not look all that different from the courthouse I had just left. I had heard foreign ambassadors remark on the power of President Clinton choosing Czech refugee Madeleine Albright to represent the United States at the UN, President Bush naming Afghan immigrant Zalmay Khalilzad, and President Obama selecting me. But immigrants defined every part of American society.

Kelly Razzouk, the human rights adviser at the Mission, was the daughter of a Lebanese man who had escaped his country's civil war as a nineteen-year-old, carrying with him just two pairs of pants. Kam Wong, the mission's longest serving administrative assistant, had worked for the State Department for twenty-five years. Her father had fled Communist China when she was an infant. After spending his family's savings on a boat ticket to America, he had worked shifts in a Chinese restaurant in Iowa until he could send for his wife and new-born daughter.

The parents of my military adviser, Colonel Mike Rauhut, were German survivors of World War II who had made their way to the

United States when the Berlin Wall went up in 1961. By coincidence, their son Mike had been stationed in Berlin when East and West Germany were unified in 1990, and on the day of reunification he had walked through Brandenburg Gate with his mother. Mike would go on to become a decorated officer, serving tours in Iraq and Afghanistan.

Wa'el Alzayat, one of my Middle East advisers, had immigrated with his family to the United States from Syria when he was a teenager. Wa'el's father, a former colonel in the Syrian Air Force, drove limousines and ice cream trucks before returning to school in his fifties to become a semiconductor testing engineer. Wa'el, meanwhile, studied at top American universities and then joined the State Department.

Maher Bitar, my deputy in Washington, was the son of a Palestinian father and an Egyptian mother who had met in Beirut before being displaced by Lebanon's civil war. Maher spoke Arabic, French, and German and had gotten his law degree at Georgetown by taking night classes while serving as an aide to Middle East peace envoys George Mitchell and David Hale. My assistant Manya-Jean Gitter's grandfather had been a prominent Jewish businessman and her grandmother a well-known psychologist in Vienna. After Hitler annexed Austria in 1938 and the Nazis began confiscating Jewish property, her grandparents, each of whom spoke six languages, fled with their young son, Manya's father, to New York City. Manya's grandparents learned after the war that their parents and many of their siblings, nieces, and nephews had been murdered in the Holocaust.

Along with María, so many of the people I relied upon every day—patriots who often worked seven days a week to promote US interests—were themselves immigrants or children of immigrants. The United States is the only country at the UN about which this is true.

IN SEPTEMBER OF 2015, the lifeless body of Alan Kurdi, a two-year-old Syrian boy in a red T-shirt and tiny Velcro shoes, was photographed after he washed up on a Turkish shore. When an inflatable dinghy bound for Greece had capsized, Alan had drowned, along with his mother and five-year-old brother. The image ran on the front page of newspapers all over the world, focusing people on the danger that refugees endured in their search for safety. By the time of Kurdi's death, some 65 million people in the world had been displaced, with an additional 34,000 people fleeing their homes each day.[46]

In the decades since the US government had slammed its doors on thousands of Jews seeking refuge from the Nazis during World War II, America had become the world's leader in responding to refugee crises, resettling more than four million people. Even after the fear brought about by the September 11th terrorist attacks, the Bush administration had still managed to resettle an average of nearly 45,000 refugees each year. Yet from the start of the Syrian civil war in 2011 until that September in 2015 when Alan Kurdi died, while the United States had admitted more than 284,000 refugees of other nationalities, we had only taken in 1,484 Syrians. This was a tiny fraction of the nearly five million people who had poured out of the country.

On trips to places like Jordan, Turkey, and Germany, I would meet Syrian refugees desperate to find somewhere safe to restart their cruelly interrupted lives. At a refugee center in Amman, I spoke with a twelve-year-old boy named Ibraheem who had lost his mother and four siblings after Assad's forces struck his home near Damascus with a barrel bomb. Because Ibraheem couldn't walk after the attack, his father had carried him in his arms for eight months in a desperate quest to find a doctor who could remove the shrapnel in Ibraheem's head, chest, and leg. Ibraheem eventually got the specialized care he needed, but only when he reached Winnipeg, Canada, where he and his father found refuge and where Ibraheem is now a high school student.

On one visit, I was introduced to an extraordinary Syrian Kurd from Aleppo named Nujeen Mustafa. Nujeen, who was seventeen years old, had cerebral palsy and needed a wheelchair to get around. Unable to attend school even before the war, she had educated herself and became fluent in English from watching American television shows like *Days of Our Lives*. In 2014, she and her family had fled Syria, and Nujeen began a 3,500-mile wheelchair journey, traversing Turkey, Greece, Macedonia, Serbia, Hungary, Croatia, Slovenia, and Austria before arriving in Germany. Her older sister Nisreen had stayed by her side, helping push her wheelchair during their sixteen-month trek. When I met the two sisters in Berlin, I asked Nujeen why so many Syrians like her risked drowning in the rough waters of the Mediterranean for an uncertain future in Europe. She explained that their motivation was elemental: "People are dying every day for the chance to brush their teeth in the morning and go to school."

In the early years of the war, Syrian refugees had not intended to resettle in faraway places like Germany or the United States. They had instead remained in Jordan, Lebanon, and Turkey so they would be nearby when the time came to return home. But as the war dragged on, many lost hope and began trying to move to Western countries, where they hoped to find work and build new lives. Not until 2015 did the UN refugee agency ask the Obama administration if the United States would be willing to resettle several thousand Syrians. Unfortunately, with Republicans caricaturing those in flight as dangerous threats, senior officials in the Department of Homeland Security and the White House claimed the political support did not exist to take in large numbers. Kurdi's death, however, became a catalyst for reopening the internal Obama administration debate over how many Syrians we could admit.

Taking in Syrian refugees wasn't mere charity; we had real national security interests at stake.[47] Most refugees were living in countries of modest means, with fragile political systems or recent histories of violence. For all the political noise generated in countries like the US, almost 90 percent of the world's refugee population had fled to low- and middle-income countries.[48] Lebanon, for example, had become home to more than a million Syrian refugees since the start of the war. By the time of Alan Kurdi's death, one in every five people in the country was a refugee—roughly the equivalent of the United States receiving *64 million* new Canadians or Mexicans. Other frontline states like Jordan were experiencing similarly huge influxes.

Despite being a cauldron of sectarian tensions, Lebanon had somehow managed to avoid returning to conflict even as its neighbor, Syria, was engulfed in flames. But Lebanon's generosity was putting an impossible strain on its infrastructure and politics. The more refugees the United States and other wealthy countries could accept, the more we could lobby other countries to do—and ultimately the lighter the load the Lebanese would carry.

The US government's first responsibility was of course to keep the American people safe, and US officials were determined to prevent violent extremist groups from planting terrorists among resettled refugees. When I served on the NSC staff, I had seen all that our counterterrorism experts had done to strengthen the screening process. The Department of Homeland Security vetted refugee applicants against multiple databases, including those maintained by the National Counterterrorism Center, the FBI, and the Department of Defense. Refugees were also interviewed, often several times, before ever being allowed to travel to the United States. For Syrians, we had even put in place an additional layer of review to ensure that US officials thoroughly interrogated even the smallest inconsistency or gap in information. A typical application took more than a year to vet. Some took much longer.

Candidate Trump repeatedly lied about this process, promoting falsehoods like, "We have no idea who [refugees] are, where they come from. There's no documentation. There's no paperwork."[49] In fact, two-thirds of all of the refugees who had come to the US in the previous decade were women and children—and we knew who they were. Of the millions of refugees admitted to the United States since the landmark Refugee Act of 1980, not one has carried out a lethal act of domestic terrorism.

Along with many others—most notably White House chief of staff Denis McDonough, who had gotten to know Vietnamese refugees through his church as a child—I urged that the administration increase the number of refugees accepted into the United States. Recognizing that the more people we admitted, the more we could reasonably urge other nations to take, President Obama increased the national "cap" on refugees from 70,000 in 2015 to 85,000 in 2016, and designated at least 10,000 spots for Syrians. In 2016, he would set the cap for the following year at 110,000 refugees—a bold message to world leaders, who typically looked to see what the United States did before themselves acting.*

Unfortunately, as our administration tried to respond to the growing need to take vetted Syrian families, prominent Republicans—perhaps eyeing Trump's political ascent—took up his cause. Two months after Kurdi's death provoked such an outpouring, coordinated terrorist attacks in Paris perpetrated by followers of ISIS killed 130 people. In the immediate wake of these attacks, thirty-one governors—thirty of them Republicans—made statements opposing the resettlement of Syrian refugees in their states. And within a week, the Republican-controlled House had passed a bill that would have effectively halted the admission of Syrians.[50]

The political battle lines were drawn, with the fate of vulnerable refugees suddenly at the center of a national debate about American identity and security. Hearteningly, I began to hear from a growing number of people—through emails, letters to the US Mission, and queries on my Twitter feed—asking what they themselves could do to help refugees.[51] Mum and Eddie were among those who felt compelled to do more; along with their neighbors, they sponsored a recently arrived Afghan father and son who moved in with them for several months while the father looked for work.

When I dropped by an International Rescue Committee office in New York to thank volunteers who were teaching English to resettled refugees, I couldn't help but notice the vast number of boxes piled in the hallways and on desks. When the office director saw my puzzlement, she explained, "It's donations. Ever since politicians started demonizing refugees, the grassroots response has been incredible. We can't keep up. Toys, clothes, money—we are overwhelmed."

---

* Despite President Obama setting the 2017 refugee cap at 110,000, President Trump's travel ban—which temporarily halted refugee admissions—meant that fewer than 54,000 refugees were actually resettled in the US during 2017. The Trump administration has since further reduced refugee admissions, resettling 22,491 refugees in 2018. From September 2015 to January 2017, the Obama administration welcomed approximately 17,000 Syrian refugees. In 2018, the Trump administration admitted 62 Syrian refugees.

Seeing this, I wondered how many more people would help if they knew what they personally could do. I asked my team whether the US government could create a website where individuals would enter their zip code to learn which nearby organizations needed help welcoming refugees into the community. Although it took months, NSC aide Ronnie Newman worked with the web designers at the White House to create *aidrefugees.gov*, a site that allowed users to easily find out how they could offer after-school tutoring or provide groceries, bed linens, or even rides to job interviews.[52]

In order to fulfill President Obama's promise to admit 10,000 vetted Syrians, Deputy National Security Advisor Avril Haines, Deputy Homeland Security Advisor Amy Pope, President Obama's human rights adviser Steve Pomper, Ronnie, and others pushed the entire administration to innovate in new ways. The US Digital Service, a team of information technology experts at the White House, computerized the paper processes and studied the data to understand the source of bureaucratic bottlenecks. For the first time, the different agencies involved in vetting sat together in a fusion cell to work through issues that arose. And once the President had announced the US goal, the Department of Homeland Security brought on new staff to its "refugee corps" in order to interview refugees and process their applications. When DHS and the intelligence community put out the call for volunteers to join the refugee processing effort, many dozens of civil servants stepped forward, working around the clock to be sure that applicants in the pipeline got a fair hearing.

My team and I also worked with Steve and others at the NSC to help organize a refugee summit, the first of its kind, which President Obama hosted during the UN General Assembly. As the United States had done during the Ebola outbreak, we used our enhanced commitments to push other countries to do more. We also made sure to recognize the extraordinary leadership shown by American partners like Germany and Canada, where Chancellor Angela Merkel and Prime Minister Justin Trudeau had boldly welcomed Syrian families in the face of domestic political backlash. By the time the summit ended, Obama had mobilized more than $4 billion in new funding for refugees, while doubling the number of displaced that countries around the world planned to admit.[53]

Recognizing that all sectors of society needed to be involved in managing the largest displacement crisis since World War II, I also partnered with Obama's senior adviser Valerie Jarrett to help the President convene at the UN several dozen CEOs, who made $650 million worth of specific pledges to support refugees. A leader in this effort was Hamdi Ulukaya, a Turkish immigrant to the United States who built his Chobani yogurt company into an industry giant while going out of his way to employ immigrants and refugees. Ulukaya pledged at Obama's business summit to take responsibility for ensuring corporate follow-through after the President left office. Through what he calls the Tent Partnership for Refugees, Ulukaya has thus far enlisted 130 companies to house, provide banking and other services for, and—most precious of all—hire refugees.

IN ORDER TO LEARN how resettled families were faring at such a politically inflamed time, I reached out to offer support to a recently arrived Syrian family. At our first meeting, Morad and Ola Al-Teibawi and their five children joined Mum, Eddie, Laura, María, and the kids for an evening together in the Waldorf residence. Rían and Rama, their young daughter of the same age, colored together, and Declan befriended the middle son, an eleven-year-old named Mohamed. Mohamed did not yet speak English, but quickly showed he was up for any sport that Declan was willing to play.

As I put Declan to bed after the dinner, he peppered me with questions about his new friend. Why, he wanted to know, did Mohamed have to leave his home in Syria?

When I said that Mohamed's home had been destroyed by Assad's warplanes, Declan asked if we could help get bricks to rebuild it.

I explained that Assad's forces would probably just bomb the house again.

"Why doesn't Obama make Assad stop?" Declan asked.

"Because America has been in two really hard wars over the last fifteen years, and he doesn't want to start another one," I said. "It is also really hard to use war to make things better and save people. Often it doesn't work."

"But then Assad will keep doing what he's doing to kids like Mohamed," Declan replied.

"And to Syrian grown-ups too," I added.

"Can't Obama at least stop the airplanes?" Declan asked.

I couldn't believe I was on the verge of debating the merits of a no-fly zone with my young son.

When I left the Waldorf each morning to take Declan to school, I picked up the *New York Times* from the guard stationed outside our apartment. Declan made a game out of grabbing the paper before me and racing down the long, carpeted hallway, daring me to catch him. As he did this, he would often glimpse whatever image was on the front page.

"Why do the kids in Syria always put white and gray powder on their faces?" he asked me one day.

Initially confused, I quickly realized that almost all the photos my son had seen of Syrian children were taken after bombings, which left them caked in dust from the debris.

Declan and Rían fortunately did not see the film of dazed and traumatized Omran Daqneesh, a five-year-old boy injured after a government air strike in a rebel-held area of Aleppo. A local activist captured footage of Omran covered in blood and dirt as he sat barefoot and alone in the back of an ambulance. As with Alan Kurdi, the image went viral, concentrating the world's attention for a fleeting moment on the agony Syrians were enduring.

When someone in the White House circulated a letter that an American boy around Declan's age had written President Obama about Omran, I decided to read it to my son.

Dear President Obama,

Remember the boy who was picked up by the ambulance in Syria? Can you please go get him and bring him to [my home]? Park in the driveway or on the street and we will be waiting for you guys with flags, flowers, and balloons. We will give him a family and he will be our brother. Catherine, my little sister, will be collecting butterflies and fireflies for him. In my school, I have a friend from Syria, Omar, and I will introduce him to Omar. We can all play together. We can invite him to birthday parties and he will teach us another language. We can teach him English too, just like my friend Aoto from Japan.

Please tell him that his brother will be Alex who is a very kind boy, just like him. Since he won't bring toys and doesn't have toys Catherine will share her big blue stripy white bunny. And I will share my bike and I will teach him how to ride it. I will teach him additions and subtractions in math. And he [can] smell Catherine's lip gloss penguin which is green. She doesn't let anyone touch it.

Thank you very much! I can't wait for you to come!

Alex

Alex lived close to New York City, so when Declan asked if I could set up a play date, I contacted his family and invited them to the UN. When Alex arrived, Declan shyly introduced himself as if he were meeting a superhero. The boys took turns sitting in the Security Council president's chair, banging the gavel used to start meetings.

As I watched Declan and Alex presiding over an imaginary meeting, it was hard to escape the thought that perhaps we would be better off with the children of the world in charge.

38

EXIT, VOICE, LOYALTY

In 2016, I met Raed Saleh, a thirty-two-year-old former electronics salesman who led Syria's fearless rescue and recovery volunteers. Known as the White Helmets, they were estimated to have helped save some 50,000 lives since their founding in 2013. More than 140 of their men had been killed in the line of duty, including dozens of Saleh's friends. Their motto was drawn from the Quran: "To save a life is to save all of humanity."[54]

The previous year, Russia had intervened militarily in Syria, sending heavy weapons, fighter jets, and thousands of soldiers in support of President Assad. Saleh was visiting New York and Washington in a desperate bid to lobby the United States government to set up a no-fly zone to protect civilians who were being killed in large numbers.[55] I was in awe of Saleh's organization. But knowing that US Syria policy was very unlikely to change, I had been dreading seeing him.

I ushered Saleh into my office at the US Mission to the UN. The walls were decorated with my children's artwork, a watercolor of the town in Ireland where I'd been married, and, near my desk, a map of Syria. On my bookshelves, alongside photos of Cass and our kids, I kept the program from Richard Holbrooke's memorial, a photo of a Liberian Ebola survivor being welcomed home by her family, and a basketball President Obama had inscribed to me.

Saleh took note of an enormous tome that stretched the width of the coffee table where we sat. Given to me by Abraham Foxman of the Anti-Defamation League, the book's pages bore the word "Jew" printed in tiny letters over and over—six million times.

Saleh spoke in Arabic while a Syrian opposition activist translated into English. He described Syrian and Russian aircraft pulverizing civilian neighborhoods, using "bunker bombs" to target people hiding in the basements of their apartment buildings. He confirmed news reports that fighter jets were deliberately hunting down the White Helmets as they tried to rescue those trapped in the wreckage. In the previous week alone, he estimated, 1,000 Syrians had been killed.

I heard myself begin, "Well, hopefully, we can . . ." But then, catching Saleh's gaze, I stopped.

He had pulled the bodies of dead children from the rubble of Assad's air strikes. He had seen the damage that chemical weapons, shattered glass, and falling cement did to the human body. He deserved more than hollow words. I just looked at him as we sat across from each other.

Instead of filling the silence, Saleh just stared back. For an entire minute, perhaps even two, neither of us said anything.

For all of the words that had been expended in the White House Situation Room and the UN Security Council, I knew that neither the United States government nor the governments of other capable countries were planning to confront a scale of evil rarely seen in this world. Syrian civilians were going to remain besieged until they surrendered to the Assad regime. And when they capitulated, even worse could follow.

While our discussion eventually resumed, it was tense. After I said goodbye to Saleh, my speechwriter Nik Steinberg reflected, "Every official in the US government should be required to sit through a meeting like that and have to justify our response."

FROM MY EARLIEST DAYS in the job, I had heard calls for my resignation over our administration's Syria policy.

"UN Ambassador Samantha Power made her reputation by denouncing Western indifference to the types of atrocities the Assad regime is committing by the day," wrote the *Wall Street Journal* editorial board. "She of all people could set a fine example here of choosing principle over power." In a *Washington Post* piece titled, "You Got Some Nerve, Madame Ambassador," opinion columnist Jennifer Rubin wrote, "In a better world, you'd resign, give back the Pulitzer and do something more constructive. Write a sequel, perhaps, about the age of genocide. You've been there, every step of the way."

Rubin did not relent, calling for me to step down in three more articles, including one in which she asserted that I was remaining in the administration out of an "unwillingness to sacrifice career or monetary benefits (or fancy New York lodging) for the sake of principle."

Opinion pieces like this were extremely upsetting to Mum and Eddie, although they had very different reactions to them. Eddie's approach was to go after the messenger. "Bastards," he would rage at some of the more caustic takedowns. "What have these columnists ever done for anybody?"

Inevitably, he would then say, "Obama should call a press conference to go out and defend you." He must have suggested this a half dozen times, despite my reminders that the President had a country to run and was himself being subjected to far more severe and damaging attacks.

My mother, an insomniac in the best of circumstances, stayed up all night every time a friend of hers carelessly forwarded an article condemning my terribleness. "Just keep doing your best, Sam," she would say.

Friends of mine seemed surprised that I wasn't more rattled by these denunciations. But if events in Syria did nothing else, they gave me perspective. Syrians are suffering unimaginable losses, I thought; I am getting some bad press.

But despite this logical response to criticisms of me personally, I was often flattened with horror by what was happening in Syria itself. When I would read the details of some new massacre, I often closed my office door and prayed for those begging for rescue, appealing also for wisdom as to how I could help. In February of 1994, when Bosnian Serbs had shelled the market in Sarajevo, killing sixty-eight shoppers and vendors, the attack had outraged people everywhere and led the world news for days. In Syria, almost as many civilians were dying every single day—attacked in their homes and schools, deliberately starved to death, shot by snipers, and executed in Syria's prisons in a depraved and methodically documented murder scheme.[56]

One of the most vocal public advocates for greater US involvement in Syria was Senator McCain. I had worked with McCain during my years at the White House, and he had supported me during my confirmation process. So when he placed a hold on Deputy National Security Advisor Antony Blinken's nomination to become Obama's Deputy Secretary of State, I volunteered to call the senator to smooth out the situation.

"McCain and I have a great relationship," I assured Blinken. "I've got this."

Our call began calmly. I told McCain that if he allowed the nomination to go forward, Blinken would become an important voice within the administration for doing more to protect Syrian civilians. As I finished my pitch, the senator erupted.

"What planet are you living on?" he shouted.

Sitting at my desk in New York, I held the receiver away from my ear. For the next several minutes, McCain did not seem to take a breath as he denounced Obama and what he deemed our administration's "complete indifference to human life."

Initially, I took notes, scribbling down McCain's points so I could respond to them. Many of his arguments about the gap between our objectives and what we were doing to realize them were ones I had made in the Situation Room, so I was achingly familiar with the rebuttals.

I started by citing Congress's opposition to the use of force in response to Assad's 2013 chemical weapons attack—a reflection of how unenthusiastic the American people were for a military engagement in Syria. McCain interrupted me.

"That is a complete cop-out!" he shouted. "Barack Obama has spent the last several years telling the American people that getting involved in Syria would be a disaster, and now he claims that he's not getting involved because the American people had the decency to listen to him!"

I tried bringing the conversation back to the importance of having Blinken in the Situation Room, where he could influence the direction of our debates. But McCain had had enough.

"You know what—not only should Blinken never be confirmed by the US Senate, but you should resign. NOW!"

The line went dead. He had hung up.

FROM THE EARLIEST STAGES of Syria's war, I had weighed the risks of any new US action against the risks of maintaining the general direction of our policy. As I considered the potential dangers in either direction—first as a White House staffer, and then as UN ambassador—I had tried not only to factor in the harms of the present, and all that could go wrong if we deepened our involvement, but also to assess what the trends in the conflict portended for Syria, the Middle East region, and the United States.

From 2012 onward, it was clear that if the United States and others did not alter the trajectory of the Syrian war, the consequences would extend well beyond the hundreds of thousands of lives that would be lost in Syria. Millions of refugees would pour into neighboring countries. Terrorists would continue to draw recruits, lured by the sectarian conflict. Foreign fighters, radicalized and battle-hardened, would eventually seek to return from Syria to the United States and Europe.*

President Obama frequently convened us to discuss options for jump-starting the stalled diplomatic process and limiting the carnage. In these meetings, I and others argued that the United States should accept greater risk in the present to prevent more horrific and extensive harm down the road. We suggested measures including air-dropping food parcels to besieged civilians being starved to death by Assad's forces, significantly increasing our support for the Syrian military opposition so they could better defend civilians from Assad's attacks, and

---

* An estimated 40,000 people from more than one hundred countries ultimately traveled to Iraq and Syria to become foreign fighters for ISIS, including approximately 5,000 residents of European Union countries and around 130 Americans.

creating a no-fly zone over select areas of Syria that were under opposition control.

Each of these proposals came with potential benefits and risks. The no-fly zone, for example, could both protect civilians and neutralize the Syrian government's singular advantage: its ability to bomb populations into submission. Unlike Qaddafi in Libya, Assad used air power as a key tool of terror and death. If government forces were unable to inflict harm from the air, they would be more likely to seriously consider peace negotiations. Hampering Assad's ability to destroy pockets of the opposition would also lead to fewer refugees fleeing the country. However, the Pentagon estimated that Syria had five times the air defense capability as Libya, meaning that the US military would first have had to destroy Syrian anti-aircraft systems before putting in place any no-fly zone.

Obama demanded and reviewed proposals such as these, and those of us advocating for new measures earnestly prepared for every meeting by refining and adapting them based on evolving battlefield and geopolitical dynamics. But ever since the President had pulled back from air strikes in August of 2013, he had been looking for lower-risk options to impact the direction of the war—which didn't exist.

Our internal debates became circular and unproductive. In meeting after meeting, participants would emerge better informed about the conflict, yet even more polarized in our respective views on what the United States should—or shouldn't—do differently.

Once, when President Obama began a Situation Room discussion on Syria by remarking, "I don't expect a solution out of today's meeting," the Chairman of the Joint Chiefs Martin Dempsey quipped, "We won't disappoint you there, sir."

Cass had introduced me to the behavioral science concept of "confirmation bias"—the inclination to hunt for, interpret, and remember information in a manner that confirms one's preexisting beliefs. None of us was immune to this tendency, which Simon and Garfunkel had so aptly summed up in "The Boxer": "A man hears what he wants to hear and disregards the rest." I would leave many meetings on Syria unable to get the song's refrain out of my head: "Lye-la-lye, lye-la-la-la-lye-la-lye, lye-la-lye . . ."

On several occasions, President Obama reprimanded me for comments he thought were dogmatic or sanctimonious.

"We've all read your book, Samantha," he snapped in one Situation Room meeting. I looked down, chastened. But fifteen minutes later, he said, "Let's get back to the point Sam made earlier . . ." He seemed to be trying to rehabilitate me, knowing that his criticisms could make me less influential in meetings he wasn't chairing.

Likewise, following a different meeting, he telephoned to complain about something I had said.

"You are trying to tutor us as to why this is such a shit show," he said. "People are heartbroken and anguished. I rack my brain and my conscience constantly. But I can't answer in practical terms what we can do."

As someone who talked often about the humanitarian dimensions of various crises, I knew the risk of coming across as self-righteous. I went out of my way to avoid impugning my colleagues or sounding strident. Even when I was an activist and outsider, I believed that making—and criticizing—US foreign policy should be done with humility. I did not think Obama's interpretation of my comments was fair, so I pulled out my notebook during our call and read to him precisely what I had said in the meeting. I wanted to demonstrate that I *had* offered a concrete recommendation and grappled with the very real constraints that he faced. I never wanted to fall into the trap of "admiring the problem."

Obama conceded the point, but added, "You don't always come across the way you think." Given the horrors happening day after day in Syria, I was not entirely surprised.

On no other issue did I see Obama so personally torn—convinced that even limited military action would mire the United States in another open-ended conflict, yet wracked by the human toll of the slaughter. I don't believe he ever stopped interrogating his choices.

While Syria brought only grim news, Obama refused to allow it to dictate his overall outlook on humanity's capacity for progress over time. He professed a distinct optimism about what the future held for the world. "We're pushing in the direction of more security, more international norms and rules, more human rights, more free speech, less religious intolerance," Obama said in a typical interview in 2015. His hopeful disposition often became intertwined with a belief that the US government could do best by avoiding foreign policy mistakes of the kind it had so often made. His memorable mantra for how he evaluated options in this arena became "don't do stupid shit."

In choosing me as UN ambassador, Obama knew he was appointing someone impatient about present-day harms. Even as I tried never to identify a problem without offering recommendations for what the United States could do about it, I was not shy about bombarding him with statistics highlighting the global decline in freedom and rise in inequality over the previous decade. When I did so, he would throw back data on the tremendous gains in maternal health, poverty, and literacy, or note that the number of democracies around the world had nearly doubled since the end of the Cold War.

While Obama told me many times, "you get on my nerves," he didn't push me away. On the rare occasions when I didn't speak during a national security debate, he would joke, "Are you sick, Power?" or draw me out by saying, "Samantha has that skeptical look again." In our very first meeting over dinner in 2005, he had said he synthesized ideas well. He seemed to want my perspective and my sense of urgency in the mix.

AFTER ASSAD'S CHEMICAL WEAPONS ATTACKS in 2013, I believe that the United States should have followed through on Obama's threats and bombed the Syrian military targets designated by the Pentagon. Even having not taken this step, before Russia intervened militarily two years later, we should have at least attempted to mobilize a group of countries to enforce a no-fly zone. If implemented, this would have offered some civilians protection from Syrian air assaults. In light of the complexity of the conflict and the vast number of factions that became involved, these steps in and of themselves would certainly not have ended the war. But they could have mitigated some of its most egregious effects and potentially helped ignite the diplomacy necessary to establish a cease-fire.

Starting in 2014, however, the Obama administration's priority in Syria shifted from ending the civil war to confronting the terrifying rise of ISIS. President Obama directed a comprehensive effort to defeat what was quickly becoming both the world's most lethal terrorist organization and an alarming threat to American national security.

After overseeing the removal of American forces from Iraq in 2011, Obama sent thousands of troops back to the country, at the behest of the Iraqi government, to take part in the fight against ISIS. By 2015, the US-led military coalition had begun to make significant headway, helping liberate territory held by ISIS in both Iraq and neighboring Syria. At the UN, my team and I helped spearhead the passage of a number of anti-ISIS resolutions in support of the coalition's efforts. We crafted new laws requiring UN member states to prevent foreign fighters from traveling to Syria to join ISIS. We made it far harder for ISIS to access funds to pay those in their ranks. And we targeted ISIS's looting and sale of Syria's highly coveted cultural artifacts, calling on Interpol to track illicit antiquity sales and requiring member states to pass laws cracking down on the international trade in these items. (Fifty countries went on to pass such laws.)

While we did this, however, the Assad regime used the world's focus on ISIS as cover to decimate Syrian civilians in opposition-held areas. The Syrian government, which had portrayed even peaceful protesters as "terrorists," now attempted to justify its brazen attacks by lumping in the entire opposition with ISIS and al-Qaeda.

Once Russia had intervened militarily in the fall of 2015, its aircraft helped the Syrian government attack population centers. With Russian soldiers now involved in the war, Obama saw that the risks of US military entanglement had further increased. Although the President initially argued that the Russians would pull back only if they paid a military price—what he called getting "a bloody nose"—he soon directed that US-backed opposition groups avoid clashes with Russian forces. The Pentagon worked assiduously to deconflict its flight patterns with those of Russian jets. In such a contested airspace, widening the American mission beyond ISIS would have created more opportunities for an accidental confrontation—and subsequent escalation—between the Russian and American militaries.

Obama's reluctance to take further action in Syria played into critiques that he was an unfeeling, "Spock"-like leader. *The New Yorker*'s David Remnick quoted a more novel, alternative assessment from a former US official, who observed, "Obama is basically a realist—but he feels bad about it."

Despite our differences over Syria, such portrayals did not ring true to me.

Obama took unprecedented steps to protect civilians in a range of circumstances. When I undertook an extensive atrocity prevention agenda at the White House, he offered unbridled support. He had such concern for Libyan civilians that he had ordered military action to protect them *despite* his goal of reducing US military deployments overseas. Although commentators frequently claimed that Obama came to view the Libya decision as the "worst mistake" of his presidency, he made publicly clear that what he regretted was "failing to plan for the day after what I think was *the right thing to do in intervening in Libya*" (italics mine).[57]

And despite the fracturing of Libya and his resistance to deeper involvement in Syria, Obama had responded quickly to ISIS's threat to wipe out the Yazidis, a Kurdish-speaking religious minority group in Iraq. In August of 2014, tens of thousands of defenseless Yazidis had fled ISIS's approaching troops and retreated to Mount Sinjar, where they were trapped without food or water. They seemed almost certain to die of starvation and dehydration or else be killed en masse by ISIS.

I joined Secretary Kerry, Ben Rhodes, and others in advocating the use of US air power to protect the Yazidis, but President Obama had already decided to order US military aircraft to begin airdropping supplies to the mountain and conducting air strikes on ISIS positions. These strikes provided cover to Kurdish ground forces, who opened up a corridor that allowed the trapped Yazidis to escape into Iraqi Kurdistan. As the President declared publicly at the time, "When we have the unique capabilities to help avert a massacre, then I believe the

United States of America cannot turn a blind eye. We can act, carefully and responsibly, to prevent a potential act of genocide. That's what we're doing on that mountain." Due to Obama's actions, an estimated 30,000 people were saved.*

However, Obama was never convinced that the United States could use military force "carefully and responsibly" in Syria.

Publicly, he defended this restraint with great conviction. Most notably, in a 2016 interview with *The Atlantic*'s Jeffrey Goldberg, Obama described himself as "very proud" of his willingness to put the brakes on air strikes during the 2013 red-line episode:

> The perception was that my credibility was at stake, that America's credibility was at stake. And so for me to press the pause button at that moment, I knew, would cost me politically. And the fact that I was able to pull back from the immediate pressures and think through in my own mind what was in America's interest, not only with respect to Syria but also with respect to our democracy, was as tough a decision as I've made—and I believe ultimately it was the right decision to make.

Obama's retrospective embrace of pulling back from his planned air strikes seemed to me a defensive overstatement—one that I believed derived from years of feeling personally blamed for the carnage in Syria. In my experience, President Obama sounded most defiant in public when he felt internally conflicted.

After reading his comments, I sent him an email, urging him to re-

---

* The Yazidi community was concentrated primarily around the Sinjar region in northwestern Iraq. For centuries, the Yazidis had been targeted for persecution due to their religious practices, which combine elements of Islam, Christianity, Judaism, and Zoroastrianism. ISIS thus considered Yazidis "infidels" who had to either convert to Islam or be killed. It was later estimated that some 10,000 Yazidis living in Sinjar were killed or taken prisoner during ISIS's invasion, which displaced the entirety of what was once a community of 400,000 people. Many of the kidnapped women and girls were held for years by ISIS fighters and subjected to unrelenting sexual violence.

consider the "distorted" account in *The Atlantic* of what had happened in August and September of 2013.

"When you decided to go to Congress, you did not expect or want to fail," I wrote Obama. "By getting Congress behind you, you expected to have a thicker base to sustain an intervention that was unpredictable." That hadn't worked out, and thanks to the President's improvisation, we had still managed to get something useful out of the crisis: the destruction of 1,300 tons of chemical weapons. Nevertheless, I did not think we could call the chapter a proud one in the annals of US foreign policy. The way Obama characterized what had happened also seemed to underestimate the negative, longer-term effects of the red-line events, which I thought damaged his credibility as President and undermined the influence of the United States. Reversing ourselves in public left us looking confused, and it exposed how constrained the President was domestically on foreign policy.

The consequences of the Syrian war went beyond the unfathomable levels of death, destruction, and displacement. The spillover of the conflict into neighboring countries through massive refugee flows and the spread of ISIS's ideology has created dangers for people in many parts of the world. Whereas in 2011 or 2012—or even after the 2013 chemical weapons attack—it may have seemed to many non-Syrians (and certainly to most Americans) that the conflict would not touch their lives, today it is much harder to make that case.

A massive population movement sent a half million Syrian refugees across Europe in 2015 alone. Presidential candidate Donald Trump and Brexit advocates used this biblical flight to help strategically demonize migrants and refugees, a key element of their successful campaigns. Of course, the widespread discontent among those harmed by globalization and inequality had far greater effects on American and European political developments than the influx of refugees. But the sense of a world gone mad gave enterprising demagogues an effective scapegoat, and one that they continue to use to this day.

All that said, I do not now—and did not then—have the bitter certitude of President Obama's critics. Because history can't be replayed, we will never know what would have happened had Obama taken a different path, for example, ordering the Pentagon to set up a no-fly zone. Perhaps tens of thousands more Syrians would be alive today and perhaps, without such a huge exodus of refugees, the xenophobic forces rising in Western countries would not have gained such traction. On the other hand, had the US military struck Syria's air defenses, Assad—sensing how little appetite there was in the United States for a fight—might have called the President's bluff and dared us to ramp up our military involvement. This escalation could have taken the United States down the very "slippery slope" that all of us sought to avoid, miring our troops in a regional conflagration with Russia on the other side of the line.

It is easy to speculate about counterfactuals, but all we can know is that those of us involved in helping devise Syria policy will forever carry regret over our inability to do more to stem the crisis. And we know the consequences of the policies we did choose. For generations to come, the Syrian people and the wider world will be living with the horrific aftermath of the most diabolical atrocities carried out since the Rwandan genocide.

WHEN I WROTE "A PROBLEM FROM HELL," my friend Jonathan Moore recommended that I read economist Albert Hirschman's book *Exit, Voice, and Loyalty*. Published in 1970, Hirschman wrote that when someone is unhappy with a policy or practice, they can choose to "exit," exercise "voice" (communicate grievances internally or through public protest), or be governed by "loyalty," which "holds exit at bay and activates voice."

Jonathan also steered me to a 1968 *Atlantic* essay written by his friend James C. Thomson, a former East Asia specialist at the State Department and NSC who had left the Johnson administration over Vietnam. In the essay, Thomson set out to explain why more of his colleagues had not dissented internally or resigned over a US-led war that ultimately killed millions of people in Vietnam, Laos, and Cambodia, and resulted in the deaths of more than 58,000 Americans. As part of his explanation, Thomson invoked what he called the "effectiveness trap." US officials unhappy with a policy, he wrote, typically deceive themselves into believing that they are doing more good by staying in government than they could by leaving.

Late one night in New York, with the kids asleep and Cass in Cambridge, I pulled up the essay online and reread it for the first time since I had joined the administration. Thomson wrote:

> The inclination to remain silent or to acquiesce in the presence of the great men—to live to fight another day, to give on this issue so that you can be "effective" on later issues—is overwhelming . . . it is easy to rationalize the decision to stay aboard. By doing so, one may be able to prevent a few bad things from happening and perhaps even make a few good things happen.

While I did not see any equivalency between the horrors that resulted from America's prosecution of the Vietnam War and the Obama administration's Syria policy, the concept of the effectiveness trap seemed applicable to many professional circumstances. I was determined not to fall into it, and every few months, rather than simply writing off those who attacked me, I would ask whether the balance of considerations still made it right to stay.

Was the President still listening to me or was he tuning me out? Could I take specific initiatives at the United Nations to try to help Syrians? Would the public reaction to my resignation make a difference in President Obama's decision-making or to the plight of Syrians? Was I making progress on other issues that mattered? If I were replaced, would someone carry those issues forward?

Depending on the day, my answers to these questions varied. When I talked to Cass, he would remind me of how often I agreed with Obama. And he would say, "If you can make one person's life better, do that."

I did what was within my power to do. I made use of my public platform at the UN to expose the ways in which Assad's government pretended to be a bulwark against terrorism while it cynically provided weapons and oil to ISIS.[58] I used public and private diplomacy (through Vitaly) to push to get Syrian political prisoners out of jail. My advocacy conceivably played a role in securing the release of human rights lawyer Mazen Darwish, a prisoner for more than three years whose wife I often met and whose court appearances I tracked.

Working with Australia, Jordan, and my European colleagues, I also secured Russia's support for a UN Security Council resolution that permitted food aid to move across international borders into opposition areas of Syria. This allowed more than two million people to receive UN assistance that the Syrian government had been blocking.

Yet next to the scale of Syrians' suffering, I knew all of this was a pittance. I would force myself to read every Syria report that crossed my desk, and nothing I and my team did diminished my sense of guilt and frustration at being unable to make a convincing case to do more to help those in desperate need.

Still, I never seriously considered leaving.

Mort was blunt, as always. "Look, I think your administration's Syria policy is terrible," he said during one of our calls. "'Don't do stupid shit' basically means, 'Don't do shit.' But what the hell are you going to accomplish for the Syrians from Cambridge? You leave and it's a one-day story. The next day nobody will give a damn. Certainly, Obama won't give a damn. There will just be more like-minded people in the Situation Room."

When I spoke with Jonathan, I reminded him that when we had first met at Carnegie, several State Department officials had just resigned to protest US inaction in the face of atrocities in Bosnia—the largest wave of resignations in the Department's history. But when we spoke about Syria, he distinguished the two situations. For those Balkans specialists, he said, staying meant that they would work only to implement a policy they abhorred, with no recourse for changing it and no other issues on which they could make a positive difference. Jonathan urged me to see how privileged I was.

"You need to keep arguing for what you believe on Syria," he insisted. "But even if it is the most important and most deadly conflict on the planet right now, you can't let Syria become the only measure of what you do. You can use your position to help a lot of people out there. The world is filled with broken places. Pick your battles, and go win some."

María Castro (below, with Obama and Rían) made it possible for me to work such punishing hours at the White House and the UN. For nine years, at great personal sacrifice, she cared for my kids with indescribable tenderness.

In June of 2013, President Obama nominated me to become US Ambassador to the UN. While Declan sat calmly in Mum's arms for the ceremony, Rían had other ideas . . .

DEVELOPING STORY
TWITTER @WallBlitzer **CRYING BABY INTERRUPTS OBAMA**
MALLOY IS EXPECTED TO SIGN BILL INTO LAW LATER THIS

After my confirmation hearing ended, four-year-old Declan jumped into my arms, and a pool of photographers descended on the hearing table to capture the shot. After this picture ran in several prominent newspapers, I received notes from women saying how heartened they were to see someone attempting a national security Cabinet role with small children in tow.

On August 2nd, 2013, Vice President Joe Biden presided over my swearing in as UN ambassador.

Presenting my credentials to UN Secretary-General Ban Ki-moon in 2013. Upon seeing this photo, the French ambassador to the UN asked me mischievously, "You wore your swimsuit to present credentials?"

Three weeks after I became UN ambassador, the Assad regime in Syria staged a massive chemical weapons attack that killed more than 1,400 people. After a Cabinet meeting on September 12th, 2013, we discussed our next steps in response.

As a former reporter, I retained the habit of bringing my notebooks everywhere and carefully detailing what I heard. Here, in October of 2013 in the North Kivu province of the Democratic Republic of Congo, I listened to an internally displaced Congolese woman describe ferocious attacks that drove her from her home.

I had many public battles with Vitaly Churkin, Russia's ambassador to the UN, but even amid our feuding, I continued to try to work with him to confront shared threats.

In June of 2015, I visited Maidan Square in Kiev, Ukraine, to pay respects to the more than one hundred people who were killed by Ukrainian security forces during the massive protests that occurred in late 2013 and early 2014.

The US Ambassador to the United Nations is immensely fortunate to be able to rely on four deputy US ambassadors, who rotated at various points during my tenure. Here, I'm pictured with ambassadors David Pressman, Michele Sison, Sarah Mendelson, and Isobel Coleman.

In October of 2014, during the height of the Ebola epidemic, I traveled to the three affected countries in West Africa. In Freetown, Sierra Leone, soldiers briefed me on how they had dramatically expanded their ability to safely bury those who had died from Ebola.

In Monrovia, Liberia, Liberian president Ellen Johnson Sirleaf and I showed off the "elbow bump" that had replaced handshakes, hugs, and kisses as a safe form of greeting throughout the region.

Obama plays soccer with Declan at a Camp David Cabinet retreat.

With Declan and Rían (left) on a typical morning. While my kids generally seemed to delight in engaging foreign ambassadors and UN officials, sometimes they were not in the mood. Here, Rían "poses" with Ban Ki-moon.

During my eight years in the Obama administration, I leaned heavily on María Castro, my parents, and friends like John Prendergast (top left), Elliot Thomson (top right), and Laura Pitter (center). As vital and loving as my support network was, Declan and Rían longed for a time when I could be with them without working on my phone or dealing with a national security intrusion.

When I arrived at the UN in 2013, women comprised 37 of the 193 ambassadors. I often invited my female colleagues for dinners, cultural events, and substantive discussions. In this gathering, we spent an evening in dialogue with feminist and political activist Gloria Steinem (center left).

Rían and I holiday shopping, with an assist from the head of my security detail.

Each September, President Obama visited New York for the UN General Assembly and carried out the presidential equivalent of speed-dating with heads of state from around the world. Here, in 2015, Obama, Deputy National Security Adviser Avril Haines, and I hurried into the US Mission to the UN, and in 2014, I spoke with Obama as he chaired a Security Council meeting on ISIS.

When I traveled overseas, I made a point of adding a stop on each trip to meet with local girls. Here, I played a game called Elle in Sri Lanka, basketball in Nigeria, and soccer in Mexico.

In September of 2015, I had the great fortune of speaking at María's naturalization as a US citizen.

In December of 2015, hearing how rhetoric toward refugees generally and Syrians in particular was growing inflamed, I invited the Al-Teibawis, a newly arrived family of Syrian refugees, to the ambassador's residence for an American dinner.

Meeting with a mother and her young child in April of 2016 at a camp in Nigeria for people displaced by Boko Haram violence. By this point, Boko Haram had forced 2.5 million people from their homes.

In August of 2016, six-year-old Alex Myteberi (left) wrote a letter to President Obama inviting a young Syrian who had survived an airstrike to come live with him in the US. Here, Declan welcomed Alex and his family to the UN for a tour.

Nujeen Mustafa (left) and her sister Nisreen (right) in Berlin in 2016. Nujeen, a Syrian Kurd from Aleppo who has cerebral palsy, rode her wheelchair more than 3,500 miles seeking asylum.

In 2016, I visited an English class for newly arrived refugees in Buffalo, New York. One of the students told me, "In America, we found peace."

The relationship between UN ambassadors and Secretaries of State has not always been easy. But Secretary of State John Kerry was a mentor, partner, and friend.

I called for the release of twenty female political prisoners in the #Freethe20 campaign. By the time I left government in January of 2017, fourteen of the twenty women we profiled had been freed. Two more would be released from jail the following month.

Even when we disagreed on issues, Vice President Biden would pass me notes in the Situation Room, encouraging me to keep raising my voice, and during tense times he could be counted on for humor and warmth.

At a state dinner in honor of French president François Hollande.

Speaking to the press on a visit to South Sudan with the UN Security Council in 2016, and walking with South Sudanese president Salva Kiir.

Casting the US vote for UN Security Council sanctions on North Korea. We also initiated the Council's first discussion of the North Korean government's brutal treatment of its own people. In Seoul, South Korea, I met inspiring young women who risked death to escape North Korea and were studying to become nurses, engineers, and lawyers.

Election night, 2016. I invited all the female ambassadors to the UN to watch the returns. By this point in the evening, I and the other ambassadors knew that the United States was not going to elect its first female president.

I brought my family on one last tour of the UN before departing my post on January 20th, 2017. We each took up a seat and pretended to stage a Council vote on whether the US should remain in the Paris climate agreement.

39

SHRINK THE CHANGE

I heard one question more than any other during my time as UN ambassador: "But what can one person do?"

Even committed, motivated people felt overwhelmed by the gravity of challenges in the world, from climate change to the refugee crisis to the global crackdown on human rights. I worried about individuals experiencing a kind of doom loop in which, because they could not single-handedly fix these large problems, they would end up opting to do nothing. Whenever my own thoughts about the state of the world headed toward a similarly bleak impasse, I would brainstorm with my team about how we might "shrink the change" we hoped to see.

I had come across this phrase in a book called *Switch: How to Change Things When Change Is Hard*, by professors Chip and Dan Heath. Cass had given me the book when I worked at the White House, and I had ordered many copies for my US government colleagues. The Heath brothers stressed that, counterintuitively, big problems "are most often solved by a sequence of small solutions, sometimes over weeks, sometimes over decades." "Shrink the change" became a kind of motto for me and my team, along with President Obama's version of the point: "Better is good."

Sometimes human achievements *were* big and sweeping—like helping end the Ebola epidemic. But more often, the changes we as individuals were able to make in the world were smaller. "Even if we can't solve the whole problem," I would say, "surely there is *something* we can do."

FROM THE BEGINNING OF MY TIME at the UN, securing the release of political prisoners seemed like an achievable and worthwhile initiative. I used private meetings with foreign ministers, public statements, and social media to call for the release of individuals being held around the world for "crimes" like exposing officials' lawbreaking or advocating for free speech.

Efforts like this naturally rankled foreign governments, so I was fortunate to have a supportive colleague in Secretary Kerry. When a foreign minister called him to complain about "Samantha's tweets," Kerry would occasionally vent to his staff that I was making his job harder. But we talked and emailed several times a week, and we met whenever we were both in Washington. He never urged me to temper my criticisms of abusive governments.

When I once raised with him the Egyptian foreign minister's objections to my advocacy, for example, Kerry just rolled his eyes. "Soon they will have no one left to lock up," he noted, and that was the end of it. My style was not his style, but we had an unspoken understanding: Kerry would try to influence governments his way, generally through private channels, while I would conduct quiet diplomacy *and* exert public pressure.

In September of 2015, Chinese president Xi Jinping planned to hold a summit at the United Nations to celebrate the twentieth anniversary of the 1995 World Conference on Women that had been hosted in Beijing. Xi's conference provided an occasion to highlight an inconvenient fact: women's voices were still being silenced in many countries, including China. Indeed, recently, the Chinese government had even locked up a group of women for having the temerity to campaign against sexual harassment. These women, who became known as the Beijing Five, had only been released after sustained international pressure.

Knowing that the Chinese-led "Beijing+20" summit would of course ignore the plight of the world's female political prisoners, my team and I decided to use the unique spotlight of a major global gathering to show solidarity with imprisoned women and to pressure governments to release them. These efforts coalesced into a campaign called #Freethe20, through which we aimed to help free twenty female political prisoners from thirteen countries.* Our list not only included prisoners in countries with which the administration had adversarial relations (like Venezuela and Syria), but also women incarcerated by governments with which the United States wanted to maintain strong ties (like China and Egypt). This balance made our stance on human rights more credible, and it comported with my view that our important relationships could withstand human rights pressure.

For each of the women we planned to profile, we reached out to their families, directly or through human rights organizations, to gauge whether they wanted their wife, sister, or daughter included. But we also needed clearances from numerous US officials, including the ambassadors posted to the countries where the women were jailed. Some resisted, worrying that a prisoner's inclusion on our list would add unnecessary tension to our dealings with the country. Even with Kerry's support, we only received sign-off for the final woman after I had put out a press release announcing the campaign's launch for the next day.

Twenty days before the Beijing+20 conference, in front of the diplomatic press corps at the State Department, I shared the story of the first prisoner, a courageous forty-four-year-old Chinese lawyer named Wang Yu. In addition to representing the Beijing Five, Wang had defended Ilham Tohti, the Uighur scholar jailed for highlighting the Chinese government's abuses against its brutalized Uighur minority. Now Wang herself was imprisoned for "subversion of state power," which carried a potential life sentence.

Thanks to the Mission's human rights adviser Kelly Razzouk, Kurtis Cooper, and others on our press team, we unearthed unforgettable details about each woman and made full use of social media to publicize their cases. Although our emphasis was on each individual pris-

---

* Nineteen of the women came from Azerbaijan, Burma, China, Egypt, Eritrea, Ethiopia, Iran, Russia, Syria, Uzbekistan, Venezuela, and Vietnam. The twentieth woman was a composite we referred to simply as a "North Korean political prisoner." At the time, North Korea held well over 100,000 political prisoners. However, Kim Jong-un's regime was so brutal that highlighting a single woman's name would have endangered her. Profiling an unnamed political prisoner in North Korea minimized the risk to any one individual, while still allowing us to draw attention to the country's mass imprisonment of its citizens in modern-day concentration camps.

oner, the women's experiences cast light on the larger judicial systems that abetted injustice: the coopted judges that presided over their trials, the draconian laws used to sentence them, the inhumane conditions in which they were imprisoned, and the persecuted organizations and movements for which they worked.

Every day for twenty days, I posted a video to Facebook in which I described the featured woman's work and the charges against her. Then we hung a jumbo picture of the woman in the large glass windows in the lobby of the US Mission, directly across the street from the entrance to UN Headquarters. Dignitaries attending the UN General Assembly, as well as anyone walking down First Avenue, had little choice but to pass this expanding series of portraits.

I reached out to Kelly Ayotte, the Republican senator from New Hampshire, who agreed to introduce a resolution in support of the campaign. The resolution, cosponsored by the then-twenty female US senators, Republican and Democrat, called for the immediate release of the prisoners. "Our message is simple," the senators said in a press release. "World leaders and foreign governments . . . should empower women, not imprison them."

On the day I hung the poster for Wang Yu, China's Ambassador to the UN, Liu Jieyi, telephoned me with "an urgent message" from Beijing. I had a respectful relationship with Liu, but he sounded mystified by what I was doing. He explained that Beijing saw our campaign as an aggressive act. He cautioned that continuing would not contribute positively to the atmosphere between our countries, and he urged me to reconsider.

I said I understood his government's perspective—and assured him that releasing Wang and China's other political prisoners in time for them to participate in the summit would do wonders to improve that atmosphere.

Soon after, I profiled Ta Phong Tan, a forty-seven-year-old Vietnamese blogger arrested in 2011. Tan, a former police officer, had written about corruption in Vietnam's judicial system and was serving a ten-year prison sentence for publishing "anti-state propaganda." Her mother had died after setting herself on fire to protest her daughter's prolonged detention.

Not long after we publicized Tan's story, I received a call from Vietnam's UN ambassador. She also expressed her government's displeasure with our decision to feature Tan and another Vietnamese prisoner named Bui Thi Minh Hang. But a few days later, we learned that Tan was going to be freed, and Kelly soon emailed me a photo of her landing in Los Angeles to start a new life.

I was amazed. When we developed the concept for the campaign, I did not expect that many of the women would actually be released. Nonetheless, I thought it worthwhile to make repressive governments pay at least a reputational cost for their actions. Yet our modest effort already seemed to be producing some tangible results.

Sanaa Seif was a twenty-one-year-old Egyptian arrested the previous year for peacefully demonstrating without a permit. Within forty-eight hours of featuring her, Kelly informed me that Sanaa had been pardoned—along with ninety-nine others. At our daily morning meeting, Kelly arrived carrying the photo of Sanaa that we had hung in the window of the Mission. Only now, the image had the word "RELEASED" stamped in large red letters across the bottom.

We would never know precisely how our campaign impacted various governments' decisions to release the women. Our efforts only supplemented ongoing advocacy by their families and lawyers. But news of a prisoner's release was exhilarating to US officials who had labored to secure the sign-off from a reluctant embassy or who had hunted down compelling details to share with the public. Unambiguous victories in government were rare. And we were all moved to know that these women, whom we felt we knew, would be reunited with their families.

In an atmosphere of repression and democratic backsliding around the world, I found it gratifying to focus less on the overall human rights "recession"—an abstraction that could be paralyzing—and more on specific people. Once freed, these women would again be able to raise their voices on behalf of important causes.

"We are up to six," Kelly told me three months after we launched the campaign.

"Now we are at twelve," she said in August of 2016, following Wang Yu's release.

By the time I left government in January of 2017, fourteen of the twenty women we profiled had been freed. Two more would be released from jail the following month.

We had made only a microscopic dent in a colossal problem. But as I said to Kelly, "For each one of these women, and those around them, it is the universe."

THE #FREETHE20 CAMPAIGN AFFIRMED what I had seen during my years in journalism: people were more likely to respond when they could focus on a specific individual—like David Rohde when he disappeared in Bosnia.

Government officials were no different. During the Ebola crisis, Jackson Niamah, the Liberian health worker, had reached typically stoic diplomats with his chilling prophecy that "if the international community does not stand up, we will all be wiped out." Likewise, we had held a succession of meetings highlighting ISIS's brutality before I invited Nadia Murad, a twenty-one-year-old Yazidi woman, to appear before the Council. When she described how ISIS had executed her mother and six of her nine brothers and then forced her into sexual slavery, her testimony drove home in a visceral way the savagery that the US-led coalition was working to end.*

When ISIS began disseminating propaganda showing executions of Iraqis and Syrians they suspected of being gay, I approached Vitaly, with whom I usually found common ground on confronting ISIS. But when I raised the possibility of collaborating in the Security Council on an effort to oppose anti-gay acts of terror, he replied, "Not possible." No matter how vocal the Russian government was about terrorism,

---

* Murad would win the 2018 Nobel Peace Prize for her work combating sexual violence in conflict.

when the victims were gay, it preferred to remain silent. And it had long used its clout to ensure the Council stayed silent as well.

Because Chile had made such strides domestically on LGBT rights, I asked its ambassador, Cristián Barros, to join the United States in convening the Council's first ever discussion of violence against LGBT people. Cristián sighed, knowing how upset some countries would be if we proceeded. Then, with a twinkle in his eye, he said, "We will do it, Samantha. We will be all alone, but we will be there."

It turned out we were not alone—around two hundred foreign diplomats participated in the informal Council meeting. Everyone sat in sober silence as we heard from two LGBT witnesses who had been terrorized by ISIS. One was a twenty-eight-year-old Syrian named Subhi Nahas, who sat next to me as he detailed the beatings he had endured, his harrowing escape to Turkey, and his eventual resettlement in San Francisco. The other was an Iraqi in his mid-twenties who was so terrified of being hunted down that he used a pseudonym ("Adnan") and spoke to the Council by telephone from an undisclosed location in the Middle East.

Subhi's and Adnan's testimonies made clear that ISIS was tapping into a deep societal hatred. Even once the terrorists were defeated, gay people would not feel secure in Iraq and Syria. Still, we had provided two young men a visible platform to tell their stories and assert their dignity. Given the heavy media coverage of the session, their words would be heard far from New York—possibly by an immigration official adjudicating an LGBT person's asylum claim, possibly even in the deepest reaches of Iraq and Syria, where many of their friends remained in hiding.

A few days later, I received an email from "Adnan." Written in English, it read:

> I was honored to take part in that historic event, it was the greatest thing I do in my life so far . . . Words cannot describe how much I am thankful to you. And I believe that I am conveying the thoughts of thousands of people in the middle east.

He signed his email with his real name, which I had not known.

Nine months later, a gunman who pledged loyalty to ISIS murdered forty-nine people at Orlando's Pulse dance club, a popular nightspot for the city's LGBT community. The massacre was the worst terrorist attack on US soil since September 11th. Digesting the news, I tried to ward off the desire to throw my hands up in disgust at the hatred in the world. Instead, I called David Pressman and said I wanted to find some way to respond in the Security Council.

We both knew that the horror of the Pulse attack might be enough to get reluctant countries in the UN to put their biases aside—even if only temporarily. After the surprising turnout for our informal Security Council session with Subhi and Adnan, we decided to test how far other countries were willing to go in opposing anti-gay violence. "I think this is the time," I said.

David, who had been playing in a local park with his twin toddler sons when I called, left his partner and kids and headed straight to the UN. After a day of furious diplomacy in New York and in capitals around the world, the UN Security Council, joined by Russia and Egypt (whose representatives did not want to be seen blocking a condemnation of ISIS), agreed to a statement that "condemned in the strongest terms the terrorist attack in Orlando . . . targeting persons as a result of their sexual orientation."

When David and I had arrived at the UN, we had fought simply to include the phrase "vulnerable populations" in Security Council resolutions—which Russia rejected as code for LGBT people. Now, for the first time in history, the Security Council had condemned attacks on the basis of sexual orientation, establishing a standard that could subsequently be invoked by persecuted LGBT people in any country.

Several days later, I convened the "Core Group" of UN ambassadors who had worked together on LGBT rights. Instead of meeting at the UN, I suggested we gather at the legendary Stonewall Inn in Greenwich Village. Tree Sequoia, Stonewall's bartender for decades, greeted our group of sixteen ambassadors, recalling what it was like when Stonewall had been raided by the New York City police in 1969. This incident sparked protests, helping launch a national gay rights movement that few people had anticipated.

Tree escorted us to a dark wood-paneled back room that reeked of the sour smell of hops. After the ambassadors had taken their seats, I kicked off the discussion by taking note of the fact that the same police force that had once raided Stonewall now participated in the New York City Pride March.

"You never know," I said. "We can only do what we can do. But one day, someone might look back on the brave testimonies of two gay men from the Middle East at the Security Council or one sentence in a UN statement condemning attacks on the LGBT community as the first step on a long road to something far more meaningful."

The other ambassadors seemed fired up. Some had been nervous about whether to pursue the creation of a UN position dedicated to protecting LGBT people. But at the Stonewall Inn, we pledged to forge ahead.

Exactly two weeks later, over the fierce resistance of the same coalition that had opposed granting benefits to the UN's LGBT staff, we secured the creation of the first UN position to monitor and publicly report on LGBT rights around the world. Human Rights Watch called it "a historic victory for the human rights of anyone at risk of discrimination and violence because of their sexual orientation or gender identity."

I viewed it as a very small step—one that built on the small steps before it.

THE ANNUAL UN GENERAL ASSEMBLY gathering in September of 2016 was a bittersweet occasion. Advising President Obama, I had attended and helped shape each of his seven previous appearances at these meetings. This would be his last.

A few days before Obama's arrival, New York City workers began erecting barriers to close off roads near the UN. As she had every year during this event, María struggled to navigate the five heavily policed blocks that separated the Waldorf and Rían's preschool. And Cass again resolved to remain in Cambridge for the week, to avoid being manhandled by security as he tried to reach our apartment.

I would not miss these disruptions after I left the UN. But when heads of state gathered for the General Assembly, I still could not shake the sense that together—as Cass's dad had written from San Francisco in 1945—we *could* accomplish something. This potential had not been realized nearly as often as I had hoped, but I would miss assembling coalitions to combat the world's hardest problems, as well as that tingling sense of possibility.

On one of the last nights of UNGA week, I had dinner with a foreign minister who had also become a friend. I had worked closely with him over the years and was grateful for the tough votes he had instructed his UN ambassador to take. He had a marvelous sense of humor that most ministers did not display, and I had grown very fond of him.

We spent the dinner discussing China, Syria, the upcoming US presidential election, and his country's ethnic tensions. Then, toward the end of the meal, I offhandedly mentioned that I had gotten permission from New York City for the UN's human rights office to paint in rainbow colors the First Avenue crosswalk that many VIPs would use to enter the UN. The Dutch ambassador had floated this idea during our Stonewall meeting. Now, foreign ministers and heads of state were traversing our rainbow "Path to Equality" as they walked into an institution that had only recently recognized LGBT rights.

For a split second, I thought I caught a flash of interest on the minister's face, but he quickly changed the subject. Despite our friendship, I had never asked him about his personal life.

As we got up to say good night, I heard myself whisper in his ear, "Any chance you would like to come see the crosswalk?"

Suddenly, he broke out in a broad, mischievous smile. In that moment, he saw that I knew and understood what he still could not advertise in his own country.

At 12:30 a.m. on a breezy September night, the minister walked slowly across the rainbow crosswalk toward the UN, where the flags of his country, my country, and all the countries of the world flew each day.

Thanks to the streetlamp, I was able to see his expression as he approached my side of First Avenue. He bore a look I had not seen before. It combined relief, delight, and a deep calm.

It was the look of someone being fully himself.

40

THE END

Early in my tenure as UN ambassador, I visited New York City mayor Mike Bloomberg in his office at City Hall. To motivate himself not to waste time, Bloomberg had hung a large digital clock counting down the days, hours, and minutes until his final term would end. In my last year on the job, as I tried to make the most of my remaining time representing the United States, I kept a version of that clock in my head.

I also passed out White House notecards to members of my team that were inscribed with President Obama's words: "We are entering the fourth quarter and really important things happen in the fourth quarter."

Sure enough, early in 2016, North Korea carried out its fourth nuclear test. Relying on our government's sanctions experts, I threw myself into mastering the technical aspects of Pyongyang's revenue streams. After nine weeks of painstaking negotiations with my Chinese counterpart—and backed by Washington's relentless high-level lobbying of Beijing—we secured a resolution that went further than any in two decades. It required all cargo to and from North Korea to be inspected. And it banned jet and rocket fuel supplies to North Korea, imposed an arms embargo, and prohibited North Korean banks from doing business in, or with, UN member states.[59]

I managed these negotiations while simultaneously initiating the Security Council's first discussion of North Korea's brutal treatment of its own people. For years, China had blocked the Council from holding sessions to condemn North Korea's vast gulag system. This time, I joined with the South Korean and Australian ambassadors to mobilize the necessary votes, allowing us to override China's opposition and finally bring North Korean human rights onto the agenda.*

I invited North Korean defectors into the chamber and included their testimonies in my remarks. I also condemned Beijing for its deplorable practice of forcing back to North Korea people who had managed to escape across the border into China. Although these forced repatriations would lead to near-certain torture or death, most governments were hesitant to call China to account.

I was moved to see the defectors' gratitude, after years of near starvation and horrendous mistreatment, at being able to tell their stories to the world. Although they knew that exposing the abuses they had endured would not make the Kim regime stop brutalizing people, they stressed that maintaining silence left both the regime and its victims with the impression that the outside world did not care. Reactions like this affirmed my view that it was generally a mistake to censor ourselves on human rights—even during the tightrope walk of high-stakes nuclear negotiations.

We faced a similar dilemma with regard to Iran, another long-time US adversary that combined dangerous nuclear ambitions with domestic repression. After Secretary Kerry concluded negotiations to secure the Iran nuclear deal, my team shepherded a resolution through the Security Council that etched its provisions into international law. Iran would be forced to eliminate 98 percent of its enriched uranium stockpile, decommission two-thirds of its centrifuges, dismantle a heavy water nuclear reactor that could have produced weapons-grade plutonium, and submit to the most extensive inspections regime ever undertaken by the International Atomic Energy Agency.

The Iran deal illustrated the importance of UN Security Council sanctions and unrelenting diplomacy—which in this case played a de-

---

* The UN Charter specifies that Security Council votes on "procedural matters" cannot be vetoed. As a result, when a country objects to putting an item on the Council's agenda, nine of the fifteen countries on the Council must vote in favor of it.

cisive role in bringing Iran to the negotiating table. The subsequent politicization of the deal was disheartening and extremely counter-productive given that the agreement achieved what both Democrats and Republicans generally agreed should be the top US priority toward Iran: stopping it from building nuclear weapons. In so doing, the deal greatly reduced the likelihood that American service members would have to put their lives on the line in another American-led military conflict in the Middle East, which had seemed an imminent possibility at various points during Obama's first term.

Unfortunately, some countries were so pleased by the nuclear agreement that they felt it was unnecessary to run an annual UN General Assembly resolution condemning Iran's human rights abuses. I insisted we proceed, lobbying frenetically to ensure that the Iranian government's deplorable treatment of its people got attention in its own right.

As all of this was happening, I also joined the rest of the Obama administration in attempting to ensure that the Paris climate accords became a reality before the clock ran out on the President's second term. While the Paris agreement had been signed to great fanfare in December of 2015, it would not become law until it was ratified by at least fifty-five countries that accounted for at least 55 percent of total global emissions. With Trump and other Republican candidates threatening to withdraw from the agreement if elected, we spent most of 2016 engaged in a relentless, full-court press to reach this 55/55 threshold before we left office.

We faced steep odds in attempting to quickly bring the agreement into force. A previous climate change agreement—the 1997 Kyoto Protocol—took eight years, while the 1982 UN Convention on the Law of the Sea had needed twelve years. We had one year.

Each week throughout 2016, the White House identified a new set of target countries and asked me, Secretary Kerry, and US diplomats everywhere to press for expedited domestic ratification processes. One month before the 2016 election, the seventy-third country ratified the agreement, and it crossed the 55 percent emissions threshold. As a result of bringing the Paris agreement into force, we had ensured that any future US withdrawal would not unravel the overall agreement.*

Amid these fourth-quarter initiatives, I started joking that I loved my job so much that, at the appointed hour for my departure, my security detail would have to transform themselves into an extraction team, donning riot gear to pull me out of my office by the ankles as I clutched the legs of the couch, determined to stay put. Knowing that US officials at the Mission would be tempted to focus on their professional futures as our time wound down, I appealed to the staff to keep going strong through the Obama administration's finish line. "When we look back on this period, let's have no regrets," I said. And when the administration's political appointees looked weary, I would remind them, "Remember, for as long as we work here, we *get to be* the United States—let's not waste that!"

In my years at the White House, I had usually managed to sleep six hours a night (when I wasn't nursing). But during the fourth quarter of my government service, I was lucky to steal four or five hours. Eddie was usually the first person to notice my exhaustion. When he saw me on TV, he would call to tell me I was overdoing it. I agreed, but would cheerfully point out, "I can sleep all I want after January 2017."

My special assistant Becca tried to encourage a bit of self-care, often passing me a hairbrush in the elevator ("Forget again?" she would ask, staring at my tangles). On several occasions, she had to chase me to finish zipping up the back of my dress as I rushed out to meet the day.

A second, parallel clock was also running in my head as the remaining months ticked away. Declan was already seven and Rían was four. María had cared for them with exceptional tenderness, and with-

---

* In June of 2017, President Trump announced that he was withdrawing the US from the Paris climate accord. According to the agreed-upon rules for exiting, however, the earliest possible date by which the US government can finalize its withdrawal is November 4th, 2020—the day after the 2020 presidential election. The rules also allow for a country that has exited to rejoin, a process that could be completed within a month of a future president formally requesting to reenter. Even if the US ultimately rejoins, what matters most is a concerted American domestic effort to meet and then exceed the commitments the Obama administration made.

out her dedication, I could never have done my job. But I felt their constant pull.

During my early years in the job, Declan had asked each morning, "Are you coming home early?" This question meant, "Is there any chance I will see you tonight?" Too often, the answer had been no. But even when I had given him an exuberant yes, by late afternoon I usually called María and asked that she tell him that an urgent matter had come up at the White House or the UN, forcing me to stay at work.

I noticed that after many disappointments, Declan had stopped asking about my plans. Rían had never started.

I wanted to be present for homework, for baseball and soccer games, and for that magic, unforeseeable moment when they divulged what had happened in school that day.

So I was torn. The slower the clock moved, the longer I could represent the United States and try to make progress on issues that mattered. And the more quickly the clock moved, the sooner I would be the mother and partner I longed to be.

In the end, of course, my conflicting inner clocks were immaterial. Time does its own work.

WHEN ELECTION DAY ARRIVED, I was worried about many potential outcomes. Would the Democrats take the Senate? Would Donald Trump concede graciously or follow through on his threats not to accept an unfavorable result? And in the event that Hillary Clinton asked me to serve in her administration, would I have the discipline to turn her down in order to be with my family?

I was not asking the more fundamental question of who would win.

Indeed, I was so unconcerned about the outcome of the presidential race that I arranged an election night party at the ambassador's residence and invited all the female ambassadors to the UN.

Diplomats have to try to build constructive relations with whoever is in power, and they do not typically reveal their preferences in another country's election. But most of my guests made no secret of their longing to see a woman become the US president. They knew the cascading effect that such a victory would have on women's empowerment globally. In addition, Trump's outward hostility to much of the rest of the world, combined with the ways he had talked about and treated women, made my election party an unusually incautious diplomatic gathering. Of course, Clinton also had a comfortable lead in the polls going into the evening, so the open partiality of my female colleagues did not seem professionally hazardous.

"At what time will we know that Hillary has won?" one ambassador from an undemocratic country asked shortly after I began welcoming guests.

Recalling the tight races between Bush and Gore in 2000, and Bush and Kerry in 2004, I told her that our system did not work like her country's—nothing was preordained. "But," I said assuredly, "we won't keep you too late."

I had invited Gloria Steinem, whose lifetime of work on behalf of women's rights seemed destined to culminate in Secretary Clinton's victory. Madeleine Albright dropped by, wearing a broach with stained glass in the shape of a ceiling being shattered. I delighted in seeing my mother—whose drive for knowledge had been so impertinently questioned by an Irish judge—chatting with these two better-known pioneers.

Cass and our children rounded out the festivities, with Declan running around the apartment telling foreign diplomats to ignore the popular vote and pay attention to who "scored 270 points."

Only when states that were expected to be shoo-ins for Clinton suddenly became nail-biters did we begin to fear that something unexpected and unwelcome might happen. Still, Trump's path to victory required undecided voters to break his way in so many places that I tried to remain a calming voice in the room even as evidence mounted that Trump was on the verge of a shocking upset.

Gloria started to lose color in her cheeks around 10:30 p.m., but she remained unfailingly courteous to foreign ambassadors, who continued to approach her with thanks for inspiring them during their younger years. She patiently inquired about their paths to the UN, all the while keeping one eye trained on the large-screen TV I had rented for the evening.

My husband took on the role of messenger of doom, carrying in his laptop like the pallbearer at a funeral. His screen showed a website depicting a jumble of pie charts, graphs, and numbers. Cass, who projected perpetual good cheer, looked stricken.

"She—" he said.

"She what?" I asked.

"She can't get there," he said, his voice trailing off. Clinton was going to lose.

Declan had fallen asleep on one of the couches in the great room, holding his stuffed snow tiger. Rían was in her pajamas, stretched out horizontally in deep sleep on my lap. She looked angelic, her pale Irish skin as white as the carpet, her long lashes fluttering while many of the adults wept openly around her.

Earlier that day, when I had sent Rían off to school with her huge backpack on her shoulders, the horizon had seemed bright and boundless. This was to be the night when young girls saw—and thus believed—that they could do anything. Instead, we were about to elect to our highest office a man who had boasted about forcing himself on women. I was deeply shaken.

Gloria and I sat on the couch watching CNN's election coverage until after two a.m., refusing to give up until the race had been officially called. After she left, I crawled into bed next to Cass and thought about the many cruel and foolish policies Trump had pledged to pursue if he became President. I eventually fell asleep for an hour or two and woke just as dawn broke to find Cass on his computer.

"Gosh," he said, when he saw I was conscious.

We each tried out a series of "Maybe it won't be as bad as we think" arguments—the same expressions of desperate hope that were being made in millions of gloomy households across America.

On its face, Trump's victory—and the 63 million votes that made it possible—seemed a repudiation of many of the central tenets of my life. I was an immigrant, someone who felt fortunate to have experienced many countries and cultures. I saw the fate of the American people as intertwined with that of individuals elsewhere on the planet. And I knew that if the United States retreated from the world, global crises would fester, harming US interests.

When I had arrived at the UN in 2013, I had hoped to make time to get out into the country to connect with Americans far from New York and Washington. I took a few such trips, including to Georgia and Kentucky, where I spoke alongside Republican Senate Majority Leader Mitch McConnell about how US security was linked with the work of the UN. But in the latter phase of the administration, a few prominent Republicans confessed privately that the party "base" would criticize them if they were seen to be collaborating with the UN ambassador. And while I certainly didn't need the company of politicians to engage skeptics of our administration's foreign policy, my responsibilities at the UN and in Washington also limited my domestic travel.

I knew I had to be careful not to overinterpret such a close election. Nonetheless, caricatures of internationalism—and fearmongering about the "other"—had clearly resonated with millions of people. But more than that, Trump had successfully spoken to deeply-felt and entirely legitimate grievances about how the globalized economy had left people behind. At least some of those who voted for Obama in 2012 and turned to Trump in 2016 had agreed with the President-elect that America's openness to the outside world had contributed to their struggles.*

WHILE I TRIED to sort through what had just happened, I recognized that my first task was to find a way to offer my support to the individuals who worked at the US Mission to the UN. "This day is going to suck," I said to Cass before we parted the morning after the election.

Declan was in a foul mood during our drive to school, and I was

---

* Among Americans who voted for President Obama in 2012, an estimated 9 percent voted for President Trump in 2016; another 7 percent did not vote; and 3 percent opted for a third-party candidate. Together, these three categories represented approximately 13 million votes in an election ultimately decided by fewer than 80,000 cast across the three critical swing states of Michigan, Pennsylvania and Wisconsin.

the target. "Mommy you told me Hillary would win," he said. "You promised you would never lie to me."

I tried to explain the difference between a lie and a mistake, but as he argued his position from his booster seat in the back of the armored SUV, I noticed his lower lip was trembling. As soon as we began to pull away from the Waldorf, he started crying, "Mi-ma. Mi-ma. I don't want Mima to go away."

Declan had heard Trump's bigoted commentary about Latinos during the campaign and was now terrified that María, his "Mima," would be deported to Mexico, where she was originally from. I pulled my son onto my lap, trying to soothe him.

"It's okay, Declan," I said. "Mima is an American citizen. Remember, we were with her when she became American and Mommy helped swear her in. She will be completely fine."

But Declan was exhausted from the late night, and, once the tears were flowing, they would not soon stop.

"But what about Mima's friends?" he cried. "Trump wants to send them back to Mexico. Mima will be so sad."

There, unfortunately, I could offer him little reassurance.

When I arrived at the US Mission, I sat down for the daily meeting I held with my "Dream Team"—a combination of political staff appointed during the Obama administration and lifelong government employees.

I felt that I had the most skilled legislative affairs adviser, the most able schedulers, the savviest press operation, the wisest Middle East experts, the most rigorous lawyers, and the finest staff in just about every position there was. Many people at the US Mission could have taken their talents into the private sector and landed more lucrative positions with far fancier titles than they had working with me. I had looked forward to lobbying the Clinton transition team so that the political appointees could find ways to continue to serve. Now, those hired by Obama faced unemployment. A few were not sure what they would do to make rent come February. Yet they didn't talk about themselves: they were far more focused on what the President-elect had promised to do.

The vast majority of the people who worked at the US Mission to the UN were career civil servants and foreign service officers who faced different challenges. They had no declared political views and were permanent US government employees. Nonetheless, many had invested mightily in such signature initiatives as securing the Iran nuclear deal, negotiating the Paris climate accord, and getting businesses and governments to do more to support refugees around the world. Trump had pledged to undo all of this progress.

Moreover, Trump's apparent affection for Vladimir Putin and other dictators boded ill for America's leadership on human rights. And because the staff at our Mission looked like our country—Latinos, African Americans, Muslim Americans, LGBT people, people with disabilities—many had felt personally demeaned by Trump's rhetoric during the campaign.

Even though I was devastated by the prospect of a Trump presidency, I knew my job was to rally the team. I called a Town Hall meeting to deliver a pep talk, rehearsing my upbeat message several times by myself before I tried it out on my team.

"I know some of you are shocked by the results of the election," I began. More than a hundred faces looked back at me, and I gave it my best shot:

> I'm certainly shocked. And I know this election opened some raw wounds for many people in this country and, presumably, at this Mission. And I want to give people the chance to talk about how they feel.

> But I also want us to stay focused on our job. We represent the most powerful country in the world—a country that gave an immigrant like me the chance to represent it at the UN, and a country that gave a businessman like Donald Trump the chance to be President. We need to show the rest of the world what it means to respect the rule of law, and to put one's country over one's particular political preferences.

People around the world are going to have questions about where America is going. We won't have the answers to those questions. But we know that our democracy is strong, our institutions are strong, and, no matter who is running this country, our greatest strength has always been our citizens. We are America. We are going to be okay, and the rest of the world needs to know that.

One of the first people who got up to speak was a talented foreign service officer. "Look," she said, "I don't agree with a lot of the things Trump has said. But he doesn't seem to have a lot of people experienced in foreign policy in his inner circle. He and his team will need us. And we will have the same duty to our country—and the same privilege of serving our country—on January twentieth as we had when we served George W. Bush and Barack Obama. We will keep serving this country. That's what we do."

One after another, the US officials in the Town Hall expressed their determination to serve the next President. Having gathered my staff thinking I was going to need to comfort them, they ended up consoling me, with their professionalism and patriotism.

FOR THE NEXT TEN WEEKS, my team and I made a mad dash to the finish line, lobbying governments to release more political prisoners, trying to bring more vetted refugees into our country, and supporting John Kerry in his efforts until the last moment to bring about a cease-fire in Syria.

Russia's multipronged attack on the US presidential election, which had been designed to bolster Donald Trump's candidacy and widen divisions in our democracy, also loomed large as the clock ticked down and the full scope of what Moscow had done began to come into view. Even though the public debate over election interference was just beginning, it was already breaking down along alarmingly partisan lines. Republican defenders of President-elect Trump insisted that those focused on Russia's meddling were simply "sore losers." This was obviously false. In focusing on Russian actions, voters could disagree mightily on who should be President of the United States but still be united in insisting that only Americans should get to decide.

On December 13th, 2016, President Obama chaired an NSC meeting on the situation in Syria that was the most somber of my time in government. Over the previous three and a half years, I had participated in countless discussions of Syria that left me sad and frustrated. But this one was the worst.

For months, Russia and the Syrian regime had been laying catastrophic siege to opposition-held Aleppo. Their tactics and destruction brought to mind Fred Cuny's description of Russia's decimation of Grozny, Chechnya. Russian and Syrian heavy weapons pummeled apartment buildings and makeshift hospitals with seemingly no regard for the 300,000 civilians trapped in the city.

The greatest superpower in the history of the world was a lame duck in the face of the systematic bombardment of innocents. *And* we were about to hand the reins to someone who had nothing but kind words for Putin.

After Obama's meeting, which I had joined by video, I walked across the street to an emergency UN Security Council session, also focusing on the assault in Aleppo. In the chamber, I listened to the secretary-general describe "scores of civilians being killed either by intense bombardment or summary executions" by Syrian government forces—with Russian and Iranian support. UN officials had begged to evacuate tens of thousands of civilians, but Syria, Russia, and Iran had refused to allow humanitarian convoys to enter the city to remove the wounded.

When my turn came, I began by reading the testimonies of people trapped in eastern Aleppo. I quoted a teacher named Abdulkafi Al-Hamdo, who had written on Twitter: "I can tweet now but I might not do it forever. Please save my daughter's life and others. This is a call from a father."

I recalled a doctor who had said to a journalist: "Remember that there was a city called Aleppo that the world erased from the map and history."

Then I put my prepared statement down and went off:

> To the Assad regime, Russia, and Iran, your forces and proxies
> are carrying out these crimes. Your barrel bombs and mortars
> and air strikes have allowed the militia in Aleppo to encircle tens
> of thousands of civilians in your ever-tightening noose. It is *your*
> noose. Three Member States of the UN contributing to a noose
> around civilians. It should shame you. Instead, by all appear-
> ances, it is emboldening you. You are plotting your next assault.

I looked up from my notes at Vitaly, and extemporaneously posed a
set of questions that I felt I urgently needed him to answer.

> Are you truly incapable of shame? Is there literally nothing that
> can shame you? Is there no act of barbarism against civilians, no
> execution of a child that gets under your skin, that just creeps you
> out a little bit? Is there nothing you will not lie about or justify?

Vitaly spoke next. He made no effort to respond to what I had said.
Instead, he did just what he and Russian officials had done regarding
the Syrian chemical weapons that killed 1,400 people, Russia's invasion
of Ukraine, and the brazen attempt to swing the election to Trump: he
dismissed, diverted, and lied.

My Russian counterpart denounced as "fabrications" all the claims
of independent observers and the UN. As always, he delivered his
statement in Russian, and I listened to the interpretation through my
earpiece.

"Propaganda, disinformation, and psychological warfare are not
new concepts," he said. "A new phenomenon, exacerbated by what we
are seeing in the Syrian conflict, is the spread of . . ."—and then he
suddenly broke into English to use a phrase I had not heard before that
moment—"fake news."

Instead of waiting for the session to end after Vitaly's remarks,
I walked out in disgust at the Russian and Syrian governments—but
also at my own impotence. By the time I got back to my office, the

statement I had made in the Council had gone viral. For some Americans who circulated the video, my question—"Are you truly incapable of shame?"—applied to Aleppo. But for many, I think, it was the question they longed to scream out loud to the President-elect.

I dedicated my last major public speech as UN ambassador to the threat posed by Russia. Once I gave the speech, I knew that I would not hear from Vitaly again. And I was relieved not to see him, given what Russia had done.

Yet leaving New York did not feel right without acknowledging the ups and downs of the years he and I had experienced together. After I had packed for our move to Massachusetts, I called his cell, and he answered on the first ring.

"Hey man," I said. "Just calling to say goodbye. I guess things didn't turn out exactly the way we had hoped."

"No, they certainly didn't," he said.

There was a long pause. Then, in unison, we each said, "We tried."

This would be the last time I ever spoke to Vitaly, who died the following month of a sudden heart attack at the age of sixty-four.

MY TIME IN GOVERNMENT would end at noon on January 20th, 2017.

Late in the evening on January 19th, I assembled a small group of those with whom I had worked most closely. We gathered in the same office vestibule where we had celebrated small victories and personal milestones. I went around and toasted each team member, recalling their quirks and all that they had personally done for their country. I also commended them for their achievements on behalf of people whom they would likely never have the chance to meet. It felt like an Irish wake—dark yet uplifting.

I left the Mission at around four a.m. after wrapping up thank-you notes and departure memos to my successor, South Carolina governor Nikki Haley, with whom I had been in touch during the transition. I labeled my office belongings for the movers and carried just one box out the door, an assortment of family photos, Declan's and Rían's drawings that I had peeled off my office walls, and copies of the UN Charter and the US Constitution. At the last minute I threw in a stash of business cards, to remind me of the time I had once been the US Ambassador to the United Nations.

When the UN opened the next morning, I returned with Mum and Eddie, Cass, Declan, Rían, and María for a last look around. Declan and Rían sat in the US chair in the Security Council, donning the earpiece I had so often used for translation. Then, as a family, we each took up a seat and pretended to stage a Council vote.

"Should Donald Trump remain in the Paris climate agreement and protect the planet from catastrophic warming?" I asked.

The resolution passed with seven out of seven delegates in favor.

AFTERWORD

On a snowy Tuesday night toward the end of January 2017, I was unpacking in our new home in Concord, Massachusetts, when the doorbell rang.

I carried a box of utensils from the kitchen to the nearby front door. A policeman stood on the stoop.

"Is this the home of Cass Sunstein?"

I had been trying to reach Cass for well over an hour and had begun envisioning various doomsday scenarios. But having imagined so many previous calamities, I was able to talk myself out of them . . . until I saw the policeman.

He began, "I'm sorry to inform you—"

"Is he alive?" I interrupted. Nothing mattered but the answer to that single question.

"I don't have the latest," the officer said. "He appears to have been hit by a car while walking home. I don't know his current status."

We were interrupted by a piercing scream from Declan. He and Rían had been obscured from the policeman's view by a stack of boxes—and the officer now looked chastened that he hadn't made sure we were alone before delivering the news. Declan began to cry, "I don't want my daddy to die." Rían could not comprehend her father's accident, but draped her arms around her big brother's midsection. "It's okay, Declan. You're going to be okay, sweet boy," she said, unwittingly using Cass's term of endearment for his only son.

The policeman handed me a piece of paper with the scribbled name of the hospital where Cass had been taken. Driving there in the snow would take at least forty-five minutes, he informed me. "Why did they take him so far away?" I asked, gesturing in the direction of Emerson Hospital, which was within walking distance. The officer mumbled something about head trauma specialists. I grasped at potential good news.

"So he *is* alive?" I said.

"I'm sorry, ma'am. It's best if you get to the hospital to talk to the doctors."

"What hospital?" I asked, forgetting the name was on the paper in my hand.

María, who had made yet another move with our family, had begun praying, and I knew she would find a way to soothe Declan and Rían.

Ten days earlier, I would have jumped into the backseat of an armored, government-owned SUV. My security detail would likely have sounded the sirens. Hospital management would have been informed that a senior US official's spouse was entering critical care in their emergency room.

But in my new life, I was once again on my own.

During the tense drive, I began to make deals with God—as I had done as a little girl when I first moved to Pittsburgh. "Just let him live," I pleaded over and over again. Cass had tremendous brain capacity, I thought, far more than he really needed. My husband would be heartbroken if he couldn't play sports or race Declan again, but as long as he survived, we would find a way forward.

I ditched the car at the curb in front of the emergency room's glass doors and dashed into the waiting area, leaving the engine running and my keys and wallet behind. I approached the receptionist behind the desk.

"I'm married to Cass Sunstein," I exclaimed, frantic. "Is he alive?"

My heart was no longer beating. My future was in her hands. "Sunstein, Sunstein, Sunstein," she said, methodically thumbing through her papers.

I wanted to scream, "It's a yes or no question. Please, please, please answer!"

Finally, she looked up serenely and said, "Oh yes, he's alive. Once you fill out these forms, I can let you back to see him."

Cass was in rough shape. Watching him sleep during our nine years of marriage, I had often marveled that he seemed to bear the trace of a smile, as if ideas—or memories of satisfying squash forehands—were coming to him in his dreams. But now his swollen face was twitching, his mouth downturned, his coloring yellow and gray from bruising and shock. The emergency room doctor explained that he had suffered severe head trauma that had left him unconscious with five broken vertebrae, multiple broken ribs, a skull fracture, and serious brain bleeding.

I snapped photos of his head X-rays and emailed them to Mum. She said they were horrific, but assured me that if he could move all of his limbs and get through the night without seizures, he would likely regain normal brain and physical function. The neurosurgeon on call offered a more detailed version of the same message.

"Thank you for your service," the doctor said at the close of our conversation. "Thank you for *your* service," I responded.

For the next several days, I stayed at the hospital. Thirty-six hours after the accident, Cass became more alert. When prompted, he was able to provide his name, address, and profession. When asked his wife's name, he painstakingly tilted his head in my direction and slowly but slyly answered, "Jeane Kirkpatrick?"

When the doctor asked me how I was holding up, I told him I felt as though I had won the lottery. "Not only has my husband survived a harrowing accident," I said. "But he has achieved the impossible: he's taken my mind off Donald Trump."

I HAVE NOW LIVED for two and a half years under a single roof with my small family. Cass, who recovered astonishingly quickly, has returned to teaching and writing. While Declan still loves baseball, he isn't sure how he feels about his mother's hands-on coaching. And now that I'm finally around to encourage him to practice the piano, he has learned to play beautifully—his manner and sounds evoking those of my late father. Rían has fallen in love with nature and spends entire afternoons surveying rocks and leaves in our backyard, while Finley and Snowy, our Labrador retrievers, follow her everywhere.

Mum is working harder than ever, forging deep and lasting ties with

her patients. Eddie, who has now been retired (and sober) for more than
a decade, is still clipping articles and sending me book recommendations. Stephen lives with his wife and young son, Malachy, in Los Angeles, and tracks politics like we once followed sports. After a year with
us in Concord, María returned to be with her family in Virginia, and
we see her several times a year. John Prendergast and I have begun a
gratitude ritual in which we email each other at night the three aspects
of the day for which we are most thankful.

If one lesson in my experience stands out above the others, it is that
the people we love are the foundation for all else. I have never found the
optimal balance between immersion in my work and the pull of home,
love, and laughter that are my fuel. But I do know that when we turn in
our White House badge—or its equivalent in other fields—what is left
is our own garden, and what we have sown and cultivated.

I have gone back to teaching at Harvard Kennedy School and Law
School, offering a course on geopolitics and one that I co-teach with
Cass on the law and politics of social change. I serve on the board of
the International Refugee Assistance Program (IRAP), which orga-
nizes lawyers and law students to provide pro bono legal representa-
tion to refugees. In January of 2017, when the Trump administration
first issued its executive order halting refugee admissions and barring
people from seven predominantly Muslim nations from coming to the
United States, IRAP organized thousands of volunteer lawyers to flock
to airports across the country. On the spot, they began representing
shell-shocked individuals who had received visas to enter the United
States but suddenly found themselves detained. IRAP also won the
very first court ruling against the travel ban, which had the effect of
allowing more than 21,000 vetted refugees to enter the United States
in 2017. While the Supreme Court lamentably upheld an amended version of Trump's travel ban in 2018, these refugees would never have
made it had his initial executive order not been challenged.

I also serve on the advisory council of the Tent Partnership, the
coalition of businesses that have agreed to hire refugees and improve
services and investment in their communities. Under the leadership of
Chobani founder Hamdi Ulukaya, Tent's companies have come to see

refugees not as victims who need charity, but as resourceful and driven people who strengthen workforces and communities. Having myself been given the chance to move to the United States, I am committed to doing what I can to support those working to ensure that refugees and immigrants are protected and treated with respect.

AS I HAVE TRAVELED around the United States and abroad since leaving office, I have heard—and asked myself—many variants of the same question: "Are we going to be okay?"

We have ample grounds for alarm. The sources of America's strength—our diversity, our embrace of individual rights and dignity, our commitment to the rule of law, and our leadership in the world—are under severe threat. The basic lessons Cass and I try to teach Declan and Rían (tell the truth, count and share your blessings, treat everyone equally) are being abused and ridiculed by the person holding the highest office in the land. President Trump's contempt and bigotry, his rage and dishonesty, and his attacks on judges, journalists, minorities, and opposition voices are doing untold damage to the moral and political foundations of American democracy. His cruel rhetoric and actions have not only unleashed vitriol toward those he has branded "enemies," but have also fueled violence by extremists within our own borders.

In late October of 2018, I received a call from the FBI's Boston field office. The agent informed me that Cesar Sayoc, the man accused of mailing more than a dozen pipe bombs to critics of President Trump, had done internet searches for the home addresses of other potential victims, including me. This call came the same week Declan and Rían had been incessantly checking our mailbox, awaiting the arrival of a mystery novel and science kit I had ordered for them.

Extremists with malicious tendencies like Sayoc have always been with us. But today our culture is saturated with misinformation. Even when falsehoods don't contribute to violence, they frighten people and turn us against one another. The decline in respect for objective truth and facts means we lack a stable underpinning on which to base our debates—and, ultimately, our decisions.

Trump and his enablers in politics and the media have been effective in fanning fear. While I once viewed the conflict in Bosnia as a last gasp of ethnic chauvinism and demagoguery from a bygone era, it now seems more of a harbinger of the way today's autocrats and opportunists exploit grievances, conjuring up some internal or external threat in order to expand their own power. Those of us who reject these tactics have yet to figure out how to convincingly reach people who are frightened by false claims.

While my generation was often told about the impending triumph of democracy and human rights, young people today are bombarded with commentary forecasting the retreat of liberal democracy—or even its demise. A growing mistrust in democratic institutions breeds cynicism about politics and America's future, and encourages an inward focus.

And while our rifts at home deepen, the world is not standing still. Gallup polling across 133 countries shows that approval of US leadership has plummeted since 2016, and that Russian president Putin and Chinese president Xi are now viewed as favorably as (or more favorably than) the American president. In the economic sphere, China's economy will likely surpass that of the United States in the next ten to fifteen years.

However, nothing is foreordained. The combined work of individuals can change a community's—and a country's—trajectory in a hurry. We have seen this often at home and abroad. In 1972, Richard Nixon was reelected president in a landslide, winning every state except Massachusetts. Two years later, a small number of dogged reporters and investigators had exposed his crimes, and he had resigned from office in disgrace. In the fall of 2014, the US government was predicting more than one million new Ebola infections in West Africa by early 2015. Yet thanks to determined efforts by people in the region and the US-led international response, a major Ebola outbreak was defeated.

America's greatest assets remain our democracy and the citizens who comprise it. The best predictor of whether we will ultimately "be okay" is if citizens who stand to benefit or lose from political decisions choose to organize and vote. I see among young people a fresh surge of interest in public service, born of the recognition that each of us has a responsibility—and an opportunity—to make the changes we seek. President Trump may have destabilized and weakened our institutions, but thus far his actions have not broken them.

The single most pressing task for Americans in the coming years is of course strengthening our democracy and governing ourselves more effectively. This requires making inroads against intense inequality, big money in politics, gerrymandering and restrictions on voting rights, corruption, polarization, racism, and exclusion—no small feats. At the same time, our engagement in the world cannot await the completion of a democratic renewal. We should deepen our investments in an area where the United States *has* achieved significant successes at minimal cost: diplomacy. Especially as US influence in the world diminishes, diplomacy will become more—not less—vital.

At the moment, military force is seen as the "go-to" tool in the US toolbox. Since September 11th, 2001, almost three million US service members have been deployed to Iraq and Afghanistan, many of them serving multiple tours. Astoundingly, US troops today are involved in counterterrorism activities in more than 40 percent of the countries in the world.[60] The burden of fighting wars and undertaking these missions is carried by US service members and their families. Such a heavy reliance on our military is neither sustainable nor desirable. It is emblematic of a militarization of US foreign policy that concerns people across the political spectrum. I heard our generals repeatedly plead in the Situation Room for the other facets of American power— reconstruction aid, economic development and investment, diplomatic mediation, economic and other pressures—to be brought to bear because military strikes and even battlefield victories could not achieve US strategic aims.

At present, the Pentagon and armed services have more than 225,000 American personnel deployed outside the United States; the State Department only around 9,000. Indeed, the Pentagon famously has only slightly fewer people serving in marching bands than the State Department has diplomats. This imbalance creates a self-fulfilling prophecy: the less we engage in diplomacy, the more chaotic the world becomes, and the harder it is to convince Americans that our international engagements are worth continuing.

Breaking out of this cycle will benefit all Americans, in the short and long term. Notwithstanding the diminishment of American influence, the United States will remain the most important country in the world for decades to come. In countless Security Council meetings, I watched foreign diplomats half-heartedly listen to the delegates from other countries, only to snap to attention when I, as the US representative, took the floor. On issue after issue, either the United States brought a game plan to the table or else the problem worsened. During my time in government, I saw US diplomats mobilize seventy countries to take on ISIS, negotiate the Paris climate agreement, get political prisoners out of jail, and build a coalition to impose such stringent sanctions on Iran that it gave up its potential nuclear weapons program. At more than 270 embassies and consulates around the world, diplomats aid American citizens when they run into trouble. They help ensure that American companies can more easily do business. And they attempt to negotiate an end to conflicts—an important task, especially now that Americans under the age of eighteen have lived in a country at war for their entire lives.

The United States is the only nation capable of standing up to foreign aggressors like Russia in Ukraine. It is the only country that, during a challenge like the Ebola crisis, could rapidly devise and launch a complex, unprecedented operation—as President Obama liked to put it, "building the airplane while flying it," while summoning other countries to the task. America's capacity for creative ambition and forging powerful coalitions remains unmatched.

If the United States steps back from leading the world—because of exhaustion, disillusionment, or internal division—American ideals, American prosperity, and American security will suffer. China will grow more aggressive in shaping the international rules of the road to its advantage. Crippling cyberattacks will cause growing harm and sow even greater divison. Right-wing extremists abroad will become more sophisticated in coordinating their efforts, backing their ideological allies in the United States and elsewhere with money and propaganda.

It is true that the foundation for US leadership abroad is the strength of our democracy at home. But it is also indisputable that the policies we pursue overseas can have huge effects—good and bad—on our daily lives.

DURING MY TIME IN GOVERNMENT, I came to better appreciate the constraints that stand in the way of making positive change. Even the most conscientious government decision-makers operate with shrouded and shifting fields of vision, deciding among wholly imperfect options. I felt the lasting damage caused by US government mistakes, particularly regarding the use of US military force. Irrespective of American intentions, the government's sins of commission—but also those of omission—underscore the immense responsibility one takes on as a public servant, and the need for humility about one's judgments.

I saw how important it is not to shun those with whom we disagree. As the theologian Reinhold Niebuhr once said, "We must always seek the truth in our opponent's error and the error in our own truth." This is just as important in our domestic politics as in our foreign dealings.

I was affirmed in my view that, when we respect human rights at home and abroad, we are stronger. This does not mean we should impose our values on other countries, pursue regime change, or end ties with governments that abuse their people. But it does mean standing up for those in need. The United States cannot dictate outcomes, but we often have more influence than we use.

I believe that dignity is an underestimated force in politics and geopolitics. Why did a Tunisian fruit vendor light himself on fire, setting off the Arab Spring? He felt humiliated. Why have many Russians supported Vladimir Putin despite their country's stagnant economy? At least partly because they believe he has restored Russia's status as a major player on the world stage. Why did millions of voters who supported Barack Obama in 2012 turn to Donald Trump in 2016? Many said that they felt ignored, as though their country was moving on without them.

Both as an activist and as a government official, I tried to stay focused on the real-world "scoreboard"—what had actually been accomplished as a result of my efforts. I would catch myself feeling satisfied by a powerful speech I had made at the UN, or a compelling argument I had put before the President. I would then excoriate myself for measuring the wrong thing. "It's not inputs that matter," I would hear in my head. "It's outcomes."

But looking back, I now see all that the scoreboard could not capture: The relief of a father who has been reunited with his son, newly free of a deadly disease. The look on a government minister's face as he traverses a rainbow crosswalk. The insistence of diplomats to go on serving their country, even when being ignored and insulted, because they know that our nation is bigger than any one leader. And the persistent attempts—after unforgivable acts—to find the humanity in one's foe.

Sometimes, no matter what we did, events unfolded in the wrong direction.

Sometimes, we moved the needle positively.

Sometimes, we believed we had no effect whatsoever, and only months or years later learned that our actions offered encouragement to those deciding whether their struggles were worth enduring.

Sometimes, we saved lives.

People who care, act, and refuse to give up may not change *the* world, but they can change many individual worlds.

June 14th, 2019
Concord, Massachusetts

ACKNOWLEDGMENTS

I am profoundly grateful to my colleagues, students, friends, and family members.

My incomparable agent Sarah Chalfant has been with me from the beginning, and her unflagging enthusiasm for this memoir gave me the fuel I needed to endure. The Wylie Agency's Rebecca Nagel also provided essential support throughout. Julia Cheiffetz and Lynn Grady, both then at Dey Street Books, were spirited early champions who offered editorial advice that changed my understanding of what the book could be. Kendra Newton, Andrea Molitor, Paula Russell Szafranski, Heidi Richter, Eliza Rosenberry, Ploy Siripant, Liate Stehlik, Ben Steinberg, Carrie Thornton, and my unflappable and deeply humane editor Jessica Sindler each put up with down-to-the-wire edits and brought much-appreciated ambition to publishing this book.

Special thanks to Noelle Campbell Sharp and the Cill Rialaig Retreat for the unforgettable stay in a restored pre-famine village on Bolus Head in Kerry, Ireland, where the majestic views and epic storms spurred great productivity.

At Harvard, Kennedy School Dean Doug Elmendorf, Law School Dean John Manning, and former Law School Dean (and close friend) Martha Minow welcomed me back to campus with open arms after my government service. The Radcliffe Institute's 2017–2018 Perrin Moorhead Grayson and Bruns Grayson Fellowship afforded me with a year to launch this project before returning to full-time teaching. Special thanks to Lizabeth Cohen, then-dean of Radcliffe Institute, fellowship program director (and insatiable omnivore) Judith Vichniac, and writer Zia Haider Rahman.

Since returning, the Kennedy School's Belfer Center for Science and International Affairs has been an ideal home. I am grateful to Graham Allison; Belfer Center Director and former Defense Secretary Ash Carter; and the dynamic duo of Eric Rosenbach and Aditi Kumar. For support with research and fact-checking, I thank Kennedy School scholar Natasha Yefimova-Trilling for her Russian language research; Sinead O'Donovan and Yan Bourke for their inquiries in Ireland; Kennedy School graduate Vafa Ghazavi; Brown University student Erin Brennan-Burke; Harvard College students Amanda Chen, Sunaina Danziger, Hank Sparks, and Matt Keating; Harvard Law School student Elise Baranouski; and joint Harvard Law School and Harvard Kennedy School student Parker White. I am indebted to Marin Stein, a superb manager who became a trusted adviser, and Ellie Hitt, who has been truly indispensable in bringing the book into the world.

I have been extraordinarily fortunate in the last decade to be able to call upon the wisdom of distinguished senior statesmen and -women, many of them accomplished authors and memoirists in their own right. I thank them for offering such candid, farsighted counsel.

Many people helped inform or inspire specific parts of the book, while others read particular sections and shared their own memories. I am grateful to Mort Abramowitz, Wa'el Alzayat, Brooke Anderson, Mary-Kate Barry Percival, Rob Berschinski, Josh Black, Tony Blinken, Steven Bourke, John Brennan, Sally Brooks, Adrian Brown, Torrance Brown, Scott Busby, Kurt Campbell, Ben Cohen, Chuck Cohen, Lenore Cohen, Roger Cohen, Kurtis Cooper, Mary DeRosa, Tom Donilon, Jon Favreau, Abe Foxman, Maggie Goodlander, Doris Kearns Goodwin, Sam Kass, John Kerry, Ron Klain, Chris Klein, Harold Koh, Melissa Kroeger, Molly Levinson, Tom Malinowski, Gideon Maltz, Kati Marton, Denis McDonough, Charlie Moore, Katie Moore, Charlotte Morgan, Tom Nides, Toria Nuland, Steve Pomper, Preston Price, Mike Rauhut, Susan Rice, David Rohde, Elizabeth Rubin, Evan Ryan, Michal Safdie, Moshe Safdie, Sia Sanneh, Roberta Seiler, Sarah Sewall, Liz Sherwood-Randall, Anne-Marie Slaughter, Mark Simonoff, Gayle Smith, Halie Soifer, Gene Sperling, Scott Stossel, Colin Thomas-Jensen, Stina Trainor, Tommy Vietor, Miro Weinberger, Jeff Zients, and Frederick Zollo.

I was daunted by the prospect of a government pre-publication review, but Anne Withers and Tom Lutte at the National Security Council, and Behar Godani, Dan Sanborn, and Anne Barbaro at the State Department managed the process with great efficiency and thoroughness.

My Irish friends and family members made themselves available to answer questions I should have asked years ago. Particular thanks to Geraldine Barniville, Susan Doody, Colm Gibson, Derry Gibson, Patricia Gibson, Gary Horgan, Karen "Chance of a Lifetime" Horgan, Marie Kirwan, Suzanne O'Reilly, Clare Pippet, and Michele Pippet.

During my time in the Obama administration, I would often marvel at the privilege of my circumstances, hearing a voice that said, "This. Is. Not. Normal." I had this same experience every time I heard back from a friend or colleague who made the time to provide detailed comments on entire drafts of this book. Heartfelt thanks to Greg Barker, Daniel Bluestein, Oskar Eustis, Jon Finer, Philip Gordon, Avril Haines, Dina Kawar, Megan Koilparampil, Cullen Murphy, Laura Pitter, John Prendergast, David Pressman, Kelly Razzouk, Ben Rhodes, John Schumann, Jake Sullivan, Stacy Sullivan, Larry Summers, Elliot Thomson, Mary Valente, Johnny Walsh, Jeremy Weinstein, and Becca Wexler.

I must also single out several friends who took what must have been weeks away from their lives to provide exhaustive, page-by-page comments and edits. Amy Bach worked late at night to help me avoid minefields I hadn't even noticed I was approaching. Sharon Dolovich gave the draft a meticulous read, offering granular suggestions while also urging me to address several key contradictions. Lukas Haynes, part of the "Mort Abramowitz's former interns" family, came like a burst of sunlight back into my life, helping me improve the telling of this story. Anna Husarska made the book one of her missions, marking up each chapter with care. Hillary Schrenell drew on her laser memory and deep empathy to offer vital suggestions. The incomparable Lee Siegel made me aspire to write a memoir that dug far deeper than I was initially prepared to go. Nik Steinberg brought his compassionate heart and exacting disposition to his painstaking review. Michael Rothschild saw a higher purpose when I doubted it, and, from beneath the snow drifts, treated every sentence as if it held the key to world peace. And if Michael's own deep involvement was not enough, he introduced me to Ida Rothschild, a brilliant line editor, who offered extensive, astute feedback when it mattered most.

Special thanks to President Barack Obama for taking the time to read and comment on the manuscript, but obviously—well beyond that—for entrusting me with the responsibility of being part of his team. Serving in his administration was the most meaningful professional experience of my life. I am grateful for his leadership—and his friendship.

Writing a memoir introduces an inevitable selection bias. The events I chose to describe dictate who—among the countless incredible people I worked with in government—makes an appearance in these pages. I hope I have made clear that those I depict embody the talent, patriotism, and dedication of all those who serve a cause larger than themselves. I learned from my colleagues every day, and I only hope I have done some justice to the spirit and integrity of the enterprise.

My partner in this project has been Adam Siegel, whose title, Research Associate, does not come close to capturing his contribution. Adam has been a ruthless editor, a world-class researcher and literary critic, a fair-minded political analyst, and, in the difficult times, a confidant and an inspiration. He has read every last sentence of every last draft of this book, and he has helped improve it immeasurably. My gratitude is boundless. Any errors of judgment or fact are of course my own.

Finally, my family. Ellyn Kail, my stepdaughter, and Stephen Power, my brother, offer me daily lessons in what one can achieve through perseverance. María Castro's arrival in our life was a miracle, and she will forever mean the world to us. Now Ana Reyes, who exudes kindness and joy, brightens our lives beyond words.

Mum and Eddie supported me as I delved into the past, even knowing the old wounds that this book would open. I am apprehensive about putting this memoir out into the world, but heartened that, by doing so, readers will get acquainted with these two remarkable individuals.

The book is dedicated to Declan, Rían, and Cass. Declan and Rían, you are hilarious, wise, fun, and big-hearted. Every day I get to hang out with you—and watch you discover the world and care for those around you—is a profound blessing.

Cass, you changed everything. I like, love, and admire you more each day.

Thank you for marrying me.

NOTES

PART ONE

1. For more on Fred's remarkable life, see Scott Anderson's *The Man Who Tried to Save the World: The Dangerous Life and Mysterious Disappearance of Fred Cuny* (New York: Doubleday, 1999).
2. *The 9/11 Commission Report* (Washington, DC: National Commission on Terrorist Attacks upon the United States, 2004), pp. 147, 155.
3. Stephen Engelberg and Tim Weiner, "Srebrenica: The Days of Slaughter," *New York Times*, October 29, 1995, with reporting from Raymond Bonner and Jane Perlez.
4. The psychologist Paul Slovic and others have conducted studies showing that human compassion actually decreases as the number of victims rises. One example of this "identifiable victim effect" is a study showing that volunteers asked to raise $300,000 to save eight children who are dying of a serious disease were willing to give significantly less than those asked to raise that sum to save a single child. See Paul Slovic, "'If I look at the mass I will never act': Psychic numbing and genocide," *Judgment and Decision Making* 2, no. 2 (2007): pp. 79–95; and Tehila Kogut and Ilana Ritov, "The 'Identified Victim' Effect: An Identified Group, or Just a Single Individual?," *Journal of Behavioral Decision Making* 18, no. 3 (2005): 157–167.
5. Gourevitch later published the book *We Wish to Inform You That Tomorrow We Will Be Killed with Our Families: Stories From Rwanda* (New York: Farrar, Straus, and Giroux, 1998).
6. Powell had sent human rights investigators to the same camps along the Sudan-Chad border that John and I had visited, and they had taken testimony from more than a thousand survivors. As evidence of genocide, the investigators combined these eyewitness accounts with satellite images showing that more than four hundred villages had been burned to the ground.
7. With the strong backing of the Bush administration, Sudanese president Bashir and southern opposition leader John Garang agreed to a peace accord in January of 2005. The Comprehensive Peace Agreement (CPA) established power and wealth sharing between Khartoum and the South while

providing a framework for ending the civil war. Significantly, the CPA mandated that a South Sudanese referendum on independence be held after a period of six years. The Bush administration viewed the CPA as a major achievement, but it did not lead to peace for Darfur. Many activists would come to believe that the administration's focus on north–south relations—and interest in keeping the North committed to the CPA—ended up limiting its willingness to pressure Khartoum to cease the continuing violence in Darfur.

8. First proposed by the academics George Kelling and James Wilson in 1982, the "broken windows" theory went on to be adopted as a crime-fighting measure by the New York City Police Department. The theory was roundly criticized, both for being ineffective and for contributing to the over-policing of minority neighborhoods. Kelling and Wilson posited that eliminating minor types of neighborhood disorder (like graffiti, abandoned cars, drinking in public, and buildings with broken windows) would help reduce occurrences of serious crime.

9. Many scandals broke out as well, which surely impacted public opinion. Soon after I arrived, in September of 2005, Representative Tom Delay stepped down as House majority leader after being indicted for violating campaign finance laws. Representative Duke Cunningham resigned two months later after pleading guilty to taking $2 million in bribes. Representative William Jefferson had his home raided by federal agents, who ended up finding $90,000 in his freezer, given to him in bribes. And in September of 2006, Representative Mark Foley resigned after he was revealed to have sent sexually explicit instant messages to House pages.

10. Richard Wolffe, *Renegade: The Making of a President* (New York: Crown Publishers, 2009), pp. 81, 97.

11. Chris Liddell-Westefeld, "They Said This Day Would Never Come," Crooked Media, January 3, 2018, https://crooked.com/articles/said-day -never-come/.

12. Ibid.

PART TWO

1. Australia was then the other, although it introduced paid maternity leave in 2011. As a result, the United States is currently the only country among the thirty-six highly developed nations in the Organization for Economic Cooperation and Development that does not offer paid maternity leave. The Family and Medical Leave Act, passed by Congress in 1993, only guarantees twelve weeks of unpaid leave, and it just applies to companies with more than fifty employees, leaving out parents employed by small businesses.

2. According to data reported in the 2016 Global Terrorism Index, 93 percent of all terrorist attacks between 1989 and 2014 occurred in countries with high incidences of state-sanctioned human rights abuses (defined as extra-judicial killing, torture, and political imprisonment without trial). Relatedly, a UN study that examined why people join terrorist groups like Boko

Haram and al-Shabaab found that "state security agency conduct is a direct trigger for recruitment in the final stages of the journey to extremism, with as many as 71 percent of [people who voluntarily joined a terrorist organization] pointing to 'government action,' including traumatic incidents involving state security forces, as the immediate reason for joining." See "Global Terrorism Index 2016," Institute for Economics and Peace, November 2016, p. 72; and "Journey to Extremism in Africa: Drivers, Incentives and the Tipping Point for Recruitment," United Nations Development Program, September 2017, p. 88.

3. Evans would later say he had been inspired to speak out by events surrounding the genocide in Darfur. In a 2015 interview, he recalled, "Colin Powell had come out and said that he thought that what was happening in Darfur in the Sudan did constitute genocide. That was a very brave thing for him to have done . . . His action emboldened me to endeavor not simply to be a bystander on a question of genocide but to stand up and say something about it. Even though it was ninety years in the past, I felt that someone needed to take a stand on this issue and call it what it was."

4. Obama's letter continued: "When State Department instructions are such that an Ambassador must engage in strained reasoning—or even an outright falsehood—that defies a common-sense interpretation of events in order to follow orders, then it is time to revisit the State Department's policy guidance on that issue." See Senator Barack Obama letter to Secretary of State Condoleezza Rice, July 28, 2006, http://armeniansforobama.com/common/pdf/Obama_letter_to_Rice_July_26_2008.pdf.

5. In her 2005 book *Team of Rivals: The Political Genius of Abraham Lincoln*, historian Doris Kearns Goodwin wrote about Abraham Lincoln's appointment of political adversaries to key positions in his administration. After wrapping up the Democratic nomination in 2008, Obama had cited President Lincoln's approach as a model, noting that "Lincoln basically pulled all the people he'd been running against into his Cabinet. Because whatever personal feelings there were, the issue was, 'How can we get the country through this time of crisis?'"

6. In 2004, the year after the Iraq War began, the US took in only 66 refugees from Iraq. In 2006, Sweden, a country of nine million, accepted 8,950 Iraqi refugees, while the United States, a country of 300 million, accepted 202. Even as displacement soared, our numbers remained miniscule. This changed in 2008, when President Bush signed into law the Refugee Crisis in Iraq Act, making it easier for certain Iraqis (like those who had worked for the US military and their families) to come to the United States. Prior to this law, which passed Congress with overwhelming bipartisan support, the Bush administration had admitted some 2,400 Iraqis since the beginning of the war. But in 2008, more than 14,000 Iraqis made it to the US.

7. In 2008, the US Holocaust Memorial Museum Genocide Prevention Task Force, chaired by former secretary of state Madeleine Albright and former secretary of defense William Cohen, had recommended the creation of this position in its report "Preventing Genocide: A Blueprint for U.S. Policy-

makers," https://www.ushmm.org/m/pdfs/20081124-genocide-prevention -report.pdf.

8. Presidential Proclamation 8697, issued in August of 2011, banned entry into the United States of those people who the State Department determined had been involved in "war crimes, crimes against humanity or other serious violations of human rights." Five years later, during the final month of his presidency, Obama would sign the Global Magnitsky Human Rights Accountability Act into law. This legislation further expanded the Executive Branch's toolkit by authorizing the President to impose visa bans on those responsible for extrajudicial killings and torture. The law also granted the President power to impose targeted sanctions on individuals found to have committed human rights violations or "acts of significant corruption."

9. The story of the search for Mladić is detailed in Julian Borger, *The Butcher's Trail: How the Search for Balkan War Criminals Became the World's Most Successful Manhunt* (New York: Other Press, 2016), pp. 139–149, 283–307.

10. Damien McElroy, "Ratko Mladić arrested: Europe's most wanted man seized in Serbia," *The Telegraph*, May 26, 2011, https://www.telegraph.co .uk/news/worldnews/europe/serbia/8539630/Ratko-Mladić-arrested-Eu ropes-most-wanted-man-seized-in-Serbia.html.

11. The Bush administration had begun providing logistical support to the Ugandan military for counter-LRA operations, but after President Obama took office, young activists, including those from Invisible Children, secured the passage of congressional legislation, which mandated the President to develop a more far-reaching strategy for defeating Kony's army.

12. When the Obama administration took office in 2009, the only UN resolution that contained the words "sexual orientation" was one condemning extrajudicial execution on a range of grounds. In 2010, we had to fight just to preserve the reference when it came up for a vote in the General Assembly. Although we ultimately prevailed, Zimbabwe's ambassador claimed that including it would bring the UN a step closer to accepting bestiality.

13. The US government added Libya to a list of state sponsors of terrorism in 1979 and closed its embassy in Tripoli in 1980. During the 1970s and 1980s, Qaddafi sent arms to groups as varied as the Irish Republican Army and the Basque militants of ETA, and he provided terrorists access to training camps in Libya. The Libyan government also aided and participated in several terrorist attacks that killed Americans, including the 1986 bombing of a German nightclub, the 1988 bombing of Pan Am Flight 103, and the 1989 bombing of UTA Flight 772. Qaddafi later curtailed his support for terrorism and sought closer ties to the West by ending his nuclear weapons program. As a result, in 2006 the Bush administration removed Libya from the terrorism list and resumed full diplomatic relations.

14. Mike Elkin, "Libya: Recovering from the horror, waiting for more," *Inter Press Service*, March 2, 2011, http://www.ipsnews.net/2011/03/libya -recovering-from-horror-waiting-for-more/; and Adrian Blomfield, "Libya: Rebels in desperate battle to hold ground," *The Telegraph*, March 2, 2011,

https://www.telegraph.co.uk/news/worldnews/africaandindianocean/libya/8357934/Libya-rebels-in-desperate-battle-to-hold-ground.html.

15. Martin Fletcher, "Just 30 miles from Tripoli, the defiant town that dares to humiliate Gaddafi," *The Times*, March 7, 2011, https://www.thetimes.co.uk/article/just-30-miles-from-tripoli-the-defiant-town-that-dares-to-humiliate-gaddafi-qsppc8bc66d; reporting from Alex Crawford of *Sky News*, recounted by Samer al-Atrush, "Kadhafi forces accused of 'massacre' as battles rage," *AFP*, March 6, 2011; and Crawford interviewed on CNN's *Anderson Cooper 360*, March 10, 2011.

16. Qaddafi himself made contradictory statements about his intentions. In his February 22nd televised address to the Libyan people, he stated, "Any Libyan who holds a weapon against Libya, his punishment is execution." Later, on March 17th, as his forces closed in on Benghazi, he again made ominous threats but also claimed that if a person handed over his weapons, "whatever he did previously, he will be pardoned, protected." Given Qaddafi's penchant for lying and his previous treatment of opponents, opposition supporters in Benghazi did not trust his last-minute assurances.

17. We rightly never discussed polling data in the Situation Room. However, the media reported varying degrees of support for the different potential US military actions in Libya. As is typical, opinions differed depending on how questions were asked. An ABC News/*Washington Post* poll conducted March 10th–March 13th found 72 percent of Americans supportive of a US-enforced no-fly zone, while a poll conducted by CNN on the same days, but with different phrasing, found only 56 percent in favor of this option. Meanwhile, the same CNN poll showed that 74 percent of Americans preferred that the United States "leave it to international organizations or allies" to take the leading role in Libya. A week later, a CNN poll found that 77 percent of Americans believed it was either "very important" (34 percent) or "somewhat important" (43 percent) to make "the removal of Moammar Gadhafi from power in Libya" a foreign policy goal of the United States.

18. George Packer, *Our Man: Richard Holbrooke and the End of the American Century* (New York: Alfred A. Knopf, 2019), p. 81.

19. In July 2011, Assistant Secretary of State for the Middle East Jeff Feltman, US Ambassador to Libya Gene Cretz, and NSC Senior Director for Strategic Planning Derek Chollet met with Qaddafi's advisers in Tunis, Tunisia, for close to three hours.

20. NATO intensified its bombing of military targets in Tripoli in mid-August. Rebel sleeper cells within the city activated on August 20th, setting in motion a series of defections among pro-Qaddafi troops, and rebel forces from outside the capital began streaming into Tripoli. By August 23rd, the rebels had assumed control of most of the capital and had seized Qaddafi's central compound. Qaddafi himself remained on the run for two more months before he was seized and murdered in October of 2011.

21. MKULTRA ended only when CIA director Richard Helms retired and destroyed most of the materials related to the program, but its sordid history emerged in a series of Senate hearings in the mid-1970s.

22. Countries like Brazil, Germany, India, Japan, and South Africa have been lobbying for years to be given permanent Security Council seats, but negotiations over reforming the Council's membership have always broken down. For the composition of the Security Council to be altered, two-thirds of the member states of the United Nations, including *all* the Council's permanent members, would need to ratify the change to the UN Charter. In the United States, this would entail securing approval by two-thirds of the Senate. As a result of these high thresholds and the inability of member states to agree on precisely how the Council should be modernized, it has only been reformed once, in 1965, when member states came together to expand the number of nonpermanent seats from six to ten.

23. Many countries spend vast sums campaigning for seats on UN bodies, engaging in vote swapping and vote buying. Winning a two-year Security Council term is particularly coveted. Although amounts are hard to verify, countries typically spend millions of dollars on the events, receptions, and lobbying that precede a vote. Over the last decade, countries have reportedly spent anywhere from $4 million (Sweden) to $25 million (Australia) campaigning to win a Security Council seat.

24. The five permanent members have used their veto power a total of 288 times. This number does not correspond to the number of resolutions vetoed, as more than one permanent member sometimes vetoes the same resolution. The USSR/Russia has cast the most vetoes (141), followed by the United States (83), the United Kingdom (32), France (18), and China (14).

25. Six years later, the Global Public Policy Institute think tank in Berlin released a report identifying at least 33 incidents of chemical weapons use in Syria between December 23rd, 2012, and August 20th, 2013. The study's authors were not able to confirm all the reported incidents with the highest degree of confidence, but their extensive research indicates that more attacks took place than the US government was aware of at the time. See "Annex: List of Confirmed Incidents (2012–2018)" in Tobias Schneider and Theresa Lütkefend, "Nowhere to Hide: The Logic of Chemical Weapons Use in Syria," Global Public Policy Institute, February 2019, https://www .gppi.net/2019/02/17/the-logic-of-chemical-weapons-use-in-syria.

26. The Iraqi government under Saddam Hussein was the last country to use chemical weapons on a large scale. Saddam's forces deployed them in the 1980s both against Iran during the Iran-Iraq War and against Iraqi Kurds. The deadliest and most notorious chemical attack against the Kurds occurred on March 16th, 1988, in the town of Halabja, where Iraqi bombs containing mustard gas, sarin, and VX gas killed five thousand Kurds and injured thousands more.

27. The War Powers Resolution came into force, during the Vietnam War, in 1973. Nonetheless, President Reagan deployed US troops to Lebanon in September of 1982 as part of a multinational peacekeeping effort, arguing that the troops were not engaged in "hostilities," despite sustaining casualties and being equipped for combat. US forces remained in Lebanon for

almost a year until Congress retroactively authorized their presence under the War Powers Resolution. President George H.W. Bush sent American troops to Somalia beginning in December of 1992, and a subset of these troops remained under President Clinton, with the last not leaving until March of 1995. Clinton's advisers assessed that their "intermittent military engagements" were not "sustained hostilities" and were therefore in compliance with the 60-day deadline imposed by the War Powers Resolution. Without congressional authorization, the Clinton administration waged an air campaign in Kosovo, which lasted 78 days. Clinton's lawyers argued that Congress's funding of the military effort showed that it "clearly intended to authorize continuing military operations in Kosovo." During the Libya intervention, Obama administration lawyers contended that the operation's "limited military mission," "limited exposure for US troops and limited risk of serious escalation" with "limited military means" meant the United States was "not in hostilities of the kind envisioned by the War Powers Resolution that was intended to trigger an automatic 60-day pullout."

28. See "Government Assessment of the Syrian Government's Use of Chemical Weapons on August 21, 2013," August 30, 2013, https://obamawhitehouse .archives.gov/the-press-office/2013/08/30/government-assessment-syrian -government-s-use-chemical-weapons-august-21.

29. Ambassador Rice and Secretary Clinton maintained a professional relationship during Obama's first term, but previous UN ambassadors and Secretaries of State had clashed. For example, Secretary of State Alexander Haig reacted to President Reagan's selection of Jeane Kirkpatrick as UN ambassador by reportedly exclaiming, "I don't know how anybody expects that I will work with that bitch." He would go on to accuse Kirkpatrick of being generally "temperamental" as well as "mentally and emotionally incapable of thinking clearly." Peter Collier, *Political Woman: The Big Little Life of Jeane Kirkpatrick* (New York: Encounter Books, 2012), p. 118.

30. As soon as it became clear that the Assad regime had illicitly retained certain capabilities and supplies, I and others in the administration called on Syria to fully comply with its commitment to end its chemical weapons program. I raised the issue repeatedly in Security Council consultations and through diplomatic channels. I was authorized to publicly make clear our grave concern over what we called the "discrepancies and omissions in Syria's original declaration." Other administration representatives registered similar concerns, including our delegation to the Organization for the Prohibition of Chemical Weapons. See "United States of America: Statement at the 82nd Session of the Executive Council," Organization for the Prohibition of Chemical Weapons, July 12, 2016, https://www.opcw.org/ec-82.

31. This study is the most detailed assessment of the US response to the CAR crisis, providing a critical look at our policies and offering a number of lessons for future atrocity prevention efforts. See Charles J. Brown, "The Obama Administration and the Struggle to Prevent Atrocities in the Central African Republic," Simon-Skjodt Center for the Prevention of Genocide, United

States Holocaust Memorial Museum, November 2016, https://www.ushmm .org/m/pdfs/20161116-Charlie-Brown-CAR-Report.pdf.

32. In the 1980s, when Vitaly worked at the Soviet embassy in Washington, he became the first Soviet diplomat to appear regularly on American television. In one telling C-SPAN clip from 1985, a caller, impressed with Vitaly's interview, said, "I think you're sort of Western-looking and a real sharp guy. How about defecting? We'd love to have you." Grinning, Vitaly replied, "I'd advise you not to spend all your time waiting for that to happen. Your life will be wasted, Madame."

33. The films Vitaly appeared in were titled *Blue Notebook* (from 1963, about Lenin on the eve of the October Revolution) and *A Mother's Heart* (from 1965, about Lenin's mother and her love for her children).

34. Ukraine ranked 144th out of 175 countries on Transparency International's corruption index—the lowest of any European country. The pillaging by Yanukovych and his cronies had left the country tens of billions of dollars in debt. Ukraine's prosecutor general later estimated that, between 2010 and 2014, Ukrainian officials stole a fifth of their country's output.

35. Although the UN General Assembly lacks the enforcement authorities of the Security Council, it has the authority to make legal pronouncements and to direct the UN secretary-general and UN staff to follow them. Some votes in the UN General Assembly require a simple majority and others a two-thirds majority of "those present and voting." An absence has the same weight as an abstention; both reduce the number of total votes needed to win. In this case, a simple majority was required.

36. In doing so, Russian forces seized billions of dollars of Ukrainian government properties and military equipment, and the Russian authorities mandated that Crimeans take Russian citizenship or forgo receiving government services and assistance.

37. The US and EU sanctions had a measurable impact on the Russian economy, which entered a two-year recession in 2014. The Russian ruble lost more than 50 percent of its value against the dollar, and foreign investment slowed considerably. By making the sanctions "targeted," the administration hoped to impose costs on the Russian leadership and other powerful entities and individuals connected to the Kremlin, who in turn would have incentive to pressure Putin to de-escalate the crisis. In addition to sanctions, the United States and its partners in the G-8 grouping of leading industrialized nations suspended Russian participation.

38. Steven Hatch, an American doctor who participated in the Ebola response in Liberia, makes a credible case that the attention Trump generated with his Ebola commentary helped set the stage for his presidential campaign and provided him with a blueprint for how stoking fear could be marshaled for political gain. See Steven Hatch, "How the Ebola Crisis Helped Launch Donald Trump's Political Career," *Mother Jones*, April 3, 2017, https://www .motherjones.com/politics/2017/04/trump-ebola-tweets/.

39. The model used by the CDC to assess a worst-case scenario of 1.4 million Ebola infections was not universally embraced. Some scientists and academ-

ics questioned the CDC's underlying assumptions, such as the likely number of unreported cases.

40. Victor Luckerson, "Watch How Word of Ebola Exploded in America," *Time*, October 7, 2014, http://time.com/3478452/ebola-twitter/.

41. Critically, research has documented that women tend to have less self-esteem than men—a "confidence gap" that therefore creates disparities and disadvantages for them in professional settings. See Kay and Shipman's *The Confidence Code: The Science and Art of Self-Assurance—What Women Should Know* (New York: HarperCollins, 2014).

42. Back in 1945, the United Kingdom sent two female delegates to San Francisco as part of the team negotiating the text of the UN Charter. Overall, only eight women were present among the 850 delegates. Frustrated that reporters kept asking them what it was like to be woman delegates, the two British women, Florence Horsbrugh and Ellen Wilkinson, would reply, "We are not 'women delegates.' We are delegates of our country and ministers of our government." See Virginia Crocheron Gildersleeve, *Many a Good Crusade* (New York: Macmillan, 1954), p. 349.

43. Collier, *Political Woman*, p. 161.

44. Seven women ran for the positon, more than twice as many women than in all the previous elections for secretary-general combined. But in the end, former Portuguese prime minister António Guterres was the candidate who rallied the most enthusiastic support, and the only one who won the necessary backing of the Security Council's five permanent members. In his campaign, Guterres promised to prioritize promoting women's equality at the UN. As of 2018, he had achieved full gender parity among UN senior managers for the first time in the organization's history. Nonetheless, the male-dominated culture at the UN will take generations to reform.

45. Finding the appropriate balance was important, since we were making difficult requests of each government. Over the course of Obama's second term, Chad would lose thirty-six peacekeepers fighting militants in Mali, a country where American diplomats and aid workers operated. Cameroon, meanwhile, had opened its borders not only to Nigerians fleeing Boko Haram, but also to more than half of the refugees who had fled the Central African Republic. At the same time, the militaries in the regional task force were committing serious abuses. Amnesty International had issued detailed reports on the Cameroonian and Nigerian security forces' violations of international humanitarian law. In the case of Nigeria, for example, Amnesty alleged that the military had extrajudicially executed more than 1,200 people, including at least 640 detainees.

46. The 65 million people displaced was the highest number since World War II. One reason the number was so high was that conflicts had begun lasting far longer than before. A conflict that ended in 1970 had lasted, on average, 9.6 years. Those that ended in 2014, however, had lasted an average of 26.7 years, meaning many people end up displaced for decades.

47. In addition to our security interest in refugee resettlement and care, research shows that refugees make positive economic contributions to American soci-

ety as well. One 2017 study found that since 1975 the median household income for refugees who have been in the US for at least 25 years is significantly higher than overall median household income. The same report also found that refugees start companies at a higher rate than both non-refugee immigrants and the US-born population. Other research has shown that refugees who come to the US as children graduate high school and enter college at the same rate as the US-born population. A 2017 study published by the State Department, which looked at economic data from 1980 to 2010, assessed that "there is no adverse long-run impact of refugees on the U.S. labor market." Notably, under President Trump, the Department of Health and Human Services prepared a draft report that found refugees brought a net benefit to the economy of $63 billion between 2005 and 2014, although the administration tried to suppress the report's findings. See "From Struggle to Resilience: The Economic Impact of Refugees in America," New American Economy, June 2017, https://research.newamericaneconomy.org/report/from-struggle-to-re silience-the-economic-impact-of-refugees-in-america/; William N. Evans and Daniel Fitzgerald, "The Economic and Social Outcomes of Refugees in the United States: Evidence from the ACS," NBER Working Paper No. 23498, June 2017, https://www.nber.org/papers/w23498; Ana María Mayda et al., "The Labor Market Impact of Refugees: Evidence from the U.S. Resettlement Program," US Department of State, Office of the Chief Economist Working Paper, August 2017, https://www.state.gov/wp-content/uploads/2018/12 /The-Labor-Market-Impact-on-Refugees-Evidence-from-the-U.S.-Resettle ment-Program-1.pdf; and Julie Hirschfeld Davis and Somini Sengupta, "Trump administration rejects study showing positive impact of refugees," *New York Times*, September 18, 2017, https://www.nytimes.com/2017/09/18 /us/politics/refugees-revenue-cost-report-trump.html.

48. According to the UN's refugee agency, the top five refugee-hosting countries in the world today are: Turkey (3.6 million), Pakistan (1.4 million), Uganda (1.1 million), Germany (1 million), and Iran (979,400).

49. Trump made this false claim on August 31st, 2016 in Arizona, and made similar statements on a number of occasions during the campaign. See "Transcript of Donald Trump's Immigration Speech," https://www.nytimes .com/2016/09/02/us/politics/transcript-trump-immigration-speech.html.

50. Concerns that groups like ISIS would take advantage of refugee flows grew in the aftermath of the Paris attacks. The attackers were not refugees, and most were European citizens. However, some of them had trained with ISIS in Syria and were able to avoid scrutiny returning home by being part of the influx of refugees occurring at the time. Yet whereas refugees in Europe were then pouring across borders in an unregulated manner, the United States admitted only those who had gone through the lengthy vetting process.

51. Recall Paul Slovic and the "identifiable victim effect": our capacity to feel is greatest when considering just one person (in this instance, a two-year-old child). Numbers and statistics, no matter how large, usually fail to spark emotion or feeling and thus fail to motivate action.

52. The site, which was shut down by the Trump administration, can still be accessed at https://obamawhitehouse.archives.gov/aidrefugees.
53. The most significant long-term pledge made at Obama's refugee summit came from World Bank president Jim Yong Kim, who announced a willingness to provide multiyear financing for refugee-hosting countries to improve their public infrastructure and education and health systems. In turn, the World Bank pushed for legal changes that have allowed refugees in many more countries to work legally and send their kids to school.
54. Khaled Omar Harrah, a painter before the war, was perhaps the best-known member of the White Helmets. In 2014, he had spent sixteen hours digging through the rubble of a bombed-out apartment building to save a ten-day-old "miracle baby" named Mahmud. But the month before I sat down with Saleh, the Syrian regime had killed Harrah while he was on a rescue mission in Aleppo.
55. On a previous visit in 2015, Saleh had briefed the Security Council, saying, "As a patriotic Syrian, I never imagined I would one day ask for a foreign intervention in my country, by land or air. But the lives of innocent women and children that we see dying in our hands every day compel us to ask for any intervention possible to stop the barbaric killing machine led by Bashar al-Assad, including preventing Syrian aircraft from flying, and especially preventing helicopters from hovering above us and dropping these bombs. Before the strongest power on this planet, all I can do is ask that you awaken your conscience and tell me what you are going to do to stop these barrel bombs." For Saleh's full remarks from the June 26, 2015, informal Security Council meeting on Syria, see https://diary.thesyriacampaign.org/as-a-patriotic-syrian-i-never-imagined-i-would-do-this/.
56. The "Caesar photos" provided gruesome and incontrovertible evidence of the widespread murder of detainees by the Syrian government. "Caesar" is the alias of a Syrian defector who worked as a photographer for the Syrian military police and, with the help of a friend, smuggled some 55,000 photos out of the country. The photos, which Caesar and other military photographers had taken between 2011 and 2013, showed the bodies of dead men, women, and children who were starved, beaten, tortured, and executed by Syrian security forces while in government detention facilities. According to Caesar (who escaped from Syria in 2013), he and his colleagues had been instructed to record the images as internal documentation, but he preserved and shared the photos as proof of the Assad regime's crimes. Multiple investigations, including one by the FBI, have confirmed the authenticity of the images.
57. President Obama gave this response during an interview with Chris Wallace on *Fox News Sunday* on April 10, 2016. He has made related points in interviews with Tom Friedman in the *New York Times* and Jeffrey Goldberg in *The Atlantic*. I myself believe the flaw in the US approach was not so much a shortage of planning—from 2011 onward, US officials had done extensive planning, but the Libyans rejected most offers of outside support. Instead, as discussed in Chapter 25, I think our mistake was a lack of sustained,

high-level diplomatic engagement in the critical 2012–2014 period after the intervention was over and Libyan society began fracturing.

58. Despite billing himself as staunchly opposed to terrorism, the actual relationship between Assad and ISIS was much murkier. By the end of 2016, the Syrian government was buying so much oil from ISIS that these purchases had become the group's largest source of revenue; Assad was thus helping sustain the operations of the terrorists that he claimed to be fighting. At various points during the war, ISIS also appeared to be the intended beneficiary of air strikes undertaken by the Syrian military. At the core of this relationship was mutual self-interest: both Assad and ISIS seemed to prioritize attacking the moderate Syrian opposition. For more on these dynamics, see Anne Barnard, "Assad's Forces May Be Aiding New ISIS Surge," *New York Times*, June 2, 2015, https://www.nytimes.com/2015/06/03/world/middle east/new-battles-aleppo-syria-insurgents-isis.html; and Benoit Faucon and Ahmed Al Omran, "Islamic State Steps Up Oil and Gas Sales to Assad Regime," *Wall Street Journal*, January 19, 2017, https://www.wsj.com/articles /islamic-state-steps-up-oil-and-gas-sales-to-assad-regime-1484835563.

59. When North Korea launched another nuclear test that September, I negotiated a second resolution that went further. The new measures banned North Korean exports of copper, nickel, silver, and zinc, and drastically reduced North Korea's coal exports. Together, these new measures slashed the regime's revenue by at least $750 million, depriving it of funds it was using to expand its nuclear program while its citizens starved.

60. See "Where We Fight," Costs of War Project, Watson Institute for International and Public Affairs, Brown University, January 2019, https://watson .brown.edu/costsofwar/.

INDEX

Index